Dr. Jackson's *Zondervan Compact Greek Lexicon* packs a wealth of information into brief compass, providing a truly "handy" lexicon for those interested in growing in their reading facility rather than pursuing deeper lexical study. Particularly winsome features include Jackson's attention to displaying the components of compound words, helpful designations of noun declensions, contextually sensitive glosses, and listing of irregular principal parts as separate entries, pointing the user to the more familiar first principal part.

David A. deSilva, Trustees' Distinguished Professor of New Testament and Greek, Ashland Theological Seminary

In the line of influential Greek scholars in the Baptist tradition like A. T. Robertson, Hersey Davis, Ray Summers, and Curtis Vaughan, Paul Jackson—assisted by consulting editor George Guthrie—has now produced this well-researched *Zondervan Compact Greek Lexicon*. This useful resource represents years of studying and teaching Greek to hundreds and hundreds of students. Though the treatment of some words and texts with disputed conclusions occasionally swerves into the interpretive sphere, overall this informative volume will be quite beneficial for both the new Greek student as well as the seasoned exegete. I am happy to recommend this important volume as a tool for students, pastors, and scholars to keep on hand.

David S. Dockery, President and Distinguished Professor of Theology, Southwestern Baptist Theological Seminary

Lexica, theological wordbooks, and theological dictionaries are essential tools for the study of biblical languages, including Koine Greek. But these tools are often overwhelming with extensive entries. Pertinent information can be hard to identify, leaving users overwhelmed and unsure of the meaning and significance of a given Greek word. On the other hand, abbreviated lexica or vocabulary lists that accompany beginning grammars simplify the lexical universe too much and lead to flattened or even distorted understandings of Greek vocabulary. This is why Paul Jackson's *Zondervan Compact Greek Lexicon* is such a valuable resource. Relevant information such as frequency in both the Greek New Testament and the LXX is clearly indicated, often providing verse references for less frequent words. Of particular note is the effort to indicate "contextually controlled meaning" rather than merely list possible glosses for a given work. Glosses are also divided into subcategories, sometimes summarizing the extensive entries in *NIDNTT* in only several lines of text. Despite the compact nature of this lexicon, relevant Greco-Roman and early-church references are cited when necessary to indicate a word's usage. Difficult, irregular forms are also listed with clear references to the lexical form. In short, this volume packs an incredible amount of essential information into a surprisingly small number of pages! I will definitely recommend this valuable tool for my students and look forward to using it in my own study.

Dana M. Harris, New Testament Professor and Department Chair, Trinity Evangelical Divinity School

The standard Greek lexica tend to be expensive and overly technical with confusing symbols and abbreviations. If a student or pastor wants to look up a New Testament Greek term quickly and easily, they will greatly benefit from this handy compact lexicon. It delivers on what it promises—accurate information in a small amount of space. Jackson manages to pack in lots of helpful information into a fraction of the size of most lexica, which is ideal for quick reference help.

Nijay K. Gupta, Julius R. Mantey Professor of New Testament, Northern Seminary

By use of an innovative set of reference and format features, Paul Jackson compiles a huge amount of data into a small space. In contrast to smaller lexicons, the *Zondervan Compact Greek Lexicon* presents the wide range of meaning for a single term (the Greek New Testament has some five thousand lexical terms with a corresponding twenty-five thousand different meanings). This is a user-friendly tool—practical and handy for both the beginning student and the advanced scholar. I recommend it to everyone who carries a Greek New Testament—take this lexicon with you.

Bruce Corley, Senior Professor of New Testament and Greek, Chancellor, B. H. Carroll Theological Seminary

ZONDERVAN

COMPACT GREEK LEXICON

PAUL N. JACKSON

GEORGE H. GUTHRIE,
Consulting Editor

ZONDERVAN ACADEMIC

ZONDERVAN ACADEMIC

Zondervan Compact Greek Lexicon

Published in Grand Rapids, Michigan, by Zondervan. Zondervan is a registered trademark of The Zondervan Corporation, L.L.C., a wholly owned subsidiary of HarperCollins Christian Publishing, Inc.

Requests for information should be addressed to customercare@harpercollins.com.

Zondervan titles may be purchased in bulk for educational, business, fundraising, or sales promotional use. For information, please email SpecialMarkets@Zondervan.com.

Library of Congress Cataloging-in-Publication Data

Names: Jackson, Paul Norman, author. | Guthrie, George H., 1959- editor.
Title: Zondervan compact Greek lexicon / Paul N. Jackson ; George H. Guthrie, consulting editor.
Description: Grand Rapids, Michigan : Zondervan Academic, 2024.
Identifiers: LCCN 2024044636 (print) | LCCN 2024044637 (ebook) | ISBN 9780310099499 (hardcover) | ISBN 9780310099505 (ebook)
Subjects: LCSH: Bible. New Testament--Language, style. | Greek language, Biblical--Dictionaries--English. | BISAC: RELIGION / Biblical Reference / Language Study | RELIGION / Biblical Studies / Exegesis & Hermeneutics | LCGFT: Dictionaries.
Classification: LCC PA881 .J26 2024 (print) | LCC PA881 (ebook) | DDC 225.4/803--dc23/eng/20241120
LC record available at https://lccn.loc.gov/2024044636
LC ebook record available at https://lccn.loc.gov/2024044637

Interior design: Kait Lamphere

Printed in the United States of America

25 26 27 28 29 LBC 5 4 3 2 1

Contents

Lexicon

Preface

Sadly, Elvis died on August 16, 1977. In that same year, I subsequently had appendicitis, a spiritual revival, a vocational redirection, a broken marital engagement, and an introduction to the Greek New Testament! Pain accompanied it all. But pain is not necessarily a bad thing. My pastor and father in the ministry, Rev. Kenneth Frank Brown, guided me through this Fire Swamp of sudden change. Not long after I walked the aisle one Sunday morning at Kirby Baptist Church to share my decision with the congregation to pursue biblical studies, he invited me to his house to receive my first Greek lesson, and then, as one would expect any good exegete to do, he assigned me a date to preach my maiden sermon. Baited, hooked, and pulled onto the shore for life! In case you did not catch it, Greek (and Hebrew, for that matter) *before* the sermon! The year 1977 proved to be consequential for me in San Antonio, Texas. Did I mention that my wife, Janet, attended the same church? Also, it is remarkable that a dozen or so members of that little church became preachers and professors due chiefly to Brown's influence. Now, almost fifty years later, his impact remains a permanent fixture in the hearts of the hundreds, if not the thousands, of us who knew him. These are just a few reasons why I heartily dedicate the *Zondervan Compact Greek Lexicon* to my first and greatest Greek professor, Kenneth Frank Brown. Exponentially sadder than the passing of Elvis, for me and so many others, Ken died July 2, 2021, at the age of 90. Impersonators are a dime a dozen, but there was only one Ken Brown.

While it took some time for me to see it, I am convinced math skills also contributed greatly to my study and acquisition of biblical Greek and Hebrew knowledge, and a half dozen other inflected languages. Hammering out translations reminded me of solving integrals in calculus, proving geometric theorems, and determining the x-intercepts of quadratic equations. If you learn the formulas and rules, whether for Greek or math, then you are off to the races!

From engineering days, I recall that the *CRC Standard Mathematical Tables and Formulas* book was affectionately known as the "CRC Math Bible." I wore mine out. Although not permitted for exams, it served as a lifeline while trudging through increasingly difficult math and engineering courses. It served faithfully as an extremely useful resource. I hope the *ZCGL* will function similarly in your study of NT Greek, no matter where you are in the journey. I believe my approach is highly intuitive. And be of good cheer! Neither the Pythagorean theorem nor the quadratic formula (as beautiful and edifying as those truly are) are required to benefit from this lexicon. Now, identifying the lexical forms in a pluperfect periphrastic construction? That is a different story.

I am a builder: houses, furniture, expansive decks, apple pie, tortilla soup, Lego kits, sermons, and yes, a Greek lexicon. Investigating 5,000+ Greek words resulted in some unexpected discoveries, some of which I did not find in a commentary or any other reference tool. Granted, that could mean I really did not find anything, as verified a couple of times by my longtime friend, Harry Lee Poe. In his unmistakable voice, he would kindly say, "Paul, this is certainly interesting; it's just not pertinent." David DeSilva reminded me to stay true to my chief guideline: "The *ZCGL* is not a commentary, but through a structured referencing system, it will provide important portals to the resources where the meanings of words are thoroughly wrestled over." Once you pay the admission fee, I can take you to the mat. While I do try to stay out of the fray, I may occasionally enter in.

Amid this project, I retired from Union University in 2021, where I taught Greek and biblical studies for about three decades. Unfortunately, Covid-19 also made its ugly appearance during this time, afflicting me with pneumonia, a sizable blood clot in my right leg, and long-term fatigue, thus hampering my progress. The Lord extended mercy to me as I plodded along. Finally, I am landing the plane! Reflecting on how this book came together, I am eternally grateful to so many passengers. First and foremost is my wife Janet, who endured the "When is he going to be finished with this?" thought bouncing around in her head while life continued to happen all around us. Make no mistake about it, she is the glue that held us all together while I wrote a Greek dictionary. Adding to the overall challenge is that many of you know how hard it is for me to sit still for extended periods of time. Office hours are my kryptonite. In addition to serving as this work's consulting editor, George H. Guthrie is one of my dearest friends in the world. When Union considered hiring me in 1993, George, serving as the dean, asked Bruce Corley, our friend and beloved seminary professor, "Which one of these guys do we want?" He answered, "Jackson, but you will need to tie him to his desk!" Many thanks to Bruce and George for having a great sense of humor and loving me anyway.

Deep thanks to the hundreds of excellent Greek students I've had the honor to teach over my long tenure at Union, including some budding language scholars who assisted me with editing, suggestions, and basic research for this lexicon. A good number of them also came to my house each week for "JackSundays" to eat pancakes and watch the latest installment of *The Walking Dead* (I still haven't convinced Guthrie of the spiritual significance of this series; see *The Zombie*

Gospel, by Danielle Strickland). Nathan Maroney, Jacob Collins, Ryan Linkous (λίνκος, ου, ὁ$_2$, ①amp **red-headed exegete**), and Steven Errico walked with me through much of this laborious process. I love these young brains! They are all pastoring, teaching, or still slugging it out in various grad schools. Maroney and Collins have also endured my teaching on two continents. And we had deep discussions on the meanings of several Greek words while being on mission in Mozambique. Steven Errico receives special attention as he is teaching Elementary Greek to two of our fifteen grandchildren, Lucy Carson and Reid Carson, at the prestigious Augustine School in Jackson, Tennessee. On top of all of these is the unmatched contribution of Gabrielle Berry. She is an incredible biblical-languages student at Union University. Gabby enrolled in my New Testament Survey class in which I frequently emphasized the importance of studying Greek and Hebrew. She worked many hours researching, tagging, editing, clarifying, and filling in a lot of blanks in this ever-burgeoning manuscript. As an elementary Greek student, she demonstrated an uncanny facility for the language. Remember her name. Thank you, Gabbs!

Of course, I am always indebted to the Zondervan team, especially Chris Beetham, who again has guided me through a Greek language project that I hope many students, professors, and pastors will find useful in their collective quest to understand the New Testament better for many years to come. I thank the Lord above all. When I followed through with what Ken Brown challenged me to do, he answered.

Jackson, Tennessee
Fall, 2023

Abbreviations

General

⟹	multi-duplicated phrase
«	by implication
«»	contrast
--›	direct causation
→	alludes to, leads to
abs.	absolute
acc.	accusative
act.	active
adj.	adjective, adjectival
adv.	adverb, adverbial
affirm.	affirmative
anarth.	anarthrous
aor.	aorist
Aram.	Aramaic
assoc.	association
astr.	astrological
astron.	astronomer, astronomy
attrib.	attributive
bus.	business
chron.	chronological
class.	classical
coll.	collated
cmpd.	compound
compar.	comparative
con	contract (*verb*)
conj.	conjunction
constr.	construction
coord.	coordinate
correl.	correlative
crucif.	crucifixion
dat.	dative
demonstr.	demonstrative
develop.	development
emph.	emphasis, emphatic
eschat.	eschatological
et al.	and the rest; and others
equiv.	equivalent
fig.	figurative
foll.	following
form.	formulaic, formula
fut.	future
G	Gospels
GA	Gospel and Acts
gen.	genitive
Gk.	Greek
GNT	Greek New Testament
gen.	genitive
geom.	geometric, geometrician
gramm.	grammatical, grammarian
Heb.	Hebrew, Hebraic
ichthyol.	ichthyology
i.e.	in other words; that is
illust.	illustrative, illustration
imp.	imperative
impf.	imperfect
impers.	impersonal

impr.	improper
ind.	indicative
indecl.	indeclinable
indef.	indefinite
inf.	infinitive
infer.	inferential
inscr.	inscription
interj.	interjection
interrog.	interrogative
intran.	intransitive
LA	Luke-Acts
lit.	literal
litt.	literature
loc.	locative
math.	mathematical
med.	medical
mid.	middle
milit.	military, militaristic
MajPr	Major Prophets (Isa, Jer, Ezek)
medic.	medical
MinPr	Minor Prophets
n	note
narr.	narrative
neg.	negative
neol.	neologism (*normally hapax created by author*)
neut.	neuter
num.	number
onoma.	onomatopoeia
opp.	opposite
opt.	optative
part.	particle
pass.	passive
Pent	Pentateuch
pf.	perfect
phil.	philosophical, philosophy
phys.	physical
pleon.	pleonastic, pleonasm (*to be excessive, redundancy*)
plpf.	pluperfect
pos.	positive
prep.	preposition
pres.	present
prob.	probable, probably
pron.	pronoun
ptc.	participle
purp. cl.	purpose clause
quot.	quotation
recipr.	reciprocal
rel.	relative
resid.	residence
Sem.	Semitic
spir.	spiritual
subj.	subject, subjective
subord.	subordinate
subst.	substantive, substantival
super.	superlative
surg.	surgical
sym.	symbolic, symbolism
Syn	Synoptic (Matt, Mark, Luke)
SynA	Synoptics and Acts
t.t.	*terminus technicus* (technical term)
temp.	temporal
theol.	theological
transfig.	transfiguration
usu.	usually
var.	variant
w/	with
WisLit	Wisdom Literature
zool.	zoological

Parsing Tags

This guide defines the superscripted parsing tags appearing for hapax legomena (words occurring once). Parsing tags can also appear when more than one term shares the same parsing scheme.

Nouns and Adjectives (Case/Gender/Number)
Verbs (Tense/Voice/Mood/Person/Number)
Participles (Tense/Voice/Participle/Case/Gender/Number)
Infinitives (Tense/Voice/Inf)

Case	**Gender**	**Number**
Nominative–n	Masculine–m	Singular–s
Genitive–g	Feminine–f	Plural–p
Dative–d	Neuter–n	
Accusative–a		
Vocative–v		

Tense	**Voice**	**Mood**	**Part of Speech**
Present–p	Active–a	Indicative–i	Participle–p
Imperfect–i	Middle–m	Subjunctive–s	Infinitive–inf
Future–f	Passive–p	Optative–o	
Aorist–a	Imperative–imp		
Perfect–pf			
Pluperfect–plpf			

Modern Sources

ABC	Anchor Bible Commentary
AGG	*Ancient Greek Grammar for the Study of the New Testament.* By Heinrich von Siebenthal. New York, 2019
APB	*All the People of the Bible.* By James C. Turner, ed. Nashville: Thomas Nelson, 1993
ASV	American Standard Version
B (Bel)	Bel and the Dragon (14th chapter in the LXX version of Daniel)
BBG	*Basics of Biblical Greek.* By William D. Mounce. 4th ed. Grand Rapids: Zondervan, 2019
BCOT	Baker Commentary on the Old Testament

BDAG	Danker, Frederick W., Walter Bauer, William F. Arndt, and F. Wilbur Gingrich, *A Greek-English Lexicon of the New Testament and Other Early Christian Literature.* 3rd ed. Chicago: University of Chicago Press, 2000
BEC	Baker Exegetical Commentary
BHGNT	Baylor Handbook on the Greek New Testament
BLXX	Brenton LXX
BNTC	Black's New Testament Commentaries
BrDAG	*The Brill Dictionary of Ancient Greek.* By Franco Montanari. Leiden: Brill, 2015
Brun[1]	Frederick Dale Bruner. *Matthew: A Commentary. Volume 1: The Christbook, Matthew 1–12.* Revised and Expanded Ed. Grand Rapids: Eerdmans, 2004
Brun[2]	Frederick Dale Bruner. *Matthew: A Commentary. Volume 2: The Churchbook, Matthew 13–28.* Revised and expanded ed. Grand Rapids: Eerdmans, 2004
BST	The Bible Speaks Today Commentary
BWIII	Ben Witherington III. *The Letters to Philemon, the Colossians, and the Ephesians: A Socio-Rhetorical Commentary on the Captivity Epistles.* Grand Rapids: Eerdmans, 2007
CGL	*The Cambridge Greek Lexicon.* Edited by J. Diggle. 2 vols. Cambridge: Cambridge University Press, 2021
CMG	*Christology in Mark's Gospel.* Edited by Anthony Le Donne. Grand Rapids: Zondervan, 2021
CSB	Christian Standard Bible
DGNT2	*Devotions on the Greek New Testament.* Edited by Paul N. Jackson. Vol. 2. Grand Rapids, 2017
DJG2	*Dictionary of Jesus and the Gospels.* Edited by Joel B. Green, Jeannine K. Brown, and Nicholas Perrin. 2nd ed. Downers Grove, IL: IVP Academic, 2013
EBC	Expositor's Bible Commentary
ECBC	Eerdmans Classic Biblical Commentaries
EDNT	*Exegetical Dictionary of the New Testament.* Edited by H. Balz and G. Schneider. 3 vols. Grand Rapids: Eerdmans, 1990–1993
EEE	E. Earle Ellis. *1 Corinthians: A Commentary.* Edited by Terry L. Wilder. New York, 2022
EGG	Exegetical Guide to the Greek New Testament
Emmet	C. W. Emmet. *The Fourth Book of Maccabees Commentary.* New York: MacMillan, 1918

GDG	*Going Deeper with New Testament Greek*. By Andreas J. Köstenberger, Benjamin L. Merkle, and Robert L. Plummer. Rev. ed. Nashville: B&H Academic, 2020
GNB	Good News Bible
GrLXX	F. C. Conybeare and St. George Stock. *Grammar of Septuagint Greek*. Boston: Ginn, 1905. Repr., Grand Rapids: Baker Academic, 2010
HCSB	Holman Christian Standard Bible
Hem	Colin Hemer. *The Book of Acts in the Setting of Hellenistic History*. Tübingen: Mohr Siebeck, 1989. Repr., Winona Lake, IN: Eisenbrauns, 1990
Héring	Jean Héring. *The First Epistle of St. Paul to the Corinthians*. Translated from the second French edition by A. W. Heathcote and P. J. Allcock. London: Epworth, 1962
Herm	Hermeneia: Critical and Historical Commentary on the Bible
HH	Harold Hoehner. *Ephesians: An Exegetical Commentary*. Grand Rapids: Baker Academic, 2002
ICC	International Critical Commentary
ICNT	International Commentary on the New Testament
IHR	*Into the Heart of Romans: A Deep Dive into Paul's Greatest Letter*. By N. T. Wright. Grand Rapids: Zondervan Academic, 2023
IL	*An Interpretive Lexicon of New Testament Greek: Analysis of Prepositions, Adverbs, Particles, Relative Pronouns, and Conjunctions*. By G. K. Beale, D. J. Brendsel, and W. A. Ross. Grand Rapids: Zondervan, 2014
ITA	*Introducing the Apocrypha: Message, Context and Significance*. By David deSilva. Grand Rapids: Baker, 2002
JBPhil	J. B. Phillips. *The New Testament in Modern English*
JG-M	Darrell L. Bock. *Jesus the God-Man: The Unity and Diversity of the Gospel Portrayals*. Grand Rapids: Baker Academic, 2016
Keen1–4	Craig Keener. *Acts: An Exegetical Commentary*. 4 vols. Grand Rapids: Baker Academic, 2012–15
Keen1P	Craig Keener. *1 Peter: A Commentary*. Grand Rapids: Baker Academic, 2021
KeenG	Craig Keener. *Galatians: A Commentary*. Grand Rapids: Baker Academic, 2019
KEL	Kregel Exegetical Library
LAGNT	*Linguistic Analysis of the Greek New Testament*. By Stanley E. Porter. Grand Rapids: Baker Academic, 2015

LEB	Lexham English Bible
LES	Lexham English Septuagint, 2nd ed.
L7	Hemer, Colin J. *The Letters to the Seven Churches of Asia in Their Local Setting*. Grand Rapids: Eerdmans, 2001
LetJ	Letter of Jeremiah
LGCa	*Lexham Geographic Commentary on the Gospels*. Edited by Barry J. Beitzel. Bellingham, WA: Lexham, 2018
LGCb	*Lexham Geographic Commentary on Acts through Revelation*. Edited by Barry J. Beitzel. Bellingham, WA: Lexham, 2019
Logos	Logos Bible Software
LSJ	Liddell, H. G., R. Scott, and H. S. Jones. *A Greek-English Lexicon*. 9th ed. with revised supplement. Oxford: Clarendon, 1996
LXX	Septuagint
Mot	J. Alec Motyer. *The Prophecy of Isaiah*. Downers Grove, IL: IVP, 1998
MSG	Eugene Peterson, *The Message*
NCBC	New Cambridge Bible Commentary
NET	New English Translation
NETS	New English Translation of the Septuagint
NGD	Newman Greek Dictionary
NIBC	New International Biblical Commentary
NICNT	New International Commentary on the New Testament
NICOT	New International Commentary on the Old Testament
NIDNTT	*New International Dictionary of New Testament Theology*. Edited by C. Brown. 4 vols. Grand Rapids: Zondervan, 1986
NIGTC	New International Greek Testament Commentary
NIV	New International Version
NRSV	New Revised Standard Version
NRSVUE	New Revised Standard Version, Updated Edition
NTIW	*The New Testament in Its World*. By N. T. Wright and Michael F. Bird. Grand Rapids: Zondervan Academic, 2019
NTWSD	*The Complete Word Study Dictionary: New Testament*. Edited by Spiros Zodhiates. Chattanooga: AMG, 1992
PaG	*Paul and Gender*. By Cynthia Long Westfall. Grand Rapids: Baker Academic, 2016
Pfit	V. C. Pfitzner. *Paul and the Agon Motif*. Supplements to Novum Testamentum 16. Leiden: Brill, 1967
PNTC	Pillar New Testament Commentary

PPE	Stanley E. Porter. *The Pastoral Epistles*. Grand Rapids: Baker Academic, 2023
PrTh	*Prepositions and Theology in the Greek New Testament*. By Murray J. Harris. Grand Rapids: Zondervan, 2012
Pseud.	Pseudepigrapha
PTW	Preaching the Word Commentary
QaR	*Questions and Rhetoric in the Greek New Testament*. By Douglas Estes. Grand Rapids: Zondervan Academic, 2017
RRU	*Revelation for the Rest of Us*. By Scot McKnight. Grand Rapids: Zondervan, 2023
Runge	Steven A. Runge. *Discourse Grammar of the Greek New Testament*. Peabody, MA: Hendrickson, 2010
SacPag	Sacra Pagina
SCS	Septuagint Commentary Series
SeptJob	*Septuagint's Job and the Testament of Job*. Scriptural Research Institute, 2020
SiM	*Studies in Matthew: Interpretation Past and Present*. By Dale C. Allison. Grand Rapids: Baker Academic, 2005
SoM	*The Sermon on the Mount and Human Flourishing*. By Jonathan T. Pennington. Grand Rapids: Baker Academic, 2017
Spicq	Ceslas Spicq. *Theological Lexicon of the New Testament*. Translated and edited by James D. Ernest. 3 vols. Peabody, MA: Hendrickson, 1994
TAB	The Amplified Bible
Tanakh	*The Tanakh: The Holy Scriptures, The New JPS Translation According to the Traditional Hebrew Text*. Philadelphia: Jewish Publication Society, 1985
TDNT	*Theological Dictionary of the New Testament*. Edited by Gerhard Kittel and Gerhard Friedrich. Translated by Geoffrey W. Bromiley. 10 vols. Grand Rapids: Eerdmans, 1964–1976
TFT	*The Septuagint: The First Translation*
Theod	Theodotion Version of the Septuagint
TNTC	Tyndale New Testament Commentary
Vogt	Peter Vogt. *Interpreting the Pentateuch*. Handbooks for Old Testament Exegesis. Grand Rapids: Kregel Academic, 2009
Wall	Daniel Wallace. *Greek Grammar Beyond the Basics*. Grand Rapids: Zondervan, 1996
Waltke	Bruce Waltke, with Cathi J. Fredericks. *Genesis*. Grand Rapids: Zondervan, 2001

WBC	Word Biblical Commentary
Wire	Antoinette Clark Wire. *The Corinthian Women Prophets.* Minneapolis: Fortress, 1991
WLC	*A Week in the Life of Corinth.* By Ben Witherington III. Downers Grove, IL: IVP, 2012
WPNT	*Word Pictures in the New Testament.* By A. T. Robertson. 6 vols. Nashville: Broadman, 1930–1933
ZEC	Zondervan Exegetical Commentary

Ancient Sources

Abbreviations for biblical books and the Old Testament Apocrypha or deuterocanonical works follow those found in *The SBL Handbook of Style*, 2nd ed. (Atlanta: SBL Press, 2014), 124–25.

Ael.	**Aelian**, *sophist, 2nd–3rd c. CE*
	N.A. *De natura animalium*
	V.H. *Varia historia*
Aeschl.	**Aeschylus**, *6th–5th c. BCE*
	Ag. *Agamemnon*
	Ch. *Choephori*
	Eum. *Eumenides*
	Pers. *Persae*
	Pr. *Prometheus vinctus*
	Sept. *Septem contra Thebas*
	Suppl. *Supplices*
Alc.	**Alceus**, *lyric poet, 7th–6th c. BCE*
Alexis	*4th–3rd c. BCE*
Amips.	**Amipsias**, *5th–4th c. BCE*
An.	**Anonymous**
	Par. *Parisinus de morbis acutis et chronicis*
Andoc.	**Andocides**
	Alc. *Against Alcibiades*
Antipho.	**Antiphon**, *5th c. BCE*
Ap.	**Apollonius Rhodius**, *3rd c. BCE*
Ap. Dys.	**Apollonius Dyscolus**, *2nd c. CE*
	Pron. *De pronominibus*
Archim.	**Archimedes**, *mathematician, 3rd c. BCE*

	Spir. *De spiralibus lineis*
Aristoph.	**Aristophanes**, *5th–4th c. BCE*
	Ach. *Acharnenses*
	Av. *Aves*
	Ec. *Ecclesiazusae*
	Eq. *Equites*
	fr. fragment in *Poetae comici Graeci* 3.2.
	Nub. *Nubes*
	Pax *Pax*
	Pl. *Plutus*
	Ran. *Ranae*
	Th. *Thesmophoriazusae*
	Ve. *Vespae*
Aristot.	**Aristotle**
	An. *De Anima*
	Cael. *De caelo*
	E.E. *Ethica Eudemia*
	E.N. *Ethica Nichomachea*
	fr. *fragmenta*
	Gen. an. *De generatione animalium*
	H.A. *Historia animalium*
	Mem. *De Memoria*
	Metaph. *Metaphysica*
	Meteor. *Meteorologica*
	Mir. *Mirabilia*
	Mund. *On the Cosmos*
	Phys. *Physica*
	Pol. *Politico*
	Pr. *Problemata*
	Rh. *Rhetorica*
	Top. *Topica*
Bacchy.	**Bacchylides**, *5th c. BCE*
	Epin. Epinicia
Callim.	**Callimicus**
	H. *Hymns*
[Callisth.]	**Pseudo-Callisthenes**, *3rd c. BCE*
Chrysip.	***Chrysippus***, *Stoic philosopher, 3rd c. BCE*
Clem. Al.	**Clement of Alexandria**
	Quis. div. *"Who Is the Rich Man Who Will Be Saved?"*

Com.	**Comic Writers**
Dem.	**Demosthenes**
Diod. Sic.	**Diodorus Siculus**
	Bib. Hist. *Bibliotheca Historica*
Dion.	**Dionysius of Halicarnassus**
	Lys. *De Lysia*
	Rom. Ant. *Roman Antiquities*
Diph.	**Diphilus**, *4th–3rd c. BCE*
Epichar.	**Epicharmus**, *5th c. CE*
Epict.	**Epictetus**
	Diatr. *Diatribai*
	Ench. *Enchiridion*
Epiph.	**Epiphanius of Cyprian**, *bishop, 4th–5th c. CE*
	Anc. *Ancoratus*
	Haer. *Panarion* or *Adversus*
Eucl.	**Euclid of Alexandria**
	El. *Elements*
Eup.	**Euphorion**, *3rd c. BCE*
Eur.	**Euripides**, *5th c. BCE*
	Alc. *Alcestis*
	Andr. *Andromacha*
	Bac. *Bacchanals*
	Hec. *Hecuba*
	Hel. *Helena*
	H.F. *Hercules furens/Madness of Heracles*
	Ion *Ion*
	I.T. *Iphigeneia at Tauris*
	Med. *Medea*
	Or. *Orestes*
	Ph. *Phoenissae*
	Tr. *Troades/Daughters of Troy*
Eus.	**Eusebius of Caesarea**, *church father and historian, 3rd–4th CE*
	Hist. eccl. *Historia ecclesiastica*
Gal.	**Galen**, *medical writer, 2nd c. CE*
	U.P. *De usu partium*
Gem.	**Geminus**, *1st c. BCE*
Greg.	**Gregory of Nazianzus**, *the theologian, church father, 4th c. CE*
	Or. *Orationes*
Hdt.	**Herodotus**

	Hist. *Histories*
Hero	**Hero**
	Diop. *Dioptra*
Hes.	**Hesiodus**, *8th–7th c. BCE*
	Sc. *Scutum*
	Th. *Theogonia*
Hippar.	**Hipparchus**, *astronomer, 2nd c. BCE*
Hippol.	**Hippolytus**
	Haer. *Refutatio omnium haeresium*
Hom.	**Homer and Homeric poetry**
	Il. *Illiad*
	Od. *Odyssey*
Hp.	**Hippocrates**, *physician, 5th c. BCE*
	Aër. *De aere, aquis et locis*
	Aph. *Aphorismi*
	Arte *Arte*
	De off. *De Officiis*
	Fist. *De fistulis*
	Fract. *De fracturis*
	Morb. *De morbis*
	Mochl. *Mochlicum*
	Nat. Mul. *De natura muliebri*
	Prorrh. *Praedicta* 1–2
Iambl.	**Iamblichus**, *novelist, 2nd c. CE*
	Myst. *De mysteriis*
Is.	**Isaeus**
Isocr.	**Isocrates**
	Archid. *Archidamus*
	Paneg. *Panegyricus*
Jos.	**Flavius Josephus**, *Jewish historian, 1st c. CE*
	A.J. *Antiquitates judaicae*
	B.I. *Bellum judaicum*
Leon.	**Leonidas of Tarentum**, *3rd c. BCE*
Luc.	**Lucianus**, *sophist, 2nd c. CE*
	Alex. *Alexander*
	Lex. *Lexipanes*
	Philopatr. *Philopatris*
Lys.	**Lysias**
	Sp. *Speeches*

Machon	**Machon**, *3rd c. BCE*
	Chr. *Chreia*
MAur.	**Marcus Aurelius Imperator**, *2nd c. CE*
Men.	**Menander**, *4th–3rd c. BCE*
	fr. *fabularum certarum*
	Gn. *Maxims*
	Perin. *Perinthia*
	Sam. *Samia*
Mnesim.	**Mnesimachus,** *4th c. BCE*
Orib.	**Oribasius**
Orph.	**Orphic Poetry**
	H. *Hymni*
	L. *Lithica*
Pall.	**Palladius**, *bishop of Helenopolis, 4th–5th c. CE*
	L. *Historia Lausiaca*
Paus.	**Pausanias**, *2nd c. CE*
Philo	**Philo of Alexandria**
	Mut. Nom. *De Mutatione Nominum*
	Spec. *De specialibus legibus*
Pind.	**Pindar**, *lyric poet, 6th–5th c. BCE*
	O. *Olympica*
Plato	**Plato**, *5th–4th c. BCE*
	Am. *Amatores*
	Ax. *Axiochus*
	Crat. *Cratylus*
	Def. *Definitiones*
	Epist. *Epistulae*
	Euthyd. *Euthydemus*
	Gorg. *Gorgias*
	H. *Hymni*
	Lach. *Laches*
	Leg. *Leges*
	Men. *Meno*
	Menex. *Menexenus*
	Phaed. *Phaedrus*
	Pol. *Politicus*
	Prot. *Protagoras*
	Rp. *Res publica*
	Soph. *Sophista*

	Symp. *Symposium*
	Theaet. *Theaetetus*
Plut.	**Plutarchus**
	Alex. fort. *De Alexandri Magni fortuna aut virtute*
	Amat. *Amatorius*
	An Seni *An seni respublica gerenda*
	CMi. *Cato minor*
	Cr. *Crassus*
	Fort. Rom. *De fortuna Romanorum*
	Frig. *De primo frigido*
	Garr. *De garrulitate*
	Isid. *De Iside et Osiride*
	Mor. *Moralia*
	Nic. *Nicias*
	Praec. *Praecepta gerendae reipublicae*
	QCon. *Quaestiones convivales*
	Sollert. *De sollertia animalium*
	Symp. *Septem sapientium convivium*
Polyb.	**Polybius**
	Hist. *Histories*
Procl.	**Proclus**
	Hyp. *Hypothesis*
Pseud.	**Old Testament Pseudepigrapha**
	1 En. *1 Enoch*
	2 En. *2 Enoch*
	4 Ezra *4 Ezra*
	Ezek. Trag. *Ezekiel the Tragedian*
	Let. Aris. *Letter of Aristeas*
	Pss. Sol. *Psalms of Solomon*
Soph.	**Sophocles**
	Ai. *Ajax*
	Ant. *Antigona*
	El. *Elektra*
	fr. *Tragicorum Graecorum Fragmenta*
	Ichn. *Ichneutae*
	O.C. *Oedipus coloneus*
	Ph. *Philoctetes*
Sotad.	**Sotades**, *scurrilous humorist and poet, 3rd c. BCE*
Strabo	**Strabo**

	Geogr. *Geographi Graeci Minores*
	Hist. *Historia*
Theocr.	**Theocritus**
Thphr.	**Theophrastus**, *4th–3rd c. BCE*
	C.P. *De causis plantarum*
	H.P. *Historia plantarum*
Thuc.	**Thucydides**, *5th–4th c. BCE*
Xen.	**Xenophon**
	An. *Anabasis*
	Cyr. *Institutio Cyri*
	Hel. *Historia Graeca*
	Hier. *Hiero*
	Hip. *De re equestri*
	Lac. *De republica Lacedaemoniorum*
	Mem. *Memorabilia*
	Oec. *Oeconomicus*
	Symp. *Symposium*
Zeux.	**Zeuxis**, *elegiac poet, 5th c. BCE*

Lexicon User Guide

Refer to this guide for instructions and illustrations for the many features that are included throughout the lexicon. Through regular use, you should quickly gain greater facility in the total functionality of these features.

Basic Noun Features

Entry and definition are in bold. Each noun's declension (specific pattern) is subscripted, whether first, second, or third. First-declension patterns are threefold, tagged as 1α, 1η or 1> (alpha, eta, or eta-shift pattern). For example, **ἁμαρτία, ας, ἡ**$_{1\alpha}$ is a first-declension, feminine, alpha-pattern noun, meaning the α is found in each ending. The noun **ἀγωγή, ῆς, ἡ**$_{1\eta}$ is a first-declension, feminine, eta-pattern noun, meaning the η is found in each ending. The noun **ᾅδης, ου, ὁ**$_{1>}$ is a first-declension, masculine, eta-shift pattern noun, meaning that the α or the η in the nominative case shifts to ου in the genitive case, then shifts back to the α or the η through the remaining cases.

Second- and third-declension nouns are indicated by a subscripted 2 or 3, with no further clues to their patterns except the inclusion of the genitive ending. Some third-declension nouns like **θρίξ, τρίχος, ἡ**$_{3}$, whose genitive form presents a morphological change difficult to detect in the biblical text, is listed with full nominative and genitive forms.

ἀγωγή, ῆς, ἡ$_{1\eta}$ ①^{dfs} {ἄγω} 2 Tim 3:10, **way of life**, **conduct**; ❻ LXX, Esth 2:20

λίθος, ου, ὁ$_{2}$ (59x; 14x Luke, 11x Matt) Matt 4:3 = Luke 4:3; Mark 5:5, John 8:7; Acts 4:11; Rev 4:3, **stone**; Rev 17:4, **jewel**; (292x LXX; 29x Exod, 22x Josh)

ψῦχος, ους, τό$_{3}$ ❸ {ψύχομαι} John 18:18; Acts 28:2; 2 Cor 11:27, **cold**; ❽ LXX, 2x Dan

θρίξ, τρίχος, ἡ$_{3}$ (15x) Matt 3:4 = Mark 1:6, *camel* **hair**; Matt 10:30 = Luke 12:7; John 11:2; Rev 1:14, **hair**; (45x LXX; 16x Lev → *hair rules*)

Rare second-declension feminine nouns follow the pattern of second-declension masculine nouns. Some elementary Greek grammars use **ὁδός, οῦ, ἡ**$_2$ as the paradigm noun for this peculiarity (e.g., *BBG*). Nouns following this pattern are thus tagged as **Αἴγυπτος, ου, ἡ**$_{2ὁδός}$.

Αἴγυπτος, ου, ἡ$_{2ὁδός}$ (25x, 15x Acts) Matt 2:13; Acts 2:10; Acts 7 (11x, *Stephen's speech*); 13:17; Heb 3:16; 11:26; Jude 5; Rev 11:8, **Egypt**; (633x LXX; 130x MajPr, 114x Exod)

Number of Occurrences

Each entry includes the number of NT occurrences as well as the number of LXX occurrences. Hapax legomena (those terms occurring only once in the NT or in the LXX) are identified by a black 1 within a clear circle along with its contextual parsing tag in a superscript. Words occurring two to nine times are indicated using white numbers within a black circle. Frequencies greater than nine are in parentheses. If there is no reference to the LXX, the term does not occur there.

ἄγγος, ους, τό$_3$ ①^{anp} Matt 13:48, **container**; ❻ LXX, 1 Kgs 17:10, **cup**

ἀγωγή, ῆς, ἡ$_{1η}$ ①^{dfs} {ἄγω} 2 Tim 3:10, **way of life**, **conduct**; ❻ LXX, Esth 2:20

ὑπομονή, ῆς, ἡ$_{1η}$ (32x, 7x Rev) {ὑπό + μένω} Luke 8:15, *with* **patient endurance**; Rom 2:7–15:5,^{6x} 2 Cor 1:6; Rev 1:9–14:12,^{7x} **steadfast endurance**; (25x LXX; 11x 4 Macc^{scs})

Contextually Controlled Meanings

Any Greek term can have multiple, contextually controlled meanings. This is especially true with prepositions. The various possible meanings are subdivided by black-circled letters (Ⓐ Ⓑ Ⓒ Ⓓ Ⓔ, etc.), each followed by a category description. If the categories are all derived from the same source, as with **ἀδελφή** below, that source will be superscripted along with an arrow signifying total inclusion (i.e., all the categories for **ἀδελφή** are derived from *NIDNTT*).

ἀπό, ἀπ', ἀφ' *prep* w/ gen. (646x, 239x LA) Ⓐ ***positional, source***; 1 Thess 1:2, **from** *God*; Ⓑ ***temporal***; 2 Cor 8:10, **since** *the creation*; Ⓒ ***figurative***; Matt 7:16, **by** *their fruits*; Acts 22:11, **because of** *the brightness*; (3,890x LXX, 910x Pent)

ἀδελφή, ῆς, ἡ$_{1η}$ (26x; 7x Matt, 6x Rev) {ἀδελφός} *NIDNTT*→ Ⓐ (8x), Matt 12:50, **spiritual sister**; Ⓑ (17x), Matt 13:56, **blood sister**; Ⓒ Mark 3:32, 35, *contrast of spiritual and blood sisters*; Ⓓ 1 Cor 9:5, **wife** (*who is a believer*) (1x) (109x LXX; 25x Gen, 20x Ezek), **sister**

Adjectival Patterns

Adjectives are listed with their respective declension patterns as subscripts. While all three genders have different forms for adjectives like **ἁγνός, ή, όν**$_{2.1.2}$ and **εἷς, μία, ἕν**$_{3.1.3}$, the masculine and feminine forms are identical for adjectives like **ἄγναφος, ον**$_{2.2}$ and **ἀκλινής, ές**$_{3.3}$.

ἁγνός, ή, όν$_{2.1.2}$ {ἅγος} *adj.* ❽ 2 Cor 7:11, **innocent**[BEC]; Phil 4:8; Titus 2:5; 1 John 3:3, **pure**; (13x LXX; 4x Prov) Lev 23:40, **goodly** *fruit of trees* (BrLXX); Prov 15:26, **pure**

εἷς, μία, ἕν$_{3.1.3}$ (345x) Ⓐ ***noun*: *one, single person or thing***; 1 John 5:8, **agreement** (*are one*); Ⓑ ***adjective*: *single unit or thing***; Matt 5:18, *a* **single** *iota* (*the smallest Greek letter*); Eph 4:5, **εἷς** κύριος, **μία** πίστις, **ἕν** βάπτισμα, **one** *Lord*, **one** *faith*, **one** *baptism*; Ⓒ ***noun*: *initial day of a block of time***; Acts 20:7, **first day**; (305x LXX; 43x Ezek, 31x Num, 26x 1 Kgs)

ἄγναφος, ον$_{2.2}$ {α + γναφεύς} *adj.* ❷ Matt 9:16 = Mark 2:21, **unshrunk** *wine skins*

ἀκλινής, ές$_{3.3}$ {α + κλίνω} *adj.* ①[afs] Heb 10:23, *adv. usage*, **unswervingly, not leaning**[WPNT]; ❷ LXX, 4 Macc 6:7, **firm**; 17:3, **unswervingly** *against the earthquake of tortures*[SCS]; *math.*, Plato *Phaed.* 109a, **fixed**[BrDAG]; *geom.*, Procl., **perpendicular**[BrDAG]

Contract Verbs and Grouped Occurrences

Contract verbs like **ἀγανακτέω** (verbs whose connecting vowels are α, ε, or ο) are superscripted with [con]. Within the GNT, these kinds of verbs are not found in their lexical, uncontracted forms.

Multiple occurrences in a document, genre, or section are referred to in parentheses immediately following the number of total occurrences. For instance, ❼ (Syn) means all seven instances of this verb appear in the Synoptic Gospels. If the meaning of the word is different in the LXX from what appears in the GNT, then that translation is included. When these differences are significant, a reference is included for elaboration.

ἀγανακτέω^{con} ❼ (Syn) {ἄγαν} Matt 20:24 = Mark 10:41; Mark 14:4, **to be angry**; ❸ LXX, 4 Macc 4:21; Wis 5:22, 12:27

Sometimes terms are concentrated in one genre (Synoptic Gospels), subgenre (parables), or metaphor/symbol (vineyard, fruit of the vine). In the case of ἀμπελών, 22 of the 23 occurrences appear in Synoptic parables. Beyond the Synoptics, only Paul uses it.

ἀμπελών, ῶνος, ὁ$_3$ (23x, 22x Syn) {ἄμπελος} *22x in Syn. parables*; *1x in Pauline illust.*; Matt 21:33 = Mark 12:1, 2 = Luke 20:9, 10; 1 Cor 9:7, **vineyard**; (97x LXX; 15x Isa, 10x 1 Kgs)

Sometimes verbs have peculiar grammatical constructions in the GNT, as with the aorist middle imperative of **ἀσπάζομαι**.

ἀσπάζομαι (59x; 40x Paul, 35x *aor. mid. imp.*) Matt 5:47; Mark 9:15; Rom 16:13–20;^{21x} 1 Cor 16:19; 3 John 15, **to greet**; Mark 15:18, **to address**; (10x LXX) Exod 18:7, **to embrace**

Terms Occurring 1–4 Times ① ❷ ❸ ❹

Every reference is included for NT terms occurring 1–4 times.

ἄγκυρα, ας, ἡ$_{1\alpha}$ ❹ Acts 27:29, 30, 40, *lit.*, **anchor**; Heb 6.19, *fig.*, **security**

Verbal Parallels

An equal sign within the Scripture references signifies a verbal parallel. These are most frequent amid Gospel references but also appear within Pauline texts (esp. Colossians and Ephesians) and elsewhere.

ἀγανακτέω^{con} ❼ (Syn) {ἄγαν} Matt 20:24 = Mark 10:41; Mark 14:4, **to be angry**; ❸ LXX, 4 Macc 4:21; Wis 5:22, 12:27

ἀνθρωπάρεσκος, ον$_{2.2}$ ❷ {ἄνθρωπος + ἀρέσκω} Eph 6:6 = Col 3:22, **people-pleasers**; ❺ LXX, Ps 52:6 (53:5) **men-pleasers**

ἀποδίδωμι (48x, 18x Matt) Matt 5:26 = Luke 12:59, **to repay**; Matt 5:33, **to keep**; 2 Tim 4:8, **to reward**; Heb 13:17, *bus. idiom*, **to give an accounting**; Rom 13:7, **to pay**; Luke 9:42, **to give back**; Acts 5:8, **to sell**; (Rom 12:17 = 1 Thess 5:15 = 1 Pet 3:9), **to return** *evil for evil*; Rev 22:2, **to yield**; 2 Tim 4:14, **to punish**; (206x LXX, 75x Pent)

Greyscale and Corresponding Roots

Greyscale is used to highlight compound words. This is helpful for pronunciation, memorization, and in some guarded cases, translation. But be careful how you assess the bare roots.*

ἀγαθοποιΐα, ας, ἡ$_{1\alpha}$ ①[dfs] {ἀγαθός + ποιέω} 1 Pet 4:19, **by doing good**[EGG]

Roots are identified in braces if the combined lexical form is altered in any way. If roots in braces are not present, it is because no alteration has occurred with the lexical form. This pattern occurs frequently in prepositionally prefixed verbs like the two listed below.

ἀποβαίνω ❹ Luke 5:2; John 21:9, **to disembark**; Luke 21:13, **to lead out**; Phil 1:19, **to lead to** *Paul's ultimate salvation*; (20x LXX, 15x Job) Job 9:20, **to prove**; 11:6, **to overlook**

ἀποβάλλω ❷ Mark 10:50, **he threw off** *his coat*; Heb 10:35, *don't* **throw away** *your confidence*; ❺ LXX, Deut 26:5, **to abandon**; Prov 28:24, **to rob**

Greco-Roman Citations and Further Study Resources

Sometimes Greco-Roman sources can shed light on a biblical term's usage, as we see with Plato's mathematical application of ἀκλινής. This is especially helpful if the biblical term is a hapax legomenon. The influence can also extend through the biblical occurrences (NT and LXX) and resurface in a post-NT occurrence, as below with Proclus, a Neoplatonist philosopher in the fifth century CE. In this case the Greco-Roman sources chronologically "sandwich" the biblical reference.

* For a discussion of the dangers of translation based on roots, see D. A. Carson, *Exegetical Fallacies*, 2nd ed. (Grand Rapids: Baker, 1996), 27–33.

ἀκλινής, ές$_{3.3}$ ①[afs] {α + κλίνω} *spir.*, Heb 10:23, *adv.*, **unswervingly, not leaning**[WPNT]; ❷ LXX, 4 Macc 6:7, **firm**; 17:3, **unswervingly** *against the earthquake of tortures*[SCS]; *math.*, Plato *Phaed* 109a, **fixed**;[BrDAG] *geom.*, Procl., **perpendicular**[BrDAG]

On occasion, Greco-Roman sources can demonstrate influence from a biblical author's "new term" (neologism). A key is provided so the reader can access unabbreviated resources. The resource highlighted here is Epiphanius's post-NT work *Ancoratus.*

ἀλλοτριεπίσκοπος, ου, ὁ$_2$ ①[nms] {ἄλλος + ἐπί + σκοπός} *neol.* 1 Pet 4:15, **troublemaker**[Keen1P!]; Epiph. *Anc.* 12.5, **snoopy busybody**[BrDAG]; Epict. *Diatr.* 3.22.97, **self-appointed censor of another's morality**[Herm.BEC.296-7]

Superscripted references are regularly provided throughout the lexicon for further study, elaboration, or clarification on various provided translations, especially when existing biblical translations are decidedly ambiguous or, in some rare cases, unsupportable by the latest research. These resources are mostly commentary series (e.g., BEC), other lexica (e.g., *BrDAG, CGL*), or an author's monograph (e.g., Keen1P). This feature provides many windows for further study. An exclamation point will follow the reference if the explanation is especially pertinent (e.g., Keen1P!).

Parsing Tags

All hapax legomena forms appear with a superscripted parsing tag. The contextual form can be found at the provided citation in the Greek New Testament.

πιέζω ①[pfmp.ans] Luke 6:38, **to press down**; ①[fai2s] LXX, Mic 6:15, **to tread** *grapes*; Hom. *Il.* 16.510, **to constrict** *a part of the body*

If a parsing is affixed to any other circled number, then the parsing is the same for each occurrence.

κοπάζω ❸[aai3s] {κόπτω} **ἐκόπασεν** ὁ ἄνεμος, Matt 14:32 = Mark 6:51; Mark 4:39, *the wind* **ceased**; (26x LXX, 4x Gen) Gen 8:1

The appearance of partitioned occurrences reveals some important peculiarities beyond the total word count; e.g., six of the seven NT occurrences of **περιβλέπω** appear in Mark, and of those six, five appear as aorist middle participles.

> περιβλέπω ❼ (6x Mark) (5x, **περιβλεψάμενος**[amp.nms]); Mark 3:34, 5:32, 9:8, 10:23; Luke 6:10 = Mark 3:5, **to look around**; ❾ LXX, 1 Kgs 21:40 (20:40), **was busy** (HCSB)

Parsing tags for nouns and adjectives are ordered as case-gender-number. So, for example, **ἀγκάλας** is an accusative-feminine-plural form found in Luke 2:28.

> **ἀγκάλη, ης, ἡ**$_{1\eta}$ ①[afp] Luke 2:28, **arms**; ❸ LXX, 1 Kgs 3:20, **embrace**

Parsing tags for verbs, participles, and infinitives are superscripted and follow an easily adaptable scheme for quick assessment. The order for verbs is tense-voice-mood-person-number. So, for example, **ἐκόπασεν** is tagged as "aorist-active-indicative-third person-singular." Tags for participles are ordered "tense-voice-participle-case-gender-number." So, for example, **πεπιεσμένον** is "perfect-middle-participle-accusative-neuter-singular."

> **πιέζω** ①[pfmp.ans] **πεπιεσμένον**

> **κοπάζω** ❸[aai3s] **ἐκόπασεν**

Difficult Forms

One of the most helpful and time-saving features of *ZCGL* is the identification and parsing of numerous difficult verbal forms in the GNT. These forms are followed by an → pointing toward the elusive lexical form, along with the reference and a translation. Once encountered, these can be committed to memory for future ease in reading the GNT.

> **οἴσει → φέρω,** *fut. act. ind. 3s,* John 21:18, *someone* **will carry**

> **στάς → ἵστημι,** *aor. act. ptc. nms,* Matt 20:32, **stopped**

A, α [*alpha*]

Α, α, τό (ἄλφα) *indecl.* **alpha**, *1st letter of the Gr. alphabet*; Rev 22:13, ἐγώ **τὸ ἄλφα** καὶ τὸ ὦ: *I am the* **Alpha** *and the Omega* ‖ *num.* α′ = 1; ͵α = 1,000

Ἀαρών, ὁ₃ *indecl.* ❺ Luke 1:5; Acts 7:40; Heb 5:4; 9:4, **Aaron**; (369x LXX; 119x Exod)

Ἀβαδδών, ὁ₃ *indecl.* ①[nms] Rev 9:11, **Abaddon**; *Heb.* **destruction**[NIGTC]

ἀβαρής, ές₃.₃ {ἀ + βάρος} *adj.* ①[ams] 2 Cor 11:9, **weightless**; *fig.*, **not burdensome**

ἀββά ❸ *Aram.* Mark 14:36; Rom 8:15; Gal 4:6; **father**; ① LXX, 2 Chr 29:1, **Abijah**

Ἅβελ, ὁ₃ *indecl.* ❹ Matt 23:35 = Luke 11:51; Heb 11:4; 12:24, **Abel**; (14x LXX; 8x Gen 4)

Ἀβιά, ὁ₃ *indecl.* ❸ Matt 1:7,[2x] **Abijah**; Luke 1:4, *priestly division of* **Abijah**; (24x LXX)

Ἀβιαθάρ, ὁ₃ *indecl.* ①[gms] Mark 2:26, **Abiathar**; (29x LXX; 16x 1–2 Sam, 9x 1 Kgs)

Ἀβιληνή, ῆς, ἡ₁η ①[gfs] Luke 3:1, **Abilene**

Ἀβιούδ, ὁ₃ *indecl.* ❷ Matt 1:13,[2x] **Abiud**; (13x LXX; 4x Exod) Exod 6:23; Lev 10:1

Ἀβραάμ, ὁ₃ *indecl.* (73x; 15x Luke) Luke 3:34; Heb 7,[6x] **Abraham**; (210x LXX; 140x Gen)

ἄβυσσος, ου, ἡ₂ὁδός {βυθίζω} ❾ (7x Rev) Luke 8:31; Rom 10:7; Rev 9:1; 20:3, **abyss**; **place of the dead, without depth, underworld**; (49x LXX) Gen 1:2; 8:2, **watery depths**

Ἅγαβος, ου, ὁ₂ ❷ Acts 11:28; 21:10, **Agabus**, *a Christian prophet* [ZEC]

ἀγαθοεργέω[con] {ἀγαθός + ἔργον} ❷ Acts 14:17, **to confer benefits**[ZEC]; 1 Tim 6:18, **to do good**

ἀγαθοποιέω[con] {ἀγαθός + ποιέω} ❾ Luke 6:9, **to do good** *or to do evil*; 1 Pet 2:15, **to do good**; 3 John 11, *subst.*, *the one who does* **good**; ❺ LXX, Num 10:32; Zeph 1:12

ἀγαθοποιΐα, ας, ἡ₁α {ἀγαθός + ποιέω} ①[dfs] 1 Pet 4:19, **by doing good**[EGG]

ἀγαθοποιός, όν₂.₂ {ἀγαθός + ποιέω} *adj.* ①[gms] 1 Pet 2:14; *subst.*, **a well-doer**; ①[nfs] LXX, Sir 42:14

ἀγαθός, ή, όν₂.₁.₂ *adj.* (102x; 21x Rom) Luke 6:45[3x]; Rom 2:7, **good**; Matt 12:34; Luke 12:19, **good things**; Matt 20:15, **generous**; Eph 2:10, **good work**; (612x LXX; 81x Prov, 77x Sir)

ἀγαθωσύνη, ης, ἡ₁η {ἀγαθός} ❹ Rom 15:14; Gal 5:22; Eph 5:9; 2 Thess 1:11, **goodness**; (14x LXX; 11x Eccl, 3x Neh) Neh 9:25, Eccl 4:8, **pleasure**

ἀγαλλίασις, εως, ἡ₃ {αγαλλιάομαι} ❺ Luke 1:14, **exultation**[ZEC]; Luke 1:44; Heb 1:9, **joy**; Acts 2:46, **glad**[ZEC]; Jude 24, **great joy**; (20x LXX; 17x Pss) Ps 29:6 (30:5), **joy**

ἀγαλλιάω[con] {αγαλλιάομαι} (11x; 8x *mid. voice*) Matt 5:12, **to be glad**; Luke 1:47; John 5:35; 1 Pet 1:6; Rev 19:7, **to rejoice**

ἄγαμος, ου, ἡ₂ὁδός {γαμέω} ❹ 1 Cor 7:8, 11, 32, 34, *all refer to the* **unmarried**; *however*, 7:11, **divorced** (*also*)[NIGTC]; ①[nmp] LXX, 4 Macc 16:9, *some* **unmarried**

ἀγανακτέω[con] {ἄγαν} ❼ (Syn) Matt 20:24 = Mark 10:41; Mark 14:4, **to be angry**; ❸ LXX, 4 Macc 4:21; Wis 5:22; 12:27

ἀγανάκτησις, εως, ἡ₃ {ἄγαν} ①[afs] 2 Cor 7:11, **indignation**[BEC]; Plato *Phaed.* 251c, **irritation, pain** *from teething*; Thuc. 2.41.3, **indignation**

ἀγαπάω[con] {ἀγάπη} (143x; 37x John, 28x 1 John) John 3:16; 21:15–20,[3x] **to love**; Eph 5:2, *Christ* **loved** *us*; 5:25–33,[6x] *mutual* **love**; 1 John 4:7–21,[15x] **loving** *one another*; Rev 20:9, *the* **beloved** *city*; (271x LXX; 44x Pss, 27x Deut, 14x Hos) 2 Sam 13:4, *the "love" that led to incestuous rape*, 13:15; Job 19:19, **ἠγαπήκειν,**^{plpfai1s} *friends* **I have loved**; Hos 3:1^{3x}

ἀγάπη, ης, ἡ$_{1η}$ (116x; 23x 1–2 Cor, 18x 1 John) Matt 24:12; Rom 5:5, **love**; 1 Cor 13,^{9x} *Paul's love chapter*; 1 John 2:5–5:3,^{18x} *John's love letter*; Jude 12, **love** *feast*; (19x LXX, 11x Song)

ἀγαπητός, ή, όν$_{2.1.2}$ *adj.* (61x; 7x Rom, 6x 2 Pet, 1 John) Matt 3:17 = Mark 1:11 = Luke 3:22, *my* **beloved** *Son*; Rom 16:5–12, *Paul greets many* **dear friends**; 1 Cor 4:14, **dear** *children*; 4:17, **dearly loved**, *Timothy*; (24x LXX; 7x Pss) Gen 22:2, 12, 16, *your* **beloved** *son*

Ἁγάρ, ἡ$_{3}$ *indecl.* ❷ Gal 4:24, 25, **Hagar**; (14x LXX; 13x Gen, 1x Bar 3:23)

ἀγγαρεύω ❸ *Roman milit.*, Matt 5:41, **to force one** *into service*; Matt 27:32 = Mark 15:21, **to force one** *to assume a heavy burden* (*carrying Jesus's cross*)

ἀγγεῖον, ου, τό$_{2}$ {ἄγγος} ①^{dnp} Matt 25:4, **container**; (24x LXX, 8x Jer) 1 Sam 25:18, *two* **skins** *of wine*

ἀγγελία, ας, ἡ$_{1α}$ ❷ {ἄγγελος} 1 John 1:5; 3:11, **message**; (13x LXX) Nah 3:19, **news**

ἀγγέλλω ①$^{pap.nfs}$ John 20:18, **to announce**; Plato *Phaed.* 242b, *not* **announcing** *war*

ἄγγελος, ου, ὁ$_{2}$ (175x; 67x Rev), Matt 1:20, *the*$^{Wall\ 252}$ **angel** *of the Lord* (4x, only in Matt) ^{ZEC}; Acts 12:7–11^{5x}; Heb 1:4, **angel**; Mark 1:2, **messenger**; 1 Cor 13:1, **angelic**; 2 Cor 11:14, *Satan*, **an angel** *of light*; 12:7, **messenger** *from Satan*; Rev 2:1–3:14, *formula*: τῷ **ἀγγέλῳ,**^{7x} *to* **the angel** . . .; (294x LXX; 54x **angel** *of the Lord*)

ἄγγος, ους, τό$_{3}$ ①^{anp} Matt 13:48, **container**; ❻ LXX, 1 Kgs 17:10, **cup**; Amos 8:1, 2, **basket**

ἀγέλη, ης, ἡ$_{1η}$ ❼ (Syn) Matt 8:30 = Mark 5:11 = Luke 8:32, **herd** *of pigs*; (10x LXX; 5x Song)

ἀγενεαλόγητος, ον$_{2.2}$ {α + γεννάω + λέγω} *adj.* ①^{nms} Heb 7:3, **without genealogy**

ἀγενής, ές$_{3.3}$ {α + γεννάω} *adj.* ①^{anp} *subst.* 1 Cor 1:28, **the insignificant**^{NIGTC}; Soph. *fr.* 84, **of low birth, ignoble**; Plato *Tim.* 27c, **unborn, uncreated**; Is., **childless**

ἁγιάζω {ἅγος} (28x; 7x Heb) Matt 6:9 = Luke 11:2, **may** *your name* **be kept sacred**^{ZEC}; 2 Tim 2:21, **to set apart**; Heb 2:11,^{2x} **to sanctify**; Rev 22:11, **to be holy**; (192x LXX)

ἁγιασμός, οῦ, ὁ$_{2}$ {ἅγος} (10x) Rom 6:19, 22; 1 Cor 1:30; 1 Thess 4:4, **sanctification**; ❾ LXX, Judg 17:3, **to consecrate**; Amos 2:11, **for consecration** (Heb. *to be Nazarites*)

ἅγιος, ία, ον$_{2.1.2}$ {ἅγος} *adj.* (233x; 53x Acts, 25x Rev) **holy**; (197x, ἅγιος + πνεῦμα; 83x Acts, 28x Luke) **Holy Spirit**; (792x LXX; 123x Lev, 84x Ezek, 66x Exod:Isa) Isa 57:15, ἅγιος ἐν ἁγίοις, **holy** *among the* **holy** *places*; Jer 4:11, **wind**; Dan 5:12, *an extraordinary* **spirit**

ἁγιότης, ητος, ἡ$_{3}$ {ἅγος} ①^{gfs} Heb 12:10, **holiness**; ①^{gfs} LXX, 2 Macc 15:2, **μεθ' ἁγιότητος**, **hallowed** *above other days*

ἁγιωσύνη, ης, ἡ$_{1η}$ {ἅγος} ❸ Rom 1:4; 2 Cor 7:1; 1 Thess 3:13, **holiness**; ❺ LXX

ἀγκάλη, ης, ἡ$_{1η}$ ①^{afp} Luke 2:28, **arms**; ❸ LXX, 1 Kgs 3:20, **embrace**

ἄγκιστρον, ου, τό$_{2}$ {ἄγκυρα} ①^{ans} Matt 17:27, **fishhook**; ❺ LXX, Isa 19:8; Hab 1:15, **hook**

ἄγκυρα, ας, ἡ$_{1α}$ ❹ Acts 27:29, 30, 40, *lit.*, **anchor**; Heb 6:19, *fig.*, **security**; Plato *Leg.* 961C, **anchor** *of salvation*; Soph. *fr.* 685, *children are a mother's* **hope** *of life*

ἄγναφος, ον$_{2.2}$ {α + γναφεύς} *adj.* ❷ Matt 9:16 = Mark 2:21, **unshrunk** *wine skins*

ἁγνεία, ας, ἡ$_{1α}$ {ἅγος} ❷ 1 Tim 4:12; 5:2, **purity**; ❹ LXX, 2 Chr 30:19, **cleansing**

ἁγνίζω {ἅγος} ❼ John 11:55; Acts 21:24, 26; Jas 4:8, **to purify**; (34x LXX; 16x 2 Chr)

ἁγνισμός, οῦ, ὁ$_{2}$ {ἅγος} ①^{gms} Acts 21:26, **purification**; ❻ LXX, 5x Num; Num 6:5, **Nazarite** *vow*

ἀγνοέω^{con} {α + γίνωσκω} (22x) Mark 9:32 = Luke 9:45; Rom 1:13; Heb 5:2, **to be unaware**;

Acts 13:27; Rom 2:4, **not to recognize**; Acts 17:23, **not to know**; 1 Thess 4:13, **to be uninformed**; (21x LXX; 7x Wis) Gen 20:4, **ignorantly** *sinning*

ἀγνόημα, ατος, τό$_3$ {α + γίνωσκω} ①[gnp] Heb 9:7, **sins of ignorance**[WPNT]; ❻ LXX

ἄγνοια, ας, ἡ$_{1α}$ {α + γίνωσκω} ❹ Acts 3:17; 17:30; Eph 4:18; 1 Pet 1:14, **ignorance**; (28x LXX; 6x Dan) Lev 5:18, **unintentional error**; 1 Sam 14:24, *trespass* **of ignorance**

ἁγνός, ή, όν$_{2.1.2}$ {ἅγος} *adj.* ❽ 2 Cor 7:11, **innocent**[BEC]; Phil 4:8; Titus 2:5; 1 John 3:3, **pure**; (13x LXX; 4x Prov) Lev 23:40, **goodly** *fruit of trees* (BrLXX); Prov 15:26, **pure**

ἁγνότης, τητος, ἡ$_3$ {ἅγος} ❷ 2 Cor 6:6; 11:3, **pure, purity**[BEC]

ἁγνῶς {ἅγος} *adv.* ① Phil 1:17, **impure**; ❸ LXX, Job 35:16, **without knowledge**

ἀγνωσία, ας, ἡ$_{1α}$ {α + γινώσκω} ❷ 1 Cor 15:34; 1 Pet 2:15, **ignorance**

ἄγνωστος, ον$_{2.2}$ {α + γινώσκω} *adj.* ①[dms] Acts 17:23, **unknown**

ἀγορά, ᾶς, ἡ$_{1α}$ (11x) Matt 11:16 = Luke 7:32, **marketplace**; (11x LXX; 5x Ezek)

ἀγοράζω (30x; 7x Matt, 6x Rev) Matt 14:15 = Mark 6:36 = Luke 9:13 = John 6:5, **to buy**; 1 Cor 7:23, **you were purchased**; 2 Pet 2:1, *deny the Master* **who bought** *them*; 1 Cor 7:30, **to transact** *commerce*[NIGTC]; Rev 3:18, *fig.*, **to buy**; 14:3, **the redeemed**; (22x LXX; 7x Gen)

ἀγοραῖος, ον$_{2.2}$ *adj.* ❷ Acts 17:5, **the agora; market people**, *spec. the crowd in the marketplace, so* **rabble**[BDAG]; 19:38, **court**

ἄγρα, ας, ἡ$_{1α}$ ❷ Luke 5:4, εἰς ἄγραν, *for* **a catch**; 5:9, **a catch** *of fish*; Hes. *Th.* 442, **game, prey, quarry**

ἀγράμματος, ον$_{2.2}$ {α + γράφω} *adj.* ①[nmp] Acts 4:13, **uneducated** *amateurs*; **unschooled**, *not* **illiterate**[BEC]; (CSB) **uneducated** *and untrained, not = an insult*[Keen2]; Xen. *Mem.* 4.2.20

ἀγραυλέω[con] {ἀγρός + αὐλή} ①[pap.nmp] Luke 2:8, **to live outdoors**[BHGNT]

ἀγρεύω {ἄγρα} ①[aas3p] Mark 12:13, **to catch in** *an unguarded statement*[BHGNT]; ❺ LXX, Job 10:16, **to hunt** *me like a lion*; Xen. *An.* 5.3.8, **to be hunted**

ἀγριέλαιος, ου, ἡ$_{2όδός}$ {ἀγρός + ἐλαία} ❷ Rom 11:17, 24, **wild olive branch**

ἄγριος, ία, ον$_{2.1.2}$ {ἀγρός} *adj.* ❸ Matt 3:4 = Mark 1:6; Jude 13, **wild**[BHGNT]; ❺ LXX, Job 5:22

Ἀγρίππας, α, ὁ$_{1α}$ (11x, all in Acts 25–26) **Herod Agrippa II**

ἀγρός, οῦ, ὁ$_2$ (36x; 35x Gs) Matt 6:28; Mark 11:8; Acts 4:37, **field**; (232x LXX; 35x 1–2 Sam, 23x Jer)

ἀγρυπνέω[con] {ἄγρα + ὕπνος} ❹ Mark 13:33; Luke 21:36; Eph 6:18, **watch out, be alert**; Heb 13:17, **to maintain pastoral care**; (11x LXX) 2 Sam 12:21, **to stay awake**

ἀγρυπνία, ας, ἡ$_{1α}$ {ἄγρα + ὕπνος} ❷ 2 Cor 6:5; 11:27, **sleepless**; (10x LXX; 9x Sir) 2 Macc 2:26, **loss of sleep**; Plato *Ax.* 368b, **time of watch**

ἄγω (67x; 39x LA, 13x John) *act.*, 1 Thess 4:14, **to bring**; *pass.*, Matt 10:18; Gal 5:18, **to be led**; John 1:42; Acts 5:26; 2 Tim 3:6, **to be led astray**; (255x LXX; 28x Isa, 25x 2 Macc)

ἀγωγή, ῆς, ἡ$_{1η}$ {ἄγω} ①[dfs] 2 Tim 3:10, **way of life, conduct**; ❻ LXX, Esth 2:20

ἀγών, ῶνος, ὁ$_3$ ❻ Phil 1:30; Col 2:1, **struggle**; 1 Thess 2:2, **opposition**; 1 Tim 6:12; 2 Tim 4:7, **fight**; Heb 12:1, **race**; (16x LXX; 5x 2 Macc, 6x 4 Macc)

ἀγωνία, ας, ἡ$_{1α}$ {ἀγών} ①[dfs] Luke 22:44, γενόμενος ἐν ἀγωνίᾳ, *becoming* **steeled for combat**[ZEC]; ❸ LXX, 2 Macc 3:14, 16; 15:19, **distress**

ἀγωνίζομαι {ἀγών} ❽ Luke 13:24, **to strain every nerve**; John 18:36, **to fight**; 1 Cor 9:25,[Pfit] **to enter as a combatant**[NIGTC]; Col 1:29; 4:12; 1 Tim 4:10, **to strive, labor**; 1 Tim 6:12; 2 Tim 4:7, **to fight** *the good fight*; ❻ LXX, 1 Macc 7:21; 4 Macc 17:13

Ἀδάμ, ὁ$_3$ *indecl.* ❾ (Heb. דם *blood*, אדם *Adam/man*, אדמה *ground*) Luke 3:38; Rom 5:14[2x];

1 Cor 15:22; 1 Tim 2:13, **Adam**; (33x LXX; 26x Gen) Gen 2–4, **the man**[20x]; 5:1–5, **Adam**[5x], *in primal genealogy*

ἀδάπανος, ον$_{2.2}$ {α+ δαπάνη} *adj.* ①[ans] 1 Cor 9:18, **free of charge**[NIGTC]

Ἀδδί, ὁ$_{3}$ *indecl.* ①[nms] Luke 3:28, **Addi**, *son of Cosam*; ❹ LXX, Num 26:25[2x]; 1 Chr 6:6

ἀδελφή, ῆς, ἡ$_{1η}$ {ἀδελφός} (26x; 7x Matt, 6x Rev) *NIDNTT*→ Ⓐ (8x) Matt 12:50, **spiritual sister**; Ⓑ (17x) Matt 13:56, **blood sister**; Ⓒ Mark 3:32, 35, *contrast of spiritual and blood* **sisters**; Ⓓ (1x) 1 Cor 9:5, **wife** (*who is a believer*); (109x LXX; 25x Gen, 20x Ezek), **sister**

ἀδελφός, οῦ, ὁ$_{2}$ (343x; 57x Acts, 39x Matt:1 Cor, 24x Luke) **brother**; *NIDNTT*→ Ⓐ (141x) **sibling believers**; 1 Cor 1:11, *my* **dear Christian family**[NIGTC]; 15:6, **Christian people**; Ⓑ (83x) **sharing the same parents**, Jude 1; Ⓒ (84x) **fellow believer**, Phlm 1; Ⓓ (19 of 21x, Acts), **fellow countryman**, Rom 9:3; Heb 7:5; Ⓔ (19x) **neighbor** Matt 7:3 = Luke 6:41; 1 John 3:14; (851x LXX; 179x Gen, 105x 1 Chr, 71x 1 Macc)

ἀδελφότης, τητος, ἡ$_{3}$ {ἀδελφός} ❷ 1 Pet 2:17; 5:9, **the spiritual family**[Keen1P]; ❼ LXX, 1 Macc 12:10; 4 Macc 9:23

ἄδηλος, ον$_{2.2}$ {α + δῆλος} *adj.* ❷ Luke 11:44, **unmarked** *tombs*; 1 Cor 14:8, **indistinct** *bugle call*; ❹ LXX, Ps 50:8 (51:6) **unclear** *and secret aspects of your wisdom*

ἀδηλότης, τητος, ἡ$_{3}$ {α + δῆλος} ①[dfs] 1 Tim 6:17, **uncertainty**

ἀδήλως {α + δῆλος} *adv.* ① 1 Cor 9:26, **aimlessly, without a goal in mind**[ZEC]

ἀδημονέω[con] ❸ Matt 26:37 = Mark 14:33; Phil 2:26, **distressed, troubled**

ᾅδης, ου, ὁ$_{1>}$ {α + εἶδος} (10x) Luke 10:15; Rev 1:18; 6:8; 20:13, 14; **Hades**, *a place of fiery torment*[ZEC]; (107x LXX; 18x Pss, 11x Prov; Isa)

ἀδιάκριτος, ον$_{2.2}$ {α + διά + κρίνω} *adj.* ① Jas 3:17, **impartial**; ①[nfp] LXX, Prov 25:1, **varied**

ἀδιάλειπτος, ον$_{2.2}$ {α + διά + λείπω} *adj.* ❷ Rom 9:2; 2 Tim 1:3, **unceasing**, **constant**

ἀδιαλείπτως *adv.* ❹ Rom 1:9; 1 Thess 1:2; 2:13; 5:17, **constantly**; ❻ LXX, 1 Macc 12:11

ἀδικέω[con] {α + δίκη} (28x) Matt 20:13, **to cheat**; Luke 10:19, **to harm**; Acts 7:26, **to do wrong**; 1 Cor 6:7, **to be deprived**[NIGTC]; 2 Cor 7:2, 12, **to mistreat with a view to harm**[ZEC]; (68x LXX; 11x Pss, 9x Isa)

ἀδίκημα, ατος, τό$_{3}$ {α + δίκη} ❸ Acts 18:14; 24:20, **wrongdoing**; Rev 18:5, **crimes**; (19x LXX; 7x MajPr) Gen 31:36; Exod 22:8, **offense**; 4 Macc 11:3, **crimes**; Isa 56:2, **evil**

ἀδικία, ας, ἡ$_{1α}$ {α + δίκη} (25x; 7x Rom) Luke 13:27, **iniquity**; Acts 8:23; 1 John 1:9, **unrighteousness**; Luke 16:9, **unrighteous** *Mammon*[ZEC]; 2 Cor 12:13, **injustice**; 2 Thess 2:12, **wickedness**[ZEC]; 2 Pet 2:13, **wrong**; (215x LXX; 43x Ezek, 28x Pss)

ἄδικος, ον$_{2.2}$ {α + δίκη} *adj.* (12x; 4x Luke) Matt 5:45; 1 Cor 6:9, **unrighteous**; Luke 16:10, 11, **not trustworthy**; 1 Cor 6:1, **crooked** *judge*; (123x LXX; 18x Prov, 16x Job, 13x Pss)

ἀδίκως {α + δίκη} *adv.* ① 1 Pet 2:19, *suffering* **unjustly**[EGG]; (26x LXX; 7x Prov, 5x Pss)

Ἀδμίν, ὁ$_{3}$ *indecl.* ①[gms] Luke 3:33, **Admin**, *son of Arni*

ἀδόκιμος, ον$_{2.2}$ {α + δοκιμάζω} *adj.* ❽ Rom 1:28, **unqualified** *for anything worthwhile*[ZEC]; 1 Cor 9:27, **ἀδόκιμος** γένωμαι, **not proven to stand the test**[NIGTC]; 2 Cor 13:5, **fails to stand up under testing**[BEC]; 2 Tim 3:8, **worthless**; Heb 6:8, **worthless** *plants*[NIGTC]; ❷[nns] LXX, Prov 25:4; Isa 1:22, **dross**

ἄδολος, ον$_{2.2}$ *adj.* ①[ans] 1 Pet 2:2, **without contamination** *of farm products,*[BDAG] *word play with* **δόλος** (2:1), *thus not deceptive, but* **pure doctrine**

Ἀδραμυττηνός, ή, όν$_{2.1.2}$ *adj.* ①[dns] Acts 27:2, **Adramyttium**[LGCb]

Ἀδρίας, ου, ὁ$_{1}$ ①[dms] Acts 27:27, **Adriatic Sea**

ἁδρότης, τητος, ἡ$_{3}$ {ἁδρός} ①[dfs] 2 Cor 8:20, *an* **abundance** *of money*[EDNT]

ἀδυνατέω[con] {α + δύναμαι} ❷[fai3s] Matt 17:20[ac] = Luke 1:37,[bc] οὐδὲν[a] (οὐκ)[b] **ἀδυνατήσει,**[c] *nothing* **will be impossible**; (12x LXX) Lev 25:35, *if your brother* **cannot** *handle it*

ἀδύνατος, ον$_{2.2}$ {α + δύναμαι} *adj.* (10x; 4x Heb) Matt 19:26; Rom 8:3; Heb 6:4, **impossible**; Acts 14:8, **not able to use**; 15:1, **the weak**; (25x LXX; 14x Job)

ᾄδω ❺ Eph 5:19 = Col 3:16; Rev 5:9; 14:3; 15:3, **to sing**; (75x LXX; 25x Pss, 16x Neh)

ἀεί {α + ἴδιος} *adv.* ❼ Acts 7:51; 2 Cor 4:11; Heb 3:10; 2 Pet 1:12, **constantly**, **always**; (14x LXX) Judg 16:20, ποιήσω καθὼς ἀεί, *as I did* **before**

ἀετός, οῦ, ὁ$_{2}$ ❺ Matt 24:28 = Luke 17:37, **vulture**; Rev 4:7; 8:13; 12:14, **eagle, majestic bird**; (28x LXX; 4x Deut) Prov 23:5, **eagle**

ἄζυμος, ον$_{2.2}$ {α + ζέω} *adj.* ❾ Matt 26:17 = Mark 14:12 = Luke 22:7; Acts 12:3; 20:6, **unleavened bread**; 1 Cor 5:7, 8, **unleavened bread** *of sincerity and truth*; (53x LXX)

Ἀζώρ, ὁ$_{3}$ *indecl.* ❷ Matt 1:13, 14, **Azor**; ❷ LXX, Josh 19:45; Jer 35:1 (28:1)

Ἄζωτος, ου, ἡ$_{2όδός}$ ①[afs] Acts 8:40, **Azotus**; (27x LXX; 11x 1 Macc) **Ashdod**

ἀήρ, έρος, ὁ$_{3}$ ❼ Acts 22:33; 1 Cor 9:26; 1 Thess 4:17; Rev 9:2, **air**; Eph 2:2, *the devil's* **air** *or* **domain**; ①[gms] LXX, 1 Chr 7:12, **Aher**

ἀθανασία, ας, ἡ$_{1α}$ {α + θνήσκω} ❸ 1 Cor 15:53, 54; 1 Tim 6:16, **immortality**; ❼ LXX (5x Wis, 2x 4 Macc) 4 Macc 14:5[SCS]

ἀθέμιτος, ον$_{2.2}$ {α + θέμις} *adj.* ❷ Acts 10:28, **unlawful**; 1 Pet 4:3, **lawless** *idolatries*[EGG]; ❹ LXX, 2 Macc 6:5, 7:1, **unlawful**

ἄθεος, ον$_{2.2}$ *adj.* ①[nmp] Eph 2:12, **alienated from the one true God**

ἄθεσμος, ον$_{2.2}$ {α + τίθημι} *adj.* ❷ 2 Pet 2:7; 3:17, **lawless**; ①[gfs] LXX, 3 Macc 5:12

ἀθετέω[con] {α + τίθημι} (16x) Mark 6:26, **to refuse**; Mark 7:9; Luke 7:30; Jude 8, **to reject**; 1 Cor 1:19; Gal 2:21, **to set aside**; (62x LXX; 12x Isa) 2 Kgs 18:20, **to rebel** *against*

ἀθέτησις, εως, ἡ$_{3}$ {α + τίθημι} ❷ Heb 7:18, 9:26, **annulment**; ① LXX, 1 Sam 24:12 (24:11)

Ἀθηναῖος, α, ον$_{2.1.2}$ {Ἀθῆναι} *adj.* ❷ *subst.*, Acts 17:21, **Athenians**; 17:22, *people* **of Athens**

ἀθλέω[con] {ἆθλον} ❷ 2 Tim 2:5,[2x] **to compete in a contest**; Soph. *O.C.* 564, *I involved myself* **in dangerous struggles**[BrDAG]

ἄθλησις, εως, ἡ$_{3}$ {ἆθλον} ①[afs] Heb 10:32, **difficult struggle**[NIVAC, EGG]

ἀθροίζω {α + θρόος} ①[pfmp.amp] Luke 24:33, **to assemble**; (15x LXX; 7x 1 Macc)

ἀθυμέω[con] {α + θυμός} ①[pas3p] Col 3:21, **to become discouraged, lose heart**[PNTC]; ❾ LXX

ἀθῷος, ον$_{2.2}$ {α + θωή} *adj.* ❷ Matt 27:4, 24, **innocent**; (54x LXX) Gen 24:41,[2x] **to be free**

αἴγειος, α, ον$_{2.1.2}$ {αἴξ} *adj.* ①[dnp] Heb 11:37, *in* **goat** *garments* (*perhaps an allusion to* Zech 13:4)[NIGTC]; ❹ LXX, Exod 25:4; 35:6, **goat** *hair*

αἰγιαλός, οῦ, ὁ$_{2}$ {ἀΐσσω = ***move quickly*** + ἁλίζω} ❻ Matt 13:24; John 21:4; Acts 21:5, 27:39, 40; **beach**, **shore**; ①[ams] LXX, Judg 5:17, **seashore**

Αἰγύπτιος, α, ον$_{2.1.2}$ {Αἴγυπτος} *adj.* ❺ Acts 7:22–28; Heb 11:29, **Egyptian**; (140x LXX)

Αἴγυπτος, ου, ἡ$_{2όδός}$ (25x; 15x Acts) Matt 2:13; Acts 2:10; 7:9–40; 13:17; Heb 3:16; 11:26; Jude 5; Rev 11:8, **Egypt**; (633x LXX; 130x MajPr, 114x Exod)

ἀΐδιος, ον$_{2.2}$ *adj.* ❷ Rom 1:20; Jude 6, **eternal**; ❷ LXX, 4 Macc 10:15; Wis 7:26

αἰδώς, οῦς, ἡ$_{3}$ {αἰδέομαι} ①[gfs] 1 Tim 2:9, **not violating the limits of womanly modesty**[NIGTC]; ❷ LXX, 3 Macc 1:19; 4:5

Αἰθίοψ, οπος, ὁ$_{3}$ ❷ Acts 8:27,[2x] **Ethiopian**

αἷμα, ατος, τό$_{3}$ (97x; 21x Heb, 19x Rev) Ⓐ ***human and divine relationships***, John 1:13, **by human procreation**; 6:53, *metaph.*, **for life through death**; Heb 2:14, *flesh and* **blood**; Ⓑ ***mortality and death***, Matt 27:24, 25, **death**; Mark 5:25, *a* **bleeding** *disorder*; Luke 13:1, **homicide**; Ⓒ ***blood symbolism and sacrifice***, Matt 26:28, *Last Supper* **blood**; Heb 9:12–25,[11x] **blood** *and Jesus's atonement*[EGG]; Rev 1:5–19:13,[NIGTC] **blood** *of the Lamb*, *passim*; Ⓓ ***consequences and betrayal,*** Matt 27:4, *Judas's* **blood** *money* (396x LXX; 82x Lev)

αἱματ**εκχυσία, ας, ἡ**$_{1α}$ {αἷμα + ἐκ + χέω} ①[gfs] Heb 9:22, **shedding of blood**

αἱμο**ρροέω**[con] {αἷμα + ῥέω} ①[pap.nfs] Matt 9:20, **afflicted with chronic bleeding**; ①[pap.dfs] LXX, Lev 15:33, **menstrual period**

Αἰνέας, ου, ὁ$_{1>}$ ❷ Acts 9:23, 24, **Aeneas**

αἴνεσις, εως, ἡ$_{3}$ {αἶνος} ①[gfs] Heb 13:15, **praise** = *sacrifice*; (64x LXX; 29x Pss)

αἰνέω[con] ❽ Luke 2:13; 19:37; Acts 2:47; Rom 15:11; Rev 19:5, **to praise**; (137x LXX)

αἴνιγμα, ατος, τό$_{3}$ {αἶνος, *deriv.*, αἰνίσσομαι, **to speak in riddles**} ①[dns] 1 Cor 13:12, *in an* **enigma**, i.e., **obscurely**, **darkly**[NIGTC]; ❾ LXX, Num 12:8, **in a puzzling way**

αἶνος, ου, ἡ$_{2ὁδός}$ ❷ Matt 21:16; Luke 18:43, **praise**; (11x LXX; 4x Pss)

Αἰνών, ἡ$_{3}$ *indecl.* ①[dfs] John 3:23, **Aenon**; ①[dfs] LXX, Josh 15:61

αἱρέομαι[con] ❸ Phil 1:22, **to prefer**; 2 Thess 2:13, Heb 11:25, **to choose**; (αἱρέω, 11x LXX)

αἵρεσις, εως, ἡ$_{3}$ {αἱρέω} ❾ (6x Acts) Acts 5:17; 15:5; 24:5, 14, **sect**, **party**; 1 Cor 11:19, **factions**; Gal 5:20, **sectarianism**, *rigid loyalties and rivalry*[KeenG]; ❹ LXX, Gen 49:5

αἱρετίζω {αἱρέω} ①[aai1s] Matt 12:18, **to choose** (*quot.* Isa 42:1); (29x LXX; 5x Pss, 4x 1 Chr)

αἱρετικός, ή, όν$_{2.1.2}$ {αἱρέω} *adj.* ①[ams] Titus 3:10, **factious**, **causing divisions**

αἴρω (101x; 85x Gs) Matt 4:6 = Luke 4:11, **to hold up**; Matt 9:6, **to get up**; 9:16, **to pull away**; 11:29, **to take upon**; Mark 16:18; Acts 20:9, **to pick up**; Acts 4:24, **to lift**; Eph 4:31, **to remove**; 1 John 3:5, **to take away** *sin*; (280x LXX; 41x 1–2 Sam:Isa)

αἰσθάνομαι ①[ams3p] Luke 9:45, **to comprehend**; (11x LXX) Prov 17:10

αἴσθησις, εως, ἡ$_{3}$ {αἰσθάνομαι} ①[dfs] Phil 1:9, **insight**; (28x LXX; 22x Prov)

αἰσθητήριον, ου, τό$_{2}$ {αἰσθάνομαι} ①[anp] Heb 5:14, **ethical discernment**; ❷ LXX, Jer 4:19, **the walls** *of my heart*[LES]; 4 Macc 2:22, **senses**; Aristot. *An.* 4.19a 26, **sensory organ**

αἰσχρο**κερδής, ές**$_{3.3}$ {αἰσχρός + κέρδος} *adj.* ❷ 1 Tim 3:8, Titus 1:7, **greedy for money**

αἰσχρο**κερδῶς** {αἰσχρός + κέρδος} *adv.* ① 1 Pet 5:2, **greedily**

αἰσχρο**λογία, ας, ἡ**$_{1α}$ {αἰσχρός + λέγω} ①[afs] Col 3:8, **filthy speech**

αἰσχρός, ά, όν$_{2.1.2}$ *adj.* ❹ 1 Cor 11:6, **shame-bringing**[NIGTC]; 1 Cor 14:35, **brings disgrace**; Eph 5:12; Titus 1:11, **shameful**; (11x LXX) Gen 41:3–21,[6x] **sickly**, **unhealthy** *cows*

αἰσχρότης, τητος, ἡ$_{3}$ {αἰσχρός} ①[nfs] Eph 5:4, **obscene** *talk or behavior*

αἰσχύνη, ης, ἡ$_{1η}$ ❻ Luke 14:9; Phil 3:19; Heb 12:12, **shame**; 2 Cor 4:2; Rev 3:18, **shameful**; Jude 13, *the* **foam** *of the sea* (**shameless deeds**)[BEC]; (79x LXX; 12x Isa, 11x Sir)

αἰσχύνομαι ❺ Luke 16:3; 2 Cor 10:8, **to be ashamed**; Phil 1:20; 1 John 2:28, **to put to shame**; 1 Pet 4:16, **to feel disgraced**[BEC, Keen1P]

αἰτέω[con] (70x; 21x LA, 14x Matt) Matt 5:42; John 16:23; 1 Pet 3:15, **to ask**; Luke 11:9–13, **to ask** *in prayer*; 1 Cor 1:22, **to demand**; Acts 9:2, **to scout**; (84x LXX; 16x 1 Kgs)

αἴτημα, ατος, τό$_{2}$ {αἰτέω} ❸ Luke 23:24, **a demand**; Phil 4:6; 1 John 5:15, **a request**; (11x LXX; 3x Esth:Pss) 1 Sam 1:17, **petition**

αἰτία, ας, ἡ$_{1α}$ (20x; 8x Acts) Matt 19:3, *for any* **reason** *whatever*; 19:10, **the relationship**[ZEC]; Matt 27:37 = Mark 15:26; John 18:38, **criminal charge, accusation**; Luke 8:47; 2 Tim 1:6; Heb 2:11, **reason**; Acts 13:28; 28:18, **cause** *deserving of death*[Keen2]; **basis** *for a death sentence*[ZEC]; (20x LXX; 13x 1–4 Macc) Job 18:14, **terror**

αἴτιος, ία, ον$_{2.1.2}$ {αἰτία} *adj.* ❺ Luke 23:4, **basis** *for a criminal charge*; 23:22, *death* **sentence**; Acts 19:40, **cause**; Heb 5:9, *Jesus is* **the source/the one responsible** *for salvation*; ❻ LXX, *in* LXX *and Hom., normally* **one who causes harm**, 2 Macc 4:47

αἰτίωμα, ατος, τό$_{3}$ {αἰτία} ①[anp] Acts 25:7, *serious* **charges**[Keen4]

αἰφνίδιος, ον$_{2.2}$ {ἄφνω} *adj.* ❷[nfs] Luke 21:34, **unexpected**; 1 Thess 5:3, **suddenness** *of birth pangs*; ❸ LXX, 2 Macc 14:17; Jos. *Vita* 253, *milit.*, **unexpected** *sneak attack*

αἰχμ**αλωσία, ας, ἡ**$_{1α}$ {ἀκή + ἅλωσις} ❷ Eph 4:8, *Christ leads* **prisoner***s of spiritual war*[HH]; Rev 13:10, *the beast takes* **prisoners**; (125x LXX) Ezek 1:1–40:1,[18x] **exiles**

αἰχμ**αλωτεύω** {ἀκή + ἅλωσις} ①[aai3s] Eph 4:18, **to lead away captive**; (39x LXX; 18x Ezek, 17x Esd)

αἰχμ**αλωτίζω** {ἀκή + ἅλωσις} ❹ Luke 21:24, **led away captive**; *post-destruction of Jerusalem*[ZEC]; Rom 7:23, *Paul's mind* **taken captive** *by sin*; 2 Cor 10:5, **taking captive** *every thought*[BEC]; 2 Tim 3:6, **to captivate** *morally weak and spiritually dwarfed women*[TAB]; (18x LXX; 5x 1 Macc)

αἰχμ**άλωτος, ώτου, ὁ**$_{2}$ {ἀκή + ἅλωσις} ①[dmp] Luke 4:18, **spiritual captives**; (24x LXX; 6x Isa) Exod 22:9, *if livestock is* **trapped** *and dies*; Isa 5:13, *to go into* **exile**

αἰών, ῶνος, ὁ$_{3}$ (122x; 26x Rev) Ⓐ ***simple constr.***, 1 Cor 1:20, **age**; Ⓑ ***in prep. phrases***, 1 Cor 8:13, **εἰς** +, **as long as I live**[NICNT]; Ⓒ ***emphatic***, John 8:51, *never taste death* **forever!**; Ⓓ ***adverbial***, 1 Tim 6:17, **present age**; Ⓔ ***unique contrast*** (***eternal*** *peace* «» ***eternal*** *chaos*), *positive*, **εἰς** + *cmpd. articular*, Rev 1:6–22:5,[12x] **forever and ever** *reigning with God*; *negative*, **εἰς** + *cmpd. anarthrous*, ***only*** *in* Rev 14:11, *torturous, restless, and chaotic existence* **forever and ever**; Ⓕ ***complex constr.***, Jude 13, *reserved* **forever**[PNTC]; (662x LXX; 201x Pss, 59x Dan)

αἰώνιος, ον$_{2.2}$ {αἰών} *adj.* (71x, 17x John) Matt 18:8; John 3:16, **eternal**; 1 Tim 6:16, **forever**; (153x LXX; 22x Isa, 18x Lev)

ἀ**καθαρσία, ας, ἡ**$_{1α}$ {α + καθαρός} (10x) 2 Cor 12:21, **filth, impurity**; Rom 1:24, 6:19; 1 Thess 4:17, **sexual immorality**[ZEC]; (62x LXX; 23x Lev, 11x Ezek)

ἀ**κάθαρτος, ον**$_{2.2}$ {α + καθαρός} *adj.* (32x; 11x Mark) Matt 10:1; Mark 1:23; Acts 5:16; Eph 5:5; Rev 16:13, **unclean**; (157x LXX; 96x Lev, 21x Num)

ἀ**καιρέομαι**[con] {α + καιρός} ①[imi2p] Phil 4:10, **you had no chance**

ἀ**καίρως** {α + καιρός} *adv.* ① 2 Tim 4:2, εὐκαίρως **ἀκαίρως**, *in season or* **out of season, whatever the circumstances**[ABC]; ① LXX, Sir 32:4, **at the wrong time** (NRSV)

ἄ**κακος, ον**$_{2.2}$ {α + κακός} *adj.* ❷ Rom 16:18, **unsuspecting**[ZEC]; Heb 7:26, **guileless, pure, innocent**[WBC]; (17x LXX; 8x Prov) *subst.* Prov 1:22, **O simple ones!**; Aeschl. *Pers.* 663, **devoid of malice**

ἄ**κανθα, ης, ἡ**$_{1>}$ (14x; 12x Syn) Matt 7:16 = Luke 6:44, **thornbushes**; Matt 13:7 = Mark 4:7; Heb 6:8, **thorns**; Matt 27:29, *crown of* **thorns**

ἀ**κάνθινος, η, ον**$_{2.1.2}$ {ἀκή} *adj.* ❷ Mark 15:17; John 19:5, **thorny** *crown* ①[nnp] LXX, Isa 34:13

ἄ**καρπος, ον**$_{2.2}$ *adj.* ❼ Matt 13:22 = Mark 4:19; 1 Cor 14:14; Titus 3:14; 2 Pet 1:8; Jude 12, **unfruitful, fruitless**; ❸ LXX, Jer 2:6, **barren**; 4 Macc 16:7; Wis 15:4, **fruitless**

ἀ**κατάγνωστος, ον**$_{2.2}$ {α + κατά + γινώσκω} *adj.* ①[ams] Titus 2:8, **not condemned**

ἀ**κατακάλυπτος, ον**$_{2.2}$ {α + κατά + καλύπτω} *adj.* ❷ 1 Cor 11:5, 13, **uncovered**[NIGTC]; ①[nfs] LXX, Lev 13:45, *the hair of his head must be* **unbound** (NET)

ἀ**κατάκριτος, ον**$_{2.2}$ {α + κατά + κρίνω} *adj.* ❷ Acts 16:37; 22:25, **uncondemned**

ἀ**κατάλυτος, ον**$_{2.2}$ {α + κατά + λύω} *adj.* ①[gfs] Heb 7:16, **indestructible, unstoppable**; ①[afp] LXX, 4 Macc 10:11, **perpetually**

ἀ**κατάπαυστος, ον**$_{2.2}$ {α + κατά + παύω} *adj.* ①[amp] 2 Pet 2:14, **restless, insatiable**[PTW]

ἀ**καταστασία, ας, ἡ**$_{1α}$ {α + κατά + ἵστημι} ❺ Luke 21:9; 2 Cor 6:5, **riot, rebellion, mob violence**; 1 Cor 14:33; 2 Cor 12:20; Jas 3:16, **chaos**; ❷ LXX, Prov 26:28, **confusion**

ἀ**κατάστατος, ον**$_{2.2}$ {α + κατά + ἵστημι} *adj.* ❷ Jas 1:8, **unstable, vacillation of the heart**[EGG]; 3:8, **uncontrollable**, *tongue is a* **restless** *evil*; ① LXX, Isa 54:11, **storm-tossed**

Ἀκελδαμάχ$_3$ *indecl., Aram.* ①[ans] Acts 1:19, **Field of Blood**[Keen1]

ἀ**κέραιος, ον**$_{2.2}$ {α + κεράννυμι} *adj.* ❸ Matt 10:16; Rom 16:19; Phil 2:15, **innocent**; ①[afs] LXX, Add Esth 8:12 (Esth 16:6), **innocent**

ἀκήκοαμεν → **ἀκούω**, *pf. act. ind. 1p* (6x) John 4:42; 1 John 1:1, **we have heard**

ἀ**κλινής, ές**$_{3.3}$ {α + κλίνω} *adj.* ①[afs] Heb 10:23, *adv. usage*, **unswervingly, not leaning**[WPNT]; ❷ LXX, 4 Macc 6:7, **firm**; 17:3, **unswervingly** *against the earthquake of tortures*[SCS]; *math.*, Plato *Phaed.* 109a, **fixed**[BrDAG]; *geom.*, Procl., **perpendicular**[BrDAG]

ἀκμάζω {ἀκή} ①[aai3p] Rev 14:18, **to ripen**; ①[pap.nms] LXX, 4 Macc 2:3; Hdt. *Hist.* 2.134.2, **to be in full vigor**; Thuc. 3.3.1, **at the height of the war**

ἀκμήν {ἀκή} *adv.* ① Matt 15:16, **still, even now**

ἀκοή, ῆς, ἡ$_{1η}$ {ἀκούω} (24x; 8x Syn) 🅐 ***communication***, Rom 10:16, **report**; Acts 28:26, **hearing**; 🅑 ***recognition***, Matt 24:6 = Mark 13:7, **rumors** *of wars*; Mark 1:28, **fame**; 🅒 ***listening and reception***, Acts 17:20, **ears**; 1 Thess 2:13, **heard**; Gal 3:2, **hearing**; 🅓 ***comprehension***, Heb 5:11, **willingness to understand**[NIGTC]; (49x LXX; 8x Jer)

ἀκολουθέω[con] {ἀκόλουθος} (90x; 79x Gs) John 1:43 and 21:22 (*inclusio* in John), *single-minded* **following**[ZEC]; Rev 6:8, **to follow** *spatially or sequentially*; 14:4, **to follow** *the Lamb wherever he goes*[ZEC]; (13x LXX) 1 Sam 25:42, **to follow, to go with**

ἀκούω (428x; 172x Syn, 46x Rev) Matt 2:9, **to hear, listen**; 2:18, **to be heard**; Acts 28:27,[2x] **to hear** *with ears*, **to understand** *with heart*; John 7:51, *grant a judicial* **hearing**; 1 Cor 14:2, **to understand**[NIGTC]; Jas 5:11, **to learn**; (1,014x LXX; 137x Jer, 88x 1–2 Sam, 87x Isa)

ἀ**κρασία, ας, ἡ**$_{1α}$ {α + κεράννυμι} ❷ Matt 23:25, **selfishness**[NAC]; 1 Cor 7:5, **lack of** *sexual* **self-control**[NIGTC]; Aristot. *Rh.* 1372b 13, **overpowered** *by what concerns all men*; Plut. *Garr.* 508b, **logorrhea** (*diarrhea of the mouth*): *blurting out secrets leads to destruction*[BrDAG]

ἀ**κρατής, ές**$_{3.3}$ {α + κεράννυμι} *adj.* ①[nmp] 2 Tim 3:3, **out of control, wild**,[ABC] **ungovernable**[ICNT]; ①[nmp] LXX, Prov 27:20; Jos. *A.J.* 16:399, **not satisfied**

ἄ**κρατος, ον**$_{2.2}$ {α + κεράννυμι} *adj.* ①[gms] Rev 14:10, **untempered strength**; ❹ LXX

ἀκρίβεια, ας, ἡ$_{1α}$ {ἀκριβής} ①[afs] Acts 22:3, **strict conformity**[ZEC, Keen4]; Thuc. 1.22.2, **meticulous attention, scrupulousness**[BrDAG] ❹ LXX, Wis 12:21; Sir 16:25, 42:4; Dan 7:16

ἀκριβής, ές$_{3.3}$ *adj.* ①[afs] Acts 26:5, *super.* **strictest**; ❽ LXX, Dan 2:45; 4:27, **certain**

ἀκριβόω[con] {ἀκριβής} ❷ Matt 2:7, 16, **to determine exactly**

ἀκριβῶς {ἀκριβής} *adv.* ❾ Matt 2:8, **exactly**; Luke 1:3, **accurately**; Acts 18:25, *taught*

accurately; *comp.*, Acts 18:26, *explained* **more accurately**; Eph 5:15, **intentionally focused**; 1 Thess 5:2, **perfectly well**; ❷ LXX, Deut 19:18, Wis 19:18, **careful**, **thorough**

ἀκρίς, ίδος, ἡ$_3$ {ἀκή} ❹ Matt 3:4 = Mark 1:6, *lit.*, **locust**; Rev 9:3, 7, *fig.*, *ghastly* **locust**[ZEC]; (33x LXX; 6x Exod, 3x Joel)

ἀκροατήριον, ου, τό$_2$ {ἀκροάομαι} ①[ans] Acts 25:23, **audience chamber**

ἀκροατής, οῦ, ὁ$_{1>}$ {ἀκροάομαι} ❹ Rom 2:13; Jas 1:22, 23, 25, **hearers**; ❷ LXX, Sir 3:29; Isa 3:3, **enchanter**; Aristot. *Pol.* 1274a, **one who listens**, **disciple**

ἀκροβυστία, ας, ἡ$_{1α}$ {ἀκή + πόσθη} (20x) Acts 11:3; Gal 2:7; Rom 4:9–12,[4x] **uncircumcised**; Rom 2:25, **gentile believers**; 1 Cor 7:18, 19, *insignificance of* **ἀκροβυστία**[NICNT]; Col 2:13, *lit. and fig.*, **uncircumcision** *of your flesh*[TNTC]

ἀκρογωνιαῖος, α, ον$_{2.1.2}$ {ἀκή + γωνία} *adj.* ❷ Eph 2:20; 1 Pet 2:6, *fig.*, **keystone**

ἀκροθίνιον, ου, τό$_2$ {ἀκή + θίς} ①[gnp] Heb 7:4, **choicest of the spoils**[WBC]; *lit.*, **top of the heap**[NIGTC]; Hdt. *Hist.* 1.86.2, **valued object** *of plunder*

ἄκρον, ου, τό$_2$ ❻ Matt 24:31 = Mark 13:27, **farthest point**; Luke 16:24, **tip of finger**; Heb 11:21, **top of staff**; Hom. *Il.* 14.292, **summit**; Alc. 34.9, **crow's nest** *of a ship*

Ἀκύλας, *acc.* **-αν, ὁ**$_1$ ❻ Acts 18:2, 18, 26; Rom 16:3; 1 Cor 16:19; 2 Tim 4:19, **Aquila**

ἀκυρόω[con] {α + κῦρος} ❸ Matt 15:6 = Mark 7:13; Gal 3:17, *jur.* **nullify**, **legally invalidate**; ①[aas3p] LXX, 1 Esd 6:31 (6:32), **to transgress**, **nullify**; Strabo *Hist.* 8.4.10, **to be abolished**

ἀκωλύτως {α + κωλύω} *adv.* ① Acts 28:31 **unhindered**[Keen4]; Plato *Crat.* 415d, **unimpeded**

ἄκων {α + ἑκών} *adv.* ① 1 Cor 9:17, **not my own initiative** (*wordplay with* **ἑκών**)[ZEC]

ἀλάβαστρος, ου, ὁ$_2$ ❹ Matt 26:7 = Mark 14:3[2x] = Luke 7:37, **alabaster jar**; ①[nms] LXX, 2 Kgs 21:13

ἀλαζονεία, ας, ἡ$_{1α}$ {ἀλαζών} ❷ Jas 4:16, **pride**, **arrogance**[PTNC]; 1 John 2:16, **braggadocio**[BEC]; Plato *Rp.* 531b, **amplification** *of the string sounds*[BrDAG]; ❼ LXX, 2x 2 Macc, 3x 4 Macc, 2x Wis

ἀλαζών, όνος, ὁ$_3$ ❷ Rom 1:30; 2 Tim 3:2, **braggart**; ❸ LXX, Job 28:8; Hab 2:5

ἀλαλάζω {ἀλαζών} ❷ Mark 5:38, **to wail**, **shriek**; 1 Cor 13:1, **to clang**; (18x LXX; 8x Pss, 4x Jer) Judg 15:14, **to shout**; Xen. *An.* 5.2.14, **to raise the war cry**[BrDAG]

ἀλάλητος, ον$_{2.2}$ {α + λάλος} *adj.* ①[dmp] Rom 8:26, **inexpressible**[NICNT]; *distinct from* **ἀλαλητός, οῦ, ὁ**$_2$ Hom. *Il.* 12.138, **cry of war** *or* **victory**

ἄλαλος, ον$_{2.2}$ *adj.* ❸ Mark 7:37; 9:17, 25, **mute**; ❷ LXX, Ps 30:19 (31:18); 37:14 (38:13) **speechless**, **deaf**; Hippol. *Haer.* 5.7.19, **indescribable**

ἅλας, ατος, τό$_3$ ❽ Matt 5:13 = Mark 9:50; Col 4:6, *fig.*, **salt**, ①[nns] LXX, Sir 39:26

ἀλείφω ❾ Matt 6:17; Mark 16:1; Luke 7:38, **to anoint**; (20x LXX; 7x Ezek) Ruth 3:3, **to apply oil**; Ezek 13:10–15,[6x] **to plaster**; Dan 10:3, **to anoint myself**

ἀλεκτοροφωνία, ας, ἡ$_{1α}$ {ἀλέκτωρ + φωνή} ①[gfs] Mark 13:35, **rooster's crow**

ἀλέκτωρ, ορος, ὁ$_3$ (12x) Matt 26:34 = Mark 14:30 = Luke 22:34 = John 13:38, **rooster** ①[nms] LXX, Prov 30:31, **rooster** *strutting courageously among the hens*

Ἀλεξανδρεύς, εως, ὁ$_3$ ❷[dmp] Acts 6:9; 18:24, **Alexandrian**; ①[dmp] LXX, 3 Macc 2:30

Ἀλεξανδρῖνος, η, ον$_{2.1.2}$ ❷ Acts 27:6; 28:11, **Alexandria**

Ἀλέξανδρος, ου, ὁ$_2$ ❻ Mark 15:21; Acts 4:6; 19:33[2x]; 1 Tim 1:20; 2 Tim 4:14, **Alexander**; *only the pastoral refs. likely refer to the same person*; (27x LXX)

ἄλευρον, ου, τό$_2$ {ἀλήθω} ❷ Matt 13:33 = Luke 13:21, **flour**; (13x LXX; 6x 1–2 Kgs)

ἀλήθεια, ας, ἡ$_{1α}$ {α + λανθάνω} (109x; 25x John, 20x 1–3 John) 1 Cor 13:6, **truth**; John 1:14–18:38,[20x] **truth**; Luke 22:59, **surely**; (179x LXX; 59x Pss, 13x Isa)

ἀληθεύω {α + λανθάνω} ❷ Gal 4:16, **to tell** *or* **speak the truth**; Eph 4:15, **to conduct oneself according to the truth**[*BrDAG*]; ❺ LXX, Isa 44:26, **to prove true**

ἀληθής, ές$_{3.3}$ {α + λανθάνω} *adj.* (26x; 14x John) Matt 22:16, **genuine**, **correctly**; John 3:33–21:24[14x] **valid**, **true**; Acts 12:9, **real**; Rom 3:4, 2 Pet 2:22, **true**; (20x LXX; 12x Wis)

ἀληθινός, ή, όν$_{2.1.2}$ {α + λανθάνω} *adj.* (28x; 10x Rev, 9x John) Luke 16:11; John 1:9; 1 Thess 1:9; Heb 10:22; Rev 3:7, **true**; (43x LXX; 10x Job, 7x Isa)

ἀλήθω ❷ Matt 24:41 = Luke 17:35, **to grind** *at a mill*; ❹ LXX, Num 11:8; Judg 16:21

ἀληθῶς {α + λανθάνω} *adv.* (18x, 7x John) Matt 14:33; 26:73, **truly**; (18x LXX; 3x 4 Macc)

ἁλιεύς, έως, ὁ$_3$ {ἅλας} ❺ Matt 4:18 = Mark 1:16, **fisherman**; Matt 4:19 = Mark 1:17, **fishers** *of men*; Luke 5:2, **fishers of men** (cf. 5:10 *now you will catch* (**ζωγρέω**) *live people*; 2 Tim 2:26, *caught* (**ζωγρέω**) *alive, the devil has snared the lost to do his will*); ❹ LXX, Job 40:31

ἁλιεύω {ἅλας} ①[painf] John 21:3, **to fish**; ①[fai3p] LXX, Jer 16:16, **they shall catch**

ἁλίζω {ἅλας} ❷[fpi3s] Matt 5:13, ἐν τίνι **ἁλισθήσεται,** *how can it* **be made salty?**; Mark 9:49,[*DGNT2*] **will be salted**; ❷ LXX, Ezek 16:4

ἀλίσγημα, ατος, τό$_3$ ①[gnp] Acts 15:20, **contaminated by idols**

ἀλλά, ἀλλ᾽ {ἄλλος} *conj.* (638x) Ⓐ ***adversative particle***, John 16:20, **but**; Luke 24:21, **ἀλλά** γε, **but even**; Phil 3:8, ἀλλὰ μενοῦνγε, **really**; Ⓑ ***redemptive emphasis in John and Paul***; John 5:30, *not* . . . **but**; Rom 5:3, *not only* . . . **but also**; Ⓒ ***intensive contrast***, Rom 12:2, *do not be* **(x) . . . but** *be* **(y)**[*EDNT*]; (557x LXX; Isa 55x, 4 Macc 50x, Job 40x)

ἀλλάσσω {ἄλλος} ❻ Acts 6:14; Gal 4:20; Heb 1:12, **to change**; Rom 1:23, **to trade away**; (37x LXX; 7x Lev, 4x Jer) Isa 40:31, **to renew strength**

ἀλλαχόθεν {ἄλλος + θεν} *adv.* ① John 10:1, **some other way**; ① LXX, 4 Macc 1:7

ἀλλαχοῦ {ἄλλος} *adv.* ① Mark 1:38; Xen. *Hel.* 2.3.20, **elsewhere**

ἀλληγορέω[con] {ἄλλος + ἀγορά} ①[pmp.nnp] Gal 4:24, **to speak allegorically**

ἁλληλουϊά$_3$ *indecl.* (= הַלְלוּ־יָהּ) *Heb.* ❹ Rev 19:1, 3, 4, 6, **Hallelujah! Praise Yah(weh)!**; (23x LXX; 21x Pss 104–150) *refrain in v. 1 of the "Five Hallelujah Psalms,"* 146–150[ABC]

ἀλλήλων, οις, ους, *recipr. plur. pron.* (100x; 15x John, 14x Rom) Matt 24:10, 25:32; Mark 9:50; Acts 4:15, **one another**; Rom 1:12, ἐν **ἀλλήλοις**, **mutual**; (42x LXX)

ἀλλογενής, ές$_{3.3}$ {ἄλλος + γίνομαι} *adj.* ①[nms] Luke 17:18, **foreigner**; (47x LXX; 11x Esd)

ἅλλομαι ❸ John 4:14, **to spring up**[ZEC]; Acts 3:8; 14:10, **to jump up**; ❼ LXX, 1 Sam 10:2, 10; Job 6:10, **to leap upon**; Callim. *H.* 3.195, **he leapt into the sea**

ἄλλος, η, ο$_{2.1.2}$ *adj.* (155x) Matt 2:12; 1 Cor 3:10; Rev 14:6, **another**; Luke 9:8; 1 Cor 3:11, **other**; Jas 5:12; (105x LXX; 18x 1–2 Macc, 13x Dan)

ἀλλοτριεπίσκοπος, ου, ὁ$_2$ {ἄλλος + ἐπί + σκοπός} ①[nms] *neol.* 1 Pet 4:15, **troublemaker**[Keen1P!]; Epiph. *Anc.* 12.5, **snoopy busybody**[*BrDAG*]; Epict. *Diatr.* 3.22.97, **self-appointed censor of another's morality**[Herm!, BEC 296–97!]

ἀλλότριος, α, ον$_{2.1.2}$ *adj.* (14x) John 10:5, **stranger**; Luke 16:12, **someone else**; Rom 14:4; Heb 9:25, **another**; 2 Cor 10:15, **other people**; 1 Tim 5:22, **others'** *sins* (161x LXX; 18x Jer, 17x Prov)

ἀλλόφυλος, ον$_{2.2}$ {ἄλλος + φύω} *adj.* ①[dms] Acts 10:28, **of a different tribe**, **gentile**; (287x LXX; 133x 1 Sam, 35x Judg); **foreigners**, **aliens**

ἄλλως {ἄλλος} *adv.* ① 1 Tim 5:25, **otherwise, in another way**; ❼ LXX, Esth 1:19

ἀλοάω[con] ❸ 1 Cor 9:9, 10; 1 Tim 5:18, **to beat** *or* **thresh grain**; (10x LXX) Deut 25:4, *you shall not muzzle a* **threshing** *ox*

ἄλογος, ον$_{2.2}$ {α + λέγω} *adj.* ❸ Acts 25:27, **unreasonable, foolish**; 2 Pet 2:12; Jude 10, *beasts* **without reason**; ❽ LXX, Exod 6:12, **without eloquence**; Num 6:12, **not reckoned**

ἀλόη, ῆς, ἡ$_{1\eta}$ ①[gfs] John 19:39, **aloe**, *aromatic tree sap*; **agalloch, aloeswood**[BrDAG]

ἁλυκός, ή, όν$_{2.1.2}$ {ἅλας} *adj.* ①[nns] Jas 3:12, **salty**; ❽ LXX, Josh 15:2, *Sea of* **Salt**

ἄλυπος, ον$_{2.2}$ {α + λυπή} *adj.* ①[nms] *compar.*, Phil 2:28, **less grieved, less sorrowful**[NIGTC]

ἅλυσις, εως, ἡ$_3$ (11x) Mark 5:3, 4 = Luke 8:29, **chain**; Acts 28:20, *fig.*, **chains** *for the hope of the resurrection*[ZEC]; Rev 20:1, **chain**; ①[dfs] LXX, Wis 17:60, **locked up** *in darkness without bars*

ἀλυσιτελής, ές$_{3.3}$ {α + λύω + τέλος} ①[nns] Heb 13:17, *commerce*, **unprofitable**

ἄλφα, τό$_3$ ❸ Rev 1:8; 21:6; 22:13, **Alpha, the beginning**

Ἁλφαῖος, ου, ὁ$_2$ ❺ Matt 10:3 = Mark 3:18 = Luke 6:15; Acts 1:13, **Alpheus**

ἀλώπηξ, εκος, ἡ$_3$ ❸ Matt 8:20 = Luke 9:58, *zool.* **Egyptian fox**[BrDAG]; Luke 13:32, *metaph.*, **fox** *as in crafty, sly, or cunning*; ❽ LXX, Judg 1:35; 15:4 (*Samson's fiery fox ploy*)

ἅλων, ωνος, ἡ$_3$ {ἀλοάω} ❷ Matt 3:12 = Luke 3:17, **threshing floor**; (24x LXX)

ἅλωσις, εως, ἡ$_3$ ①[afs] 2 Pet 2:12, εἰς ἅλωσιν, *for* **capture**; ①[gfs] LXX Jer 27:46, **capture**

ἅμα (10x) Ⓐ ***impr. prep. w/ dat.***, Matt 13:29, **at the same time**; 20:1, **together with**; Ⓑ ***adverb***, Acts 24:26; 1 Thess 4:17; Phlm 22, **at the same time**; (119x LXX; 38x Isa) Jonah 4:8, **ἅμα** τῷ ἀνατεῖλαι τὸν ἥλιον, **as soon as** *the sun arose*

ἀμαθής, ές$_{3.3}$ {α + μανθάνω} *adj.* ①[nmp] 2 Pet 3:16, **ignorant, oblivious, uninstructed**[TNTC]

ἀμαράντινος, η, ον$_{2.1.2}$ {α + μαραίνω} *adj.* ①[ams] 1 Pet 5:4, *fig.*, **unfading, indestructible**

ἀμάραντος, ον$_{2.2}$ {α + μαραίνω} *adj.* ①[afs] 1 Pet 1:4, *fig.*, **imperishable, spiritual heredity**[BrDAG]; ①[nfs] LXX, Wis 6:12, *wisdom is* **unfading**

ἁμαρτάνω (43x; 10x 1 John) Matt 18:15, 21; Luke 15:18, 21; John 5:14; Rom 3:23; 1 Cor 6:15; 8:12; 1 John 1:10; 5:16, **to sin, to do wrong**; (258x LXX; 29x Lev, 18x 1 Sam, 15x Job)

ἁμάρτημα, ατος, τό$_2$ {ἁμαρτάνω} ❹ Mark 3:28, 29; Rom 3:25; 1 Cor 6:18, **sin, error, failing**; (36x LXX; 6x Wis) Gen 31:36, **crime, error**

ἁμαρτία, ας, ἡ$_{1\alpha}$ {ἁμαρτάνω} (173x; 39x Rom, 24x Heb, 12x 1 John) Matt 1:21; Rom 3:9; Heb 1:3; Jas 1:15; 1 John 1:7–9,[3x] **sin, error, failing**; (526x LXX; 99x Lev, 56x Num, 52x Sir)

ἀμάρτυρος, ον$_{2.2}$ *adj.* ①[ams] Acts 14:17, **lacking witness**

ἁμαρτωλός, όν$_{2.2}$ {ἁμαρτάνω} *adj.* (47x; 18x Luke) Matt 9:10; Jude 15, **sinner**; John 9:16; Rom 7:13, **sinful**; (142x LXX; 69x Pss, 40x Sir); Pseud., 35x Pss. Sol.

ἄμαχος, ον$_{2.2}$ {α + μάχη} *adj.* ❷ 1 Tim 3:3; Titus 3:2, **noncombative, peaceful**[NIGTC]

ἀμάω[con] ①[aap.gmp] Jas 5:4, **reaped, mowed, harvested**[KEL]; ❺ LXX, Mic 6:15, **to reap**

ἀμέθυστος, ου, ἡ$_{2\acute{o}\delta\acute{o}\varsigma}$ {α + μεθύω} ①[nfs] Rev 21:20, **amethyst**; ❸ LXX, Exod 28:19; 36:19 (39:12); Ezek 28:13

ἀμελέω[con] {α + μέλω} ❹ Matt 22:5, **to make light of**; 1 Tim 4:14, **to neglect**; Heb 2:3, **to be heedless, to reject** *God's purposes*[ABC]; 8:9, **I paid no attention** *to them*[ABC]; ❹ LXX, 2 Macc 4:14; Wis 3:10; Jer 4:17; 38:32 (31:32)

ἄμεμπτος, ον$_{2.2}$ {α + μέμφομαι} *adj.* ❺ Luke 1:6, **blameless**; 1 Thess 3:13, *eschat.*, **blameless** = Phil 2:15, *presently* **ethically blameless**[ABC!]; 3:6, **exceptional merit**[BDAG]; Heb 8:7, **faultless**; (16x LXX; 11x Job) Gen 17:1; Job 1:1; 2:3, **blameless**

ἀμέμπτως {α + μέμφομαι} *adv.* ❷ 1 Thess 2:10; 5:23, **blamelessly**; ① LXX, Esth 13:4

ἀμέριμνος, ον$_{2.2}$ {α + μεριμνάω} *adj.* ❷ Matt 28:14, *keeping one* **out of trouble** (HCSB); 1 Cor 7:32, **free from anxieties**[NIGTC!]; ❷ LXX, Wis 6:15; 7:23, **carefree**

ἀμετάθετος, ον$_{2.2}$ {α + μετά + τίθημι} *adj.* ❷ Heb 6:17, 18, **irrevocable, unchanging**; ❷ LXX, 3 Macc 5:1, 12, **intractable, uncompromising**

ἀμετακίνητος, ον$_{2.2}$ {α + μετά + κίνεω} *adj.* ①[nmp] 1 Cor 15:58, **immovable**[NIGTC]

ἀμεταμέλητος, ον$_{2.2}$ {α + μετά + μέλω} *adj.* ❷ Rom 11:29, **irrevocable**; 2 Cor 7:10, **with no regrets**[BEC]

ἀμετανόητος, ον$_{2.2}$ {α + μετά + νοῦς} *adj.* ①[afs] Rom 2:5, **unrepentant**

ἄμετρος, ον$_{2.2}$ {α + μέτρον} *adj.* ❷ 2 Cor 10:13, 15, **excessively, to an excessive degree**[BEC]; Epict. *Ench.* 33, **excessive** *swashbuckler tales at a party*

ἀμήν (254x; 50x John, 31x Matt) *Aram./Heb. term*; Ⓐ ***for verification***, Luke 18:29, **"I tell you the truth!"** Ⓑ ***emph. phrase***, *only in John*, 1:51, ἀμὴν ἀμήν (*25 pairs = 50x*), **"I assure you!"**[ZEC] Ⓒ ***voicing approval***, Rev 22:20, **Amen!**; (10x LXX) Neh 5:13

ἀμήτωρ, τορος, ὁ$_3$ {α + μήτηρ} ①[nms] Heb 7:3, **motherless**; Soph *El.* 1154, μήτηρ **ἀμήτωρ**, *mother that is* **not a mother**

ἀμίαντος, ον$_{2.2}$ {α + μιαίνω} *adj.* ❹ Heb 7:26; 13:4; Jas 1:27; 1 Pet 1:4, **undefiled, uncontaminated**[TLNT]; ❺ LXX, 2 Macc 14:36; Wis 3:13; Bacchyl. *Epin.* 3.86, **uncontaminated** *ether*

Ἀμιναδάβ, ὁ$_2$ ❸ Matt 1:4[2x] = Luke 3:33, **Amminidab**; (27x LXX; 10x 1 Chr) 1 Chr 2:10[2x]

ἄμμος, ου, ἡ$_{2\ ὁδός}$ ❺ Matt 7:26, **sand**; Rom 9:27; Heb 11:12; Rev 12:18; 20:8, **sand** *of the sea*; (32x LXX; 6x Gen); Xen. *Mem.* 3.3.6, **sandy ground**, *for running*

ἀμνός, οῦ, ὁ$_2$ ❹ John 1:29, 36; Acts 8:32; 1 Pet 1:19, **lamb**; (101x LXX; 55x Num, 12x Lev)

ἀμοιβή, ῆς, ἡ$_{1η}$ ①[afp] 1 Tim 5:4, **repayment, make some return**[NIGTC]

ἄμπελος, ου, ἡ$_{2ὁδός}$ ❾ Matt 26:29 = Mark 14:25 = Luke 22:18; John 15:1; Rev 14:18, **vine**; Jas 3:12, **grapevine**; Rev 14:19, **grape harvest**; (67x LXX; 9x Isa, 7x Ezek)

ἀμπελουργός, οῦ, ὁ$_2$ {ἄμπελος + ἔργον} ①[ams] Luke 13:7, **vinedresser**; ❹ LXX, Isa 61:5

ἀμπελών, ῶνος, ὁ$_3$ {ἄμπελος} (23x; *22x in Synoptic parables*; *1x in Pauline illust.*) Matt 21:33 = Mark 12:1, 2 = Luke 20:9, 10; 1 Cor 9:7, **vineyard**; (97x LXX; 15x Isa, 10x 1 Kgs)

Ἀμπλιᾶτος, ου, ὁ$_2$ ①[ams] Rom 16:8, **Ampliatus**

ἀμύνομαι ①[ami3s] Acts 7:24, **strongly moved to defend, intervene**; (10x LXX) Josh 10:13, **to avenge oneself**; Ps 117:10 (118:10), **to destroy**

ἀμφιβάλλω ①[pap.amp] Mark 1:16, **to cast a net**; ①[fai3s] LXX, Hab 1:17, **ἀμφιβαλεῖ** τὸ ἀμφίβληστρον αὐτοῦ, **to cast** *his fishing net*

ἀμφίβληστρον, ου, τό$_2$ {ἀμφί + βάλλω} ①[ans] Matt 4:18, **fishing net**; ❺ LXX, Hab 1:15–17

ἀμφιέζω {*var. form of* **ἀμφιέννυμι**} {ἀμφί + ἕννυμι} ①[pai3s] Luke 12:28, **to clothe**

ἀμφιέννυμι {ἀμφί + ἕννυμι} ❸ Matt 6:30, **to clothe** *the grass*; Matt 11:8 = Luke 7:25, **to be dressed**; ❷ LXX, 2 Kgs 17:9, **to clothe**; Job 40:10, **to put on** *glory and honor*

Ἀμφίπολις, εως, ἡ$_3$ ①[afs] Acts 17:1, **Amphipolis**[Keen3]

ἄμφοδον, ου, τό$_2$ {ἀμφί, *on both sides* + ὁδός} ①[gns] Mark 11:4, **street**; ❷ LXX, Jer 17:27, **citadels** (CSB); **fortified dwellings** (NET); **palaces and all** (MSG)

ἀμφότεροι, αι, α$_{2.1.2}$ {ἄμφω} *adj.*, *plural only* (14x) Matt 9:17; 13:30; 15:14 = Luke 6:39; Acts 8:38; Eph 2:14, **both**; (129x LXX; 20x Exod)

ἀμώμητος, ον$_{2.2}$ {α + μῶμος} *adj.* ①[nmp] 2 Pet 3:14, **spotless, unblemished**[ABC!]

ἄμωμον, ου, τό$_2$ ①[ans] Rev 18:13, **spice**[ABC]

ἄμωμος, ον$_{2.2}$ *adj.* ❽ Eph 1:4; Phil 2:15; Col 1:22, **without blemish**; (83x LXX; 23x Lev)

Ἀμώς, ὁ$_2$ *indecl.* ❸ Matt 1:10[2x]; Luke 3:25, **Amos**

ἄν *part. that injects uncertainty* (166x; 119x Gs) 🅐 ἄν + ***aor.***[a]***/impf.***[b] ***indicative***; Mark 6:56,[a] **whoever** *touched it*; Acts 2:45,[b] **as any** *had need*; 🅑 ἄν + ***subjunctive after a rel. clause***; 2 Cor 3:15, **whenever**; 🅒 ὅπως ἄν ***in purpose clause***; Luke 2:35, **so that** *the thoughts*; 🅓 ἄν + ***optative***; Acts 26:29, **εὐξαίμην ἄν, I wish**; (619x LXX; 84x Lev, 76x Deut)

ἀνά *prep. only w/ acc.* (13x) 🅐 Matt 13:25, **among**; 🅑 Matt 20:9; 1 Cor 14:27; Rev 4:8, **each**; 🅒 Mark 7:31, **in**; 🅓 Luke 9:3,[EGG!] **only one** *tunic*; 🅔 Luke 10:1, *with numbers*, **in groups of**[BDAG]; 🅕 1 Cor 6:5, **between**; 🅖 Rev 7:17, **the center**; (362x LXX; 67x Gen)

ἀνα**βαθμός, οῦ, ὁ**$_2$ {ἀνά + βαίνω} ❷ Acts 21:35, 40, **flight of stairs, steps**; (27x LXX)

ἀνα**βαίνω** (82x; 19x Acts) Luke 5:19, **to come up**; Matt 13:7, **to grow up**; John 10:1, **to climb into**; Eph 4:8, **to ascend**; Rev 17:8, **to rise**; (614x LXX; 56x Judg)

ἀνα**βάλλω** ①[ami3s] Acts 24:22, **to adjourn**[Herm]; ❻ LXX; Thuc. 4.90.2, **to dig and throw off** *dirt from a ditch*; Aristot. *Pr.* 876a 31, **to roll the eyes**[Keen4]

ἀνα**βιβάζω** {ἀνά + βαίνω} ①[aap.nmp] Matt 13:48, **to drag on** *shore*; (39x LXX; 7x Exod)

ἀνα**βλέπω** (25x, GA) Matt 11:5, **to receive sight**; 14:19 = Mark 6:41 = Luke 9:16, **to look up**; Mark 8:24, **to regain sight**; Matt 20:34 = Mark 10:52 = Luke 18:43, **to see** *immediately*; (31x LXX; 13x Gen)

ἀνά**βλεψις, εως, ἡ**$_3$ {ἀνά + βλέπω} ①[afs] Luke 4:18, **regaining of sight** *to the blind*; ①[afs] LXX, Isa 61:1; Aristot. *Phys.* 247b 8, **act of looking up**

ἀνα**βοάω**[con] {ἀνά + βοή} ①[aai3s] Matt 27:46, **to cry out with a loud voice**; (44x LXX)

ἀνα**βολή, ῆς, ἡ** {ἀνά + βάλλω} ①[afs] Acts 25:17, **deferment, delay**; ❸ LXX, 1 Chr 19:4, **garments**; Ezek 5:3, *tie them up in your* **skirts** (Tanakh)

ἀνά**γαιον, ου, τό**$_2$ {ἀνά + γῆ} ❷ Mark 14:15 = Luke 22:12, **upper room**

ἀνα**γγέλλω** {ἀνά + ἄγγελος} (14x) John 4:25, **to explain**; 5:15, **to tell**; 2 Cor 7:7, **to report**; Acts 19:18, **to admit, divulge**; 1 Pet 1:12, **to proclaim**; (230x LXX)

ἀνα**γεννάω**[con] {ἀνά + γεννάω} ❷ 1 Pet 1:3, **to birth anew**[Keen1P]; 1:23, **to be reborn**[Keen1P]

ἀνα**γινώσκω** (32x) Matt 12:3; Rev 1:3, **to read**; Acts 8:30, *do you understand what* **you are reading**?; (60x LXX; 18x Jer)

ἀναγκάζω {ἀνάγκη} ❾ Matt 14:22, **to impel, force**[ZEC]; 2 Cor 12:11, **to force into extreme measures**[BEC!]; Acts 26:11, **to force one** *into blasphemy*[Keen4]; Acts 28:19, **to be compelled**; Gal 2:3; 6:12, **to force** *believers to be circumcised*[Herm!]; (19x LXX) 2 Macc 6:18, **to force open** *Eleazar's mouth to eat swine's flesh*[SCS]

ἀναγκαῖος, α, ον$_{2.1.2}$ {ἀνάγκη} *adj.* ❽ Acts 10:24, **close** *friends*; Heb 8:3, **necessity**; 1 Cor 12:22, **essential**[NIGTC]; Titus 3:14, **urgent**; ❺ LXX, 2 Macc 4:23, **essential** *business*

ἀναγκαστῶς {ἀνάγκη} *adv.* ① 1 Pet 5:2, **like something you are forced to do**[Keen1P]

ἀνάγκη, ης, ἡ$_{1\eta}$ {ἀναγκάζω} (17x; 4x Heb) Matt 18:7, **inevitable**; Luke 14:18, **legal obligation**[NIGTC]; Rom 13:5, **moral obligation**[ABC]; 2 Cor 6:4, **crises**; 9:7, **pressure**[BEC]; (41x LXX, 10x 4 Macc), 2 Macc 15:2, **κατὰ ἀνάγκην,** *with* **compulsion**; Hp. *Fract.* 15, *medic.*, **mechanical constraint** *of a joint*[BrDAG]

ἀνα**γνωρίζω** {ἀνά + γινώσκω} ①[api3s] Acts 7:13, **to be revealed**; ①[imi3s] LXX, Gen 45:1

ἀνάγνωσις, εως, ἡ$_3$ {ἀνά + γινώσκω} ❸ Acts 13:15; 2 Cor 3:14; 1 Tim 4:13, **reading**; ❹ LXX, Neh 8:8; 1 Esd 9:48

ἀνάγω {ἀνά + ἄγω} (23x; 17x Acts) Matt 4:1 = Luke 4:5, **to lead**; Luke 2:22; Acts 12:41; Rom 10:7, **to bring**; Luke 8:22; *naut.*, **to set out** *across the lake*; Acts 28:11, *naut.*, **to put out to sea, set sail**[NICTC]; Heb 13:20, **to bring up** *from the dead*; (111x LXX)

ἀναδείκνυμι ❷ Luke 10:1, **to appoint**; Acts 1:24, **to show clearly**; (19x LXX; 7x 2 Macc, 6x 1 Esd)

ἀνάδειξις, εως, ἡ$_3$ {ἀνά + δείκνυμι} ①[gfs] Luke 1:80, *until the time he* **was made known**[ZEC]; ①[afs] LXX, Sir 43:6, **a proclamation**

ἀναδέχομαι ❷ Acts 28:7, **to welcome**; Heb 11:17, **to receive**; ❷[amp.nms] LXX, 2 Macc 6:19

ἀναδίδωμι ①[aap.nmp] Acts 23:33, to deliver; ❷ LXX, 2 Macc 13:15

ἀναζάω[con] ❷ Luke 15:24; Rom 7:9, **to spring to life again**; *see* **ἀναζωπυρέω** *below*

ἀναζητέω[con] ❸ Luke 2:44, 45; Acts 11:25, **to look for**; ❸ LXX, Job 3:4; 10:6, **to seek out**

ἀναζώννυμι ①[amp.nmp] *metaph.*, 1 Pet 1:13, **to keep** *one's mind* **ready**, *lit.*, **girding up** *the waist of your mind*[Keen1P!]; ①[amp.nfs] LXX, Prov 31:17

ἀναζωπυρέω[con] {ἀνά + ζάω + πύρ} ①[painf] 2 Tim 1:6, **to rekindle, to revivify**[ABC]; ❷ LXX, 1 Macc 13:7, **to revive** *the spirit*; Aristot. *On Spirit* 484A, **to reset the flame**

ἀναθάλλω {ἀνά + θηλάζω} ①[aai2p] Phil 4:10, **to restore to a previous state**[ABC]; ❾ LXX, Ps 27:7 (28:7), **to revive** *my flesh*; Ael. *V.H.* 5.4, **to rebloom**

ἀνάθεμα, ατος, τό$_3$ {ἀνά + τίθημι} ❻ Acts 23:14, **a solemn oath**[ZEC!]; Rom 9:3, **cursed and cut off** *from Christ*; 1 Cor 12:3, **accursed**; Gal 1:8, 9, **devoted to God for total destruction**[EGG]; (25x LXX; 12x Josh) Deut 13:16, *anathema*, **to devote to slaughter**; Josh 6:17–7:13,[11x] **devoted** *to God for annihilation*

ἀναθεματίζω {ἀνά + τίθημι} ❹ Mark 14:71, **to swear**[PNTC]; Acts 23:12, 21, **to put a death curse upon oneself**; 23:14, ἀναθέματι **ἀνεθεματίσαμεν, we cursed ourselves** *with a curse*[Keen3]; (13x LXX; 3x Num) Num 21:2, 3, **to destroy utterly**; Deut 20:17, ἀναθέματι **ἀναθεματιεῖτε, you shall annihilate** *them*

ἀναθεωρέω[con] {ἀνά + θεάομαι} ❷ Acts 17:23, **to examine carefully**; Heb 13:7, **to reflect carefully**; Thphr. *H.P.* 1.5.1, **to examine in depth**

ἀνάθημα, ατος, τό$_3$ {ἀνά + τίθημι} ①[dnp] Luke 21:5, **gifts consecrated to God**[ZEC]; ①[dnp] LXX, 3 Macc 3:17, **votive offerings**

ἀναίδεια, ας, ἡ$_{1α}$ {α + αἰδέομαι} ①[afs] Luke 11:8, **shamelessness**[ZEC]; ①[nfs] LXX, Sir 25:22, **audacity**; Soph. *El.* 607, **total lack of consideration**[BrDAG]

ἀναίρεσις, εως, ἡ$_3$ {ἀνά + αἱρέω} ①[dfs] Acts 8:1, **execution**, **murder**; ❹ LXX, Num 11:15, **by slaying**; Judg 15:17, Ἀναίρεσις σιαγόνος, *Jawbone's* **Slaying**

ἀναιρέω[con] {ἀνά + αἱρέω} (24x; 19x Acts) Matt 2:16; Luke 22:2; Acts 2:23, **to kill**, **execute**; Acts 7:21, **to raise up**, **rear**; 2 Thess 2:8, **to destroy**; Heb 10:9, **to nullify**; (81x LXX; 11x Isa:Jer) Exod 2:10, **to draw out**, *connected to Heb.* מֹשֶׁה (Moses)

ἀναίτιος, ον$_{2.2}$ {α + αἰτία} *adj.* ❷ Matt 12:5, 7, **guiltless**, **innocent**; ❺ LXX, Deut 19:10

ἀνακαθίζω {ἀνά + κατά + ἵζω} ❷[aai3s] Luke 7:15; Acts 9:40, **to sit up** *from the dead*

ἀνακαινίζω {ἀνά + καινός} ①[painf] Heb 6:6, **to renew**, **to restore** *as in conversion*; ❺ LXX, 1 Macc 6:9, *deep disappointment* . . . **gripped** *him*; Ps 38:3 (39:2), **to intensify**; Lam 5:21, **to renew**

ἀνα**καινόω**[con] {ἀνά + καινός} ❷ 2 Cor 4:16; Col 3:10, *pass.*, **to be renewed**

ἀνα**καίνωσις, εως,** ἡ$_3$ {ἀνά + καινός} ❷ Rom 12:2; Titus 3:5, **renewal**

ἀνα**καλύπτω** ❷ 2 Cor 3:14, 18, **to uncover**; (25x LXX; 9x Isa) Job 28:11, **to reveal**

ἀνα**κάμπτω** ❹ Matt 2:12; Luke 10:6; Acts 18:21; Heb 11:15, **to return**; (14x LXX; 4x Jer)

ἀνά**κειμαι** (14x Gs) Matt 9:10; 26:7; Mark 14:18; 16:14, **to recline**; Matt 22:10; Mark 6:26, **those reclining to eat**; John 6:11; 13:28, **seated**; ①[ppi3s] LXX, 1 Esd 4:11, **to recline**

ἀνα**κεφαλαιόω**[con] {ἀνά + κεφαλή} *pass.* ❷ Rom 13:9, **to summarize**; Eph 1:10, **to bring everything under the headship** *of Christ*; Dion. *Lys.* 9.4, *mid.*, **to recapitulate**

ἀνα**κλίνω** ❻ Matt 8:11 = Luke 13:29, **to recline**; Mark 6:29, **to sit down**; Luke 2:7, **to lay** *Jesus* **down**; ①[aainf] LXX, 3 Macc 5:16, **to recline**

ἀνα**κόπτω**[LXX] ❸ 4 Macc 1:35; 13:6, **to hinder, restrain**[SCS]; Wis 18:23, **to hold back**

ἀνα**κράζω** ❺ Mark 1:23; 6:49; Luke 4:33; 23:18, **to cry out**; (14x LXX) Josh 6:5, **to shout**

ἀνα**κρίνω** (16x; 10x 1 Cor) Luke 23:14; Acts 4:9; 28:18, **to examine**; 12:19, **to interrogate**; 1 Cor 2:14; 4:3, **to judge, discern**; 1 Cor 9:3, **to evaluate**; 14:25, **to be judged**[NIGTC!]; ❹ LXX, 1 Sam 20:12, **to question carefully**

ἀνά**κρισις, εως,** ἡ$_3$ {ἀνά + κρίνω} ①[gfs] Acts 25:26, **preliminary examination** *before trial*[ZEC, Kccn4]; ①[gfs] LXX, 3 Macc 7:5, **careful enquiry**

ἀνα**κύπτω** ❹ Luke 13:11, **to straighten up**; 21:38, **to stand up**; John 8:7, 10, **to rise** *after bending down to write*; ❷ LXX, Job 10:15, **to lift up** *my head*; Sus 35, **to look up**

ἀνα**λαμβάνω** (13x; 8x Acts) 1 Tim 3:16, **to take up**; Acts 20:13, **to board** *a ship*; 23:31, **to take**; Eph 6:13, *fig.*, **to take up** *arms*; 2 Tim 4:11, **to bring**; (94x LXX; 12x Ezek)

ἀνά**λημψις, εως,** ἡ$_3$ {ἀνά + λαμβάνω} ①[gfs] Luke 9:51, **ascension, death**; Pseud., Pss. Sol. 4.18, **death, removal**; *comp.* ἔξοδον in Luke 9:31[ZEC]; Aristot. *Mem.* 451a 20, **recovery**

ἀν**αλίσκω**[LXX] {ἀνά + ἅλωσις} (19x, 4x Ezek) Gen 41:30; Joel 2:3, **to consume** *the land*; **to be wasted**; Prov 23:28, **to be destroyed**; Ezek 5:12, **to be dispensed** *by death*

ἀνα**λογία, ας,** ἡ$_{1α}$ {ἀνά + λέγω} ①[afs] Rom 12:6, **proportion**

ἀνα**λογίζομαι** {ἀνά + λέγω} ①[ami] Heb 12:3, **carefully consider**; ❸ LXX, Isa 44:19, 3 Macc 7:7

ἄν**αλος, ον**$_{2.2}$ {α + ἅλας} *adj.* ①[nns] Mark 9:50, *if salt becomes* **unsalty**[ZEC, DGNT2]

ἀναλόω[con] ❷ Luke 9:54, **to obliterate** *them*[ZEC]; Gal 5:15, **to devour** *one another*

ἀνά**λυσις, εως,** ἡ$_3$ {ἀνά + λύω} ①[gfs] 2 Tim 4:6, **departure, death**

ἀνα**λύω** ❷ Luke 12:36, **to return**; Phil 1:23, **to depart, to die**; (18x LXX; 10x 2–3 Macc); Polyb. *Hist.* 3.69.14, **to raise anchor**, *to sail on*[ABC]; 5.28.8, **to break camp**

ἀν**αμάρτητος, ον**$_{2.2}$ {α + ἁμαρτάνω} *adj.* ①[nms] John 8:7, **without sin**; ❹ LXX, Deut 29:18

ἀνα**μένω** ①[painf] 1 Thess 1:10, **to await**; (10x LXX; 3x Sir, 2x Job) Job 2:9a, *I will* **hang on**

ἀνα**μιμνήσκω** {ἀνά + μιμνήσκομαι} ❻ Mark 11:21; 2 Cor 7:15; Heb 10:32, **to cause to recall, remember**; 1 Cor 4:17; 2 Tim 1:6, **to remind**; (10x LXX; 7x Ezek) Gen 41:9

ἀνά**μνησις, εως,** ἡ$_3$ {ἀνά + μιμνήσκομαι} ❹ Luke 22:19; 1 Cor 11:24, 25, **remembrance**[NIGTC]; Heb 10:3, **reminder**; ❹ LXX, Lev 24:7, **remembrance**

ἀνα**νεόω**[con] {ἀνά +νέος} ①[ppinf] Eph 4:23, **to be renewed** *in spirit*; (10x LXX; 7x 1 Macc)

ἀνα**νήφω** ①[aas3p] 2 Tim 2:26, **to regain control of oneself** *from the trap of the devil*; **to become sober**[PPE]

Ἀνανίας, ου, ὁ$_2$ (11x, Acts) Ⓐ **Ananias**, 5:1, 3, 5, *Christian in Jerusalem*; Ⓑ 9:10,[2x] 12, 13, 17; 22:12, *Christian in Damascus*; Ⓒ 23:2; 24:1, *the high priest*

ἀναντίρρητος, ον$_{2.2}$ {α + ἀντί + ῥῆμα} *adj.* ①[gnp] Acts 19:36, **indisputable**

ἀναντιρρήτως {α + ἀντί + ῥῆμα} *adv.* ① Acts 10:29, **without making objections**

ἀνάξιος, ον$_{2.2}$ {α + ἄξιος} *adj.* ①[nmp] 1 Cor 6:2, **unfit**[NIGTC]; ❹ LXX, Jer 15:19, **worthless**

ἀναξίως {α + ἄξιος} *adv.* ① 1 Cor 11:27, **careless manner**[NIGTC]; ① LXX, 2 Macc 14:42

ἀνάπαυσις, εως, ἡ$_3$ {ἀνά + παύω} ❺ Matt 11:29, **rest** *for your souls*; Matt 12:43 = Luke 11:24, **to seek rest**[ZEC]; Rev 4:8, *no* **cessation** *from praising God;* 14:11, *no* **cessation** *from suffering apart from God*; (61x LXX) Lev 16:31, **Sabbath rest**

ἀναπαύω (12x)[EDNT] Matt 11:28, **to provide rest**; Mark 6:31, *mid.*, **to take rest**; Luke 12:19, **to take it easy**[ZEC]; Phlm 7, *pass.*, **to be refreshed**; 2 Cor 7:13, *pass.*, **to be relieved of hard labor**[BEC]; 1 Pet 4:14, **to rest upon**; Rev 14:13, *blessed martyr's* **rest**[ZEC!]; (71x LXX; 17x Isa) Isa 14:2, *to enter the kingdom of* **shalom/rest**; Xen. *Cyr.* 2.4.3, **to stop** *an enemy*[BrDAG]

ἀναπείθω ①[pai3s] Acts 18:13, **to induce, to stir up by persuasion**[WPNT]; ❸ LXX, 1 Macc 1:11; Jer 36:8 (29:8) **to persuade**

ἀνάπειρος, ον$_{2.2}$ *adj.* ❷[amp] Luke 14:13, 21, **maimed, crippled**; ①[amp] LXX, 2 Macc 8:24

ἀναπέμπω ❺ Luke 23:7, 11, 15; Acts 25:21; Phlm 12, **to send**

ἀναπηδάω[con] ①[aap.nms] Mark 10:50, **to spring up**[NIGTC]; ❻ LXX, 1 Sam 25:9, **to wait**

ἀναπίπτω (12x; 5x John) Matt 15:35 = Mark 8:6; John 6:10; 13:10; 21:20, **to sit down**; Luke 11:37; 14:10; 17:7; 22:14, **to recline**; ❺ LXX, Gen 49:9, **to crouch**

ἀναπληρόω[con] ❻ Matt 13:14, **to be fulfilled**; *subst. ptc.*, 1 Cor 14:16, **the uninitiated,**[NIGTC] **those who are ungifted**[JBPhil]; (13x LXX) Gen 2:21, **to fill up**

ἀναπολόγητος, ον$_{2.2}$ {α + ἀπό + λέγω} *adj.* ❷ Rom 1:20; 2:1, **without excuse**; Dion. *Rom. Ant.* 7.46.4, *one* **who does not defend himself** *in court*

ἀναπτύσσω ①[aap.nms] Luke 4:17, **to unroll**; ❺ LXX, Deut 22:17, **to spread out** *a garment*; Soph. *El.* 639, *fig.*, **to put into the light, expose**

ἀνάπτω {ἀνά + πτύσσω} ❷ Luke 12:49, **to cast fire**; Jas 3:5, **to kindle**; (24x LXX; 7x Jer)

ἀναρίθμητος, ον$_{2.2}$ {α + ἀριθμός} *adj.* ①[nms] Heb 11:12, **innumerable**; (13x LXX; 3x Job)

ἀνασείω ❷ Mark 15:11; Luke 23:5, **to stir up, to agitate, to incite**;[NIGTC] Thuc. 4.38.1, *dropping shields and then* **waving** *the hands seeking a truce*

ἀνασκευάζω {ἀνά + σκεῦος} ①[pap.nmp] Acts 15:24, **to upset**; Thuc. 4.116.2, **to devastate**

ἀνασπάω[con] ❷ Luke 14:5, **to pull out**; Acts 11:10, **to pull up**; ❸ LXX, Amos 9:2, **to pull out** *of Sheol*; Hab 1:15, **to pull up** *with a fishhook*; Thuc. 4.9.1, **to ground a ship on land**

ἀνάστασις, εως, ἡ$_3$ {ἀνά + ἵστημι} (42x; 12x Syn, 11x Acts) Luke 2:34; John 5:29[2x]; 1 Cor 15:12; Phil 3:10, **resurrection**; Rev 20:5, *the first* **resurrection**; ❻ LXX, 2 Macc 7:14

ἀναστατόω[con] {ἀνά + ἵστημι} ❸ Acts 17:6, *hyperbole* **to cause trouble everywhere,**[TNTC]; 21:38, **to raise a rebellion**; Gal 5:12, **to subvert**[NIGTC]; ①[fai3s] LXX, Dan 7:23; P. Oxy. 119.10, *Theon,* **after upsetting** *Theon's mother, she expelled Theon from home*

ἀνασταυρόω[con] ①[pap.amp] Heb 6:6, **to crucify again**; Hdt. *Hist.* 3.125.3, **to hoist on a pole**

ἀναστενάζω {ἀνά + στένος} ①[aap.nms] Mark 8:12, **to sigh deeply in frustration**[ZEC]; ❸ LXX, 2 Macc 6:30; Lam 1:4, **to groan aloud**

ἀναστρέφω ❾ Acts 5:22, **to return**; 2 Cor 1:12, *mid.*[WPNT] **to live** *a principled life*[BEC]; Eph 2:3, *mid.*, **to live** *in spiritual darkness*; 1 Tim 3:15, *mid.*, **to practice**[NIGTC]; Heb 10:33, **to treat**; 2 Pet 2:18, *mid.*, **to live** *in error*; (106x LXX; 27x 1–2 Sam)

ἀναστροφή, ῆς, ἡ$_{1η}$ {ἀνά + στρέφω} (13x; 8x 1–2 Pet) *reprehensible* **way of life, conduct**; 2 Pet

2:7; *praiseworthy* **conduct**; 1 Tim 4:12; Jas 3:13; 1 Pet 1:15[Herm n61]; 2 Pet 3:11, **way of life, conduct, lifestyle**; 1 Pet 1:15; 3:1, **behavior**; ❷ LXX, Tob 4:14; 2 Macc 6:23

ἀνα**τάσσομαι** {ἀνά + τάσσω} ①[aminf] Luke 1:1, **to put together in order**

ἀνα**τέλλω** ❾ Matt 4:16; 2 Pet 1:19, **to dawn** (*Isa 9:1–2*); Matt 5:45, **to cause to rise**; 13:6 = Mark 4:6, **to rise**; Heb 7:14, **to descend, to spring from**; (58x LXX; 14x Isa, 6x Pss)

ἀνα**τίθημι** ❷ Acts 25:14, **to explain**; Gal 2:2, **to present**; ❾ LXX, Lev 27:28, **to dedicate**

ἀνα**τολή, ῆς, ἡ**$_{1\eta}$ (11x, 5x Matt) Matt 2:1; 24:27; Luke 13:29; Rev 21:13; **the east**; Luke 1:78, **the Dawn**; Rev 7:2, **rising**; (181x LXX; 54x Ezek), Zech 3:8; 6:12, **"The Branch"**

ἀνα**τρέπω** ❸ John 2:15, *lit.*, **to overturn** *tables*; 2 Tim 2:18; Titus 1:11, *fig.*, **to throw into confusion**[ABC]; ❾ LXX, Prov 10:3, **to thwart**; Gal. *U.P.* 12.911, *medic.*, **to wrangle the stomach**[BrDAG]

ἀνα**τρέφω** ❸ Acts 7:20, 21 (*Moses*); 22:3 (*Paul*), **to make grow by nourishing education**[BrDAG]; ❸ LXX, 4 Macc 10:2; Aeschl. *Eum.* 523, **to raise the morale** *of the troops*

ἀνα**φαίνω** ❷ Luke 19:11, **to appear**; Acts 21:3, *a ship* **to come in sight**; ❻ LXX, 4x Job

ἀνα**φέρω** (10x; 4x Heb) Matt 17:1 = Mark 9:2, **to lead up**; Luke 24:51, **to carry up**; Heb 7:27,[2x] 13:15; Jas 2:21, **to offer up**; Heb 9:28, **to take away**; 1 Pet 2:24, **to carry** *our sins*[Keen1P]; (155x LXX; 26x Lev) Gen 22:2, **to offer** *him as a sacrifice*

ἀνα**φωνέω**[con] ①[aai3s] Luke 1:42, **to shout, cry out**; ❺ LXX (1–2 Chr), 1 Chr 15:28, **to play loudly**; 2 Chr 5:13, **to speak out**; Aristot. *Mir.* 400a 18, **to say emphatically**

ἀναχθῆναι → **ἀνάγω**, *aor. pass. inf.*, Acts 21:1; 27:12, **to set sail**

ἀνά**χυσις, εως, ἡ**$_3$ {ἀνά + χέω → *to pour*} ①[afs] 1 Pet 4:4, *fig.*, **torrent, flood**, *wild* **excess** *of degeneracy*[ABC]

ἀνα**χωρέω**[con] (14x; 10x Matt) Matt 2:12; 4:12; John 6:15; Acts 26:31, **to withdraw, leave**; Acts 23:19, **to draw aside**; (14x LXX) Exod 2:15, **to flee**

ἀνά**ψυξις, εως, ἡ**$_3$ {ἀνά + ψύχω} ①[gfs] Acts 3:20, **refreshment**,[Keen2] **relief**[ZEC]; ①[nfs] LXX, Exod 8:11, **relief** *from frog deluge*; Hp. *De medico* 3.5, **relief** *from physical pain*

ἀνα**ψύχω** ①[aai3s] 2 Tim 1:16, **to revive, refresh, cool off**; ❼ LXX, Exod 23:12

ἀνδρα**ποδιστής, οῦ, ὁ**$_{1>}$ {ἀνήρ + πούς} ①[dmp] 1 Tim 1:10, **kidnapper**; Lys. *Sp.* 10.10, **snatcher**[BrDAG]

Ἀνδρέας, ου, ὁ$_2$ (13x) Matt 10:2 = Mark 3:18 = Luke 6:14; Acts 1:13, **Andrew**

ἀνδρίζομαι {ἀνήρ} ①[pmimp2p] 1 Cor 16:13, **to show mature courage**[NIGTC]; (24x LXX)

Ἀνδρόνικος, ου, ὁ$_2$ ①[ams] Rom 16:7, **Andronicus**

ἀνδρο**φόνος, ου, ὁ**$_2$ {ἀνήρ + φόνος} ①[dmp] 1 Tim 1:9, **murderer**; ① LXX, 2 Macc 9:28

ἀνέ**γκλητος, ον**$_{2.2}$ {α + ἐν + καλέω} *adj.* ❺ 1 Cor 1:8; Col 1:22, *jur.* **unimpeachable**; 1 Tim 3:10; Titus 1:6, 7, **beyond reproach**; ①[gmp] LXX, 3 Macc 5:31, **no ground for complaint** Plato *Leg.* 737a, **that makes no room for protests**[BrDAG]

ἀνεθέμην → **ἀνατίθημι**, *aor. mid. ind. 1s*, Gal 2:2, **presented** *the gospel to them*

ἀν**εκδιήγητος, ον**$_{2.2}$ {α + ἐκ + διά + ἄγω} *adj.* ①[dfs] 2 Cor 9:15, **indescribable**; Pseud., Let. Aris. 99, **a wonder beyond description**

ἀν**εκλάλητος, ον**$_{2.2}$ {α + ἐκ + λάλος} *adj.* ①[dfs] 1 Pet 1:8, **inexpressible, unutterable**[Keen1P]

ἀνέ**κλειπτος, ον**$_{2.2}$ {α + ἐκ + λείπω} *adj.* ①[ams] Luke 12:33, **totally inexhaustible**[ZEC]

ἀν**εκτός, όν**$_{2.2}$ {ἀνά + ἔχω} *adj.* ❺ Matt 10:15 = Luke 10:12; Matt 11:22 = Luke 10:14, **bearable, tolerable**; Plato *Theaet.* 154c, οὐκ ἀνεκτόν, **it is unbearable**

ἀν**ελεήμων, ον**$_{2.2}$ {α + ἔλεος} *adj.* ①[amp] Rom 1:31, **impious, cruel**; (11x LXX; 5x Prov) Prov 5:9, **merciless**; 11:17, **the one doing harm**

ἀνέλεος, ον$_{2.2}$ {α + ἔλεος} *adj.* ①[nfs] Jas 2:13, **merciless**

ἀνελήμφθη → **ἀναλαμβανω,** *aor. pass. ind. 3s* ❺ Mark 16:19, **he was taken up**

ἀνεμίζω {ἄνεμος} ①[ppp.dms] *neol.*[WPNT] Jas 1:6, **driven by the wind**

ἄνεμος, ου, ὁ$_2$ (31x; 20x Syn) Matt 7:25; Mark 4:37; Rev 6:13, **wind**; (64x LXX)

ἀνένδεκτος, ον$_{2.2}$ {α + ἐν + δέχομαι} *adj.* ①[nns] Luke 17:1, **inevitable**

ἀνενέγκας (*kappa aor.*)[BBG] → **ἀναφέρω,** *aor. act. ptc. nms,* Heb 7:27, **offering** *himself*

ἀνεξεραύνητος, ον$_{2.2}$ {α + ἐκ + ἔρομαι} *adj.* ①[nnp] Rom 11:33, **unsearchable**

ἀνεξίκακος, ον$_{2.2}$ {ἀνά + ἔχω + κακός} *adj.* ①[ams] 2 Tim 2:24, **extraordinary patience in the face of evil**[NIGTC]

ἀνεξιχνίαστος, ον$_{2.2}$ {ἀν + ἔχω + ἴχνος} *adj.* ❷ Rom 11:33[NAC]; Eph 3:8, **unsearchable, impossible to find**; ❹ LXX, [NAC] Job 5:9; 9:10; 34:24, **inscrutable** *mysteries of creation*

ἀνεπαίσχυντος, ον$_{2.2}$ {α + ἐπί + αἶσχος} *adj.* ①[ams] 2 Tim 2:15, **unashamed**

ἀνεπίλημπτος, ον$_{2.2}$ {α + ἐπί + λαμβάνω} *adj.* ❸ 1 Tim 3:2; 5:7; 6:14, **above reproach**

ἀνέρχομαι {ἀνά + ἔρχομαι} ❸ John 6:3; Gal 1:17, 18, **to go up**; ①[aai3s] LXX, 1 Kgs 13:12

ἄνεσις, εως, ἡ$_3$ {ἀνά + ἵημι → *to send, set in motion*} ❺ Acts 24:23, **freedom**; 2 Cor 2:13; 7:5; 8:13[BEC], *phys.* **rest, relief**; 2 Thess 1:7, *eschat.*, **relief, rest, ease**; ❻ LXX, Ezra 4:22, **remiss**

ἀνετάζω {ἀνά + ἐτάζω} ❷ Acts 22:24, 29, **to examine** μάστιξιν, *with a whip,*[ZEC] *under torture*[BrDAG]; ①[iai3p] LXX, Judg 6:29, **they investigated** *the matter thoroughly*

ἄνευ *impr. prep. w/gen.* ❸ Matt 10:29; 1 Pet 3:1; 4:9,[Keen1P] **apart, without**; (44x LXX; 9x Job)

ἀνεύθετος, ον$_{2.2}$ {α + εὖ + τίθημι} *adj.* ①[gms] Acts 27:12, **unsuitable**

ἀνευρίσκω {ἀνά + εὑρίσκω} ❷ Luke 2:16; Acts 21:4, **to locate, find**; ①[amp.nmp] LXX, 4 Macc 3:14, **having boldly discovered**

ἀνέχω {ἀνά + ἔχω} *only mid.* (15x; 5x 2 Cor) Matt 17:17 = Mark 9:19 = Luke 9:41; 2 Cor 11:1, 4, 19, 20,[BEC] **to put up with**; 2 Thess 1:4, **to endure**; Eph 4:2 = Col 3:13, *imp. sense,* **to put up** *with each other*[ZEC]; Acts 18:14, *legal t.t.*, **to agree to hear a case**[Keen3]; 2 Tim 4:3[NIGTC]; Heb 13:22,[NIGTC] **to listen willingly** *to sound teaching*; (17x LXX; 5x Isa) *act.*, Hag 1:10; *mid.*, Isa 1:13; *pass.* 4 Macc 1:35

ἀνεψιός, οῦ, ὁ$_2$ ①[nms] Col 4:10, **cousin**; ❷ LXX, Num 36:11; Tob 7:2

ἀνεῴχθη → **ἀνοίγω,** *aor. pass. ind. 3s,* Luke 1:64, *his mouth* **was opened**

ἄνηθον, ου, τό$_2$ ①[ans] Matt 23:23, **dill**

ἀνήκω {ἀνά + ἥκω} ❸ Eph 5:4, *to be not* **appropriate**[ZEC]; Col 3:18, *to* **be fitting**; *subst.*, Phlm 8, **fitting thing**[IPT 71]; ❾ LXX, Josh 23:14, **concerning things**

ἀνήμερος, ον$_{2.2}$ {α + ἥμερος → *tame*} *adj.* ①[nmp] 2 Tim 3:3, **undomesticated, wild, savage**; Anacr. 1.7, **wild** *citizens*; Aeschl. *Pr.* 716, *avoid* **the savage** *Chalybes*

ἀνήρ, ἀνδρός, ὁ$_3$ (216x; 100x Acts, 32x 1 Cor) Matt 1:6, **husband**; 7:24, 12:41, **man, men**; Acts 1:16, **brothers**; (1,673x LXX; 290x 1–2 Sam, 208x Judg, 146x Prov)

ἀνηρέθη → **ἀναιρέω,** *aor. pass. ind. 3s,* Acts 5:36, **he was killed**

ἀνήφθη → **ἀνάπτω,** *aor. pass. ind. 3s,* Luke 12:49, *I wish it were already* **kindled**

ἀνθέξεται → **ἀντέχομαι,** *fut. mid. ind. 3s,* Matt 6:24, **he will be devoted**

ἀνθίστημι {ἀντί + ἵστημι} (14x) Matt 5:39; Luke 21:15; Acts 6:10; Rom 9:19; Jas 4:7; 1 Pet 5:9, **to resist**; Gal 2:11; 2 Tim 3:8, **to oppose**; (71x LXX; 7x Wis, 6x Deut)

ἀνθομολογέομαι[con] {ἀντί + ὁμός + λέγω} ①[imi3s] Luke 2:38, **to give thanks**; ❻ LXX; 2x Dan

ἄνθος, ους, τό$_3$ ❹ Jas 1:10, 11; 1 Pet 1:24,[2x] **flower**; (26x LXX; 9x Isa)

ἀνθρακιά, ᾶς, ἡ$_{1α}$ {ἄνθραξ} ❷[afs] John 18:18; 21:9, **charcoal fire**; ❷ LXX, 4 Macc 9:20; Sir 11:32

ἄνθραξ, ακος, ὁ$_{3}$ ①[amp] Rom 12:20, **coal**; (30x LXX; 6x Isa)

ἀνθρωπάρεσκος, ον$_{2.2}$ {ἄνθρωπος + ἀρέσκω} *adj.* ❷ Eph 6:6; Col 3:22, **people-pleasers**; ❺ LXX, Ps 52:6 (53:5)

ἀνθρώπινος, η, ον$_{2.1.2}$ {ἄνθρωπος} *adj.* ❼ Acts 17:25; Rom 6:19; 1 Pet 2:13, **human**; 1 Cor 10:13, **part and parcel of being human**[NIGTC]; Jas 3:7, **humankind**; (14x LXX)

ἀνθρωποκτόνος, ου, ὁ$_{2}$ {ἄνθρωπος + κτείνω} ❸ John 8:44, 1 John 3:15,[2x] **murderer**

ἄνθρωπος, ου, ὁ$_{2}$ {ἀνήρ + ὤψ = *man-faced*} (550x; 325x Gs, 25x Rev) Ⓐ ***anthropological*** (*general*) Rev 9:15, **humankind**; John 1:9, **everyone**; (*human nature*) Rev 9:7, **human**; 2 Tim 3:2, **people**; Ⓑ ***sociocultural***, Matt 4:4, **man/male**; Matt 13:52, *dat. of ref.*, ἀνθρώπῳ οἰκοδεσπότῃ, **owner of a house**; Ⓒ ***theological*** (*messianic title*) Mark 8:31, **the Son of Man**; (*inner spiritual state*) Eph 4:22, 24, **old self** «» **new self**; 2 Thess 2:3, **man** *of lawlessness*; 1 Pet 3:4, **inner person**; Ⓓ ***developmental***, John 16:21, **newborn child**; Ⓔ ***philosophical***, 1 Cor 2:11[3x], **man, man, spirit** (1,372x LXX; 313x Pent, 118x Sir)

ἀνθύπατος, ου, ὁ$_{2}$ ❺ Acts 13:7, 8; 13:12; 18:12; 19:38, **proconsul**

ἀνίημι {ἀνά + ἵημι → *set in motion*} ❹ Acts 16:26, **to come loose**; 27:40, **to cut away**; Eph 6:9, **to eliminate**; Heb 13:5, **to abandon, desert**[NIGTC]; (43x LXX; 13x Isa)

ἄνιπτος, ον$_{2.2}$ {α + νίπτω} *adj.* ❷[dfp] Matt 15:20; Mark 7:2, **unwashed**

ἀνίστημι {ἀνά + ἵστημι} *narr. verb* (108x, 101x GA) Matt 9:9 = Mark 2:14, **to get up**; 1 Thess 4:14, **to rise up**; Luke 4:38, **to depart**; John 6:39, **to raise up** *the dead*; Acts 5:6, **to come** *for the dead*; Heb 7:11, *messianic assoc.*, **to appear**[EGG] (473x LXX; 112x 1–2 Sam)

Ἄννα, ας, ἡ$_{1α}$ ①[nfs] Luke 2:36, **Anna**, *a prophetess*; (20x LXX; 11x 1 Sam) **Hannah**

Ἄννας, α, ὁ$_{1α}$ ❹ Luke 3:2; John 18:13, 24; Acts 4:6, **Annas**

ἀνόητος, ον$_{2.2}$ {α + νοῦς} *adj.* ❻ Luke 24:25; Rom 1:14; Titus 3:3, **foolish**; (13x LXX)

ἄνοια, ας, ἡ$_{1α}$ {α + νοῦς} ❷ Luke 6:11, **senseless wrath**; 2 Tim 3:9, **stupidity**[ABC]; (11x LXX) Ps 21:3 (22:2), **relentless grief**; Plato *Tim.* 86b, **madness**

ἀνοίγω (77x; 27x Rev) John 10:3, **to allow**; Rev 3:7, **to open**[BEC]; 10:2, **to unroll**; 1 Cor 16:9; 2 Cor 2:12; Rev 3:8, *doors to be* **opened** *for ministry opportunity*[BEC]; Rev 5:2–9:2,[12x] **to open** *scroll, seals*; (165x LXX; 17x Isa, 15x Pss); *naut.*, Xen. *Hel.* 1.1.2, *to reach* **open** *sea*

ἀνοικοδομέω[con] {ἀνά + οἶκος + δῶμα} ❷[fai1s] Acts 15:16,[2x] **to rebuild**[BST]; (20x LXX)

ἄνοιξις, εως, ἡ$_{3}$ {ἀνοίγω} ①[dfs] Eph 6:19 (= Col 4:3[verb]), **great opportunity**[ZEC, PNTC]

ἀνομία, ας, ἡ$_{1α}$ {α + νόμος} (15x; 4x Matt) 2 Cor 6:14; **lawlessness**; Matt 13:41, **lawless**; 2 Thess 2:3, *man* **of lawlessness**; 1 John 3:4,[2x] **law breaker**; (224x LXX; 80x Pss, 49x Ezek)

ἄνομος, ον$_{2.2}$ ❾ Luke 22:37, **outlaw**; 1 Cor 9:21,[4x] **those outside the law**[NIGTC]; 2 Thess 2:8, *man* **of lawlessness**; 1 Tim 1:9; 2 Pet 2:8, **lawless** *deeds*; (102x LXX; 20x Isa)

ἀνόμως {α + νόμος} *adv.* ❷ Rom 2:12,[2x] **without law**[ZEC]; ① LXX, 2 Macc 8:17, **unjustly**

ἀνορθόω[con] {ἀνά + ὀρθός} ❸ Luke 13:13, **to be straightened**; Acts 15:16, **to restore**; Heb 12:12, **to strengthen**; (11x LXX) 2 Sam 7:13, 16, **to establish**

ἀνόσιος, ον$_{2.2}$ {α + ὅσιος} *adj.* ❷ 1 Tim 1:9; 2 Tim 3:2, **unholy**; ❼ LXX, Ezek 22:9, **obscene**

ἀνοχή, ῆς, ἡ$_{1η}$ {ἀνά + ἔχω} ❷ Rom 2:4, **tolerance**, **patience**; 3:26, **forbearance**; ①[afs] LXX, 1 Macc 12:25, **delay** *of some days;* Xen. *Mem.* 4.4.17, **truce**[BrDAG]

ἀνταγωνίζομαι {ἀντί + ἀγών} ①[pmp.nmp] Heb 12:4, **to strive against**; ①[imi3s] LXX, 4 Macc 17:14, *Antiochus who* **antagonized** *true "athletes"*[NIGTC, SCS!]

ἀντ**άλλαγμα, ατος, τό**$_2$ {ἀντί + ἄλλος} ❷ Matt 16:26 = Mark 8:37, **to exchange**; ❼ LXX, Ruth 4:7, **a transaction**; Ps 54:20 (55:19), *refuse* **to change**

ἀντ**αναπληρόω**[con] {ἀντί + ἀνά + πληρόω} ①[pai1s] Col 1:24, **to complete, fulfill**; Dem. 14.17, **to balance or reconcile** *the numbers*

αποδίδωμι {ἀντί + ἀπό + δίδωμι} ❼ Luke 14:14,[2x] **to compensate**; *positive*, 1 Thess 3:9, **to repay** *thanks*; *negative*, 2 Thess 1:6, *the Lord* **repays** *affliction for affliction*; (87x LXX)

ἀντ**απόδομα, ατος, τό**$_2$ {ἀντί + ἀπό + δίδωμι} ❷ Luke 14:12, **repayment**; Rom 11:9, **repayment, retribution**; (22x LXX) Sir 12:2, **recompense**

ἀντ**απόδοσις, εως, ἡ**$_3$ {ἀντί + ἀπό + δίδωμι} ①[afs] Col 3:24, **a giving in place of**[PNT n209]; (14x LXX) Ps 18:12 (19:11), *rich* **reward**

ἀντ**αποκρίνομαι** {ἀντί + ἀπό + κρίνω} ❷ Luke 14:6, **to give an answer**; Rom 9:20, **to answer back**; ❸ LXX, Judg 5:29, **to answer**; Job 16:18, **to confront**

ἀντ**έχω** {ἀντί + ἔχω} *mid.* ❹ Matt 6:24 = Luke 16:13, **to be devoted to**; 1 Thess 5:14, **to support**; Titus 1:9, **to cling**; (19x LXX; 5x Isa) Prov 3:18, **to grasp**; Isa 56:2, **to commit oneself**

ἀντί *prep. w/ gen.* (22x) Ⓐ ***substitutionary positioning***; Matt 2:22, Jas 4:15, **in place of, instead of**; Ⓑ ***reciprocal justice***; Matt 5:38,[2x] *an eye* **for** *an eye*; Ⓒ ***advocacy***; Matt 17:27, **in behalf of**; Ⓓ ***reciprocal evil***; Rom 12:17 = 1 Thess 5:15 = 1 Pet 3:9[2x], *evil* **for** *evil*; Ⓔ ***causation***; **ἀνθ᾽** ὧν, Luke 1:20; Acts 12:23; 2 Thess 2:10, **because**; Ⓕ ***purpose***; Heb 12:2, **for the sake of**[NIGTC]; (386x LXX; 71x 1–2 Kgs, 40x Ezek, 28x Gen)

ἀντι**βάλλω** ①[pai2p] Luke 24:17, **to discuss**, *implying* **conflicting opinions**[EGG]; ①[pap.nms] LXX, *mid.*, 2 Macc 11:13, **to reflect to oneself**; Thuc. 7.25.6, **to return** *arrow* **fire**; Plut. *Nic.* 25.3, **to respond** *with* **spear attack**; Luc. *Lex.* 5 **to beat against** *a punching bag*[BrDAG]

ἀντι**διατίθημι** ①[pmp.amp] 2 Tim 2:25, **to offer resistance, oppose**

ἀντί**δικος, ου, ὁ** {ἀντί + δίκη} ❺ Matt 5:25[2x] = Luke 18:3; 1 Pet 5:8, **adversary**; ❾ LXX, Hos 5:11, **adversary**; Plato *Phaed.* 273c, **opponent in a trial**; Aeschl. *Ag.* 41, **enemy**

ἀντί**θεσις, εως, ἡ**$_3$ {ἀντί + τίθημι} ①[dfp] 1 Tim 6:20, **opposing arguments or ideas**[NIGTC]; Plato *Soph.* 257e, **opposition**

ἀντι**καθίστημι** {ἀντί + κατά + ἵστημι} ①[aai2p] Heb 12:4, **to resist** *to the point of shedding blood*; ❷ LXX, Deut 31:21; Josh 5:7

ἀντι**καλέω**[con] ①[aas3p] Luke 14:12, **to invite** *in expectation of a return*; Plut. *QCon.* 612D, *illust. the friend-making power of the table*[ZEC]

ἀντί**κειμαι** ❽ Luke 13:17; Phil 1:28, *subst.* **adversaries**; Gal 5:7, **to oppose**; 2 Thess 2:4, **the one who opposes**; 1 Tim 1:10, **to be contrary to** *sound teaching*; 1 Tim 5:14, **the Accuser**; (15x LXX; 4x Isa) Job 13:15, **to set against**; Plut. *Frig.* 952b, **expels** *the heat*

ἄντικρυς {ἀντί} *adv.* ①Acts 20:15, **opposite** *Chios*; ① LXX, 3 Macc 5:16, **opposite** *him*

ἀντι**λαμβάνω** ❸ Luke 1:54[BEC]; Acts 20:35, **to support**; 1 Tim 6:2, *subst.*, **those who take part in receiving**[BEC]

ἀντι**λέγω** (11x; 7x LA) Luke 2:34, **to take hostile action against**[ZEC]; 20:27, **to contradict**; Acts 28:19, **to object to**; Titus 2:9, **to talk back**; (11x LXX; 3x Job:Isa)

ἀντί**λημψις, εως, ἡ**$_3$ {ἀντί + λαμβάνω} ①[afp] 1 Cor 12:28, **administrative supports** (*lexicographical and exegetical minefield*[NIGTC]) (17x LXX; 6x Ps) Ps 21:20 (22:19), *come quickly to my* **aid**!; Ps 82:9 (83:8), εἰς **ἀντίλημψιν**, εἰς + *acc.*, for **strength**; Hp. *De off.* 743, *medic.*, **support** *with bandages*; Thphr. *C.P.* 2.18.2, *hort.*, **rooting**, *of plants* ἀντι**λογία, ας, ἡ**$_{1\alpha}$ {ἀντί + λέγω} ❹ Heb 7:7, **dispute**; 12:3; Jude 11, **verbal and hostile action**; (20x LXX) Deut 17:8, *between* **contradiction** *and* **contradiction**

ἀντι**λοιδορέω**[con] {ἀντί + λοίδορος} ①[iai3s] 1 Pet 2:23, **to abuse back**[Keen1P]

ἀντί**λυτρον, ου, τό**$_2$ {ἀντί + λύω} ①[ans] 1 Tim 2:6, **ransom**; Orph. *L.* 593, **antidote**

ἀντι**μετρέω**[con] {ἀντί + μέτρον} ①[fpi3s] Luke 6:38, **to measure in return**

ἀντι**μισθία, ας, ἡ**$_{1\alpha}$ {ἀντί + μισθός} ❷[afs] Rom 1:27; **punishment**; 2 Cor 6:13, τὴν δὲ αὐτὴν **ἀντιμισθίαν, as a fair return on our investment**[BEC]

Ἀντιόχεια, ας, ἡ$_{1\alpha}$ (18x) 🅐 Acts 11:19–13:1[7x]; 14:26–18:22[6x]; Gal 2:11, **Syrian Antioch**; 🅑 Acts 13:14–14:21[3x]; 2 Tim 3:11, **Pisidian Antioch**

Ἀντιοχεύς, έως, ὁ$_3$ ①[ams] **an inhabitant of Antioch**

ἀντι**παρέρχομαι** {ἀντί + παρά + ἔρχομαι} ❷[aai3s] Luke 10:31, 32, **to pass by on the other side of the road**; ①[aai3s] LXX, Wis 16:10, **to go get help**

Ἀντιπᾶς, ᾶ, ὁ$_1$ ①[nms] Rev 2:13, **Antipas**

Ἀντιπατρίς, ίδος, ἡ$_3$ ①[afs] Acts 23:31, **Antipatris**

ἀντι**πέρα** *impr. prep. w/gen.* ① Luke 8:26, **on the opposite shore**

ἀντι**πίπτω** ①[pai2p] Acts 7:51, **to fall against, resist**[ZEC]; ❸ LXX, Exod 26:5, 17, **to be opposite**; Num 27:14, **to resist** (Acts 7:51); Aristot. *Pr.* 915b 18, **to crash into**

ἀντι**στρατεύομαι** *milit.* ①[pmp.ams] Rom 7:23, **to wage war against**; Xen. *Cyr.* 8.8.6, **go to war**[4x]; Diod. Sic. *Bib. Hist.* 22.13.2; Ios. 2.240, **to make an expedition** *against*

ἀντι**τάσσω** *mid.* ❺ Acts 18:6; Rom 13:2; Jas 4:6; 5:6; 1 Pet 5:5, **to oppose, resist**; ❽ LXX, 1 Kgs 11:34,[2x] **ἀντιτασσόμενος ἀντιτάξομαι, since opposing, I will oppose**

ἀντί**τυπος, ον**$_{2.2}$ *adj.* ❷ Heb 9:24, **the lesser of two counterparts** (*Moses*)[NIGTC]; 1 Pet 3:21, **the greater of two counterparts** (*Jesus*)[Keen1P]

ἀντί**χριστος, ου, ὁ**$_2$ {ἀντί + χρίω} ❺ 1 John 2:18,[2x] 22; 4:3; 2 John 1:7, **antichrist**

ἀντλέω[con] ❹ John 2:8, 9; 4:7, 15, **to draw** *water*; ❻ LXX, Exod 2:16, **to draw** *water*

ἄντλημα, ατος, τό$_3$ {ἀντλέω} ①[ans] John 4:11, **bucket** *for drawing water*

ἀντ**οφθαλμέω**[con] {ἀντί + ὀφθαλμός} ①[painf] Acts 27:15, *naut.*, **to face** *the wind*[ZEC, WPNT] ①[aainf] LXX, Wis 12:14, **to look into the face**[CGL]

ἄν**υδρος, ον**$_{2.2}$ {α + ὕδωρ} *adj.* ❹ Matt 12:43 = Luke 11:24, **waterless**; 2 Pet 2:17, *springs* **without waters**; Jude 12, **waterless** *clouds* (*life-threatening situations*)[BEC]; (24x LXX; 8x Pss); Eur. *Tr.* 1085, *of a dead person* **deprived of lustral ablution** (*ceremony of purification by water*)[BrDAG]

ἀν**υπόκριτος, ον**$_{2.2}$ {α + ὑπό + κρίνω} *adj.* ❻ Rom 12:9; 2 Cor 6:6; 2 Tim 1:5; Jas 3:17; 1 Pet 1:22, **genuine, without pretense**; ❷[afs] LXX, Wis 5:18, **true**

ἀν**υπότακτος, ον**$_{2.2}$ {α + ὑπό + τάσσω} *adj.* ❹ 1 Tim 1:9; Titus 1:6, **undisciplined, rebellious**; Titus 1:10, **unruly**, *likely false teachers*; Heb 2:8, **not made subject**[EGG]

ἀνῶ → **ἀνίημι,** *aor. act. sub 1s*, Heb 13:5, **I** *will never* **leave** *you*

ἄνω {ἀνά} *adv.* ❾ John 2:7, **brim**; 8:23; Acts 2:19; Col 3:1, **above**; John 11:41; Heb 12:15, **up**; Phil 3:14, **upward**; (40x LXX; 6x Deut:1Kgs, 5x Isa)

ἄνωθεν {ἀνά + θεν} *adv.* (13x; 5x John) Matt 27:51; Luke 1:3, **long time**; John 3:3, 7, **again**; 3:31; Jas 3:15, 17, **above**; Acts 26:5, **first**; Gal 4:9, **over**; (23x LXX; 7x Exod)

ἀνωτερικός, ή, όν$_{2.1.2}$ {ἀνά} *adj.*①[anp] Acts 19:1, **upper, inland**

ἀνώτερος, έρα, ον$_{2.1.2}$ {ἀνά} *adj.* ❷ Luke 14:10, *fig.*, **a more worthy seat**[ZEC]; Heb 10:8, **above**; ❹ LXX, 2x Ezek

ἀνωφελής, ές$_{3.3}$ {α + ὠφελέω} *adj.* ❷ Titus 3:9; Heb 7:18, **unprofitable**; ❺ LXX, Prov 28:3, *fig.*, *torrential rain that delivers* **havoc**[TOTC]; Isa 44:10, **worthless** *things*

ἀξίνη, ης, ἡ$_{1η}$ ❷ Matt 3:10 = Luke 3:9, **ax**; ❼ LXX, Isa 10:15; Jer 26:22

ἄξιος, α, ον$_{2.1.2}$ {ἀξιόω} *adj.* (41x; 15x LA) Rev 3:4–5:12,[6x] **worthy**; Matt 10:10, **deserving**; 2 Thess 1:3, **fitting**; 1 Cor 16:4, **fit, right**[NIGTC]; Rom 8:18, **worth**; (40x LXX)

ἀξιόω[con] {ἄξιος} ❼ Luke 7:7; Heb 3:3, **consider worthy**; Acts 15:38, **consider it fitting**; Acts 28:22, **to be anxious**; Heb 10:29, **to be worthy** *of judgment*; (48x LXX; 17x 2 Macc)

ἀξίως {ἄξιος} *adv.* ❻ Eph 4:1; Phil 1:27; Col 1:10; 1 Thess 2:12; 3 John 6, **worthily**; Rom 16:2, **deservingly**; ❸ LXX, Wis 7:15; Sir 14:11, **worthily, due**

ἀόρατος, ον$_{2.2}$ {α + ὁράω} *adj.* ❺ Rom 1:20; Col 1:15, 16; 1 Tim 1:17; Heb 11:27, **invisible**; ❸ LXX, Gen 1:2, *the earth was* **unseen** *and unprepared*[Waltke]; Heb. תֹהוּ וָבֹהוּ, **unformed** *and void*[ABC]; 2 Macc 9:5, **invisible** *plague*

ἀπαγγέλλω {ἀπό + ἄγγελος} (45x, 26x LA) Matt 2:8; 8:33 = Mark 5:14; Acts 4:23–28:21[14x]; 1 Thess 1:9, **to report**; Luke 9:36, **to tell**; Acts 26:20, **to declare**; (232x LXX)

ἀπάγχω {ἀπό + ἄγχω → *to squeeze, strangle*} ①[ami3s] Matt 27:5, **to hang oneself** (*Judas Iscariot*); ❷ LXX, 2 Sam 17:23 (*Ahithophel the Gilonite*)

ἀπάγω {ἀπό + ἄγω} (15x; 12x Syn) Matt 7:13, 14, **to depart** *either to destruction or to life*; 26:57; Acts 12:19, *idiom*, **to be led off**, i.e., *to be executed*; 1 Cor 12:2, **to be led astray**; (44x LXX) Gen 31:18, 26, **to take away**; Demosth. 22.27, **to haul** *before the court*

ἀπαίδευτος, ον$_{2.2}$ {παιδεύω} *adj.* ①[afp] 2 Tim 2:23, **uneducated, ignorant**; (18x LXX; 7x Prov) Prov 5:23, **uninstructed**; Plato *Gorg.* 510b, **rude, boorish**

ἀπαίρω {ἀπό + αἴρω} ❸ **ὅταν ἀπαρθῇ**[aps3s] (*Synoptic hapax*) Matt 9:15 = Mark 2:20 = Luke 5:35 (*echo from* Isa 53:8, αἴρω[2x])[CGNT], *pass.*, **to be taken away**; (118x LXX; *milit.*, 56x Num, 23x 1 Macc) Gen 12:9, **to depart**; 26:21, 22, **to take away** *dirt*, **to dig** *a well*; Num 9:17, *milit.*, **to march**[ABC] (*to the Jordan*); Num 33:1–49,[46x] **ἀπῆραν** . . . παρενέβαλον, **they marched, departed** . . . *they encamped* (*like Abram in Gen 12:9*)

ἀπαιτέω[con] {ἀπό + αἰτέω} ❷ Luke 6:30, **to demand in return**; 12:20, **to demand, require**; (11x LXX; 4x Isa) Deut 15:2, **to ask for repayment**; Isa 3:12; 14:4, *subst.* **the extortioner(s)**

ἀπαλγέω[con] {ἀπό + ἀλγέω → feel pain} ①[pfap.nmp] Eph 4:19, **to lose the capacity to feel shame**[PNTC]; Thuc. 2.61.4.6, **to dismiss sorrow, grief**

ἀπαλλάσσω {ἀπό + ἄλλος} ❸ Luke 12:58, **to strike a deal**; Acts 19:12, *evil spirits* **departed**; Heb 2:15, **to liberate**; (15x LXX; 7x Job) Job 3:10, **to hide**; 7:15, **to choose strangling** (NRSV); 9:12, **to snatch away**

ἀπαλλοτριόω[con] {ἀπό + ἄλλος} ❸[pfmp] Eph 2:12 = Col 1:21, **to alienate**; Eph 4:18, **to be separated**; (11x LXX) Hos 9:10; Ezek 14:5, **to estrange**; Jer 19:4, **to profane**

ἁπαλός, ή, όν$_{2.1.2}$ *adj.* ❷ Matt 24:32 = Mark 13:28, **tender** *fig branch*; ❾ LXX, Gen 18:7

ἀπαντάω[con] {ἀπό + ἀντί} ❷ Mark 14:13; Luke 17:2, **to meet**; (45x LXX; 11x 1 Macc)

ἀπάντησις, εως, ἡ$_{3}$ {ἀπό + ἀντί} ❸ (εἰς *w/acc.*) Matt 25:6; Acts 28:15; 1 Thess 4:17, **to meet**; (43x LXX; 31x εἰς *w/acc.*; 12x 1 Sam, 8x Judg)

ἅπαξ *adv.* (14x; 8x Heb) 2 Cor 11:25; Phil 4:16; Heb 6:4; Jude 3, 5, **once**; 1 Thess 2:18, **time** *and again*; (42x LXX; 9x Judg, 8x 1–2 Sam) Lev 16:34, **once** *in the year*

ἀπαράβατος, ον$_{2.2}$ {ἀπό + παρά + βαίνω} *adj.* ①[afs] Heb 7:24, **permanent**[EGG]

ἀπαρασκεύαστος, ον$_{2.2}$ {α + παρά + σκεῦος} *adj.* ①[amp] 2 Cor 9:4, **unprepared**[BEC]

ἀπαρνέομαι {ἀπό + ἀρνέομαι} (11x Syn) Matt 16:24 = Mark 8:34; Matt 26:34 = Mark 14:30, **to disown**, **deny**; ①[fmi3p] LXX, Isa 31:7, **to renounce** *their silver idols*

ἀπαρτισμός, οῦ, ὁ$_2$ {ἀπό + ἄρτι} ①[ams] Luke 14:28, **completion**

ἀπαρχή, ῆς, ἡ$_{1\eta}$ {ἀπό + ἄρχω} ❾ Rom 8:23; 1 Cor 15:20; 2 Thess 2:13; Rev 14:4, **firstfruits**; Rom 16:5; 1 Cor 16:15, **first convert(s)**; (75x LXX; 22x Ezek) **firstfruits**

ἅπας, ασα, αν$_{3.1.3}$ (*alt form of* πᾶς) *adj.* (34x; 23x LA) Acts 2:7, **all**; Eph 6:13, **everything**; Mark 11:32, **everyone**; 1 Tim 1:16, **complete**; (77x LXX; 17x Jer, 13x 3 Macc)

ἀπασπάζομαι {ἀπό + ἀσπάζομαι} ①[ami1p] Acts 21:6, **goodbye**[ZEC]

ἀπατάω[con] {ἀπάτη} ❸ Eph 5:6; 1 Tim 2:14; Jas 1:26, **to deceive**; (38x LXX; 7x Jer; 6x 2 Chr)

ἀπάτη, ης, ἡ$_{1\eta}$ ❼ Matt 13:22 = Mark 4:19; Heb 3:13, **deceitfulness**; Eph 4:22; Col 2:8, **deceit**[Spicq]; 2 Thess 2:10, **deception**; 2 Pet 2:13, **deceitful**; ❺ LXX, Jdt 9:3, 10, 13; 16:8

ἀπάτωρ, ορος, ὁ, ἡ$_3$ {α + πατήρ} ①[nms] Heb 7:3, **fatherless**

ἀπαύγασμα, ατος, τό$_3$ {ἀπό + αὐγή} ①[nns] Heb 1:3, **radiance**; ①[nns] Wis 7:26

ἀπαχθῆναι → **ἀπάγω**, *aor. pass. inf.*, Acts 12:19, **to be led away** (*for execution*)

ἀπείθεια, ας, ἡ$_{1\alpha}$ {α + πείθω} ❼ Eph 5:6 = Col 3:6; Heb 4:6, 11, **disobedience**; ❸ LXX, 4 Macc 12:3[SCS]; Pseud., Pss. Sol. 17.20

ἀπειθέω[con] {α + πείθω} (14x; 5x Rom) John 3:36, **to reject**; Rom 2:8; 1 Pet 2:8, **to disobey**; Acts 14:2; Rom 15:31, **unbelieving Jews**; (49x LXX; 13x Isa) Num 20:10, *subst.* **rebels**

ἀπειθής, ές$_{3.3}$ {α + πείθω} *adj.* ❻ Luke 1:17; Acts 26:19; Rom 1:30; 2 Tim 3:2; Titus 1:16; 3:3, **disobedient**; ❼ LXX, Deut 21:18, **rebellious**

ἀπειλέω[con] {ἀπό + εἴλω → *strike, press hard*} ❷ Acts 4:17, **to warn**; 1 Pet 2:23, **to threaten**[Keen1P]; ❾ LXX, Nah 1:4, **to rebuke**; Isa 66:14, **to reveal wrath**

ἀπειλή, ῆς, ἡ$_{1\eta}$ {ἀπό + εἰλέω} ❸ Acts 4:29; 9:1; Eph 6:9, **threat(s)**; (24x LXX)

ἄπειμι[1] {ἀπό + εἰμί} ❼ 1 Cor 5:3; 2 Cor 10:1; Phil 1:27; Col 2:5, **to be absent, away**; ❼ LXX, Exod 33:8; 2 Macc 13:22; Prov 25:10; Job 6:13; Wis 9:6; 11:11; 14:17; Hos 5:3, **to be absent, away, to withdraw, to be hidden**

ἄπειμι[2] {ἀπό + εἰμί} ①[aai3p] Acts 17:10, **to go, travel**[ZEC]; ❹ LXX, 2 Macc 12:1; 4 Macc 4:8; Wis 19:2, **to return**

ἀπεῖπον {ἀπό + εἶπον → *aor. of* λέγω} ①[ami1p] 2 Cor 4:2, **we turn our backs** *on shameful things people hide*[BEC]; ①[ami2s] LXX, Job 10:3, **to reject**; Eur. *Alc.* 737, **to renounce**

ἀπείραστος, ον$_{2.2}$ {α + πεῖρα} *adj.* ①[nms] Jas 1:13, *God is* **untemptable**

ἄπειρος, ον$_{2.2}$ {α + πεῖρα} *adj.* ①[nms] Heb 5:13, **unskillful**; ❹ LXX, Zech 11:15, **foolish** *shepherd*; Jer 2:6, **desert**, **impassable**; Aristot. *Phys.* 207a.2, **without an end**, **circular**

ἀπεκατεστάθη → **ἀποκαθίστημι**, *aor. pass. ind. 3s*, Matt 12:13, **it was restored**

ἀπεκδέχομαι {ἀπό + ἐκ + δέχομαι} *mid.* ❽ *eschat.*, Rom 8:19; Gal 5:5; Phil 3:20; Heb 9:28, **to wait for, to eagerly await** *the parousia*; 1 Pet 3:20, **God waited** *patiently*

ἀπεκδύομαι {ἀπό + ἐκ + δύω} *mid.* ❷ *act.*, Col 2:15, **to disarm** *the princes and the powers*; *mid.*, 3:9, **to strip oneself completely**[BrDAG]

ἀπέκδυσις, εως, ἡ$_3$ {ἀπό + ἐκ + δύω} ①[dfs] Col 2:11, **putting off** *the body of flesh*[ZEC]

ἀπελαύνω {ἀπό + ἐλαύνω} ①[aai3s] Acts 18:16, **to drive off, expel**[Keen3]; ❸ LXX, 1 Sam 6:8

ἀπελεγμός, οῦ, ὁ$_2$ {ἀπό + ἐλέγχω} ①[ams] Acts 19:27, **criticism pertaining to discreditable behavior, ill repute**[Keen3]; **εἰς ἀπελεγμὸν ἐλθεῖν**, *Latinism*, *fall into contempt*

ἀπελεύθερος, ου, ὁ$_2$ {ἀπό + ἐλεύθερος} ①^{nms} 1 Cor 7:22, **a freedperson to the Lord**[NIGTC]; Is. 4.9; Plato *Leg.* 930a, **emancipated slave**

ἀπεληλύθεισαν → ἀπέρχομαι, *plpf. act. ind. 3p, the disciples* **had gone**

Ἀπελλῆς, οῦ, ὁ$_2$ ①^{ams} Rom 16:10, **Apelles**

ἀπελπίζω {ἀπό + ἐλπίς} ①$^{pap.nmp}$ Luke 6:35, **to expect nothing back**[WPNT]; ❻ LXX, Isa 29:19, *subst.* **they who had no hope**[NAC]; Diod. Sic. *Bib. Hist.* 1.25.5, **declared a hopeless case** *by the doctors*

ἀπέναντι {ἀπό + ἐν + ἀντί} *impr. prep. w/gen.* ❺ Matt 27:24; Rom 3:18, **before**; Matt 27:61, **opposite**; Acts 3:16, **in the presence of**; 17:7, **contrary to, in opposition to**; (94x LXX)

ἀπένεγκε → ἀποφέρω, *aor. act. imp. 2s,* Num 17:11, **carry it away** *quickly!*

ἀπέραντος, ον$_{2.2}$ {ἀπό + πέραν} *adj.* ①^{dfp} 1 Tim 1:4, **endless**; ❷ LXX, Job 36:26, **infinite**

ἀπερισπάστως {α + περί + σπάω} *adv.* ① 1 Cor 7:35, **undistracted** *devotion*

ἀπερίτμητος, ον$_{2.2}$ {α + περί + τόμος} ①^{vmp} Acts 7:51, **uncircumcised** *in heart and ears*[Keen2]; (34x LXX; 12x Ezek, 5x 1 Sam) Lev 26:41, **uncircumcised** *hearts* → Acts 7:51

ἀπέρχομαι {ἀπό + ἔρχομαι} (117x; 99x Gs, 108x aor. *narr. verb*) *act.*, Jas 1:24, **to go, depart**; Matt 4:24, **to spread**; Rom 15:28, **to visit**; Jude 7, **to pursue**; John 4:8, *plpf. act. ind 3p,* **ἀπεληλύθεισαν**, *the disciples* **had gone**; *mid.*, Matt 25:46, **they will go away**; John 6:68, *to whom* **will we go?**; *pass. nuance.*, Matt 5:30; Rev 11:14; 21:4, **to be cast away, pass away**; (217x LXX; 42x 1–2 Sam, 27x Gen, aor. *narr. verb*)

ἀπέστησεν → ἀφίστημι, *aor. act. ind. 3s,* Acts 5:37, **attracted**

ἀπέχω (19x; 11x Syn) Phil 4:18, **to receive**; Matt 14:24; Luke 15:20, **to be at some distance from a position**[BDAG]; Matt 15:8, **far, far from me**[BHGNT]; Mark 14:41, **Enough** *sleeping*! → **Is it far off?,**[ZEC] **Is it wrong?**[BrDAG]; Acts 15:20; 1 Thess 4:3; 1 Tim 4:3, **to abstain**; Phlm 15, *so* **you might have** *him forever*; (41x LXX; 12x Ezek, 5x 1 Sam) Gen 43:23

ἀπῄεσαν → ἄπειμι,[2] *impf. act. ind. 3p,* Acts 17:10, **they went** *into*

ἀπήνεγκαν → ἀποφέρω, *aor. act. ind. 3p,* Mark 15:1, **they led** *him* **away**

ἀπιστέω[con] {α + πιστεύω} ❽ Mark 16:11; 1 Pet 2:7, **to refuse to believe**; Rom 3:3; 2 Tim 2:13, **to lack faith**; ❺ LXX, 2 Macc 8:13, **to distrust**

ἀπιστία, ας, ἡ$_{1α}$ {α + πιστεύω} (11x; 4x Rom, 3x Mark) Matt 13:58; Mark 6:6; Rom 3:3; 1 Tim 1:13; Heb 3:19, **unbelief**; 3:12, **unbelieving**; ①^{nfs} LXX, Wis 14:25

ἄπιστος, ον$_{2.2}$ *adj.* (23x; 14x 1–2 Cor) Matt 17:17; John 20:27; Titus 1:15; Rev 21:8, **unfaithful, unbelieving**; Acts 26:8, **unbelievable**; 1 Cor 6:6, **unbeliever(s)**; ❸ LXX, Isa 17:10

ἁπλότης, ητος, ἡ$_3$ ❽ Rom 12:8, **generosity**; 2 Cor 1:12–11:3,[5x] **personal integrity**[BEC]; Eph 6:5 = Col 3:22, **sincerity of heart**[PNTC]; ❼ LXX, 1 Chr 29:17, **upright**

ἁπλοῦς, ῆ, οῦν$_{2.1.2}$ {ἁπλότης} *adj.* ❷ Matt 6:22 = Luke 11:34, **healthy**; ❼ LXX, 1 Chr 29:17

ἁπλῶς {ἁπλότης} *adv.* ① Jas 1:5, **with pure thoughts**[Herm]; ❸ LXX, Prov 10:9, **integrity**

ἀπό, ἀπ᾽, ἀφ᾽ *prep. w/gen.* (646x; 239x LA) Ⓐ ***positional, source***, 1 Thess 1:2, **from** *God*; Ⓑ ***temporal***, 2 Cor 8:10, **since** *the creation*; Ⓒ ***figurative***, Matt 7:16, **by** *their fruits*; Acts 22:11, **because of** *the brightness*; (3,890x LXX; 910x Pent, 703x MajPr, 247x Pss)

ἀποβαίνω ❹ Luke 5:2; John 21:9, **to disembark**; Luke 21:13, **to lead out**; Phil 1:19, **to lead to** *Paul's ultimate salvation*; (20x LXX; 15x Job) Job 9:20, **to prove**; 11:6, **to overlook**

ἀποβάλλω ❷ Mark 10:50, **he threw off** *his coat*; Heb 10:35, *don't* **throw away** *your confidence*; ❺ Deut 26:5, **to abandon**; Prov 28:24, **to rob**; Eur. *Bac.* 692, *subst.* **chasing** *sleep* **from** *eyes*

ἀπο**βλέπω** ①[iai3s] Heb 11:26, **to look away** *from Egypt,*[NIGTC] **to look ahead**; ❽ LXX, Judg 9:37, *the* **Diviner's** *Oak Tree*; Hos 3:1, **to turn to**

ἀπό**βλητος, ον**$_{2.2}$ {ἀπό + βάλλω} *adj.* ①[ans] 1 Tim 4:4, **rejected**; Hom. *Il.* 2.362, **to lay aside**

ἀπο**βολή, ῆς, ἡ**$_{1η}$ {ἀπό + βάλλω} ❷[nfs] Acts 27:22, **a loss**; Rom 11:15, **a casting away**

ἀπο**γίνομαι** ①[amp.nmp] 1 Pet 2:24 = Thuc. 1.39.3, **having no part** *in wrongdoing*[ABC]

ἀπο**γραφή**$_{1η}$ {ἀπό + γράφω} ❷ Luke 2:2; Acts 5:37, **census, registration**; ❻ LXX, 4x 3 Macc

ἀπο**γράφω** ❹ *mid.*, Luke 2:1, 3, 5, **to be registered**; Heb 12:23, *names* **are inscribed** *in heaven*; ❻ LXX, Judg 8:14, **to write down** *the names*

ἀπο**δείκνυμι** ❹ Acts 2:22, **to show, to appoint**; 25:7, **to prove**; 1 Cor 4:9, **to put on exhibit**[NIGTC]; 2 Thess 2:4, **to display** *himself*; (10x LXX) Job 33:21, **to protrude**

ἀπό**δειξις, εως, ἡ**$_3$ {ἀπό + δείκνυμι} ①[dfs] 1 Cor 2:4, **transparent truth**[NIGTC]; ❷ LXX

ἀπο**δεκατόω**[con] {ἀπό + δεκά} ❹ Matt 23:23 = Luke 11:42; Luke 18:12; Heb 7:5, **to tithe**; ❻ LXX, Gen 28:22; Exod 14:22, **to set aside** *a tenth*

ἀπό**δεκτος, ον**$_{2.2}$ {ἀπό + δέχομαι} *adj.* ❷[nns] 1 Tim 2:3; 5:4, **acceptable, pleasing**

ἀπο**δέχομαι** ❼ Luke 8:40; Acts 21:17; 28:30, **to welcome**; 2:4, **to receive**; ❽ LXX

ἀπο**δημέω**[con] {ἀπό + δῆμος} ❻ Matt 21:33; 25:14; Luke 15:13, **to leave on a journey**

ἀπό**δημος, ον**$_{2.2}$ *adj.* ①[nms] Mark 13:34, **sojourner**

ἀπο**δίδωμι** (48x; 18x Matt) 🅐 *financial transactions and obligations*, Matt 18:23–34[7x]; Matt 5:26 = Luke 12:59; Rom 13:7, **to pay, repay**; Luke 9:42, **to give back**; Acts 5:8, **to sell**; 🅑 *commitments and promises*, Matt 5:33, **to keep**; Rev 22:2, **to yield**; 🅒 *rewards and consequences*, 2 Tim 4:8, **to reward**; 4:14, **to punish**; 🅓 *moral and ethical conduct*, Rom 12:17 = 1 Thess 5:15 = 1 Pet 3:9, **to return** *evil for evil*; 🅔 *accountability and stewardship, bus. idiom*, Luke 16:2; Heb 13:17, **to give an accounting** (206x LXX; 75x Pent, 16x Pss)

ἀπο**διορίζω** {ἀπό + ὅρος} ①[pap.nmp] Jude 19, **to divide, to create division**[TNTC]

ἀπο**δοκιμάζω** ❾ Matt 21:42 = Mark 12:10 = Luke 20:17; 1 Pet 2:4, **to reject**; (10x LXX)

ἀπο**δοχή, ῆς, ἡ**$_{1η}$ {ἀπό + δοκιμάζω} ❷ 1 Tim 1:15; 4:9, **acceptance**

ἀπό**θεσις, εως, ἡ**$_3$ {ἀπό + τίθημι} ❷ 1 Pet 3:21, **the removal** *of dirt from the body*; 2 Pet 1:14, **to lay aside** *my tent*; Aristot. *Pol.* 1335b 19, **exposure** *of infants*[BrDAG]

ἀπο**θήκη, ης, ἡ**$_{1η}$ {ἀπό + τίθημι} ❻ Matt 3:12 = Luke 3:17; Matt 6:26 = Luke 12:24; Luke 12:18, **barn**; (12x LXX; 5x 1 Chr) Exod 16:32, εἰς **ἀποθήκην**, *keep an omer of manna for* **posterity sake** (Tanakh); Deut 28:5, **basket**

ἀπο**θησαυρίζω** ①[pap.amp] 1 Tim 6:19, **to lay up treasure**[NIGTC]; ①[pap.nms] LXX, Sir 3:4

ἀπο**θλίβω** ①[pai3p] Luke 8:45, **to crowd in upon**; ①[aai3s] LXX, Num 22:25, **to squeeze**

ἀπο**θνῄσκω** (111x; 28x John, 23x Rom) Matt 8:32; John 11, *Lazarus saga*[9x], Acts 7:4, Rom 5:6–8[4x]; 1 Cor 15:22; 1 Thess 4:14; Rev 3:2, **to die**; 1 Cor 15:31, *from day to day*, **I court fatality**[NIGTC]; Jude 12, **dead**; (546x LXX; 182x Pent, 62x 1–2 Sam, 52x 1–2 Kgs)

ἀπο**καθίστημι** {ἀπό + κατά + ἵστημι} ❽ Matt 12:13 = Mark 3:5 = Luke 6:10; Mark 8:25; Acts 1:6; Heb 13:19, **to restore, reinstate**; (44x LXX; 6x Jer) Job 5:18, **to bandage**

ἀπο**καλύπτω** (26x; 10x Gs) Matt 10:26 = Luke 12:2; John 12:38; Rom 1:18; Gal 3:23; 1 Pet 5:1, **to reveal**; (100x LXX; 27x Lev) Gen 8:13, **to remove**; Lev 18:6–20:21,[27x] **to uncover** *nakedness*; Prov 27:5, **open** *reprimand*

ἀπο**κάλυψις, εως, ἡ**$_3$ (18x) Luke 2:32; Rom 2:5; 1 Cor 1:7; Gal 1:12; 1 Pet 4:13, **revelation, unveiling** ❹ LXX, 1 Sam 20:30, *your mother's* **nakedness**

ἀποκαραδοκία, ας, ἡ$_{1\alpha}$ {ἀπό + κάρα + δοκέω} ❷ Rom 8:19; Phil 1:20, **eager expectation**, *stretching the head forward*[TDNT, PNTC]

ἀποκαταλλάσσω {ἀπό + κατά + ἄλλος} ❸ Eph 2:16 = Col 1:20, 22, **to reconcile**[ABC]

ἀποκατάστασις, εως, ἡ$_3$ {ἀπό + κατά + ἵστημι} ①[gfs] Acts 3:21, **restoration**[EDNT]; Polyb. *Hist.* 3.99.6, **hostages return to homeland, restoration of health, cure**[BrDAG]

ἀπόκειμαι ❹ Luke 19:20, *lit.*, **to lay aside**; Col 1:5; 2 Tim 4:8, *fig.*, **to store for future use**; Heb 9:27, **to be ordained**; ❹ LXX, 4 Macc 8:11 (8:9), *death is* **ordained**[TDNT]

ἀποκεφαλίζω {ἀπό + κεφαλή} ❹ Matt 14:10; Mark 6:16, 27; Luke 9:9, **to behead**; ①[aai1s] LXX, Ps 151:7,[ITA 330] *reflection on David's* **beheading** *of Goliath* (NRSVUE)

ἀποκλείω ①[aas3s] Luke 13:25, **to close**; (32x LXX) Judg 3:22, *Eglon's fat* **closed over**

ἀποκόπτω ❻ Mark 9:43; John 18:10, 26; Acts 27:32, **to chop off, to cut away**; Gal 5:12, *mid.*, **to castrate themselves**; ❼ LXX, Deut 23:2, **to castrate oneself**[BEC]

ἀπόκριμα, ατος, τό$_3$ {ἀπό + κρίνω} ①[ans] 2 Cor 1:9, **an official decision, verdict**; MSG: **"We felt like we'd been sentenced to death row."**[BEC]

ἀποκρίνομαι {ἀπό + κρίνω} (231x; 229x GA) Col 4:6; Rev 7:13, **to answer**; (18x Matt) *pleon.*, ὁ δὲ **ἀποκριθεὶς** εἶπεν, but/and **he answered**[EGG]; (246x LXX)

ἀπόκρισις, εως, ἡ$_3$ ❹ Luke 2:47; 20:26; John 1:22; 19:9, **an answer**; (13x LXX; 7x Job)

ἀποκρύπτω ❹ Luke 10:21, **you have hidden**; ❸[pfpp] 1 Cor 2:7; Eph 3:9; Col 1:26, **hidden**; (18x LXX; 4x Sir, 2x Isa) Zeph 3:5, *not* **hidden**

ἀπόκρυφος, ον$_{2.2}$ {ἀπό + κρύπτω} *adj.* ❸ Mark 4:22 = Luke 8:17; Col 2:3, **hidden, secret**; (23x LXX; 7x Pss) Deut 27:15, *crafts and keeps an idol* **in secret**

ἀποκτείνω (74x; 54x GA, 15x Rev) Luke 13:4; Acts 7:52; 1 Thess 2:15; Rev 19:21, **to kill, put to death**; (206x LXX; 56x Pent, 20x 1 Macc)

ἀποκυέω {ἀπό + κύω} ❷ Jas 1:15, *fig.*, *desire* **gives birth** *to sin*; 1:18, *spir. God* **gave us birth** *by the word*; ①[aap] LXX, 4 Macc 15:17, **to bring forth** *perfect holiness*

ἀποκυλίω ❹ Matt 28:2 = Mark 16:3, 4 = Luke 24:2, **to roll away** *the stone*; ❹ LXX, Gen 29:3, 8, 10, **to roll** *the stone from the opening*; Jdt 13:9, **to roll** *his body off the bed*

ἀπολαμβάνω (10x; 5x Luke) Mark 7:33, **to take aside**; Luke 6:34; 15:27; 16:25; 23:41; Rom 1:27; Gal 4:5; Col 3:24; 2 John 8, **to receive**; ❺ LXX, Num 34:14, **to receive**

ἀπόλαυσις, εως, ἡ$_3$ {ἀπολαύω} ❷ 1 Tim 6:17; Heb 11:25, **pleasure, enjoyment**; ①[afs] LXX, 3 Macc 7:16, **enjoyment**; Thuc. 2.38.2, **fruition, enjoyment**

ἀπολείπω {ἀπό + λαμβάνω} ❼ 2 Tim 4:13, 20; Titus 1:5, **to leave behind**[Spicq]; Heb 4:6, 9; 10:26, **to remain**; Jude 6, **to desert**; (25x LXX) Exod 5:19, **to reduce**

ἀπόλλυμι {ἀπό + ὄλλυμι} (90x; 66x Gs) Matt 2:13; Jude 5, **to kill, destroy**; Matt 5:29; Rev 18:14, **to lose**; Matt 8:25, **to perish**; Luke 15:17, **dying** *of hunger*; John 6:12, **to waste**; 2 Cor 4:9, **to terminate**[BEC]; (366x LXX; 40x Isa, 28x Sir:Jer)

Ἀπολλύων, ονος, ὁ$_3$ ①[nms] Rev 9:11, **Apollyon**

Ἀπολλωνία, ας, ἡ$_{1\alpha}$ ①[afs] Acts 17:1, **Apollonia**

Ἀπολλῶς, ῶ, ὁ$_3$ (10x) Acts 18:24; 19:1; 1 Cor 1:12–16:12[7x]; Titus 3:13, **Apollos**

ἀπολογέομαι {ἀπό + λέγω} (10x) Luke 12:11; 21:14; Acts 19:33–26:24[6x]; Rom 2:15; 2 Cor 12:19, **to defend**; ❸ LXX, 2 Macc 13:26; Jer 12:1; 38:6 (31:6)

ἀπολογία, ας, ἡ$_{1\alpha}$ {ἀπό + λέγω} ❽ Acts 22:1; 2 Cor 7:11; Phil 1:7; 2 Tim 4:16; 1 Pet 3:15, **defense**; ①[afs] LXX, Wis 6:10, *to find an answer* **in defense**

ἀπολούω ❷ *metaph.* Acts 22:16, **to wash away**; 1 Cor 6:11, *to have your sins* **washed away** *for you*[NIGTC]; ①[ams1s] LXX, Job 9:30, **to wash myself** *with snow*

ἀπολύτρωσις, εως, ἡ$_3$ {ἀπό + λύω} (10x) Luke 21:28; Rom 3:24; 1 Cor 1:30; Eph 1:7; Col 1:14; Heb 9:15, **deliverance, redemption**; ①[gfs] LXX, Dan 4:34, **to restore**

ἀπολύω (66x; 65x GA) Matt 1:19; 5:31, 32, **to divorce**; 14:15; **to send away**; Luke 2:29, **to let die**; 6:37, **to forgive**; 23:16; Acts 16:35, **to release**; 13:3, **to commission**; Heb 13:23, **to be set free**; (27x LXX; 17x 1–4 Macc[SCS]) Exod 33:11, **to return**

ἀπομάσσω {ἀπό + μαστιγάω} ①[pmi1p] Luke 10:11, **to wipe off** *in protest*

ἀπονέμω ①[pap.nmp] 1 Pet 3:7, **to attribute, assign**; ❸ LXX, Deut 4:19, **to allot, portion**

ἀπονίπτω ①[ami3s] Matt 27:24, **to wash** *one's hands of guilt*[EBC]; ❸ LXX, Prov 30:12

ἀποπίπτω ①[aai3p] Acts 9:18, **to fall**; (10x LXX) Lev 19:9, *subst.* **the gleanings**

ἀποπλανάω[con] {ἀπό + πλανάω} ❷ Mark 13:22; 1 Tim 6:10, **to deceive, seduce**; ❼ LXX, 3x Sir; 2 Chr 21:1, **to lead astray**; Plut. *Sollert.* 962e, **to digress, ramble**

ἀποπλέω[con] ❹ Acts 13:4; 14:26; 20:15; 27:1, **to set sail**

ἀποπνίγω ❷ Luke 8:7, **to choke**; 8:33, **to drown**; ❷ LXX, Nah 2:13 (2:12)

ἀπορέω[con] {ἀπό + πορεύομαι} ❻ Mark 6:20, **to be totally perplexed** *about John*; Luke 24:4; Acts 25:20, **to be at a loss**[ZEC]; John 13:22, **to be speechless**[ZEC]; 2 Cor 4:8, **to be baffled**[BEC]; Gal 4:20, **to be bewildered**[KeenG]; (14x LXX; 3x Isa) Gen 32:8, **to be perplexed**

ἀπορία, ας, ἡ$_{1\alpha}$ {ἀπό + πορεύομαι} ①[dfs] Luke 21:25, **perplexity, anxiety**; (11x LXX; 3x Isa) Lev 26:16, **wasting disease**; Antipho. 2.4.2, **difficulty** *finding a killer*

ἀπορίπτω ①[aap.amp] Acts 27:43, **to jump overboard**[ZEC]; (45x LXX; 10x Jer) Jonah 2:4

ἀπορφανίζω {ἀπό + ὀρφανός} ①[app.nmp] 1 Thess 2:17, **to be orphaned**

ἀποσκίασμα, ατος, τό$_3$ {ἀπό + σκιά} ① Jas 1:17, **shadow**; Greg. *Or.* 30.17.16, **trick**

ἀποσπάω[con] ❹ Matt 26:51, **to draw** *a sword*; Luke 22:41, **to withdraw**; Acts 20:30, **to draw away**[ZEC]; 21:1, **to tear ourselves away**[ZEC]; ❽ LXX, Josh 8:6, **to draw away**

ἀποστασία, ας, ἡ$_{1\alpha}$ {ἀπό + ἵστημι} ❷ Acts 21:21, **abandonment** *from Moses*; 2 Thess 2:3, **rebellion, apostasy**; ❹ LXX, Josh 22:22, **rebellion**; 2 Chr 29:19, **unfaithful**

ἀποστάσιον, ου, τό$_2$ {ἀπό + ἵστημι} ❸ Matt 5:31; Matt 19:7 = Mark 10:4, **divorce papers**; ❹ LXX, Deut 24:1, 3, *to write a* **divorce** *certificate* {βιβλίον}

ἀποστεγάζω {ἀπό + στέγω} ①[aai3p] Mark 2:4, **to uncover, unroof**

ἀποστέλλω (132x; 120x GA) Matt 2:16; Mark 4:29; John 3:17; Acts 5:21; 1 John 4:9; Rev 1:1; 2 Tim 4:12; 1 Pet 1:12, **to send, send out**; (651x LXX; 87x 1–2 Sam, 96x 1–2 Kgs, 52x 1–2 Chr, 62x Jer, 75x 1 Macc)

ἀποστερέω[con] {στρέω → **to deprive, rob**} ❻ Mark 10:19, **to defraud**; 1 Cor 6:7, 8, **to be defrauded**[NIGTC]; 1 Cor 7:5, **to cheat, deprive**; 1 Tim 6:5, **to be robbed**; Jas 5:4, **to withhold** *wages*; ❽ LXX, 5x Sir; Deut 24:14, **to defraud purposefully**

ἀποστολή, ῆς, ἡ$_{1\eta}$ {ἀπό + στέλλω} ❹ Acts 1:25; Rom 1:5; 1 Cor 9:2; Gal 2:8, **apostleship**; (11x LXX) Deut 22:7, *with cognate verb*, **to go free**; Eccl 8:8, **discharge** *during battle*

ἀπόστολος, ου, ὁ$_2$ {ἀπό + στέλλω} (81x; 29x Acts) Matt 10:2 = Mark 3:14; Luke 24:10; 1 Pet 1:1; Rev 21:14, **apostle**; Rom 1:1; 2 Cor 8:23; Phil 2:25, **messenger(s)**; Rom 16:7; 1 Cor 15:7, **apostles**; Gal 1:17, 19, **commissioned agents**[KeenG]; 2 Cor 11:5, *extraordinary* **apostles**[BEC!]; Plato *Epist.* 346a, **dispatched** *merchant ships*

ἀποστοματίζω {ἀπό + στόμα} ①[painf] Luke 11:53–54, **ἀποστοματίζειν . . . στόματος, to interrogate** *intensely*,[BEC] *to be hostile and* **to lecture** *him*[BHGNT!]

ἀποστρέφω ❾ Matt 5:42; Rom 11:26, **to turn away**; Luke 23:14, **to subvert**[NIGTC]; 2 Tim 1:15; Titus 1:14,[ABC] **to abandon**; Heb 12:25, **to repudiate**; (450x LXX; 134x MajPr, 37x Pss)

ἀποστυγέω[con] ①[pap.nmp] Rom 12:9, **to loathe**[ZEC!]; Callim. *H.* 4.223, **to chase away**

ἀποσυνάγωγος, ον$_{2.2}$ {ἀπό + σύν + ἄγω} *adj.* ❸ John 9:22; 12:42; 16:2, **expelled from the synagogue**

ἀποτάσσω ❻ *mid.*, Mark 6:46 = Luke 9:61; Acts 18:18; 2 Cor 2:13, **to say goodbye**

ἀποτελέω[con] {ἀπό + τέλος} ❷ Luke 13:32, **to perform**; Jas 1:15, **to be full grown**; ①[pai3s] LXX, 2 Macc 15:29, **to enhance** *one's enjoyment* (NRSV)

ἀποτίθημι ❾ *aor. mid.*, Matt 14:3, **to put** *into prison*; Acts 7:58, **to disrobe**; Rom 13:12; Eph 4:25 = Col 3:8; Heb 12:1; 1 Pet 2:1, **to rid oneself**; (15x LXX; 4x Num) Lev 16:23

ἀποτινάσσω {ἀπό + τείνω} ❷ Luke 9:5, **to shake off** *dust*; Acts 28:5, **to shake off** *a snake*; ❸ LXX, Judg 16:20, **shake myself** *free*; Lam 2:7, **to repudiate**

ἀποτίνω ①[fai1s] Phlm 19, **to pay, repay**; (30x LXX; 16x Exod)

ἀποτολμάω[con] ①[pai3s] Rom 10:20, **to be bold**

ἀποτομία, ας, ἡ$_{1α}$ {ἀπό + τομός} ❷ Rom 11:22,[2x] **severity**; [Callisth.] 2.12.5, **pure madness**

ἀποτόμως {ἀπό + τομός} *adv.* ❷ 2 Cor 13:10, **harshly**[BEC]; Titus 1:13, **sharply**[NIGTC]; ① LXX, Wis 5:22, **cruelly**

ἀποτρέπω ①[pmimp2s] 2 Tim 3:5, **to avoid**; ❸ LXX, 3 Macc 1:23, **to deflect**

ἀπουσία, ας, ἡ$_{1α}$ {ἀπό + εἰμί} ① Phil 2:12, **absence** (*the opposite of* παρουσία)

ἀποφέρω ❻ *act.*, 1 Cor 16:3, **carry** *your gift*; Mark 15:1, **the chief priests led him away**; *pass.*, Rev 17:3; 21:10, *then* **he carried me away** *in the spirit*; (32x LXX; 7x 1 Esd) Lev 20:19, **to bear** *their iniquity*; Num 17:11, **to carry away**

ἀποφεύγω ❸ 2 Pet 1:4; 2:18, 20, **to escape**; ①[fmi3s] LXX, Sir 22:22, **will depart**

ἀποφθέγγομαι ❸ *mid.*, Acts 2:4, **to speak** *in tongues*; 2:14, **to speak** *with inspiration*; 26:25, **to speak** *soberly*[Keen4]; ❻ LXX, 1 Chr 25:1, **to speak inspired thoughts**; Ps 58:8 (59:7), **to spew out**; Mic 5:12; Ezek 13:9, **idolaters**

ἀποφορτίζομαι {ἀπό + φέρω} ①[pmp.nns] Acts 21:3, **to unload** *ship's cargo*

ἀπόχρησις, εως, ἡ$_{3}$ {ἀπό + χράομαι} ①[dfs] Col 2:22, **use, consumption**[NIGTC]

ἀποχωρέω[con] ❸ Matt 7:23, **Depart!**; Luke 9:39; Acts 13:13, **to leave**

ἀποψύχω ①[pap.gmp] Luke 21:26, *lit.*, **to stop breathing, to faint**; ①[pap.nms] LXX, 4 Macc 15:18, **breathing out his soul**; Luc. *Philopatr.* 1, **to die of fright**

Ἄππιος, ου, ὁ$_{2}$ ①[gms] Acts 28:15, **Appius**, Ἀππίου Φόρον, *Forum* **of Appius**

ἀπρόσιτος, ον$_{2.2}$ {α + πρός + εἶμι → to come, go} *adj.* ①[ans] 1 Tim 6:16, **unapproachable**

ἀπρόσκοπος, ον$_{2.2}$ {α + πρός + κόπτω} *adj.* ❸ Acts 24:16, **blameless**; 1 Cor 10:32, **inoffensive**[NIGTC]; Phil 1:10, **unfailing**[NIGTC]; ❷ LXX, 3 Macc 3:8; Sir 32:21, **blameless**

ἀπροσωπολήμπτως *adv.* {α + ὁράω + λαμβάνω} ① 1 Pet 1:17, *lit.*, **not regarding someone's face**, *to judge* **fairly**[Keen1P]

ἄπταιστος, ον$_{2.2}$ {α + πταίω} *adj.* ①[amp] Jude 24, **free from stumbling**; ①[amp] LXX, 3 Macc 6:39, **unharmed**; Xen. *Hip.* 1.6, *sure-footed horse that* **does not stumble**

ἅπτω (39x; 33x Syn) 35x *mid.*, Luke 11:33; Acts 28:2, **to light** *a fire*; Mark 10:13; Luke 7:39, **to touch**; Col 2:21, **to partake of**; 1 Cor 7:1, **to have sexual intercourse**; 1 John 5:18,

to take hold of[ZEC]; (122x LXX) Gen 3:3, **to touch**; Lev 6:20–22:4,[28x] **touching** *rules, guidelines*

Ἀπφία, ας, ἡ$_{1\alpha}$ ①[dfs] Phlm 2, **Apphia**

ἀπωθέω[con] {ἀπό + ὠθέω} ❻ *mid.*, Acts 7:27, 39, **to repudiate**; Acts 13:46; 1 Tim 1:19, **to reject**; (60x LXX; 16x Pss, 12x Ezek) Judg 6:13, **to abandon**; Ps 88:39 (89:38), **to reject**

ἀπώλεια, ας, ἡ$_{1\alpha}$ {ἀπό + ὄλλυμι} (18x) Matt 7:13; Acts 8:20; 1 Tim 6:9, **destruction**; Matt 26:8, **waste**; John 17:12; 2 Thess 2:3, *the son of* **destruction**; Heb 10:39, *supernatural* **destruction**[NIGTC]; 2 Pet 2:1[2x]; 3:7, **destruction**; (116x LXX; 15x Prov, 11x Ezek)

ἀρά, ᾶς, ἡ$_{1\alpha}$ ①[gfs] Rom 3:14, **imprecation, curse**; (31x LXX) Num 5:21; Deut 30:7, **curse**

ἄρα *infer. part.* (49x) Ⓐ ***inference***, 2 Cor 2:17, **then**; Ⓑ ***result***, Rom 5:18; 1 Thess 5:6, **as a result, consequently**; Ⓒ ***potential***, Mark 4:41; Acts 5:8, **perhaps**

ἆρα, *part. injecting suspense*[AGG 427] ❸ Luke 18:8; Acts 8:30; Gal 2:17,[KeenG] **then . . . ?**

Ἀραβία, ας, ἡ$_{1\alpha}$ ❷ Gal 1:17; 4:25, **Arabia**; (13x LXX) Gen 45:10, *Goshen* **of Arabia**

Ἀράμ, ὁ$_2$ ❷ Matt 1:3, 4, **Ram**; (11x LXX; 4x 1 Chr:Isa) Gen 10:22, 23

ἄραφος, ον$_{2.2}$ {α + ῥαφίς} *adj.* ①[nms] John 19:23 (*cf.* Ps 22:18), **seamless**, *of Jesus's tunic*

Ἄραψ, βος, ὁ$_3$ ①[nmp] Acts 2:11, **Arabians**; (15x LXX; 4x 2 Chr:1 Macc)

ἀργέω[con] {α + ἔργον} ①[pai3s] 2 Pet 2:3, to **idle**; ❻ LXX, 1 Esd 2:26, **to stop**

ἀργός, η, ον$_{2.1.2}$ {α + ἔργον} *adj.* ❽ Matt 12:36, **careless**; 20:3, 6; 1 Tim 5:13[2x]; Titus 1:12, **lazy**[NIGTC!]; Jas 2:20, **useless**; 2 Pet 1:8, **ineffective**; ❹ LXX, 1 Kgs 6:7, **finished** *stones*

ἀργύριον, ου, τό$_2$ {ἄργυρος} (20x; 19x GA) Matt 25:18; Mark 14:11, **money**; Acts 3:6–20:33; 1 Pet 1:18, **silver**; (383x LXX; 86x Pent)

ἀργυροκόπος, ου, ὁ$_2$ ①[nms] Acts 19:24, **silversmith**; ①[nms] LXX, Jer 6:29

ἄργυρος, ου, ὁ$_2$ ❺ Matt 10:9; Acts 17:29; 1 Cor 3:12; Jas 5:3; Rev 18:12, **silver**; (11x LXX; 3x Prov); Plato *Pol.* 303e, *proper.* **white metal**

Ἄρειος, α, ον$_{2.1.2}$ *adj.* ❷ Acts 17:19, 22, **Areopagus**

Ἀρεοπαγίτης, ου, ὁ$_{1>}$ ①[nms] Acts 17:34, *Dionysius the* **Areopagite**

ἀρεσκεία, ας, ἡ$_{1\alpha}$ {ἀρέσκω} ①[afs] Col 1:10, **fully pleasing**; ①[nfp] LXX, Prov 31:30

ἀρέσκω (17x) Matt 14:6 = Mark 6:22; Acts 6:5; Rom 8:8; 1 Cor 7:32; 10:33; 1 Thess 2:4; 2 Tim 2:4, **to please**; (54x LXX; 6x Esth) Gen 19:8, *do as* **it may please** *you*

ἀρεστός, ή, όν$_{2.1.2}$ {ἀρέσκω} *adj.* ❹ John 8:29; Acts 12:3; 1 John 3:22, **pleasing**; Acts 6:2, **desirable**; (32x LXX; 6x Deut) Gen 3:6; Lev 10:19, **pleasing**

Ἀρέτας, α, ὁ$_1$ ①[gms] 2 Cor 11:32, **Aretas**, *Aretas IV, king of Nabatean Arabia*

ἀρετή, ῆς, ἡ$_{1\eta}$ {ἀρέσκω} ❺ Phil 4:8; 2 Pet 1:5, **moral excellence** *of humans*; 1 Pet 2:9, 2 Pet 1:3, **wonderful deeds, excellence** *of God*; (32x LXX) 4 Macc 1:2, **virtue**

ἀρήν, ἀρνός, ὁ$_3$ {ἀρνίον} ①[amp] Luke 10:3, **lamb**

ἀριθμέω[con] {ἀριθμός} ❸ Matt 10:30 = Luke 12:7; Rev 7:9, **to count**; (37x LXX; 9x 1–2 Chr)

ἀριθμός, οῦ, ὁ$_2$ {ἀριθμέω} (18x; 10x Rev) Luke 22:3; John 6:10; Acts 4:4; 16:5; Rom 9:27; Rev 5:11; 20:8, **number**; (167x LXX; 33x Num, 31x 1–2 Chr)

Ἀριμαθαία, ας, ἡ$_{1\alpha}$ ❹ Matt 27:57 = Mark 15:43 = Luke 23:51 = John 19:38, *Joseph of* **Arimathea**

Ἀρίσταρχος, ου, ὁ$_2$ ❺ Acts 19:29; 20:4; 27:2; Col 4:10; Phlm 24, **Aristarchus**

ἀριστάω[con] {ἄριστος} ❸ Luke 11:37, **to dine**; John 21:12, 15, **to eat breakfast**; ❸ LXX

ἀριστερός, ά, όν$_{2.1.2}$ {ἀριστάω} *adj.* ❹ Matt 6:3; Mark 10:37; Luke 23:33; 2 Cor 6:7, **left hand**; (58x LXX; 6x 1 Chr) Jonah 4:11, *between their right and* **left**

Ἀριστόβουλος, ου, ὁ$_{2}$ ①[gms] Rom 16:10, **Aristobulus**

ἄριστον, ου, τό$_{2}$ ❸ Matt 22:4; Luke 11:38; 14:12, **banquet**; ❻ LXX, 2 Sam 24:15, **noon**

ἀρκετός, ή, όν$_{2.1.2}$ {ἀρκέω} *adj.* ❸ Matt 6:34; 10:25; 1 Pet 4:3, **enough**, **sufficient**

ἀρκέω[con] ❽ Matt 25:9; John 6:7, **to be enough**; Luke 3:14, **be satisfied**; 2 Cor 12:9,[BEC] **is sufficient**; 1 Tim 6:8; Heb 13:5; 3 John 10, **is content**; (12x LXX) Exod 12:4, **to suffice**

ἄρκος, οῦ, ὁ$_{2}$ ①[gms] Rev 13:2, **bear**; (15x LXX) Judg 1:35; 1 Sam 17:34, **bear**

ἅρμα, ατος, τό$_{3}$ ❹ Acts 8:28, 29, 38, **carriage**; Rev 9:9, **war chariots**; (170x LXX)

Ἁρμαγεδών, τό$_{3}$ *indecl.* ①[nns] Rev 16:16, *fig.*, **Armageddon**; *non-geographical*[NIGTC]

ἁρμόζω ①[ami1s] 2 Cor 11:2, **to betroth**[BEC]; (10x LXX; 3x Prov) 2 Sam 6:5, **tuned** *instruments*; Prov 17:7, **to suit**; Hom. *Od.* 5.248, *carpentry*, **to fit together a mortice joint**

ἁρμός, οῦ, ὁ$_{2}$ {ἁρμόζω} ①[gmp] Heb 4:12, **joint**; ❷ LXX, 4 Macc 10:5; Sir 27:2

ἀρνέομαι[con] (33x; 18x GA) Matt 26:70 = Mark 14:68; John 1:20; 2 Pet 2:1; 1 John 2:22; Jude 4, **to deny** *Jesus*; Acts 7:35, **to reject**; Heb 11:24, **to renounce**, **refuse**; 1 Tim 5:8; Rev 2:13, **to deny** *the faith*; ❻ LXX, 3x Wis; Gen 18:15, **to deny**

Ἀρνί, ὁ$_{2}$ ①[gms] Luke 3:33, **Arni**[NIGTC]

ἀρνίον, ου, τό$_{2}$ {ἀρήν} (30x; 29x Rev) John 21:15, **lambs**[ZEC]; Rev 13:11, *anti-Messianic* **lamb** *of Satan*; 5:6–22:3,[28x] *messianic* **Lamb** *of God*[ZEC]; ❺ LXX, Ps 113:4 (114:4)

ἀροτριάω[con] {ἄροτρον} ❸ Luke 17:7; 1 Cor 9:10,[2x] **to plow**; (14x LXX; 6x Isa) Job 1:14

ἄροτρον, ου, τό$_{2}$ ①[ans] Luke 9:62, **plow**; ❺ LXX, 1 Chr 21:23, **threshing sledge**

ἁρπαγή, ῆς, ἡ$_{1\eta}$ {ἁρπάζω} ❸ Matt 23:25 = Luke 11:39, **greed**; Heb 10:34, **forcible seizure**[NIGTC]; Eus. *Hist. eccl.* 3.17, *Domitian sponsored* **seizure of property**; ❽ LXX, Lev 6:2

ἁρπαγμός, οῦ, ὁ$_{2}$ {ἁρπάζω} ①[ams] Phil 2:6, **a prize to be held on to**[ICC, ABC!]

ἁρπάζω (14x) Matt 11:12, *attempted* **forceful entry and seizure** *of the kingdom*[KeenM]; Matt 12:29, **to snatch** *something*; 2 Cor 12:2[BEC]; 1 Thess 4:17; Jude 23, **to snatch up**, **away**; John 6:15, **to take by force**; 10:12, *the wolf* **attacks**; Rev 12:5, **to catch up** *as in resurrection*[NIGTC]; (37x LXX; 8x Ezek) Ps 7:2 (7:3), **to be snatched away** *by a wild animal*

ἅρπαξ, αγος, ὁ$_{3}$ {ἁρπάζω} ❺ Matt 7:15, **ravenous** *wolves*; Luke 18:11, **greedy**; 1 Cor 5:10, 11, **one who practices extortion**; 6:10, **swindlers**[NIGTC]; ①[nms] LXX, Gen 49:27

ἀρραβών, ῶνος, ὁ$_{3}$ ❸ 2 Cor 1:22; 5:5; Eph 1:14, **pledge**; ❸ LXX, Gen 38:17

ἄρρητος, ον$_{2.2}$ {α + ῥῆμα} *adj.* ①[anp] 2 Cor 12:4, **not permitted to speak**[BEC]

ἄρρωστος, ον$_{2.2}$ {α + ῥώννυμι} *adj.* ❺ Matt 14:14; Mark 6:5; 1 Cor 11:30, **sick**; ❷ LXX

ἀρσενοκοίτης, ου, ὁ$_{1>}$ {ἄρσην + κοίτη = men + bed} ❷ 1 Cor 6:9, **those males who sexually penetrate males**[NIGTC, EEE]; 1 Tim 1:10, **male homosexual**[NIGTC]

ἄρσην, εν$_{3.3}$ *adj.* ❾ Matt 19:4; Rom 1:27; Gal 3:28; Rev 12:5, 13, **man**, **male**; (52x LXX)

Ἀρτεμᾶς, ᾶ, ὁ$_{1}$ ①[ams] Titus 3:12, **Artemas**, *friend of Paul the apostle*

Ἄρτεμις, ιδος, ἡ$_{3}$ ❺ Acts 19:24, 27, 28, 34, 35, **Artemis**

ἀρτέμων, ῶνος, ὁ$_{3}$ ①[ams] Acts 27:40, **top sail, foresail**

ἄρτι *adv.* (36x; 12x John) Matt 3:15, **for now**[NIGTC]; 1 Cor 4:13, **up to this moment**; Matt 23:39, **from now on**[NIGTC]; 1 Cor 15:6, **still**; 16:7, **incidentally**[NIGTC]; 1 John 2:9, **currently**; Rev 14:13, *the* **now** *of redemption*[BEC]; Matt 9:18, **a moment ago**; (12x LXX)

ἀρτιγέννητος, ον$_{2.2}$ {ἄρτι + γίνομαι} *adj.* ①[nnp] 1 Pet 2:2, **just-born** *babies*[Keen1P]

ἄρτιος, α, ον$_{2.1.2}$ {ἄρτι} *adj.* ①[nms] 2 Tim 3:17, **capable to meet all demands**; Plato *Gorg.* 451 c3, **even** *and odd numbers*, Thphr. *H.P.* 2.5.5, **sound**, *of mind and body*

ἄρτος, ου, ὁ$_2$ (97x; 86x GA) Matt 14:17 = Mark 6:37, 38 = Luke 9:13 = John 6:5; 1 Cor 11:27, **bread**; John 6,[21x] (**bread** « flesh « Jesus); 2 Cor 9:10, **bread** = **God's word**[BEC]; 2 Thess 3:8, **food**; (295x LXX; 25x Lev:1 Sam)

ἀρτύω ❸ Mark 9:50[DGNT2, 28–32] = Luke 14:34, **to restore flavor**; Col 4:6, **to season** *with the salt of conversation*[Herm.Col]; Plut. *QCon.* 5.10.2

Ἀρφαξάδ, ὁ$_3$ *indecl.* ①[gms] Luke 3:36, **Arphaxad**, *son of Shem*; (12x LXX; 6x Gen, 5x Jdt)

ἀρχάγγελος, ου, ὁ$_2$ {ἄρχω + ἀγγέλλω} ❷ 1 Thess 4:16; Jude 9, **archangel**

ἀρχαῖος, α, ον$_{2.1.2}$ {ἄρχω} *adj.* (11x) Matt 5:21, 33; Acts 15:7; 2 Cor 5:17, **old**; Luke 9:8; Acts 15:21; 2 Pet 2:5, **ancient**; 21:16, **early**; Rev 12:9; 20:2, **ancient** *serpent*; (26x LXX)

Ἀρχέλαος, ου, ὁ$_2$ ①[nms] Matt 2:22, **Archelaus**, *a son of Herod the Great*

ἀρχή, ῆς, ἡ$_{1\eta}$ {ἄρχω} (55x; 8x John, 8x 1 John) John 1:1, **the beginning**[WBC]; John 2:11, **first**; Acts 10:11, **ends**; Rom 8:38, **ruler**; 1 Cor 15:24, **dominion**; Eph 6:12, **supernatural rulers**[HH]; Jude 6, **domain of authority**; Phil 4:15, **early**; Heb 5:12, **foundation**; Rev 21:6, **origin**; *math.* Archim. *Spir.* 11 *def.* 2, **origin** *of a curve*[BrDAG]; (215x LXX; 25x Isa)

ἀρχηγός, οῦ, ὁ$_2$ {ἄρχω + ἄγω} ❹ *Jesus is referent*; Acts 3:15, **founder** *of life*, 5:31, **leader**; Heb 2:10; 12:2, **author**, **captain**[KJV]; (28x LXX; 7x Num)

ἀρχιερατικός, όν, τό$_2$ {ἄρχω + ἱερός} ①[gns] Acts 4:6, **pertaining to the chief priest**

ἀρχιερεύς, έως, ὁ$_3$ {ἄρχω + ἱερός} (122x; 105x GA) Matt 28:11; Luke 24:20; Acts 26:12, **chief priest**; Matt 26:3, 65; Luke 22:50; Heb 13:11, **high priest**; (44x LXX)

ἀρχιποίμην, ενος, ὁ$_3$ {ἄρχω + ποιμαίνω} ①[gms] 1 Pet 5:4, **chief shepherd**

Ἄρχιππος, ου, ὁ$_2$ ❷[dms] Col 4:17; Phlm 2, **Archippus**

ἀρχισυνάγωγος, ου, ὁ$_2$ {ἄρχω + σύν + ἄγω} ❾ Mark 5:22, 35, 36, 38; Luke 13:14; Acts 13:15; 18:8, 17, **ruler of the synagogue**[WLC 95]

ἀρχιτέκτων, ονος, ὁ$_3$ {ἄρχω + τέκτων} ① 1 Cor 3:10, *skilled* **master builder**; ❸ LXX, Isa 3:3, *skilled* **artisan**

ἀρχιτελώνης, ου, ὁ$_{1>}$ {ἄρχω + τελέω} ①[nms] Luke 19:2, **chief tax collector**

ἀρχιτρίκλινος, ου, ὁ$_2$ {ἄρχω + τρεῖς + κλίνω} ❸ John 2:8, 9,[2x] **chief servant**

ἄρχω (86x; 83x GA, 78x *aor. mid*) Matt 26:74; Mark 1:45; John 8:9; 1 Pet 4:17, **to begin**; Mark 10:42, **to rule**; (81x LXX; 17x Judg, 10x Isa)

ἄρχων, οντος, ὁ$_3$ {ἄρχω} (37x; 19x LA) Matt 9:34; Mark 3:22; Eph 2:2, **demonic powers**; Luke 8:41–Acts 23:5[22x]; 1 Cor 2:6, 8[Héring]; Eph 2:2; Rev 1:5, **high-level earthly ruler(s)**; *never employed for the church, family, or husband*; (624x LXX; 93x 1 Chr, 80x Num)

ἄρωμα, ατος, τό$_3$ ❹ Mark 16:1 = Luke 23:56; 24:1; John 19:40, **spices**; (17x LXX)

ἀσάλευτος, ον$_{2.2}$ {α + σάλος} *adj.* ❷ Acts 27:41, **immovable**; Heb 12:28, **unshakable**; ❸ LXX, Exod 13:16; Deut 6:8; 11:18, **symbol** *on your forehead*

Ἀσάφ, ὁ$_2$ ❷ Matt 1:7, 8, **Asaph**; (48x LXX) Pss 73–83, *psalms attributed to* **Asaph**

ἄσβεστος, ον$_{2.2}$ {α + σβέννυμι} *adj.* ❸ Matt 3:12 = Luke 3:17; Mark 9:43, **unquenchable**

ἀσέβεια, ας, ἡ$_{1\alpha}$ {α + σέβω} ❻ Rom 1:18; 11:26; 2 Tim 2:16; Titus 2:12; Jude 15, **godlessness**; (73x LXX; 17x Ezek, 10x Amos, 8x Prov)

ἀσεβέω[con] {α + σέβω} ❷ Jude 15; 2 Pet 2:6, **to live in an ungodly manner**; (37x LXX)

ἀσεβής, ές$_{3.3}$ {α + σέβω} *adj.* ❾ Rom 4:5; 1 Tim 1:9; 2 Pet 2:5; Jude 1:4, 15, **ungodly**; 1 Pet 4:18, **irreverent**[Keen1P]; (242x LXX; 90x Prov, 37x Job, 19x Pss)

ἀσέλγεια, ας, ἡ$_{1\alpha}$ {ἀσελγής} (10x) Mark 7:22, **open flaunting**[ABC]; Jude 4, **debauchery**[ABC]; 2 Cor 12:21, **rank promiscuity**[BEC]; 1 Pet 4:3, **uninhibited**[Keen1P]; ❷ LXX

ἄσημος, ον$_{2.2}$ {α + σημεῖον} *adj.* ①[gfs] Acts 21:39, *lit., a citizen of no* **obscure** *city* (*i.e., Tarsus*); ❸ LXX, Job 42:11, **unstamped** *gold.*

Ἀσήρ, ὁ$_3$ *indecl.* ❷[gms] Luke 2:36; Rev 7:6, *the tribe of* **Asher**; (43x LXX; 12x Num)

ἀσθένεια, ας, ἡ$_{1\alpha}$ {α + σθενόω} (24x; 8x 1–2 Cor) Matt 8:17; Gal 4:13; Heb 11:34, **illness, disease**; John 5:5, **lame**[ZEC]; Rom 6:19; 8:26; 2 Cor 13:4, **weakness**; ❼ LXX

ἀσθενέω[con] {α + σθενόω} (33x, 9x 1–2 Cor) Ⓐ Mark 6:56, **the sick**; John 11:1; Acts 9:37; Jas 5:14, **to be sick**; Ⓑ 1 Cor 8:11, **the spiritually immature**; Ⓒ[BEC] ***varied pictures of weakness***; 2 Cor 11:21, **to be unwilling to pressure**; 11:29, **to be pastorally burdened**; 12:10, **various persecutions**; 13:3, **ineffectiveness**; 13:4, 9, **vulnerability** *and* **nonretaliation**; (67x LXX; 11x Pss, 7x Hos)

ἀσθένημα, ατος, τό$_3$ {α + σθενόω} ①[anp] Rom 15:1, **frailties**[ZEC]

ἀσθενής, ές$_{3.3}$ {α + σθενόω} *adj.* (26x; 11x 1 Cor) Matt 25:43; Acts 4:9, **sick**; 26:41; Rom 5:6,[ZEC] **morally weak**; 1 Thess 5:14, **without adequate faith**; 2 Cor 10:10; 1 Pet 3:7,[BEC!] **physical weakness**; Heb 7:18, **impotent**, **ineffective**; (21x LXX; 5x Prov, 3x Wis)

Ἀσία, ας, ἡ$_{1\alpha}$ (18x) Acts 2:9–27:2[12x]; Rom 16:5; 2 Tim 1:15; 1 Pet 1:1, **Asia,** ❾ LXX

Ἀσιανός, οῦ, ὁ$_2$ ①[nmp] Acts 20:4, *someone from the Roman province of* **Asia**

Ἀσιάρχης, ου, ὁ$_{1>}$ ①[gmp] Acts 19:31, **Asiarch**

ἀσιτία, ας, ἡ$_{1\alpha}$ {α + σῖτος} ①[gfs] Acts 27:21, **not eating** *due to seasickness*[Keen4]

ἄσιτος, ον$_{2.2}$ *adj.* ①[nmp] Acts 27:33, **not eating** *due to seasickness* or *anxiety*[Keen4]

ἀσκέω[con] ①[pails] Acts 24:16, **to do my best**[ZEC]; ①[painf] LXX, 2 Macc 15:4, **to celebrate**; Xen. *Cyr.* 2.1.20, **to train** *the bodies to strength*

ἀσκός, οῦ, ὁ$_2$ (12x) Matt 9:17[4x] = Mark 2:22[4x] = Luke 5:37–38,[4x] **wineskins**; (15x LXX)

ἀσμένως {ἥδομαι} *adv.* ① Acts 21:17, **warmly**; ❸ LXX, 2 Macc 4:12, **gladly**

ἄσοφος, ον$_{2.2}$ *adj.* ①[nmp] Eph 5:15, **unwise**

ἀσπάζομαι (59x; 40x Paul, 35x *aor. mid. imp.*) Matt 5:47; Mark 9:15; Rom 16:13–20[21x]; 1 Cor 16:19; 3 John 15, **to greet**; Mark 15:18, **to address**; (10x LXX) Exod 18:7, **to embrace**

ἀσπασμός, οῦ, ὁ$_2$ (10x; 5x Luke) Matt 23:7; Mark 12:38; 2 Thess 3:17, **greeting**

ἄσπιλος, ον$_{2.2}$ {σπιλόω} *adj.* ❹ 1 Tim 6:14; Jas 1:27; 1 Pet 1:19; 2 Pet 3:14, **undefiled**

ἀσπίς, ίδος, ἡ$_3$ ①[gfp] Rom 3:13, **cobra**; *milit.*, Hom. *Il.* 2.389, **shield**; Eur. *Ph.* 78, *armed with* **shields** (*cf. the cobra's shield-like hood*); (31x LXX) Deut 32:33, **cobra**; 1 Chr 5:18, **shield**

ἄσπονδος, ον$_{2.2}$ {α + σπένδω} *adj.* ①[gfp] 2 Tim 3:3, **unforgiving**

ἀσσάριον, ου, τό$_2$ ❷ Matt 10:29 = Luke 12:6, **a Roman copper coin**

ἆσσον *adv.* ① Acts 27:13, **nearer**

Ἆσσος, ου, ἡ$_2$ ❷ Acts 20:13, 14, **Assos**

ἀστατέω[con] {α + ἵστημι} ①[pailp] 1 Cor 4:11, **no fixed abode**[NIGTC]; Plut. *Cr.* 17.1, **to be in constant motion, be agitated**[BrDAG]

ἀστεῖος, α, ον$_{2.1.2}$ {ἄστυ → *city, urbane*} *adj.* ❷ Acts 7:20; Heb 11:23, **well-bred, beautiful**; ❻ LXX, Exod 2:2, **handsome**; *but* Judg 3:17, *Eglon*, **well-fed**, *not necessarily fat*[KEL]; Alexis 194, **pleasing to the eye**

ἀστήρ, έρος, ὁ$_3$ {ἄστρον} (24x; 14x Rev) Matt 2:2; 1 Cor 15:41; Rev 1:16, **star**; Jude 13, *wandering* **stars**, *i.e., godless false teachers*[BEC]; (20x LXX; 5x Gen) Gen 22:17

ἀστήρικτος, ον$_{2.2}$ {α + στηρίζω} *adj.* ❷ 2 Pet 2:14, 3:16, **unstable**
ἄστοργος, ον$_{2.2}$ {α + στέργω} *adj.* ❷ Rom 1:31; 2 Tim 3:3, **unloving**
ἀστοχέω[con] {α + στόχος} ❸ 1 Tim 1:6; 6:21; 2 Tim 2:18, **to miss the mark**, *concerning the truth*; ❷ LXX, Sir 7:19; 8:9
ἀστραπή, ῆς, ἡ$_{1η}$ ❾ Matt 24:27; Luke 10:18; Rev 4:5; 8:5; 16:18, **lightning**; Luke 11:36, **ray of light**; (24x LXX) Exod 19:16, **lightning** *on Mt. Sinai*
ἀστράπτω {ἀστραπή} ❷ Luke 17:24, **to flash**; 24:4, **to dazzle**; ❷ LXX
ἄστρον, ου, τό$_{2}$ {ἀστήρ} ❹ Luke 21:25; Acts 7:43; 27:20; Heb 11:12, **star**; (38x LXX)
Ἀσύγκριτος, ου, ὁ$_{2}$ ①[ams] Rom 16:14, **Asyncritus**, *the incomparable one*
ἀσύμφωνος, ον$_{2.2}$ {α + σύν + φωνή} *adj.* ①[nmp] Acts 28:25, **in disagreement with**; ❷ LXX
ἀσύνετος, ον$_{2.2}$ {α + σύν + ἵημι} ❺ Matt 15:16 = Mark 7:18; Rom 1:21; 10:19, **dull**, **slow**; (13x LXX; 6x Sir) Deut 32:21, **devoid of understanding**
ἀσύνθετος, ον$_{2.2}$ {α + σύν + τίθημι} *adj.* ①[amp] Rom 1:31, **untrustworthy**; ❹ LXX, Jer 3:7, 8, 10, 11, **treacherous** *sister Judah* (ESV)
ἀσφάλεια, ας, ἡ$_{1α}$ {α + σφάλλω} ❸ Luke 1:4, **certainty**; Acts 5:23, *prison* **securely locked**; 1 Thess 5:3, **peace**[BEC!]; (19x LXX) Lev 26:5, **securely**
ἀσφαλής, ές$_{3.3}$ {α + σφάλλω} *adj.* ❺ Acts 21:34, **truth**; 22:30, **exactly**; 25:26, **definite**; Phil 3:1, *someth. providing* **steadfastness**[Spicq]; Heb 6:19, **anchor**[EGG]; ❻ LXX, Prov 3:18
ἀσφαλίζω {α + σφάλλω} ❹ *mid./pass.* Matt 27:64, 65, 66, **to make secure**; Acts 16:24, **to fasten** *their feet*; ❹ LXX, Isa 41:10, **to establish**
ἀσφαλῶς {α + σφάλλω} *adv.* ❸ Mark 14:44, **under guard**; Acts 2:36, **with certainty**[ZEC]; 16:23, **securely**, **under close guard**; ❻ LXX, Gen 34:25, **unsuspecting**
ἀσχημονέω[con] {α + σκῆμα} ❷ 1 Cor 7:36; 13:5, **to behave inappropriately**[NIGTC]; ❺ LXX
ἀσχημοσύνη, ης, ἡ$_{1η}$ {α + σκῆμα} ❷ Rom 1:27, **shameless act**; Rev 16:15, *his* **shame**; (44x LXX; 32x Lev) Lev 18:6–20:21, **brazen acts** *of certain sexual practices*
ἀσχήμων, ον$_{3.3}$ {α + σκῆμα} *adj.* ①[npn] 1 Cor 12:23, **unpresentable**, *private parts*[NIGTC]; ❹ LXX, Gen 34:7, *commit an* **outrage** (*rape*); Deut 24:1, **an unbecoming thing**
ἀσωτία, ας, ἡ$_{1α}$ {σῴζω} ❸ Eph 5:18, **drunkenness**; Titus 1:6, **not saved**, **reckless**[ABC]; 1 Pet 4:4, **wasteful excesses**[Keen1P]; ❷ LXX, 2 Macc 6:4, **riotous behavior**
ἀσώτως {α + σῴζω} *adv.* ① Luke 15:13, **reckless orgy of spending**, **wasteful** *living*
ἀτακτέω[con] {α + τάσσω} ①[aai1p] 2 Thess 3:7, **to be idle**
ἄτακτος, ον$_{2.2}$ {α + τάσσω} *adj.* ①[amp] 1 Thess 5:14, **disruptive**; ①[ams] LXX, 3 Macc 1:19, **disorderly**; Isocr. *Paneg.* 150.8, *soldiers who lost all* **stamina** *for war*
ἀτάκτως {α + τάσσω} *adv.* ❷ 2 Thess 3:6, 11, **disorderly fashion**, **rank breaker**[NIGTC]
ἄτεκνος, ον$_{2.2}$ {α + τίκτω} *adj.* ❷ Luke 2:28, 29, **childless**; ❻ LXX, Gen 15:2; Lev 20:20
ἀτενίζω {α + τείνω → *to stretch out fully*} (14x; 12x LA) Luke 4:20; Acts 1:10–23:1,[10x] **to gaze upon intently**; 2 Cor 3:7, 13, **attentive and prolonged visual observation of an object**[BEC]; ❸ LXX, 1 Esd 6:27, **to look diligently**
ἄτερ *impr. prep. w/ gen.* ❷ Luke 22:6, **away from**; 22:35, **without**; ① LXX, 2 Macc 12:15
ἀτιμάζω {α + τιμάω} ❼ Mark 12:4; Rom 2:23; Jas 2:6, **to dishonor**; Acts 5:41, **counted worthy to be dishonored**; Rom 1:24, **to degrade**; (33x LXX; 9x Prov, 7x Sir)
ἀτιμία, ας, ἡ$_{1α}$ {α + τιμή} ❼ Rom 1:26; 1 Cor 11:14; 2 Tim 2:20, **dishonor**, **disgrace**; 1 Cor 15:43, **weakness**; 2 Cor 6:8, **disrespect**; (55x LXX; 11x Prov, 8x Sir:Song)

ἄτιμος, ον$_{2.2}$ {α + τιμή} *adj.* ❹ Matt 13:57, **without honor**; 1 Cor 4:10, **disgraced**; 12:23, *comp.* **dishonored**; (11x LXX; 5x Wis) Job 30:4, **dishonorable**

ἀτμίς, ίδος, ἡ$_3$ {ἄω} ❷ Acts 2:19; Jas 4:14, **vapor, mist**; (11x LXX; 4x Sir)

ἄτομος, ον$_{2.2}$ {α + τομός} *adj.* ①[dns] 1 Cor 15:52, **indivisible**; ἐν ἀτόμῳ, **in an instant**[NIGTC]

ἄτοπος, ον$_{2.2}$ *adj.* ❹ Luke 23:41; Acts 25:5, *jurid.* **wrong**; Acts 28:6, **unusual**; *no ill effects from poisonous snake bite*; 2 Thess 3:2, **out of place; evil, wrong, improper**[BDAG]; ❽ LXX, Prov 30:20, *done nothing* **wrong**; Job 4:8, **injustice**

Ἀττάλεια, ας, ἡ$_{1α}$ ①[afs] Acts 14:25, **Attalia**[LGCb]

αὐγάζω {αὐγή} ①[aainf] 2 Cor 4:4, **to see**[BEC]; ❼ LXX, Lev 13:14–14:56, **bright** *spots*

αὐγή, ῆς, ἡ$_{1η}$ ①[gfs] Acts 20:11, **dawn**; ❷ LXX, 2 Macc 12:9, **light** *of the fire*; Isa 59:9, **brightness**

Αὐγοῦστος, ου, ὁ$_2$ ①[gms] Luke 2:1, **Augustus**

αὐθάδης, ες$_{3.3}$ {αὐτός + ἥδομαι} *adj.* ❷ Titus 1:7; 2 Pet 2:10, **self-willed, arrogant**; ❸[nms] LXX, Gen 49:3, 7; Prov 21:24, **stubborn**

αὐθαίρετος, ον$_{2.2}$ {αὐτός + αἱρέω} *adj.* ❷ 2 Cor 8:3, 17, **voluntarily, of one's own accord**

αὐθεντέω[con] {αὐτός + ἔντεα → ***instruments, gear***[NGD]} ①[painf] 1 Tim 2:12, **to tyrannize**[WestPG 290]; **to teach in a domineering fashion**[TNTC 90–98]; **to have abusive authority** *over a man*[PPE 250]; Aeschl. *Eum.* 40, **to have full authority**

αὐλέω[con] ❸ Matt 11:17 = Luke 7:32; 1 Cor 14:7, **to play the double oboe**[LAGNT 67]

αὐλή, ῆς, ἡ$_{1η}$ (12x, 11x Gs) Matt 26:3; Rev 11:2, **courtyard**; Luke 11:21, **estate, dwelling**; John 10:1, 16, **sheep pen**; (181x LXX; 51x Ezek) Ezek 8:7–48:1, **court**

αὐλητής, οῦ, ὁ$_{1>}$ {αὐλέω} ❷ Matt 9:23; Rev 18:22, **double-oboe players**[LAGNT 67]

αὐλίζομαι {αὐλή} ❷ Matt 21:17; Luke 21:37, **to spend the night, to lodge**; (43x LXX; 8x Job) Judg 19:6; Job 11:14, *don't allow injustice* **to dwell** *in your tents*

αὐλός, οῦ, ὁ$_2$ {αὐλέω} ①[nms] 1 Cor 14:7, **double oboe**[LAGNT 67]; (12x LXX, 3x Isa:Jer) Isa 30:29

αὐτοῦ {αὐτός} *adv.* ❹ Matt 26:36; Luke 9:27; Acts 18:19; 21:4, **there**; ❾ LXX, Gen 22:5

αὐξάνω {αὔξησις} (21x; 8x LA) Matt 6:28; 2 Pet 3:18, **to grow**; John 3:30, **to increase**, *of Jesus and John* (*cf.* **waxing** *and waning of heavenly lights*[ABC]); Acts 6:7, **to spread**; Eph 4:15, **to grow** *in faith*; 1 Pet 2:2, **to grow** *toward salvation*[Keen1P]; (37x LXX; 19x Gen) Gen 1:22

αὔξησις, εως, ἡ$_3$ {αὐξάνω} ❷ Eph 4:16; Col 2:19, **growth**; ①[afs] 2 Macc 5:16

αὔξω {αὐξάνω} ❷[pai3s] Eph 2:21 = Col 2:19, **to grow**; ❷ Isa 61:11, **to increase**

αὔριον *adv.* (14x; 8x LA) Matt 6:30; Acts 23:20; 1 Cor 15:32; Jas 4:13, **tomorrow**; (62x LXX)

αὐστηρός, ά, όν$_{2.1.2}$ *adj.* ❷ Luke 19:21, 22, **harsh**; ①[ams] LXX, 2 Macc 14:30, **churlish**

αὐτάρκεια, ας, ἡ$_{1α}$ {αὐτός + ἀρκέω} ❷ 2 Cor 9:8, *having* **everything you need**[BEC]; 1 Tim 6:6, **contentment**; Pseud., Pss. Sol. 5.16, **self-sufficiency**

αὐτάρκης, ες$_{3.3}$ {αὐτός + ἀρκέω} *adj.* ①[nms] Phil 4:11, **contentment**; ❻ LXX, Prov 30:8, **need**

αὐτοκατάκριτος, ον$_{2.2}$ {αὐτός + κατά + κρίνω} *adj.* ① Titus 3:11, **self-condemned**

αὐτόματος, η, ον$_{2.1.2}$ {αὐτός} *adj.* ❷ Mark 4:28; Acts 12:10, **of itself**[BEC]; ❻ LXX, Lev 25:5

αὐτόπτης, ου, ὁ$_{1>}$ {αὐτός + ὄψομαι, *fut.* of ὁράω} ①[nmp] Luke 1:2, **eyewitness**

αὐτός, ή, ό$_{2.1.2}$ (5,597x; 4,340x GA, 441x Rev; 4,845x → masc; 1,321x → Jesus)[GDG 12] Ⓐ ***emphatic***, Matt 3:14, **he!, she!, it!**; Eph 4:10, **he is!**[NIGTC]; Ⓑ ***intensive***, 1 Thess 4:16; Heb 11:11, **himself, herself, itself**; Ⓒ ***identical***, Jas 3:10; 1 Pet 4:1, **same**; (27,398x LXX)[Logos]

αὐτοῦ {αὐτός} *adv.* ❹ Matt 26:36; Luke 9:27; Acts 18:19; 21:4, **there**; ❾ LXX

αὐτό**φωρος, ον**$_{2.2}$ {αὐτός + φώρ → *thief*} *adj.* ①[dns] John 8:4, ἐν **αὐτοφώρῳ, in the act**
αὐτό**χειρ, ος, ὁ**$_{3}$ ①[nmp] Acts 27:19, **with one's own hands**
αὐχέω[con] {αὐχήν → *lift up the neck*} ①[pai3s] Jas 3:5, **to boast**[LSJ]; **αὐχήεις, braggart**[KEL]
αὐχμηρός, ά, όν$_{2.1.2}$ {αὐστηρός} *adj.* ①[dms] 2 Pet 1:19, **dark**; *the squalor and gloom of a dungeon*[BST]; Pseud., 4 Ezra 12.42, *like a haven for a ship saved from a* **storm**
ἀ**φαιρέω**[con] {ἀπό + αἱρέω} (10x) Matt 26:51 = Mark 14:47 = Luke 22:50, **to cut off**; Luke 1:25; Rom 11:27; Rev 22:19, **to take away**; (165x LXX; 36x Isa) Gen 21:25, **to seize**
ἀ**φανής, ές**$_{3.3}$ {α + φαίνω} *adj.* ①[nfs] Heb 4:13, **hidden**; ❹ LXX, Job 24:20, **to vanish**
ἀ**φανίζω** {α + φαίνω} ❺ Matt 6:16, **to disfigure** *their faces*[KeenM]; 6:19, **to destroy**; Acts 13:41, **to perish** *due to disbelief*[ZEC]; Jas 4:14, **to disappear**; (88x LXX; 16x Ezek)
ἀ**φανισμός, οῦ, ὁ**$_{2}$ {α + φαίνω} ①[gms] Heb 8:13, *it will soon* **pass away**; (56x LXX; 18x Jer, 5x Zeph) Jer 9:10–28:62, εἰς **ἀφανισμόν,**[16x] **for desolation, destruction**
ἄ**φαντος, ον**$_{2.2}$ {α + φαίνω} *adj.* ①[nms] Luke 24:31, **vanished**[ZEC]; Hom. *Il.* 6.60, *ships* **sank**
ἀ**φεδρών, ῶνος, ὁ**$_{3}$ {ἀπό + ἕζομαι} ❷[ams] Matt 15:17 = Mark 7:19, **latrine**, **sewer**, *lit.*, *and goes out into the toilet*[HCSB]
ἀ**φειδία, ας, ἡ**$_{1α}$ {φείδομαι} ①[dfs] Col 2:23, **harsh control**, i.e., **severity**, **rigor** *in dealing with the body*[BrDAG]; Plato *Def.* 412c; Plut. *Amat.* 762e, **generosity**, **prodigality**[BrDAG]
ἀ**φελότης, τητος, ἡ**$_{3}$ {α + φελλός → stone} ①[dfs] Acts 2:46, **simplicity** *of heart*[ZEC]
ἄ**φεσις, εως, ἡ**$_{3}$ (17x; 10x LA) Matt 26:28; Mark 1:4 = Luke 3:3; Acts 2:38; 26:18; Eph 1:7 = Col 1:14, *appos. w/ redemption*; Heb 9:22; 10:18, **forgiveness**; Luke 4:18, **release**, **liberty**; (50x LXX; 22x Lev) Lev 25:10–27:24, *laws for the* **redemption** *of people and property*
ἁφή, ῆς, ἡ$_{1η}$ {ἅπτω} ❷ Eph 4:16 = Col 2:19, **ligament**, **joint**; (69x LXX; 61x Lev) Lev 13:2–14:54, *ritual status and treatment of* **skin impurities**
ἀ**φθαρσία, ας, ἡ**$_{1α}$ {φθείρω} ❼ 2 Tim 1:10, **immortality**; 1 Cor 15:42, 53, **decay's reversal**, *flourishing in fullness of life*[NIGTC]; Eph 6:24, **undying** *love*[PNTC]; ❺ LXX, 3x Wis; 2x 4 Macc
ἄ**φθαρτος, ον**$_{2.2}$ {φθείρω} *adj.* ❽ Mark 16:8[HGT]; Rom 1:23; 1 Tim 1:17, **incorruptible**; 1 Cor 9:25; 1 Pet 1:4, 23; 3:4, **imperishable**; ❷ LXX, Wis 12:1; 18:4
ἀ**φθορία, ας, ἡ**$_{1α}$ {α + φθείρω} ①[afs] Titus 2:7, **purity of motive**[ICC, WBC]
ἀ**φίημι** {ἀπό + ἵημι} (143x; 127x GA) Rev 11:9, **to allow**, **permit**; 1 John 1:9, **to forgive**; John 14:27, **to leave**; Matt 9:2, **to be forgiven**; Matt 15:14, **to leave alone**; Rev 2:4, **to abandon**; 1 Cor 7:11, 12, 13, **to divorce**; Mark 12:19, **to orphan**; Matt 18:27, **to cancel** *a debt*; 27:50, **to give up** *his spirit*; (125x LXX; 21x 1 Macc, 12x Lev)
ἀ**φικνέομαι** {ἀπό + ἱκανός} ①[ami3s] Rom 16:19, **to be known**; (14x LXX) Gen 28:12
ἀ**φιλάγαθος, ον**$_{2.2}$ {α + φίλος + ἀγαθός} *adj.* ①[nmp] 2 Tim 3:3, **not loving the good**[ABC]
ἀ**φιλάργυρος, ον**$_{2.2}$ {α + φίλος + ἄργυρος} *adj.* ❷ 1 Tim 3:3; Heb 13:5, **not loving money**
ἄ**φιξις, εως, ἡ**$_{3}$ {ἀπό + ἱκανός} ①[afs] Acts 20:29, **departure**; ①[afs] LXX 3 Macc 7:18
ἀ**φίστημι** {ἀπό + ἵστημι} (14x; 10x LA) Acts 12:10, **to leave**; 15:38, **to desert**; 19:9, **to withdraw**; 2 Cor 12:8, **to remove** *thorn in the flesh*; Luke 8:13, **to fall away**; 2 Tim 2:19, **to keep away from** *unrighteousness*[PPE]; Acts 5:37, **to incite** *rebellion*[ZEC]; Heb 3:1, **to defect**, **to abandon** *God*[NIGTC]; (218x LXX; 26x Sir, 23x 2 Kgs) Xen. *Cyn.* 3.3, **to withdraw** *from the sun into the shade*; Procl. *Hyp.* 6.7, *geom*, **to cut** *a line*
ἄφνω *adv.* ❸ Acts 2:2; 16:26; 28:6, **suddenly**; (10x LXX; 3x 1 Macc:Jer) Prov 1:27, **suddenly** *strikes you like a storm*

ἀφόβως {α + φόβος} *adv.* ❹ Luke 1:74; 1 Cor 16:10; Phil 1:14, **without fear**; Jude 12, **arrogantly**; ❷ LXX, Prov 1:33, **to be undisturbed**

ἀφομοιόω[con] {ἀπό + ὁμός} ①[pfmp.nms] Heb 7:3, **to resemble**; ❹ LXX, 4x LetJ

ἀφοράω[con] {ἀπό + ὁράω} ❷ Phil 2:23, **to see**; Heb 12:2, **to look to**; ❹ LXX, 4 Macc 17:10, **to fix one's eyes** *upon God amid persecution*; Jonah 4:5, **to perceive**

ἀφορίζω {ἀπό + ὅρος} (10x) Matt 13:49, **to separate**; Gal 1:15, **to set apart**; 2 Cor 6:17, **to distance oneself**[BEC]; Gal 2:12, **to retreat**[NIGTC]; (87x LXX; 41x Josh, 18x Lev) Lev 10:15, **forever**; Lev 13:11, **to quarantine**; Josh 21, τὰ **ἀφωρισμένα**,[36x] **to apportion** *land*

ἀφορμή, ῆς, ἡ$_{1η}$ {ἀπό + ὁρμή} ❼ *Pauline term*, Rom 7:8, 11; 2 Cor 5:12; 11:12; Gal 5:13; 1 Tim 5:12, **occasion, opportunity**; ❸ LXX, Prov 9:9, *give an* **instruction**

ἀφρίζω {ἀφρός} ❷ Mark 9:18, 20, **to foam at the mouth**

ἀφρός, οῦ, ὁ$_2$ ①[gms] Luke 9:39, **foam**

ἀφροσύνη, ῆς, ἡ$_{1η}$ {α + φρήν} ❹ Mark 7:22; 2 Cor 11:1, 17, 21, **foolishness, lacking good judgment**[BEC]; (35x LXX; 9x Prov, 8x Eccl) Prov 5:5, 23, **folly**

ἄφρων, ον$_{3.3}$ {α + φρήν} *adj.* (11x) Luke 11:40; 12:20; Rom 2:20; Eph 5:17; 1 Pet 2:15, **fool, foolish**; (133x LXX; 74x Prov) Ps 73:22 (74:22); Prov 1:22; 10:1, **foolish**

ἀφυπνόω[con] {ἀπό + ὕπνος} ①[aai3s] Luke 8:23, **to fall asleep**

ἄφωνος, ου, ὁ$_2$ {α + φωνή} ❹ Acts 8:32; 1 Cor 12:2, *idols* **incapable of speech**[NIGTC]; 14:10, **without meaning**; 2 Pet 2:16, **speechless**; ❸ LXX, 2 Macc 3:29, **speechless**

Ἀχάζ, ὁ$_2$ ❷ Matt 1:9,[2x] **Ahaz**; (38x LXX; 17x 2 Kgs, 12x 1–2 Chr, 6x Isa)

Ἀχαΐα, ας, ἡ$_{1α}$ (10x) Acts 18:12; Rom 15:26; 1 Cor 16:15; 2 Cor 9:2; 1 Thess 1:7, **Achaia**

Ἀχαϊκός, οῦ, ὁ$_2$ ①[gms] 1 Cor 16:17, **Achaicus**

ἀχάριστος, ον$_{2.2}$ {χαρίζομαι} *adj.* ❷ Luke 6:35; 2 Tim 3:2, **ungrateful**; ❹ 4 Macc 9:10

ἀχειροποίητος, ον$_{2.2}$ {α + χείρ + ποιέω} *adj.* ❸ Mark 14:48; 2 Cor 5:1; **not made with hands**, *i.e., an immortal body*; Col 2:11, *circumcision* **not performed by human hands**

ἀχθῆναι → ἄγω, *aor. pass. inf.*, Luke 18:40, **to be brought**

Ἀχίμ, ὁ$_3$ *indecl.* ❷ Matt 1:14,[2x] **Achim**; ①[nms] LXX, 1 Chr 11:35, **Ahiam**

ἀχλύς, ύος, ἡ$_3$ ①[nfs] Acts 13:11, **mist**

ἀχρεῖος, ον$_{2.2}$ {α + χράομαι} *adj.* ❷ Matt 25:30, **worthless**; Luke 17:10, **unworthy**; ❷ LXX

ἀχρειόω[con] {α + χράομαι} ①[api3p] Rom 3:12, **to become worthless**; ❼ LXX, 2x Pss:Dan

ἄχρηστος, ον$_{2.2}$ {α + χράομαι} *adj.* ①[ams] Phlm 11, **of no use**; (10x LXX; 5x Wis) 2 Macc 7:5

ἄχρι, ἄχρις *impr. prep. w/ gen.* (49x; 19x LA, 11x Rev) Ⓐ ***abrupt event***, Matt 24:38 = Luke 17:27; Gal 3:19; Rev 2:10, **until** *the very day, time, or event*; Ⓑ ***directional***, Acts 11:5, **right down** *to me* (NASB); Rev 14:20, **up to**; Ⓒ ***spatial***, Heb 4:12, **even to the point of** (NET) Ⓓ ***chron.***, Acts 20:6, **within** (NET); Acts 27:33, **when**; Rom 5:13, **before**; ❸ LXX, Ⓐ 2 Macc 14:10, *for* **as long as** *Judas lives*; Ⓓ 14:15, ἄχρι αἰῶνος, **forever**; Job 32:11, **while**

ἄχυρον, ου, τό$_2$ ❷ Matt 3:12 = Luke 3:17, **chaff**; (21x LXX; 8x Exod 5, 4x Isa) Gen 24:25, **straw**; Exod 5:7–18, *Pharaoh's* **straw** *decree*; Isa 65:25, *lion will eat* **straw**

ἀψευδής, ές$_{3.3}$ {α + ψεύδομαι} *adj.* ①[nms] Titus 1:2, *God* **never lies**; ①[afs] LXX, Wis 7:17

ἄψινθος, ου, ἡ$_2$ ❷ Rev 8:11,[2x] **Wormwood, wormwood**

ἄψυχος, ον$_{2.2}$ {α + ψύχω} *adj.* ①[nnp] 1 Cor 14:7, **lifeless**; ❷ LXX, Wis 13:17; 14:29

B, β [*bēta*]

B, β, τό (βῆτα) *indecl.* **beta**, *2nd letter of the Gr. alphabet* ‖ *num.* β′ = 2; ,β = 2,000

βαβυλών, ῶνος, ἡ$_3$ (12x; 6x Rev, 4x Matt)[*RRU* 37–62] Matt 1:11, 12, 17,^{2x} *exile to* **Babylon**; Rev 14:8–18:21,^{6x} **Babylon** *the Great*[NIGTC]; (276x LXX; 132x Jer, 32x 2 Kgs)

βαθμός, οῦ, ὁ$_2$ {βαίνω} ①^{ams} 1 Tim 3:13, *good* **standing** ❼ LXX, 2 Kgs 20:9–11^{5x}

βάθος, ους, τό$_3$ {βαθύς} ❽ Matt 13:5 = Mark 4:5; Luke 5:4, **deep** *water*; 1 Cor 2:10, **depth**, *greatness of God*; 2 Cor 8:2, **extreme** *poverty*[BEC]; **rock-bottom** *poverty*[BNTC]; Eph 3:18, **depth** *of God's love*; (23x LXX; 7x Ezek)

βαθύνω ①^{aainf} Luke 6:48, **to dig deeper**[BEC]; ❸ LXX, Ps 91:6 (92:5), **great depths**; Jer 30:2, **lie low**; Xen. *Cyr.* 6.3.23, *milit.*, **to extend a phalanx in depth**

βαθύς, εῖα, ύ$_{3.1.3}$ *adj.* ❹ Luke 24:1, **deep** *dawn*[BEC]; John 4:11; Acts 20:9, **deep**; Rev 2:24, **deep things** *of Satan*[NIGTC]; (23x LXX) Prov 22:14, *the mouth . . . is a* **deep** *pit*

βάϊον, ου, τό$_2$ ①^{anp} John 12:13, **branches**; ①^{gnp} 1 Macc 13:51

βαλαάμ, ὁ$_3$ *indecl.* ❸ *neg. narr.* 2 Pet 2:15; Jude 11; Rev 2:14, **Balaam**[*APB*]; (62x LXX; 55x Num) **Balaam**, *son of Beor*; Num 22:5–31:16, *the Balaam chronicle*

βαλάκ, ὁ$_3$ *indecl.* ①^{dms} Rev 2:14, **Balak**; (52x LXX; 41x Num) **Balak**, *king of Moab*

βαλλάντιον, ου, τό$_2$ ❹ Luke 10:4; 12:33; 22:35,^{2x} **money-bag**; ❷ LXX, Job 14:17

βάλλω (122x; 34x Matt, 28x Rev) Matt 3:10 = Luke 3:9; Rev 18:19, **to throw**, **cast**; Matt 9:17 = Mark 2:22 = Luke 5:37, **to pour**; Acts 27:14, *fierce wind* **rushed down**; Jas 3:3, **to put**, **place**; Rev 8:7, **to hurl**; (54x LXX; 6x Ezek) Judg 20:16, *stone*-**slingers**

βαπτίζω {βάπτω} (177x; 31x LA, 13x Mark:Luke) Matt 3:6 = Mark 1:4; John 1:25, **to baptize** *with water*; Luke 12:50, **to be immersed in disaster** (*the coming passion*)[WBC]; Acts 1:5,^{2x} *John* **baptized** *in water, but* **you will be baptized** *with the Holy Spirit*; 1 Cor 1:13–17,^{6x} **to baptize**; Plato *Euthyd.* 277d, **to drown**; *Symp.* 176b, **immersed** *in wine*, **drunk**

βάπτισμα, ματος, τό$_3$ {βάπτω} (19x; 6x Acts) Matt 3:7; 21:25 = Mark 11:30 = Luke 20:4, **baptism**; Mark 10:38, 39; Luke 12:50, **baptism** *of suffering and death*[ZEC]; Rom 6:4, *metaph. through that* **plunge** *into death*[ZEC]

βαπτισμός, οῦ, ὁ$_2$ {βάπτω} ❹ Mark 7:4; Heb 6:2; 9:10, **washings**; Col 2:12, **baptism**

βαπτιστής, οῦ, ὁ$_{1>}$ {βάπτω} (12x) Matt 16:14 = Mark 8:28 = Luke 9:19, *John* **the Baptizer**

βάπτω ❹ Luke 16:24; John 13:26^{2x}; Rev 19:13, **to dip**; (16x LXX; 7x Lev) Exod 12:22

βαραββᾶς, ᾶ, ὁ$_{1α}$ (11x) Matt 27:20–21 = Mark 15:11 = Luke 23:18 = John 18:40, **Barrabas**

βαράκ, ὁ$_3$ *indecl.* ①^{gms} Heb 11:32, **Barak**; (14x LXX; 13x Judg) Judg 4:6–5:12

βαραχίας, ου, ὁ ①^{gms} Matt 23:35, **Barachiah**; ❺ LXX, 2 Chr 28:12; Neh 3:4; Zech 1:1

βάρβαρος, ον$_{2.2}$ *adj.* ❻ Acts 28:2, 4, **natives** *of Malta*; Rom 1:14, **barbarian** (*not pejorative*); 1 Cor 14:11, **an alien** *to the speaker*; ❼ LXX, 2 Macc 2:21, **barbarous hordes**

βαρέω^{con} {βαρύς} ❻ Luke 9:32, **heavy-lidded** *with sleep*[ZEC]; Luke 21:34; 2 Cor 5:4, **to be burdened**; 2 Cor 1:8, **we were oppressed**[BEC]; ①^{pfpi3s} LXX, Exod 7:14, **weighed down**

βαρέως {βαρύς} *adv.* ❷ Matt 13:15 = Acts 28:27 = (Isa 6:10), **hard** *of hearing*; ❺ LXX, 2 Macc 11:1, *being* **deeply** *displeased*; Xen. *Cyr.* 5.3.37, **heavily** *armed forces*

βαρθολομαῖος, ου, ὁ$_2$ ❹ Matt 10:3 = Mark 3:18 = Luke 6:14; Acts 1:13, **Bartholomew**

βαριησοῦς, οῦ, ὁ$_3$ ①[gms] Acts 13:6, *Aram.* **son of Jesus, son of Joshua**[ZEC]

βαριωνᾶ, ὁ$_3$ *indecl.* ①[vms] Matt 16:17, *Aram. Simon*, **son of Jonah**[ZEC]

βαρναβᾶς, ᾶ, ὁ$_{1α}$ (28x, 23x Acts) Acts 4:36, **Barnabas**

βάρος, ους, τό$_3$ {βαρύς} ❻ Matt 20:12; Gal 6:2, **burden**; 2 Cor 4:17, **tonnage** *of glory*[BEC]; 1 Thess 2:7, **harsh demands**;[ABC] ❸ LXX, 2 Macc 9:10, *unbearable* **oppressiveness** *of smell*; Mnesim. 4.62, **aromatic** *plant*; Soph. *Ant.* 1256, **weight** *of silence*

βαρσαββᾶς, ᾶ, ὁ$_{1α}$ ❷ Acts 1:23; 15:22, **Barsabbas**

βαρτιμαῖος, ου, ὁ$_2$ ①[nms] Mark 10:46, **Bartimaeus**

βαρύς, εῖα, ύ$_{3.1.3}$ *adj.* ❻ 1 John 5:3, **burden**; Matt 23:23, **weightier matters**[EGG]; Acts 20:29, **fierce** *wolves*[Keen3]; Acts 25:7, **serious**; 2 Cor 10:10, **intimidating**[BEC]; (46x LXX)

βαρύτιμος, ον$_{2.2}$ {βαρύς + τιμή} *adj.* ①[gns] Matt 26:7, **expensive**

βασανίζω {βάσανος} (12x) Ⓐ Matt 8:6, **suffering** *horribly*; Ⓑ Matt 8:29; Luke 8:28; 2 Pet 2:8; Rev 11:10, **to torment**; Ⓒ Matt 14:24 = Mark 6:48, **battered** *by the waves*; Ⓓ Rev 12:2, **in agony**; (29x LXX; 19x 4 Macc) 1 Sam 5:3, **to plague**; 4 Macc 6:5–16:15, **to be tortured**[SCS]

βασανισμός, οῦ, ὁ$_2$ {βάσανος} ❻ Rev 14:11, **torment**; ❷ LXX, 4 Macc 9:6; 11:2[SCS]

βασανιστής, οῦ, ὁ$_{1>}$ {βάσανος} ①[dmp] Matt 18:34, **torturers**[ZEC]

βάσανος, ου, ἡ$_2$ ❸ Matt 4:24, **tormentor**; Luke 16:23, 28, **in torment**; (61x LXX; 41x 4 Macc, 7x Ezek) 4 Macc 4:26–18:20, *vile* **torture** *leading to victorious death*[SCS]

βασιλεία, ας, ἡ$_{1α}$ {βασιλεύς} (162x; 121x Syn) Matt 4:8 = Luke 4:5, **kingdoms**, *earthly*; Matt 3:2; 18:3, **kingdom** *of heaven* (39x, only Matt)[ZEC]; Matt 6:33; 2 Thess 1:5, **kingdom** *of God* (64x); Matt 8:11–12, *many gentiles will enter* **the kingdom**, *but the (putative) sons of the* **kingdom** *will be thrown out into outer darkness*[EGG]; see Matt 7:21, *not everyone who says to me*, 'Lord, Lord,' *will enter* **the kingdom** of heaven; Rev 11:15, **the kingdom** *of the world has become* **the kingdom** *of our Lord and of his Christ* (363x LXX; 61x 1–2 Chr)

βασίλειος, ον$_{2.2}$ {βασιλεύς} *adj.* ❷ Luke 7:25, **royal palaces**[ZEC]; 1 Pet 2:9, **royal** *community of priests*; ❹ LXX, Exod 19:6; 23:22, **kingdom** *of priests*; 4 Macc 3:8,[SCS] **royal**

βασιλεύς, έως, ὁ$_3$ (115x; 81x GA) Matt 1:6, **King** *Herod*; 2:2; John 18:33–19:21,[12x] **King** *of the Jews*; Rev 15:3; 17:14, **βασιλεὺς βασιλέων, King** *of* **kings**; (3,181x LXX; 678x 1–2 Kgs, 292x 2 Sam, 275x 2 Chr) Gen 14:1–21, *the battle of the* **kings**

βασιλεύω {βασιλεύς} (12x) Matt 2:22; Luke 19:14, **to rule over**; Rom 5:14; 1 Cor 4:8,[2x] **to reign**; (389x LXX; 242x 1 Kgs–2 Chr) Gen 37:8, **Are you indeed to reign?**

βασιλικός, ή, όν$_{2.1.2}$ {βασιλεύς} *adj.* ❺ John 4:46, 49, **royal official**; Acts 12:20, *from the* **royal** *supply*; Acts 12:21, **royal**; (389x LXX; 153x 1–2 Kgs) Num 20:17, **King's** *Highway*

βασίλισσα, ης, ἡ$_{1η>}$ ❹ Matt 12:42 = Luke 11:31; Acts 8:27; Rev 18:7, **queen**; (39x LXX)

βάσις, εως, ἡ$_3$ {βαίνω} ①[nfp] Acts 3:7, **feet**; (70x LXX; 40x Exod, 11x Lev)

βασκαίνω {βάσκανος} ①[aai3s] Gal 3:1, **to cast a spell**[KeenG]; ❷ LXX, Deut 28:54, 56, **to disparage**; Aristot. *Pr.* 926b 24, **to give the evil eye, bewitch**[BrDAG]

βαστάζω {βάσκανος} (27x; 9x LA) Matt 3:11, **to remove**; 8:17, **to bear**; Luke 7:14, *subst.* **the pallbearers**; John 10:31, **to pick up**; Gal 6:2, **to carry**; Rom 11:18, **to support**; Rev 2:2, **to tolerate**; ❹ LXX, Ruth 2:16,[2x] **to lift up**[ABC]

βάτος, ου, ἡ$_1$/ὁ$_2$ ❺ Matt 12:26 = Luke 20:37 = Acts 7:30, 35, **burning bush**; Luke 6:44, **thornbush**; ❼ LXX, (5x) Exod 3:2–4, **thornbush**

βάτος, ου, ὁ$_2$ ①[amp] Luke 16:6, **measure**[ZEC]

βάτραχος, ου, ὁ$_2$ ①[nmp] Rev 16:13, **frogs**; (15x LXX; 12x Exod), Exod 7:27–8:9, **frog(s)** *plague*

βατταλογέω[con] {βάττος + λέγω} ①[aas2p] Matt 6:7, **to babble**[TNTC]

βδέλυγμα, ατος, τό$_3$ {βδελύσσω} ❻ Matt 24:15 = Mark 13:14, *the* **abomination** *of desolation*; Luke 16:15, **revulsion**; Rev 17:4, **devastation**; (120x LXX; 19x Deut) Gen 43:32

βδελυκτός, ή, όν$_{2.1.2}$ {βδελύσσω} *adj.* ①[nmp] Titus 1:16, **detestable**; ❷ LXX, 2 Macc 1:27

βδελύσσομαι {βαίνω} ❷ Rom 2:22, **to detest**; Rev 21:8, *subst.* **the detestable**; (50x LXX; 8x Pss, 7x Lev) Gen 26:29, **to loathe**; Job 9:31, *my own clothes* **despised** *me*

βέβαιος, α, ον$_{2.1.2}$ *adj.* {βαίνω} ❽ Rom 4:16, **confirmed**; 2 Cor 1:7, **firmly grounded**[BEC]; Heb 9:17, *jur.* **legally binding**; Heb 3:14, **firmly**; 2 Pet 1:19, *compar.*, **strongly confirmed**; ❺ LXX, 2x 3 Macc; Plato *Symp.* 182c, **guaranteed** *friendship*

βεβαιόω[con] {βαίνω} ❽ Heb 2:3, **to confirm**; 2 Cor 1:21, **to strengthen**; Col 2:7, **to establish**; ❷ LXX, Ps 40:13 (41:12); 118:28 (119:28), **to secure**, **strengthen**

βεβαίωσις, εως, ἡ$_3$ {βαίνω} ❷ Phil 1:7, **confirmation**; Heb 6:16, *for* **a guarantee**[NIGTC]; ❷ LXX, Lev 25:23; Wis 6:1

βέβηλος, ον$_{2.2}$ {**βεβηλόω**} *adj.* ❺ 1 Tim 1:9; Heb 12:16, **irreverent**; 1 Tim 4:7, **godless**; 6:20, **empty talk**; (15x LXX) 1 Sam 21:5, **common**; Ezek 21:30 (21:25), **profane one**

βεβηλόω[con] {**βέβηλος**} ❷ Matt 12:5, **to violate**; Acts 24:6, **to desecrate**; (86x LXX; 29x Ezek)

βεελζεβούλ, ὁ$_3$ *indecl.* ❼ (Syn) Matt 12:24 = Mark 3:22 = Luke 11:15, **Beelzebul**

Βελιάρ, ὁ$_3$ *indecl.* ①[ams] 2 Cor 6:15, **Belial**[BEC]

βελόνη, ης, ἡ$_{1η}$ ①[gfs] Luke 18:25, **a needle**[ZEC]

βέλος, ους, τό$_3$ {βάλλω} ①[anp] Eph 6:16, *flaming* **arrows**; (43x LXX; 12x Pss)

βελτίων, ον$_{3.3}$ *comp adv.* ① 2 Tim 1:18, **very well**

Βενιαμίν, ὁ$_3$ *indecl.* ❹ Acts 13:21; Rom 11:1; Phil 3:5; Rev 7:8, **Benjamin**; (180x LXX; 46x Judg, 17x Gen)

Βερνίκη, ης, ἡ$_{1η}$ ❸ Acts 25:13, 23; 26:30, **Bernice**, *a daughter of Herod Agrippa I*

Βέροια, ας, ἡ$_{1α}$ ❷ Acts 17:10, 13, **Berea**

Βεροιαῖος, α, ον$_{2.1.2}$ *adj.* ①[nms] Acts 20:4, **Berean**

Βηθανία, ας, ἡ$_{1α}$ (12x, Gs) Matt 26:6 = Mark 14:3 = John 12:1, **Bethany**

Βηθζαθά, ἡ$_3$ *indecl.* ①[nfs] John 5:2, **Bethzatha**, *pool in northeast Jerusalem*[LGCa]

Βηθλέεμ, ἡ$_3$ *indecl.* ❽ (5x Matt) Matt 2:16; Luke 2:4, 15; John 7:42, **Bethlehem**[LGCa]

Βηθσαϊδά, ἡ$_3$ *indecl.* ❼ (Gs) Matt 11:21 = Luke 10:13; John 1:44, **Bethsaida**[LGCa]

Βηθφαγή, ἡ$_3$ *indecl.* ❸ Matt 21:1 = Mark 11:1 = Luke 19:29, **Bethphage**[LGCa]

βῆμα, ατος, τό$_3$ (12x, 8x Acts) John 19:13, **judgment seat**; Acts 7:5, *not even a* **foot's length**[ZEC]; 12:21, **platform**[ZEC]; 18:16, **judicial bench**;[WLC 97] Rom 14:10, **tribunal**; 2 Cor 5:10, **judgment seat** *of Christ*; ❻ LXX, Deut 2:5, **a foot's length**

βήρυλλος, ου, ὁ$_2$, ἡ$_2$ ①[nms] Rev 21:20, **beryl**, ①[dfs] LXX, Tob 13:17, **precious stone**

βία, ας, ἡ$_{1α}$ ❸ Acts 5:26; 27:41, **force**; 21:35, **violence**[ZEC]; (30x LXX; 6x Wis)

βιάζω {βία} ❷[ppi3s] *pass.*, Matt 11:12,[ZEC] **to be the object of violence**[ZEC]; Luke 16:16, **to be pressed**[ABC, WBC]; **violence** *is contrary to the nature of the kingdom*[Spicq]; Aeschl. *Sept.* 1042, *I beg you not* **to visit such violence** *upon the city*[BrDAG]

βίαιος, α, ον$_{2.1.2}$ {βία} *adj.* ①[gfs] Acts 2:2, **violent** *rushing wind*[ZEC]; (12x LXX) Exod 14:21, **powerful** *wind*; Ps 47:8 (48:7) ἐν πνεύματι **βιαίῳ**, *with* **a violent** *blast*

βιαστής, οῦ, ὁ$_{1>}$ {βία} ①[nmp] Matt 11:12, **violent people**

βιβλαρίδιον, ου, τό$_2$ {βίβλος} ❸ Rev 10:2, 9, 10, **little scroll**[NIGTC]

βιβλίον, ου, τό$_2$ {βίβλος} (34x; 23x Rev) Matt 19:7 = Mark 10:4, **certificate** *of divorce*; Rev 22,[7x] **book**; Luke 4:17; Rev 1:11–10:8,[10x] **scroll**; (183x LXX; 61x 1–2Kgs)

βίβλος, ου, ἡ$_{2όδός}$ (10x) Matt 1:1,[EGG] **βίβλος** γενέσεως, **record** *of the genealogy*; Mark 12:26; Phil 4:3; Rev 3:5, **book**; Acts 19:19, *magic* **books**; (24x LXX; 5x Esd)

βιβρώσκω ①[pap.dmp] John 6:13, **those who had eaten**; (40x LXX) Lev 6:9–22:30, (13x)[fpi3s] **it will** (*or will not*) **be eaten**

Βιθυνία, ας, ἡ$_{1α}$ ❷ Acts 16:7; 1 Pet 1:1, **Bithynia**[LGCb]

βίος, ου, ὁ$_2$ (10x, 5x Luke) Matt 12:44 = Luke 21:4, *all she had to* **live on**; Luke 8:14, **life**; Luke 15:30, **estate**; (69x LXX) 2 Macc 5:5, *changed his* **life** (*i.e., died*)

βιόω ①[aainf] 1 Pet 4:2, **to live**[Keen1P]; ❼ LXX, Prov 7:2, *keep my commands and* **live**

βίωσις, εως, ἡ$_3$ {βίος} ① Acts 26:4, **the life I spent**[ZEC]; ①[gfs] LXX, Sir 10 .

βιωτικός, ή, όν$_{2.1.2}$ {βίος} *adj.* ❸ Luke 21:34, *worries of* **life**; 1 Cor 6:3, 4, *subst.* **matters of everyday life**[NIGTC]

βλαβερός, ά, όν$_{2.1.2}$ {βλάπτω} *adj.* ①[afp] 1 Tim 6:9, **harmful**; ①[nns] LXX, Prov 10:26

βλάπτω ❷ Mark 16:18; Luke 4:35, **to harm**, **hurt**; ❻ LXX, 2 Macc 12:22

βλαστάνω {βλαστός} ❹ Matt 13:26; Mark 4:27, **to sprout**; Heb 9:4, **to blossom**[ABC]; Jas 5:18, **to produce** *its fruit*; Pind. *O.* 7.69, *Rhodes* **was born** *from the sea*

Βλάστος, ου, ὁ$_2$ ①[amp] Acts 12:20, **Blastus**

βλασφημέω[con] {βλάπτω + φήμι} (34x; 13x Syn) Matt 9:3[EGG] = Mark 2:7; Jas 2:7, **to speak irreverently** (*about God*); Acts 19:37, **blasphemers** *of our goddess*[EGG]; Matt 27:39 = Mark 15:29, **to demean through speech**[BHGNT]; Matt 27:44 = Luke 23:39, **to taunt**[ZEC]; 1 Cor 10:30, **to suffer defamation of character**[NIGTC]; Titus 2:5; 2 Pet 2:12, **to slander**; 1 Pet 4:4, **to say terrible things about you**[Keen1P]; ❼ LXX, 2 Kgs 19:4, **to rebuke**; 19:6, **to revile**

βλασφημία, ας, ἡ$_{1α}$ {βλάπτω + φήμι} (18x) Matt 12:31 = Mark 3:28; Rev 13:5, **blasphemy**; Eph 4:31 = Col 3:8; Rev 2:9, **slander**; ❺ LXX, 1 Macc 2:6, **blasphemies**

βλάσφημος, ον$_{2.2}$ {βλάπτω + φήμι} *adj.* ❹ Acts 6:11, **blasphemous** *words*[NIGTC]; 1 Tim 1:13; 2 Tim 3:2, **abusive** *language*; 2 Pet 2:11, **slanderous**

βλέμμα, ατος, τό$_3$ ①[dns] 2 Pet 2:8, **by hearing**

βλέπω (132x, 81x GA) *phys. sight*, Matt 5:28, **to look at**; 6:4, **to see**; *phys./spir. sight*, 13:13,[2x] *although* **looking**, *they do not* **see**; Mark 4:12, *in order that* **seeing** *they may* **see** *and not perceive*[BHGNT]; *idiom.*, Matt 22:16, *you are not* **swayed**[EGG]; (123x LXX; 37x Ezek, 9x 1 Sam)

βλητέος, α, ον$_{2.1.2}$ {βάλλω} *adj.* ①[nns] Luke 5:38, **to be put**

Βοανηργές$_3$ *indecl.* ①[amp] Mark 3:17, **Boanerges**, *sons of thunder*

βοάω[con] (12x; 7x LA) Matt 3:3 = Mark 1:3 = Luke 3:4 = John 1:23; Acts 8:7, **to cry out**; Gal 4:27, **to shout**[KeenG]; (133x LXX; 23x Isa, 12x 2 Kgs, 10x 2 Chr)

Βόες, ὁ$_3$ *indecl.* ❷ Matt 1:5, **Boaz**

βοή, ἡ$_{1η}$ {βοάω} ①[nfp] Jas 5:4, **cries**[KEL]; (17x LXX; 4x 3 Macc, 3x 1 Sam), Exod 2:23, *their* **cry for help** *rose to God*; Aristoph. *Nub.* 11.53, **βοὰν βοᾶν, to let out** *a shout*

βοήθεια, ας, ἡ$_{1α}$ ❷ Acts 27:17, **supports, undergirding**[ZEC]; Heb 4:16, **need**; (67x LXX)

βοηθέω[con] ❽ (5x *imp.*) Matt 15:25; Mark 9:24; Acts 16:9, **help!**; (106x LXX; 20x Pss)

βοηθός, όν$_{2.2}$ *adj.* ①[nms] Heb 13:6, **helper**; (56x LXX; 26x Pss); Hdt. *Hist.* 5.77.1, **auxiliary, defender**

βόθυνος, ου, ὁ$_2$ ❸[ams] Matt 12:11; 15:14 = Luke 6:39, **pit**; (12x LXX); 2 Kgs 3:16

βολή, ῆς, ἡ$_{1η}$ {βάλλω} ①[afs] Luke 22:41, *a stone's* **throw**; ❸ LXX, Gen 21:16

βολίζω ❷[aap.nmp] Acts 27:28,[2x] **to take a depth sounding**

Βόος, ὁ$_3$ *indecl.* ①[gms] Luke 3:32, **Boaz**; (28x LXX; 26x Ruth, 2x 1 Chr)

βόρβορος, ου, ὁ$_2$ ①[gms] 2 Pet 2:22, **mud, filth**; ❷ LXX, Jer 45:6 (38:6)[2x], **mire**

βορρᾶς, ᾶ, ὁ$_1$ ❷[gms] Luke 13:29; Rev 21:13, **north**; (146x LXX; 47x Ezek, 19x Josh)

βόσκω ❾ Matt 8:30 = Mark 5:11 = Luke 8:32; John 21:15, **to feed**; Matt 8:33 = Mark 5:14 = Luke 8:34, **to tend**; (28x LXX; 11x Ezek) Gen 29:7, **to graze**

Βοσόρ, ὁ$_3$ *indecl.* ①[gms] 2 Pet 2:15, *Balaam, the son of* **Bosor**; (12x LXX) Josh 21:36, **Bezer**

βοτάνη, ης, ἡ$_{1η}$ {βόσκω} ①[afs] Heb 6:7, **vegetation**; (16x LXX) Gen 1:11; Exod 9–10[4x]

βότρυς, υος, ὁ$_3$ ①[amp] Rev 14:18, **clusters** *of grapes*; (14x LXX), Deut 32:32, **clusters**

βουλευτής, οῦ, ὁ$_{1>}$ {βούλομαι} ❷ Mark 15:43 = Luke 23:50, **council member**

βουλεύω {βούλομαι} ❻ *mid.*, Luke 14:31; John 11:53; 2 Cor 1:17,[2x] **to plan**; (85x LXX)

βουλή, ῆς, ἡ$_{1η}$ {βούλομαι} (12x; 9x LA) Luke 7:30; Acts 2:23; Eph 1:11, **plan**; Acts 27:12, *reached* **a decision**; 1 Cor 4:5, **the motivations** *of the heart*[NIGTC]; (170x LXX; 32x Isa)

βούλημα, ατος, τό$_3$ {βούλομαι} ❸ Acts 27:43, **plan**; Rom 9:19, **will**; 1 Pet 4:3, *to live* **the way** *the gentiles* **want to**[Keen1P]; ❷ LXX, 2 Macc 15:5; 4 Macc 8:18, **counsel, design**

βούλομαι (37x; 14x Acts) Matt 1:19, **to decide**; 11:27 = Luke 10:22, **to desire**; 2 Cor 1:15, **to plan**; Jas 1:18, **having desired**[KEL]; (121x LXX; 32x 1–4 Macc, 10x Exod) Exod 4:23, **to allow**

βουνός, ου, ὁ$_2$ ❷ Luke 3:5; 23:30, **hill**; (96x LXX; 14x Isa, 12x 1 Sam) 1 Sam 10:5, **heap**

βοῦς, ός, ὁ$_3$ ❽ Luke 13:15; 1 Cor 9:9; 1 Tim 5:18, **ox**; John 2:14, **oxen**; (175x LXX)

βραβεῖον, ου, τό$_2$ {βραβεύω} ❷[ans] 1 Cor 9:24; Phil 3:14, **prize**; Men. *Gn.* 124, **prize**

βραβεύω ①[paimp3s] Col 3:15, **to rule**; ①[aai3s] LXX, Wis 10:12

βραδύνω {βραδύς} ❷ 1 Tim 3:15; 2 Pet 3:9, **to delay**; ❹ LXX, Gen 43:10; Deut 7:10

βραδυπλοέω[con] {βραδύς + πλέω} ①[pap.nmp] Acts 27:7, **to sail slowly**

βραδύς, εῖα, ύ$_{3.1.3}$ *adj.* ❸ Luke 24:25; Jas 1:19,[2x] **slow**

βραδύτης, ητος, ἡ$_3$ {βραδύς} ①[afs] 2 Pet 3:9, **delay, slowness**

βραχίων, ονος, ὁ$_3$ ❸ Luke 1:51; John 12:38; Acts 13:17, *metaph.*, **arm**; (122x LXX; 17x Isa)

βραχύς, εῖα, ύ$_{3.1.3}$ *adj.* ❼ Luke 22:58, **μετὰ βραχύ,** *after* **a little while**; Acts 5:34, **a little while**; John 6:7; Acts 27:28, **a little**; Heb 2:7, 9, *for a* **short** *time*[EGG]; (18x LXX), Exod 18:22, *subst.*, **minor case**

βρέφος, ους, τό$_3$ ❽ (5x Luke) Luke 1:41, **baby**; Acts 7:19; 2 Tim 3:15, *from* **your infancy**; 1 Pet 2:2, *just-born* **babies**[Keen1P]; ❺ LXX, 1 Macc 1:61; 2 Macc 6:10, **babies**

βρέχω ❼ Matt 5:45, **to send rain**; Luke 7:38, 44, **to wash** *his feet*; Luke 17:29, *fig.*, *fire and sulfur* **rained** *from heaven*; Jas 5:17; Rev 11:6, **to rain**; (16x LXX) Gen 2:5, **to rain**

βροντή, ῆς, ἡ$_{1η}$ (12x, 10x Rev) Mark 3:17, *sons of* **thunder**; John 12:29; Rev 4:5; 11:19, **thunder**; ❾ LXX, Job 26:14, **thunder**; Amos 4:13[Herm]

βροχή, ῆς, ἡ$_{1η}$ {βρέχω} ❷ Matt 7:25, 27, **rain**; ❷ LXX, Ps 67:10 (68:9)

βρόχος, ου, ὁ$_2$ ①[ams] 1 Cor 7:35, *not to throw* **a tight rein** *over you;*[NIGTC] ❹ LXX, 3 Macc 4:8, **noose**; Dem. 24.139, *fig., proposes a law while he has* **a rope** *around his neck*

βρυγμός, οῦ, ὁ$_2$ ❼ (6x Matt) Matt 8:12, **gnashing** *of teeth;* ❷ LXX, Prov 19:12, **growling**

βρύχω ①[iai3p] Acts 7:54, **gnashed** *their teeth;* ❺ LXX, Ps 34:16 (35:16)

βρύω ①[pai3s] Jas 3:11, **to pour forth**; Aeschl. *Ch.* 69, **full** *of evil*

βρῶμα, ατος, τό$_3$ {βιβρώσκω} (17x; 6x 1 Cor) 1 Cor 6:13, *lit.*, **food**; John 4:34, *metaph. my* **food** *is to do my Father's will;* Rom 14:15, *offended by* **what you eat**; 1 Cor 3:2, **solid food** (*change of perspective, not diet*)[NIGTC!]; (73x LXX; 17x Gen)

βρώσιμος, ον$_{2.2}$ {βιβρώσκω} *adj.* ①[ans] Luke 24:41, *idiom.* ἔχετέ τι **βρώσιμον**, *do you have something* **to eat**; ❸ LXX, Lev 19:23; Neh 9:25; Ezek 47:12

βρῶσις, εως, ἡ$_3$ (11x; 4x John) John 4:32; 6:55, **food**; Rom 14:17, *kingdom is not* **eating** *and drinking*; 1 Cor 8:4, *eating* **food**; Heb 12:16, *a single* **meal**; Matt 6:19, 20, **eating** (*poss. by vermin*) (41x LXX; 8x Gen)

βυθίζω {βυθός} ❷ Luke 5:7, *lit.*, **to sink**; 1 Tim 6:9, *fig.*, **to plunge** *into ruin and destruction;* ①[aai3p] LXX, 2 Macc 12:4, **they drowned** *them at sea*

βυθός, οῦ, ὁ$_2$ ①[dms] 2 Cor 11:25, **open sea**; ❼ LXX, Exod 15:5, **the deep**

βυρσεύς, έως, ὁ$_3$ ❸ Acts 9:43; 10:6, 32, *Simon* **the tanner**

βύσσινος, η, ον$_{2.1.2}$ {βύσσος} *adj.* ❺ Rev 18:12; 19:14, **fine linen**; (17x LXX) Gen 41:42

βύσσος, οῦ, ἡ$_2$ ①[afs] Luke 16:19, **fine linen**; (40x LXX; 33x Exod) Exod 25:4

βωμός, οῦ, ὁ$_2$ {βαίνω} ①[ams] Acts 17:23, **altar**; (46x LXX; 9x Num) Exod 34:13

Γ, γ [*gamma*]

Γ, γ, τό (γάμμα) *indecl.* **gamma**, *3rd letter of the Gr. alphabet* ‖ *num.* γʹ = 3; ͵γ = 3,000
Γαββαθᾶ$_3$ *indecl.* ①[ans] John 19:13, *Aram.*, **Gabbatha**
Γαβριήλ, ὁ$_3$ *indecl.* ❷ Luke 1:19, 26, *the angel* **Gabriel**; ❷ LXX, Dan 8:16; 9:21
γάγγραινα, ης, ἡ$_{1\eta}$ ①[nfs] 2 Tim 2:17, **gangrene**; Hp. *Mochl.* 33, **spreading decay**
Γάδ, ὁ$_3$ *indecl.* ①[gms] Rev 7:5, **Gad**; (79x LXX; 22x Josh, 21x Num)
Γαδαρηνός, ή, όν$_{2.1.2}$ *adj.* ①[gmp] Matt 8:28, **Gadarene**, *from Gadara*[LGC 227]
Γάζα, ης, ἡ$_{1\eta>}$ ①[afs] Acts 8:26, **Gaza**; (22x LXX) Gen 10:19; 1 Sam 6:17
γάζα, ης, ἡ$_{1\eta>}$ ①[gfs] Acts 8:27, **treasury**; ❻ LXX, Ezra 5:17, **treasure**
γαζο**φυλάκιον, ου, τό**$_2$ {γάζα + φυλάσσω} ❺ Mark 12:41 = Luke 21:1, **treasury**; (25x LXX; 9x Neh, 6x 2 Macc) 2 Kgs 23:11; Ezra 10:6
Γάϊος, ου, ὁ$_2$ ❺ **Gaius** Ⓐ Acts 19:29, *Christian arrested with Paul*; Ⓑ Acts 20:4, *from Derbe* Ⓒ Rom 16:23; 1 Cor 1:14, *one baptized by Paul* Ⓓ 3 John 1, *addressee of 3 John*[APB]
γάλα, γάλακτος, τό$_3$ ❺ 1 Cor 3:2[Hook!]; Heb 5:12; 1 Pet 2:2, **milk**; 1 Cor 9:7, **milk** *from the flock*; (47x LXX; 9x Deut, 6x Exod) Exod 3:8; *land flowing with* **milk** *and honey*
Γαλάτης, ου, ὁ$_{1>}$ ❷[vmp] Gal 1:0, *to the* **Galatians**; 3:1, **Galatians**
Γαλατία, ας, ἡ$_{1\alpha}$ ❹ 1 Cor 16:1; Gal 1:2; 2 Tim 4:10; 1 Pet 1:1, **Galatia**
Γαλατικός, ή, όν$_{2.1.2}$ *adj.* ❷[afs] Acts 16:6; 18:23, **Galatian**
γαλήνη, ης, ἡ$_{1\eta}$ ❸ Matt 8:26 = Mark 4:39 = Luke 8:24, **calmness** *of the sea of Galilee*
Γαλιλαία, ας, ἡ$_{1\alpha}$ (61x, 58x Gs)[LGCa 134] Matt 4:18 = Mark 1:16, *Sea of* **Galilee**; (25x LXX)
Γαλιλαῖος, α, ον$_{2.1.2}$ *adj.* (11x, 8x LA) Matt 26:69 = Mark 14:70; Acts 1:11, **Galilean**
Γαλλίων, ῶνος, ὁ$_3$ **Acts** ❸ 18:12, 14, 17, **Gallio**, *proconsul of Achaia*
Γαμαλιήλ, ὁ$_3$ *indecl.* ❷ Acts 5:34; 22:3, **Gamaliel**; ❺ LXX (Num), 1:10, *son of Pedahzur*
γαμέω[con] {γάμος} (28x; 9x 1 Cor 7) Matt 5:32; 22:30 = Mark 12:25 = Luke 20:34; 1 Cor 7:9–39; 1 Tim 5:11, **to marry**; ❹ LXX, Esth 10:6; 4 Macc 16:9
γαμίζω {γάμος} ❼ *act.*, 1 Cor 7:38,[2x] **to marry** Matt 22:30 = Mark 12:25 = Luke 20:35, *pass.*, **to be given in marriage**
γαμίσκω {γάμος} ①[ppi3p] Luke 20:34, **to be given in marriage**
γάμος, ου, ὁ$_2$ (16x; 9x Matt) Matt 22:2–12,[8x] *parable of the wedding feast*; John 2:1, **wedding**; Rev 19:9, **marriage** *of the Lamb*; (19x LXX; 8x Tob)
γάρ *clarif. conj.* (1,041x[EDNT!]) Ⓐ (*main usage*)[Runge 51] ***explanatory***, *introduces bolstering material*; Matt 10:19; Luke 17:21; Heb 6:7, **for, then, because**; Ⓑ ***conclusion***, 1 Cor 9:19; 2 Cor 11:5, **therefore, thus, so, then**; (1,522x LXX; 171x Job, 157x Wis)
γαστήρ, γαστρός, ἡ$_3$ ❾ (6x Syn) Matt 1:18; Luke 1:31; 1 Thess 5:3; Rev 12:2, ἐν **γαστρί,**[dfs] **with child, pregnant**; Titus 1:12, **gluttons**; (67x LXX; 15x Job) ἐν **γαστρί**[36x]
γε *enclitic part.* (26x) **1.** ***fixed combinations*** Ⓐ (8x) εἰ δὲ μή γε, Matt 6:1, **otherwise**; Ⓑ (6x) εἴ γε, Rom 5:6, **if indeed**, Ⓒ (3x) ἄρα γε, Matt 7:20, **therefore**; Ⓓ (3x) εἰ ἄρα γε, Acts 17:27a, **whether**; Ⓔ (1x) ἆρά γε *in a question*, Acts 8:30, **So**, *do you know . . . ?*[QaR 97] **2.** ***fixed***

cmpds.[EDNT] 🅐 (7x) μήγε, **not**, *alternate reading, occurring only in the expression* εἰ δὲ μήγε *instead of* εἰ δὲ μή γε, **otherwise**, Matt 6:1; 9:17; Luke 5:36f.; 10:6; 13:9; 14:32; 2 Cor 11:16; 🅑 (3x) καίτοιγε, John 4:2, **though**; 🅒 (3x) μενοῦνγε, Rom 9:20, **on the contrary**; 🅓 (1x) εὖγε, Luke 19:17, **Well done!**; (164x LXX; 59x Eccl, 28x 2 Sam)

Γεδεών, ὁ$_3$ *indecl.* ①[gms] Heb 11:32, **Gideon,** *son of Joash*; (45x LXX; 44x Judg)

γέεννα, ης, ἡ$_{1η>}$ (12x; 7x Matt) Matt 5:29, 30 = Mark 9:43, 44; Jas 3:6, **hell**, **Gehenna**

Γεθσημανί$_3$ *indecl.* ❷ Matt 26:36 = Mark 14:32, **Gethsemane**

γείτων, ονος, ὁ, ἡ$_3$ {γῆ} ❹ Luke 14:12; 15:6, 9; John 9:8, **neighbor**; (16x LXX; 6x Pss)

γελάω[con] ❷ Luke 6:21, **to laugh** *last*; 6:25, **to laugh** *first*[ZEC]; (15x LXX) Gen 17:17

γέλως, ωτος, ὁ$_3$ {γελάω}①[nms] Jas 4:9, **laughter**; (20x LXX) Prov 10:23: Job 8:21

γεμίζω {γέμω} ❽ Mark 4:37; Luke 14:23; John 2:7; Rev 8:5, **to fill**; ❷ LXX, Gen 45:17

γέμω (11x; 7x Rev) Matt 23:25 = Luke 11:39; Rom 3:14; Rev 4:8, **to be full**; ❼ LXX, Gen 37:25, **to be loaded**; Ps 9:28 (10:7) **full** *of cursing*

γενεά, ᾶς, ἡ$_{1α}$ {γίνομαι} (43x; 15x Luke, 13x Matt) Matt 1:17[4x]; 12:39 = Luke 11:29, **generation**; (255x LXX) Ps 44:18 (45:17), *idiom.* **γενεᾷ** καὶ **γενεᾷ**, **forever and ever**

γενεα**λογέω**[con] {γίνομαι + λέγω} ①[pmp.nms] Heb 7:6, **to trace one's descent**[NIGTC]; ①[api3s] LXX, 1 Chr 5:1, **to be listed in the genealogy**

γενεα**λογία, ας, ἡ**$_{1α}$ {γίνομαι + λέγω} ❷[dfp] 1 Tim 1:4; Titus 3:9, **genealogies**

γενέσια, ίων, τά$_2$ {γίνομαι} ❷[dnp] Matt 14:6 = Mark 6:21, *Herod's* **birthday**

γένεσις, εως, ἡ$_3$ {γίνομαι} ❺ Matt 1:1, **genealogy**; Luke 1:14, **birth**; Jas 1:23, *Semitism for* **natural** *face*[ZEC]; Jas 1:26, *course* **of existence** (*circle of life*); (57x LXX; 15x Gen, 12x 1 Chr)

γενετή, ῆς, ἡ$_{1η}$ {γίνομαι} ①[gfs] John 9:1, ἐκ **γενετῆς**, *from* **birth**; ❷ LXX, Lev 25:47; Esth 4:17

γενηθήτω[7x] → **γίνομαι**, *aor. pass. imp. 3s*, Matt 6:10, *your will* **be done**

γένημα, ατος, τό$_3$ {γίνομαι} ❹ Matt 26:29 = Mark 14:25 = Luke 22:18, **fruit** *of the vine*; 2 Cor 9:10, **harvest**; (76x LXX; 17x Deut, 11x Lev)

γεννάω[con] {γίνομαι} (97x, 45x Matt) **ἐγέννησεν**[aai3s], *act.*, Matt 1:2–16a,[39x] **to father**; *pass.*, John 1:13, **born** *of God*; John 3:3–8,[8x] **to be born** *again*; Phlm 10, **I became his father**; Heb 11:12, **were born**; (251x LXX; 89x 1 Chr, 77x Gen)

γέννημα, ατος, τό$_3$ {γίνομαι} ❹ Matt 3:7 = Luke 3:7, **offspring** *of vipers*; ❷ LXX, Judg 1:10; Sir 10:18

Γεννησαρέτ, ἡ$_3$ *indecl.* ❸ Matt 14:34 = Mark 6:53; Luke 5:1, **Gennesaret**[LGCa]

γεννητός, ή, όν$_{2.1.2}$ {γίνομαι} *adj.* ❷ Matt 11:11 = Luke 7:28, **born** *of women*; ❺ LXX, (Job)

γένος, ους, τό$_3$ {γίνομαι} (20x; 9x Acts) Matt 13:47; 1 Cor 12:10, **kind**, **type**; Mark 7:26; Acts 4:36, **birth**; 13:26, **race**; 7:13, **family**; 18:2, 24, **native**; 2 Cor 11:26, *dangers from my own* **people**; Phil 3:5, **nation**; Rev 22:16, **descendant** *of David*; (112x LXX; 27x Gen)

Γερασηνός, ή, όν$_{2.1.2}$ *adj.* ❸ Mark 5:1; Luke 8:26, 37, **Gerasene**

γερουσία, ας, ἡ$_{1α}$ {γέρων} ①[afs] Acts 5:21, **council of elders**[ZEC]; (35x LXX; 16x Deut)

γέρων, οντος, ὁ$_3$ ①[nms] John 3:4, **old man**; (20x LXX; 12x 4 Macc)

γεύομαι (15x) Matt 16:28 = Mark 9:1 = Luke 9:27; John 8:52, **to taste** *death*; Luke 14:24; Col 2:21, **to taste**; Acts 10:10; 23:14, **to eat**; Heb 6:4, **to taste** *the heavenly gift*

γε**ωργέω**[con] {γῆ + ἔργον} ①[pmpi3s] Heb 6:7, **to farm**, **cultivate**; ❸ LXX, 1 Chr 27:26

γε**ώργιον, ου, τό**$_2$ {γῆ + ἔργον} ①[nns] 1 Cor 3:9, **field**[NIGTC]; ❽ (5x Prov) LXX

γε**ωργός, οῦ, ὁ**$_2$ {γῆ + ἔργον} (19x) Matt 21:33–35[4x] = Mark 12:1–7[4x] = Luke 20:9–14[4x]; 2 Tim 2:6; Jas 5:7, **farmer**; John 15:1, **gardener**; ❾ LXX, Gen 9:20, **soil-tiller**

γῆ, γῆς, ἡ$_{1η}$ (250x) Matt 24:35 = Mark 13:31 = Luke 21:33; Jas 5:7; Rev 1:5, **earth**; Matt 2:6; Acts 7:3–4[4x]; Heb 11:29, **land**; Luke 22:44, **ground**; Matt 13:5 = Mark 4:5, **soil**; Col 3:2, **earthly**; (3,042x LXX; 359x Gen) Gen 1:1–2:19[38x]; 6:1–9:20[57x]

γῆρας, γήρως (ους), τό$_3$ {γέρων} ①[dns] Luke 1:36, **old age**; (44x LXX; 10x Gen)

γηράσκω {γέρων} ❷ John 21:18; Heb 8:13, **to grow old**; (20x LXX; 4x Gen)

γίνομαι (669x; 256x LA, 75x Matt) 🅐 ***literal sense***, 1 Cor 9:22, **to be**, **become**; Mark 9:3, **to be** (= εἰμί) 🅑 ***graphic verbal***, Luke 4:25, *a famine devastated* [ἐγένετο] *the land* (NLT); 🅒 ***Hebraism*** **(60x) καὶ ἐγένετο**, Matt 7:28, *and* **when**; Rev 8:7, *and* **there came**; 🅓 ***emphatic idiom*** (15x, 10x Rom) **μὴ γένοιτο**,[amo3s] Luke 20:16, **never!**[ZEC]; Rom 3:4; 11:1; 1 Cor 6:15, **perish the thought!**[NIGTC]; (2,077x LXX) Gen 1:3,[2x] **"Let there be** *light!"* *and* **there was** *light*[NIDNTT]

γινώσκω (222x; 57x John) 🅐 ***cognition***, 1 Cor 2:14, **to understand**; 14:9, **to comprehend**[NIGTC]; 2 Cor 2:9, **to see**; 🅑 ***perception***, 1 Cor 4:19, **to discover**; 14:7, **to recognize**; Heb 10:34, **to become aware**[ZEC]; 🅒 ***knowledge acquisition***, Matt 24:32; Rev 3:9, **to know**; Mark 6:38, **to check**[ZEC]; 🅓 ***carnal knowledge***, Matt 1:25; 🅔 ***language and communication***, Acts 21:37, *Do you* **speak** *Greek?*; (690x LXX) Gen 4:1, 17, **to have sexual relations**

γλεῦκος, ους, τό$_3$ ①[gns] Acts 2:13, **sweet new wine**[ZEC]; ①[gns] LXX, Job 32:19

γλυκύς, εῖα, ύ$_{3.1.3}$ *adj.* ❹[ans] Jas 3:11, 12; Rev 10:9, 10, **sweet**; (15x LXX) Prov 16:21

γλῶσσα, ης, ἡ$_{1η>}$ (50x; 21x 1 Cor) Rev 16:10, *physical* **tongue**; Acts 2:3, **tongues** *like flames of fire*; 19:6, *speak in* **tongues**; 1 Cor 12:10, *spiritual gift* **of tongues**; 14:2–39,[15x] *evaluation of prophecy and tongues*; 1 John 3:18, **speech**; (160x LXX; 37x Pss, 26x Sir)

γλωσσόκομον, ου, τό$_2$ {γλῶσσα + κομέω} ❷[ans] John 12:6, 13:29, **money box**; ❹[ans] LXX, 2 Chr 24:8, 10, 11,[2x] **the money box** *of Joash*

γναφεύς, έως, ὁ$_3$ ①[nms] Mark 9:3, **clothing specialist**[ZEC]; ❸ LXX, Isa 7:3; 36:2

γνήσιος, α, ον$_{2.1.2}$ {γίνομαι} *adj.* ❹ 2 Cor 8:8, *subst.*, **genuineness**; Phil 4:3, **loyal**[BEC]; 1 Tim 1:2; Titus 1:4, **loyal**; ❷ LXX, 3 Macc 3:19, **reasonable**; Sir 7:18, **faithful**

γνησίως {γίνομαι} *adv.* ① Phil 2:20, **genuinely**; ❷ LXX, 2 Macc 14:8; 3 Macc 3:23

γνόφος, ου, ὁ$_2$ ①[dms] Heb 12:18, **darkness**; (27x LXX; 6x Job) Exod 10:22, *thick* **darkness**

γνώμη, ης, ἡ$_{1η}$ {γίνομαι} ❾ Acts 20:3, **he decided**; 1 Cor 1:10; Phlm 14, **consent**; 2 Cor 8:10, **opinion**; Rev 17:13, 17, **purpose**; (32x LXX; 18x Ezra)

γνωρίζω {γινώσκω} (25x; 6x Eph) Luke 2:15; Rom 9:22, **to make known**; 1 Cor 15:1, **I give you to understand**[NIGTC]; 2 Cor 8:1, **to be aware**; (48x LXX; 12x Pss)

γνωσθήσεται[4x] → **γινώσκω**, *fut. pass. ind. 3s*, 1 Cor 14:7, *how* **will anyone know**?

γνῶσις, εως, ἡ$_3$ {γινώσκω} (29x; 16x 1–2 Cor) Luke 1:77; Rom 2:20; 1 Cor 1:5; 8:1; 2 Cor 2:4, **knowledge**; (60x LXX; 15x Prov) 1 Sam 2:3; Prov 2:6; Eccl 2:21, **knowledge**

γνώστης, ου, ὁ$_{1>}$ {γινώσκω} ①[ams] Acts 26:3, **an expert**[EGG]; ❹ LXX, 1 Sam 28:3, **wizards** (BrLXX), **familiar spirits** (Tanakh); 2 Chr 35:19, **a divining spirit**

γνωστός, ή, όν$_{2.1.2}$ {γινώσκω} *adj.* (15x, 10x Acts) Luke 23:49; John 18:15, **acquainted with**; Rom 1:19, **known**; (22x LXX; 5x Pss) Gen 2:9, **knowledge** *of good and evil*

γογγύζω ❽ Matt 20:11; John 6:41, *onoma.* **to grumble**; 1 Cor 10:10, **μηδὴ γογγύζετε**, *stop your* **querulous moaning**[NIGTC]; (15x LXX; 6x Num) Isa 29:24, *subst.* **the murmurers**

γογγυσμός, οῦ, ὁ$_2$ {γογγύζω} ❹ John 7:12, **whispering**; Acts 6:1, **complaint**; Phil 2:14; 1 Pet 4:9, **grumbling**; (13x LXX) Exod 16:7; Num 17:20, **murmuring**

γογγυστής, οῦ, ὁ$_{1>}$ {γογγύζω} ①^{nmp} Jude 16, **grumbler**

γόης, ητος, ὁ$_{3}$ ①^{nmp} 2 Tim 3:13, **impostor**; Hdt. *Hist.* 2.33.1, **enchanter**, **magician**

Γολγοθᾶ, ἡ$_{3}$ *part. decl.* ❸ Matt 27:33 = Mark 15:22 = John 19:17,[LGCa] **Golgotha**

Γόμορρα, ων, τά$_{2}$ ❹ Matt 10:15; Rom 9:29; 2 Pet 2:6; Jude 7, **Gomorrah**[LGCb]; (21x LXX; 10x Gen) Gen 10:19–19:28

γόμος, ου, ὁ$_{2}$ {γέμω} ❸ Acts 21:3; Rev 18:11, 12, **cargo** ❷ LXX, Exod 23:5, **load**

γονεύς, έως, ὁ$_{3}$ {γίνομαι} (20x) Matt 10:21 = Mark 13:12 = Luke 21:16; John 9:2; Rom 1:30; 2 Cor 12:142x; 2 Tim 3:2, **parents**; (14x LXX) Esth 2:7

γόνυ, ατος, τό$_{3}$ (12x, 4x Acts) Mark 15:19; Luke 5:8; Acts 7:60; Rom 11:4; Eph 3:14, **knees**; Acts 20:36, **θεὶς τὰ γόνατα** αὐτοῦ, *idiom.*, **knelt down**; Phil 2:10, *every* **knee**; (32x LXX) Judg 7:5, *to kneel down upon his* **knees**

γονυπετέω {γόνυ + πίπτω} ❹ Matt 17:14; Mark 1:40, **to kneel**

γράμμα, ατος, τό$_{3}$ {γράφω} (14x) Luke 16:6, **contract**; 2 Cor 3:6, **letter**, **writing**; Gal 6:11, *large* **letters**[WLC 43]; (23x LXX) Lev 19:28, *tattoo* **marks**; Dan 1:4, *teach them* **letters**

γραμματεύς, έως, ὁ$_{3}$ {γράφω} (63x; 57x Syn, only 1x after Acts) Matt 5:20; Mark 2:16 = Luke 5:30; John 8:3; Acts 6:12; 1 Cor 1:20, **scribe**; (84x LXX; 16x Ezra:Neh, 8x Jer)

γραπτός, ή, όν$_{2.1.2}$ {γράφω} *adj.* ①^{ans} Rom 2:15, **written** *on their hearts*

γραφή ῆς, ἡ$_{1\eta}$ {γράφω} (50x; 12x John) Matt 21:42 = Mark 12:10; Luke 24:27; John 2:22; Acts 1:16; Rom 9:17: Gal 3:8, **Scripture(s)** (Tanakh); (41x LXX; 11x Dan)

γράφω (191x; 40x Syn, 29x Rev) (69x) **γέγραπται**^{ppi3s} Matt 4:4–10^{4x} = Luke 4:1–13^{3x}; John 20:31; 2 Cor 8:15, **it is written**; Mark 12:19; Luke 1:3; John 8:8, **to write**; John 19:22,^{2x} *what* **I have written, I have written**; 1 John 2:1–26,^{11x} *multi-purpose writing*; Rev 1:11–3:14,^{11x} **to write** *to the seven churches*; (291x LXX; 30x 1 Kgs:1 Macc)

γραώδης, ες$_{3.3}$ {γραῖα + εἶδος} *adj.* ①^{amp} 1 Tim 4:7, **silly** *myths*

γρηγορέω^{con} {ἐγείρω} (22x; 7x Syn) Matt 24:42; 1 Pet 5:8, **to be alert**; Matt 26:40 = Mark 14:37; 1 Thess 5:6, **to stay awake**; ❽ LXX, Jer 5:6, *the leopard has* **stalked**

γυμνάζω {γυμνός} ❹ 1 Tim 4:7; Heb 5:14; 12:11; 2 Pet 2:14, **to train**, **be trained**; ①^{iai3p} LXX, 2 Macc 10:15, **to harass**

γυμνασία, ας, ἡ$_{1\alpha}$ {γυμνός} ①^{nfs} 1 Tim 4:8, **physical training**; ①^{afs} LXX, 4 Macc 11:20

γυμνιτεύω {γυμνός} ①^{pai1p} 1 Cor 4:11, **to be poorly clothed**[NIGTC]

γυμνός, ή, όν$_{2.1.2}$ *adj.* (15x; 4x Matt) Matt 25:36; Mark 14:51; Jas 2:15, **naked**; 1 Cor 15:37, **bare** *seed*; Heb 4:13, *metaph.* **exposed**; (35x LXX; 7x Job, 6x Ezek)

γυμνότης, ητος, ἡ$_{3}$ {γυμνός} ❸ Rom 8:35; 2 Cor 11:27; Rev 3:18, **nakedness**, ①^{dfs} LXX, Deut 28:48

γυναικάριον, ου, τό$_{2}$ {γυνή} ①^{anp} 2 Tim 3:6, **childish women**[NIGTC]

γυναικεῖος, α, ον$_{2.1.2}$ {γυνή} *adj.* ①^{dns} 1 Pet 3:7, **female (wife)**[EGG]; ❻ LXX, Gen 18:11, γίνεσθαι τὰ γυναικεῖα, *lit.*, *Sarah no longer* **experienced the cycle of women**[Waltke]

γυνή, αικός, ἡ$_{3}$ (215x; 60x LA, 41x 1 Cor) Matt 14:3 = Mark 6:17 = Luke 3:19; 1 Cor 7:1; Eph 5:22, **wife**; Matt 26:7 = Mark 14:3 = Luke 37; Rev 2:20, **woman**; Rom 7:2, ὕπανδρος **γυνή**, *married* **woman**; Eph 5:22–33,^{9x} **wives**; Rev 19:7, **bride**; (967x LXX; 151x Gen)

Γώγ, ὁ$_{3}$ *indecl.* ①^{ams} Rev 20:8, Gog *and Magog*; (14x LXX; 12x Ezek 38–39)[TOTC]

γωνία, ας, ἡ$_{1\alpha}$ ❾ Matt 6:5; Acts 26:26; Rev 7:1, **corner**; Matt 21:42[ZEC] = Mark 12:10 = Luke 20:17 = Acts 4:11 = 1 Pet 2:7 = Ps 117:22 (118:22), **cornerstone**; (31x LXX) Exod 26:23

Δ, δ [*delta*]

Δ, δ, τό (δέλτα) *indecl.* **delta**, *4th letter of the Gr. alphabet* ‖ *num.* δʹ = 4; ͵δ = 4,000

δαιμονίζομαι {δαιμόνιον} (13x) Matt 4:24; Mark 5:15; John 10:21, **the demon-possessed**

δαιμόνιον, ου, τό$_2$ (63x; 23x Luke, 13x Mark) Matt 7:22; 9:33; Luke 4:33; John 10:20; Acts 17:18; 1 Cor 10:20, 21[4x]; Jas 2:19; Rev 18:2, **demon(s)**; (17x LXX; 7x Tob, 1x Pent)

δαιμονιώδης, ες$_{3.3}$ {δαιμόνιον + εἶδος} *adj.* ①[nfs] Jas 3:15, **demonic**

δαίμων, ονος, ὁ$_3$ {δαιμόνιον} ①[nmp] Matt 8:31, **demon, evil spirit**; ①[dms] LXX, Isa 65:11, **demon**; Aristoph. *Ve.* 525, ἀγαθὸς **δαίμων**, *good* **spirit**[BrDAG]

δάκρυον, ου, τό$_2$ {δάκρυ} (10x) Luke 7:38; Acts 20:19; 2 Cor 2:4; Rev 21:4, **tear** (*from eye*)

δακρύω {δάκρυ} ①[aai3s] John 11:35, *Jesus* **wept**; ❾ LXX, Job 3:24; Mic 2:6

δακτύλιος, ου, ὁ$_2$ {δείκνυμι} ①[ams] Luke 15:22, **ring**; (41x LXX; 24x Exod)

δάκτυλος, ου, ὁ$_2$ {δείκνυμι} ❽ Matt 23:4; Mark 7:33; John 8:6, **finger**; (40x LXX)

Δαλμανουθά, ἡ$_3$ *indecl.* ①[gfs] Mark 8:10, **Dalmanutha**[LGCa]

Δαλματία, ας, ἡ$_{1α}$ ①[afs] 2 Tim 4:10, **Dalmatia**[LGCa]

δαμάζω ❹ Mark 5:4, **to subdue**; Jas 3:7,[3x] **to tame**; ①[pap.nms] LXX, Dan 2:40, **to shatter**

δάμαλις, εως, ἡ$_3$ {δαμάζω} ①[gfs] Heb 9:13, *the red* **heifer**; (40x LXX; 17x Num)

Δάμαρις, ιδος, ἡ$_3$ ①[nfs] Acts 17:34, **Damaris**

Δαμασκηνός, ή, όν$_{2.1.2}$ *adj.* ①[gmp] 2 Cor 11:32, *the city of* **Damascus**

Δαμασκός, οῦ, ὁ$_2$ (15x; 13x Acts) Acts 9:2; Gal 1:17, **Damascus**[LGCb]; (47x LXX; 14x MajPr)

δανείζω {δάνος} ❹ Matt 5:42, **to borrow**; Luke 6:34,[2x] 35, **to lend**; (23x LXX) Deut 15:6

δάνειον, ου, τό$_2$ {δάνος} ①[ans] Matt 18:27, **loan**; ❹ LXX, Deut 15:8; 4 Macc 2:8

Δανιήλ, ὁ$_3$ *indecl.* ①[gms] Matt 24:15, **Daniel**, *the prophet*; (127x LXX; 79x Dan)

δανιστής, οῦ, ὁ$_{1>}$ {δάνος} ①[dms] Luke 7:41, **moneylender**

δαπανάω[con] {δαπάνη} ❺ Mark 5:26; Luke 15:14; Jas 4:3; 2 Cor 12:15, **to spend**; Acts 21:24, **to pay the expenses**; (10x LXX) 1 Macc 14:32

δαπάνη, ης, ἡ$_{1η}$ ①[afs] Luke 14:28, *the* **cost**; ❽ LXX, Ezra 6:4, **cost**; 1 Macc 3:30, **expense**

Δαυίδ, ὁ$_3$ *indecl.* (59x) Matt 1:1; Mark 10:47; John 7:42[2x]; Acts 1:16, **David**; (1,090x LXX)

δέ *conj.* (2,791x; 1,096x LA, 494x Matt) *development marker*[Runge 28–36] Ⓐ ***temp.***, Matt 2:1–10[6x], **now**; **and**; **so**; **after**; **now**; Ⓑ ***logical***, 1 Cor 12:4,[2x] **δέ . . . δέ, now . . . but**; 12:6, καί . . . δέ, and . . . **now**; Ⓒ ***key point***, Rom 8:28, we know, **in fact**;[IHR 156] Ⓓ ***authorial intent develop.***, Matt 14:22–27[5x]; (4,837x LXX; 855x Gen, 740x Job)

δέησις, εως, ἡ$_3$ {δέομαι} (18x) Luke 1:13; Rom 10:1; Heb 5:7, **prayer**; (79x LXX; 27x Pss)

δεθῆναι → **δέω**, *aor. pass. inf.*, Acts 21:13, 33, **to be bound**

δεῖ {δέω} (101x; 40x LA) Matt 16:21; 1 Cor 11:19, **it is necessary**; Matt 24:6; Rev 1:1, **must**; Acts 25:10, **I ought**; Rom 1:27, ἔδει,[iai3s] **it is fitting**[EGG]; (45x LXX; 10x 1–4 Macc)

δεῖγμα, ατος, τό$_3$ {δείκνυμι} ①[ans] Jude 7, **example**

δειγματίζω {δείκνυμι} ❷ Matt 1:19; Col 2:15, **to disgrace publicly**

δείκνυμι (18x; 7x Rev) Matt 4:8 = Luke 4:5; Jas 2:18; Rev 22:1, **to show**; (121x LXX)

δεικνύω ❸ Matt 16:21; John 2:18; Rev 22:8, **to show**

δειλία, ας, ἡ$_{1\alpha}$ {δέος} ①^{gfs} 2 Tim 1:7, **fear**; ❾ LXX, Lev 26:36, **faintness**

δειλιάω^{con} {δέος} ①^{paimp3s} John 14:27, **to be fearful**; (17x LXX) Deut 1:21, **to be afraid**

δειλός, ή, όν$_{2.1.2}$ *adj.* {δέος} ❸ Matt 8:26 = Mark 4:40; Rev 21:8, **afraid**; (10x LXX) Deut 20:8, **fearful**

δεῖνα, ος, ὁ$_3$ ①^{ams} Matt 26:18, **a certain man**

δεινῶς {δέος} *adv.* ❷ Matt 8:6, **horribly**; Luke 11:53, **vehemently**^{ZEC}; ❹ LXX, Job 10:16

δειπνέω^{con} {δεῖπνον} ❹ Luke 17:8; Rev 3:20, **to eat**; Luke 22:20; 1 Cor 11:25, *after* **supper**; ❸ LXX, Tob 8:1; Prov 23:1; Dan 11:27, **to dine**

δεῖπνον, ου, τό$_2$ (16x; 5x Luke) Matt 23:6; Mark 6:21; Luke 14:16, **banquet**; 1 Cor 11:20, *the Lord's* **Supper**; Rev 19:9, *marriage* **feast**; 19:17, **supper** *of God*; ❺ LXX, 4x Dan

δεισι**δαιμονία, ας, ἡ**$_{1\alpha}$ {δέος + δαιμόνιον} ①^{gfs} Acts 25:19, **religion**

δεισι**δαίμων, ον**$_{3.3}$ {δέος + δαιμόνιον} *adj.* ①^{amp} Acts 17:22, **extremely religious**

δέκα *indecl.* (25x; 11x Luke, 9x Rev) Matt 20:24; Acts 25:6; Rev 2:10, **ten**; Luke 14:31, **ten** *thousand*; (293x LXX; 56x 1–2 Chr, 27x Num)

δεκα**οκτώ** *indecl.* ❷ Luke 13:4, 11, **eighteen**

δεκα**πέντε** *indecl.* ❸ John 11:18; Acts 27:28; Gal 1:18, **fifteen**

Δεκά**πολις, εως, ἡ**$_3$ ❸ Matt 4:25; Mark 5:20; 7:31, **Decapolis**

δεκα**τέσσαρες, ων**$_{3.3}$ *indecl. adj.* ❺ Matt 1:17^{3x}; 2 Cor 12:2; Gal 2:1, **fourteen**

δέκατος, η, ον$_{2.1.2}$ {δέκα} *adj.* ❼ John 1:39; Heb 7:2; Rev 11:13, **tenth**

δεκατόω^{con} {δέκα} ❷ Heb 7:6, 9, **to collect a tenth** *or* **a tithe**

δεκτός, ή, όν$_{2.1.2}$ {δέχομαι} *adj.* ❺ Luke 4:19, **favor**; 4:24; 2 Cor 6:2; Phil 4:18, **acceptable**; (34x LXX; 10x Prov) Exod 28:38; Lev 1:3

δελεάζω {δόλος} ❸ Jas 1:14, **to entice**; 2 Pet 2:14, 18, **to seduce**

δένδρον, ου, τό$_2$ (25x) Matt 7:17–19^{5x}; Mark 8:24; Jude 12, **tree(s)**; (32x LXX; 6x Dan)

δεξιο**λάβος, ου, ὁ**$_2$ {δεξιός + λαμβάνω} ①^{amp} Acts 23:23, **lancers**

δεξιός, ιά, ιόν$_{2.1.2}$ {δέχομαι} *adj.* (54x) Matt 27:38 = Mark 15:27 = Luke 23:33, **right**; Acts 7:55; Rom 8:34; Col 3:1; 1 Pet 3:22, *seated at the* **right hand** *of God*; (220x LXX)

δέομαι^{con} (22x; 15x LA) Matt 9:38 = Luke 10:2; Acts 4:31, **to pray**; Luke 5:12; Acts 26:3; 2 Cor 8:4, **to beg**; Rom 1:10, *subst.* **prayers**; 2 Cor 5:20, **to plead**^{BEC}; (91x LXX)

δέος, ους, τό$_3$ ①^{gns} Heb 12:28, **uneasy fear**^{ABC}; ❺ LXX, 2 Macc 3:17, **terror**

Δερβαῖος, α, ον$_{2.1.2}$ *adj.* ①^{nms} Acts 20:4, **Derbean**

Δέρβη, ης, ἡ$_{1\eta}$ ❸ Acts 14:6, 20; 16:1, **Derbe**

δέρμα, ατος, τό$_3$ {δέρω} ①^{dnp} Heb 11:37, **goatskins**; (78x LXX; 49x Lev, 11x Exod)

δερμάτινος, η, ον$_{2.1.2}$ {δέρω} *adj.* ❷^{afs} Matt 3:4 = Mark 1:6, **leather**; (14x LXX; 7x Num)

δέρω (15x; 8x LA) Matt 21:35 = Mark 12:3, 5 = Luke 20:10, 11, **to beat**; John 18:23, **to strike**; Acts 5:40, **to flog**; 1 Cor 9:26, **to shadowbox**^{NIGTC}; 2 Cor 11:20, **to slap** *in the face*; ①^{aainf} LXX, 2 Chr 29:34, **to flay**

δεσμεύω {δέω} ❸ Matt 23:4; Luke 8:29, **to bind**; Acts 22:4, **to arrest**; ❽ LXX, Gen 37:7

δέσμη, ης, ἡ$_{1\eta}$ {δέω} ①^{afp} Matt 13:30, **bundles**; ①^{afs} LXX, Exod 12:22, **cluster**

δέσμιος, ου, ὁ$_2$ {δέω} (16x; 6x Acts) Matt 27:15, 16 = Mark 15:6; Acts 16:25, *jailed* **prisoner**; Eph 3:1; Phlm 1, **prisoner** *of Jesus Christ*; ❾ LXX, Zech 9:11, 12

δεσμός, οῦ, ὁ$_2$ {δέω} (18x; 7x LA) Mark 7:35, *tongue* **was set free**; Luke 8:29, **restraints**; 13:16, bondage; Acts 16:26, **chains**; Phil 1:7; Phlm 13, **imprisonment**; (48x LXX) Gen 42:27, **bundle**; Lev 26:13, **bond**; Judg 16:11, **binding**

δεσμο**φύλαξ, ακος, ὁ**$_3$ {δέω + φυλάσσω} ❸ Acts 16:23, 27, 36, **jailer**; ①[dms] LXX, Gen 40:3, *in custody* **of the chief jailer**

δεσμωτήριον, ου, τό$_2$ {δέω} ❹ Matt 11:2; Acts 5:21, **jail**; ❻ LXX, Gen 39:22, 23[3x]

δεσμώτης, ου, ὁ$_{1>}$ {δέω} ❷[ams] Acts 27:1, 42, **prisoners**; ❹ LXX, Gen 39:20; Jer 24:1

δεσπότης, ου, ὁ$_{1>}$ {δέω} (10x) Acts 4:24; 1 Pet 2:18, **master**; (56x LXX; 7x Dan)

δεῦρο *interj.* ❾ Matt 19:21 = Mark 10:21 = Luke 18:22; Acts 7:34, **come!**; John 11:43, Λάζαρε, **δεῦρο** ἔξω, *Lazarus,* **come** *out*!; (68x LXX; 16x 2 Kgs) Gen 31:44; Exod 3:10

δεῦτε {δεῦρο} *interj.* (10x) Matt 4:19 = Mark 1:17, **Come** *after me*! John 4:29, **Come** *see a man*; Rev 19:17, **Come,** *gather together*; (41x LXX; 8x Pss) Gen 11:3; Exod 1:10

δευτεραῖος, α, ον$_{2.1.2}$ {δύο} *adj.* ①[nmp] Acts 28:13, **the second day**

δεύτερος, α, ον$_{2.1.2}$ {δύο} *adj.* (45x) Matt 22:26 = Mark 12:21; Rev 2:11, **second**; (217x)

δέχομαι (56x; 13x Rev, 9x Syn) Matt 10:14 = Mark 6:11 = Luke 9:5; 1 Thess 1:6, **to welcome**; Acts 3:21; 7:59; Jas 1:21, **to receive**; (62x LXX; 11x Prov)

δέω[con] (43x; 12x Acts, 10x Matt) Matt 12:29 = Mark 3:27; John 11:44, **to bind**; Acts 21:11, **to tie**; 24:27, *left Paul* **a prisoner**; (58x LXX; 13x Judg)

δή *part.* ❺ Matt 13:23, *who* **indeed** *bears fruit*; Luke 2:15, **Indeed**, *let us go*; (293x LXX)

δῆλος, η, ον$_{2.1.2}$ *adj.* ❸ 1 Cor 15:27; Gal 3:11, **it is clear**; Matt 26:73, *accent* **makes clear**; ❾ LXX, Num 27:21; Deut 33:8; 1 Sam 28:6, *subst. the* **clear ones** = **Urim**; Hos 3:4, **manifestations**

δηλόω[con] {δῆλος} ❼ 1 Cor 1:11, **to make clear**; 3:13, **to become apparent**; Col 1:8, **to tell**; 1 Pet 1:11[Keen1P], **to announce**; (36x LXX; 15x Dan) Exod 33:12, **to disclose**; Dan 2:5, **to interpret**

Δημᾶς, ᾶ, ὁ$_{1α}$ ❸ Col 4:14; 2 Tim 4:10; Phlm 24, **Demas**

δημ**ηγορέω** {δῆμος + ἀγορά} ①[iai3s] Acts 12:21, **to speak publicly**; ❷ LXX, 4 Macc 5:15

Δημήτριος, ου, ὁ$_2$ ❸ Acts 19:24, 38; 2 John 12, **Demetrius**

δημι**ουργός, οῦ, ὁ**$_2$ {δῆμος + ἔργον} ①[nms] Heb 11:10, **maker**; ①[nms] LXX, 2 Macc 4:1

δῆμος, οῦ, ὁ$_2$ ❹ Acts 12:22; 17:5; 19:30, 33, **people**; (208x LXX; 151x Num)

δημόσιος, α, ον$_{2.1.2}$ {δῆμος} *adj.* ❹ Acts 5:18; 16:37, **public**; ❸ LXX, 2 Macc 6:10

δηνάριον, ου, τό$_2$ (16x; 12x Syn) Matt 18:28; John 6:7, **denarii**; 20:2, **denarius**

δήπου *indef. adv.* ① Heb 2:16, *for* **it is clear; one would agree**[BDAG]

διά *prep.* (668x, 91x Rom)[PrTh 32] Ⓐ ***w/ gen.–spatial***, Luke 6:1, **through** *the grainfields*; ***w/ gen.—temporal***, Acts 24:17, **after** *several years*; ***w/ gen.—instrumental***, Acts 15:27, **by** *word of mouth*; 2 John 12, *not* **with** *paper*; Ⓑ ***w/ acc.—spatial***, Luke 17:11, **after**; ***w/ acc.—basis***, John 7:13, **for** *fear of the Jews*; ***w/ inf.*** + ***subj. acc.***, Luke 2:4, **because he was**; (1,391x LXX; 218x Pent, 134x Isa, 109x 4 Macc)

δια**βαίνω** ❸ Luke 16:26; Heb 11:29, **to cross**; Acts 16:9, **to come over**; (123x LXX)

δια**βάλλω** ①[api3s] Luke 16:1, **to bring charges**; ❸ LXX, Dan 3:8, **to denounce**

δια**βεβαιόομαι**[con] {διά + βαίνω} ❷ 1 Tim 1:7; Titus 3:8, **to speak confidently**

δια**βλέπω** ❸ Mark 7:5; 8:25; Luke 6:42, **to see clearly**

διά**βολος, ον**$_{2.2}$ {διά + βάλλω} *adj.* (37x) Matt 4:1 = Luke 4:2, 3; Acts 13:10; Eph 6:11; Heb 2:14; 1 John 3:8[3x]; Rev 20:10, **devil**; 1 Tim 3:11, **slanderers**; (22x LXX; 13x Job) δια**γγέλλω** {διά + ἄγγελος} ❸ Luke 9:60; Acts 21:26; Rom 9:17, **to proclaim**; ❾ LXX

δια**γίνομαι** ❸ Mark 16:1, **to be over**; Acts 25:13; 27:9, **to pass**; ①[pms3p] LXX, 2 Macc 11:26, **to conduct, live**

δια**γινώσκω** ❷ Acts 23:15; 24:22, **to investigate**; ❾ LXX, Deut 8:2, **to discern**

διά**γνωσις, εως, ἡ**$_{3}$ {διά + γινώσκω} ①[afs] Acts 25:21, **trial**; ①[gfs] LXX, Wis 3:18

δια**γογγύζω** ❷[iai3p] Luke 15:2, **complain**; 19:7, **they began grumbling**[HBGNT]; (10x LXX; 7x Exod–Num)

δια**γρηγορέω** ①[aap.nmp] Luke 9:32, **when they became fully awake**

δι**άγω** {διά + ἄγω} ❷ 1 Tim 2:2, **to lead**; Titus 3:3, **to live**; (21x LXX) 2 Kgs 16:3

δια**δέχομαι** ①[amp.nmp] Acts 7:45, **to receive**; ❾ LXX, 1 Chr 26:18, **deputies**

διά**δημα, ατος, τό**$_{3}$ {διά + δέω} ❸[anp] Rev 12:3; 13:1; 19:12, **crown**; (17x LXX; 8x 1 Macc)

δια**δίδωμι** ❹ Luke 11:22; 18:22; Acts 4:35, **to divide**; (11x LXX) Gen 49:27, **to distribute**

διά**δοχος, ου, ὁ**$_{2}$ {διά + δέχομαι} ①[ams] Acts 24:27, *received* **as successor**; ❼ LXX

δια**ζώννυμι** ❸ John 13:4, 5; 21:7, **to wrap around**

δια**θήκη, ης, ἡ**$_{1η}$ {διά + τίθημι} (33x; 17x Heb) Rom 9:4; Heb 7:22, **covenant**; (345x LXX)

δι**αίρεσις, εως, ἡ**$_{3}$ {διά + αἱρέω} ❸ 1 Cor 12:4, 6, **different apportionings**[NIGTC]; 12:5, **varieties**[NIGTC]; (33x LXX; 22x 1 Chr) Josh 19:51, **portions**

δι**αιρέω** {διά + αἱρέω} ❷ Luke 15:12, **distributed**; 1 Cor 12:11, **apportioning**; (38x LXX)

δια**καθαίρω** {διά + καθαρός} ①[aainf] Luke 3:17, **to clean out**

δια**καθαρίζω** {διά + καθαρός} ①[fai3s] Matt 3:12, **to clean**

δια**κατελέγχομαι** {διά + κατά + ἐλέγχω} ①[imi3s] Acts 18:28, **to refute**

δια**κονέω**[con] {διά + κόνις} (37x; 10x LA, 6x Matt) Mark 10:45[2x]; John 12:2; 2 Cor 3:3; Phlm 13, **to serve**; Acts 6:2, **διακονεῖν** τραπέζαις, **to serve** *tables*; 1 Pet 4:10, **managers**[Keen1P]; Aristot. *Pol.* 1333a 8, **to do servant's work**

δια**κονία, ας, ἡ**$_{1α}$ {διά + κόνις} (34x; 11x 2 Cor, 8x Acts) Rev 2:19, **service**; Acts 1:17; Col 4:17, **ministry**; Acts 6:1, *daily* **distribution**; 2 Cor 11:8; Heb 1:14, **to minister**; ①[afs] LXX, 1 Macc 11:58, **table utensils**

διά**κονος, ου, ὁ** *or* **ἡ**$_{2}$ {διά + κόνις} (29x) Matt 20:26 = Mark 10:43; Rom 13:4,[2x] **servants**; 2 Cor 3:6, **ministers**; Gal 2:17, **facilitator**[KeenG]; 1 Tim 3:8, **deacons**; ❻ LXX

δι**ακόσιοι, αι, α**$_{2.1.2}$ {δύο + ἑκατόν} *adj.* ❽ Mark 6:37 = John 6:7, **two hundred**; (89x LXX)

δι**ακούω** {διά + ἀκούω} ①[fmi1s] Acts 23:35, **I will give** *you* **a hearing**; ❷ LXX, Deut 1:16

δια**κρίνω** (19x; 5x 1 Cor) Matt 16:3, *you know how* **to interpret**; Matt 21:21 = Mark 11:23, **to doubt**; Acts 11:2, **to take issue with**; Jas 2:4, **to make a distinction**; 1 Cor 4:7, **to see a difference**; 6:5, **to arbitrate**; 11:29, **to recognize**; 14:29, **to sift** *what is said*[NIGTC]; Jude 9, **to argue over**; 22, **to dispute**[BEC]; (28x LXX; 5x Job:Ezek) Exod 18:16, **to decide**

διά**κρισις, εως, ἡ**$_{3}$ {διά + κρίνω} ❸ Rom 14:1, **to argue**; 1 Cor 12:10, **discernment**; Heb 5:14, **to distinguish between**; ①[afs] LXX, Job 37:16, **hovering**

δια**κωλύω** ①[iai3s] Matt 3:14, **to prevent** *from doing something*; ❷ LXX, Jdt 4:7; 12:7, **to hinder**; Antipho. 3.2.7, **having been prevented** *from reaching his goal*[BrDAG]

δια**λαλέω** {διά + λάλος} ❷ Luke 1:65, **to talk about**; 6:11, **to talk it over**

δια**λέγομαι** {διά + λέγω} (13x; 10x Acts) Mark 9:34, **to argue**; Acts 17:2, **to engage**; 19:8, **to convince**; 24:25, **to discuss**; Jude 9, **to dispute**; ❻ LXX, Exod 6:27, **to negotiate**

δια**λείπω** ①[aai3s] Luke 7:45, **to cease**; (12x LXX; 6x Jer) Jer 9:4, **to cease** *producing fruit*

δι**άλεκτος, ου, ἡ**$_{2}$ {διά + λέγω} ❻ Acts 1:19; 2:6, 8, **language**; 21:40, Ἑβραΐδι **διαλέκτῳ**, *Hebrew* **dialect**, *i.e., Aramaic*; ❷ LXX, Esth 9:26, **language**; Dan 1:4, *Chaldean* **dialect**

δι**αλλάσσομαι** {διά + ἄλλος} ①[apimp2s] Matt 5:24, **to be reconciled**

δια**λογίζομαι** {διά + λέγω} (16x) Matt 16:7 = Mark 8:16; Luke 20:14, **to discuss**; (12x LXX; 7x Pss) Ps 9:23 (10:2) **to devise**

δια**λογισμός, οῦ, ὁ**$_{2}$ {διά + λέγω} (14x; 6x Luke) Matt 15:19 = Mark 7:21; Luke 5:22; Jas 2:4, **thoughts**; Luke 9:46, **argument**; Rom 1:21, **reasoning processes**[ZEC]; Rom 14:1, **differing opinions**; 1 Cor 3:2, **reasonings**[ZEC]; (19x LXX; 7x Pss) 1 Macc 2:63, **plans**

δια**λύω** ①[api3p] Acts 5:36, **were dispersed**; (11x LXX) Judg 15:14, *his bonds* **melted**

δια**μαρτύρομαι** {διά + μάρτυς} (15x, 9x Acts) 2 Tim 2:14, **to warn**; Acts 2:40; 20:21, **to bear witness**; (26x LXX; 5x Deut) Exod 18:20, **to inform** *them*

δια**μάχομαι** {διά + μάχη} ①[imi3p] Acts 23:9, **they sharply contended**[EGG]; ❹ LXX, 3x Sir

δια**μένω** ❺ Luke 1:22; 22:28, **to remain**; Gal 2:5; 2 Pet 3:4, **to continue**; (20x LXX; 8x Pss)

δια**μερίζω** {διά + μέρος} (11x; 6x Luke) Matt 27:35 = Mark 15:24; Luke 12:52, 53, **to divide**; (19x LXX; 5x Pss) Gen 10:25; Deut 32:8; Ps 21:19 (22:18)

δια**μερισμός, οῦ, ὁ**$_{2}$ {διά + μέρος} ①[ams] Luke 12:51, **division**; ❸ LXX, Mic 7:12,[2x] **dividing**

δια**νέμω** {διά + νέμω} ①[aps3s] Acts 4:17, **to spread**; ①[aai3s] LXX, Deut 29:25, **to distribute**

δια**νεύω** ①[pap.nms] Luke 1:22, **to make a sign**; ❷ LXX, Ps 34:19 (35:19), **to wink**

δια**νόημα, ατος, τό**$_{3}$ {διά + νοῦς} ①[anp] Luke 11:17, **thoughts**; (13x LXX; 7x, Sir)

δι**άνοια, ας, ἡ**$_{1\alpha}$ (12x) Matt 22:37 = Mark 12:30 = Luke 10:27, **mind**; (69x LXX; 9x Exod)

δι**ανοίγω** {διά + ἀνοίγω} ❽ *act.*, Luke 2:23, *every male who* **opens** *the womb*; *pass.*, Acts 7:56, *the heavens* **opened**; Mark 7:34, **be opened!**; (36x LXX; 6x Exod) Gen 3:5, 7; Exod 13:2

δια**νυκτερεύω** {διά + νύξ} ①[pap.nms] Luke 6:12, **spent the whole night**; ①[pap.nms] LXX, Job 2:9

δια**νύω** ①[aap.nmp] {διά + ἀνύω} Acts 21:7, **we continued**; ①[aai3p] LXX, 2 Macc 12:17

δια**παρατριβή, ῆς, ἡ**$_{1\eta}$ ①[nfp] 1 Tim 6:5, **to irritate thoroughly**[PPE]

δια**περάω**[con] {διά + πέραν} ❻ Matt 14:34 = Mark 6:53; Acts 21:2, **to cross over**; ❾ LXX

δια**πλέω**[con] ①[aap.nmp] Acts 27:5, **sailing through**[Keen4]

δια**πονέομαι**[con] {διά + πόνος} ❷ Acts 4:2; 16:18, **to be annoyed**

δια**πορεύομαι** ❺ Luke 6:1, **to pass through**; Acts 16:4, **to travel**; (43x LXX; 9x Pss)

δια**πορέω**[con] {διά + πορεύομαι} ❹ Luke 9:7; Acts 2:12; 5:24; 10:17; **to be perplexed**

δια**πραγματεύομαι** {διά + πράσσω} ①[ami3p] Luke 19:15, **to earn**

δια**πρίω** {διά + πρίων} ❷[ipi3p] Acts 5:33; 7:54, **they were infuriated**; ①[aai3s] LXX, 1 Chr 20:3, **he hacked** *them* (Tanakh); or **he tore (it) asunder** *with a saw, iron picks, and axes*[ABC]

διαρήσσετο → διερρήγνυμι, *impf. pass. ind. 3s*, Luke 5:6, **began to tear**

δι**αρπάζω** {διά + ἁρπάζω} ❸ Matt 12:29 = Mark 3:27,[2x] **to plunder**; (37x LXX; 9x Pss)

δια**ρήγνυμι** ❺ Matt 26:65 = Mark 14:63; Luke 5:6; Acts 14:14, **to tear**; Luke 8:29, **to break** *the restraints*; (85x LXX; 11x 2 Kgs, 10x 2 Sam) Gen 37:29; Lev 10:6; 2 Kgs 2:12

δια**σαφέω**[con] {διά + σαφής} ❷ Matt 13:36, **to explain**; 18:31, **to report** *the details*; (10x LXX; 7x 2 Macc) Deut 1:5; 2 Macc 7:6, **to declare**

δια**σείω** ①[aas2p] Luke 3:14, **to shake violently**,[EGG] **to take money by force** (CSB); ①[app.nmp] LXX, 3 Macc 7:21, **abused** *of their belongings*

δια**σκορπίζω** ❾ (*all in* GA) Matt 25:24, **to scatter** *seed*; Luke 15:13, **to squander**; John 11:52, **the scattered** *children of God*; (50x LXX; 15x Jer, 13x Ezek) Num 10:34; Neh 1:8

διασπάω ❷ *act.*, Mark 5:4, **to tear apart**; *pass.*, Acts 23:10, *lest Paul* **be torn apart**; (10x LXX)

διασπείρω ❸ Acts 8:1, 4; 11:19, **to scatter**; (67x LXX; 15x Ezek, 8x Jer)

διασπορά, ᾶς, ἡ$_{1\alpha}$ {διά + σπείρω} ❸ John 7:35; Jas 1:1; 1 Pet 1:1, **the dispersed**; (12x LXX) Deut 28:25; Neh 1:9, **in dispersion**

διαστέλλω ❽ (5x Mark) Mark 5:43, **to give a strict order**; Acts 15:24, *without* **orders** *from us*; (57x LXX; 11x Ezek) Ezek 3:18–21[6x], **to warn**

διάστημα, ατος, τό$_{3}$ {διά + ἵστημι} ①[nns] Acts 5:7, **interval**; (16x LXX; 10x Ezek)

διαστολή, ῆς, ἡ$_{1\eta}$ {διά + στέλλω} ❸ Rom 3:22; 10:12; 1 Cor 14:7; **distinction**; ❺ LXX, Num 19:2

διαστρέφω ❼ Luke 23:2, **to corrupt**; Acts 13:8, **to mislead**; 20:30, **to pervert**[BDAG]; Matt 17:17 = Luke 9:41, **perverse** *generation*; (35x LXX; 6x Ezek) Ezek 16:34, **to be opposite**

διασῴζω ❽ Matt 14:36, **to heal**; Acts 23:24, **to be delivered safely**; 28:5, **to escape**; 1 Pet 3:20, **were saved** *through water*[Keen1P]; (69x LXX; 9x Josh) Gen 19:19, **to escape**

διαταγή ῆς, ἡ$_{1\eta}$ {διά + τάσσω} ❷ Acts 7:53, **transmitted**[ZEC]; Rom 13:2, **decree**; ①[nfs] LXX, Ezra 4:11, **text**

διάταγμα, ατος, τό$_{3}$ {διά + τάσσω} ①[ans] Heb 11:23, **edict**; ❸ LXX, Ezra 7:11

διαταράσσω ①[api3s] Luke 1:29, **was deeply troubled**, Xen. *Mem.* 4.2.40, **to perturb**, **upset**

διατάσσω (16x; 11x LA) Matt 11:1, **to instruct**; Luke 8:55, **to command**; 18:2; 22:31, **to order**; 1 Cor 7:17, **I lay down this charge**; 11:34, **I will set in order**; 16:1, **as I directed**[NIGTC]; Gal 3:19, **to appoint**; (20x LXX; 7x 1–4 Macc, 4x Ezek) Judg 5:9, **commanders**

διατελέω[con] ①[pai2p] Acts 27:33, **having gone** *without food*; ❺ LXX, Deut 9:7, **to continue**

διατηρέω[con] ❷ Luke 2:51; Acts 15:29, **to keep**; (24x LXX) Gen 17:19, **to maintain**

διατίθημι ❼ Luke 22:29, **to bestow upon**; Heb 8:10, **to make** *a covenant*; (86x LXX)

διατρίβω {διά + τρίβος} ❾ John 3:22; Acts 12:19, **to spend time**; ❻ LXX, Lev 14:8

διατροφή, ῆς, ἡ$_{1\eta}$ {διά + τρέφω} ①[afp] 1 Tim 6:8; **food**; ①[nfp] LXX, 1 Macc 6:49

διαυγάζω {διά + αὐγή} ①[aas3s] 2 Pet 1:19, *until the day* **dawns**

διαυγής, ές$_{3.3}$ {διά + αὐγή} *adj.* ①[nfs] Rev 21:21, **transparent**

διαφέρω (13x; 6x Syn) Matt 6:26 = Luke 12:24, **to be worth**; Mark 11:16, **to carry through**; Acts 13:49, **to spread**; 1 Cor 15:41, **to differ**; Phil 1:10, **things that really matter**[BEC]; (16x LXX; 4x Dan) 2 Macc 3:4, **to quarrel with**[Herm]

διαφεύγω ①[aas3s] Acts 27:42, **to escape**; (15x LXX; 4x Josh) Deut 2:36; Josh 8:22

διαφημίζω {διά + φημί} ❸ Matt 9:31; 28:15; Mark 1:45, **to spread**

διαφθείρω ❻ Luke 12:33, **to destroy**; 2 Cor 4:16, **to waste away**; 1 Tim 6:5, *subst.* **depraved** *minds*; Rev 11:18, **to destroy** *those who* **destroy** *the earth*; (65x LXX; 12x 1–2 Sam)

διαφθορά, ᾶς, ἡ$_{1\alpha}$ {διά + φθείρω} ❻ **(Acts)** 2:27, 31; 13:34–37,[4x] **decay**; (20x LXX; 7x Pss)

διάφορος, ον$_{2.2}$ {διά + φέρω} *adj.* ❹ Rom 12:6, **different**; Heb 1:4, *more* **excellent**; 8:6, **superior**; 9:10, **various**; (11x LXX) Lev 19:19; Deut 22:9, **different**

διαφυλάσσω ①[aainf] Luke 4:10, **to protect**; (30x LXX; 6x 2 Macc)

διαχειρίζω {διά + χείρ} ❷ Acts 5:30; 26:21, **to murder**, **kill**

διαχλευάζω ①[pap.nmp] Acts 2:13, **to scoff**[ZEC]

διαχωρίζω {διά + χωρίς} ①[pminf] *simul.* Luke 9:33, **were departing**; (23x LXX; 10x Gen)

διδακτικός, ή, όν$_{2.1.2}$ {διδάσκω} *adj.* ❷ 1 Tim 3:2; 2 Tim 2:24, **able to teach**

διδακτός, ή, όν$_{2.1.2}$ {διδάσκω} *adj.* ❸ John 6:45, **taught** *by God*; 1 Cor 2:13,[2x] *not* **taught** *by humans . . . but the Spirit* **teaches**[NIGTC]; ❸ LXX, 1 Macc 4:7, **instructed** *for war*

διδασκαλία, ας, ἡ$_{1α}$ {διδάσκω} (21x; 11x 1–2 Tim) Matt 15:9 = Mark 7:7, **doctrines**; Rom 12:7; Eph 4:14; 1 Tim 1:10, **teaching**; ❹ LXX, Prov 2:17, **teaching**

διδάσκαλος, ου, ὁ$_{2}$ {διδάσκω} (59x) Matt 8:19; Mark 4:38; John 3:10, **teacher**; ❷ LXX

διδάσκω (97x; 74x GA) Matt 4:23 = Luke 4:15; John 7:14; Acts 15:1, **to teach**; (103x LXX)

διδαχή, ῆς, ἡ$_{1η}$ {διδάσκω} (30x) Matt 7:28 = Mark 1:22 = Luke 4:32; Acts 2:42; Rom 6:17; 2 John 9–10,[3x] **teaching**; ①[nfs] LXX, Ps 59:1 (60:0), *a Davidic miktam* **for teaching**

δίδραχμον, ου, τό$_{2}$ {δύο + δράσσομαι} ❷ Matt 17:24,[2x] **two-drachma temple tax**[ZEC]; (26x LXX; 10x Lev) Gen 20:14, **didrachma**[WBC]; Exod 30:13[4x]

Δίδυμος, ου, ὁ$_{2}$ {δύο} ❸ (John) 11:16; 20:24; 21:2, *Thomas, called* **Twin**; ❻ LXX, Gen 25:24

δίδωμι (415x; 230x Gs, 58x Rev) Matt 4:9; John 17:2–24[17x]; Rev 13:2–16,[10x] **to give**; Matt 13:8 = Mark 4:7, **to produce**; (1,991x LXX; 169x Ezek, 147x Deut) Gen 3:6, 12,[2x] **to give**

δι**εγείρω** {διά + ἐγείρω} ❻ Mark 4:39 = Luke 8:24, **to wake up**; John 6:18, **to begin stirring**[ZEC]; 2 Pet 1:13; 3:1, **to rouse** *you*[BEC]; ❺ LXX, 2 Macc 15:10, **to arouse**

διέζωσατο → διαζώννυμι, *aor. mid. ind. 3s*, John 21:7, **he wrapped around**

διεῖλεν → διαιρέω, *aor. act. ind. 3s*, Luke 15:12, **he distributed**

διεληλυθότα → διέρχομαι, *pf. act. ptc. ams*, Heb 4:14, **who has passed through**

δι**ενθυμέομαι**[con] {διά + ἐν + θυμός} ①[pmp.gms] Acts 10:19, **pondering**

δι**έξοδος, ου, ἡ**$_{2}$ {διά + ὁδός} ①[afp] Matt 22:9, **exit points**[ZEC] (26x LXX; 13x Josh)

δι**ερμηνευτής, οῦ, ὁ**$_{1>}$ {διά + ἑρμηνεύω} ①[nms] 1 Cor 14:28, **cannot express**[NIGTC]

δι**ερμηνεύω** {διά + ἑρμηνεύω} ❻ Luke 24:27, **to interpret**; Acts 9:36, *which* **is translated**; 1 Cor 12:30, *Do all* **put** *secret things* **into articulate speech?**[NIGTC] 14:27, *let the one who speaks* **put it into words**[NIGTC]; ①[ppi3s] LXX, ὃ **διερμηνεύεται**, 2 Macc 1:36, *which* **means**

δι**έρχομαι** {διά + ἔρχομαι} (43x; 31x LA) Matt 12:43 = Luke 11:24, **to roam through**; Matt 19:24 = Mark 10:25, **to go through**; Luke 5:15, **to spread**; Acts 11:22, **to travel**; 13:14, **to continue** *their journey*; (146x LXX; 16x Pss, 13x Josh) Josh 18:4, **to go throughout**

δι**ερωτάω**[con] {διά + ἐρωτάω} ①[aap.nmp] Acts 10:17, **to ask**

διεστραμμένα → διαστέφω, *pf. mid. ptc. anp*, Acts 20:30, **perverse things**

δι**ετής, ές**$_{3.3}$ {δύο + ἔτος} *adj.* ①[gms] Matt 2:16, **two years old**; ①[ams] 2 Macc 10:3

δι**ετία, ας, ἡ**$_{1α}$ {δύο + ἔτος} ❷ Acts 24:27; 28:30, **two years**

δι**ηγέομαι**[con] {διά + ἄγω} ❽ Mark 5:16; Acts 8:33, **to describe**; Mark 9:9; Luke 8:39; Heb 11:32, **to tell**; (63x LXX; 19x Pss, 10x Sir) Gen 24:66; Exod 10:2

δι**ήγησις, εως, ἡ**$_{3}$ {διά + ἄγω} ①[afs] Luke 1:1, **narrative**; (11x LXX; 7x Sir)

δι**ηνεκής, ές**$_{3.3}$ {διά + φέρω} *adj.* ❹ Heb 7:3; 10:12, 14, **forever**; 10:1, **continually**

δι**θάλασσος, ον**$_{2.2}$ {δύο + ἅλας} *adj.* ①[ams] Acts 27:41, *a place* **of two seas, sandbar**[Keen4]

δι**ϊκνέομαι** {διά + ἱκανός} ①[pmp.nms] Heb 4:12, **penetrating**; ①[pmimp3s] Exod 26:28, **let it reach** *from one side to the other*

δι**ΐστημι** {διά + ἵστημι} ❸ Luke 22:59, **to pass**; 24:51, **to part**; Acts 27:28, *after* **they sailed a little farther**; (10x LXX) Exod 15:8, *the water* **separated**

δι**ϊσχυρίζομαι** {διά + ἰσχύς} ❷ Luke 22:59; Acts 12:15, **to insist**

δικαιο**κρισία, ας, ἡ**$_{1α}$ {δίκη + κρίνω} ①[gfs] Rom 2:5, **righteous judgment**

δίκαιος, α, ον$_{2.1.2}$ {δίκη} *adj.* (79x; 17x Matt) Matt 1:19; 2 Thess 1:5, **righteous**; Matt 20:4, **right**; John 5:30, **just**; Acts 3:14, *subst. the* **Righteous One**; (421x LXX; 104x Prov, 53x Pss)

δικαιοσύνη, ης, ἡ$_{1\eta}$ {δίκη} (92x; 34x Rom) Matt 3:15; Gal 3:6; Rev 22:11, **righteousness**; Acts 13:10, *all* **that is right**; Rev 19:11, **justice**; (336x LXX; 82x Pss, 52x Isa)

δικαιόω^{con} {δίκη} (39x; 15x Rom) *act.*, Matt 11:19 = Luke 7:35, **to vindicate**; *pass.*, Matt 12:37; Rom 2:13, **to be justified**; (49x LXX; 11x Sir, 8x Isa)

δικαίωμα, ατος, τό$_{3}$ {δίκη} (10x; 5x Rom) Luke 1:6, **requirements**; Rom 1:32, **righteous decree**; 5:18; Rev 15:4, **righteous act**; (140x LXX; 34x Pss, 28x Deut) Ezek 44:24, **statutes**

δικαίως {δίκη} *adv.* ❺ 1 Pet 2:23, **justly**; 1 Cor 15:24, ἐκνήψατε **δικαίως**, *Come to your senses*; **wake up and sober up!**[NIGTC!]; 1 Thess 2:10, **righteously**; (12x LXX; 3x 2 Macc)

δικαίωσις, εως, ἡ$_{3}$ {δίκη} ❷ Rom 4:25; 5:18, **justification**; ❷ LXX, Lev 24:22, **standard** (Tanakh)

δικαστής, οῦ, ὁ$_{1>}$ {δίκη} ❷ Acts 7:27, 35, **judge**; (13x LXX) Exod 2:14; Josh 24:1

δίκη, ης, ἡ$_{1\eta}$ ❸ Acts 28:4, **justice**; 2 Thess 1:9, **penalty**; Jude 7, *undergo* **punishment**[BEC]; (39x LXX; 11x 4 Macc)

δίκτυον, ου, τό$_{2}$ (12x, Gs) Matt 4:20 = Mark 1:18; Luke 5:2; John 21:6, 8, 11,^{2x} **net(s)**; (22x LXX; 6x 1 Kgs, 4x Ezek) 1 Kgs 7:5 (7:17), **latticework**

δίλογος, ον$_{2.2}$ {δύο + λέγω} *adj.* ①^{amp} 1 Tim 3:8, **indulging in double talk**[NIGTC]

διό {διά + ὅς} *coord. conj.* (53x) Matt 27:8; Rom 13:5; 2 Cor 4:13,^{2x} **therefore**; Luke 7:7; Acts 10:29; Rom 15:22, **that is why**; Acts 24:26, **so**; (24x LXX)

διοδεύω {διά + ὁδός} ❷ Luke 8:1, **he went about**; Acts 17:1, **they traveled through**; (19x LXX; 7x 2 Macc:Job) Gen 12:6; Wis 5:7, **to journey through**

Διονύσιος, ου, ὁ$_{2}$ ①^{nms} Acts 17:34, **Dionysius** *the Areopagite*

διόπερ {διά + ὅς + περ} *emph. log. conn.* ❷ 1 Cor 8:13, **for this very reason**[NIGTC]; 10:14, **so then**; ❻ (5x 2 Macc) LXX, Jdt 8:17, **for this reason**; 2 Macc 5:20, **therefore**

διοπετής, ές$_{3.3}$ {Ζεύς (Διός) + πίπτω} *adj.* ①^{gns} Acts 19:35, **fallen from heaven**[ZEC]

διόρθωμα, ατος, τό$_{3}$ {διά + ὀρθός} ①^{gnp} Acts 24:2, **political reforms**[ZEC]

διόρθωσις, εως, ἡ$_{3}$ {διά + ὀρθός} ①^{gfs} Heb 9:10, *time of* **correction**[ABC]; Aristot. *Pol.* 1321b 21, **renovating** *a building*[BrDAG]

διορύσσω {διά + ὀρύσσω} ❹ Matt 6:19, 20; 24:43 = Luke 12:39, **to break in;** ❹ LXX

Διόσκουροι, ων, οἱ$_{2}$ {Ζεύς (Διός) + κοῦροι} ①^{dmp} Acts 28:11, **the Dioscuri**[ZEC!]

διότι {διά + ὅτι} (23x) Luke 1:13, **because**[EGG]; Rom 1:19, **since**; 1 Cor 15:9, **for**; (335x LXX)

Διοτρέφης, φους, ὁ$_{3}$ ①^{nms} 3 John 9, **Diotrephes**

διπλοῦς, ῆ, οῦν$_{2.1.2}$ *adj.* {δύο + πλοῦς} ❹ Matt 23:15, **twice**; 1 Tim 5:17; Rev 18:6,^{2x} **double**; (27x LXX; 10x Exod; 7x Gen)

διπλόω {δύο + πλοῦς} ①$^{\text{aaimp2p}}$ Rev 18:6, **mix** *her a double portion*[ZEC]

δίς {δύο} *adv.* ❻ Mark 14:30; Luke 18:12; Jude 12, **twice**; 1 Thess 2:18, *time and* **again**; (17x LXX) Gen 41:32, **twice**; Deut 9:13, ἅπαξ καὶ **δίς**, *once and* **twice**

δισμυριάς, άδος, ἡ$_{3}$ {δύο + μυρίος} ①^{nfp} Rev 9:16, **200 million**

διστάζω {δύο + στάζω} ❷ Matt 14:31; 28:17, **to hesitate**[ZEC]

δίστομος, ον$_{2.2}$ {δύο + στόμα} *adj.* ❸ Heb 4:12; Rev 1:16, 2:12, **double-edged**; ❹ LXX

δισχίλιοι, αι, α$_{2.1.2}$ {δύο + χίλιοι} *adj.* ①^{nmp} Mark 5:13, **two thousand**; (46x LXX)

διϋλίζω {διά + ὕλη} ①$^{\text{pap.nmp}}$ Matt 23:24, **to strain out**; ①$^{\text{ppp.ams}}$ LXX, Amos 6:6, **thoroughly filtered** *wine*

διχάζω {δύο} ①^{aainf} Matt 10:35, **to turn against**

διχοστασία, ας, ἡ$_1$ {δύο + ἵστημι} ❷ Rom 16:17; Gal 5:20, **divisions**; ①^{gfs} LXX, Macc 3:29

διχοτομέω^{con} {δύο + τομός} ❷$^{\text{fai3s}}$ Matt 24:51 = Luke 12:46, **to cut in two**; ①$^{\text{fai2s}}$ LXX, Exod 29:17, **to divide limb by limb**

διψάω^{con} {δίψος} (16x) Matt 5:6; John 4:13; Rom 12:20; **to thirst**; (36x LXX; 16x Isa)

δίψος, ους, τό$_3$ ①^{dns} 2 Cor 11:27, **in thirst**; (15x LXX) Deut 32:10, **desert**

δίψυχος, ον$_{2.2}$ {δύο + ψύχω} *adj.* ❷ Jas 1:8; 4:8, **double-minded**

διωγμός, οῦ, ὁ$_2$ {διώκω} (10x) Matt 13:21 = Mark 4:17; Acts 8:1; 2 Cor 12:10, **persecution**; ❸ LXX, 2 Macc 12:23; Prov 11:19, **pursuit**; Lam 3:19, **persecution**

διώκτης, ου, ὁ$_{1>}$ {διώκω} ①^{ams} 1 Tim 1:13, **persecutor**

διώκω (45x) Matt 5:10; Acts 9:4; Phil 3:6, **to persecute**; Rom 9:30; Phil 3:12; 1 Thess 5:15, **to pursue**; Rom 12:13 «» 12:14, **to pursue «» to persecute**; (104x LXX; 14x 1 Macc) Lev 26:7–8,$^{\text{3x}}$ **to give chase** *to enemies*; Hdt. *Hist.* 6.82.2, *jurid.*, ὁ διώκων, **the accuser**$^{\textit{BrDAG}}$

δόγμα, ατος, τό$_3$ {δοκέω} ❺ Luke 2:1; Acts 17:7, **decree**; 16:4, **decisions**; Eph 2:15 = Col 2:14, **regulations**; ❻ LXX, Dan 6:13, **decrees**

δογματίζω {δοκέω} ①$^{\text{pmi2p}}$ Col 2:20, **to submit to**; ❼ LXX, Dan 2:13, 15, **to decree**

δοκέω^{con} (62x; 18x LA, 10x Matt) Matt 3:9, **to presume**; Acts 15:22, **to decide**; 1 Cor 3:18, **to think**; 12:22, **to seem**; 2 Cor 11:16, **to suppose**; (55x LXX; 25x 1–4 Macc, 7x Prov)

δοκιμάζω {δόκιμος} (22x) Luke 12:56,$^{\text{2x}}$ **to evaluate**; Rom 1:28, **to deem worthwhile**; 12:2; Eph 5:10, **to discern**; 2 Cor 8:8; 1 John 4:1, **to test**; 1 Cor 11:28, **to examine one's genuineness**^{NIGTC}; 1 Pet 1:7, *even though fire* **proves**$^{\text{Keen1P!}}$; (36x LXX; 8x Pss, 7x Jer)

δοκιμασία, ας, ἡ$_{1α}$ **{δόκιμος}** ①^{dfs} Heb 3:9, *tested me* **with proving**; ❷ LXX, Sir 6:21

δοκιμή, ῆς, ἡ$_{1η}$ **{δόκιμος}** ❼ (Pauline) Rom 5:4$^{\text{2x}}$; 2 Cor 2:9, **obedience**^{BEC}; 8:2, *a severe* **test**; 9:13, **proven character**^{BEC}; 13:3, *demanding* **proof**

δοκίμιον, ου, τό$_2$ **{δόκιμος}** ❷ Jas 1:3, **testing**; 1 Pet 1:7, *these* **testings**$^{\text{Keen1P}}$; ❷ LXX

δόκιμος, ον$_{2.2}$ *adj.* ❼ Rom 14:18, **approval**; 1 Cor 11:19, **tried and true**; 2 Tim 2:15, *as* **one approved**; ❻ LXX, Gen 23:16, **certified**; Zech 11:13, **genuine**

δοκός, οῦ, ἡ$_{2\text{ὁδός}}$ {δέχομαι} ❻ Matt 7:3–5$^{\text{3x}}$ = Luke 6:41–42,$^{\text{3x}}$ **log**; (10x LXX) Gen 19:8

δόλιος, α, ον$_{2.1.2}$ {δόλος} *adj.* ①^{nmp} 2 Cor 11:13, **deceitful**^{BEC}; (27x LXX; 11x Pss)

δολιόω^{con} {δόλος} ①$^{\text{iai3p}}$ Rom 3:13, **to speak deceit**; ❻ LXX, Num 25:18

δόλος, ου, ὁ$_2$ (11x) Mark 7:22; Acts 13:10; 1 Thess 2:3, **deceit**; (54x LXX; 8x Pss)

δολόω^{con} {δόλος} ①$^{\text{pap.nmp}}$ 2 Cor 4:2, *not* **twisting** *God's word*; ❷ LXX, Ps 14:3 (15:3)

δόμα, ατος, τό$_3$ {δίδωμι} ❹ Matt 7:11 = Luke 11:13; Eph 4:8; Phil 4:17, **gift**; (55x LXX)

δόξα, ης, ἡ$_{1η>}$ {δοκέω} (166x; 31x 1–2 Cor, 19x John) Matt 4:8, **splendor**; 16:27 = Mark 13:26; John 1:14$^{\text{2x}}$; Acts 7:2; 1 Cor 2:7, **glory**; (438x LXX; 68x Isa, 56x Pss, 53x Sir)

δοξάζω {δοκέω} (61x, 23x John) *act.*, Matt 5:16; Rom 1:21, **to give glory**; 1 Cor 6:20, **to show forth** *God's* **glory**; *pass.*, Matt 6:2, **to receive glory**; John 7:39, **to be glorified**; (136x LXX; 32x Sir, 17x Isa)

Δορκάς, άδος, ἡ$_3$ ❷ Acts 9:36, 39, **Dorcas**

δός → **δίδωμι**, *aor. act. imp. 2s*, Matt 6:11, **give**

δόσις, εως, ἡ$_3$ {δίδωμι} ❷ Phil 4:15, **giving**; Jas 1:17, **gift**; (22x LXX; 17x Sir)

δότης, ου, ὁ$_{1>}$ {δίδωμι} ①^{ams} 2 Cor 9:7, **giver**; ①^{ams} Prov 22:8, **generous**

δουλαγωγέω^{con} {δοῦλος + ἄγω} ①^{pai1s} 1 Cor 9:27, **to strictly serve my purposes**^{NIGTC}

δουλεία, ας, ἡ$_{1α}$ {δοῦλος} ❺ Rom 8:15, 21; Gal 4:24; 5:1; Heb 2:15, **slavery** (45x LXX; 9x Ezra–Neh) Exod 6:6; 13:3

δουλεύω {δοῦλος} (25x; 7x Rom) *act.*, Matt 6:24,^{2x} **to serve**; Luke 15:29, *I've* **slaved** *for you*; Gal 4:8, *pass.*, **to be enslaved**; Rom 7:6; Eph 6:7, **to serve**; (143x LXX; 15x Gen) Gen 14:4

δούλη, ης, ἡ$_{1η}$ {δοῦλος} ❸ Luke 1:38, 48, **female servant**; Acts 2:18, *male and female* **servants**; (50x LXX, 42x 1–2 Sam) 1 Sam 1:11

δοῦλος, ου, ὁ$_2$ (126x; 30x Matt) Matt 8:9; Mark 12:2; Luke 2:29; John 4:51; Acts 4:29; **servant(s)**; 1 Cor 7:21–23^{4x}; Gal 4:7; Eph 6:5, **slave**; (370x LXX; 106x 1–2 Sam, 96x 1–2 Kgs)

δουλόω^{con} {δοῦλος} ❽ Acts 7:6; Rom 6:18; 2 Pet 2:19, **to enslave**; 1 Cor 7:15, **to remain in slavery**^{NIGTC}; 1 Cor 9:19, **I put myself into slavery**; ❻ LXX, Gen 15:13, **to enslave**

δοχή, ῆς, ἡ$_{1η}$ {δέχομαι} ❷^{afs} Luke 5:29; 14:13, **banquet**; (10x LXX; 6x Esth) Gen 21:8

δράκων, οντος, ὁ$_3$ (13x, Rev) 12:3, **dragon**; (36x LXX) Job 40:25 (41:1) **Leviathan**

δράσσομαι ①$^{pmp.nms}$ 1 Cor 3:19, **he catches** *the wise*; ❽ LXX, Lev 2:2, **to take** *a handful*; Theocr. 24.28, **having grabbed** *him by the throat*

δραχμή, ῆς, ἡ$_{1η}$ {δράσσομαι} ❸ Luke 15:8–9,^{3x} **drachma, coin**; ❼ LXX, Exod 39:3

δρέπανον, ου, τό$_2$ ❽ Mark 4:29; Rev 14:14–19,^{7x} **sickle**; (12x LXX) Deut 16:9; Mic 4:3

δρόμος, ου, ὁ$_2$ {τρέχω} ❸ Acts 13:25; 20:24, **course**, **mission**; 2 Tim 4:7, **race**; ❾ LXX

Δρούσιλλα, ης, ἡ$_{1η>}$ ①^{dfs} Acts 24:24, **Drusilla**

δύναμαι (210x; 144x GsA) Heb 2:18; Jas 4:12; Jude 24, **to be able**; John 1:46, **Can** *anything good come out of Nazareth?*; Rom 8:7, **cannot** *please God*; Phil 3:21, **to enable**; 1 Thess 2:7, *although* **we could have**; (305x LXX; 22x Gen:Jer, 19x Isa)

δύναμις, εως, ἡ$_3$ {δύναμαι} (119x; 25x LA, 1–2 Cor) Matt 7:22, **mighty deeds**; 11:20; Mark 9:39, **miracle(s)**; Matt 22:29; Mark 5:30 = Luke 8:46; Heb 6:5, **power**; 1 Cor 12:10, **effective deeds of power**^{NIGTC}; 2 Cor 1:8, **ability**; (563x LXX; 102x 1 Macc, 60x Num)

δυναμόω^{con} {δύναμαι} ❷ Col 1:11; Heb 11:34, **to gain strengthen**; ❸ LXX, Eccl 10:10

δυνάστης, ου, ὁ$_{1>}$ {δύναμαι} ❸ Luke 1:52, **mighty**; Acts 8:27, **court official**^{BEC}; 1 Tim 6:15, *only* **Sovereign**; (73x LXX) Gen 49:24, *hands of* **the Mighty One of Jacob**

δυνατέω^{con} {δύναμαι} ❸^{pai3s} Rom 14:4; 2 Cor 9:8, **is able**; 2 Cor 13:3, **to show power**^{BEC}

δυνατός, ή, όν$_{2.1.2}$ {δύναμαι} *adj.* (32x; 12x Syn) Matt 26:39 = Mark 14:36; Gal 4:15, **possible**; Luke 14:31; Rom 4:21, *he is* **able**; (179x LXX; 48x 1–2 Chr, 24x 1–2 Sam)

δύνω ❷ Mark 1:32 = Luke 4:40, **to set** (*the sun*)

δύο (135x) Matt 27:38 = Mark 15:27 = Luke 23:32 = John 19:18; 1 Cor 6:16; Rev 11:3, **two**; (645x LXX; 70x Exod, 69x 1–2 Kgs) Gen 1:16; Ps 61:12 (62:11), *I heard this* **twice**

δυσβάστακτος, ον$_{2.2}$ {δυσ- + βαστάζω} *adj.* ❷ Matt 23:4 = Luke 11:46, **hard to carry**; ①^{nns} LXX, Prov 27:3, **a burden**

δυσεντέριον, ου, τό$_2$ {δυσ- + ἔντερον} ①^{dns} Acts 28:8, **dysentery**

δυσερμήνευτος, ον$_{2.2}$ {δυσ- + ἑρμηνεύω} *adj.* ① Heb 5:11, **difficult to explain**

δύσις, εως, ἡ$_3$ ①^{gfs} Mark 16:8, *from east to* **west**; ①^{afs} LXX, Ps 103:19 (104:19)

δύσκολος, ον$_{2.2}$ {δυσ- + κωλύω} *adj.* ①^{nns} Mark 10:24, **hard**; ①^{anp} LXX, Jer 30:2 (49:8)

δυσκόλως {δυσ- + κωλύω} *adv.* ❸ Matt 19:23 = Mark 10:23 = Luke 18:24, **hard**, **difficult**

δυσμή, ῆς, ἡ$_{1η}$ {δύω} ❺ Matt 8:11 = Luke 13:29, Rev 21:13, **west**; (61x LXX; 8x Josh) Gen 15:12, ἡλίου **δυσμάς, sunset**

δυσνόητος, ον$_{2.2}$ {δυσ- + νοῦς} *adj.* ①^{nnp} 2 Pet 3:16, **to understand**

δυσφημέω^{con} {δυσ- + φημί} ①$^{ppp.nmp}$ 1 Cor 4:13, **to slander**; ①^{aai3p} LXX, 1 Macc 7:41

δυσφημία, ας, ἡ$_{1α}$ {δυσ- + φημί} ①^{gfs} 2 Cor 6:8, **slander**; ❷ LXX, 1 Macc 7:38; 3 Macc 2:26

δώδεκα {δύο + δέκα} (75x; 40x Syn, 23x Rev) **twelve**; Matt 9:20 = Mark 5:25 = Luke 8:43, *years*; Matt 10:1 = Mark 3:14 = Luke 9:1, *disciples*; (94x LXX) Gen 14:4; Exod 24:4

δωδέκατος, η, ον$_{2.1.2}$ {δύο + δέκα} *adj.* ①^{nms} Rev 21:20, **twelfth**; (25x LXX) Num 7:78

δωδεκάφυλον, ου, τό$_2$ {δύο + δέκα + φύω} ①^{nns} Acts 26:7, **twelve tribes**

δῶμα, ατος, τό$_3$ ❼ Matt 24:17 = Mark 13:15; Luke 5:19; Acts 10:9, **housetop**; (27x LXX)

δωρεά, ᾶς, ἡ$_{1α}$ {δίδωμι} (11x; 4x Acts) John 4:10; Acts 2:38; Eph 3:7, **gift**; ❼ LXX

δωρεάν {δίδωμι} *adv.* ❾ Matt 10:8^{2x}; Rev 21:6, **freely**; John 15:25, **without reason**; 2 Cor 11:7; 2 Thess 3:8, **free of charge**; Gal 2:21, **for nothing**; (26x LXX; 6x Pss)

δωρέομαι^{con} {δίδωμι} ❸ Mark 15:45, **to give**; 2 Pet 1:3, 4, **to bestow upon**; ❽ LXX

δώρημα, ατος, τό$_3$ {δίδωμι} ❷ Rom 5:16; Jas 1:17, **gift**; ①^{nnp} LXX, Sir 34:18, **offering**

δῶρον, ου, τό$_2$ {δίδωμι} (19x) Matt 2:11; Mark 7:11; Luke 21:4; Eph 2:8; Heb 5:1; Rev 11:10, **gift**, (170x LXX, 44x Lev) Num 5:15, **gift**; Exod 23:7–8,^{3x} **bribe**

δῶτε → **δίδωμι**, *aor. act. sub 2p*, Matt 7:6, **give**

Ε, ε [*epsilon*]

Ε, ε, τό (ἒ ψιλόν) *indecl.* **epsilon,** *5th letter of the Gr. alphabet* ‖ *num.* ε′ = 5; ͵ε = 5,000

ἔα *interj.* ① Luke 4:34, **Ah!**[BHB]; ❸ LXX, Job 15:16; 19:5; 25:6

ἐάν *conj.* {εἰ + ἄν} (350x) 🅐[BDAG] ***functioning alone***, *w/ subj.*, Rom 2:26, **if**; *w/ ind.*, 1 John 5:15, **if** *we know*; *certain part of future time,* John 12:32, **when** *I am lifted up*; *simple possibility*[WSD]; 1 Cor 16:6, **wherever** *I go*; 🅑 ***in conj. with other particles,***[WSD] Matt 18:17, *and* **if** *also*; Gal 2:16, **but instead**[KeenG]; (1,315x LXX; 557x Pent, 139x MajPr)

ἐάν**περ** {εἰ + ἄν + περ} *conj.* ❸ Heb 3:6, 14, 6:3

ἑαυτοῦ, ῆς$_1$ (319x; 140x Gs) 🅐 ***3rd person refl. pron.,*** Matt 8:22, **their own**; Luke 9:25, *forfeits* **himself**; 🅑 ***1st and 2nd person gen. refl. pron.,*** 1 Cor 11:31, **we ourselves**; 🅒 ***reflexive,*** Col 3:13, **to one another**; 🅓 ***in tandem with another preposition,***[WSD] Matt 13:21, ἐν **ἑαυτῷ, in himself**; 1 Cor 16:2, παρ᾽ **ἑαυτῷ, by himself**; (630x LXX; 84x Prov, 40x Gen)

ἐάω[con] (11x; 7x Acts) Matt 24:43; 1 Cor 10:13, **to allow**; Acts 27:40, **to leave**; (26x LXX)

ἑβδομ**ήκοντα**$_3$ {ἑπτά} *indecl.* ❺ (LA) Acts 23:23, **seventy**; (111x LXX; 26x Num)

ἑβδομ**ηκοντάκις** {ἑπτά} *adv.* ① Matt 18:22, **seventy times**; ① LXX, Gen 4:24

ἕβδομος, η, ον$_{2.1.2}$ {ἑπτά} *adj.* ❾ John 4:52, **seventh** *hour*; Heb 4:4,[2x] **seven**; (129x LXX)

Ἔβερ, ὁ$_3$ *indecl.* ①[gms] Luke 3:35, **Eber**; ❽ LXX; 7x Gen

Ἑβραῖος, ου, ὁ$_2$ ❺ Acts 6:1, **Jews,** *i.e., in contrast to the Greeks*; 2 Cor 11:22, **Hebrews**; **Ἑβραῖος** ἐξ **Ἑβραίων, a Hebrew** *born* **of Hebrews**; (40x LXX; 13x Exod)

Ἑβραΐς, ΐδος, ἡ$_3$ ❸[dfs] Acts 21:40; 22:2; 26:14, **in Aramaic**; ❷ LXX; 4 Macc 12:7; 16:15

Ἑβραϊστί *adv.* ❼ John 5:2, 19:13; Rev 9:11; 16:16, **in Hebrew**; ① LXX, Sir 0:22

ἐγγίζω {ἐγγύς} (42x; 18x Luke) Acts 23:15; Phil 2:30, **to come, draw near**; Matt 3:2 = Mark 1:15, **to break into** *to stay*[JG-M 34]; Heb 10:25, *the day* **approaching**; (148x LXX; 23x Isa)

ἐγ**γράφω** {ἐν + γράφω} ❸ (*all perfect tense*) Luke 10:20; 2 Cor 3:2, 3, **are written**; ❸ LXX, Exod 36:21 (39:14), **engraved**

ἔγ**γυος, ον**$_{2.2}$ {ἐν + γύαλον} *adj.* ①[nms] Heb 7:22, **guarantor**[Herm] ❸ LXX, 2 Macc 10:28, **pledge**

ἐγγύς *adv.* (31x; 11x John) Matt 24:32, 33 = Mark 13:28, 29 = Luke 21:30, 31; Rom 10:8; Phil 4:5; Rev 1:3, **near**; Heb 8:13, **about to be** *obliterated*[NIGTC]; (58x LXX; 7x Pss, 5x Deut:Jer)

ἐγείρω (144x; 36x Matt, 31x LA) 🅐 ***in relation to sleep,*** Matt 8:25 = Mark 4:38, **to (rise) wake**; Matt 27:52; **to wake up** *from sleep of death*; 🅑 ***non-sleep sense,*** John 11:29, **to rise**; Luke 14:15, **to pull** *the ox*; 🅒 ***metaph.,*** Eph 5:14, **Awake,** *O sleeper!*; Phil 1:17, **to add** *pressure*[BEC]; (71x LXX) Job 14:12

ἔγερσις, εως, ἡ$_3$ {ἐγείρω} ①[afs] Matt 27:53, *after his* **resurrection**; ❸ LXX, Judg 7:19

ἐγ**κάθετος, ον**$_{2.2}$ {ἐν + κατά + ἵημι} *adj.* ①[amp] Luke 20:20, *subst.* **spies,** *hired* **to lie in wait;**[EGG] ❷ LXX, Job 19:12, *subst.*, **spies**; 31:9, *pred. subst.*, **ἐγκάθετος** ἐγενόμην, **encamping**; Plato *Ax.* 368e, *subst.*, **introduced secretly**

ἐγ**καίνια, ων, τά**$_2$ {ἐν + καινός} ① John 10:22, **Jewish Feast of Dedication, Hanukkah**; ❹ LXX, Ezra 6:16, 17; Neh 12:27,[2x] **dedication**

ἐγκαινίζω {ἐν + καινός} ❷ Heb 9:18; 10:20, **to inaugurate**; (15x LXX; 4x 1 Macc)

ἐγκακέω[con] {ἐν + κακός} ❻ Luke 18:1, **to lose heart**; 2 Cor 4:1, **to give up**; Gal 6:9, **to get discouraged**[KeenG]; 2 Thess 3:13, **to grow weary**

ἐγκαλέω[con] {ἐν + καλέω} ❼ (6x Acts) Acts 19:38, **let them bring charges**[EGG]; 23:28, **to accuse**; 23:29, **accusations**; Rom 8:33, **to bring an accusation**; ❻ **LXX,** Exod 22:8

ἐγκαταλείπω (10x) Matt 27:46 = Mark 15:34, **to forsake**; 2 Cor 4:9, **to abandon**; Rom 9:29, **to leave**; 2 Tim 4:10, **to desert**; Heb 10:25, **to give up**; (179x LXX; 21x Pss, 2 Chr 20x)

ἐγκατοικέω {ἐν + κατά + οἶκος} ①[pap.nms] 2 Pet 2:8, **to live, dwell**

ἐγκαυχάομαι ①[pminf] 2 Thess 1:4, **to pride oneself**; ❹ LXX, Ps 51:3 (52:1)

ἐγκεντρίζω {ἐν + κεντέω} ❻ (Rom) 11:17, 19, 23–24,[4x] **to graft in**; ①[ipi3p] LXX, Wis 16:11

ἔγκλημα, ατος, τό$_3$ {ἐν + καλέω} ❷ (Acts) 23:39; 25:16, **charge**

ἐγκομβόομαι ①[amimp2p] 1 Pet 5:5, **clothe yourselves** *with humility*

ἐγκοπή, ῆς, ἡ$_1$ {ἐν + κόπτω} ①[afs] 1 Cor 9:12, *milit., avoiding* **cutting into** *or* **up**[NIGTC!]

ἐγκόπτω ❺ *act.*, Acts 24:4, **to impose**[ZEC]; Gal 5:7, **to cut off**[KeenG]; 1 Thess 2:18; 1 Pet 3:7, **to hinder**; Rom 15:22, *pass.*, **to be prevented**

ἐγκράτεια, ας, ἡ$_{1α}$ {ἐν + κράτος} ❹ Acts 24:25; Gal 5:23; 2 Pet 1:6,[2x] **self-control**; ①[vfs] LXX, 4 Macc 5:34

ἐγκρατεύομαι {ἐν + κράτος} ❷ (1 Cor) 7:9, **to have power over passions**[NIGTC]; 9:25, **to exercise self-control**; ❷ **LXX,** Gen 43:31; 1 Sam 13:12

ἐγκρατής, ές$_{3.3}$ {ἐν + κράτος} *adj.* ①[ams] Titus 1:8, **disciplined**; ❾ LXX; 4x 2 Macc:Sir

ἐγκρίνω ①[aainf] 2 Cor 10:12, **to classify**

ἐγκρύπτω ❷[aai3s] Matt 13:33 = Luke 13:21, **to mix**; ❼ **LXX,** Josh 7:21

ἐγχρίω ①[aainf] Rev 3:18, **to anoint**; ❸ LXX, Jer 4:30, **to rub** *powder on your eyes*

ἐγώ *1st person pron.* (2,664x) 🅐 ***simple identification***, Acts 17:3, **I** *proclaim*; 🅑 ***Jesus, the true interpreter of Torah***, Matt 5:22–48,[6x] *but* **I** *say*; 🅒 ***Jesus, the*** Ἐγὼ εἰμί ***in John*** (7x), 6:35, **I am** *the bread of life*; 🅓 ***Paul: law and sin*** (26x), Rom 7:7–25[ZEC] (11,918x LXX)

ἐδαφίζω {ἔδαφος} ①[fai3p] Luke 19:44, **to dash to the ground**; ❻ LXX, Hos 10:14, **to destroy**

ἔδαφος, ους, τό$_3$ ①[ans] Acts 22:7, **ground**; (179x LXX; 21x Pss, 20x 2 Chr)

ἐδόθη → **δίδωμι**, *aor. pass. ind. 3s*, Matt 14:11, **given**

ἑδραῖος, αία, αῖον$_{2.2}$ {ἕζομαι} *adj.* ❸ 1 Cor 7:37; Col 1:23, **steadfast**

ἑδραίωμα, ατος, τό$_3$ {ἕζομαι} ①[nns] 1 Tim 3:15, **foundation**

ἔδωκα (*kappa aor.*) → **δίδωμι**, *aor. act. ind. 1s*, John 13:15, **I have given**

Ἑζεκίας, ου, ὁ$_{1>}$ ❷ Matt 1:9, 10, **Hezekiah**; (133x LXX; 43x 2 Kgs, 42x 2 Chr, 30x Jer)

ἐθελοθρησκία, ας, ἡ$_{1α}$ {θέλω + θρησκός} ①[dfs] Col 2:23, **self-imposed worship**

ἐθίζω {ἔθος} ①[pmp.ans] Luke 2:27, **what was customary**; ❷ LXX, 2 Macc 14:30

ἐθνάρχης, ου, ὁ$_{1>}$ {ἔθνος + ἄρχω} ①[nms] 2 Cor 11:32, **ethnarch, governor**[BEC]; ❸ LXX, 1 Macc 14:47; 15:1, 2

ἐθνικός, ή, όν$_{2.1.2}$ *adj.* {ἔθνος} ❹ Matt 5:47; 6:7; 18:17; 3 John 7, **pagans**

ἐθνικῶς *adv.* {ἔθνος} ① Gal 2:14, *act* **like a gentile**[KeenG]

ἔθνος, ους, τό$_3$ (162x; 43x Acts, 29x Rom, 23x Rev) 🅐 ***general sense***, Acts 8:9, **people** *in Samaria*; 🅑 ***distinctive sense***, Matt 20:25 = Mark 10:42, *rulers of* **the gentiles**; 🅒 ***pejorative sense (Jewish sense)***, Matt 4:15, *Galilee of* **the gentiles**; 🅓 ***inclusive sense***, 1 Cor 10:32, *Jews and* **gentiles** *and the church of God*[NIBC!]; (992x LXX; 102x Isa, 101x Ezek)

ἔθος, ους, τό$_3$ (12x; 10x LA) Luke 1:9; John 19:40; Acts 6:14, **custom**; ❺ LXX

εἰ *part.* (502x; 100x 1–2 Cor, 88x LA, 55x Matt) Ⓐ ***first-class conditional***,[GDG] Matt 18:8; 1 Thess 4:14, **if** (*least iffy*: εἰ + *ind. mood*); Ⓑ ***second-class conditional***, Matt 11:23, **if** (*contrary-to-fact*); Ⓒ ***fourth-class conditional***, 1 Pet 3:14, **if** (*most iffy*: εἰ + *opt. mood*); (761x LXX; 83x Job, 57x Gen)

εἰδέα, ας, ἡ$_1$ {εἶδος} ①[nfs] Matt 28:3, **appearance**

εἶδον → ὁράω, *aor. act. ind. 3p*, Matt 2:9, **they saw**

εἶδος, ους, τό$_3$ ❺ Luke 3:22, *bodily* **form**; 9:29; John 5:37, **appearance**; 2 Cor 5:7, *not by* **what can be seen**; 1 Thess 5:22, **form** *of evil*; (52x LXX; 9x Gen)

εἰδωλεῖον, ου, τό$_2$ {εἶδος} ①[dns] 1 Cor 8:10, **in the actual place of an idol**[NIGTC]

εἰδωλόθυτος, ον$_{2.2}$ {εἶδος + θύω} *adj.* ❾ (5x 1 Cor) Acts 15:29; 1 Cor 8:1–10:19, **meat associated with offerings to pagan deities**[NIGTC]; ①[gnp] LXX, 4 Macc 5:2

εἰδωλολάτρης, ου, ὁ$_{1>}$ {εἶδος + λατρεύω} ❼ 1 Cor 5:10; Eph 5:5; Rev 21:8, **one who practices idolatry**

εἰδωλολατρία, ας, ἡ$_{1\alpha}$ {εἶδος + λατρεύω} ❹ 1 Cor 10:14; Gal 5:20; Col 3:5; 1 Pet 4:3, **idolatry**

εἴδωλον, ου, τό$_2$ {εἶδος} (11x) Acts 7:41; Rom 2:22; 2 Cor 6:16, **idol**; (90x LXX; 12x Ezek)

εἰκῇ *adv.* ❻ Rom 13:4, **in vain**; 1 Cor 15:2, εἰ μὴ εἰκῇ, **without coherent consideration**[NIGTC]; Gal 3:4,[2x] **pointlessly**[KeenG]; ① LXX, Prov 28:25

εἴκοσι$_3$ *indecl.* (11x; 6x Rev) Luke 14:31, **twenty**; Rev 4:4, **twenty**-*four*; (277x LXX)

εἴκω ①[aai1p] Gal 2:5, *we didn't let them* **subjugate** *us*[KeenG]; ❷ LXX, 4 Macc 1:6

εἰκών, όνος, ἡ$_3$ (23x; 10x Rev) Matt 22:20 = Mark 12:16 = Luke 20:24; 1 Cor 11:7; 2 Cor 3:18; Rev 13:14, **image**; (40x LXX; 15x Dan, 8x Wis)

εἰλικρίνεια, ας, ἡ$_{1\alpha}$ {ἥλιος + κρίνω} ❸ 1 Cor 5:8; 2 Cor 1:12; 2:17, **purity**

εἰλικρινής, ές$_{3.3}$ {ἥλιος + κρίνω} *adj.* ❷ Phil 1:10, **pure**; 2 Pet 3:1, **sincere**; ① LXX, Wis 7:25

εἰμί (2,462x)[NIDNTT]→ Ⓐ ***fixed formula/general usage***, *cf.* ἐγώ; ἐγώ εἰμί, (48x, 24x John) Matt 14:27 = Mark 6:50 = John 6:20, **it is I, I am he**; Ⓑ ***seven formal "I am" embodiments***, John 6:35, **I am** *the bread of life*[ZEC]; Ⓒ ***periphrastic usage***, εἰμί + *participle*,[GDG] Eph 2:8, **you are being** *saved*; Matt 7:29, *for* **he was** *teaching*; (6,476x LXX; 1,713x Pent) Ⓐ ***fixed formula*** ἐγώ εἰμί, Deut 32:39; (6x Isa) 43:10, 13; 46:4, אֲנִי הוּא, **I am** *he*; Ⓑ ***original "I am" divine embodiment***, Exod 3:14, **I am** *the existing One*

εἵνεκεν *impr. prep.* ❷ Luke 4:18, **because**; 2 Cor 3:10, **since**; ❾ LXX (4x Gen)

εἴπερ *intens. conj.* ❻ Rom 3:30, 8:9, **if after all**[EGG]; 8:17, **provided that**[EGG]; 1 Cor 8:5, **if there really exists**[NIGTC]; 1 Cor 15:15, εἴπερ . . . ἄρα, **if really** *as they* **indeed** *say*[NIGTC]; 2 Thess 1:6, **since indeed**; ① LXX, Jdt 6:9

εἶπον → **λέγω**, *aor. act. ind. 1s/3p*, Mark 8:7, **to speak, tell**[BHGNT]

εἰρηνεύω {εἰρήνη} ❹ Mark 9:50; Rom 12:18; 2 Cor 13:11; 1 Thess 5:13, **to live in peace**; (19x LXX; 5x Job)

εἰρήνη, ης, ἡ$_1$ (92x; 14x Luke) Matt 10:13,[2x] **blessing of pronounced peace**[EGG]; Mark 5:34; Luke 2:14; Rom 5:1; Phlm 3; Rev 1:4, **peace**[EGG]; (275x LXX; 29x Isa, 24x Pss:Jer)

εἰρηνικός, ή, όν$_{2.1.2}$ {εἰρήνη} *adj.* ❷ Heb 12:11; Jas 3:17, **peaceful**; (49x LXX; 8x 1 Macc, 7x Gen)

εἰρηνοποιέω[con] {εἰρήνη + ποιέω} ①[aap.nms] Col 1:20, **making peace**; ①[pai3s] LXX, Prov 10:10

εἰρηνοποιός, όν$_{2.2}$ {εἰρήνη + ποιέω} *adj.* ①[nmp] Matt 5:9, **peacemaker**

εἰς *prep. w/ acc.* (1,764x; 1,099x GA, 119x Rom) Ⓐ ***interch. with* πρός**, 2 Cor 1:15–16, **to**; Ⓑ ***interch. with* ἐν**, Rev 22:19, **ἐν τῷ βιβλίῳ, in** *a book*; Rev 1:11, **(εἰς) to** *the seven churches*, εἰς[7x] Ἔφεσον, **to** Ephesus . . . **to**; Ⓒ ***purposive***, Eph 1:10, **as** *a plan*[ZEC]; Ⓓ ***result***, Rom 4:18, **so that** *he might become*; Ⓔ ***causal***, 2 Cor 10:16, **about** *work*[BEC]; Ⓕ ***significant and ambiguous***[PrTh 92]; (6,926x LXX; 492x Jer, 464x Pss)

εἷς, μία, ἕν$_{3.1.3}$ (345x) Ⓐ ***noun: one, single person or thing***; 1 John 5:8, **agreement** (*are* **one**); Ⓑ ***adjective: single unit or thing***; Matt 5:18, *a* **single** *iota* (*the smallest Greek letter*); Eph 4:5, **εἷς** κύριος, **μία** πίστις, **ἓν** βάπτισμα, **one** *Lord*, **one** *faith*, **one** *baptism*; Ⓒ ***noun: initial day of a block of time***; Acts 20:7, **first day**; (305x LXX; 43x Ezek, 31x Num, 26x 1 Kgs)

εἰσ**άγω** (11x; 9x LA) Luke 2:27; John 18:16; Acts 7:45; Heb 1:6, **to bring**; (153x LXX)

εἰσ**ακούω** ❺ Matt 6:7; Acts 10:31; 1 Cor 14:21, **to hear**; (238x LXX; 51x Pss, 28x Exod)

εἰσ**δέχομαι** ①[fmi1s] 2 Cor 6:17, **to welcome**; (19x LXX; 6x Ezek)

εἰσδραμοῦσα → εἰστρέχω, *aor. act. ptc. nfs*, Acts 12:14, **ran in**

εἴσ**ειμι** ❹ Acts 3:3; 21:18, 26; Heb 9:6, **to go**; ❻ LXX, Exod 28:29

εἰσενέγκῃς → εἰσφέρω, *aor. act. subj. 2s*, Matt 6:13, **to lead**

εἰσ**έρχομαι** (194x; 84x LA) Ⓐ ***literal or figurative***, Rev 3:20, **to come in** *to him*; Ⓑ ***a state or condition***, Matt 26:41 = Mark 14:38 = Luke 22:40, **to enter** *into temptation*; Ⓒ ***initiation***, Luke 9:46, **to start** *an argument*; Ⓓ ***divine awareness***, Jas 5:4, **has reached** *the ears*[BEC]; Ⓔ ***baptism*** *to ascension*, Acts 1:21, **went in** *and went out*; (653x LXX)

εἰσῄει → εἴσειμι, *impf. act. ind. 3s*, Acts 21:18, 26, **went into**

εἰσ**καλέομαι** ①[amp.nms] Acts 10:23, **to invite**

εἴσ**οδος, οῦ, ἡ**$_{2όδός}$ ❺ Acts 13:24, *his* **entrance**;[EGG] 1 Thess 1:9; 2:1, **entrance**; Heb 10:19, εἰς τὴν **εἴσοδον**, **to enter**; 2 Pet 1:11, **entry**; (48x LXX; 8x Ezek)

εἰσ**πηδάω**[con] ①[aai3s] Acts 16:29, **to rush in**; ①[aas3s] LXX, Amos 5:19, **to rush** *home*

εἰσ**πορεύομαι** (18x) Matt 15:17; Luke 11:33, **to go into, to enter**; Acts 9:28, **went in** *and went out*, **moved about freely**[NAC] (*cf.* Acts 1:21!); (157x LXX; 20x Deut, 19x Ezek)

εἱστήκειν → ἵστημι, *plpf. act. ind. 3s*, Matt 13:2, **stood**[NIV]

εἰσ**τρέχω** ①[aap.nfs] Acts 12:14, **ran in**; ①[aap.nms] LXX, 2 Macc 5:26, **to rush into**

εἰσ**φέρω** ❽ Matt 6:13 = Luke 11:4, **to lead**; Acts 17:20; 1 Tim 6:7, **to bring**; (90x LXX)

εἶτα *adv.* (15x) Mark 4:17 = Luke 8:12; John 13:5; 1 Tim 3:10, **then**; Heb 12:9, **besides** *this*; (20x LXX; 12x Job)

εἴτε (65x; 27x 1 Cor, 14x 2 Cor) Ⓐ ***or*** (29x), 1 Cor 3:22[7x]; Col 1:16[3x]; Ⓑ ***whether*** (18x), 1 Cor 3:22; 12:13[2x]; 1 Pet 2:13; Ⓒ ***if*** (11x), 2 Cor 5:13[2x]; Ⓓ ***as*** (4x), 1 Cor 13:8[3x]; Ⓔ ***as for*** (1x), 2 Cor 8:23; Ⓕ ***either*** (1x), 2 Thess 2:15; ❾ LXX, 2x Josh

εἴωθα ❹ **εἰώθει**[plpfai3s], Matt 27:15; Mark 10:1, **to be accustomed**; **εἰωθός**[pap.ans] Luke 4:16; Acts 17:2, *as* **was his custom**

ἐκ, ἐξ *prep. w/ gen.* (914x; 171x LA, 165x John) [PrTh 103–13] → Ⓐ ***origin***, John 7:52, **from** *Galilee*; Phil 3:5; Ⓑ ***source***, 2 Cor 2:4; Ⓒ ***agency***, Matt 3:15, *to be baptized* **by** *him*; Ⓓ ***basis***, 1 Cor 7:5, **by** *mutual agreement*[NIGTC]; Ⓔ ***cause***, 2 Cor 7:9, **because** *of us*; Ⓕ ***means***, Rev 3:18, **by means** *of fire*; Ⓖ ***partitive***, 1 Cor 9:7, **some** *of the milk*; Ⓗ ***crucial constructions employing* ἐκ**[PrTh 105]; (3,651x LXX; 249x Num, 243x Exod)

ἕκαστος, η, ον$_{2.1.2}$ *adj.* (82x; 22x 1 Cor) Matt 16:27, **each person**; 1 Cor 1:12; 2 Cor 5:10, **each one**; Luke 2:3, **each**; 16:5, ἕνα **ἕκαστον**, **one by one**; (352x LXX; 42x Jer, 28x Exod)

ἑκάστοτε {ἕκαστος + ὅς + τέ} *adv.* ① 2 Pet 1:15, **on any occasion**[BEC]

ἑκατόν (17x; 10x Syn) Matt 13:8 = Mark 4:8, **hundredfold**; Luke 15:4, **hundred** *sheep*; Rev 7:4, **one hundred** *forty-four thousand*; (237x LXX; 29x Gen, 21x 1 Esd, 20x Num)

ἑκατονταετής, ές$_{3.3}$ {ἑκατόν + ἔτος} *adj.* ①^{nms} Rom 4:19, **a hundred years old** ①^{dms} LXX, Gen 17:17, **a hundred-year-old man**

ἑκατονταπλασίων, ον$_{3.3}$ {ἑκατόν} *adj.* ❸ Matt 19:29 = Mark 10:30, **hundredfold**; ①^{anp} LXX, 2 Sam 24:3, *multiply the troops* **a hundred times more**

ἑκατοντάρχης, ου, ὁ$_{1>}$ {ἑκατόν + ἄρχω} (20x; 13x Acts) Matt 8:5 = Luke 7:2; Acts 10:22; 22:5, **centurion**; ❷ LXX, 2 Kgs 11:10, 15, **commanders of hundreds**

ἐκβαίνω ①^{aai3p} Heb 11:15, **had gone out**; (10x LXX) Isa 24:18, **to escape from**

ἐκβάλλω (81x; 66x Syn) Ⓐ ***forceful urgency***, Mark 1:12, *the Spirit* **drove** *him*[EGG]; Ⓑ ***forceful separation***, Matt 21:12 = Mark 11:15, **to drive out**; Ⓒ ***symbolic removal***, Mark 9:47, **to gouge** *it* **out**; Ⓓ ***eternal punishment***, Matt 22:13, **to throw** *into darkness*; (96x LXX)

ἔκβασις, εως, ἡ$_{3}$ {ἐκ + βαίνω} ❷ 1 Cor 10:13, **exit**[NIGTC]; Heb 13:7, **outcome**; ❸ LXX

ἐκβληθήσονται → **ἐκβάλλω**, *fut. pass. ind. 3p*, Matt 8:12, **will be thrown into**

ἐκβολή, ῆς, ἡ$_{1}$ {ἐκ + βάλλω} ①^{afs} Acts 27:18, *began* **to jettison** *the cargo*[ZEC]; ❷ LXX, Exod 11:1, ἐκβαλεῖ ὑμᾶς **ἐκβολῇ**, *he will expel you* **with expulsion**; Jonah 1:5, **they threw** *the ship's cargo overboard*

ἔκγονος, ον$_{2.2}$ {ἐκ + γίνομαι} *adj.* ①^{anp} 1 Tim 5:4, **grandchildren**; (33x LXX; 11x Deut, 8x Isa)

ἐκδαπανάω^{con} {ἐκ + δαπάνη} ①^{fpi1s} 2 Cor 12:15, **to be spent**

ἐκδέχομαι ❻ Acts 17:16; 1 Cor 11:33; Heb 10:13, **to wait for**; (15x LXX; 4x Sir)

ἔκδηλος, ον$_{2.2}$ *adj.* ①^{nfs} 2 Tim 3:9, **quite evident**[NIGTC]; ❷ LXX, 3 Macc 3:19; 6:5

ἐκδημέω^{con} {ἐκ + δῆμος} ❸ 2 Cor 5:6, 8,^{2x} **to be absent**; Hdt. *Hist.* 1.30, **to be on one's travels**

ἐκδίδωμι ❹ Matt 21:33 = Mark 12:1 = Luke 20:9; Matt 21:41, **to rent, lease**; (16x LXX)

ἐκδιηγέομαι^{con} {ἐκ + διά + ἄγω} ❷ Acts 13:41, 15:3, **to tell, inform**; (14x LXX; 10x Sir)

ἐκδικέω^{con} {ἐκ + δίκη} ❻ Luke 18:3, **to secure justice**; Rom 12:19, **to take revenge**; 2 Cor 10:6, **to punish**; Rev 6:10, **to bring justice**; (89x LXX; 16x Jer, 10x Ezek)

ἐκδίκησις, εως, ἡ$_{3}$ {ἐκ + δίκη} ❾ Luke 18:7, **justice**; 2 Thess 1:8, **vengeance**; Acts 7:24, ἐποίησεν **ἐκδίκησιν**, *lit.*, *he made* **justice**, *or* **avenged**[ZEC]; Rom 12:19, **vengeance** *is mine*; 2 Cor 7:11, *your* **execution of justice**; 1 Pet 2:14, εἰς **ἐκδίκησιν**, **to punish**; (79x LXX)

ἔκδικος, ον$_{2.2}$ *adj.* ❷ Rom 13:4; 1 Thess 4:6, **avenger**; ❸ LXX, 4 Macc 15:29

ἐκδιώκω ①$^{aap.gmp}$ 1 Thess 2:15, *who* **persecuted** *us*; (12x LXX; 5x Pss)

ἔκδοτος, ον$_{2.2}$ *adj.* ①^{ams} Acts 2:23, *this one* **was given up**[EGG]

ἐκδοχή, ῆς, ἡ$_{1}$ ①^{nfs} Heb 10:27, **expectation** *of judgment*; Polyb. *Hist.* 3.29.4, **understanding**

ἐκδύω ❺ Matt 27:31 = Mark 15:20; Luke 10:30, **to strip**; 2 Cor 5:4, *mid.*, **to be undressed**[BEC]; (27x LXX; 4x Ezek)

ἐκεῖ *adv.* (105x) Matt 5:24; Luke 15:13; Jas 3:16; Rev 21:25, **there**; (757x LXX)

ἐκεῖθεν *adv.* (37x) Matt 4:21; Mark 6:1; Luke 9:4; Acts 7:4, **from there**; (139x LXX)

ἐκεῖνος, η, ο$_{2.1.2}$ {ἐκεῖ} (265x, 120x Syn, 75x John) Ⓐ ***in tandem with subst.***, John 21:7, **that** *disciple*; Ⓑ ***gen. of place*** (*understood* ὁδοῦ),[*EDNT*] Luke 19:4, **that place**; Ⓒ ***subst.***

distinction, Luke 18:14, *this one* [οὗτος] *is more upright than* **that one [ἐκεῖνον]**[ZEC]; Ⓓ ***Jesus, the "well-known person" in John***, 1:18; 5:37; 10:1; (683x LXX; 165x Pent, 55x Isa)

ἐκεῖσε {ἐκεῖ} *adv.* ❷ Acts 21:3; 22:5, **there**; ① LXX, Job 39:29

ἐκ**ζητέω**[con] ❼ Luke 11:50, **to be required**[BEC]; Acts 15:17; Heb 11:6, **to seek**; (131x LXX)

ἐκ**ζήτησις, εως, ἡ**$_{3}$ {ἐκ + ζητέω} ①[afp] 1 Tim 1:4, **useless speculation**[NIGTC]

ἐκ**θαμβέω**[con] {ἐκ + θάμβος} ❹ (Mark) 9:15, **to be greatly amazed**; 14:33, **to be deeply distressed**; 16:5, 6, **to be alarmed**; ①[fai3s] LXX, Sir 30:9, **will terrorize you**

ἔκ**θαμβος, ον**$_{2.2}$ *adj.* ①[nmp] Acts 3:11, *the people* **were utterly astonished**

ἐκ**θαυμάζω** ①[iai3p] Mark 12:17, **they marveled**; ❷ LXX, Sir 27:23, 43:18

ἔκ**θετος, ον**$_{2.2}$ {ἐκ + τίθημι} *adj.* ①[anp] Acts 7:19, τοῦ ποιεῖν τὰ βρέφη **ἔκθετα**, **to expose**, *euph. for the practice of leaving newborns in the open to die*[EGG]

ἐκ**καθαίρω** {ἐκ + καθαρός} ❷ 1 Cor 5:7; 2 Tim 2:21, **to clean out**; ①[aai1s] LXX, Deut 26:13, **to remove**

ἐκ**καίω** ①[api3p] Rom 1:27, **burned** *in their strong desire*; (51x LXX; 13x Sir, 8x Pss)

ἐκ**κεντέω**[con] {ἐκ + κέντρον} ❷[aai3p] John 19:37; Rev 1:7, **to pierce**; ❽ LXX, Num 22:39

ἐκ**κλάω** ❸[api3p] Rom 11:17, 19, 20,[2x] **to break off**; ①[fai3s] LXX, Lev 1:17, **to tear open**

ἐκ**κλείω** ❷ Rom 3:27; Gal 4:17, **to lock out**[KeenG]

ἐκ**κλησία, ας, ἡ**$_{1α}$ {ἐκ + καλέω} (114x; 23x Acts) Matt 16:18[/G-M 124–25]; 18:17[2x]; Acts 5:11; Rev 2–3,[15x] **church**[WLC 150]; Acts 7:38, *exodus* **assembly**; 19:32, *riotous* **assembly**; (100x LXX; 32x 1–2 Chr, 13x Sir) Deut 4:10, *the day* **of gathering**; *then in verbal form only in LXX*

ἐκκλησιάζω ①[aaimp2s], **ἐκκλησίασον** πρός με τὸν λαόν, **assemble** *the people before me*

ἐκ**κλίνω** ❸ Rom 3:12; 16:17, **to steer clear**[ZEC]; 1 Pet 3:11, **to let them turn**[Keen1P]; (146x LXX; 18x Pss:Prov, 11x Judg)

ἐκ**κολυμβάω**[con] ①[aap.nms] Acts 27:42, **swimming away**

ἐκ**κομίζω** ①[imi3s] Luke 7:12, *a dead man* **was being carried out**

ἐκ**κόπτω** (10x; 4x Matt) Matt 5:30, **to chop off**; Rom 11:22, **to cut off**; (48x LXX; 6x Jer)

ἐκ**κρεμάννυμι** ①[imi3s] Luke 19:48, **were hanging on** *him*; **were captivated** (HCSB)

ἐκ**λαλέω**[con] {ἐκ + λάλος} ①[aainf] Acts 23:22, *don't* **tell** *anyone*; ①[aai3s] LXX, Jdt 11:9

ἐκ**λάμπω** ①[fai3p] Matt 13:43, **will shine**; ❻ LXX, 2 Sam 22:29

ἐκ**λανθάνομαι** ①[pmi2p] Heb 12:5, **you have forgotten**

ἐκ**λέγομαι** {ἐκ + λέγω} (22x; 11x LA) Mark 13:20; Luke 14:7; John 15:16[2x]; Acts 1:2; 1 Cor 1:27,[2x] **to choose**; (67x LXX; 11x Isa)

ἐκ**λείπω** ❹ Luke 16:9, **to fail**[EGG]; Heb 1:12, τὰ ἔτη σου οὐκ **ἐκλείψουσιν**, *your years* **will never end**[EGG]; (187x LXX; 32x Pss, 28x Jer)

ἐκ**λεκτός, ή, όν**$_{2.1.2}$ {ἐκ + λέγω} *adj.* (22x) Matt 24:22 = Mark 13:20; Rom 8:33, **the chosen**; Luke 23:35, *the* **Chosen One**; 1 Tim 5:21, **the elect** *angels*; (97x LXX; 12x Isa, 10x Pss)

ἐκ**λογή, ῆς, ἡ**$_{1η}$ ❼ Acts 9:15, **chosen**; Rom 9:11, **elect**; 2 Pet 1:10, **election**; Pseud., Pss. Sol. 9.4, 18.5

ἐκ**λύω** ❺ Matt 15:32 = Mark 8:3, **to collapse**; Gal 6:9, μὴ **ἐκλυόμενοι**, *without* **growing faint**; Heb 12:3, **to give up**[EGG]; 12:5, **to lose heart**[EGG]

ἐκ**μάσσω** ❺ Luke 7:38 = John 11:2; Luke 7:44; John 12:3; 13:5, **to wipe**; ❸ LXX, Sir 12:11

ἐκ**μυκτηρίζω** ❷[iai3p] Luke 16:14; 23:35, **to scoff**; ❹ LXX, Ps 2:4

ἐκνεύω ①[aai3s] John 5:13, **to slip away** (*unnoticed*);[EGG] ❽ LXX, Judg 4:18,[3x] **to turn aside**

ἐκνήφω ①[aaimp2p] 1 Cor 15:34, **ἐκνήψατε** δικαίως, **Come to your senses; wake up and sober up!**[NIGTC]; ❻ LXX, Gen 9:24, *when Noah* **awoke** *from his wine*

ἑκούσιος, α, ον$_{2.1.2}$ {ἑκών} *adj.* ①[ans] Phlm 14, κατὰ **ἑκούσιον**, **willingly**; (15x LXX; 4x Ezra)

ἑκουσίως *adv.* ❷ Heb 10:26, **deliberately**; 1 Pet 5:2, **willingly**; ❺ LXX, Exod 36:2

ἔκπαλαι {ἐκ + παλαιός} *adv.* ❷ 2 Pet 2:3; 3:5, **long ago**

ἐκπειράζω {ἐκ + πεῖρα} ❹ Matt 4:7 = Luke 4:12; 1 Cor 10:9, **to test**; ❺ LXX, Deut 6:16

ἐκπέμπω ❷ Acts 13:4; 17:10, **to be sent out, away**; ❾ LXX, Gen 24:54, **to send back**

ἐκπερισσῶς {ἐκ + περί} *adv.* ① Mark 14:31, **emphatically**

ἐκπετάννυμι {ἐκ + πέτομαι} ①[aai1s] Rom 10:21, **to stretch out**; (19x LXX) Exod 9:29, 33

ἐκπηδάω ①[aai3p] Acts 14:14, **to rush**; ❼ LXX, Deut 33:22, **that leaps forth** *from Bashan*

ἐκπίπτω (10x; 5x Acts) Acts 12:7; 27:32; 1 Pet 1:24, **to fall off**; Acts 27:17, **to run aground**; Rom 9:6, **to fail**; Gal 5:4, **to fall away**; (15x LXX; 5x Isa)

ἐκπλέω[con] ❸ Acts 15:39; 18:18; 20:6, **to sail away**

ἐκπληρόω[con] ①[pfai3s] Acts 13:33, **to fulfill**; ❸ LXX, 3 Macc 1:2

ἐκπλήρωσις, εως, ἡ$_3$ {ἐκ + πληρόω} ①[afs] Acts 21:26, **completion**; ①[afs] LXX, Macc 6:14, **full measure** *of their sins*

ἐκπλήσσω {ἐκ + πληρόω} (13x; 12x Syn) Matt 7:28 = Mark 1:22 = Luke 2:48; Acts 13:12, **astonished to the point of being overwhelmed**[BHGT]; ❺ LXX, 2 Macc 7:12, **astonished**; Eur. *Tr.* 183, **seized by trembling** *in my heart*

ἐκπνέω[con] ❸ Mark 15:37 = Luke 23:46, **to expire**[ZEC]; Mark 15:39, οὕτως **ἐξέπνευσεν**, *the way* **he breathed**; Aristot. *Rh.* 1409a 32, *athl.*, **to lose one's breath** (*of a runner*); Soph. *Ai.* 1148, *great storm* **that blows** *from a little cloud*

ἐκπορεύομαι (33x; 11x Mark) Matt 3:5 = Mark 1:5; John 5:29, **to go out**; (161x LXX)

ἐκπορνεύω {ἐκ + πόρνη} ①[aap.nfp] Jude 7, **to commit sexual sin**; (44x LXX; 7x Hos)

ἐκπτύω ①[aai2p] Gal 4:14, **to reject**[KeenG]; Hom. *Od.* 5.322, **to spit out**

ἐκριζόω[con] {ἐκ + ῥίζα} ❹ Matt 13:29; Jude 12, **to uproot**; ❾ LXX, Jer 1:10, **to pluck up**

ἔκστασις, εως, ἡ$_3$ {ἐκ + ἵστημι} ❼ Mark 5:42, *great* **amazement**[ZEC]; Luke 5:26, **astounded**; Acts 10:10, **a trance**[ZEC]; (28x LXX) Gen 2:21; 15:12, **a deep sleep**

ἐκστρέφω ①[pmi3s] Titus 3:11, **to go astray**; ❺ LXX, Deut 32:20, *a* **perverse** *generation*

ἐκταράσσω ①[pai3p] Acts 16:20, *men* **throw** *our city* **into confusion**; ❺ LXX, Wis 17:3

ἐκτείνω (16x; 12x Syn) Matt 8:3 = Mark 1:41 = Luke 5:13, **to reach out**; Matt 12:13; John 21:18, **to stretch out**; Acts 27:30, **to lay out** *anchors*; (137x LXX; 23x Exod, 19x Ezek)

ἐκτελέω[con] {ἐκ + τέλος} ❷[aainf] Luke 14:29, 30, **to finish**; ❸ LXX, 2 Macc 15:9, **to win**

ἐκτένεια, ας, ἡ$_{1a}$ {ἐκ + τείνω} ①[dfs] Acts 26:7, **earnestly**; ❹ LXX, 2 Macc 14:38, **zealously**

ἐκτενής, ές$_{3.3}$ {ἐκ + τείνω} *adj.* ①[afs] 1 Pet 4:8, **devotedly**; ❷ LXX, 3 Macc 3:10, **earnest**

ἐκτενῶς *adv.* ❸ Luke 22:44, **more fervently**; Acts 12:5, **fervently**; 1 Pet 1:22, **from the bottom of your hearts**[Keen1P]; ❹ LXX, Jonah 3:8, *to cry* **mightily**

ἐκτίθημι ❹ *act.*, Acts 11:4; 18:26, **to explain**; 28:23, **to expound**; *pass.*, Acts 7:21, *gen. abs.* **ἐκτεθέντος** δὲ αὐτοῦ, *when he* **was exposed**; (13x LXX; 9x Esth)

ἐκτινάσσω {ἐκ + τείνω} ❹ Matt 10:14 = Mark 6:11, **to shake off**; (20x LXX; 5x Neh)

ἐκτός {ἐκ} *adv.* ❽ Ⓐ ***prep. with gen.***, Matt 23:26, **outside**; Ⓑ ***conj.***, 1 Cor 14:5, **unless**; 15:27, **nothing but**[EDNT] Ⓒ ***the exterior, outside***, 2 Cor 12:2, **outside** *the body*

ἕκτος, η, ον$_{2.1.2}$ {ἕξ} *adj.* (14x) Ⓐ ***chronological***, Matt 27:45 = Mark 15:33 = Luke 23:44, *the* ***sixth*** *hour* (*i.e., noon*); Ⓑ ***numerical***, Luke 1:26; Rev 6:12; Rev 9:13, **the sixth**
ἐκτρέπω ❺ (4x Pastorals) 1 Tim 1:6, **have turned themselves aside**[NIGTC]; 1 Tim 6:20, **to avoid**; Heb 12:13, **to be dislocated**[EGG]; ①[pap.nms] LXX, Amos 5:8, **to turn**
ἐκτρέφω ❷ Eph 5:29, **to nourish**; 6:4, **to bring up**; (26x LXX) Gen 45:11, **to provide for**
ἔκτρωμα, ατος, τό$_3$ {ἐκ + τραῦμα} ①[dns] 1 Cor 15:8, *as though* **an aborted fetus**[NIGTC]; ❸ LXX, Num 12:12; Eccl 6:3; Job 3:16, **stillborn child**
ἐκφέρω ❽ (4x Acts) 1 Tim 6:7, **to take out**; Luke 15:22, **to bring out**; Acts 5:6, 9, 10, **to carry out**; Heb 6:8, **to produce**; (82x LXX; 7x Ezra, 6x Lev)
ἐκφεύγω ❽ Luke 21:36; 2 Cor 11:33, **to escape**; Acts 19:16, **to run away**; (21x LXX), 5x Sir
ἐκφοβέω {ἐκ + φόβος} ①[painf] 2 Cor 10:9, **to terrify** *you*; (14x LXX; 3x Ezek)
ἔκφοβος, ον$_{2.2}$ *adj.* ❷ Mark 9:6, **terrified**; Heb 12:21, **so frightening**; ❷ LXX, Deut 9:19
ἐκφύω ❷ Matt 24:32 = Mark 13:28, **to sprout leaves**
ἐκχέω (16x) Matt 9:17, **to spill out**; John 2:15; Acts 2:17; Titus 3:6; Rev 16:1–17,[9x] **to pour out**; Rom 3:15, **to shed** *blood*; (140x LXX; 25x Ezek, 15x Pss)
ἐκχύννομαι (11x, 6x LA) Matt 23:35, **to shed** *blood*; 26:28 = Mark 14:24 = Luke 22:20, **to pour out**; Acts 1:18, **spilled out**; Jude 11, **they have rushed** *for profit*[NTC]
ἐκχωρέω[con] ①[paim3p] Luke 21:21, **to depart**; ❺ LXX, Amos 7:12
ἐκψύχω ❸[aai3s] Acts 5:5, 10; 12:23, **to die**; ❷ LXX, Judg 4:21; Ezek 21:12 (21:7)
ἑκών, οῦσα, όν$_{3.1.3}$ *adj.* ❷ Rom 8:20; 1 Cor 9:17, **willingly**; ❷ LXX, Exod 21:13; Job 36:19
ἐλαία, ας, ἡ$_{1α}$ (15x; 10x Syn) Matt 21:1 = Mark 11:1 = Luke 19:29, *Mount of* **Olives**; Rom 11:17; Rev 11:4, **olive tree(s)**; Jas 3:12, **olives**; (33x LXX; 5x Zech)
ἔλαιον, ου, τό$_2$ (11x) Mark 6:13; Luke 7:46; Jas 5:14; Rev 6:6, **oil**; (196x LXX; 41x Lev)
ἐλαιών, ῶνος, ὁ$_3$ ①[gms] Acts 1:12, *Mount of* **Olives**; ❾ LXX, Jer 5:17
Ἐλαμίτης, ου, ὁ$_{1>}$ ①[nmp] Acts 2:9, **Elamites**
ἐλάσσων, ον$_{3.3}$ {ἐλαχύς} *adj.* ❹ John 2:10, **cheaper**; Rom 9:12, **smaller**; 1 Tim 5:9, **at least**; Heb 7:7, *the* **inferior** *is blessed by the superior*
ἐλαττονέω[con] {ἐλαχύς} ①[aai3s] 2 Cor 8:15, **to have too little**; ❼ LXX, Gen 8:3, 5, **to abate**
ἐλαττόω[con] {ἐλαχύς} ❸ John 3:30, **decrease**; Heb 2:7, 9, **you made** *him* **lower**; (27x LXX)
ἐλαύνω ❺ Mark 6:48, *inf. of cont. time*, ἐν τῷ **ἐλαύνειν**, *straining* **at the oars**[EGG]; John 6:19, **to row**; *pass.*, Luke 8:29; 2 Pet 2:17, **to be driven**; ❽ LXX, *act. inf.*, 1 Kgs 9:27, ναυτικοὺς **ἐλαύνειν** εἰδότας θάλασσαν, *sailors* **familiar** *with the sea* (NRSV)
ἐλαφρία, ας, ἡ$_{1α}$ {ἐλαφρός} ①[dfs] 2 Cor 1:17, **being wishy-washy**[BEC]
ἐλαφρός, ά, όν$_{2.1.2}$ *adj.* ❷ Matt 11:30, **light**; 2 Cor 4:17, **light** *bundle*[BEC]; ❺ LXX
ἐλάχιστος, η, ον$_{2.1.2}$ {ἐλαχύς} *adj.* (14x; 5x Matt) Matt 2:6, **least**; Luke 12:26, **a little thing**; 1 Cor 4:3, *counts for* **very little**[NIGTC]; 6:2, **small** *claims*; Jas 3:4, **small** *rudder*
Ἐλεάζαρ, ὁ$_3$ *indecl.* ❷ Matt 1:15,[2x] **Eleazar**
ἐλεάω[con] {ἔλεος} ❹ Rom 9:16; 12:8; Jude 22, 23, **mercy**; (10x LXX; 4x Prov)
ἐλεγμός, ου, ὁ$_2$ {ἐλέγχω} ①[ams] 2 Tim 3:16, **refuting error**; (21x LXX; 6x Num:Sir)
ἔλεγξις, εως, ἡ$_3$ {ἐλέγχω} ①[afs] 2 Pet 2:16, **rebuke**; ❷ LXX, Job 21:4; 23:2, **complaint**
ἔλεγχος, ου, ὁ$_2$ {ἐλέγχω} ① Heb 11:1, **the proof**; (31x LXX; 14x Prov)
ἐλέγχω (17x) *act.*, Matt 18:15, **to reprove and convict**[ZEC]; Luke 3:19; Titus 1:13, **to rebuke**; 1 Cor 14:24; Jude 15, **to convict**; John 3:20; *pass.*, Eph 5:11, **to be exposed**; (65x LXX; 12x Job)

ἐλεεινός, ή, όν$_{2.1.2}$ {ἔλεος} *adj.* ❷ 1 Cor 15:19, **we are more to be pitied**; Rev 3:17, **pitiful**; ❸ LXX, Dan 9:23, *you are* **one who has received mercy** (LES)

ἐλεέω^{con} {ἔλεος} (28x) Matt 5:7; 2 Cor 4:1, **to be shown mercy**; Matt 9:27, **Have mercy** *on us!*; Rom 9:18, **to have mercy**; 1 Pet 2:10, **to receive mercy**; (132x LXX; 20x Pss:Isa)

ἐλεημοσύνη, ης, ἡ$_{1\eta}$ {ἔλεος} (13x; 8x Acts) Matt 6:2–4,^{3x} *when you give* **to the needy**; Acts 3:2, **giving alms**^{ZEC}; Acts 3:10, **asking for alms**; 10:31, **charitable giving**; (56x LXX)

ἐλεήμων, ον$_{3.3}$ {ἔλεος} *adj.* ❷ Matt 5:7; Heb 2:17, **merciful**; (31x LXX; 6x Pss)

ἔλεος, ους, τό$_{3}$ (27x; 6x Luke) Matt 9:13; Rom 9:23; Gal 6:16, **mercy**; (334x LXX; 124x Pss)

ἐλευθερία, ας, ἡ$_{1\alpha}$ {ἐλεύθερος} (11x) Rom 8:21; Gal 2:4; Jas 1:25, **freedom**; ❼ LXX

ἐλεύθερος, α, ον$_{2.1.2}$ *adj.* (23x) Matt 17:36; John 8:33; Rom 6:20; 1 Cor 7:21, **free**; (30x LXX)

ἐλευθερόω^{con} {ἐλεύθερος} ❼ John 8:32, **to set free**; Rom 6:18; 8:2, **to be freed**; Gal 5:1, **to liberate**^{KeenG}; ❸ LXX, 2 Macc 1:27; 2:22; Prov 25:10

ἔλευσις, εως, ἡ$_{3}$ ①^{gms} Acts 7:52, *the* **coming** *of the Righteous One*

ἐλεφάντινος, η, ον$_{2.1.2}$ {ἐλέφας, **elephant**} *adj.* ①^{ans} Rev 18:12, **made of ivory**; (10x LXX)

ἐλήλυθας → **ἔρχομαι**, *pf. act. ind. 2s*, John 3:2, *who* **has come**

Ἐλιακίμ, ὁ$_{3}$ *indecl.* ❸ Matt 1:13^{2x}; Luke 3:30, **Eliakim**, *son of Hilkiah*; (12x LXX)

Ἐλιέζερ, ὁ$_{3}$ *indecl.* ①^{gms} Luke 3:29, **Eliezer**; (14x LXX; 7x 1 Chr)

Ἐλιούδ, ὁ$_{3}$ *indecl.* ❷ Matt 1:14, 15, **Eliud**

Ἐλισάβετ, ἡ$_{3}$ *indecl.* ❾ (Luke) 1:5–57, **Elizabeth**, *wife of Zechariah*

Ἐλισαῖος, ου, ὁ$_{2}$ ①^{gms} Luke 4:27, **Elisha**

ἑλίσσω ❷ Heb 1:12, Rev 6:14, **to roll up**; ❷ LXX, Job 18:8, **to be entangled** (LES)

ἑλιχθείη → **ἑλίσσω**, *aor. pass. opt. 3s*, Job 18:8, **may** *snares* **entrap** *him*

ἕλκος, ους, τό$_{3}$ ❸ Luke 16:21; Rev 16:2, 11, **sores**; (15x LXX; 6x Lev)

ἑλκόω^{con} ①$^{pmp.nms}$ Luke 16:20, **covered with sores**

ἕλκω ❽ John 6:44; 18:10, **to draw**; 21:6; Jas 2:6, **to drag**; (25x LXX; 3x Job:Jer)

Ἑλλάς, άδος, ἡ$_{3}$ ①^{afs} Acts 20:2, **Greece**; ❹ LXX, 1 Macc 1:1; Isa 66:19

Ἕλλην, ηνος, ὁ$_{3}$ (25x) John 7:35; Acts 14:1; Rom 1:14, **a Greek person**; (13x LXX)

Ἑλληνικός, ή, όν$_{2.1.2}$ *adj.* ①^{dfs} Rev 9:11, **in Greek language**; ❺ (5x 2 Macc)

Ἑλληνίς, ίδος, ἡ$_{3}$ ❷ Mark 7:26, **gentile woman**; Acts 17:12, **Greek women**; ①^{afp} LXX, 2 Macc 6:8, **Greek**

Ἑλληνιστής, οῦ, ὁ$_{1>}$ ❸ Acts 6:1; 9:29; 11:20, **Hellenistic**

Ἑλληνιστί *adv.* ❷ John 19:20, **in Greek language**; Acts 21:37, *Do you know the* **Greek language**?

ἐλλογέω^{con} {ἐν + λέγω} ❷ *pass.*, Rom 5:13, *is not* **invoiced**^{ZEC}; Phlm 18, **charge** *it to me*

Ἐλμαδάμ, ὁ$_{3}$ *indecl.* ①^{gms} Luke 3:28, **Elmadam**

ἐλπίζω {ἐλπίς} (31x; 8x 1–2 Cor) Matt 12:21, **to place hope**; Luke 6:34; Acts 24:26; Rom 8:24; 1 Cor 13:7; Phlm 22; 3 John 14, **to hope**; (114x LXX; 73x Pss, 11x Isa)

ἐλπίς, ίδος, ἡ$_{3}$ (53x) Acts 2:26; 1 Cor 9:10^{2x}; 2 Cor 10:15; Eph 4:4, **hope**; (114x LXX; 18x Pss, 16x Isa)

Ἐλύμας, α, ὁ$_{1}$ ①^{nms} Acts 13:8, **Elymas**

ἐλωΐ *Aram.*, *indecl.* ❷ Mark 15:34, **ἐλωΐ, ἐλωΐ, My God, my God!**

ἐμαυτοῦ, ῆς, οῦ$_{2.1.2}$ {ἐγώ + αὐτός} (37x, 16x John) Matt 8:9; Luke 7:8; John 5:30; Acts 20:24, **my**; Luke 7:7; John 8:14; 1 Cor 4:3, **on my own**; Acts 24:10; Phlm 13, **me**; (58x LXX; 9x Job) ἐμ**βαίνω** (16x Gs) Matt 8:23 = Luke 8:22, **he boarded**; ❹ LXX, Jonah 1:3

ἐμ**βάλλω** {ἐν + βάλλω} ①^{aainf} Luke 12:5, **to throw** *people* **into** *hell*; (75x LXX; 10x Dan) Dan 3:6–20, **to be thrown into** *the furnace*

ἐμ**βάπτω** {ἐν + βάπτω} ❷ Matt 26:23 = Mark 14:20, **to dip**

ἐμ**βατεύω** {ἐν + βαίνω} ①$^{pap.nms}$ Col 2:18, **to enter**; ❼ LXX (4x 1 Macc)

ἐμ**βιβάζω** {ἐν + βαίνω} ①^{aai3s} Acts 27:6, **to put aboard**; ①^{pai1s} LXX, Prov 4:11, **I have led**

ἐμ**βλέπω** {ἐν + βλέπω} (11x; 4x Mark) Matt 6:26, **to look at**; Acts 1:11, **looking** *into heaven*; (22x LXX; 9x Isa)

ἐμ**βριμάομαι**^{con} {ἐν + βρίμη} ❺ Matt 9:30[EGG] = Mark 1:43, **to warn sternly**; 14:5, **to scold indignantly**[BHGNT]; John 11:33, 38, **he was outraged** *in himself*[EGG!]; ①^{fmi3p} LXX, Dan 11:30, **raging** (Tanakh); Aeschl. *Sept.* 461, **to breathe heavily, snort** (*horses*)

ἐμέω^{con} ①^{aainf} Rev 3:16, **to vomit**; ❷ LXX, Sir 31:21; Isa 19:14

ἐμ**μαίνομαι** {ἐν + μαίνομαι} ①$^{pmp.nms}$ Acts 26:11, **furiously enraged** *with them*[ZEC]

Ἐμμανουήλ$_3$ *indecl.* ①^{ams} Matt 1:23, **God with us**; ①^{ams} LXX, Isa 7:14, Heb. עִמָּנוּ אֵל **Immanuel**

Ἐμμαοῦς, ου, ἡ$_3$ ①^{nfs} Luke 24:13, **Emmaus**

ἐμ**μένω** {ἐν + μένω} ❹ Acts 14:22, **to persevere**[ZEC]; 28:30, **to live**; Gal 3:10, **to keep doing**[KeenG]; Heb 8:9, **to remain faithful to**; (21x LXX; 6x Sir)

Ἐμμώρ, ὁ$_3$ *indecl.* ①^{gms} Acts 7:16, **Hamor**

ἐμός, ἐμή, ἐμόν$_{2.1.2}$ (76x) Matt 18:20; John 4:34, **my**; (104x LXX; 38x Prov, 11x Gen)

ἐμ**παιγμονή, ῆς, ἡ**$_{1η}$ {ἐν + παῖς} ①^{dfs} 2 Pet 3:3, **scoffers**

ἐμ**παιγμός, οῦ, ὁ**$_2$ {ἐν + παῖς} ①^{gmp} Heb 11:36, **mockings**; ❽ LXX, 2 Macc 7:7

ἐμ**παίζω** {ἐν + παῖς} (13x Syn) *pass.*, Matt 2:16, **to be deceived, outwitted**; 20:19 = Mark 10:34 = Luke 18:32, **to be mocked**; (28x LXX; 4x Judg)

ἐμ**παίκτης, ου, ὁ**$_{1>}$ {ἐν + παῖς} ❷^{nmp} 2 Pet 3:3; Jude 18, **scoffers**; ①^{nmp} LXX, Isa 3:4

ἐμ**περιπατέω**^{con} ①^{fai1s} 2 Cor 6:16, **to walk around**[BEC]; ❽ LXX, Lev 26:12, **to walk**

ἐμπέσῃ → ἐμ**πίπτω**, *aor. act. subj. 3s*; Matt 12:11, **if** *a sheep* **fell**

ἐμ**πίπλημι** ❺ Luke 1:53; John 6:12, **to satisfy**; Luke 6:25, **those who are full**; Acts 14:17, **to fill**; Rom 15:24, *once I have first* **enjoyed your company**[EGG]; (146x LXX; 23x Isa)

ἐμ**πίμπρημι** ①^{aai3s} Matt 22:7, **to set** *their city* **on fire**

ἐμ**πίπτω** ❼ Matt 12:11; Luke 6:39; 1 Tim 6:9; Heb 10:31, **to fall**; 1 Tim 3:6, **to fall** *into the judgment reserved for the devil* (**διαβόλου**, *obj. gen.*)[ABC]; 3:7, **to fall** *into disgrace and the trap set by the devil* (**διαβόλου**, *subj. gen.*)[ABC]; (51x LXX; 10x Sir)

ἐμ**πλέκω** {ἐν + πλέκω} ❷ 2 Tim 2:4; 2 Pet 2:20, **to become entangled, interwoven**; ❷ LXX; 2 Macc 15:17; Prov 28:18

ἐμ**πλοκή, ῆς, ἡ**$_{1η}$ {ἐν + πλέκω} ①^{gfs} 1 Pet 3:3, *such as* **braiding** *your hair*[Keen1P]

ἐμ**πνέω**^{con} {ἐν + πνέω} ①$^{pap.nms}$ Acts 9:1, **breathing** *threats*; (11x LXX; 9x Josh)

ἐμ**πορεύομαι** ❷ Jas 4:13, **to do business**; 2 Pet 2:3, **to exploit**[BEC]; (11x LXX; 3x Gen)

ἐμ**πορία, ας, ἡ**$_{1α}$ {ἐν + πορεύομαι} ①^{afs} Matt 22:5, **business**; (11x LXX; 7x Ezek)

ἐμ**πόριον, ου, τό**$_2$ {ἐν + πορεύομαι} ①^{gns} John 2:16, **marketplace**; ❸ LXX, Isa 23:17

ἔμ**πορος, ου, ὁ**$_2$ {ἐν + πορεύομαι} ❺ (4x Rev) Rev 18:3, **merchant**; (25x LXX; 13x Ezek)

ἔμ**προσθεν** {ἐν + πρός + θεν} *adv.* (48x; 18x Matt) 🅐 ***near spatial***, Acts 18:17, **in front**; 1 John 3:19, **presence**; 🅑 ***remote spatial***, John 3:28, **ahead**; 🅒 ***temporal***, Phil 3:13, *what is* **to come**[BEC]; 🅓 ***rank***,[PrTh 259] John 1:15, 30, **has surpassed** *me*; (149x LXX; 23x 1–2 Sam) ἐμ**πτύω** {ἐν + πτύω} ❻ (Syn) Matt 26:67 = Mark 14:65, **to spit**; ❷ LXX, Num 12:14

ἐμ**φανής, ές**$_{3.3}$ {ἐν + φαίνω} *adj.* ❷ *pred.*, Acts 10:40, **to be seen**; *pred.*, Rom 10:20, **to become visible**[ZEC]; ❼ LXX, Wis 6:22, εἰς τὸ **ἐμφανὲς**, εἰς τὸ + *acc.*, *purp.* **to make clear**

ἐμ**φανίζω** {ἐν + φαίνω} (10x; 5x Acts) Heb 9:24, **to appear**; John 14:21, 22, **to reveal oneself**; Acts 23:22, **to inform**; Heb 11:14, **to make clear**; (10x LXX), Exod 33:13

ἔμ**φοβος, ον**$_{2.2}$ {ἐν + φόβος} *adj.* ❺ Luke 24:5; Rev 11:13, **to be terrified**; Acts 24:25, **to be alarmed**; ①[nms] LXX, Sir 19:24

ἐμ**φυσάω**[con] {ἐν + φύω} ①[aai3s] John 20:22, **to breathe upon**; ❼ LXX, Gen 2:7

ἔμ**φυτος, ον**$_{2.2}$ {ἐν + φύω} *adj.* ①[ams] Jas 1:21, **implanted**; ①[nfs] LXX, Wis 12:10

ἐν *prep.* (2,752x; 640x LA)[PrTh 115–36] 🅐 ***locative***, 1 Thess 3:1, **in** *Athens*; Matt 9:4, **in** *his heart*; 2:6, **among**; 🅑 ***temporal***, 1 Thess 2:19, **at** *his coming*; Matt 11:22, **on** *the day of judgment*; 🅒 ***means***, Matt 3:11, **with** *water*; 🅓 ***agency***, Mark 12:36, **by** *the Holy Spirit*; 🅔 ***basis***, Matt 6:7, **because of** *their many words*; 🅕 ***association***, Col 2:12, *buried* **with** *him*; 🅖 ***reference***, 1 Tim 2:7, **regarding** *faith*; Jas 1:4, *lacking* **in** *nothing*; 🅗 ***interpretive challenges***, 1 Cor 7:15; Col 3:4, 16; 🅘 **ἐν** (τῷ) **Χριστῷ** (Pauline; 170x *if* ἐν αὐτῷ *and* ἐν ᾧ *are included*) **in Christ**[PrTh 122–28], Col 1:16, ἐν αὐτῷ (= ἐν Χριστῷ) (13,462x LXX; 1,017x Pss, 853x, Ezek, 728x, Jer)

ἐν**αγκαλίζομαι** {ἐν + ἀγκαλή} ❷[amp.nms] Mark 9:36; 10:16, **to take in one's arms**; ❷ LXX, Prov 6:10; 24:33, **to fold** *one's hands in sleep*

ἐν**άλιος, ον**$_{2.2}$ {ἐν + ἅλας} *adj.* ①[gnp] Jas 3:7, **sea creature**

ἔν**αντι** *prep. w/ gen.* ❷ Luke 1:8, Acts 8:21, **before**; (262x LXX; 76x Num, 61x Lev)

ἐν**αντίον** {ἐν + ἀντί} *prep. w/ gen.* ❽ (LA) Luke 1:6; Acts 7:10, **before**; (428x LXX; 76x Gen)

ἐν**αντίος, α, ον**$_{2.1.2}$ {ἐν + ἀντί} ❽ Matt 14:24 = Mark 6:48, **against**; (60x LXX; 11x 1–2 Sam)

ἐν**άρχομαι** {ἐν + ἄρχω} ❷ Gal 3:3, **after you began with**[KeenG]; Phil 1:6, **who inaugurated** *a good work*[ABC]; (11x LXX), Deut 2:24, **to begin**

ἔνατος, η, ον$_{2.1.2}$ {ἐννέα} *adj.* (10x) Matt 20:5 = Mark 15:33 = Luke 23:44; Acts 3:1, *the* **ninth** *hour* (*i.e., 3 p.m.*); Rev 21:20, *the* **ninth** *topaz*; (32x LXX; 6x 2 Kgs, 5x Jer)

ἐν**δεής, ές**$_{3.3}$ *adj.* ①[nms] Acts 4:34, **needy**; (24x LXX; 15x Prov)

ἔν**δειγμα, ατος, τό**$_{1}$ {ἐν + δέομαι} ①[nns] 2 Thess 1:5, **evidence**

ἐν**δείκνυμι** (11x; 3x Rom) Rom 2:15; Titus 3:2, **to show**, **demonstrate**; Rom 9:17; Eph 2:7, **to display**; 2 Cor 8:24, **display** *the proof of your love openly*[BEC]; (13x LXX; 4x Josh)

ἔν**δειξις, εως, ἡ**$_{3}$ ❹ *purp.* Rom 3:25 (εἰς), 26 (πρός), **to demonstrate**; 2 Cor 8:24, *cog. w/* ἐνδείκνυμι, *display* **the proof** *of your love openly*[BEC]; Phil 1:28, *will be* **a sign**[BEC]

ἕν**δεκα**$_{3}$ {ἕν + εἷς} *indecl.* ❻ Matt 28:16 = Mark 16:14 = Luke 24:9; Acts 1:26; 2:14, *the* **eleven** *disciples*; (15x LXX) Gen 32:23, **eleven** *children*

ἐν**δέκατος, η, ον**$_{2.1.2}$ {ἕν + εἷς} *adj.* ❸ Matt 20:6, 9, *the* **eleventh** *hour* (*5 p.m.*); Rev 21:20, *the* **eleventh** *jacinth*; (15x LXX) Gen 8:5, **first day of the tenth** *month*

ἐν**δέχομαι** ①[pmi3s] Luke 13:33, **it is possible**; ❷ LXX, 2 Macc 11:18; Dan 2:11

ἐν**δημέω**[con] {ἐν + δῆμος} ❸ 2 Cor 5:6, 8, 9, **to be at home**

ἐν**διδύσκω** {ἐν + δύω} ❷ Mark 15:17, **to put on**; Luke 16:19, **he dressed himself**; ❹ LXX, 2 Sam 1:24, **to clothe**

ἔν**δικος, ον**$_{2.2}$ {ἐν + δίκη} *adj.* ❷ Rom 3:8, **just**; Heb 2:2, **based on what is right**[NIGTC]

ἐν**δοξάζομαι** {ἐν + δοκέω} ❷ 2 Thess 1:10, 12, **to be glorified**; (11x LXX; 4x Exod)

ἔνδοξος, ον$_{2.2}$ {ἐν + δοκέω} *adj.* ❹ Luke 7:25; 13:17, **splendidly**; 1 Cor 4:10, **to be honored**[NIGTC]; Eph 5:27, **glorious**; (66x LXX; 17x Isa)

ἔνδυμα, ατος, τό$_3$ ❽ (7x Matt) Matt 3:4; 6:25 = Luke 12:23, **clothing**; (12x LXX)

ἐνδυναμόω[con] ❼ *pass.*, Acts 9:22, **to grow stronger**; Rom 4:20; Eph 6:10; Phil 4:13; 2 Tim 4:17, **to be strengthened**

ἐνδύνω {ἐν + δύω} ①[pap.nmp] 2 Tim 3:6, **to creep in**; Hom. *Il.* 19.367, **to enter** *his heart*

ἔνδυσις, εως, ἡ$_3$ {ἐν + δύω} ①[gfs] 1 Pet 3:3, **putting on clothes**; ❷ LXX, Job 41:5 (41:13)

ἐνδύω (27x; 10x Syn, 4x 1 Cor) Mark 1:6, **to wear**; Rev 1:13, **to be dressed**; Matt 27:31 = Mark 15:20, **to clothe**; Luke 24:49, **clothed** *with power*; Rom 13:12, **to put on** *the armor of light*; 1 Cor 15:53–54,[4x] **become clothed**[NIGTC]; Gal 3:27, **clothed yourselves**; Col 3:12, **to put on** *compassion*; (113x LXX; 15x Ezek, 12x Lev, 11x Pss)

ἐνδώμησις, εως, ἡ$_3$ {ἐν + δῶμα} ①[nfs] Rev 21:18, **the building material**

ἐνέδρα, ας, ἡ$_1$ {ἐν + ἕζομαι} ❷[afs] Acts 23:16; 25:3, **ambush**; ❸ LXX, Josh 8:7

ἐνεδρεύω {ἐν + ἕζομαι} ❷ Luke 11:54; Acts 23:21, **to lie in wait, ambush**; (28x LXX)

ἐνειλέω[con] {ἐν + εἴλω} ①[aai3s] Mark 15:46, **to wrap in**; ①[pfpp.nfs] LXX, Wis 12:10

ἔνειμι ❼ (1x **ἐνόντα**) Luke 11:41, **what is inside**[ZEC]; (6x **ἔνι**, *emph. equiv. of* **ἐστίν**)[NIGTC] Gal 3:28, οὐκ ἔνι, **there is** *neither*; ❽ LXX, 1 Kgs 10:17; 1 Macc 5:5

ἕνεκα *impr. prep. w/gen.* (21x; 16x Syn) Ⓐ ***cause,*** 2 Cor 3:10, **because**; Mark 8:35, **for** *my* ***sake***; Ⓑ ***cause and purpose contrast,*** 2 Cor 7:12,[3x] οὐχ **ἕνεκα** . . . οὐδὲ **ἕνεκα** . . . ἀλλ᾽ **ἕνεκα**, *not* **because of . . .** *neither* **for the sake of** . . . *but* **so that**[BEC]; (126x LXX; 25x Pss, 17x Gen)

ἐνενήκοντα$_3$ *indecl.* ❹ τὰ **ἐνενήκοντα** ἐννέα, Matt 18:12 = Luke 15:4; Matt 18:13 = Luke 15:7, *the* **ninety**-*nine*; (22x LXX; 5x Gen)

ἐνεός, ά, όν$_{2.1.2}$ *adj.* ①[nmp] Acts 9:7, **speechless**; ❸ LXX, Prov 17:28; Isa 56:10

ἐνέπλησεν → **ἐμπίπλημι**, *aor. act. ind. 3s*, Luke 1:53, **he has satisfied**

ἐνέργεια, ας, ἡ$_{1α}$ {ἐν + ἔργον} ❽ Eph 1:19; 2 Thess 2:9, **working**; Phil 3:21, **power**; Col 1:29, **strength**; 2 Thess 2:11, *God sent a* **strong** *delusion*; ❽ LXX (4x Wis)

ἐνεργέω[con] {ἐν + ἔργον} (21x; 4x Gal:Eph) Matt 14:2 = Mark 6:14; Eph 2:2, **is at work**; Rom 7:5, **used to work**; 1 Cor 12:6, **brings about**; 12:11, **activates**; Jas 5:16, **has** *powerful* **effects**; ❼ LXX, Num 8:24; Prov 21:6

ἐνέργημα, ατος, τό$_3$ {ἐν + ἔργον} ❷ 1 Cor 12:6, 10, **what activates effects**[NIGTC]

ἐνεργής, ές$_{3.3}$ *adj.* ❸ 1 Cor 16:9; Phlm 6; Heb 4:12, **effective**

ἐνευλογέω[con] {ἐν + εὖ + λέγω} ❷[fpi3p] Acts 3:25; Gal 3:8, **will be blessed**; ❽ LXX; 5x Gen

ἐνέχω ❸ Mark 6:19, **nursed a grudge**[ZEC]; Luke 11:53, **held an** *intense* **grudge**; Gal 5:1, **to be subjected to**; ❹ LXX, Gen 49:23, **to embitter, provoke**[Waltke]

ἐνθάδε {ἔνθα} *adv.* ❽ (5x Acts) Acts 10:18, **there**; 16:28 **here**; ① LXX, 3 Macc 6:25

ἔνθεν *adv.* ❷ Matt 17:20; Luke 16:26, **here**; (74x LXX; 44x Ezek!)

ἐνθυμέομαι {ἐν + θυμός} ❷ Matt 1:20, **to reflect on**[ZEC]; 9:4, **to think**; (21x LXX)

ἐνθύμησις, εως, ἡ$_3$ ❹ Matt 9:4; 12:25; Heb 4:12, **thoughts**; Acts 17:29, **imagination**

ἔνι {ἐν + εἰμί} ❻ 1 Cor 6:5, **there is found**[NIGTC]; Gal 3:28,[3x] **there is** *neither . . . nor* = Col 3:11, **there is** *not*; Jas 1:17, **does** *not change*; ❷ LXX, 4 Macc 4:22; Sir 37:2

ἐνιαυτός, οῦ, ὁ$_2$ {ἕνος + αὔτος} (14x) John 11:49; Acts 11:26; Gal 4:10; Rev 9:15, **year**; Heb 10:3, κατ᾽ **ἐνιαυτόν**, **year** *after* **year**[NIGTC]; (150x LXX; 17x Lev, 16x 1 Kgs)

ἐνίστημι ❼ Rom 8:38, **things present**; 1 Cor 7:26, **impending**[NIGTC]; 2 Thess 2:2, **has**

comeNIGTC; Polyb. *Hist.* 1.71.4, **to be confronted**ZEC; (13x LXX; 9x 1–4 Macc, **to be at war**)

ἐν**ισχύω** ❷ Luke 22:43; Acts 9:19, **to strengthen**; (54x LXX; 8x Judg, 7x Gen)

ἐννέα$_3$ *indecl.* ❺ Matt 18:12 = Luke 15:4; Matt 18:13 = Luke 15:7, *ninety-***nine**; (37x LXX)

ἐν**νεύω** ①iai3p Luke 1:62, **they were making signs**ZEC; ❷ LXX, Prov 6:13; 10:10, **to wink** *the eye*; Aristoph. *fr.* 77, **to nod, give a signal**

ἔν**νοια, ας, ἡ**$_{1\alpha}$ {ἐν + νοῦς} ❷ Heb 4:12, **intentions**; 1 Pet 4:1, **hearts**Keen1P; (13x LXX; 12x Prov)

ἔν**νομος, ον**$_{2.2}$ *adj.* ❷ Acts 19:39, **regular**; 1 Cor 9:21, **subject to the law**; ①gfs LXX, Sir 14

ἔν**νυχος, ον**$_{2.2}$ {ἐν + νύξ} ① *adv.* Mark 1:35, (*three advs*) πρωῒ **ἔννυχα** λίαν, *lit.*, *early morning*, **at night**, *very*BHGNT; ①afs *adj.*LXX, 3 Macc 5:5, **through the night**

ἐν**οικέω**con {ἐν + οἶκος} ❺ Rom 8:11; 2 Cor 6:16; 2 Tim 1:14, **to live**; 1:5, *faith that first* **lived**; (39x LXX; 22x Isa, 6x Jer)

ἐνόντα → **ἔνειμι**, *pres act. ptc. nmp*, Luke 11:41, *what* **is within**, τὰ **ἐνόντα**

ἐν**ορκίζω** {ἐν + ὅρκος} ①pai1s 1 Thess 5:27, **I charge** *you*

ἑ**νότης, ητος, ἡ**$_3$ ❷afs Eph 4:3, 13, **unity**

ἐν**οχλέω**con {ἐν + ὄχλος} ❷ Luke 6:18, **unhinged**; Heb 12:15, **causing trouble**, ❻ LXX

ἔν**οχος, ον**$_{2.2}$ {ἐν + ἔχω} *adj.* (10x; 5x Matt) Matt 5:21–22,4x **subject to**; Mark 3:29, **guilty**; 14:64, **worthy** *of death*; 1 Cor 11:27, *will be* **held accountable**NIGTC; Heb 2:15, **who were held** *in slavery*EGG; Jas 2:10, *has become* **answerable**ZEC; (22x LXX; 6x Lev)

ἔν**ταλμα, ατος, τό**$_3$ {ἐντολή} ❸anp Matt 15:9; Mark 7:7; Col 2:22, **commands**; ❹ LXX

ἐν**ταφιάζω** {ἐν + θάπτω} ❷ Matt 26:12, **to prepare for burial**; John 19:40, **burial** *custom*; ❷ LXX, Gen 50:2,2x **to embalm**

ἐν**ταφιασμός, οῦ, ὁ**$_2$ {ἐν + θάπτω} ❷ Mark 14:8; John 12:7, **burial**

ἐν**τέλλω** {ἐντολή} (15x; 11x Gs) Matt 4:6 = Luke 4:10, **to give orders**; John 8:5, **to command**; Heb 9:20, **to ordain**EGG; 11:22, **had given instructions**

ἐν**τεῦθεν** {ἔνθα} *adv.* (10x; 6x John) Luke 4:9, **from here**; John 2:16, **of here**; (28x LXX; 8x Exod)

ἔν**τευξις, εως, ἡ**$_3$ {ἐν + τυγχάνω} ❷ 1 Tim 2:1, **appeal**; 4:5, **prayer of thanksgiving**NIGTC; ①gfs LXX, 2 Macc 4:8, **prayer**

ἔν**τιμος, ον**$_{2.2}$ {ἐν + τιμή} *adj.* ❺ Luke 7:2, **valuable**; 14:8, **more distinguished**; Phil 2:29, *to hold* **in esteem**BEC; 1 Pet 2:4, **priceless**; 2:6, **invaluable**Keen1P; (30x LXX; 7x Neh)

ἐν**τολή, ῆς, ἡ**$_{1\eta}$ (67x) Luke 1:8; Rom 7:8–136x; Eph 6:2, **commandment(s)**; Mark 7:8; 1 John 2:7–84x; Rev 12:17, **command(s)**; Acts 17:15, **instructions**; (230x LXX; 44x Pss, 40x Deut)

ἐν**τόπιος, α, ον**$_{2.1.2}$ {ἐν + τόπος} *adj.* ①nmp Acts 21:12, **local** *believers*ZEC

ἐντός *impr. prep.* ❷ Matt 23:26, **inside** *of the cup*; Luke 17:21, **in** *your grasp*;*JG-M* 33 ❼ LXX; 1 Macc 4:48; Ps 38:4 (39:3), **within**

ἐν**τρέπω** ❾ Matt 21:37 = Mark 12:6 = Luke 20:13; Heb 12:9, **to respect**; 1 Cor 4:14, **to bring you to shame**NIGTC; 2 Thess 3:14; Titus 2:8, **to be ashamed**; (46x LXX; 8x 2 Chr:Pss:Isa)

ἐν**τρέφω** ①pmp.nms 1 Tim 4:6, *mid.*, **to be nourished**

ἔν**τρομος, ον**$_{2.2}$ *adj.* ❸ Acts 7:32 **ἔντρομος** δὲ γενόμενος, *began* **to tremble**; 16:29; Heb 12:21, *hend.*, ἔκφοβός εἰμι καὶ **ἔντρομος**, *I am* **trembling** *with fear*; ❹ LXX, 1 Macc 13:2

ἐντροπή, ῆς, ἡ$_{1η}$ {ἐν + τρέπω} ❷[afs] 1 Cor 6:5; 15:34, *I say this to your* **shame** ❼ LXX, 6x Pss

ἐντρυφάω[con] {ἐν + τρυφή} ①[pap.nmp] 2 Pet 2:13, **to revel**[BEC]; ❺ LXX, Hab 1:10, **to scoff**

ἐντυγχάνω ❺ Acts 25:24, **to petition**; Rom 8:27, 34; Heb 7:25, **to intercede**; (13x LXX)

ἐντυλίσσω ❸ Matt 27:59 = Luke 23:53, **to wrap in**; John 20:7, **folded up**

ἐντυπόω[con] ①[pfmp.nfs] 2 Cor 3:7, **to be engraved**

ἐνυβρίζω ①[aap.nms] Heb 10:29, **to insult**

ἐνυπνιάζομαι {ἐν + ὕπνος} ❷ Acts 2:17; Jude 8, **to dream**; (17x LXX; 6x Gen)

ἐνύπνιον, ου, τό$_2$ ①[dnp] Acts 2:17, **dreams**; (78x LXX; 24x Gen, 18x Dan)

ἐνώπιον {ἐν + ὁράω} *impr. prep.* (94x) Ⓐ ***proximity***, Rev 4:10, **before** *the throne*; John 20:30, **in the presence** *of his disciples*; Ⓑ ***perception***, Acts 6:5, **in the opinion of**; Ⓒ ***advocacy***, Rev 13:14, **on behalf** *of the beast*; Ⓓ ***moral accountability***, Luke 15:21, *I have sinned* **against** *heaven*; (489x LXX; 99x 1–2 Sam)

Ἐνώς, ὁ$_3$ *indecl.* ①[gms] Luke 3:38, **Enos**; ❼ LXX, Gen 4:26–5:11[6x]; 1 Chr 1:1

ἐνωτίζομαι ①[amimp2p] {ἐν + οὖς} Acts 2:14, **to pay close attention to**; (35x LXX; 11x Pss)

Ἑνώχ, ὁ$_3$ *indecl.* ❸ Luke 3:37; Heb 11:5; Judg 1:14, **Enoch**; (19x LXX; 11x Gen)

ἕξ$_3$ *indecl.* (13x) Matt 17:1 = Mark 9:2, **six**; Rev 13:18, ἑξακόσιοι ἑξήκοντα **ἕξ**, *six hundred sixty*-**six**

ἐξαγγέλλω {ἐκ + ἄγγελος} ❷ Mark 16:8; 1 Pet 2:9, **to proclaim**; (12x LXX; 8x Pss)

ἐξαγοράζω {ἐκ + ἀγορά} ❹ Gal 3:13; 4:5, **to purchase our deliverance**[KeenG]; Eph 5:16 = Col 4:5, **making the most** *of the time*; ①[pai2p] LXX, Dan 2:8, **stalling** *for time*[LES]

ἐξάγω {ἐκ + ἄγω} (12x; 8x Acts) Mark 15:20; John 10:3; Acts 7:36; Heb 8:9, **to lead out**; (216x LXX; 33x Exod, 25x Deut, 19x Ezek)

ἐξαιρέω[con] {ἐκ + αἱρέω} ❽ Matt 5:29, **to gouge out**; Acts 7:10; 12:11; Gal 1:4, **to deliver, rescue**; (140x LXX; 16x Pss, 12x Isa)

ἐξαίρω {ἐκ + αἴρω}①[aaimp2p] 1 Cor 5:13, **banish** *the evil man!*[NIGTC]; (213x LXX; 35x Num)

ἐξαιτέω {ἐκ + αἰτέω} ①[ami3s] Luke 22:31, *Satan* **has asked**

ἐξαίφνης {ἐκ + ἄφνω} *adv.* ❺ Mark 13:36; Luke 2:13; Acts 9:3, **suddenly**; (10x LXX)

ἐξακολουθέω[con] {ἐκ + ἀκόλουθος} ❸ 2 Pet 1:16; 2:2, 15, **to follow**; ❼ LXX, Job 31:9

ἑξακόσιοι, αι, α$_{2.1.2}$ ❷ Rev 13:18, **ἑξακόσιοι** ἑξήκοντα ἕξ, **six hundred** *sixty-six*; 14:20, χιλίων **ἑξακοσίων**, *one thousand* **six hundred** *stadia*; (75x LXX; 14x Num, 11x 2 Chr)

ἐξαλείφω {ἐκ + ἀλείφω} ❺ Acts 3:19, **to be wiped out**; Col 2:14, **to blot out**[WPNT]; Rev 3:5, *never* **erase** . . . *from the book*; Rev 7:17, **to wipe away** *every tear*; (48x LXX) Exod 32:32, 33, **to erase** *me from the book*; Xen. *Hel.* 2.3.51, **to strike** *him* **off** *the roll*

ἐξάλλομαι {ἐκ + ἅλλομαι} ①[pmp.nms] Acts 3:8, **jumped up**; ❻ LXX, 1 Macc 13:44

ἐξανάστασις, εως, ἡ$_3$ {ἐκ + ἵστημι} ①[afs] Phil 3:11, **resurrection**; ①[afs] LXX, Gen 7:4, **the heights** *that I created* (LES)

ἐξανατέλλω {ἐκ + ἀνά + τέλλω} ❷[aai3s] Matt 13:5 = Mark 4:5, **to spring up**; ❺ LXX; 4x Pss

ἐξανίστημι {ἐκ + ἵστημι} ❸ Mark 12:19, **to raise up**; Luke 20:28, **to produce**; Acts 15:5, **to belong to**; (39x LXX; 5x Gen)

ἐξαπατάω[con] {ἐκ + ἀπάτη} ❻ *act.*, Rom 7:11; 2 Cor 11:3; 2 Thess 2:3; **to deceive**; *mid.*, 1 Cor 3:18, **to deceive oneself**; *pass.*, 1 Tim 2:14, **to be deceived**; ①[aainf] LXX, Exod 8:25 (8:29)

ἐξάπινα {ἐκ + ἄφνω} *adv.* ① Mark 9:8, **suddenly**; (15x LXX) Lev 21:4; Num 4:20

ἐξαπορέω[con] {ἐκ + ἀπό + πορεύομαι} ❷ 2 Cor 1:8; 4:8, **to experience deep despair**[BEC]

ἐξαποστέλλω {ἐκ + ἀπό + στέλλω} (13x; 10x LA) Gal 4:4, **to send**; Luke 20:10, **to send away**; Acts 11:22, **to send out**; (268x LXX; 44x Exod, 23x Judg)

ἐξαρτίζω {ἐκ + ἄρτι} ❷ Acts 21:5, *when our time* **was up**[ZEC]; 2 Tim 3:17, **having been fully equipped**[NIGTC]

ἐξαστράπτω {ἐκ + ἀστραπή} ①[pap.nms] Luke 9:29, **to flash like lightning**: *became* **dazzling** *white*; ❹ LXX, Nah 3:3; Ezek 1:4, 7; Dan 10:6

ἐξαυτῆς {ἐκ + αὐτός} *adv.* ❻ Mark 6:25, **right now**; Acts 11:11, **immediately**; Phil 2:23, **at that very moment**[ABC]

ἐξεγείρω {ἐκ + ἐγείρω} ❷ Rom 9:17; 1 Cor 6:14, **to raise up**; (82x LXX; 15x Pss, 9x Isa)

ἔξελε → ἐξαιρέω, *aor. act. imp. 2s,* Matt 5:29, **tear** *it* **out**

ἐξέλκω ①[pmp.nms] Jas 1:14, **dragging away**[KEL]; ❻ LXX, Gen 37:28, **yanked** *Joseph out of the pit*; Eur. *Hec.* 544, **extract** *the sword from the sheath*[BrDAG]

ἐξέραμα, ατος, τό$_3$ ①[ans] 2 Pet 2:22, **vomit**

ἐξεραυνάω[con] {ἐκ + ἔρομαι} ①[aai3p] 1 Pet 1:10, **to try hard**[Keen]; ①[aaim2p] LXX, Judg 18:2

ἐξέρχομαι {ἐκ + ἔρχομαι} (218x; 186x GA) Luke 1:22; Jas 3:10, **to come out**; Matt 5:26, *you will never* **get out**; 1 Thess 1:8, **has gone out**; Heb 13:13, **to go**; (669x LXX; 176x Pent)

ἔξεστιν *impers. verb* (31x; 20x Syn) Matt 12:2 = Mark 2:24 = Luke 6:2; John 5:10, **lawful**; Acts 2:29, **confidently**; 1 Cor 6:12[2x] = 10:23,[2x] **liberty to do** *all things* (*assertive autonomy; Corinthian maxim*)[NIGTC]; 2 Cor 12:4, **permitted**

ἐξετάζω {ἐκ + ἐτάζω} ❸ Matt 2:8; 10:11, **to inquire** *carefully*[EGG]; John 21:12, *no one dared* **to question**[EGG]; (12x LXX; 5x Sir) Deut 19:18, *make a careful* **investigation**

ἐξηγέομαι[con] {ἐκ + ἄγω} ❻ Luke 24:35, **to relate** *the things*; John 1:18, **to reveal**; Acts 10:8, **to tell**; 15:12, **to describe**; ❽ LXX, Lev 14:57, **to determine**

ἑξήκοντα$_3$ *indecl.* ❾ Matt 13:8, 23 = Mark 4:8, 20; 1 Tim 5:9, **sixty**; Luke 24:13, **sixty** *stadia*; Rev 13:18, ἑξακόσιοι **ἑξήκοντα** ἕξ, *six hundred* **sixty**-*six*; (77x LXX; 11x Num, 10x Gen)

ἐξήνεγκεν → ἐκφέρω, *aor. act. ind. 3s,* Mark 8:23, **to bring out**

ἑξῆς *adv.* ❺ Luke 7:11, **afterward**; Acts 21:1; 27:18, **the next day**; ❻ LXX, Deut 2:34

ἐξηχέω[con] {ἐκ + ἠκή} ①[pfai3s] 1 Thess 1:18, **to sound forth**; ❸ LXX, 3 Macc 3:2

ἕξις, εως, ἡ$_3$ {ἔχω} ①[afs] Heb 5:14, **ἕξιν, a mature state or condition**[EGG; NIVAC]; ❽ LXX, Dan 1:15, ἡ **ἕξις** τοῦ σώματος, **healthier**; Aristot. *E.N.* 1098b 33, **acquired condition**

ἐξίστημι {ἐκ + ἵστημι} (17x; 8x Acts) Mark 2:12; Acts 2:7, **to be amazed, astounded**; Mark 3:21, **He is out of his mind**[BHGNT]; 2 Cor 5:13, **to be out of one's mind**[BEC]; (68x LXX)

ἐξισχύω {ἐκ + ἰσχύς} *w/ inf.* ①[aas2p] Eph 3:18, **to be able**

ἔξοδος, οῦ, ὁ$_2$ {ἐκ + ὁδός} ❸ Luke 9:31, *his* **exodus**[ZEC]; Heb 11:22, *the* **exodus**; 2 Pet 1:15, *my* **departure**; (67x LXX); Aristoph. *Ve.* 582, *theatr.* **song of departure**, **finale**

ἐξοίσουσιν → ἐκφέρω, *fut. act. ind. 3p,* Acts 5:9; Lev 4:12, **to bring outside**

ἐξολεθρεύω {ἐκ + ὄλλυμι} ①[fpi3s] Acts 3:23, **shall be utterly rooted out**; (214x LXX)

ἐξομολογέω[con] {ἐκ + ὁμός + λέγω} (10x) Matt 3:6 = Mark 1:5; Phil 2:11; Jas 5:16, **to confess**; Luke 10:21; Rom 14:11, **to praise**; Luke 22:6, **to promise**; (121x LXX; 68x Pss)

ἐξορκίζω {ἐκ + ὅρκος} ①[pai1s] Matt 26:63, **I put you under solemn oath**[NIGTC]; ❷ LXX

ἐξορκιστής, οῦ, ὁ$_{1>}$ {ἐκ + ὅρκος} ①[gmp] Acts 19:13, **exorcists**

ἐξορύσσω {ἐκ + ὀρύσσω} ❷ Mark 2:4, **having dug through** (*the roof*); Gal 4:15, **you would have ripped** *your eyes* **right out**[KeenG]; ❸ LXX, Judg 16:21, **to gouge out**

ἐξουδενέω[con] {ἐκ + οὐδέ + εἷς} ①[aps3s] Mark 9:12, **to be rejected**; ❼ LXX

ἐξουθενέω[con] {ἐκ + οὔτε + εἷς} (11x) Gal 4:14, **to disdain**; 1 Cor 16:11, **to treat with contempt**; Acts 4:11, **to reject**; 1 Cor 1:28; 1 Thess 5:20, **to despise**; 1 Cor 6:4, *subst.*, **people of no esteem**; 2 Cor 10:10, *his speaking* **is disgraceful**[BEC]; ❽ LXX

ἐξουσία, ας, ἡ$_{1\alpha}$ {ἐκ + εἰμί} (102x; 21x Rev, 16x Luke) Ⓐ ***ability, freedom, power***, Acts 8:19; Ⓑ ***power of choice***, 2 Thess 3:9; Ⓒ ***entrusted authority***, Heb 13:10; Ⓓ ***dominant authority***, Jude 25; Rev 17:12; Ⓔ ***debatable rights***, 1 Cor 8:9, *this* **right** (*to choose*)[NIGTC]; Ⓕ Rom 13:1–3,[4x] *governing* **authorities**[TNTC]; Ⓖ 1 Cor 11:10, *to keep* **control** *of her head*-[NIGTC]; Ⓗ ***apocalyptic enclosure***, Rev 2:26, **will have authority**; (66x LXX; 22x Dan!)

ἐξουσιάζω {ἐκ + εἰμί} ❹ Luke 22:25, **to wield authority**; 1 Cor 6:12, **to take liberties** *with me*; 7:4,[2x] *does not* **have exclusive rights**; (14x LXX; 10x Eccl)

ἐξοχή, ῆς, ἡ$_{1\eta}$ {ἐκ + ἔχω} ①[afs] Acts 25:23, κατ' **ἐξοχήν**, **prominent** *men*; ① LXX, ἐπ' **ἐξοχῇ**, Job 39:28, *on a* **prominent point, cliff**

ἐξυπνίζω {ἐκ + ὕπνος} ①[aas1s] John 11:11, **to wake** *Lazarus* **up** *from* **κεκοίμηται**, *the sleep of death*; ❷ LXX, Job 14:12, **they will** *not* **stir** *from sleep* (ὕπνου)

ἔξυπνος, ον$_{2.2}$ {ἐκ + ὕπνος} *adj.* ①[nms] Acts 16:27, **to wake up**; ①[nms] LXX, 1 Esd 3:3

ἔξω {ἐκ} (63x; 52x GsA) Ⓐ ***adverb of place***, (44x) Matt 5:13, **out**; *subst.* Mark 4:11; Col 4:5; 1 Thess 4:12, **outsiders** = **unbelievers**; *anarth.* Rev 3:12,[L7 52] **outsiders**; *adj.* Acts 26:11, *the* **outside** *cities*; Ⓑ ***impr. prep.*** *w/ gen.*, (19x) Matt 12:46 = Mark 3:31 = Luke 8:20, **outside**; (104x LXX; 20x Lev, 13x Num)

ἔξωθεν {ἐκ + θεν} (13x) Ⓐ ***prepositional use of adv. of place*** (3x); Rev 11:2; 14:20, **outside**; (*possibly*) Matt 23:25, *the* **outside** *of the cup*[PrTh]; Ⓑ ***adverbial***, (10x); Luke 11:40, *he who made* **the outside**; 2 Cor 7:5, *conflicts* **on the outside**; (45x LXX; 12x Jer, 10x Ezek)

ἐξωθέω[con] {ἐκ + ὠθέω} ❷ Acts 7:45; 27:39, **to drive out**; (29x LXX; 11x Jer, 10x Ezek)

ἐξώτερος, α, ον$_{2.1.2}$ {ἐκ} ❸ τὸ **ἐξώτερον**[ans] Matt 8:12; 22:13; 25:30, **outer**; (22x LXX)

ἔοικα {εἰκών} ❷[pfai3s] Jas 1:6, 23, **to be like**; ❷ LXX, Job 6:3, 25

ἑορτάζω {ἑορτή} ①[pas1p] 1 Cor 5:8, *So*, **let us celebrate the Passover festival**; (16x LXX)

ἑορτή, ῆς, ἡ$_{1\eta}$ (25x; 17x John) Matt 26:5 = Mark 14:2; John 2:23, **feast**; (120x LXX)

ἐπαγγελία, ας, ἡ$_{1\alpha}$ {ἐπί + ἄγγελος} (52x) Acts 1:4; 13:23, **promise**; 23:21, **consent**; ❽ LXX, Esth 4:7; Amos 9:6

ἐπαγγέλλομαι {ἐπί + ἄγγελος} (15x; 4x Heb) Mark 14:11; Rom 4:21; Heb 6:13; Jas 2:5, **to promise**; 1 Tim 2:10; 6:21, **to profess, lay claim to**; (13x LXX; 4x 2 Macc)

ἐπάγγελμα, ατος, τό$_{3}$ {ἐπί + ἄγγελος} ❷ 2 Pet 1:4; 3:13, **promises**

ἐπάγω {ἐπί + ἄγω} ❸ Acts 5:28, ἐπαγαγεῖν ἐφ' ἡμᾶς, **to make** *us* **guilty**; 2 Pet 2:1, **will bring** *swift destruction*; 2:5, **he brought** *the flood*; (143x LXX; 23x Jer, 16x Ezek)

ἐπαγωνίζομαι {ἐπί + ἀγών} ①[pminf] Jude 3, **to contend** *for the faith*

ἐπαθροίζω {ἐπί + θρόος} ①[pmp.gmp] Luke 11:29, *when the crowds* **were increasing**

Ἐπαίνετος, ου, ὁ$_{2}$ ①[ams] Rom 16:5, **Epaenetus**

ἐπαινέω[con] {ἐπί + αἶνος} ❻ Rom 15:11, **to praise**; 1 Cor 11:2, **I give you full credit**[NIGTC]; 11:17, **continue** *my* **commendation**; 11:22,[2x] **to congratulate**; (28x LXX)

ἔπαινος, ου, ὁ$_{2}$ {ἐπί + αἶνος} (11x; 3x Eph) Rom 2:29; 1 Pet 1:7, **praise**; Rom 13:3, **approval**; 2 Cor 8:18, *subst.*, *is universally* **praised**[BEC]; Phil 4:8, **praiseworthy**; (10x LXX)

ἐπαίρω (19x; 11x LA) {ἐπί + αἴρω} *act.*, John 17:1, **to look up**; Luke 11:27, **to raise**; John 4:35,

to open; Acts 14:11; 22:22, **shouted** (*raised their voices*); 27:40, **hoisted** *the foresail*[BEC]; 2 Cor 11:20, *mid.*, **puts on airs** *around you*[BEC]; 1 Tim 2:8, **to lift up**; Acts 1:9, *pass.*, **to be taken up** (*the ascension*); (80x LXX; 14x Pss)

ἐπαισχύνομαι {ἐπί + αἶσχος} (11x; 3x 2 Tim) Mark 8:38[2x] = Luke 9:26[2x]; Rom 1:16; 2 Tim 1:8; Heb 2:11, **to be ashamed**; ❸ LXX, Job 34:19; Isa 1:29

ἐπαιτέω[con] {ἐπί + αἰτέω} ❷ Luke 16:3; 18:35, **to beg**; ❷ LXX, Ps 108:10 (109:10); Sir 40:28

ἐπακολουθέω[con] {ἐπί + ἀκόλουθος} ❹ Mark 16:20, **accompanying**; 1 Tim 5:10, **to devote oneself**; 1 Pet 2:21, **to follow**; (16x LXX; 4x Josh)

ἐπακούω {ἐπί + ἀκούω} ①[aai1s] 2 Cor 6:2, **to listen to**; (102x LXX; 23x Pss)

ἐπακροάομαι[con] {ἐπί + ἀκροάομαι} ①[imi3p] Acts 16:25, **were listening**

ἐπάν {ἐπί + ἄν} *temp. conj.* ❸ Matt 2:8; Luke 11:22, 34, **when**; ① LXX, Bel 11

ἐπάναγκες {ἐπί + ἀνάγκη} *adv.* ① Acts 15:28, **essentials**

ἐπανάγω {ἐπί + ἀνά + ἄγω} ❸ Matt 21:18, **to return**; Luke 5:3, 4, **to put out** (*from shore*); ❺ LXX, 2 Macc 9:21; Zeph 4:12

ἐπαναμιμνήσκω {ἐπί + ἀνά + μιμνήσκομαι} ①[pap.nms] Rom 15:15, **to remind**

ἐπαναπαύομαι[con] {ἐπί + ἀνά + παύω} ❷ Luke 10:6, **to rest**; Rom 2:17, **to rely on**; (10x LXX; 4x 2 Kgs)

ἐπανέρχομαι {ἐπί + ἀνά + ἔρχομαι} ❷ Luke 10:35; 19:15, **to return**; ❻ LXX, Gen 50:5

ἐπανίστημι {ἐπί + ἀνά + ἵστημι} ❷ Matt 10:21 = Mark 13:12, **to rebel**[ZEC]; (28x LXX)

ἐπανόρθωσις, εως, ἡ$_{3}$ {ἐπί + ἀνά + ὀρθός} ①[afs] 2 Tim 3:16, **correction**; ❷ LXX

ἐπάνω {ἐπί + ἀνά} *impr. prep.* (19x; 8x Matt) Ⓐ ***prep. w/gen.*** (16x) Matt 21:7, *Jesus sat* **upon** *their cloaks*; Luke 19:17, *you shall have authority* **over** *ten cities*[BDAG 359c]; Rev 6:8, (***Death***) *was sitting* **atop** it (*the pale horse*)[BEC]; Ⓑ ***adverbial*** (3x) Luke 11:44, *walk* **over** *them* **(graves)**; John 3:31[2x], *from the realm* **above**[EGG]; 1 Cor 15:6, *he appeared to* **over** *five hundred brothers*; (121x LXX; 35x Num, 11x Gen)

ἐπάρατος, ον$_{2.2}$ {ἐπί + ἀρά} *adj.* ①[nmp] John 7:49, **under God's curse**[EGG]

ἐπαρκέω[con] {ἐπί + ἀρκέω} ❸ 1 Tim 5:10, 16,[2x] **to help**; ❷ LXX, 1 Macc 8:26, 11:35

ἐπαρχεία, ας, ἡ$_{1α}$ {ἐπί + ἀρκέω} ❷ Acts 23:34; 25:1, **province**

ἔπαυλις, εως, ἡ$_{3}$ {ἐπί + αὐλή} ①[nfs] Acts 1:20, **homestead**[ZEC]; (39x LXX; 9x Josh, 8x Num)

ἐπαύριον {ἐπί + αὔριον} *adv.* (17x; 10x Acts, 5x John) Matt 27:62; Mark 11:12; John 1:29; Acts 10:23; 20:7, **on the next day**[IL]; (23x LXX) Gen 19:34

Ἐπαφρᾶς, ᾶ, ὁ$_{1α}$ ❸ Col 1:7; 4:12; Phil 1:23, **Epaphras**

ἐπαφρίζω {ἐπί + ἀφρός} ①[pap.nnp] Jude 13, **foaming up**

Ἐπαφρόδιτος, ου, ὁ$_{2}$ ❷ Phil 2:25; 4:18, **Epaphroditus**

ἐπεγείρω {ἐπί + ἐγείρω} ❷ Acts 13:50; 14:2, **to stir up**; (18x LXX; 5x Isa)

ἐπέθηκαν → **ἐπιτίθημι**, *aor. act. ind. 3p*, Matt 21:7, **they laid** *their clothes*

ἐπεί *conj.* (26x; 9x Heb, 7x 1–2 Cor) Ⓐ ***causal***, Mark 15:42, **since**; Heb 4:6, **ἐπεὶ οὖν**, **since** *therefore*[EGG]; Heb 9:26, **otherwise**[EGG]; Ⓑ ***temporal***, *var. reading*, Luke 7:1, **after** (38x LXX)

ἐπειδή {ἐπί + δή} *conj.* (10x) Luke 7:1, **when**; 1 Cor 1:21, **since**; (20x LXX; 6x Gen)

ἐπειδήπερ {ἐπί + δέ + περ} *conj.* ① Luke 1:1, **inasmuch as**[EGG]

ἐπεῖδεν → **ἐφοράω**, *aor. act. ind. 3s*, Luke 1:25, **looked favorably upon me**[ZEC]

ἔπειμι {ἐπί + εἰμί} ❺[pap.dfs] (Acts) *lit.*, **be next**; 7:26, **on the following** *day*; 23:11, **on the following** *night*; (10x LXX) Exod 8:18; 9:3

ἐπεισαγωγή, ῆς, ἡ$_{1η}$ {ἐπί + εἰς + ἄγω} ①[nfs] Heb 7:19, *a better hope* **is introduced**

ἐπεισέρχομαι ①[fmi3s] Luke 21:35, **to come upon**; ①[aai3p] LXX, 1 Macc 16:16, **to rush in**

ἔπειτα {ἐπί + εἶτα} *adv.* (16x) Ⓐ[1] ***simple sequential***,[EDNT] Gal 1:18, 21; 2:1, **then**; Ⓐ[2] ***ambig. content or temporal series linkage***, 1 Cor 12:28, *first, second, third,* **then**; 15:5–8, **then** . . . , **then** . . . ; *and* **then** *last*; Ⓑ ***temporal or content linkage***, 1 Cor 15:23, *first* . . . , **then** . . . , **then** (*time sequence*); Heb 7:2, *first* . . . , *and* **then** (*subject sequence*); ❷ LXX, 4 Macc 6:3; Isa 16:2

ἐπέκεινα {ἐπί + ἐκεῖ} *impr. prep.* ① Acts 7:43, **beyond** *Babylon*; (17x LXX)

ἐπεκτείνομαι {ἐπί + ἐκ + τείνω} ①[pmp.nms] Phil 3:13, **to reach forward**

ἐπενδύομαι {ἐπί + ἐν + δύω} ❷[aminf] 2 Cor 5:2, 4, **to put on**

ἐπενδύτης, ου, ὁ$_{1>}$ {ἐπί + ἐν + δύω} ①[ams] John 21:7, **garment**; ①[amp] LXX, 2 Sam 13:18

ἐπενεγκεῖν → **ἐπιφέρω**, *aor. act. inf.*, Jude 9, **to bring**

ἐπέρχομαι {ἐπί + ἔρχομαι} ❾ (4x Acts) Luke 1:35; Jas 5:1, **to come upon**; Luke 11:22, **to attack**[EGG]; Acts 8:24; 13:40, **to happen**; Eph 2:7, **coming** *ages*

ἐπερωτάω[con] {ἐπί + ἐρωτάω} (56x; 25x Mark, 17x Luke) Matt 12:10; Mark 5:9; Luke 2:46; John 9:23; Acts 5:27; Rom 10:20; 1 Cor 14:35, **to ask**; (68x LXX; 13x 1–2 Sam, 5x Ezek)

ἐπερώτημα, ατος, τό$_{3}$ {ἐπί + ἐρωτάω} ①[nns] 1 Pet 3:21, **commitment**

ἐπέχω {ἐπί + ἔχω} ❺ Luke 14:7, **to notice**; Acts 3:5; 1 Tim 4:16, **to fix one's attention on**; Acts 19:22, **to stay**; Phil 2:16, **to hold firm to**; (22x LXX; 9x Sir)

ἐπηρεάζω ❷ Luke 6:28, **to mistreat**; 1 Pet 3:16, **to slander**[Keen1P]

ἐπί, ἐπ', ἐφ' *prep.* (890x; 330x LA) Ⓐ ***grounds***, 1 Tim 5:19, **based on**; Ⓑ ***cause***, Phlm 7, **because of**; Ⓒ ***reference***, 1 Cor 9:10, **regarding**; Ⓓ ***oversight***, Luke 12:44, **in charge of**; Ⓔ ***ascensive***, 2 Cor 7:13, **in addition to**[BEC!]; Ⓕ ***purpose***, Matt 3:7, **for** *baptism*; Ⓖ ***theologically notable***,[PrTh!] Acts 4:26, **in** *the same place*[Keen1]; Rom 5:12, **ἐφ' ᾧ, because** *all have sinned*[ZEC, BHGNT]; (6,973x LXX; 559x Ezek, 496x Jer, 397x Pss)

ἐπιβαίνω ❻ Matt 21:5, **to ride**; Acts 20:18, **to set foot**; 21:2, **to board**; (58x LXX; 7x Jer)

ἐπιβάλλω (18x; 9x LA) Matt 9:16 = Luke 5:36, **to put on** *a patch*; Luke 15:12, *the share that* **belongs** *to me*; John 7:30, **to lay** *a hand on*[EGG]; Acts 4:3, **they seized** *them*; 12:1, **to arrest**; 1 Cor 7:35, *not* **to throw** *a tight rein*; (71x LXX; 9x Num:Deut:Isa)

ἐπιβαρέω[con] {ἐπί + βαρύς} ❸ 2 Cor 2:5[BEC]; 1 Thess 2:9; 2 Thess 3:8, **to burden**

ἐπιβιβάζω {ἐπί + βαίνω} ❸ Luke 10:34, **to put on**; 19:35, **to throw on**; Acts 23:24, **to ride**; (12x LXX; 4x 1 Kgs)

ἐπιβλέπω ❸ Luke 1:48; 9:38; Jas 2:3, **to look on with favor**; (108x LXX; 16x Pss, 11x 1 Sam)

ἐπίβλημα, ατος, τό$_{3}$ {ἐπί + βάλλω} ❹ Matt 9:16 = Mark 2:21 = Luke 5:36,[2x] **garment**; ①[anp] LXX, Isa 3:22, **the festal robes**

ἐπιβουλή, ῆς, ἡ$_{1η}$ {ἐπί + βούλομαι} ❹ (Acts) 9:24; 20:19; 23:30, **plot**; ❽ LXX; 3x 3 Macc

ἐπιγαμβρεύω {ἐπί + γάμος} ①[fai3s] Matt 22:24, **to marry**; ❾ LXX, 4x 1 Sam

ἐπίγειος, ον$_{2.2}$ {ἐπί + γῆ} *adj.* ❼ 1 Cor 15:40; Phil 3:19; Jas 3:15, **earthly**; *subst.*, Phil 2:10, **earth**

ἐπιγίνομαι ①[amp.gms] Acts 28:13, *a south wind* **sprang up**; ❷[pmp.dmp] LXX, 3 Macc 2:5; Ep. Jer. 47, **to come afterward**

ἐπιγινώσκω (44x; 20x LA) Matt 7:16; Acts 3:10, **to recognize**; Matt 11:27[2x]; Mark 2:8; 1 Cor 12:12[2x]; 2 Pet 2:21, **to know**; Acts 22:29, **to realize**; 28:1, **to find out**; 2 Cor 1:13–14,[3x] **to understand**[BEC]; 13:5, **to examine**; (144x LXX; 29x Ezek, 14x Sir, 12x Gen)

ἐπίγνωσις, εως, ἡ$_{3}$ {ἐπί + γινώσκω} (20x) Rom 1:28, ἔχειν ἐν ἐπιγνώσει, *idiom.*, **to recognize** *God*[BDAG]; Rom 3:20; Eph 1:17; Heb 10:26; 2 Pet 2:20, **knowledge**; Phlm 6, *by* **knowing**; ❼ LXX, Prov 2:5

ἐπιγραφή, ῆς, ἡ$_{1η}$ {ἐπί + γράφω} ❺ Matt 22:20 = Mark 12:16 = Luke 20:24; Mark 15:26 = Luke 23:38, **inscription**

ἐπιγράφω ❺ *act.*, Heb 8:10, 10:16, **I will write**; *pass.*, Mark 15:26, **written**; Acts 17:23; Rev 21:12, **was/were inscribed**; ❺ LXX, Num 7:3

ἔπιδε → ἐφοράω, *aor. act. imp. 2s*, Acts 4:29, **looked favorably upon me**[ZEC]

ἐπιδείκνυμι ❼ Matt 16:1; Luke 17:14; Acts 9:39; Heb 6:17, **to show**; (13x LXX; 6x 4 Macc)

ἐπιδέχομαι ❷ 3 John 9, **to receive**; 10, **to welcome**; (21x LXX; 11x 1 Macc)

ἐπιδημέω[con] {ἐπί + δῆμος} ❷[pap.nmp] Acts 2:10, **visitors**; 17:21, **foreigners**[ZEC]

ἐπιδιατάσσομαι {ἐπί + διά + τάσσω} ①[pmi3s] Gal 3:15, **that has been validated**[KeenG]

ἐπιδίδωμι ❾ (5x Luke) Matt 7:9, 10 = Luke 11:1; Acts 27:15, **to give**; 15:30, **to deliver**; (12x LXX; 4x Sir)

ἐπιδιορθόω[con] {ἐπί + διά + ὀρθός} ①[ams2s] Titus 1:5, **that you might set right**[NIGTC]

ἐπιδύω ①[paimp3s] Eph 4:26, **don't let** *the sun* **go down**; ❸ LXX, Deut 24:15, **sunset**

ἐπιείκεια, ας, ἡ$_{1η}$ {ἐπί + εἰκῶν} ❷ Acts 24:4, **customary graciousness**[ZEC]; 2 Cor 10:1, **clemency** *of Christ*[BEC]; (10x LXX; 2x Dan)

ἐπιεικής, ές$_{3.3}$ {ἐπί + εἰκῶν} *adj.* ❺ Phil 4:5, **graciousness**; Jas 3:17; 1 Pet 2:18, **gentle**; Titus 3:2, **gentleness**; ❹ LXX, Ps 85:5 (86:5), **forgiving**

ἐπιζητέω[con] (13x; 5x LA) Matt 6:32, **to strive for**[ZEC]; Heb 11:14, **to seek**; Matt 16:4, **to demand**; Luke 4:42, **to search for**; Acts 12:19, **to organize a search**[ZEC]; Acts 13:7, **to wish**[ZEC]; (16x LXX; 5x 2 Kgs)

ἐπιθανάτιος, ον$_{2.2}$ {ἐπί + θνῄσκω} *adj.* ①[amp] 1 Cor 4:9, **doomed to die**[NIGTC]; ①[gmp] LXX, Bel 31

ἐπίθες → ἐφιτίθημι, *aor. act. imp. 2s*, Matt 9:18, **lay** *your hands*

ἐπίθεσις, εως, ἡ$_{3}$ {ἐπί + τίθημι} ❹ Acts 8:18; 1 Tim 4:14; 2 Tim 1:6; Heb 6:2, **laying on** *of hands*; ❺ LXX, 2 Chr 25:27; 2 Macc 4:41

ἐπιθυμέω[con] {ἐπί + θυμός} (16x; 4x Luke) Matt 5:28, **to lust**; 13:17; Jas 4:2, **to desire**; Luke 22:15, **I** *greatly* **desired**; Acts 20:33, **to covet**; 1 Cor 10:6, **to crave**[NIGTC]; 1 Pet 1:12, **want** *to investigate*[Keen1P]; Rev 9:6, **to long to**[NICNT]; (55x LXX; 7x Deut, 6x Isa) Exod 20:17

ἐπιθυμητής, οῦ, ὁ$_{1>}$ {ἐπί + θυμός} ①[amp] 1 Cor 10:6, εἰς τὸ μὴ εἶναι ἡμᾶς **ἐπιθυμητὰς** κακῶν; *purp.* **εἰς** *with art. inf.* **τὸ εἶναι** *and the acc. of gen. ref. with* **ἐπιθυμητάς** *in the predicate* (*functions like a verb*); *so that we might not* **crave** *evil*; ❸ LXX, Ezek 26:12

ἐπιθυμία, ας, ἡ$_{1α}$ {ἐπί + θυμός} (38x; 8x 1–2 Pet) Jude 16, **desire(s)**; Luke 22:15, **ἐπιθυμίᾳ** ἐπεθύμησα, *I* **greatly** *desired*; Phil 1:23, **I long** *to depart*; (74x LXX; 14x 4 Macc)

ἐπικαθίζω {ἐπί + κατά + ἵζω} ①[aai3s] Matt 21:7, **to sit upon**; ❽ LXX, Gen 31:34

ἐπικαλέω[con] (30x; 20x Acts) Matt 10:25; Acts 7:59; 1 Cor 1:2, **to call**; Acts 4:36, **named**; 1 Pet 1:17, **to appeal to**; Jas 2:7, *pass.*, **to be called** *upon you*; (184x LXX; 30x Pss)

ἐπικάλυμμα, ατος, τό$_{3}$ {ἐπί + καλύπτω} ①[ans] 1 Pet 2:16, **cloak**; ❹ LXX, Exod 26:14

ἐπικαλύπτω ①[api3p] Rom 4:7, **to be covered**; (19x LXX; 3x Gen) Gen 7:19

ἐπικατάρατος, ον$_{2.2}$ {ἐπί + κατά + ἀρά} *adj.* ❷ Gal 3:10, 13, **is cursed**; (44x LXX; 19x Deut)

ἐπίκειμαι ❼ Luke 5:1, **to swarm around**; 23:23, **to keep demanding**[ZEC]; John 11:38, **to lie**

against it; 21:9, *fish* **lying on it**; Acts 27:20, **to press upon**; Heb 9:10, **to impose**; ❼ LXX, 1 Macc 6:57, **to press urgently**

ἐπι**κέλλω** {ἐπί + κελεύω} ①[aai3p] Acts 27:41, **to run aground**

Ἐπικούρειος, ου, ὁ$_{2}$ ①[gmp] Acts 17:18, **Epicurean**

ἐπι**κουρία, ας, ἡ**$_{1α}$ {ἐπί + κείρω} ①[gfs] Acts 26:22, **help**; ①[gfs] LXX, Wis 13:18

ἐπι**κρίνω** ①[aai3s] Luke 23:24, **to decree**; ❷ LXX, 2 Macc 4:2

ἐπι**λαμβάνομαι** {ἐπί + λαμβάνω} (19x) Matt 14:31, **to grab**; 1 Tim 6:12, **to take hold of**; Luke 20:20, **to trap**[ZEC]; Acts 21:30, **to seize**; Heb 2:16,[2x] **to reach out** (*first occurrence*), **to help** (*second occurrence*)

ἐπι**λανθάνομαι** {ἐπί + λανθάνω} ❽ (3x Heb) Matt 16:5 = Mark 8:14; Phil 3:13; Heb 6:10; Jas 1:24, **to forget**; Heb 13:16, **to neglect**; (121x LXX; 36x Pss, 14x Jer)

ἐπι**λέγω** ❷ John 5:2, **called**; Acts 15:40, **chose**; (23x LXX; 13x 1 Macc)

ἐπι**λείπω** ①[fai3s] Heb 11:32, *time* **is too short**

ἐπι**λείχω** ①[iai3p] Luke 16:21, **to lick**

ἐπιλελησμένον → **ἐφιλανθάνομαι**, (*periphr*) *pf. mid. ptc. nms*, Luke 12:6, **is forgotten**

ἐπι**λησμονή, ῆς, ἡ**$_{1η}$ {ἐπί + λανθάνω} ①[gfs] Jas 1:25, **forgetful**; ①[gfs] LXX, Wis 13:18

ἐπί**λοιπος, ον**$_{2.2}$ {ἐπί + λείπω} *adj.* ① 1 Pet 4:2, *the* **rest** *of their lives*; (23x LXX; 7x 1 Macc)

ἐπί**λυσις, εως, ἡ**$_{3}$ ①[gfs] 2 Pet 1:20, **interpretation**

ἐπι**λύω** ❷ Mark 4:34, **he explained**; Acts 19:39, **to resolve, decide, settle**

ἐπι**μαρτυρέω**[con] ①[pap.nms] 1 Pet 5:12, **to testify**; ①[ami1s] LXX, Neh 13:15, **to warn**

ἐπι**μέλεια, ας, ἡ**$_{1α}$ {ἐπί + μέλω} ①[gfs] Acts 27:3, **care**; (10x LXX; 4x Prov)

ἐπι**μελέομαι**[con] {ἐπί + μέλω} ❸ Luke 10:34, 35, **to take care of** (*a victim*); 1 Tim 3:5, **to take care of** (*God's church*); ❺ LXX, Gen 44:21

ἐπι**μελῶς** {ἐπί + μέλω} *adv.* ① Luke 15:8, **carefully**; (15x LXX; 6x 1 Esd)

ἐπι**μένω** (16x; 6x Acts) Rom 6:1, **to continue**; Gal 1:18, **to stay**; 1 Cor 16:7, **to spend**; 1 Tim 4:16, **to persevere**; ①[aainf] LXX, Exod 12:39, **to wait**

ἐπι**νεύω** ①[aai3s] Acts 18:20, οὐκ **ἐπένευσεν**, **he declined**; ❺ LXX, 1 Macc 6:57

ἐπί**νοια, ας, ἡ**$_{1η}$ {ἐπί + νοῦς} ① Acts 8:22, **intent**; ❽ LXX, 2 Macc 12:45, **thought**

ἐπι**ορκέω**[con] {ἐπί + ὅρκος} ①[fai2s] Matt 5:33, **to swear falsely**; ❷ LXX, Wis 14:28

ἐπί**ορκος, ον**$_{2.2}$ *adj.* ①[dmp] 1 Tim 1:10, **perjurers**; ①[nms] LXX, Zech 5:3

ἐπιούσῃ[5x] → **ἔπειμι**, (*Acts only*) *pres ptc. dfs*, Acts 23:11, **to stand by**; **to be present**

ἐπι**ούσιος, ον**$_{2.2}$ *adj.* ❷[ams] Matt 6:11 = Luke 11:3, **daily**

ἐπι**πίπτω** (11x; 8x Acts) Mark 3:10, **to push forward**; Luke 1:12; Rev 11:11, **to fall upon**; Acts 19:17, **to come upon**; 20:10, **to throw onself**; (52x LXX; 6x Gen)

ἐπι**πλήσσω** ①[aas2s] 1 Tim 5:1, **do not sharply rebuke**[NIGTC]

ἐπι**ποθέω**[con] {ἐπί + πόθος} ❾ Phil 2:26; 2 Tim 1:4, **to long for**; 2 Cor 5:2, **greatly desiring**[BEC]; 9:14, **feeling deep affection**[BEC]; Jas 4:5, **to yearn**; (13x LXX) Jer 13:14

ἐπι**πόθησις, εως, ἡ**$_{3}$ {ἐπί + πόθος} ❷[afs] 2 Cor 7:7, 11, **deep desire**[BEC]

ἐπι**πόθητος, ον**$_{2.2}$ {ἐπί + πόθος} *adj.* ①[vmp] Phil 4:1, **longed for**

ἐπι**ποθία, ας, ἡ**$_{1α}$ {ἐπί + πόθος} ①[afs] Rom 15:23, **ἐπιποθίαν** δὲ ἔχων, *idiom.*, **strongly desired**

ἐπι**πορεύομαι** ①[pmp.gmp] Luke 8:4, **journeyed** *to him*[ZEC]; ❺ LXX, Lev 26:33

ἐπι**ράπτω** {ἐπί + ῥαφίς} ①[pai3s] Mark 2:21, **to sew**

ἐπι**ρίπτω** ❷[aap.nmp] Luke 19:35, **throwing** *their clothes*; 1 Pet 5:7, **casting** *all your cares*

ἐπί**σημος, ον**$_{2.2}$ {ἐπί + σημεῖον} *adj.* ❷ Matt 27:16, **notorious**; Rom 16:7, **popular**; ❾ LXX

ἐπι**σιτισμός, οῦ, ὁ**$_{2}$ ①[ams] Luke 9:12, **provisions**; (13x LXX; 4x Josh)

ἐπι**σκέπτομαι** {ἐπί + σκοπός} (11x; 7x LA) Heb 2:6, **to care for**; Jas 1:27, **to visit**; Acts 6:3, **to look for**; 15:14, **to intervene**; (164x LXX; 49x Num, 19x Jer)

ἐπι**σκευάζομαι** {ἐπί + σκεῦος} ①[amp.nmp] Acts 21:15, **to get ready**

ἐπι**σκηνόω**[con] {ἐπί + σκηνή} ①[aas3s] 2 Cor 12:9, **might take up residence**[BEC]

ἐπι**σκιάζω** {ἐπί + σκιά} ❺ Matt 17:5 = Mark 9:7 = Luke 9:34, **enveloped** *them*; Acts 5:15, ἡ σκιὰ **ἐπισκιάσῃ**, *his shadow* **might shadow** *them*; ❹ LXX, Exod 40:35, **to settle upon**

ἐπι**σκοπέω**[con] {ἐπί + σκοπός} ❷[pap.nmp] Heb 12:15, **make sure**[EGG]; 1 Pet 5:2, **to watch over**[Keen1P]; ❹ LXX, Deut 11:12, *God* **cares for**

ἐπι**σκοπή, ῆς, ἡ**$_{1\eta}$ {ἐπί + σκοπός} ❹ Luke 19:44, **visitation**; Acts 1:20, **place of responsibility**[ZEC]; 1 Tim 3:1, **overseer**; 1 Pet 2:12, **when he comes**[Keen1P]; (45x LXX)

ἐπί**σκοπος, ου, ὁ**$_{2}$ ❺ Acts 20:28; Phil 1:1; 1 Tim 3:2; Titus 1:7, **overseers**; 1 Pet 2:25, **the Overseer**

ἐπι**σπάω**[con] ①[pmimp3s] 1 Cor 7:18, *mid.*, **let him** *not* **cover over his circumcision**[NIGTC]

ἐπι**σπείρω** ①[aai3s] Matt 13:25, **to sow**

ἐπί**σταμαι** {ἐπί + ἵστημι} (14x; 9x Acts) Mark 14:68; Jude 10, **to understand**; Acts 10:28, **to be well aware**; 18:25; 26:26; Heb 11:8; Jas 4:14, **to know**; (59x LXX; 9x Job, 8x Isa)

ἐπί**στασις, εως, ἡ**$_{3}$ {ἐπί + ἵστημι} ❷ Acts 24:12, *idiom.*, **ἐπίστασιν** ποιοῦντα ὄχλου, **causing the stop** *of a crowd*[EGG]; **to organize a crowd**[ZEC]; 2 Cor 11:28, **the daily weight**[BEC]

ἐπι**στάτης, ου, ὁ**$_{2>}$ {ἐπί + ἵστημι} ❼[vms] (Luke) 5:5; 8:24[2x] 17:13, **Master!**; (12x LXX)

ἐπι**στέλλω** ❸ Acts 15:20; 21:25; Heb 13:22, **to write**

ἐπι**στήμων, ον**$_{3.3}$ {ἐπί + ἵστημι} *adj.* ①[nms] Jas 3:13, **understanding**; (14x LXX; 5x Sir)

ἐπι**στηρίζω** ❹ Acts 14:22; 15:32, 41; 18:23, **to strengthen**; (13x LXX) Gen 28:13, *the Lord* **stood** *beside him*

ἐπι**στολή, ῆς, ἡ**$_{1\eta}$ {ἐπί + στέλλω} (24x) Acts 9:2; Rom 16:22; 2 Cor 3:1; Col 4:16; 2 Thess 2:2, **letter(s)**; (62x LXX; 20x 1 Macc)

ἐπι**στομίζω** {ἐπί + στόμα} ①[painf] Titus 1:11, **to silence**; Aristoph. *Eq.* 845, **to put on the bridle**

ἐπι**στρέφω** (36x; 18x LA) Matt 10:13; 2 Pet 2:22, **to return**; Mark 4:12; Acts 3:19; Jas 5:19, **to turn back**; 2 Cor 3:16, **to turn** *to the Lord*; (497x LXX; 83x 1–2 Kgs, 40x Pss:Jer)

ἐπι**στροφή, ῆς, ἡ**$_{1\eta}$ {ἐπί + στρέφω} ①[afs] Acts 15:3, **conversion**; (10x LXX) Ezek 42:11

ἐπι**συνάγω** ❽ (Syn) Matt 23:37 = Luke 13:34, **to gather together**; Matt 24:31 = Mark 13:27, **to gather**; Mark 1:33, **to assemble**; (47x LXX; 14x 1 Macc, 6x 1 Esd)

ἐπι**συναγωγή, ῆς, ἡ**$_{1\eta}$ {ἐπί + σύν + ἄγω} ❷ 2 Thess 2:1; Heb 10:25, **to gather together**; ①[afs] LXX, 2 Macc 2:7

ἐπι**συντρέχω** ①[pai3s] Mark 9:25, **to gather quickly**

ἐπι**σφαλής, ες**$_{3.3}$ {ἐπί + σφάλλω} *adj.* ①[gms] Acts 27.9, **dangerous**; ①[nfp] LXX, Wis 9:14

ἐπι**σχύω** {ἐπί + ἰσχύς} ①[iai3p] Luke 23:5, **to grow strong**; ❷ LXX, 1 Macc 6:6; Sir 29:1

ἐπι**σωρεύω** ①[fai3p] 2 Tim 4:3, **will multiply** *teachers*

ἐπι**ταγή, ῆς, ἡ**$_{1\eta}$ {ἐπί + τάσσω} ❼ Rom 16:26; 1 Cor 7:6; 2 Cor 8:8; 1 Tim 1:1; Titus 1:3, **ἐπιταγήν**[afs], **command**; Titus 2:15, **authority**; ❼ LXX, Wis 14:17

ἐπι**τάσσω** (10x) Mark 1:27 = Luke 4:36; Acts 23:2; Phlm 8, **to command**; (34x LXX) ἐπι**τελέω**[con] {ἐπί + τέλος} (10x) Heb 8:5, **to finish, complete**; 2 Cor 7:1; Phil 1:6, **to bring to completion**; 2 Cor 8:11,[2x] **finish** *what you started*[BEC]; Gal 3:3, **Are you completing yourselves** *with flesh*?[KeenG]; 1 Pet 5:9, **to be accomplished**; (29x LXX)

ἐπι**τήδειος, εία, ον**$_{2.1.2}$ {ἐπιτηδές} *adj.* ①[anp] Jas 2:16, *subst.*, **the needs** *of the body*; ❾ LXX, (7x 1–3 Macc)

ἐπι**τίθημι** (39x; 20x Syn) Acts 6:6, **to lay**; Matt 27:37, **to place**; Mark 3:16, **to give**; 1 Tim 5:22, **to appoint** (*to lay hands on*); Rev 22:18, **to add**; (264x LXX; 155x Pent)

ἐπι**τιμάω**[con] {ἐπί + τιμή} (29x; 27x Syn) Matt 8:26 = Mark 4:39 = Luke 8:24; 2 Tim 4:2; Jude 9, **to rebuke**; Mark 10:48, **to warn**; (11x LXX; 4x Pss)

ἐπι**τιμία, ας, ἡ**$_{1\alpha}$ ①[nfs] 2 Cor 2:6, **punishment**; ①[afs] LXX, Wis 3:10

ἐπι**τρέπω** (18x; 9x LA) Mark 5:13 = Luke 8:32; Heb 6:3, **to allow, permit**; 1 Cor 14:34, **to allow for** *silence*[NIGTC!]; 1 Tim 2:12, **I do** *not* **allow** *a woman to teach or control her husband*[PaG 298–312!]; ❽ LXX, 4 Macc 5:26

ἐπι**τροπή, ῆς, ἡ**$_{1\eta}$ {ἐπί + τρέπω} ①[gfs] Acts 26:12, **commission**; ①[afs] LXX, 2 Macc 13:14, **committing**

ἐπί**τροπος, ου, ὁ**$_2$ {ἐπί + τρέπω} ❸ Matt 20:8, **foreman**; Luke 8:3, **steward**; Gal 4:2, **guardian**; ❸ LXX, 2 Macc 11:1

ἐπι**τυγχάνω** ❺ Rom 11:7[2x]; Jas 4:2, **to obtain**; Heb 6:15; 11:33, **to receive**; ❷ LXX

ἐπι**φαίνω** ❹ Luke 1:79, **to give light**; Acts 27:20; Titus 2:11; 3:4, **to appear**; (24x LXX)

ἐπι**φάνεια, ας, ἡ**$_{1\alpha}$ {ἐπί + φαίνω} ❻ 2 Thess 2:8; 1 Tim 6:14; 2 Tim 1:10; 4:1, 8; Titus 2:13, **appearing**; (12x LXX; 6x 2 Macc) 2 Sam 7:23

ἐπι**φανής, ές**$_{3.3}$ {ἐπί + φαίνω} *adj.* ①[afs] Acts 2:20, **glorious**; (21x LXX; 7x 2 Macc)

ἐπι**φαύσκω** {ἐπί + φαίνω} ①[fai3s] Eph 5:14, **will shine**; ❸ LXX, Job 25:5; 31:26, **to shine**; 41:10, *light* **shines forth** *at its sneezing* (NETS)

ἐπι**φέρω** ❷ Rom 3:5, **to bring upon**; Jude 9, **to pronounce**; (17x LXX; 6x 1 Sam)

ἐπι**φωνέω**[con] {ἐπί + φωνή} ❹ Luke 23:21; Acts 12:22; 21:34; 22:24, **to shout**; ❸ LXX, 2 Macc 1:23, **to respond**

ἐπι**φώσκω** {ἐπί + φαίνω} ❷ Matt 28:1, **dawning**; Luke 23:54, **was about to begin**

ἐπι**χειρέω**[con] {ἐπί + χείρ} ❸ Luke 1:1, **undertaken**; Acts 9:29, **who kept attempting**; 19:13, **tried to evoke**; (12x LXX; 4x 2 Macc)

ἐπι**χέω** ①[pap.nms] Luke 10:34, **to pour on**; (22x LXX; 9x 1 Lev)

ἐπι**χορηγέω**[con] {ἐπί + χορός + ἄγω} ❺ 2 Cor 9:10; 2 Pet 1:11, **to provide**; Gal 3:5, **to supply**; Col 2:19, **to nourish**; 2 Pet 1:5, **to supplement**; ①[aas3s] LXX, Sir 25:22

ἐπι**χορηγία, ας, ἡ**$_{1\alpha}$ {ἐπί + χορός + ἄγω} ❷ Eph 4:16, **supporting**; Phil 1:19, **help**

ἐπι**χρίω** ❷[aai3s] John 9:6, 11, **to spread**

ἐπ**οικοδομέω**[con] {ἐπί + οἶκος + δῶμα} ❼ 1 Cor 3:10,[2x] 12, 14, **to build**; Eph 2:20, **having been built**[ZEC]; Jude 20, *as* **you build** *yourselves up*

ἐπ**ονομάζω** {ἐπί + ὄνομα} ①[pmi2s] Rom 2:17, *if* **you call yourself**; (35x LXX; 13x Gen)

ἐπ**οπτεύω** {ἐπί + ὁράω} ❷ 1 Pet 2:12; 3:2, **to see**

ἐπ**όπτης, ου, ὁ**$_2$ {ἐπί + ὁράω} ①[nmp] 2 Pet 1:16, **eyewitnesses**; ❹ LXX, 2 Macc 3:39

ἔπος, ους, τό$_3$ {ἔπω} ①[ans] Heb 7:9, ὡς **ἔπος** εἰπεῖν, **so to speak**; ①[anp] LXX, Sir 44:5

ἐπ**ουράνιος, ον**$_{2.2}$ {ἐπί + οὐρανός} *adj.* (19x; 6x Heb) 1 Cor 15:40,[2x] **heavenly**; Eph 1:3, *in* **the heavenly places** (ἐπουρανίοις[5xEph])[BWIII]; Phil 2:10, **in heaven**; ❺ LXX, 2 Macc 3:39

ἑπτά (88x; 55x Rev!, 9x Matt:Mark) Matt 16:10 = Mark 8:20^{2x}; Matt 15:36–37 = Mark 8:5–6; Acts 19:14; Rev 1:4,$^{2x\ \text{NIGTC!}}$ **seven**; (351x LXX; 62x Gen, 34x Num, 33x Lev)

ἑπτάκις {ἑπτά} *adv.* ❹ Matt 18:21–22^{2x} = Luke 17:4,^{2x} **seven times**; (24x LXX; 7x Lev)

ἑπτακισχίλιοι, αι, α$_{2.1.2}$ {ἑπτά + χίλιοι} ①^{amp} Rom 11:4, **seven** *thousand*; (15x LXX)

Ἔραστος, ου, ὁ$_2$ ❸ Acts 19:22; Rom 16:23; 2 Tim 4:20, **Erastus**

ἐραυνάω^{con} {ἔρομαι} ❻ Rev 2:23, **to scrutinize**; John 7:52; 1 Pet 1:11, **to search**

ἐργάζομαι {ἔργον} (41x; 8x John) Matt 7:23, *subst.*, **workers** *of lawlessness* Rom 4:4; 1 Cor 4:12, **to work**; Gal 6:10, **to be accomplished**; Mark 14:6, **to do**; 1 Cor 9:13, **to perform**^{NIGTC}; 2 Cor 7:10, **to produce**; Jas 2:9, **to practice**; (120x LXX; 23x Pss, 12x Sir:Jer)

ἐργασία, ας, ἡ$_{1\alpha}$ {ἔργον} ❻ Luke 12:58, *make* **an effort**^{EGG}; Acts 16:19, **profit**; Eph 4:19, **to accomplish**^{ZEC}; (45x LXX; 17x 1–2 Chr, 7x Sir)

ἐργάτης, ου, ὁ$_{1>}$ {ἔργον} (16x; 6x Matt) Matt 9:37 = Luke 10:2; Acts 19:25; 2 Cor 11:13; Phil 3:2; 1 Tim 5:18; Jas 5:4, **workers**; ❹ LXX, 1 Macc 3:6, *evil* **doers**

ἔργον, ου, τό$_2$ (169x; 27x John, 20x Rev) John 4:34; Rom 2:6; 1 Cor 15:58; Phil 2:30; 1 Tim 6:18; Jas 2:17, **work(s)**; (574x LXX; 75x Exod, 65x Sir, 54x Pss)

ἐρεθίζω {ἐρέθω} ❷ 2 Cor 9:2, **to stir up**; Col 3:21, **to provoke**; ❼ LXX, Deut 21:20

ἐρείδω ①$^{\text{aap.nfs}}$ Acts 27:41, *the bow* **became jammed**^{ZEC}; (11x LXX; 9x Prov)

ἐρεύγομαι ①$^{\text{fmi1s}}$ Matt 13:35, **I will declare**; ❻ LXX, Lev 11:10; 1 Macc 3:4

ἐρημία, ας, ἡ$_{1\alpha}$ {ἔρημος} ❹ Matt 15:33 = Mark 8:4, **desolate place**; 2 Cor 11:26, **wilderness**; Heb 11:38, **deserts**; ❻ LXX, Isa 60:12, **to lay waste**

ἔρημος, ον$_{2.2}$ *adj.* (48x) Matt 3:3 = Mark 1:3 = Luke 3:4 = John 1:23; Rev 12:6, *subst.* **wilderness**; Acts 1:20, *become* **desolate**; Gal 4:27, *the* **deserted** *woman*; (375x LXX; 55x Num!)

ἐρημόω^{con} {ἔρημος} ❺ Matt 12:25 = Luke 11:17, **to be made desolate**; Rev 17:16, **to make desolate**; (74x LXX; 16x Ezek, 15x Isa)

ἐρήμωσις, εως, ἡ$_3$ {ἔρημος} ❸ Matt 24:15 = Mark 13:14 = Luke 21:20, *abomination* (Matt:Mark) **of desolation**; (21x LXX; 7x Dan, 6x Jer)

ἐρίζω {ἔρις} ①$^{\text{fai3s}}$ Matt 12:19, **to quarrel**^{ZEC}; ❻ LXX, Gen 26:35; 1 Sam 12:14, **to rebel**

ἐριθεία, ας, ἡ$_{1\alpha}$ {ἔρις} ❼ Rom 2:8, **selfishness**; 2 Cor 12:20; Jas 3:16, **selfish ambitions**

ἔριον, ου, τό$_2$ ❷ Heb 9:19; Rev 1:14, **wool**; ❾ LXX, Deut 22:11

ἔρις, ιδος, ἡ$_3$ ❾ Rom 1:29; 1 Tim 6:4, **quarrels**; 1 Cor 1:11; 3:3, **discord(s)**^{NIGTC}; Gal 5:21, **factional divisions**^{KeenG}; Phil 1:15, **rivalry**; ❸ LXX, Sir 28:11; 40:4, 9

ἐρίφιον, ου, τό$_2$ {ἐρίφιος} ①^{anp} Matt 25:33, **goats**; ①^{nns} LXX, Tob 2:13

ἔριφος, ου, ὁ$_2$ ❷ Matt 25:32; Luke 15:29, **goat(s)**; (26x LXX; 6x Gen, 5x Judg)

Ἑρμᾶς, ᾶ, ὁ$_1$ ①^{ams} Rom 16:14, **Hermas**

ἑρμηνεία, ας, ἡ$_{1\alpha}$ {ἑρμηνεύω} ❷ 1 Cor 12:10; 14:26, **interpretation**; ❸ LXX, Sir 47:17, **interpretation**

ἑρμηνεύω ❸ John 1:42; 9:7, *pass.*, *which* **is translated**; Heb 7:2, **meaning**; ❸ LXX, Ezra 4:7

Ἑρμῆς, οῦ, ὁ$_{1>}$ ❷^{ams} Acts 14:12; Rom 16:14, **Hermes**

Ἑρμογένης, ους, ὁ$_3$ ①^{nms} 2 Tim 1:15, **Hermogenes**

ἑρπετόν, οῦ, τό$_2$ {ἕρπω} ❹ Acts 10:12; 11:6; Rom 1:23; Jas 3:7, **reptile**; (44x LXX)

ἐρυθρός, ά, όν$_{2.1.2}$ *adj.* ❷ Acts 7:36; Heb 11:29, *the* **Red** *Sea*; ❷ LXX, Exod 10:19; 13:18

ἔρχομαι (632x; 157x John, 114x Matt, 101x Luke) Matt 2:2; John 1:11; 1 Cor 11:34; Jude 14; Rev 1:4, **to come, go**; (978x LXX; 119x 1–2 Sam, 86x Gen, 69x 1 Macc)

ἐρωτάω[con] (63x; 28x John, 22x LA) Matt 15:23, **to urge**; 1 Thess 5:12, **to ask**; John 8:7, **to question**; Luke 16:27, **to beg**; John 17:9–20[4x]; 1 John 5:16, **to pray**; (61x LXX)

ἐσθής, ῆτος, ἡ$_{3}$ {ἕννυμι} ❽ Luke 23:11; Acts 1:10, **clothing**; Jas 2:2–3,[3x] **clothes**; ❹ LXX

ἐσθίω (158x) Mark 7:3, **to eat**; 1 Cor 11:28, **to eat** *of the bread*; 2 Thess 3:12, **to eat** *their own bread*[NIGTC]; Matt 11:18, *not* **eating** *and drinking* (*not living as other people*); Heb 10:27, **to consume, devour**[EGG]; (607x LXX; 253x Pent)

Ἑσλί, ὁ$_{3}$ *indecl.* ①[gms] Luke 3:25, *son of* **Esli**

ἔσοπτρον, ου, τό$_{2}$ {εἰς + ὁράω} ❷ 1 Cor 13:12, **mirror** *indirectly*[NIGTC]; Jas 1:23, **mirror**; ❷ LXX, Wis 7:26

ἑσπέρα, ας, ἡ$_{1α}$ {ἕσπερος} ❸ Luke 24:29; Acts 4:3; 28:23, **evening**; (121x LXX; 34x Lev)

Ἑσρώμ, ὁ$_{3}$ *indecl.* ❸ Matt 1:3[2x]; Luke 3:33, **Hezron**; ①[ams] LXX, 1 Kgs 11:14

ἑσσόομαι[con] {ἥσσων} ①[api2p] 2 Cor 12:13, **Were you treated worse?**[BEC]

ἑστηκότων → ἵστημι, *pf. act. ptc. gmp*, Matt 27:47, **standing** *there*

ἑστώτων → ἵστημι, *pf. act. ptc. gms*, Matt 16:28, **are standing**

ἔσχατος, η, ον$_{2.1.2}$ *adj.* (52x; 10x Matt, 7x John) John 6:39; Acts 1:8; 2 Pet 3:3, **last**; Jude 18, **end** *time*; Rev 1:17, *I am the First and* **the Last**; (145x LXX; 19x Sir, 14x Jer)

ἐσχάτως *adv.* ① Mark 5:23, ἐσχάτως ἔχει, *idiom. she has* **finally** (*i.e., she is at the point of death*)[BHGNT]; Hp. *Arte* 8, **extremely, in excess**

ἔσω *impr. prep.* ❾ Ⓐ ***adverb of place***, Matt 26:58 = Mark 14:54; Acts 5:23; 1 Cor 5:12, **inside**; 2 Cor 4:16; Eph 3:16, **inner** *being*; Ⓑ ***preposition***, Mark 15:16, **into**; (14x LXX)

ἔσωθεν *adv.* (12x) {εἰς + θεν} Matt 7:15, **inwardly**; Rev 4:8, **inside**; Mark 7:21; 2 Cor 7:5, **within**; (24x LXX; 11x Ezek)

ἐσώτερος, α, ον$_{2.1.2}$ *adj.* {ἔσω + τερος} ❷ Acts 16:24; Heb 6:19, **inner**; (35x LXX; 20x Ezek)

ἑταῖρος, ου, ὁ$_{2}$ ❸[vms] Matt 20:13; 22:12; 26:50, **Friend!**; (25x LXX; 6x 2 Sam)

ἑτερόγλωσσος, ον$_{2.2}$ {ἕτερος + γλῶσσα} *adj.* ①[dmp] 1 Cor 14:21, **foreign tongue**

ἑτεροδιδασκαλέω[con] {ἕτερος + διδάσκω} ❷ 1 Tim 1:3; 6:3, **to teach false doctrine**

ἑτεροζυγέω[con] {ἕτερος + ζυγός} ①[pap.nmp] 2 Cor 6:14, *stop* **being in incompatible relationships**[BEC]

ἕτερος, α, ον$_{2.1.2}$ (98x; 49x LA) **other, another of a different kind**; Ⓐ ***articular and defined***, Matt 6:24, *love* **the other**; Ⓑ ***anarthrous and undefined***, Matt 8:21, **another** *of his disciples*; Gal 1:6, *a* **different** *gospel*; (240x LXX; 25x Deut, 19x Exod)

ἑτέρως *adv.* ① Phil 3:15, *think* **differently**

ἔτι *adv.* (93x; 22x Rev, 16x Luke) Ⓐ ***durative***, Matt 12:46, **while** *he was speaking*; John 4:35, *there are* **yet**; Ⓑ ***accessive***, Heb 11:32, *What* **more** *should I say?*; (516x LXX; 49x Deut, 44x Jer)

ἑτοιμάζω {ἕτοιμος} (40x; 14x Luke) Matt 3:3 = Mark 1:3 = Luke 3:4; 1 Cor 2:9; Phlm 22, **to prepare**; Acts 23:23; Rev 8:6, **make ready**; (173x LXX; 35x 1–2 Chr, 20x Pss)

ἑτοιμασία, ας, ἡ$_{1α}$ ①[dfs] Eph 6:15, **readiness**; ❽ LXX, Ezra 2:68

ἕτοιμος, η, ον$_{2.1.2}$ *adj.* (17x; 8x Syn) Matt 22:4; Mark 14:15; Luke 22:33; John 7:6; Acts 23:15; 2 Cor 9:5; Titus 3:1; 1 Pet 3:15, **ready**; (61x LXX; 9x Pss)

ἑτοίμως *adv.* ❸ Acts 21:13; 2 Cor 12:14; 1 Pet 4:5, **ready**; ❹ LXX, Ezra 7:17, 26; Dan 3:15

ἔτος, ους, τό$_{3}$ (49x; 26x LA) Matt 9:20 = Mark 5:25; John 2:20; Luke 3:1; Acts 4:22; Rom 15:23; Gal 2:1; Heb 3:10; 2 Pet 3:8; Rev 20:7, **years**; (674x LXX; 127x 1–2 Kgs)

εὖ *adv.* ❺ Matt 25:21, 23, **well done**; Mark 14:7, *show* **kindness**; Acts 15:29; Eph 6:3, *you will do* **well**; (59x LXX; 16x Deut, 7x Sir)

Εὕα, ας, ἡ$_{1\alpha}$ ❷ 2 Cor 11:3; 1 Tim 2:13, **Eve**; ❸ LXX, Gen 4:1, 25; Tob 8:6

εὐαγγελίζω {εὖ + ἄγγελος} (54x; 25x LA) *act.*, 1 Thess 3:6, **to bring good news**; Acts 8:4, **to proclaim** *the word*; 2 Cor 10:16, **to proclaim the good news**; Rev 14:6, *eternal gospel* **to proclaim**; *pass.*, Matt 11:5, **to be given the good news**; (23x LXX; 7x 2 Sam)

εὐαγγέλιον, ου, τό$_2$ {εὖ + ἄγγελος} (76x; 16x 1–2 Cor) Matt 4:23; Acts 15:7; Rom 1:1; 1 Cor 4:15; 2 Cor 2:12; Phil 1:12; Phlm 13; Rev 14:6, **gospel**; ①[anp] LXX, 2 Sam 4:10, **news**

εὐαγγελιστής, οῦ, ὁ$_{1>}$ ❸ Acts 21:8; Eph 4:11; 2 Tim 4:5, **evangelist**

εὐαρεστέω[con] {εὖ + ἀρέσκω} ❸[aap.nms] Heb 11:5, 6; 13:6, **to please**

εὐάρεστος, ον$_{2.2}$ {εὖ + ἀρέσκω} *adj.* ❾ Rom 12:1; 2 Cor 5:9; Heb 13:21, **pleasing**; ❷ LXX

εὐαρέστως {εὖ + ἀρέσκω} *adv.* ① Heb 12:28, **acceptable**

Εὔβουλος, ου, ὁ$_2$ ①[nms] 2 Tim 4:21, **Eubulus**

εὖγε {εὖ + γέ} *adv.* ① Luke 19:17, **Well done!** (14x LXX; 8x Pss, 4x Ezek)

εὐγενής, ές$_{3.3}$ {εὖ + γίνομαι} *adj.* ❸ Luke 19:12, **a nobleman**; Acts 17:11, **open-minded**[ZEC]; 1 Cor 1:26, **born to high status**[NIGTC]; ❽ LXX, 2 Macc 10:13; 4 Macc 6:5

εὐδία, ας, ἡ$_{1\alpha}$ {εὖ + Ζεύς [Διός]} ①[nfs] Matt 16:2, **fair weather**; ①[nfs] LXX, Sir 3:15

εὐδοκέω[con] (21x) Matt 3:17 = Mark 1:11 = Luke 3:22, **to take pleasure**; Gal 1:15, **to be pleased**; 2 Cor 5:8, **we would rather**[BEC]; 12:10, **I am delighted**[BEC]; (55x LXX; 14x Pss)

εὐδοκία, ας, ἡ$_{1\alpha}$ {εὖ + δοκέω} ❾ Eph 1:9, **good pleasure**; Luke 2:14, **those favored** *by God*; Rom 10:1, **desire**; Phil 1:15, **goodwill**[BEC]; 2 Thess 1:11, *every good* **intention**[NIGTC]; (28x LXX; 14x Sir, 8x Pss)

εὐεργεσία, ας, ἡ$_{1\alpha}$ {εὖ + ἔργον} ❷ Acts 4:9, **act of kindness**; 1 Tim 6:2, **a good deed**

εὐεργετέω[con] {εὖ + ἔργον} ①[pap.nms] Acts 10:38, **doing good**; (10x LXX) 2 Macc 10:38

εὐεργέτης, ου, ὁ$_{1>}$ {εὖ + ἔργον} ①[nmp] Luke 22:25, **benefactors**; ❼ LXX; 2x Esth

εὔθετος, ον$_{2.2}$ {εὖ + τίθημι} *adj.* ❸ Luke 9:62; 14:35, **fit**; Heb 6:7, **useful**[EGG]; ①[dms] LXX, Ps 31:6 (32:6), **suitable** *time*

εὐθέως {εὐθύς} *adv.* (36x; 13x Matt, 9x Acts) Matt 4:20; Mark 7:35; Luke 5:13; John 5:9; Rev 4:2, **immediately, at once**; Gal 1:16, **my first action** *was not to check*[KeenG]; (15x LXX)

εὐθυδρομέω[con] {εὐθύς + τρέχω} ❷ Acts 16:11; 21:1, **to plot a straight course**

εὐθυμέω[con] {εὖ + θυμός} ❸ Acts 27:22, 25, **to take courage**; Jas 5:13, **to be in good spirits**[EGG]

εὔθυμος, ον$_{2.2}$ {εὖ + θυμός} *adj.* ①[nmp] Acts 27:36, **encouraged**; ①[nmp] LXX, 2 Macc 11:26

εὐθύμως {εὖ + θυμός} *adv.* ① Acts 24:10, **cheerfully**

εὐθύνω ❷ John 1:23, **make straight**; Jas 3:4, **the one directing, pilot**

εὐθύς *temp. adv.* (51x; 41x Mark![NIGTC]) Matt 14:31; John 13:30, **immediately**; Rev 4:2, **at once**; Mark 15:1, **as soon as**; Acts 10:16, **suddenly**; (66x LXX; 24x Pss, 7x Prov:Isa)

εὐθύς, εῖα, ύ$_{3.1.3}$ *adj.* ❽ Matt 3:3 = Mark 1:3 = Luke 3:4; 2 Pet 2:15, **straight**

εὐθύτης, ητος, ἡ$_3$ {εὐθύς} ①[gfs] Heb 1:8, **justice**; (23x LXX) Ps 10:7 (11:7), **the upright**

εὐκαιρέω[con] {εὖ + καιρός} ❸ Mark 6:31, **to have a chance**; Acts 17:21, **used to spend time** *in nothing else*[EGG]; 1 Cor 16:12, *as soon as* **the time is right**[NIGTC]

εὐκαιρία, ας, ἡ$_{1\alpha}$ {εὖ + καιρός} ❷ Matt 26:16 = Luke 22:6, **opportunity**; ❺ LXX

εὔκαιρος, ον$_{2.2}$ *adj.* ❷ Mark 6:21, **opportunity**; Heb 4:16, **in time of need**; ❺ LXX εὐ**καίρως** {εὖ + καιρός} *adv.* ❷ Mark 14:11; **opportunity**; 2 Tim 4:2, **favorable**; ① LXX, Sir 18:22

εὔ**κοπος, ον**$_{2.2}$ {εὖ + κόπτω} *adj.* ❼ Matt 9:5 = Mark 2:9 = Luke 5:23, **easier**; ❷ LXX

εὐ**λάβεια, ας, ἡ**$_{1α}$ {εὖ + λαμβάνω} ❷ Heb 5:7; 12:28, **reverence**; ❸ LXX, Josh 22:24, **caution**

εὐ**λαβέομαι**[con] {εὖ + λαμβάνω} ①[app.nms] Heb 11:7, **respected**; (38x LXX; 9x Sir)

εὐ**λαβής, ές**$_{3.3}$ {εὖ + λαμβάνω} *adj.* ❹ Luke 2:25; Acts 2:5; 8:2; 22:12, **devout**; ❷ LXX

εὐ**λογέω**[con] {εὖ + λέγω} (41x) Matt 14:19 = Mark 6:41; Acts 3:26; Rom 12:14[2x]; Gal 3:9; Jas 3:9, **to bless**; (442x LXX; 62x Gen, 58x Pss, 34x Deut)

εὐ**λογητός, ή, όν**$_{2.1.2}$ {εὖ + λέγω} *adj.* ❽ Mark 14:61, *subst.* **the Blessed One**; Rom 1:25, **blessed**; 2 Cor 1:3; Eph 1:3; 1 Pet 1:3, **Blessed** *be the God . . .*; (80x LXX; 16x Pss, 12x Tob)

εὐ**λογία, ας, ἡ**$_{1α}$ {εὖ + λέγω} (16x; 4x 2 Cor) Rom 16:18[ZEC!]; Gal 3:14; Heb 6:7; Jas 3:10; Rev 5:12, **blessing**; 2 Cor 9:5,[2x] **generous gift**; 9:6[2x], ὁ σπείρων ἐπ᾽ **εὐλογίαις** ἐπ᾽ **εὐλογίαις**, *the one who sows with* **generosity** *will reap with* **generosity** (95x LXX; 19x Sir, 16x Gen)

εὐ**μετάδοτος, ον**$_{2.2}$ {εὖ + μετά + δίδωμι} *adj.* ①[amp] 1 Tim 6:18, **generous**

Εὐνίκη, ῆς, ἡ$_{1}$ ①[dfs] 2 Tim 1:5, **Eunice**

εὐ**νοέω**[con] {εὖ + νοῦς} ①[pap.nms] Matt 5:25, *come* **to terms**; ❸ LXX, Dan 2:43, **to bond**

εὔ**νοια, ας, ἡ**$_{1α}$ {εὖ + νοῦς} ①[gfs] Eph 6:7, **enthusiasm**; (18x LXX; 7x 2 Macc)

εὐ**νουχίζω** {εὐνή + ἔχω} ❷ *lit.*, **someone who takes care of the nuptial chamber, a chamberlain**; *pass.*, Matt 19:12,[2x] **to be made eunuchs**[ZEC]

εὐ**νοῦχος, ου, ὁ**$_{2}$ {εὖ + ἔχω} ❽ Matt 19:12[3x]; Acts 8:27–39,[5x] **eunuch(s)**; (38x LXX)

εὔξαίμην → **εὔχομαι** *aor. mid. opt. 1s*, Acts 26:29, **I wish** *before God*

Εὐοδία, ας, ἡ$_{1α}$ ①[afs] Phil 4:2, **Euodia**

εὐ**οδόω**[con] {εὖ + ὁδός} ❹ Rom 1:10, **I might succeed**; 1 Cor 16:2, **with how you may fare**[NIGTC]; 3 John 2,[2x] **to go well**; (68x LXX; 11x 2 Chr, 9x Gen)

εὐ**πάρεδρος, ον**$_{2.2}$ *adj.* ①[ans] 1 Cor 7:35, **undistracted devotion**[NIGTC]

εὐ**πειθής, ές**$_{3.3}$ {εὖ + πείθω} *adj.* ①[nfs] Jas 3:17, **willing to yield**

εὐ**περίστατος, ον**$_{2.2}$ {εὖ + περί + ἵστημι} *adj.* ①[afs] Heb 12:1, **so easily ensnares**[EGG]

εὐ**ποιΐα, ας, ἡ**$_{1α}$ {εὖ + ποιέω} ①[gfs] Heb 13:16, *don't neglect* **to do what is good**[EGG]

εὐ**πορέω**[con] {εὖ + πορεύομαι} ①[imi3s] Acts 11:29, **each according to one's ability**; ❹ LXX, Lev 25:26, 28, 49, **finds sufficient means**

εὐ**πορία, ας, ἡ**$_{1α}$ {εὖ + πορεύομαι} ①[nfs] Acts 19:25, **wealth**

εὐ**πρέπεια, ας, ἡ**$_{1α}$ {εὖ + πρέπω} ①[nfs] Jas 1:11, **beauty**; (17x LXX; 4x Pss)

εὐ**πρόσδεκτος, ον**$_{2.2}$ {εὖ + πρός + δέχομαι} *adj.* ❺ Rom 15:16, 31; 2 Cor 6:2; 8:12[BEC]; 1 Pet 2:5[Keen1P], **acceptable, pleasing**

εὐ**προσωπέω**[con] {εὖ + πρός + ὁράω} ①[aainf] Gal 6:12, **to show a good face**[KeenG]

εὐρα**κύλων, ωνος, ὁ**$_{3}$ {εὖ + ῥάκνυμι} ①[nms] Acts 27:14, **northeaster**

εὑρίσκω (176x; 80x LA) Luke 1:30; 2 Cor 2:13; Phil 2:7, **to find**; Acts 13:6, **to come across**; (572x LXX; 56x Gen, 48x Sir)

εὐρύ**χωρος, ον**$_{2.2}$ {εὐρύς + χωρέω} *adj.* ①[nfs] Matt 7:13, **broad**; (11x LXX) Judg 18:12

εὐ**σέβεια, ας, ἡ**$_{1α}$ {εὖ + σέβω} (15x; 8x 1 Tim) Acts 3:12, **piety**; 1 Tim 2:2; 6:3; 2 Tim 3:5; Titus 1:1; 2 Pet 1:6, **godliness**; (57x LXX; 46x 4 Macc)

εὐ**σεβέω**[con] {εὖ + σέβω} ❷ Acts 17:23, **to worship**; 1 Tim 5:4, **to live piously**; ❺ LXX

εὐ**σεβής, ές**$_{3.3}$ {εὖ + σέβω} *adj.* ❸ Acts 10:2, 7; 2 Pet 2:9, **devout, godly**; (34x LXX; 14x Sir)

εὐσεβῶς {εὖ + σέβω} *adv.* ❷ 2 Tim 3:12; Titus 2:12, **godly**

εὔσημος, ον$_{2.2}$ {εὖ + σημεῖον} *adj.* ①^{ams} 1 Cor 14:9, **readily intelligible**[NIGTC]; ①^{dfs} LXX Ps 80:4 (81:3)

εὔσπλαγχνος, ον$_{2.2}$ {εὖ + σπλάγχνον} *adj.* ❷^{nmp} Eph 4:32; 1 Pet 3:8, **tenderhearted**; ①^{nms} LXX, Pr Man 1:7

εὐσχημόνως {εὖ + ἔχω} *adv.* ❸ Rom 13:13, **honorably**; 1 Cor 14:40, **fittingly**[NIGTC]; 1 Thess 4:12, *live* **becomingly**[NIGTC]

εὐσχημοσύνη, ῆς, ἡ$_{1η}$ {εὖ + ἔχω} ①^{afs} 1 Cor 12:23, *have greater* **adornment to make them presentable**[NIGTC]; ①^{dfs} LXX, 4 Macc 6:2, **gracefulness**

εὐσχήμων, ον$_{2.2}$ {εὖ + ἔχω} *adj.* ❺ Mark 15:43, **respected**; Acts 13:50, **prominent**; 1 Cor 7:35, **well suited**[NIGTC]; 12:24, **more presentable**; ①^{nms} LXX, Prov 11:25

εὐτόνως {εὖ + τείνω} ❷ Luke 23:10; Acts 18:28, **vigorously**; ① LXX, Josh 6:8

εὐτραπελία, ας, ἡ$_{1α}$ {εὖ + τρέπω} ①^{nfs} Eph 5:4, **dirty jokes**[ZEC]; Aristot. *Rh.* 1389b 11, *a* **witty remark** *is an excess tempered by good education*[BrDAG]

Εὔτυχος, ου, ὁ$_{2}$ ①^{nms} Acts 20:9, **Eutychus**

εὐφημία, ας, ἡ$_{1α}$ {εὖ + φημί} ①^{gfs} 2 Cor 6:8,[BEC] **good report**

εὔφημος, ον$_{2.2}$ {εὖ + φημί} *adj.* ①^{nnp} Phil 4:8, **respectable**[BEC]

εὐφορέω^{con} {εὖ + φέρω} ①^{aai3s} Luke 12:16, **produced a good crop**[ZEC]

εὐφραίνω {εὖ + φρήν} (14x; 8x LA) Luke 12:19, **be merry**; 15:23–32,^{4x} **to celebrate**; Gal 4:27, **to rejoice**; Luke 16:19, **to feast**; Acts 2:26, *heart* **was glad**; 2 Cor 2:2, **to cheer**; (246x LXX; 57x Pss, 31x Isa)

Εὐφράτης, ου, ὁ$_{1>}$ ❷ Rev 9:14; 16:12, *the great river* **Euphrates**; (27x LXX; 8x Jer)

εὐφροσύνη, ῆς, ἡ$_{1η}$ {εὖ + φρήν} ❷^{gfs} Acts 2:28; 14:17, **gladness**; (170x LXX; 34x Isa)

εὐχαριστέω^{con} {εὖ + χάρις} (38x; 6x 1 Cor) Matt 15:36 = Mark 8:6; Luke 18:11; John 6:11; Rom 1:8; 2 Cor 1:11; Eph 1:16; Phil 1:3, **to give thanks**; ❻ LXX, 2 Macc 1:11; 12:31

εὐχαριστία, ας, ἡ$_{1α}$ {εὖ + χάρις} (15x) Acts 24:3; 1 Cor 14:16; Phil 4:6, **gratitude, thanksgiving**; ❺ LXX, 2 Macc 2:27; Sir 37:11, **kindness**

εὐχάριστος, ον$_{2.2}$ {εὖ + χάρις} *adj.* ①^{nmp} Col 3:15, *be* **thankful**; ①^{nfs} LXX, Prov 11:16

εὐχή, ῆς, ἡ$_{1η}$ {εὔχομαι} ❸ Acts 18:18; 21:23, **vow**; Jas 5:15, **prayer**; (89x LXX; 32x Num)

εὔχομαι ❼ Acts 26:29; 2 Cor 13:7; Jas 5:16; 3 John 2, **to pray**; Rom 9:3, **I could almost wish**[ZEC]; (84x LXX; 16x Num, 9x 1 Esd)

εὔχρηστος, ον$_{2.2}$ {εὖ + χράομαι} *adj.* ❸ 2 Tim 2:21; 4:11; Phlm 11, **useful**; ❷ LXX, Prov 31:13

εὐψυχέω^{con} {εὖ + ψύχω} ①^{pas1s} Phil 2:19, **to find comfort**[BEC]

εὐωδία, ας, ἡ$_{1α}$ {εὖ + ὄζω} ❸ 2 Cor 2:15, **aroma**; Eph 5:2, **fragrant**; Phil 4:18, *a beautiful* **fragrance**; (57x LXX; 20x Num, 18x Lev)

εὐώνυμος, ον$_{2.2}$ *adj.* ❾ (5x Matt) Matt 20:21; Mark 10:40; Acts 21:3; Rev 10:2, **left**; (19x LXX)

ἐφάλλομαι {ἐπί + ἅλλομαι} ①$^{amp.nms}$ Acts 19:16, **leaped**; ❸ LXX, 1 Sam 10:6; 11:6

ἐφάπαξ *adv.* ❺ Rom 6:10; 1 Cor 15:6; Heb 7:27; 9:12; 10:10, **once for all**

Ἐφέσιος, α, ον$_{2.1.2}$ *adj.* ❻ (5x Acts) Acts 19:28, 34–35^{3x}; 21:29; Eph 1:0 (= *title*), **Ephesian(s)**

Ἔφεσος, ου, ἡ$_{2όδός}$ (16x, 8x Acts) Acts 18:19; 1 Cor 15:32; 2 Tim 1:18, **Ephesus**

ἐφευρετής, οῦ, ὁ$_{1>}$ {ἐπί + εὑρίσκω} ①^{amp} Rom 1:30, **inventors** *of evil*

ἔφη^{14xMatt} → **φημί** *aor. act. ind. 3s*, Matt 4:7, *Jesus* **told** *him*

ἐφημερία, ας, ἡ$_{1α}$ {ἐπί + ἡμέρα} ❷^{gfs} Luke 1:5, 8, **division**; (23x LXX; 17x 1–2 Chr)

ἐφήμερος, ον$_{2.2}$ {ἐπί + ἡμέρα} *adj.* ①[gfs] Jas 2:15, **daily**
ἐφικνέομαι[con] {ἐπί + ἱκανός} ❷ 2 Cor 10:13, **to reach**; 10:14, **to overextend**[BEC]
ἐφίστημι {ἐπί + ἵστημι} (21x; 18x LA) Luke 2:9, 38, **to stand before**; 20:1, **to come with**; Acts 4:1, **to come to**; 6:12, **to confront**; 2 Tim 4:2, **be ready**; 4:6, *my departure* **is imminent**[NIGTC]; (72x LXX; 9x Jer, 5x Lev:Isa)
ἐφοράω[con] {ἐπί + ὁράω} ❷ Luke 1:25, **to gaze upon**[EGG]; Acts 4:29, **to look at**; (36x LXX)
Ἐφραίμ, ὁ$_3$ *indecl.* ①[ams] John 11:54, **Ephraim**; (199x LXX; 39x Hos, 28x Judg)
ἐφφαθά *Aram.* ① Mark 7:34, "**Ephphatha**!" *that is, be opened!*
ἐχθές *adv.* ❸ John 4:52; Acts 7:28; Heb 13:8, **yesterday**; (34x LXX; 6x Exod, 5x Gen)
ἔχθρα, ας, ἡ$_{1α}$ {ἐχθρός} ❻ Luke 23:12, **enemies**; Rom 8:7, **hostile**; Gal 5:20, **instances of enmity**[KeenG]; Eph 2:4; Jas 4:4, **hostility**; (22x LXX; 5x Prov)
ἐχθρός, ά, όν$_{2.1.2}$ *adj.* (32x) Matt 5:43; Acts 2:35; Heb 1:13; Rev 11:5, **enemy**; (436x LXX)
ἔχιδνα, ης, ἡ$_{1>}$ ❺ Matt 3:7 = Luke 3:7; Matt 12:34, *brood* **of vipers**; Acts 28:3, **viper**
ἔχω (708x; 308x Gs, 100x Rev) Ⓐ ***possession***, Matt 11:18 = Luke 5:33, **to have**; Matt 1:18, **to be** *with child*; Rev 1:16, **to hold**; Ⓑ ***spatial proximity***, Mark 1:38, *to the* **neighboring** *town*[BHGNT]; Ⓒ ***idiom.***, Mark 5:23, *"she* ***has*** *finally"* (*i.e.*, **to be** *at the point of death*[BHGNT]); (458x LXX; 53x 2 Macc)
ἕως *conj.* (146x; 50x LA, 49x Matt) Ⓐ ***adverb***, 1 Tim 4:13, **until**; John 9:4, **while** *it is day*; Ⓑ ***preposition* w/ *gen.***, Mark 15:33, **until** *the ninth hour*; Matt 1:17, *from Babylon* **to** *Christ*; 11:23, **unto** *heaven*; (1,431x LXX; 302x Pent, 92x Josh, 83x Pss)

Z, ζ [*zēta*]

Z, ζ, τό (ζῆτα) *indecl.* **zeta**, *6th letter of the Gr. alphabet* ‖ *num.* ζʹ = 7; ͵ζ = 7,000

Ζαβουλών, ὁ$_3$ *indecl.* ❸ Matt 4:13, 15; Rev 7:8, **Zebulun**; (46x LXX; 11x Num, 7x Judg)

Ζακχαῖος, ου, ὁ$_2$ ❸ Luke 19:2, 5, 8, **Zacchaeus**; ①[ams] LXX, Macc 10:19

Ζάρα, ὁ$_3$ *indecl.* ①[ams] Matt 1:3, **Zerah**; (14x LXX; 5x 1 Chr, 4x Josh) *5 men in LXX:* Gen 36:13; 38:30; Num 26:13; 1 Chr 6:21; 2 Chr 14:9

Ζαχαρίας, ου, ὁ$_2$ (11x; 10x Luke) Matt 23:25; Luke 1:40, **Zechariah**, *father of John the Baptist*; (44x LXX; 9x 1 Esd, 7x 2 Chr) *thirty-two different persons*[APB]

ζάω[con] (140x; 23x Rom, 17x John) **to live**; Ⓐ ***biologically***, Rom 7:1; Ⓑ ***spiritually***, 1 Pet 4:6; Ⓒ ***believer's conduct***, Gal 2:19–20[5x]; Ⓓ ***to possess vigor***, John 4:10, 11, **living** *water*; Ⓔ ***to produce authentic life***, Acts 7:38, **living**; (528x LXX, 74x Gen, 46x Ezek, 42x Pss)

Ζεβεδαῖος, ου, ὁ$_2$ (12x; 6x Matt, 4x Mark) Matt 4:21; John 21:2, **Zebedee**

ζεστός, ή, όν$_{2.1.2}$ *adj.* {ζέω} ❸ Rev 3:15,[2x] 16, **hot**, *as the medicinal waters from Hierapolis*[L7 186–90]; (see also **ψυχρός**)

ζεῦγος, ους, τό$_3$ {ζυγός} ❷ Luke 2:24, **a pair**; 14:19, **a yoke**; (13x LXX) Lev 5:11

ζευκτηρία, ας, ἡ$_{1α}$ ①[apf] Acts 27:40, **pennants** *of the steering oars*[ZEC, Keen4]

Ζεύς, *gen.* **Διός,** *acc.* **Δία, ὁ$_3$** ❷ Acts 14:12, 13, **Zeus**; ❸ LXX, 2 Macc 6:2[2x]; 11:21, **Zeus** *of Mount Olympus*; **Zeus**-*the-Friend-of-Strangers shrine*; *Corinthian* **Zeus**[ABC]

ζέω[con] ❷ Acts 18:25, **being fervent** *in spirit*[ZEC]; Rom 12:11, **being ardent** *in spirit*[ZEC]; ❹ LXX, 4 Macc 18:20, **seething** *rage*; Ezek 24:5,[2x] **boil** *its* **boilings**!

ζηλεύω {ζέω} ①[paimp2s] Rev 3:19, **be zealous**; Demosth. 2.15, **to seek with enthusiasm**

ζῆλος, ου, ὁ$_2$ {ζέω} (16x; 5x 2 Cor) *positive*, John 2:17; Acts 5:17, **zeal**[ZEC]; 2 Cor 7:7, 11, **enthusiastic concern**[BEC]; 11:2, **with a jealousy** *from God*[BEC]; *negative*, Rom 13:13; Jas 3:14, **jealousy**; 1 Cor 3:3, **strife**; (40x LXX; 6x Isa:Ezek)

ζηλόω[con] {ζέω} (11x; 4x 1 Cor) *negative*, Acts 7:9, **to be envious**; 1 Cor 13:4, *love never* **boils with jealousy** (CBW); Gal 4:17,[2x] **to pursue** *with impure motives*[KeenG!]; Jas 4:2, **to covet**; *positive*, 1 Cor 12:31, **continue to be zealously concerned**[NIGTC]; 14:1, **avidly desire**[SacPag]; Gal 4:18, **to be pursued** *in a good way*[KeenG]; (49x LXX; 6x Num)

ζηλωτής, οῦ, ὁ$_{1>}$ {ζέω} ❽ (4x LA) Luke 6:15; Acts 1:13, *Simon, the* **Zealot**; Acts 21:20, *subst.*, **zealous**; 1 Cor 14:12, **a burning concern** *about the powers of the spirit*[NIGTC]; ❻ LXX (= *Heb.* קנא, *to burn with zeal*), Exod 20:5, **jealous**

ζημία, ας, ἡ$_{1α}$ ❹ Acts 27:10, 21, **loss, damage**; Phil 3:7, 8, **a loss**; ❺ LXX, 2 Kgs 23:33

ζημιόω[con] {ζημία} ❻ Matt 16:26 = Mark 8:36 = Luke 9:25, **to lose, forfeit**; 1 Cor 3:15, **to suffer loss**[NIGTC]; Phil 3:8, **to suffer loss of wealth**; ❼ LXX, Exod 21:22

Ζηνᾶς, *acc.* **ᾶν, ὁ$_3$** ①[ams] Titus 3:13, **Zenas**, *the lawyer*

ζητέω[con] (117x; 35x LA, 34x John) Matt 2:13; Acts 17:5, **to search for**; 9:11, **to ask for**; Rom 11:3, **trying to take** *my life*; 1 Cor 4:2, **it is required**[NIGTC]; 13:5, *is not* **self-seeking**;

Gal 1:10, **to strive**; Heb 8:7, *would not* **have sought**[NIGTC]; 1 Pet 5:8, **to look for**[Keen1P]; (302x LXX; 37x 1–2 Sam)

ζήτημα, ατος, τό$_3$ {ζητέω} ❺[ZEC] (Acts) 15:2, *a very serious* **argument**; 18:15; 23:29; 25:19; 26:3, **disputes**

ζήτησις, εως, ἡ$_3$ {ζητέω} ❼ John 3:25, **discussion**[ZEC]; Acts 15:2, 7, **controversy**[ZEC]; Acts 25:20, **matters**; Titus 3:9, **controversial questions**[NIGTC]

ζιζάνιον, ου, τό$_2$ ❽ (Matt 13:25–40) **zizanium**, **darnel**, *a troublesome weed*[ZEC]

Ζοροβαβέλ, ὁ$_3$ *indecl.* ❸ Matt 1:12, 13; Luke 3:27, **Zerubbabel**; (34x LXX; 11x 1 Esd, 7x Hag, 4x Zech) 1 Chr 3:19, **Zerubbabel**, *a Judean exile who returned to Jerusalem*[APB]

ζόφος, ου, ὁ$_2$ ❺ Heb 12:18, **darkness**; 2 Pet 2:4, **utter darkness**; 2:17, **gloom**; Jude 6, **under gloom**[BHGNT]; Jude 13, **ὁ ζόφος** τοῦ σκότους, **the deepest** *darkness*

ζυγός, ου, ὁ$_2$ ❻ Matt 11:29, 30, **yoke**[ZEC]; Acts 15:10; 1 Tim 6:1, *metaph.* **yoke**, *oppressed*; Rev 6:5, **scales** (*see* Lev 19:35, **volume, quantity**)[NIGTC]; (65x LXX) Zeph 3:9, **purpose**

ζύμη, ης, ἡ$_{1η}$ {ζέω} (13x; 8x Syn, 4x 1 Cor) Ⓐ *positive*, Matt 13:33, *kingdom like* **leaven** *in dough*; Ⓑ *negative*, Matt 16:6 = Mark 8:15 = Luke 12:1, **leaven, the spreading of evil teaching**[ZEC]; 1 Cor 5:6–8[4x NIGTC!]; Gal 5:9, *negative effects of* **leaven**[KeenG]; (10x LXX; 7x Exod) Exod 12:15[2x]

ζυμόω[con] {ζέω} ❹ Matt 13:33 = Luke 13:21; 1 Cor 5:6; Gal 5:9, **to leaven**, ❺ LXX, Exod 12:34

ζωγρέω[con] {ζάω + ἄγρα} *metaph.* ❷ Luke 5:10, **to catch** *people* **alive** *for Christ*; 2 Tim 2:26, **are captured alive** *by Satan*;[NIGTC] ❽ LXX, Josh 2:13, 6:25, 9:25, **to spare a life**

ζωή, ῆς, ἡ$_{1η}$ (135x; [36x John, 17x Rev, 13x 1 John], 14x Rom) Matt 18:8 = Mark 9:43; John 3:15, 16; Luke 12:15, **life**; John 6:27–68,[11x] *Bread of Life Discourse*; 1 Cor 3:22, *physical* **life**; *one of the tyrannies of existence*[NICNT]; (282x LXX) Gen 3:20, **Eve**

ζώνη, ῆς, ἡ$_{1η}$ {ζώννυμι} ❽ Matt 3:4 = Mark 1:6, *leather* **belt**; Acts 3:15; Matt 10:9 = Mark 6:8, **money belt**; Acts 21:11,[2x] **belt**; Rev 1:13; 15:6, *golden* **sash**; (19x LXX; 5x Exod)

ζώννυμι ❸ John 21:18, **you dressed** *yourself*; Acts 12:8, **fasten your belt**[Keen2]

ζῳογονέω {ζάω + γίνομαι} ❸ Luke 17:33, **to keep** *one's life*; Acts 7:19, **to remain alive**; 1 Tim 6:13, **to give life**; (12x LXX) Exod 1:17, 22, **to let live**

ζῷον, ου, τό$_2$ {ζάω} (23x; 20x Rev) Jude 10, **animal**; Rev 4:6–19:4[14x], **living**, **celestial beings**[BEC]; (38x LXX; 12x Ezek, 11x Wis) Ezek 1:5 (= Rev 4:6), τεσσάρων **ζῴων**, *four* **living creatures**; 1:13–47:9, **living creature(s)**[11x]

ζῳοποιέω {ζάω + ποιέω} (11x) John 5:21,[2x] **to restore life**; 1 Cor 15:22, 36, **to be made alive**; 2 Cor 3:6, *the Spirit* **produces life**[BEC]; Gal 3:21, **to give life**; ❺ LXX, Neh 9:6

H, η [ēta]

H, η, τό (ἦτα) *indecl.* **eta**, *7th letter of the Gr. alphabet* || *num.* η′ = 8; ͵η = 8,000

ἤ (343x) Ⓐ ***particle***, Matt 5:17, **or**; Ⓑ ***disjunctive***, Matt 6:24, ἤ . . . ἤ, **either . . . or**; Ⓒ ***comparative***, John 3:19, μᾶλλον . . . ἤ, *rather* **than**; Matt 1:18, πρὶν ἤ, **before**; 1 Cor 14:19, θέλω . . . ἤ, *I would* **rather**; Ⓓ ***w/ other particles***, Luke 11:12, ἢ καί, **or** *even*; (970x LXX)

ἡγεμονεύω {ἄγω} ❷$^{pap.gms}$ Luke 2:2; 3:1, **to govern**

ἡγεμονία, ας, ἡ$_{1α}$ {ἄγω} ①^{gfs} Luke 3:1, **reign**; ❼ LXX, Num 1:52, **military men** (LES)

ἡγεμών, όνος, ὁ$_3$ {ἄγω} (20x; 10x Matt, 8x LA) Matt 2:6, **ruler**; Luke 20:20; 1 Pet 2:14, **governor**; (84x LXX; 42x Gen, 14x Jer)

ἡγέομαι {ἄγω} (28x; 6x Phil) Matt 2:6; Acts 7:10, *subst.*, **ruler**; Luke 22:26, **to lead**; Acts 14:12, *the* **leading** *speaker*; 2 Cor 9:5; Phil 2:3; 2 Thess 3:15, **to consider**; Heb 10:29, **to regard**; Heb 13:7, 17, 24, **leaders**; (160x LXX; 28x 1–2 Chr)

ᾔδεισαν → **οἶδα**, *plpf. act. ind. 3p*, Mark 1:34, **they knew** *him*

ἡδέως {ἥδομαι} *adv.* ❺ Mark 6:20; 12:37, **ἡδέως** αὐτοῦ ἤκουεν, *hearing him* **gladly**; 2 Cor 11:19, **cheerfully**; 12:9, **very gladly**[NIGTC]; (10x LXX) 2 Macc 2:27

ἤδη *temp. adv.* (61x; 16x John, 10x Luke) Matt 3:10 = Luke 3:9; John 3:18; 1 Cor 4:8; Phil 3:12[2x]; 1 John 2:8, **already**; (55x LXX; 28x 2–4 Macc)

ἡδονή, ης, ἡ$_{1η}$ ❺ Luke 8:14; Titus 3:3; Jas 4:1; 2 Pet 2:13, **pleasure**; (15x LXX; 11x 4 Macc)

ἡδύοσμον, ου, τό$_2$ {ἡδύς + ὀσμή} ❷^{ans} Matt 23:23 = Luke 11:42, **mint** (*the herb*)

ἦθος, ους, τό$_3$ {ἔθος} ①^{anp} 1 Cor 15:33, **lifestyles**[NIGTC]; ❼ LXX (5x 4 Macc[SCS])

ἥκω (26x; 14x Syn) Matt 8:11; 23:36; Rom 11:26; Heb 10:9; Rev 3:9, **to come**; Luke 15:27, **is here**; (242x LXX; 42x Isa, 37x Jer)

ἠλί ❷ *from Heb.* אֵל, **God**, *and 1st per. pron. suffix*, **my God**, Matt 27:46 = Ps 22:2

Ἠλί, ὁ ① Luke 3:23, **Eli**; (36x LXX; 34x 1 Sam)

Ἠλίας, ου, ὁ$_1$ (29x; 25x Syn) Matt 17:13 = Mark 9:4 = Luke 9:30; John 1:25; Rom 11:2; Jas 5:17, **Elijah**; ❾ LXX, (3x 2 Kgs) 9:36; 10:10, 17

ἡλικία, ας, ἡ$_{1α}$ ❽ Matt 6:27 = Luke 12:25, **moment**, **hour**; Luke 2:52; Eph 4:13, **stature**; Luke 19:3, τῇ **ἡλικίᾳ μικρὸς** ἦν, *he was a* **small** *man*; John 9:23, **ἡλικίαν** ἔχει, *he has* **years** (*i.e., he is old enough*); (22x LXX; 18x 2–4 Macc)

ἡλίκος, η, ον$_{2.1.2}$ *adj.* ❸ Col 2:1, **how greatly**; Jas 3:5,[2x] **ἡλίκον** πῦρ **ἡλίκην** ὕλην ἀνάπτει, **What-sized** *fire kindles* **what-sized** *forest?*[WPNT]; Men. *Sam.* 255, **How you babble!**[BrDAG]

ἥλιος, ου, ὁ$_2$ (36x; 13x Syn) Matt 24:29 = Mark 13:24 = Luke 21:25 = Acts 2:20 = Rev 6:12 = Joel 2:10; 1 Cor 15:41; Jas 1:11, **sun**; (201x LXX; 36x Eccl, 17x Josh)

ἦλος, ου, ὁ$_2$ ❷ John 20:25,[2x] **nail**; ❽ LXX, Josh 23:13, **sharp stick**

ἡμέρα, ας, ἡ$_{1α}$ (389x; 177x LA, 45x Matt) Matt 24:36 = Mark 13:32; John 4:40; Acts 3:24; Rom 13:12, **day**; 1 Cor 4:3, *human* **court of judgment**[NIGTC]; (2,419x LXX)

ἡμέτερος, α, ον$_{2.1.2}$ {ἐγώ} *adj.* ❼ Acts 2:11; Rom 15:4; 1 John 1:3, **our**; (22x LXX) ἡμι**θανής, ές**$_{3.3}$ {ἥμισυς + θνήσκω} *adj.* ①^{ams} Luke 10:30, **half dead**; ① LXX, 4 Macc 4:11

ἥμισυς, εια, υ$_{3.1.3}$ *adj.* ❺ Mark 6:23; Luke 19:8; Rev 11:9; 12:14, **one half**; (132x LXX; 33x)

ἡμι**ώριον, ου, τό**$_2$ {ἥμισυς + ὥρα} ①^{ans} Rev 8:1, **half-hour**

ἠνεῴχθησαν → **ἀνοίγω**, *pf. pass. ind. 3p*, Matt 3:16, **opened**

ἠνέχθη → **φέρω**, *aor. pass. ind. 3s*, Matt 14:11; 2 Pet 1:21, **to bring, to come**

ἡνίκα *adv.* ❷ 2 Cor 3:15, **whenever**; 3:16, *but* **whenever**; (102x LXX; 31x Gen, 14x Exod)

ἤ**περ** ① John 12:43, μᾶλλον **ἤπερ**, *more* **than**; ❷ LXX, 2 Macc 14:42; 4 Macc 15:16

ἤπιος, α, ον$_{2.1.2}$ *adj.* ①^{ams} 2 Tim 2:24, **gentle**

Ἤρ, ὁ *Heb.* עֵר ①^{gms} Luke 3:28, **Er**; (11x LXX; 5x Gen)

ἤρεμος, ον$_{2.2}$ *adj.* ①^{ams} 1 Tim 2:2, **tranquil**

ἤρθη → **αἴρω**, *aor. pass. ind. 3s*, Luke 9:17, **they picked up**

Ἡρῴδης, ου, ὁ$_1$ (43x) **Herod** Ⓐ *the Great*, Matt 2:1–22^{9x}; Ⓑ *Antipas*, Matt 14:1; Ⓒ *Agrippa the Elder*, Acts 12:1; Ⓓ *Agrippa the Younger*, Acts 25:13; 26:1

Ἡρῳδιανοί, ῶν, οἱ$_2$ ❸ Matt 22:16; Mark 3:6; 12:13, **Herodians**

Ἡρῳδιάς, άδος, ἡ$_1$ ❻ Matt 14:3, 6; Mark 6:17, 19; Luke 3:19, **Herodias**

Ἡρῳδίων, ωνος, ὁ$_3$ ①^{ams} Rom 16:11, **Herodion**

Ἠσαΐας, ου, ὁ$_2$ (22x; 6x Matt) Matt 3:3 = Mark 1:2 = Luke 3:4 = John 1:23; Acts 8:28; Rom 9:27, **Isaiah**; (36x LXX; 17x Isa, 12x 2 Kgs)

Ἠσαῦ, ὁ *indecl.* ❸ Rom 9:13; Heb 11:20; 12:16, **Esau**; (109x LXX; 81x Gen, 7x Obad)

ἥσσων, ον$_{3.3}$ (*gen.* **ονος**) *adj.* ❷ 1 Cor 11:17; 2 Cor 12:15, **less**; (13x LXX) Job 5:4, **crushed**

ἡσυχάζω {ἥσυχος} ❺ Luke 14:4; Acts 11:18, **to be silent**; Luke 23:56, **to rest**; Acts 21:14, **to refrain**;^{ZEC} 1 Thess 4:11, **to live peaceably**; (42x LXX; 8x Job, 6x Judg; 1 Macc)

ἡσυχία, ας, ἡ$_{1a}$ {ἥσυχος} ❹ Acts 22:2, **quieter**; 2 Thess 3:12, **quietness**; 1 Tim 2:11,^{2x} **non-disruptive**^{PaG}; (12x LXX) 1 Chr 4:40, **peaceful**

ἡσύχιος, ον$_{2.2}$ {ἥσυχος} *adj.* ❷ 1 Tim 2:2; 1 Pet 3:4, **quiet**; ❷ LXX, Isa 66:2, **submissive**

ἤ**τοι** {ἤ + τοι} *part.* ① Rom 6:16, **either**; ① LXX, Wis 11:18

ἡττάομαι {ἥσσων} ❷ 2 Pet 2:19, 20, **to defeat**

ἥττημα, ατος, τό$_3$ {ἥσσων} ❷ Rom 11:12, **loss**; 1 Cor 6:7, **moral defeat**^{NIGTC}; ①^{ans} LXX, Isa 31:8, **forced labor**

ἠχέω^{con} {ἠχή} ①$^{pap.nms}$ 1 Cor 13:1, **noisy** *gong*; (23x LXX) Exod 16:11, **to throb**

ἦχος, ου, ὁ$_2$ {ἠχή} ❹ Luke 4:37, **news**; 21:25, **roaring**; Acts 2:2, **sound**; Heb 12:19, **blast**; (23x LXX) 1 Sam 14:19, **panic, tumult**

Θ, θ [*thēta*]

Θ, θ, τό (θῆτα) *indecl.* **theta**, *8th letter of the Gr. alphabet* ‖ *num.* θʹ = 9; ͵θ = 9,000

Θαδδαῖος, ου, ὁ$_2$ ❷ Matt 10:3 = Mark 3:18, **Thaddaeus**

θάλασσα, ης, ἡ$_{1\eta>}$ {ἅλας} (91x; 26x Rev, 19x Mark) Matt 4:18 = Mark 1:16, **Sea** *of Galilee*; Matt 14:26 = Mark 6:48 = John 6:19, *Jesus walking on the* **sea** (*of Galilee*); Acts 4:24, 27:30 **sea** (*in general*); (432x LXX; 55x Ezek, 50x Josh, 36x Exod)

θάλπω ❷ Eph 5:29, **to cherish**; 1 Thess 2:7, ὡς ἐὰν τροφὸς **θάλπῃ**, *as a wet-nurse might* **cherish**;[ZEC] ❹ LXX, Deut 22:6, *mother hen* **warming** *her young birds or eggs* (LES)

Θαμάρ, ἡ ①[gfs] Matt 1:3, **Tamar**; ❽ LXX, Gen 38:6–26[6x]

θαμβέω[con] {θάμβος} ❸ *act.*, Mark 10:24, **to astonish**; *pass.*, Mark 1:27, 32, **to be astonished**; ❻ LXX, Judg 9:4, **reckless men**; 1 Sam 14:15, **to be terrified**

θάμβος, ους, τό$_3$ {θαμβέω} ❸ Luke 4:36, **amazement**; 5:9, *seized* **with awe**[ZEC]; Acts 3:10, *filled with* **awe**; ❻ LXX, 1 Sam 26:12, **deep sleep**; Ezek 7:18, **horror**

θανάσιμος, ον$_{2.2}$ {θνῄσκω} *adj.* ①[ans] Mark 16:18, **deadly poison**

θανατηφόρος, ον$_{2.2}$ {θνῄσκω + φέρω} *adj.* ①[gms] Jas 3:8, **deadly**; ❺ LXX, Job 33:23

θάνατος, ου, ὁ$_2$ {θνῄσκω} (120x; 22x Rom, 19x Rev) Matt 10:21 = Mark 13:12; John 5:24; Rom 5–8[21x]; Rev 1:18, **death**; 21:8, *the second* **death**; (351x LXX; 28x Pss)

θανατόω[con] {θνῄσκω} (11x) Matt 10:21 = Mark 13:12, *lit.*, **put to death**; Rom 7:4; 8:13, *fig.*, **put to death**; 2 Cor 6:9, *not* **being killed**[BEC]; (151x LXX; 81x 1 Sam–2 Kgs, 13x Lev)

θάπτω (11x) Matt 8:21, 22 = Luke 9:59, 60; Acts 2:29; 1 Cor 15:4, **to bury**; (151x LXX)

Θάρα, ὁ$_3$ *indecl.* ①[gms] Luke 3:34, **Terah**; (11x LXX; 9x Gen) Gen 11:24

θαρρέω[con] {θρασύς} ❻ (5x 2 Cor) 2 Cor 5:6, 8; Heb 13:6, **to be confident**; ❸ LXX, Dan 6:17 (6:16), **be courageous!**

θαρσέω[con] {θρασύς} ❼ Matt 9:2; 14:27 = Mark 6:50; John 16:33; Acts 23:11, **"Have courage!"** (24x LXX) Gen 35:17

θάρσος, ους, τό$_3$ {θρασύς} ①[ans] Acts 28:15, **courage**; ❹ LXX, 2 Chr 16:8; Job 4:4

θαῦμα, ατος, τό$_3$ {θαυμάζω} ❷[nns] 2 Cor 11:14, *no* **wonder**!; Rev 17:6, **I marveled greatly!**[NIGTC]; ❷ LXX, Job 17:8, **appalled**; 18:20, **in horror**

θαυμάζω (43x) Matt 8:10 = Luke 7:9; Rev 17:7, **to be astounded**; Gal 1:6, **I am shocked**[KeenG]; 2 Thess 1:10, **to marvel at**[ZEC]; 1 John 3:13, **to be surprised**; (56x LXX)

θαυμάσιος, α, ον$_{2.1.2}$ {θαυμάζω} *adj.* ①[anp] Matt 21:15, *subst.*, **the wonderful things**; (58x LXX; 32x Pss)

θαυμαστός, ή, όν$_{2.1.2}$ {θαυμάζω} *adj.* ❻ Matt 21:42 = Mark 12:11, **wonderful**; John 9:30; 1 Pet 2:9, **amazing**[Keen1P]; Rev 15:1, 3, **wondrous** *sign*[NIGTC]; (41x LXX; 11x Pss)

θεά, ᾶς, ἡ$_{1\alpha}$ ①[gfs] Acts 19:27, **goddess**; ❷ LXX, Isa 2:16, **sight**; 27:11, **spectacle**

θεάομαι[con] (22x; 15x Gs) Matt 6:1; Luke 7:24; Acts 1:11; 1 John 1:14, **to see**; ❽ LXX

θεατρίζω {θεάομαι} ①[pmp.nmp] Heb 10:33, **to expose to ridicule**[NIGTC]; Pall. *L.* 37.3, *neutral use*, **to represent in the theater**

θέατρον, ου, τό$_2$ {θεάομαι} ❸ Acts 19:29, 31, **amphitheater**; 1 Cor 4:9, **spectacle**
θεῖναι → **τίθημι**, *aor. act. inf.*, Luke 5:18, **to appoint**
θεῖον, ου, τό$_2$ ❼ (6x Rev) Luke 17:29; Rev 9:17; 21:8, **sulfur**; ❽ LXX, Gen 19:24
θεῖος, α, ον$_{2.1.2}$ {θεός} *adj.* ❸ Acts 17:29; 2 Pet 1:3, 4, **divine**; (34x LXX; 24x 4 Macc)
θειότης, ητος, ἡ$_3$ {θεός} ①^{nfs} Rom 1:20, **divine nature**; ①^{gfs} Wis 18:9
θειώδης, ες$_{3.3}$ {θεῖον + εἶδος} *adj.* ①^{amp} Rev 9:17, **sulfurous**
θέλημα, ατος, τό$_3$ {θέλω} (62x, 10x John) Matt 6:10; 12:50 = Mark 3:35; 1 Pet 2:15; Rev 4:11, **will**; 1 Cor 16:12, οὐκ ἦν **θέλημα**, *he was not* **willing**; (44x LXX; 12x Pss)
θέλησις, εως, ἡ$_3$ {θέλω} ①^{afs} Heb 2:4, **will**; ❾ LXX, 2 Chr 15:15, *with their whole* **will**
θέλω (208x; 62x Paul, 42x Matt) (100+ *w/ comp. inf.*) Matt 1:19; Mark 3:13; Rom 7:15–21^{7x}; Phlm 14, **to want**; Matt 2:18; 11:14; Acts 26:5; Jas 2:20, **to will**; (152x LXX; 20x Pss)
θεμέλιον, ου, τό$_2$ {τίθημι} ①^{anp} Acts 16:26, **foundation**; (44x LXX; 11x Pss)
θεμέλιος, ου, ὁ$_2$ (15x) Luke 6:48; 1 Cor 3:10–12^{3x}; Rev 21:19, **foundation**; ❾ LXX
θεμελιόω^{con} {τίθημι} ❺ Matt 7:25, **to be grounded**; Eph 3:17; Heb 1:10; 1 Pet 5:10,^{Keen1P} **to establish**; Col 1:23, **firmly grounded**; (40x LXX; 11x Pss) Josh 6:26; **to lay a foundation**
θεοδίδακτος, ον$_{2.2}$ {θεός + διδάσκω} *adj.* ①^{nmp} 1 Thess 4:9, **God-taught**
θεομάχος, ον$_{2.2}$ {θεός + μάχη} *adj.* ①^{nmp} *subst.*, Acts 5:39, **God-opposing, fighting against God**
θεόπνευστος, ον$_{2.2}$ {θεός + πνέω} *adj.* ①^{nfs} 2 Tim 3:16, **God-breathed**
θεός, ου, ὁ$_2$ (1,317x; 289x LA, 153x Rom) Matt 1:23, μεθ' ἡμῶν ὁ **θεός**, **God** *with us*; Matt 16:16, ὁ υἱὸς **τοῦ θεοῦ**,^{17x} *the Son of* **God**; (3,777x LXX; 462x Pss, 441x Deut)
θεοσέβεια, ας, ἡ$_{1α}$ {θεός + σέβω} ①^{afs} 1 Tim 2:10, **reverence for God**; ❼ LXX
θεοσεβής, ές$_{3.3}$ {θεός + σέβω} *adj.* ①^{nms} John 9:31, **God-fearing**; ❼ LXX, Exod 18:21
θεοστυγής, ές$_{3.3}$ {θεός + στυγέω} *adj.* ①^{amp} Rom 1:30, **God-hater**
θεότης, ητος, ἡ$_3$ {θεός} ①^{gfs} Col 2:9, **divine nature**
Θεόφιλος, ου, ὁ$_2$ {θεός + φίλος} ❷ Luke 1:3; Acts 1:1, **Theophilus**
θεραπεία, ας, ἡ$_{1α}$ {θεράπων} ❸ Luke 9:11, *those who needed* **healing**^{EGG}; 12:42, **servant staff**; Rev 22:2, **healing** *of the nations*; ❻ LXX, Joel 1:14; 2:15, **sacred** *assembly*
θεραπεύω {θεράπων} (43x; 19x LA) Matt 4:23; Mark 1:34; Rev 13:12, **to heal**; (24x LXX)
θεράπων, οντος, ὁ$_3$ {θεραπεύω} ①^{nms} Heb 3:5, **servant**; (64x LXX; 28x Exod) *inclusio*, Exod 4:20 = 14:31, *Moses your* **servant**; 5:21–14:8,^{26x} *Pharaoh and his* **officials**
θερίζω {θέρμη} (21x) Matt 6:26 = Luke 12:24; 2 Cor 9:6,^{2x} **to reap**; Jas 5:4, **the harvesters**; Rev 14:15, **harvested**; (27x LXX; 7x Ruth)
θερισμός, οῦ, ὁ$_7$ {θέρμη} (13x; 6x Matt) Matt 9:37–38^{3x} = Luke 10:2; John 4:35;^{2x} Rev 14:15, **harvest**; (34x LXX; 8x Lev)
θεριστής, οῦ, ὁ$_{1>}$ {θέρμη} ❷ Matt 13:30, 39, **harvester**; ①^{amp} Bel 33, **reaper**
θερμαίνω {θέρμη} ❻ Mark 14:54, **to warm oneself**; Jas 2:16, **stay warm**; (13x LXX)
θέρμη, ης, ἡ$_{1η}$ ①^{gfs} Acts 28:3, **heat**
θέρος, ους, τό$_3$ {θέρμη} ❸ Matt 24:32 = Mark 13:28 = Luke 21:30, **summer**; ❽ LXX; 3x Prov
Θεσσαλονικεύς, έως, ὁ$_3$ ❹ Acts 20:4; 27:2; 1 Thess 1:1, 2 Thess 1:1, **Thessalonian**
Θεσσαλονίκη, ης, ἡ$_{1η}$ ❺ Acts 17:1, 11; Phil 4:16, **Thessalonica**
θέτε → **τίθημι**, *aor. act. imp. 2p*, Luke 21:14, **make up** *your minds*
Θευδᾶς, ᾶ, ὁ$_1$ ①^{nms} Acts 5:36, **Theudas**

θεωρέω[con] {θεάομαι} (58x; 24x John) Matt 27:55 = Mark 15:40, **to watch** *from a distance*; Matt 28:1 = Mark 16:4, **to look**; John 2:23; Acts 3:16; Rev 11:11, **to see**; (53x LXX; 11x Dan)

θεωρία, ας, ἡ$_{1α}$ {θεάομαι} ①[afs] Luke 23:48, **spectacle**; ❹ LXX, Dan 5:7, **mysterious writing**

θήκη, ης, ἡ$_{1η}$ {τίθημι} ①[afs] John 18:11, **sheath**; ❸ LXX, Exod 25:27, **holder**

θηλάζω ❺ Matt 24:19 = Mark 13:17 = Luke 21:23, **to nurse**; (30x LXX) Exod 2:7

θῆλυς, εια, υ$_{3.1.3}$ {θηλάζω} *adj.* ❺ Matt 19:4 = Mark 10:6; Gal 3:28, **female**; Rom 1:26, 27, **women**; (36x LXX; 12x Lev, 10x Gen) Gen 1:27; 6:19; Lev 3:1

θήρα, ας, ἡ$_{1α}$ {θήρ} ①[afs] Rom 11:9, **trap**; (29x LXX) Gen 27:3–27:33,[8x] **game, prey**

θηρεύω {θήρ} ①[aainf] Luke 11:54, **to trap**; (19x LXX; 4x Pss, 3x Gen:Jer:Lam) Gen 27:3

θηριομαχέω[con] {θήρ + μάχη} ①[aai1s] 1 Cor 15:32, **to fight wild animals**[*WLC* 28]

θηρίον, ου, τό$_{2}$ {θήρ} (46x; 39x Rev) Mark 1:13, **wild animal**; Rev 11:7, **wild thing**,[*RRU* 14] **beast** *out of the abyss*; 13:1–18,[16x] *1st and 2nd* **beast**; 20:10, **beast** (*alongside devil and false prophet*); (141x LXX; 20x 1–3 Macc, 19x Gen, 17x Ezek:Dan)

θησαυρίζω {τίθημι} ❽ Matt 6:19; Rom 2:5; 2 Pet 3:7, **to store up**; 1 Cor 16:2, **to put aside**[NIGTC]; 2 Cor 12:14, **to save up**[BEC]; Jas 5:3, **to store up treasure**; (14x LXX; 4x Prov)

θησαυρός, οῦ, ὁ$_{2}$ {τίθημι} (17x; 9x Matt) Matt 2:11; 6:19; 2 Cor 4:7; Col 2:3; Heb 11:26, **treasure**; (91x LXX; 19x 1–2 Chr)

θήσω → τίθημι, *fut. act. ind. 1s*, Matt 12:18, **I will put**

θιγγάνω ❸ Col 2:21; Heb 11:28; 12:20, **to touch**; ①[aainf] Exod 19:12, **to touch** *the mountain*

θλίβω (10x) *act.*, Mark 3:9, **to press**; *pass.*, Matt 7:14, **to be confined**[ZEC]; 2 Cor 1:6; Heb 11:37, **to be afflicted**; 2 Cor 7:5, **hounded by trouble in every way**[BEC]; (97x LXX)

θλῖψις, εως, ἡ$_{3}$ {θλίβω} (45x; 9x 2 Cor) Matt 13:21 = Mark 4:17, **trouble**; Matt 24:29 = Mark 13:24, **tribulation**; John 16:21, **suffering**; Rom 2:9; 2 Cor 4:17; Rev 2:22, **affliction**; 2 Cor 2:4, **gut-wrenching**[BEC]; Jas 1:27, **difficulty**[KEL]; (132x LXX; 35x Pss)

θνήσκω ❾ Matt 2:20, **to die**; John 11:44, **ὁ τεθνηκώς**, **the dead man**; (93x LXX; 18x 1 Kgs)

θνητός, ή, όν$_{2.1.2}$ {θνήσκω} *adj.* ❻ Rom 6:12; 1 Cor 15:53; 2 Cor 4:11, **mortal**; ❾ LXX

θορυβάζω {θόρυβος} ①[ppi2s] Luke 10:41, **to fret**[ZEC]

θορυβέω[con] ❹ Matt 9:23[ZEC] = Mark 5:39,[ZEC] **to be in an uproar**; Acts 17:5, **they started a riot**; 20:10, *don't* **be alarmed!** ❺ LXX, Nahum 2:4 (2:3), **to quiver**

θόρυβος, ου, ὁ$_{2}$ ❺ Matt 26:5, **riot**; Mark 5:38, **commotion**; Acts 20:1, **turmoil**; (12x LXX)

θραύω ①[pfmp.amp] Luke 4:18, **to be set free**[EGG]; (24x LXX) Exod 15:6, **to shatter**

θρέμμα, ατος, τό$_{3}$ {τρέφω} ①[nnp] John 4:12, **livestock**

θρηνέω[con] {θρόος} ❹ Matt 11:17 = Luke 7:32; 23:27, **to sing a lament**; John 16:20, **to mourn**; (27x LXX; 6x Ezek)

θρησκεία, ας, ἡ$_{1α}$ {θρησκός} ❹ Acts 26:5; Jas 1:26, 27, **religion**; Col 2:18, **worship** *of angels*; ❹ LXX, 4 Macc 5:7, 13

θρησκός, ον$_{2.2}$ *adj.* ①[nms] Jas 1:26, **religious**

θριαμβεύω ❷ 2 Cor 2:14, **to lead in triumphal procession**[BEC!]; Col 2:15, **to triumph over**; Strabo *Geogr.* 12.3.6, *pass.*, *Adiatorix* **was led in triumph** *and slain together with his son*

θρίξ, τρίχος, ἡ$_{3}$ (15x) Matt 3:4 = Mark 1:6, *camel* **hair**; Matt 10:30 = Luke 12:7; John 11:2; Rev 1:14, **hair**; (45x LXX; 16x Lev → *hair rules*)

θροέω[con] ❸ Matt 24:6 = Mark 13:7, **to be alarmed**; 2 Thess 2:2, **to be disturbed**; ①[api3s] LXX, Song 5:4, *feelings* **were stirred** *for him*

θρόμβος, ου, ὁ$_2$ {τρέφω} ①^{nmp} Luke 22:44, **drops** *of blood*

θρόνος, ου, ὁ$_2$ (62x, 47x Rev) Matt 5:34; Acts 2:30; Heb 1:8,^{NIGTC} **throne**; Rev 4:2–5:13,^{19x} *throne room vision*$^{BEC, NCBC}$; (160x LXX; 33x 1 Kgs, 18x Pss)

Θυάτειρα, ων, τά$_3$ ❹ Acts 16:14; Rev 1:11; 2:18, 24, **Thyatira**

θυγάτηρ, τρος, ἡ$_3$ (28x; 19x Syn) Matt 15:22; Mark 6:22; Luke 1:5; Acts 7:21; 2 Cor 6:18, **daughter**; Matt 21:5 = John 12:15, **Daughter** *of Zion*; (585x LXX; 102x Gen, 41x Ezek)

θυγάτριον, ου, τό$_2$ {θυγάτηρ} ❷ Mark 5:23; 7:25, **little daughter**

θύελλα, ης, ἡ$_{1η>}$ {θύω} ①^{dfs} Heb 12:18, **windstorm**; ❸ LXX, Exod 10:22, **furious storm**

θύϊνος, η, ον$_{2.1.2}$ {θύω, θυίω → *to smell good*} *adj.* ①^{ans} Rev 18:12, **citron** *wood*

θυμίαμα, ατος, τό$_3$ {θύω, θυίω → *to smell good*} ❻ (4x Rev) Luke 1:10; Rev 5:8, **incense**; (78x LXX; 21x Num, 15x Exod)

θυμιατήριον, ου, τό$_2$ {θύω, θυίω → *to smell good*} ①^{ans} Heb 9:4, **incense**; ❸ LXX, 2 Chr 26:19, **censer**

θυμιάω^{con} {θύω, θυίω → *to smell good*} ①^{aainf} Luke 1:9, **to burn incense**; (69x LXX; 19x Jer)

θυμομαχέω^{con} {θύμος + μάχη} ①$^{pap.nms}$ Acts 12:20, **to be infuriated**

θυμός, ου, ὁ$_2$ (18x; 10x Rev) Luke 4:26, **enraged**; Acts 19:28, *filled* **with fury**; Rev 14:8, **wrath**; 19:15, **the fierce** *anger of God*; (630x LXX; 45x Isa, 31x Ezek)

θυμόω^{con} {θύμος} ①^{api3s} **ἐθυμώθη** λίαν, Matt 2:16, **to be violently enraged**^{WPNT}; (63x LXX; 10x 1–2 Sam) Gen 6:7; 1 Sam 11:6

θύρα, ας, ἡ$_{1α}$ (39x) Matt 6:6; Luke 11:7; Acts 5:9; 1 Cor 16:9; Rev 3:8, **door**; Matt 27:60, **entrance**; John 10:1; Acts 3:2, **gate**; (206x LXX; 27x Lev, 24x Exod)

θυρεός, οῦ, ὁ$_2$ {θύρα} ①^{ams} Eph 6:16, **shield**; (22x LXX; 10x 2 Chr)

θυρίς, ίδος, ἡ$_3$ {θύρα} ❷ Acts 20:9; 2 Cor 11:33, **window**; (34x LXX; 12x Ezek); Ezek 40:16–41:26, **windows** *in Ezekiel's vision of the future temple*

θυρωρός, οῦ, ὁ$_2$ {θύρα} ❹ Mark 13:34; John 18:16, 17, **doorkeeper**; 10:3, **gatekeeper**; (10x LXX; 7x 1 Esd)

θυσία, ας, ἡ$_{1α}$ {θύω, θυίω → *to smell good*} (28x; 15x Heb) Matt 9:13; Mark 12:33; Rom 12:1; Heb 7:27; 10:26; 1 Pet 2:5, **sacrifice**; (386x LXX; 84x Num, 78x Lev)

θυσιαστήριον, ου, τό$_2$ {θύω, θυίω → *to smell good*} (23x; 8x Rev) Matt 5:23; Luke 1:11; Rom 11:3; 1 Cor 10:18; Heb 7:13; Rev 11:1, **altar**; (424x LXX; 89x Lev, 55x Exod)

θύω (14x; 8x LA) Matt 22:4, **to slaughter** *cattle*; Mark 14:12; 1 Cor 5:7; 10:20, **to sacrifice**; Luke 15:23, 27, 30, **to slaughter** *the fattened calf*; John 10:10; Acts 10:13; 11:7, **to kill**; (134x LXX; 18x Exod, 15x 1 Sam)

θῶ → τίθημι, *aor. act. subj. 1s*, ❺ Matt 22:44 = Mark 12:36 = Luke 20:43, *until* **I put**

Θωμᾶς, ᾶ, ἡ$_{1α}$ (11x; 7x John) Matt 10:3 = Mark 3:18 = Luke 6:15; John 11:16, **Thomas**

θώραξ, ακος, ἡ$_3$ ❺ Eph 6:14; 1 Thess 5:8; Rev 8:9; 9:17, **breastplate**; (16x LXX; 3x 1 Macc) 1 Sam 17:5,^{2x} **coat** *of mail*

Ι, ι [*iōta*]

Ι, ι, τό (ἰῶτα) *indecl.* **iota**, *9th letter of the Gr. alphabet* ‖ *num.* ιʹ = 10; ͵ι = 10,000; *usu. subscript in diphthongs*, ᾳ, ῃ, or ῳ. Matt 5:18, **ἰῶτα** ἓν ἢ μία κεραία οὐ μὴ παρέλθῃ ἀπὸ τοῦ νόμου, *not* **the smallest letter** *or stroke of a letter will pass from the law*

Ἰάϊρος, ου, ὁ$_2$ ❷ Mark 5:22 = Luke 8:41, **Jairus**

Ἰακώβ, ου, ὁ$_3$ (27x; 12x LA) Mark 12:26 = Luke 20:37, **Jacob**; (404x LXX; 200x Gen) Gen 25:26

Ἰάκωβος, ου, ὁ$_2$ (42x; 15x Mark, 15x LA) **James**; Ⓐ *son of Zebedee*, Matt 4:21 = Mark 1:19 = Luke 5:10; Ⓑ *son of Alphaeus*, Matt 10:3; Ⓒ *James the Less*, Acts 15:13; Gal 1:19

ἴαμα, ατος, τό$_3$ {ἰάομαι} ❸[nnp] 1 Cor 12:9, 28, 30, **healing**; (10x LXX) Isa 26:19, **healing** (*resurrection?*)[NAC, Mot]; 58:8, **recovery**

Ἰαμβρῆς, οῦ, ὁ$_1$ ①[nms] 2 Tim 3:8, **Jambres**

Ἰανναί, ὁ$_3$ *indecl.* ①[gms] Luke 3:24, **Jannai**

Ἰάννης, ου, ὁ$_1$ ①[nms] 2 Tim 3:8, **Jannes**

ἰάομαι[con] (26x; 15x LA) Matt 15:28 = Mark 5:29 = Luke 8:47, **to heal**; (66x LXX; 10x Isa)

Ἰάρετ, ὁ$_3$ *indecl.* ①[gms] Luke 3:37, **Jared**; ①[nms] LXX, 1 Chr 1:2

ἴασις, εως, ἡ$_3$ {ἰάομαι} ❸ Luke 13:32; Acts 4:22, 30, **healing**; (28x LXX; 8x Sir)

ἴασπις, ιδος, ἡ$_3$ ❹ Rev 4:3; 21:11, 18, 19, **jasper**; ❹ LXX, Ezek 28:13, **emerald**

Ἰάσων, ονος, ὁ$_3$ ❺ **Jason**, *Paul's host at Thess.*, Acts 17:5, 6, 7, 9; Rom 16:21; (15x LXX; 1–4 Macc) *3 men in LXX*, 1 Macc 8:17; 2 Macc 2:23; 4:7

ἰατρός, οῦ, ὁ$_2$ {ἰάομαι} ❼ Matt 19:12 = Mark 2:17 = Luke 5:31, **physician**; (13x LXX; 5x Sir)

ἴδε {εἶδος} *interj.* (29x; 15x John) Matt 25:20, **Behold! See!**; John 18:21, **Look!**

ἰδέα, ας, ἡ$_{1α}$ ❺ LXX, Gen 5:3; Ep Jer 62; 2 Macc 3:16; 4 Macc 1:14, 18, **likeness**; Hdt. *Hist.* 1.80.4, **aspect, appearance**[*BrDAG*]

ἴδιος, α, ον$_{2.1.2}$ *adj.* (114x; 22x LA, 16x 1 Cor) 1 Cor 3:8; 14:35, **own**; (79x LXX; 20x 1–2 Macc)

ἰδιώτης, ου, ὁ$_1$ ❺ Acts 4:13; **amateurs**[ZEC] (≠ idiots); 1 Cor 14:16, 23, 24, **uninitiated**[NIGTC]; 2 Cor 11:6, **amateur**[BEC]; ①[nmp] LXX, Prov 6:8, *kings and* **commoners**

ἰδού → **ὁράω**, *aor. mid. imp. 2s*; Ⓐ ***demonstr. particle***, (200x; 80x LA, 62x Matt) Matt 20:18 = Mark 10:33 = Luke 18:31, **to see**; Ⓑ ***dramatic usage***, **Look!**; (1092x LXX; 123x Jer, 101x Ezek, 86x Gen) *serves as enlivening narrative device*[Runge 163–77]

Ἰδουμαία, ας, ἡ$_{1α}$ ①[gfs] Mark 3:8, **Idumea**[*LGCa* 123]; (54x LXX; 7x Jer) Gen 36:16, Josh 15:1

ἱδρώς, ῶτος, ὁ$_3$ ① Luke 22:44, **sweat**; ❸ LXX, Gen 3:19, **sweat** *of your brow*

ἰδών → **ὁράω**, *aor. act. ptc. nms*, (61x) Matt 2:16, **when he saw**

Ἰεζάβελ, ἡ$_3$ *indecl.* ①[afs] Rev 2:20, **Jezebel**; (22x LXX) 1 Kgs 16:31–2 Kgs 9:37, **Jezebel**

Ἱεράπολις, εως, ἡ$_3$ ①[dfs] Col 4:13, **Hierapolis**[*LGCb* 686]

ἱερατεία, ας, ἡ$_{1α}$ {ἱερός} ❷ Luke 1:9, **priesthood**; Heb 7:5, **priestly office**; (17x LXX)

ἱεράτευμα, ατος, τό$_3$ ❷ 1 Pet 2:5, *a consecrated* **community of priests**[Keen1P]; 2:9, *a royal* **community of priests**[Keen1P]; ❸ LXX, Exod 19:6; 23:22, **royal priesthood**

ἱερατεύω ①painf Luke 1:8, **to serve as priest**; (27x LXX; 10x Exod) Exod 28:1–40:15, *the birth of the Aaronic priesthood*

Ἰερεμίας, ου, ὁ$_1$ ❸ Matt 2:17; 16:14; 27:9, **Jeremiah**; (121x LXX; 97x Jer)

ἱερεύς, έως, ὁ$_3$ {ἱερός} (31x; 14x Heb) Matt 8:4 = Mark 1:44 = Luke 5:14, **priest**; Heb 7:1–10,[2x] *Melchizedek, the royal* **priest**; Heb 7:11–28,[7x] *Jesus, eternal* **priest**; (881x LXX; 211x Lev, 90x 2 Chr, 70x Num) **priest**, Lev 1:5–27:3, *passim*

Ἰεριχώ, ἡ$_3$ *indecl.* ❼ Matt 20:29 = Mark 10:46; Luke 10:30; Heb 11:30, **Jericho**; (63x LXX; 29x Josh) Josh 2:1–24:11, *the Jericho campaign*

ἱερόθυτος, ον$_{2.2}$ {ἱερός + θύω} *adj.* ①nns 1 Cor 10:28, **offered in sacrifice**

ἱερόν, οῦ, τό$_2$ {ἱερός} (72x; 39x LA) Matt 26:55 = Mark 14:49 = Luke 22:52; John 2:14; Acts 2:46; 1 Cor 9:13, **temple**; (75x LXX; 26x 2 Macc, 25x 1 Esd)

ἱεροπρεπής, ές$_{3.3}$ {ἱερός + πρέπω} *adj.* ①afp Titus 2:3, **reverent**; ❷ LXX, 4 Macc 9:25

ἱερός, ά, όν$_{2.1.2}$ *adj.* ❸ Mark 16:8b (*short ending of Mark*),[BHGNT 283] **sacred** *preaching*; 1 Cor 9:13, **sacred duties**[NIGTC]; 2 Tim 3:15, **sacred** *scriptures* (39x LXX; 15x 4 Macc, 12x 1 Esd)

Ἱεροσόλυμα, τά *or* **ἡ**$_{1α}$ {ἱερός} *indecl.* (62x; 25x Syn, 22x Acts) Matt 20:17 = Mark 10:32 = Luke 22:52; John 10:22; Acts 1:4, **Jerusalem**; (43x LXX; 24x 2 Macc[ABC])

Ἱεροσολυμίτης, ου, ὁ$_{1>}$ ❷ Mark 1:5; John 7:25, **Jerusalemite**; ❸ LXX, 4 Macc 4:22, **inhabitants of Jerusalem**

ἱεροσυλέω {ἱερός + συλάω} ①pai2s Rom 2:22, **to rob a temple**; ①painf LXX, 4 Macc 9:2

ἱερόσυλος, ου, ὁ$_1$ {ἱερός + συλάω} ①amp Acts 19:37, **temple-robbers**, ①ams LXX, 2 Macc 4:42

ἱερουργέωcon {ἱερός + ἔργον} ①pap.ams Rom 15:16, **priestly service**

Ἰερουσαλήμ, ἡ$_3$ *indecl.* (77x; 64x LA) Luke 2:25; Acts 1:8, **Jerusalem**[*LGCb* 395]; (838x LXX)

ἱερωσύνη, ῆς, ἡ$_{1η}$ {ἱερός} ❸ Heb 7:11, 12, 24, *Levitical* **priesthood**; ❽ LXX, 1 Chr 29:22; 1 Esd 5:38; 1 Macc 2:54

Ἰεσσαί, ὁ$_3$ *indecl.* ❺ Matt 1:5 = Luke 3:32; Acts 13:22; Rom 15:12, **Jesse**; (38x LXX; 20x 1 Sam) 1 Sam 16:1, *Jesse's son, David, enters the narrative*

Ἰεφθάε, ὁ$_3$ *indecl.* ①gms Heb 11:32, **Jephthah**; (31x LXX; 30x Judg, 1x 1 Sam) Judg 11:1–12:7, *the Jephthah saga/cycle*; 1 Sam 12:11, *the Lord sent* . . . **Jephthah**

Ἰεχονίας, ου, ὁ$_1$ ❷ Matt 1:11, 12, **Jeconiah**, *alt. form of* **Jehoiachin**; (16x LXX) Jer 24:1

Ἰησοῦς, ου, ὁ$_1$ (917x; 244x John, 157x LA, 152x Matt) Matt 3:16 = Mark 1:9 = Luke 3:21 = John 1:29, **Jesus**; (272x LXX; 172x Josh) **Joshua**

ἱκανός, ή, όν$_{2.1.2}$ *adj.* (39x; 27x LA) Matt 3:11 = Mark 1:7 = Luke 3:16, **worthy**; Luke 22:38, **Enough!**[ZEC!]; Luke 23:8, *a* **long** *time*; Acts 12:12, **many**; 1 Cor 15:9, **competent**[NIGTC]; 2 Cor 2:6, **sufficient**[BEC]; (47x LXX; 6x 2 Macc) Gen 30:15, *isn't it* **enough?**

ἱκανότης, ητος, ἡ$_3$ {ἱκανός} ①nfs 2 Cor 3:5, *not that we are* **qualified**[BEC]

ἱκανόωcon {ἱκανός} ❷ *act.*, Col 1:12, **who has qualified** *you*; 2 Cor 3:6, *pass.*, **made** *us* **competent**[BEC]; (15x LXX) 2 Sam 19:4, **I've had enough!** (*same sentiment as Jesus in Luke 22:38*)

ἱκετηρία, ας, ἡ$_{1α}$ {ἱκανός} ①afp Heb 5:7, **urgent supplication**[NIGTC]; ❷ LXX, Job 40:27, **petition**; Hdt. *Hist.* 5.51.1, *olive branch of* **supplication**

ἰκμάς, άδος, ἡ$_3$ ①afs Luke 8:6, *lacked* **moisture**[EGG]; ❷ LXX, Job 26:14, *how* **faint**; Jer 17:8, **moist**; *medic.*, Hp. *Aër.* 8, *the sun extracts the most* **subtle** *part of a man's humor*

Ἰκόνιον, ου, τό$_2$ ❻ Acts 13:51; 14:1, 19, 21; 2 Tim 3:11, **Iconium**[*LGCb* 301]

ἱλαρός, ά, όν$_{2.1.2}$ {ἵλεως} *adj.* ①^{ams} 2 Cor 9:7, **cheerful**; ❻ LXX, Prov 19:12, **favor**; 22:8, **cheerful**; Xen. *Mem.* 2.7.12, **hilarious, glad, jolly**

ἱλαρότης, ητος, ἡ$_{3}$ {ἵλεως} ①^{dfs} Rom 12:8, **cheerfulness**; ❸ LXX, Prov 18:22, **gladness**

ἱλάσκομαι {ἵλεως} ❷ Luke 18:13, **to be merciful**; Heb 2:17, **to remove impurity**[EGG!]; (10x LXX; 4x Pss) 2 Kgs 5:18, **to pardon**

ἱλασμός, οῦ, ὁ$_{2}$ {ἵλεως} ❷ 1 John 2:2; 4:10, **atoning sacrifice**[ZEC]; ❻ LXX, Lev 25:9, *Day of Atonement*; Ps 129:4 (130:4), **forgiveness**[NIDNTT]

ἱλαστήριον, ου, τό$_{2}$ {ἵλεως} ❷ Rom 3:25[ZEC]; Heb 9:5, **the mercy seat**; (28x LXX) Exod 25:17–22^{7x}; Lev 16:2–15,^{7x} *the ark's* **atonement** *cover*, **the mercy seat**

ἵλεως, ων$_{2.2}$ *adj.* ❷ Matt 16:22, ἵλεώς σοι, **Far be it** *from you, Lord!*[ZEC]; Heb 8:12, *I will* **forgive** *their wrongdoings*; (34x LXX) 2 Sam 23:17, **Forbid me**, *Lord*!

Ἰλλυρικόν, οῦ, τό$_{2}$ ①^{gns} Rom 15:19, **Illyricum**

ἱμάς, άντος, ὁ$_{3}$ ❹ Mark 1:7 = Luke 3:16 = John 1:27; Acts 22:25, *sandal* **strap**; ❺ LXX, Job 39:10, *ox* **harness**; Isa 5:18, 27, *yoke* **strap**

ἱματίζω {ἱμάτιον} ❷$^{pfmp.ans}$ Mark 5:15 = Luke 8:35, **fully clothed**

ἱμάτιον, ου, τό$_{2}$ (60x; 35x Syn) Matt 27:35 = Mark 15:24 = Luke 23:34 = John 19:23, **garments, clothes**; (215x LXX; 46x Lev, 19x Num)

ἱματισμός, ου, ὁ$_{2}$ {ἱμάτιον} ❺ Luke 7:25; 9:29; John 19:24; 1 Tim 2:9, **clothes**; (30x LXX; 4x Exod) Exod 3:22

ἵνα *conj.* (663x; 149x Syn, 145x John, 42x Rev)[NTWSD] Ⓐ ***telic***, **1.** *w/ subj., foll. pres/aor.*; Acts 16:30, **so that**; **2.** *w/ opt.*, Eph 1:17, *volitive*, **that** *God . . . may give*[WPNT]; **3.** *w/ ind.*, Rev 22:14, **so that**; Ⓑ ***result only w/ subj.***, **1.** *foll. pres.*, Luke 22:30; **2.** *foll. imper.*, 1 John 2:28; **3.** *foll. fut.*, Phil 1:26; **4.** *foll. aor/impf*, Rom 5:20^{aor}; Mark 6:41,^{impf} **that, so that**; Ⓒ ***demonstrative*** = ὅτι, **that**; Mark 9:12; Rom 4:23 (603x LXX; 57x Deut, 50x Gen: Exod)

ἱνατί {ἵνα + τίς} *conj.* ❻ Matt 9:4; Luke 13:7; 1 Cor 10:29, **why?**

Ἰόππη, ης, ἡ$_{1\eta}$ (10x, Acts) 9:36–11:13, **Joppa**[LGCb 238f]; (16x LXX; 10x 1 Macc) Jonah 1:3

Ἰορδάνης, ου, ὁ$_{1>}$ (15x) Matt 3:5 = Mark 1:5 = Luke 3:3, **Jordan**[LGCa 42–48]; (205x LXX; 73x Josh)

ἰός, οῦ, ὁ$_{2}$ ❸ Rom 3:13, **venom** *of asps*; Jas 3:8, **poison**; Jas 5:3, **rust**[BEC]; (11x LXX; 5x Ezek) Prov 23:32, **viper**; Ezek 24:6, **scum**; 24:11, 12, **corrosion**

Ἰουδαία, ας, ἡ$_{1\alpha}$ (43x; 22x LA, 8x Matt) Matt 2:1; Luke 3:1; Acts 1:8; Rom 15:31, **Judea**[LGC 46a-b]; (126x LXX; 29x 1 Macc, 23x 1 Esd)

Ἰουδαϊκός, ή, όν$_{2.1.2}$ *adj.* ①^{dmp} Titus 1:14, **Jewish**; ①^{gfs} LXX, 2 Macc 13:21

Ἰουδαϊκῶς, *adv.* ① Gal 2:14, **like a Jew**

Ἰουδαῖος, αία, αῖον$_{2.1.2}$ *adj.* (194x; 84x LA, 70x John) Matt 27:11 = Mark 15:2 = Luke 23:3 = John 18:33, **Jewish**; (209x LXX; 124x 1–3 Macc)

Ἰουδαϊσμός, οῦ, ὁ$_{2}$ ❷^{dms} Gal 1:13, 14, **Judaism**; ❺ LXX, 2 Macc 2:21; 4 Macc 4:26

Ἰούδας, α, ὁ$_{1}$ (44x; 39x GA, *9 diff ind*) Ⓐ **Judas** *Iscariot*, Matt 26:47 = Mark 14:43 = Luke 22:47 = John 18:2; Ⓑ *the author of Jude*, Jude 1; Ⓒ *seven other individuals in NT*; (901x LXX; 149x 2 Chr, 145x Jer), **Judah**

Ἰουλία, ας, ἡ$_{1\alpha}$ ①^{afs} Rom 16:15, **Julia**

Ἰούλιος, ου, ὁ$_{2}$ ❷ Acts 27:1, 3, **Julius**

Ἰουνιᾶς, ᾶ, ὁ$_{1}$ ①^{ams} Rom 16:7, **Junias**

Ἰοῦστος, ου, ὁ$_{2}$ ❸ Acts 1:23; 18:7; Col 4:11, **Justus**

ἱππεύς, έως, ὁ$_3$ {ἵππος} ❷^{amp} Acts 23:23, 32, **horsemen**; (67x LXX; 10x 1–2 Kgs, 9x 2 Macc)

ἱππικός, ή, όν$_{2.1.2}$ *adj.* ①^{gns} Rev 9:16, *subst.*, **cavalry, horseman**; ❷ LXX, 1 Macc 15:38; 3 Macc 1:1, *subst.*, **horsemen**; Plato *Leg.* 949a, *gymnastic and equestrian competition*

ἵππος, ου, ὁ$_2$ (17x; 16x Rev) Jas 3:3; Rev 6:2–8; 19:11–21, **horse**; (204x LXX; 36 1–2 Kings)

ἶρις, ιδος, ἡ$_3$ ❷ Rev 4:3; 10:1, **rainbow**; ①^{gfs} LXX, Exod 30:24, **cassia**

Ἰσαάκ, ὁ$_3$ *indecl.* (20x; 7x LA) Matt 22:32 = Mark 12:26 = Luke 20:37, **Isaac**; (131x LXX; 87x Gen)

ἰσάγγελος, ον$_3$ {ἴσος + ἀγγέλλος} *adj.* ①^{nmp} Luke 20:36, **equal to angels**;

ἴσθι → **εἰμί**, *pres act. imp. 2s*, (5x) Matt 2:13, **Remain** *there*!

Ἰσκαριώθ, ὁ$_3$ *indecl.* ❸ Mark 3:19; 14:10; Luke 6:16, *Judas* **Iscariot**

Ἰσκαριώτης, ου, ὁ$_1$ ❽ Matt 10:4; 26:14; Luke 22:3; John 6:71; 12:4; 13:2, *Judas* **Iscariot**; John 14:22, Ἰούδας, οὐχ ὁ **Ἰσκαριώτης**, *Judas, not* **Iscariot**

ἴσος, η, ον$_{2.1.2}$ *adj.* ❽ Rev 21:16, **equal**; Mark 14:56, **agree**; Luke 6:34, **τὰ ἴσα**, **the same amount**^{ZEC}; Acts 11:17, *the* **same** *gift*; Phil 2:6, **equality** *with God*; (40x LXX; 13 Job, 11x Ezek)

ἰσότης, ητος, ἡ$_3$ ❸ 2 Cor 8:13, 14, **equality**^{BEC}; Col 4:1, **fairness**; ❸ LXX, Job 36:29, **as though it were**; Plato *Leg.* 733b, *political* **equality**; Luc. *Zeuxis* 5, **harmonic equilibrium**; Plato *Gorg.* 508a, *geom.* **equality**

ἰσότιμος, ον$_{2.2}$ {ἴσος + τιμή} *adj.* ①^{afs} 2 Pet 1:1, **equal standing**

ἰσόψυχος, ον$_{2.2}$ {ἴσος + ψύχω} *adj.* ①^{ams} Phil 2:20, **like-minded**; ①^{vms} LXX, Ps 54:14 (55:13)

Ἰσραήλ, ὁ$_3$ *indecl.* (68x; 27x LA, 12x Matt, 11x Rom) Matt 27:42 = Mark 15:32; Rom 9:6; 2 Cor 3:13, **Israel**; (2,748x LXX; 358x 1–2 Kgs, 292x 1–2 Chr, 269x 1–2 Sam, 187x Ezek)

Ἰσραηλίτης, ου, ὁ$_{1>}$ ❾ (5x Acts) John 1:47; Acts 2:22, **Israelite**; (11x LXX) Lev 24:10

Ἰσσαχάρ, ὁ$_3$ *indecl.* ①^{gms} Rev 7:7, **Issachar**; (40x LXX; 11x Num)

ἴστε → **οἶδα**, *pf. act. imp. 2p*, (3x) Eph 5:5, **be sure!** Heb 12:17, **you know!** (*unquestioned fact*)^{EGG}; Jas 1:19, **take note of this!**^{EGG}

ἵστημι (154x; 61x LA, 21x Rev) Matt 12:25 = Mark 3:24 = Luke 11:18; Rev 3:20, **to stand**; Mark 10:49, **to stop**; Acts 7:60, **to hold**; Heb 10:9, **to establish**; (698x LXX; 133x Pent)

ἱστορέω^{con} {ἱστορία} ①^{aainf} Gal 1:18, **to get to know**; ❸ LXX, 1 Esd 1:31, **reported**

ἰσχυρός, ά, όν$_{2.1.2}$ {ἰσχύς} *adj.* (29x; 9x Rev) Matt 3:11 = Mark 1:7 = Luke 3:16; 1 Cor 1:25, **stronger**; 1 John 2:14, **strong**; 2 Cor 10:10, **powerful**; (143x LXX; 13x Dan, 11x 1 Chr) Gen 41:31, **very grievous**; Prov 21:14, **fierce** *rage*; Job 37:5, *thunders* **wondrously**

ἰσχύς, ύος, ἡ$_3$ (10x) Mark 12:30 = Luke 10:27; Eph 6:10; Rev 5:12, **strength**; (326x LXX; 39x Isa, 24x Job, Ezek) Job 6:11, **strength**; Ruth 2:1, **noble character**

ἰσχύω (28x; 14x LA) Matt 5:13, **to have value**^{ZEC}; 8:28, *nothing* **(is strong enough)**; Phil 4:13, **I am strong enough** *for all these things*^{BEC}; Matt 9:12 = Mark 2:17, *those* **who are well**; John 21:6, *not* **able**; Jas 5:16, **powerful**; (100x LXX; 22x Isa) Isa 1:24

ἴσως *adv.* ① Luke 20:13, **perhaps**; ❾ LXX, Gen 32:21; Jer 5:4; 33:3 (26:3)

Ἰταλία, ας, ἡ$_{1α}$ ❹ Acts 18:2; 27:1, 6; Heb 13:24, **Italy**

Ἰταλικός, ή, όν$_{2.1.2}$ *adj.* ①^{gfs} Acts 10:1, **Italian** *Cohort*

Ἰτουραῖος, αία, αῖον$_{2.1.2}$ *adj.* ①^{gfs} Luke 3:1, *subst.*, **Iturea**; ①^{gmp} LXX, 1 Chr 5:19, *subst.*, **Itourites**

ἰχθύδιον, ου, τό$_2$ {ἰχθύς} ❷ Matt 15:34 = Mark 8:7, **small fish**

ἰχθύς, ύος, ὁ$_3$ (20x, 19x Gs) Matt 14:19 = Mark 6:41 = Luke 9:16, **fish**; (35x LXX; 9x Tob, 7x Ezek)

ἴχνος, ους, τό$_3$ ❸ Rom 4:12; 2 Cor 12:18; 1 Pet 2:21, **steps**; (35x LXX) Gen 42:9

Ἰωαθάμ, ὁ$_3$ *indecl.* ❷ Matt 1:9,^{2x} *King* **Jotham**; (23x LXX; 7x 2 Kgs, 6x 2 Chr) 🅐 Judg 9:5, *Gideon's youngest son*; 🅑 2 Kgs 15:32, *king of Judah*, 750–742 BCE 🅒 1 Chr 2:47, *son of Jahdai*

Ἰωανάν, ὁ$_3$ *indecl.* ①^{gms} Luke 3:27, **Joanan**, *the son of Rhesa*; (23x LXX; 12x Jer) **Johanan**

Ἰωάννα, ας, ἡ$_{1α}$ ❷ Luke 8:3; 24:10, **Joanna**, *disciple of Jesus*

Ἰωάννης, ου, ὁ$_{1>}$ (140x; 131x GA, 5x Rev) **John**; 🅐 John 1:42, *father of Peter, also known as Jonah*; 🅑 Matt 3:1, *the Baptist*; 🅒 Matt 10:2, *the apostle*; 🅓 Acts 12:12, **John** *Mark, son of Mary; author of Second Gospel?*; 🅔 *the Evangelist, author of Fourth Gospel; same as* 🅒 *and* 🅕*?*; 🅕 Rev 1:1, *author of the Apocalypse*^{NIGTC}; Acts 4:6, *a member of a priestly family*; (15x LXX; 13x 1 Macc)

Ἰώβ, ὁ$_3$ *indecl.* ①^{gms} Jas 5:11, **Job**; (63x LXX; 61x Job, 2x Ezek)

Ἰωβήδ, ὁ$_3$ *indecl.* ❸ Matt 1:5^{2x} = Luke 3:32, **Obed**

Ἰωδά, ὁ$_3$ *indecl.* ①^{gms} Luke 3:26, **Joda**; ①^{gms} LXX, 1 Esd 5:58, **Joda**, *son of Iliadun*

Ἰωήλ, ὁ$_3$ *indecl.* ①^{gms} Acts 2:16, **Joel**; (25x LXX; 18x 1 Chr), *12 different men in* LXX

Ἰωνάμ, ὁ$_3$ *indecl.* ①^{gms} Luke 3:30, **Jonam**

Ἰωνᾶς, ᾶ, ὁ$_1$ ❾ Matt 12:39–41^{4x} = Luke 11:29–32,^{4x} **Jonah**; (22x LXX; 20x Jonah, 2x Tob)

Ἰωράμ, ὁ$_3$ *indecl.* ❷ Matt 1:8,^{2x} **Joram**; (53x LXX; 29x 2 Kgs, 17x 2 Chr), *six different men in* LXX

Ἰωρίμ, ὁ$_3$ *indecl.* ①^{gms} Luke 3:29, **Jorim**

Ἰωσαφάτ, ὁ$_3$ *indecl.* ❷ Matt 1:8,^{2x} **Jehoshaphat**; (90x LXX; 42x 2 Chr, 29x), *five different men in* LXX

Ἰωσῆς, ῆτος, ὁ$_3$ ❸ **Joses**; 🅐 Mark 6:3, *half-brother of Jesus*; 🅑 Mark 15:40, *brother of James the Younger*; 🅒 Matt 27:56, *alternate name of James the son of Zebedee*

Ἰωσήφ, ὁ$_3$ *indecl.* (35x; 15x LA, 11x Matt) 🅐 **Joseph**, Matt 1:6, *husband of Mary*; 🅑 *6 additional*, Matt 13:55; Mark 15:40, 43; Luke 3:24; Acts 1:23, 4:36; (226x LXX; 166x Gen) *7 different men*

Ἰωσήχ, ὁ$_3$ *indecl.* ①^{gms} Luke 3:26, **Josech**

Ἰωσίας, ου, ὁ$_1$ ❷ Matt 1:10, 11, *boy king* **Josiah**; (53x LXX; 19x 2 Chr, 15x 1 Esd, 14x 2 Kgs)

ἰῶτα, τό$_3$ *indecl.* ①^{nns} Matt 5:18, **iota**, *smallest letter in Greek alphabet*^{TNTC}

K, κ [*kappa*]

Κ, κ, τό (κάππα) *indecl.* **kappa**, *10th letter in Gr. alphabet* ‖ *num.* κʹ = 20; ͵κ = 20,000

κἀγώ {*crasis*, καί + ἐγώ} *adv.* (83x; 30x John, 19x 1–2 Cor) Matt 2:8; 2 Cor 2:10, **I too**; Matt 10:28; John 15:9, **I also**; Matt 11:28, **and I**

καθά {κατά + ὅς} *conj.* ① Matt 27:10, **as, just as**; (112x LXX; 20x Num, 19x Gen)

καθαίρεσις, εως, ἡ$_3$ {κατά + αἱρέω} ❸[afs] 2 Cor 10:4, 8; 13:10, **to tear down**[BEC]; ❷ LXX, Exod 23:24, **demolition**; 1 Macc 3:43, **ruination**

καθαιρέω {κατά + αἱρέω} ❾ (6x LA) Mark 15:46 = Luke 23:53, **to take down**; Luke 1:52, **to topple**; 12:18, **to tear down**; Acts 13:19, **to conquer**[EGG]; 2 Cor 10:4, **we dismantle** *arguments*[BEC]; (87x LXX; 21x Exod, 10x 4 Macc)

καθαίρω {κατά + αἴρω} ① John 15:2, **to prune**; ❷ LXX, 2 Sam 4:6, **cleaning** *wheat*

καθάπερ {κατά + ὅς + περ} *comp. conj.* (13x) Rom 4:6, **likewise**; 1 Cor 12:12, **just as**[NIGTC]; (82x LXX; 21x Exod, 10x 4 Macc)

καθάπτω {κατά + ἅπτω} ①[aai3s] Acts 28:3, **fastened itself on**; Soph. *Ant.* 1222, **fastened** *by a noose*

καθαρίζω {καθαρός} (31x; 18x Syn) Matt 8:2–3[3x] = Mark 1:40–42[3x] = Luke 5:12–13,[2x] **to cleanse, be cleansed** (*cultically*); Matt 23:25 = Luke 11:39, **to clean** (*cultically*); 2 Cor 7:1; Eph 5:26; Heb 9:14, **to cleanse, be cleansed** (*spiritually*); (124x LXX; 39x Lev)

καθαρισμός, οῦ, ὁ$_2$ {καθαρός} ❼ Mark 1:44 = Luke 5:14; 2 Pet 1:9, **cleansing**; John 2:6, **purification**; Heb 1:3, **cleansing** *from sin through Christ's death*[EGG]; (18x LXX; 5x 2 Macc), Exod 30:10, **ritual cleansing**

καθαρός, ά, όν$_{2.1.2}$ *adj.* (27x; 6x Rev, 4x John) 1 Tim 1:5, **pure**; Matt 27:59, **clean**; John 13:10,[2x] **clean**; 13:11, *not* **clean** (*Judas*); Acts 18:6, **innocent**; (155x LXX; 35x Lev, 19x Job)

καθαρότης, ητος, ἡ$_3$ ①[afs] Heb 9:13, **purification**; ①[afs] LXX, Wis 7:24, **pureness**

καθέδρα, ας, ἡ$_{1α}$ {κατά + ἕζομαι} ❸ Matt 21:12 = Mark 11:15; Matt 23:2, **seat**; (16x LXX) 1 Sam 20:18, 25[2x]

καθέζομαι {κατά + ἕζομαι} ❼ (3x John) Matt 26:55; Luke 2:46; Acts 6:15, **sitting**; John 4:6, **to sit down**; ❹ LXX, Lev 12:5; Ezek 26:16

καθεξῆς {κατά + ἔχω} *versatile adv.* ❺ (only LA)[EGG] Luke 1:3, *orderly* **sequence**; 8:1, **soon afterward**; Acts 3:24, **subsequent**; 11:4, **in order**; 18:23, **successively**

καθεύδω {κατά + εὕδω} (22x; 17x Syn, 4x 1 Thess) 1 Thess 5:7,[2x] **to sleep** (*physically*); 1 Thess 5:6 (*spiritually*); Matt 9:24 = Mark 5:39 = Luke 8:52; 1 Thess 5:10, **to sleep** (*sleep of death*); (33x LXX; 15x 1–2 Sam) Gen 39:10, **to sleep** (*intercourse*); 1 Sam 3:2, **to lie down**

καθηγητής, οῦ, ὁ$_{1>}$ {κατά + ἄγω} ❷ Matt 23:10,[2x] **instructor**

καθήκω {κατά + ἥκω} ❷ Acts 22:22, *he should not* **be allowed** *to live*; Rom 1:28, **τὰ μὴ καθήκοντα, things** *not* **fitting**[ZEC]; (30x LXX; 6x Exod)

κάθημαι {κατά + ἧμαι→ **to sit, be seated**[BrDAG]} (91x; 43x Syn, 33x Rev) Matt 4:16[2x] = Luke 1:79, **living** *in darkness*; Matt 9:9 = Mark 2:14 = Luke 5:27, **sitting** *in the tax office*;

Acts 2:2, **staying**; Rev 4:2, 3, **seated** *on the throne*; 6:5, 8, 9, *subst.*, *its* **rider**; (192x LXX; 24x Jer); Gen 18:1; Exod 11:5, **to sit**; 19:30, **to settle** *in the hills*; Job 38:40, **to lie** *in wait*

καθημερινός, ή, όν$_{2.1.2}$ {κατά + ἡμέρα} *adj.* ①[dfs] Acts 6:1, **daily distribution**; ①[afs] LXX, Jdt 12:17, **daily use**

καθίζω {κατά + ἵζω} (46x; 23x Syn) *trans.*, Matt 20:21 = Mark 9:35, **to sit**; 1 Cor 6:4, **to set** *those* **upon** *judgment seats*[NIGTC]; Eph 1:20; Rev 20:4, **to seat**; *intrans.*, Matt 5:1, **to sit down**; 2 Thess 2:4, **to take his seat**[ABC]; (209x LXX; 20x Jer, 19x 1 Sam)

καθίημι {κατά + ἵημι} ❹ (LA) *act.*, Luke 5:19; Acts 9:25, **to lower**; *pass.*, Acts 10:11; 11:5, **being lowered**; ❸ LXX, Exod 17:11, *mid.*, **to put** *his hands* **down**; Zech 11:13, **to place into**

καθίστημι {κατά + ἵστημι} (21x; 8x LA) Matt 24:45 = Luke 12:42, **to put in charge**; Acts 6:3, **to appoint**; Rom 5:19,[2x] **to render**[ZEC]; Jas 3:6, *mid.*, **appoints itself**[EGG]; Jas 4:4, *mid.*, **makes himself**[EGG]; (205x LXX; 16x 1 Sam:2 Chr)

καθό {κατά + ὅς} *adv.* ❹ Rom 8:26; 1 Pet 4:13, **as**; 2 Cor 8:12[2x], **according to**; ❸ LXX, Lev 9:5; 1 Esd 1:48; Jdt 3:3, **what**

καθόλου {κατά + ὅλος} *adv.* ① Acts 4:18, *not* **at all**; ❻ LXX, Amos 3:3, **at all**

καθοπλίζω {κατά + ὁπλίζω} ①[pfmp.nms] Luke 11:21, **fully armed**; ❾ LXX (5x 4 Macc)

καθοράω[con] {κατά + ὁράω} ①[pmi3s] Romans 1:20, **to clearly see**; ❽ LXX; 2x Job

καθότι {κατά + ὅτι} *conj.* ❻ (4x Acts) Luke 1:7; Acts 2:24, **because**; (64x LXX; 14x Deut, 8x Josh)

καθώς {κατά + ὡς} *adv.* (182x; 31x John:1–2 Cor) Ⓐ ***compar. part.***, 1 Thess 4:13; 1 John 3:12, **as** *others*; Ⓑ ***subord. conj.***, Acts 11:29, **just as**; Rom 1:28, **insofar**; Ⓒ ***intertextual OT comp. formula***, **καθὼς** γὰρ ἐγένετο, Luke 11:30, **just as** *it was with Jonah*; 17:26, **just as** *in the days of Noah*; Ⓓ ***formula introducing OT citation***, **καθὼς** γέγραπται, Acts 7:42, **as** *it is written*; Ⓔ ***Johannine spir. relationships***, John 5:30, **as** *I hear, I judge*; (260x LXX; 47x 1–2 Kgs, 26x Ezek)

καθώσπερ {κατά + ὡς + περ} *conj.* ① Heb 5:4, **just as**

καί *coord. conj.* (9,162x; 3,777x Syn, 1,128x Rev) Ⓐ ***simple coord.***, Jas 1:21–24; Rev 22:15[6x], **and** *connects a sevenfold list of those* ἔξω; Ⓑ ***contrasting equal coord.***, 1 Thess 2:18,[ZEC] **but** *Satan prevented us*; Ⓒ ***straight extended narrative***, Mark 5:14–19; Luke 2:41–52,[24x] **and . . . and . . . and**[Runge 27]; Ⓓ ***adverbial***, Matt 5:39, **also**; Ⓔ ***unusual***, Matt 3:14, **and**, *signals sudden surprise*[EGG]; (57,771x LXX; 11,721x Pent, 4,922x 1–2 Chr, 4,700x 1–2 Kgs)

Καϊάφας, α, ὁ$_{1>}$ ❾ (5x John) Matt 26:3; Luke 3:2; John 11:49, **Caiaphas**

Κάϊν, ὁ$_3$ *indecl.* ❸ Heb 11:4; 1 John 3:12; Jude 11, **Cain**; (17x LXX; 16x Gen, 1x 4 Macc)

Καϊνάμ, ὁ$_3$ *indecl.* ❷ Luke 3:36, 37, **Cainan**

καινός, ή, όν$_{2.1.2}$ *adj.* (42x; 14x Syn, 9x Rev) Matt 9:17 = Mark 2:21–22 = Luke 5:36–38; John 13:34; 1 Cor 11:25; Eph 2:15; Rev 21:1–5, **new**; (55x LXX; 12x Isa, 6x Pss)

καινότης, ητος, ἡ$_3$ {καινός} ❷[dfs] Rom 6:4; 7:6, **in newness**; ❷[gfs] Ezek 47:12

καίπερ *conj.* ❺ (3x Heb) Phil 3:4; Heb 12:17, **although, even though**; (13x LXX; 8x 4 Macc)

καιρός, οῦ, ὁ$_2$ (85x; 13x Luke) Matt 26:18, **appointed time** *is near*; 1 Cor 4:5, **the proper time**[NIGTC]; 7:5, **a specific span of time**; Matt 11:25, **at that time**; 13:30, *at harvest* **time**; 1 Thess 2:17, *for a short* **time**; (419x LXX; 63x Sir, 39x Eccl, 34x Dan)

Καῖσαρ, αρος, ὁ$_3$ (29x; 17 LA) Matt 22:21 = Mark 12:16 = Luke 20:24; Acts 25,[6x] **Caesar**

Καισάρεια, ας, ἡ$_{1α}$ (17x; 15x Acts) Acts 8:40; 25:13, **Caesarea**[LGCb]

καίτοι *subord. conj.* ❷ Acts 14:17; Heb 4:3, **although, even though**; ❹ LXX (4 Macc)

καίτοιγε {καίτοι + γε} *infer. part.* ① John 4:2, **and yet indeed**[IL 57, WPNT]

καίω (11x; 5x Rev) Matt 5:15, **to light**; Luke 24:32, **to burn**; John 5:35; Rev 4:5, *subst.*, **burning**; (78x LXX; 17x Isa, 12x Jer)

κἀκεῖ {*crasis*, καί + ἐκεῖ} (10x; 5x Acts) Matt 5:23; John 11:54, **and there**

κἀκεῖθεν {*crasis*, καί + ἐκεῖ + θεν} (10x; 8x Acts) Mark 9:30; Acts 20:15, **from there**

κἀκεῖνος, η, ο$_{2.1.2}$ {*crasis*, καί + ἐκεῖνος} (22x; 5x John) Matt 15:18, **and this**; 23:23, **the others**; Luke 11:7, **and from** *inside*[BHGNT]; John 6:57, **also that one**[BHGNT]; Rom 11:23, **and they**; 1 Cor 10:6, **even as those people**

κακία, ας, ἡ$_{1α}$ {κακός} (11x) Matt 6:34, **trouble**; Acts 8:22; Rom 1:29, **wickedness**; (142x LXX; 15x 1 Sam, 13x Jer)

κακοήθεια, ας, ἡ$_{1α}$ {κακός + ἔθος} ①[gfs] Rom 1:29, **mean-spirited**; (6x LXX; 4x 3–4 Macc)

κακολογέω[con] {κακός + λέγω} ❹ Matt 15:4 = Mark 7:10; 9:39; Acts 19:9, **to speak evil of, to revile**; (6x LXX) Exod 21:16; 1 Sam 3:13

κακοπάθεια, ας, ἡ$_{1α}$ {κακός + πάσχω} ①[gfs] **suffering**; ❷ LXX, Mal 1:13, **much toil**

κακοπαθέω[con] {κακός + πάσχω} ❸ 2 Tim 2:9; 4:5; Jas 5:13, **to suffer**; ①[aai2s] LXX, Jonah 4:10, **to labor**

κακοποιέω[con] {κακός + ποιέω} ❹ Mark 3:4 = Luke 6:9; 1 Pet 3:17; 3 John 11, **to do evil**; (26x LXX; 4x Prov)

κακοποιός, οῦ, ὁ$_{2}$ {κακός + ποιέω} ❸ (1 Pet) 2:12, 14; 4:15, **evildoer**; ❷ LXX, Prov 12:4; 24:19

κακός, ή, όν$_{2.1.2}$ *adj.* (50x; 15x Rom) Matt 21:41; Rom 1:30; 12:17[2x]; Jas 3:8; Rev 2:2, **evil**; John 18:23, *about* **the wrong**[ZEC]; Acts 16:28; 2 Tim 4:14, **harm**; (381x LXX; 62x Jer, 33x Pss)

κακοῦργος, ου, ὁ$_{2}$ {κακός + ἔργον} ❹ Luke 23:32, 33, 39; 2 Tim 2:9, **criminal**; ❹ LXX

κακουχέω[con] {κακός + ἔχω} ❷ Heb 11:37; 13:3, **mistreated**; ❷ LXX, 1 Kgs 2:26[2x]

κακόω[con] ❻ (5x Acts) Acts 7:6, 19, **to mistreat**[ZEC]; 1 Pet 3:13, **to wrong**[Keen1P]; (61x LXX)

κακῶς *adv.* (16x; 7x Matt) Matt 4:24; Luke 5:31, **sick**; Matt 15:22, **severely tormented**[ZEC]; John 18:23, **wrongly**; Jas 4:3, **with wrong motives**[EGG]; (15x LXX; 3x Lev:Wis)

κάκωσις, εως, ἡ$_{3}$ ①[afs] Acts 7:34, **mistreatment**; (18x LXX) Exod 3:17

καλάμη, ης, ἡ$_{1η}$ ①[afs] 1 Cor 3:12, **straw**; (18x LXX) Exod 5:12; Job 24:24

κάλαμος, ου, ὁ$_{2}$ (12x; 5x Matt) Matt 11:7 = Luke 7:24, **reed**; Mark 15:19, **wooden stick**[ZEC]; 3 John 13, **pen** *and ink*; Rev 11:1, **measuring reed**; (28x LXX; 18x Ezek)

καλέω[con] (148x; 61x LA, 26x Matt) *act.*, Matt 1:21, **you will call** *his name*; *pass.*, Acts 9:11, **named**; Luke 14:7, *those* **invited**; Luke 15:19; 1 Pet 5:10, **to be called**; (467x LXX; 84x Gen)

καλλιέλαιος, ου, ἡ$_{2}$ {καλός + ἐλαία} ①[afs] Rom 11:24, **cultivated olive tree**

καλοδιδάσκαλος, ον$_{2.2}$ {καλός + διδάσκω} *adj.* ①[afp] *neol.*, Titus 2:3, *subst.*, **teachers of what is right**; *opp. of* **κακοδιδασκαλειν**, 1 Clem. 10.5, **to teach evil**

καλοποιέω[con] ①[pap.nmp] 2 Thess 3:13, **to do what is good**

καλός, ή, όν$_{2.1.2}$ (101x; 21x Syn, 16x 1 Tim) Matt 3:10; Jas 3:13, **good**; Matt 18:8–9[2x] = Mark 9:42–47,[4x] **better**; Acts 27:8, **Fair** *Havens*[LGCb 404]; 2 Cor 8:21, *what is* **noble**[BEC!]; 13:7, *what is* **right**[BEC!]; (221x LXX; 41x Gen, 20x Prov)

κάλυμμα, ατος, τό$_3$ ❹ 2 Cor 3:13–16, **veil**[BEC]; (19x LXX; 10x Num)

καλύπτω ❽ *act.*, Luke 8:16; 23:30; Jas 5:20; 1 Pet 4:8, **to cover**; *pass.*, Matt 8:24, **to be engulfed**[NIGTC]; 2 Cor 4:3,[2x, pfmp.nns] **is hidden**; (89x LXX; 14x Exod, 11x Pss)

καλῶς {καλός} *adv.* (37x; 6x Mark) Matt 12:12, **good**; 15:7; Heb 13:18, **correctly**; Mark 7:9, **very good**[ZEC]; Mark 7:37; 1 Cor 7:37; Gal 5:7; 3 John 6, **well**; Acts 28:25, **right**; Rom 11:20, **true**[ABC]; 2 Cor 11:4, **splendidly**[BEC]; (34x LXX; 9x 1–4 Macc)

κάμηλος, ου, ὁ$_2$ *or* **ἡ**$_{2ὁδός}$ ❻ Matt 19:24 = Mark 10:25, **camel**; (58x LXX; 24x Gen)

κάμινος, ου, ἡ$_{2>}$ ❹ Matt 13:42, 50; Rev 1:15; 9:2; *blazing* **furnace**; (44x LXX; 22x Dan)

καμμύω ❷ Matt 13:15, 50; Acts 28:27, **to shut** *the eyes*; ❹ LXX, Isa 6:10; 29:10

κάμνω ❷ Heb 12:3, **to grow weary**; Jas 5:15, **the one who is physically ill**[EGG]; ❻ LXX

κάμπτω ❹ Rom 11:4; 14:11; Eph 3:14; Phil 2:10, **to bow, kneel**; (18x LXX; 4x Sir)

κἄν {*crasis*, καί + ἐάν} *conj.* (16x; 12x Gs) Matt 21:21; John 8:14, **even if**; Mark 5:28, **if only**[BHGNT]; Luke 12:38[2x]; 1 Cor 13:3, **and if**; Acts 5:15, **at least**

Κανά, ἡ$_3$ *indecl.* ❹ John 2:1, 11; 4:46; 21:2, **Cana**

Καναναῖος, ου, ὁ$_2$ ❷ (*from Aram.* קַנְאָן) Matt 10:4; Mark 3:18, **the Zealot** (≠ Κανά)

Κανδάκη, ης, ἡ$_{1η}$ ①[gfs] Acts 8:27, **Candace**

κανών, όνος, ὁ$_2$ ❹ 2 Cor 10:13, 15 **assignment**[BEC]; 10:16, **sphere of ministry**[BEC]; Gal 6:16, **just-mentioned standard**[KeenG]; ❸ LXX, 4 Macc 7:21, **rule**

καπηλεύω ①[pap.nmp] 2 Cor 2:17, **hucksters who peddle** *the word of God*[BEC]; Philo of Byzantium, *Bel.* 2.394, **to trade one's body**, *lit.*, **to trade** *in the flower of their youth*[BrDAG]

καπνός, οῦ, ὁ$_2$ (13x; 12x Rev) Acts 2:19; Rev 9:2–3,[4x] **smoke**; (28x LXX) Exod 19:18[2x]

Καππαδοκία, ας, ἡ$_{1α}$ ❷ Acts 2:9; 1 Pet 1:1, **Cappadocia**; ❷ LXX, Amos 9:7

καρδία, ας, ἡ$_{1α}$ (156x; 49x Syn, 20x Acts) *only fig. in NT*, **heart**; Ⓐ ***seat of the emotions***, Matt 5:8; Heb 3:8; 2 Cor 7:3; 1 Pet 3:4; Ⓑ ***core of the intellect***, Matt 13:15; Rom 2:15; 1 John 3:20 Ⓒ ***sphere of God's inspiration***, Rom 1:21; Eph 3:17; Ⓓ ***the core of something***, Matt 12:40; (912x LXX; 137x Pss, 86x Sir, 77x Prov, 56x Jer)

καρδιογνώστης, ου, ὁ$_{1>}$ {καρδία + γινώσκω} ❷ Acts 1:24, **knower of hearts**[EGG]; 15:8, **ὁ καρδιογνώστης, who knows the human heart**[ZEC]

Κάρπος, ου, ὁ$_2$ ①[dms] 2 Tim 4:13, **Carpus**

καρπός, οῦ, ὁ$_2$ (67x; 19x Matt, 12x Luke) Mark 4:29, **crop**; Matt 7:16–20[7x]; John 15:2–16[8x]; 1 Cor 9:7, **fruit**; Phil 1:22, **fruitful**; Luke 1:42, **fruit** *of the womb*; (124x LXX; 15x Prov)

καρποφορέω[con] {καρπός + φέρω} ❽ Matt 13:23 = Mark 4:20; Rom 7:4–5; Col 1:6, **to bear fruit**; ❸ LXX, Hab 3:17

καρποφόρος, ον$_{2.2}$ {καρπός + φέρω} *adj.* ①[amp] Acts 14:17, **fruitful**; ❸ LXX; 2x Pss

καρτερέω[con] {καράννυμι} ①[aai3s] Heb 11:27, *for* **he persevered**; (10x LXX; 5x 4 Macc)

κάρφος, ους, τό$_3$ ❻ Matt 7:3–5[3x] = Luke 6:41–42,[3x] **speck of sawdust**[ZEC]; ①[ans] LXX, Gen 8:11, **plucked-off** *olive leaf* (Tanakh); **twig**; **plucked** (CSB)

κατά, κατ', καθ' *prep.* (477x; 134x LA, 50x Rom, 41x Heb)[PrTh 148–60] → Ⓐ ***w/ gen.***, **1. *directional***, Matt 8:32, **down from**; Acts 9:42, **throughout**; **2. *opposition***, 2 Cor 8:2, **extreme** *poverty*[BEC!]; 2 Cor 13:8, **against** *the truth*; Ⓑ ***w/ acc.***, **1. *location***, Luke 8:39, **throughout**; **2. *temporal***, 2 Cor 1:17, **κατὰ** σάρκα, **impulsively**; **3. *distributive***, Heb 9:25, **κατ'** ἐνιαυτόν, **year by year**; **4. *purpose***, Titus 1:1, *apostle* **for** *the faith*; **5. *correlation***, 1 Cor 3:8, **according to** *each one's labors*; Luke 22:22, **as** *it has been ordained*; **6. *reason***,

Eph 3:3, **on the basis of**; 7. ***relationship***, Acts 24:22, **with respect to**; Col 2:8,[3x] **derived, centered, based on**; (2,069x LXX; 274x Num)

καταβ**αίνω** (81x; 32x LA, 17x John) Matt 3:16 = Mark 1:10 = Luke 3:22 = John 1:32; 1 Thess 4:16, **to descend**; Matt 7:25, **to fall**; Rev 21:10, **to come down**; (318x LXX; 1–2 Sam 44x)

κατα**βάλλω** ❷[pmp.nmp] 2 Cor 4:9, **to knock down**; Heb 6:1, **to lay down**; (46x LXX; 11x Ezek)

κατα**βαρέω** ①[aai1s] 2 Cor 12:16, **to burden**

κατα**βαρύνω** ①[pmp.nmp] Mark 14:40, *their eyes* **were heavy**; ❸ LXX, 2 Sam 14:26

κατά**βασις, εως, ἡ**$_3$ {κατά + βαίνω} ①[dfs] Luke 19:37, **the way down**; (11x LXX)

κατα**βιβάζω** (11x LXX; 5x Ezek) Deut 21:4, **to cause to go down**

κατα**βοάω**[con] {κατά + βοή} ❺ LXX, Exod 5:15, **to cry out**

κατα**βολή, ῆς, ἡ**$_{1η}$ {κατά + βάλλω} (11x) Matt 13:35; John 17:24; Eph 1:4; Heb 4:3, **foundation**; ①[gfs] LXX, 2 Macc 2:29

κατα**βραβεύω** ①[paimp3s] Col 2:18, **to decide against**[NIGTC] (*as an umpire*)

κατ**αγγελεύς, έως, ὁ**$_3$ {κατά + ἄγγελος} ①[nms] Acts 17:18, **preacher**

κατ**αγγέλλω** {κατά + ἄγγελος} (18x; 11x Acts) Acts 3:24, **to predict**[ZEC]; 4:2; Rom 1:8; 1 Cor 2:1, **to proclaim**; ❷ LXX, 2 Macc 8:36; 9:17, **to proclaim**

κατα**γελάω**[con] ❸[pap.nms] Matt 9:24 = Mark 5:40 = Luke 8:53, **to laugh at**; (21x LXX; 8x Job)

κατα**γινώσκω** ❸ Gal 2:11; 1 John 3:20, 21, **to condemn**; ❹ LXX, Deut 25:1; Prov 28:11

κατ**άγνυμι** {κατά + ἀξίνη} ❹ Matt 12:20; John 19:31–33,[3x] **to break**; ❻ LXX, Deut 33:11, **to crush**

κατα**γράφω** ①[iai3s] John 8:6, **to write down**; (11x LXX) Exod 17:14

κατ**άγω** {κατά + ἄγω} ❾ (7x Acts) Luke 5:11, **to put in to**; Acts 9:30, **to lead down**; (68x LXX; 10x Gen)

κατ**αγωνίζομαι** {κατά + ἀγών} ①[ami3p] Heb 11:33, **to conquer**

κατα**δέω**[con] ①[aai3s] Luke 10:34, **to bandage**; ❽ LXX, 1 Kgs 21:38 (20:38), **to disguise**

κατά**δηλος, ον**$_{2.2}$ *adj.* ①[nns] Heb 7:15, **clearer**; Thuc. 4.44.4, **manifest, visible**[BrDAG]

κατα**δικάζω** {κατά + δίκη} ❺ Matt 12:7; Luke 6:37; Jas 5:6, **to condemn**; (10x LXX)

κατα**δίκη, ης, ἡ**$_{1η}$ ①[afs] Acts 25:15, **guilty verdict**[Keen4]; ①[gfs] LXX, Wis 12:27, **sentence**

κατα**διώκω** ①[aai3s] Mark 1:36, **to search for**; (90x LXX; 19x Pss) Gen 14:14, **to pursue**

κατα**δουλόω**[con] {κατά + δοῦλος} ❷ 2 Cor 11:20; Gal 2:4, **to enslave**; (10x LXX)

κατα**δυναστεύω** {κατά + δύναμαι} ❷ Jas 2:6, *act.*, **to oppress** *the poor*; Acts 10:38, *pass.*, **to be oppressed** *by the devil*; (34x LXX; 7x Ezek) Exod 1:13, **to work ruthlessly**

κατά**θεμα, ατος, τό**$_3$ {κατά + τίθημι} ①[nns] Rev 22:3, **curse**

κατα**θεματίζω** {κατά + τίθημι} ①[painf] Matt 26:74, **to curse**

κατ**αισχύνω** {κατά + αἶσχος} (13x; 7x 1–2 Cor) Luke 13:17, **to humiliate**; Rom 5:5, **to bring shame**[BEC]; 1 Cor 1:27,[2x] **to shame**; 2 Cor 7:14; 1 Pet 2:6, *pass.*, **to be shamed**; (34x LXX)

κατα**καίω** (12x; 5x Rev) Matt 3:12 = Luke 3:17, **to burn** *with fire*; Rev 8:7,[3x] **κατεκάη**[api3s], **to be burned up**; (97x LXX; 18x Lev, 14x Jer, 11x Isa)

κατα**καλύπτω** ❸ 1 Cor 11:6,[2x] 7, **to cover**; (25x LXX; 5x Lev)

κατα**καυχάομαι** ❹ Rom 11:18[2x]; Jas 2:13; 3:14, **to boast against**; ❸ LXX, Zech 10:12

κατά**κειμαι** (12x; 4x Mark) *mid.*, Mark 1:30, **to lie in bed**; 14:3, **to recline at the table**; John 5:3, **to lie down**; 1 Cor 8:10, **seated at table**[NIGTC]; *pass.*, Acts 9:33, **to be bedridden**; ❹ LXX, Prov 6:9, *How long* **will you stay in bed**?

κατα**κλάω**[con] ❷[aai3s] Mark 6:41 = Luke 9:16, **to break**; ①[api3s] LXX, Ezek 19:12, **to uproot**
κατα**κλείω** ❷ Luke 3:20; Acts 26:10, **to lock up** *in prison*; ❺ LXX, Jer 39:3 (32:3)
κατα**κληρονομέω**[con] ①[aai3s] {κατά + κληρόω + νόμος} Acts 13:19, **to give as an inheritance**; (61x LXX; 15x Deut, 10x Josh)
κατα**κλίνω** ❺ Luke 7:36; 9:14, **to recline at table**; 14:8, **to sit**; ❻ LXX, Exod 21:18, *pass.*, **to be confined** *to bed*; 3 Macc 1:3, **to sleep** *in the tent*
κατα**κλύζω** ①[app.nms] 2 Pet 3:6, *pass.*, **was flooded**; ❾ LXX, Ezek 13:11, *subst.*, **torrential** *rain*
κατα**κλυσμός, οῦ, ὁ**$_2$ ❹ Matt 24:38, 39 = Luke 17:27 = 2 Pet 2:5, **flood**; (22x LXX; 12x Gen)
κατ**ακολουθέω**[con] ❷ Luke 23:55; Acts 16:17, **to follow**; ❺ LXX, Jer 17:16; Dan 9:10
κατα**κόπτω** ①[pap.nms] Mark 5:5, **to cut himself**; (20x LXX) Gen 14:5, **to cut to pieces**
κατα**κρημνίζω** {κατά + κρεμάννυμι} ①[aainf] Luke 4:29, **to throw off a cliff**; ❹ LXX, 2 Chr 25:12
κατά**κριμα, ατος, τό**$_3$ ❸ Rom 5:16, 18; 8:1, **condemnation**
κατα**κρίνω** (18x; 9x Syn, 4x Rom) Matt 20:18 = Mark 10:33; Rom 2:1; 1 Cor 11:32, **to condemn**; ❺ LXX, Esth 2:1
κατά**κρισις, εως, ἡ**$_3$ ❷ 2 Cor 3:9; 7:3, **condemnation**
κατα**κύπτω** ①[aap.nms] John 8:8, **to stoop down**; ❷ LXX, 2 Kgs 9:32, **to look down**
κατα**κυριεύω** {κατά + κύριος} ❹ Matt 20:25 = Mark 10:42; 1 Pet 5:3, **to exercise lordship over**; Acts 19:16, **to overpower**; (16x LXX; 7x Pss)
κατα**λαλέω**[con] {κατά + λάλος} ❺ Jas 4:11,[3x] **to speak against**[ZEC]; 1 Pet 2:12; 3:16, **to slander**[Keen1P]; (13x LXX; 4x Pss) Gen 19:19, **to overtake**; Exod 15:9, **to pursue**
κατα**λαλιά, ᾶς, ἡ**$_{1a}$ {κατά + λάλος} ❷ 2 Cor 12:20; 1 Pet 2:1, **slander**; ①[gfs] LXX, Wis 1:11
κατά**λαλος, ου, ὁ**$_2$ ①[amp] Rom 1:30, **slanderer**
κατα**λαμβάνω** (15x; 4x John) Mark 9:18, **to throw down**; John 1:5; 1 Thess 5:4, **to overcome**; John 8:3, **to be caught** *in adultery*; Acts 4:13, **to realize**; 25:25, **to discover**[ABC]; Rom 9:30, **to pursue**; 1 Cor 9:24, **make the prize yours**[NIGTC]; Phil 3:12,[2x] **to take hold of**[Herm]; (118x LXX; 18x 1 Macc)
κατα**λέγω** ①[pmimp3s] 1 Tim 5:9, **to be enrolled on the list**; ❷ LXX, Deut 19:16; 2 Macc 7:30
κατα**λείπω** (24x; 12x Syn) Matt 4:13; Mark 10:76; Luke 5:28, **to leave**; (279x LXX; 46x Isa)
κατα**λιθάζω** {κατά + λίθος} ①[fai3s] Luke 20:6, **to stone**
κατ**αλλαγή, ῆς, ἡ**$_{1\eta}$ {κατά + ἄλλος} ❹ Rom 5:11[TNTC]; 11:15; 2 Cor 5:18, 19, **reconciliation**[IPT 57, 156]; ❷ LXX, 2 Macc 5:20, **reconciliation**; Isa 9:4 (9:5), **exchange**
κατ**αλλάσσω** {κατά + ἄλλος} ❻ *act.*, 2 Cor 5:20, **to reconcile**; *pass.*, Rom 5:10[2x]; 1 Cor 7:11; 2 Cor 5:18–19,[2x] **to be reconciled**; ❹ LXX, 2 Macc 1:5; 7:33; 8:29; Jer 31:39 (48:39), **to reverse drastically**[Spicq]
κατά**λοιπος, ον**$_{2.2}$ {κατά + λείπω} *adj.* ①[nmp] Acts 15:17, **the rest** *of humanity*; (96x LXX; 20x Jer, 10x Ezra)
κατά**λυμα, ατος, τό**$_3$ {κατά + λύω} ❸ Mark 14:14; Luke 2:7; 22:11, **guest room**; (14x LXX) Exod 15:13, *your holy* **abode**; 1 Sam 1:18, **quarters**; 2 Sam 7:6, **tent**
κατα**λύω** (17x, 5x Matt) Matt 5:17[2x]; 2 Cor 5:1, **to destroy**; Matt 24:2 = Mark 13:2 = Luke 21:6, **to be thrown down**; Acts 5:38, **to fail**; 5:39, **to overthrow**; (65x LXX; 13x 4 Macc)
κατα**μανθάνω** ①[aaimp2p] Matt 6:28, **study closely**[NIGTC]; ❽ LXX, Gen 24:21; 34:1
κατα**μαρτυρέω**[con] ❸ Matt 26:62 = Mark 14:60; Matt 27:13, **to testify against**; ❻ LXX
κατα**μένω** ①[pap.nmp] Acts 1:13, **to stay**; ❼ LXX, Gen 6:3, **to abide**

καταναλίσκω {κατά + ἀνά + ἅλωσις} ①[pap.nns] Heb 12:29, **consuming**; (18x LXX; 3x Deut)

καταναρκάω[con] ❸ 2 Cor 11:9; 12:13, 14, **to burden**

κατανεύω ①[aai3p] Luke 5:7, **to signal**

κατανοέω[con] {κατά + νοῦς} (14x; 5x Matt) Matt 7:3 = Luke 6:41, **to ignore**; Luke 12:24; Heb 3:1, **to consider**; Jas 1:23, **to scrutinize carefully**[EGG]; (29x LXX; 8x Pss)

καταντάω[con] {κατά + ἀντί} (13x; 9x Acts) Acts 16:1, **to go**; 18:19, **to reach**; 18:24; 20:15, **to arrive**; ❺ LXX, 2 Sam 3:29, **to swirl over**

κατάνυξις, εως, ἡ$_3$ {κατά + νύσσω} ①[gfs] Rom 11:8, **stupor**; ❷[gfs] LXX, Isa 29:10

κατανύσσομαι {κατά + νύσσω} ①[api3p] Acts 2:37, **to be stunned**[ZEC]; (16x LXX; 4x Pss)

καταξιόω[con] {κατά + ἄξιος} ❸ *pass.*, Luke 20:35; Acts 5:41; 2 Thess 1:5, **to be counted worthy**; ❺ LXX, 2 Macc 13:12; 3 Macc 4:11

καταπατέω[con] ❺ Matt 5:13; Luke 8:5; Heb 10:29, **to trample on**; (51x LXX; 15x Isa, 6x Pss)

κατάπαυσις, εως, ἡ$_3$ {κατά + παύω} ❾ Acts 7:49, **resting**; Heb 3:11; 4:1–11,[6x] **rest**;[NIGTC] (13x LXX) Exod 35:2, **solemn rest**

καταπαύω ❹ Acts 14:18, **to stop**; Heb 4:4, 8, 10, **to rest**; (66x LXX; 10x Exod, 8x Josh)

καταπέτασμα, ατος, τό$_3$ {κατά + πέτομαι} ❻ Matt 27:51 = Mark 15:38, **curtain** *of the sanctuary*; Heb 10:20, **curtain**, *that is, his flesh*; (38x LXX; 21x Exod, 7x Lev)

καταπίνω ❼ Matt 23:24; 1 Cor 15:54, **to swallow**; (40x LXX; 7x Pss)

καταπίπτω ❸ Luke 8:6; Acts 26:14, **to fall**; 28:6, **to drop** *dead*[LGCb 404]; ❼ LXX, Neh 8:11, **to be downcast**

καταπλέω[con] ①[aai3p] Luke 8:26, **to sail**

καταπονέω[con] {κατά + πόνος} ❷ Acts 7:24; 2 Pet 2:7, **to be oppressed**; ❷ LXX, 3 Macc 2:2, 13

καταποντίζω {κατά + πόντος} ❷ Matt 14:30, **to sink**; 18:6, **to drown**; (12x LXX; 3x Exod)

κατάρα, ας, ἡ$_{1a}$ ❻ (3x Gal) Gal 3:10, **curse**; Jas 3:10, **cursing**; (40x LXX; 10x Deut)

καταράομαι[con] {κατά + ἀρά} ❺ Matt 25:41, **to be cursed**; Luke 6:28; Rom 12:14; Jas 3:9, **to curse**; (71x LXX; 12x Num, 9x Sir)

καταργέω[con] (27x, 13x 1–2 Cor) Luke 13:7, **to waste**; Rom 3:3, **to cancel**[BEC]; 1 Cor 6:13, **to do away with**; 13:8,[2x] **to bring to an end**; 15:24, **to annihilate**[NIGTC]; 2 Cor 3:7–14,[4x] **to make inoperative**[BEC]; Gal 3:17, **to invalidate**; 5:4, **to be cut off**; 5:11, **to be nullified**[KeenG]; Heb 2:14, **to destroy**; ❹ LXX, Ezra 5:5, **to stop**

καταριθμέω[con] {κατά + ἀριθμός} ①[pfmp.nms] Acts 1:17, **to be counted**[EGG]; ❸ LXX, Gen 50:3, **to reckon**

καταρτίζω {κατά + ἄρτι} (13x; 9x 1 Cor, 6x Rom) *act.*, Matt 4:21 = Mark 1:19, **to mend** *their nets*; Rom 9:22, **to prepare**; Luke 6:40, **to train**; *pass.*, 1 Cor 1:10, **to be knitted together again**[NIGTC]; 2 Cor 13:11, **to be restored**[BEC]; 1 Pet 5:10, **to restore**; (17x LXX; 10x Pss)

κατάρτισις, εως, ἡ$_3$ {κατά + ἄρτι} ①[afs] 2 Cor 13:9, **restoration**

καταρτισμός, οῦ, ὁ$_2$ {κατά + ἄρτι} ①[ams] Eph 4:12, **to equip**

κατασείω ❹ Acts 12:17; 13:16, **to motion** *with the hand*; ①[pap.nmp] LXX, 1 Macc 6:38

κατασκάπτω ❷ Acts 15:16, *from its* **ruins**; Rom 11:3, **to tear down**; (33x LXX; 7x Judg)

κατασκευάζω (11x; 6x Heb) Matt 11:10 = Mark 1:2 = Luke 7:27, **to prepare**; Heb 3:3, 4[2x]; 1 Pet 3:20, **to build**; Heb 9:2, **to set up**; (28x LXX) Num 21:27, *pass.*, **to be established**

κατασκηνόω[con] {κατά + σκηνή} ❹ Matt 13:32 = Mark 4:32 = Luke 13:19, **to nest**; Acts 2:26, **to live**; (63x LXX; 20x Pss) κατα**σκήνωσις, εως, ἡ**$_{3}$ {κατά + σκηνή} ❷ Matt 8:20 = Luke 9:58, **nest**; ❹ LXX, 1 Chr 28:2

κατα**σκιάζω** {κατά + σκιά} ①[pap.nnp] Heb 9:5, **to overshadow**; Hes. *Th.* 716, **they covered** *the Titans with their missiles*

κατα**σκοπέω**[con] {κατά + σκοπός} ①[aainf] Gal 2:4, **to spy against**; ❷ LXX, 2 Sam 10:3

κατά**σκοπος, ου, ὁ**$_{2}$ ①[amp] Heb 11:31, **spies**; (10x LXX) Gen 42:9–34[6x]

κατα**σοφίζομαι** {κατά + σοφός} ❸[amp.nms] Acts 7:19, **to take advantage**; ❸ LXX

κατα**στέλλω** ❷ Acts 19:35, 36, **to calm down**; ❷ LXX, 2 Macc 4:31, **to settle**

κατά**στημα, ατος, τό**$_{3}$ ①[dns] Titus 2:3, **restrained demeanor**

κατα**στολή, ῆς, ἡ**$_{1η}$ {κατά + στέλλω} ①[dfs] 1 Tim 2:9, **clothing**; ①[afs] LXX, Isa 61:3

κατα**στρέφω** ❷[aai3s] Matt 21:12 = Mark 11:15, **to overturn**; (40x LXX; 7x Job)

κατα**στρηνιάω**[con] {κατά + στρῆνος} ①[aas3p] 1 Tim 5:11, **to feel the impulse of sexual desire**[NIGTC]

κατα**στροφή** {κατά + στρέφω} ❷[dfs] 2 Tim 2:14; 2 Pet 2:6, **ruin, destruction**; (18x LXX)

κατα**στρώννυμι** {κατά + στρωννύω} ①[api3p] 1 Cor 10:5 (Num 14:16), *their corpses* **were strewn** *in the desert*; (10x LXX; 7x Job)

κατα**σύρω** ①[pas3s] Luke 12:58, **to drag**; ❸ LXX, Dan 11:26, *pass.*, **to be swept away**

κατα**σφάζω** ①[aaimp2p] Luke 19:27, **to slaughter**; (10x LXX; 8x 2 Macc)

κατα**σφραγίζω** {κατά + σφραγίς} ①[pfmp.ans] Rev 5:1, **sealed**; ❷ LXX, Job 9:7; 37:7

κατά**σχεσις, εως, ἡ**$_{3}$ {κατά + ἔχω} ❷ Acts 7:5, 45, **possession**; (68x LXX; 19x Ezek)

κατα**τίθημι** ❷[aminf] Acts 24:27, **to grant**[ZEC]; 25:9, **to do** *a favor*; ❻ LXX, 1 Chr 21:27, **to put** *the sword* **back** *into its sheath* (LES)

κατα**τομή, ῆς, ἡ**$_{1η}$ ①[afs] Phil 3:2, **a ritual characterized as mutilation**[BEC]

κατα**τοξεύω** ❻ LXX, *act.*, Num 24:8, **to strike**; 2 Kgs 9:16, **to shoot**; *pass.*, Exod 19:13, **to be shot through** *with an arrow*

κατα**τρέχω** ①[aai1p] Acts 21:32, **to run down**; ❺ LXX, Lev 26:37; 1 Kgs 19:20

κατ**αυγάζω** {κατά + αὐγή} ❷ LXX 1 Macc 6:39; Wis 17:5, **to illuminate**

κατα**φέρω** ❹ *act.*, Acts 25:7, **to bring** *charges* **against**; 26:10, *lit.*, **I brought** *my stone* **against** *them* (*i.e.*, **I cast** *my vote* **against** *them*)[BHGNT]; *pass.*, Acts 20:9,[2x] **sank into** *a deep sleep*, **to fall** *sound asleep*[Keen3]; (11x LXX) Gen 37:2, **to bring down**

κατα**φεύγω** ❷ Acts 14:6, **to flee**; Heb 6:18, **to flee for refuge**[EGG]; (20x LXX; 4x Isa)

κατα**φθείρω** ①[pfpp.nmp] 2 Tim 3:8, **corrupted** *in mind*[WPNT]; (26x LXX; 6x 2 Chr, 5x Gen)

κατα**φιλέω**[con] {κατά + φίλος} ❻ Luke 15:20; Acts 20:37, **to kiss**; (18x LXX; 4x 1 Sam, 3x Gen)

κατα**φρονέω**[con] {κατά + φρήν} ❾ Matt 6:24 = Luke 16:13; Rom 2:4, **to despise**; 1 Cor 11:22, **to show contempt for**[NIGTC]; Heb 12:2, (*sole pos. usage*) **to disdain** *disgrace*[ABC]; (22x LXX; 7x Prov, 5x 4 Macc)

κατα**φρονητής, οῦ, ὁ**$_{1>}$ {κατά + φρήν} ①[nmp] Acts 13:41, **scoffers**; ❸ LXX, Hab 2:5

κατα**χέω**[con] ❷[aai3s] Matt 26:7 = Mark 14:3, **to pour over**; ❺ LXX, Gen 39:21, **to pour down**

κατα**χθόνιος, ον**$_{2.2}$ *adj.* ①[gmp] Phil 2:10, **under the earth, subterranean**

κατα**χράομαι**[con] ❷ 1 Cor 7:31, **to be engrossed** *in the world*[NIGTC!]; 9:18, **to gratuitously forego** *my right in the gospel*[NIGTC!]; ❸ LXX, 3 Macc 4:5; 5:22, **to make full use of**

κατα**ψύχω** ①[aas3s] Luke 16:24, **to cool off** *my tongue*; ①[paimp2p] Gen 18:4, **to rest**

κατέδραμεν → **κατατρέχω**, *aor. act. ind. 3s*, Acts 21:32, **he ran down**

κατ**είδωλος, ον**$_{2.2}$ {κατά + εἶδος} *adj.* ①[afs] Acts 17:16, **full of idols**

κατειλημμένην → καταλαμβάνω, *pf. mid. ptc. afs,* John 8:3, **having been caught**

κατείληπται → καταλαμβάνω, *pf. mid. ind. 3s,* John 8:4, **was caught**

κατέναντι {κατά + ἐν + ἀντί} *impr. prep. w/gen.* ❽ Matt 21:2 = Mark 11:2 = Luke 19:30, **ahead** *of you*; Mark 12:41, **across from**; Rom 4:17, **in the presence** *of God*; 2 Cor 2:17, **before** *God*[BEC]; (80x LXX; 14x Ezek, 11x Sir)

κατενεχθείς → καταφέρω, *aor. pass. ptc. nms,* Acts 20:9, **when he was overcome**

κατενώπιον {κατά + ἐν + ὁράω} *impr. prep. w/gen.* ❸ Eph 1:4 = Col 1:22, **before** *him*; Jude 24, **in the presence of**; ❺ LXX, Lev 4:17; Josh 1:5; 3:7; 21:44; 23:9

κατεξουσιάζω {κατά + ἐκ + εἰμί} ❷[pai3p] Matt 20:25 = Mark 10:42, **to rule over**

κατεργάζομαι {κατά + ἔργον} (23x; 11x Rom) Rom 4:15, **to produce**; 7:8–20,[6x] **to do**; 1 Cor 5:3, **to perpetrate**; Eph 6:13, **to prepare**; Phil 2:12, **to work out** *one's salvation*[BEC!]; (13x LXX, 3x Exod) Exod 35:33, **to carve** *the wood*; Aeschl. *Ag.* 526, **to subdue** *the land for cultivation*; Xen. *Hier.* 2.2, **to work out** *one's fate, i.e.,* **to die**[BrDAG]

κατέρχομαι (16x; 13x Acts) Luke 4:31; Acts 15:1, **to go down**; 18:5, **to arrive**; 18:22, **to land**; ❹ LXX, 2 Macc 11:29, **to return**; Wis 11:22, **to fall**

κατεσθίω (14x; 6x Syn, 5x Rev) Matt 13:4 = Mark 4:4 = Luke 8:5, **to eat**; Gal 5:15, **to devour**; Rev 11:5, **to consume**; 2 Cor 11:20, **to eat up** *your resources*; (147x LXX; 15x Jer, 12x Amos)

κατευθύνω {κατά + εὐθύς} ❸ Luke 1:79, **κατευθῦναι,**[aainf] **to guide**; 1 Thess 3:11; 2 Thess 3:5, **κατευθύναι,**[aao3s] **may** *the Lord* **direct**; (65x LXX; 13x Pss, 9x Prov)

κατευλογέω[con] {κατά + εὖ + λέγω} ①[iai3s] Mark 10:16, **to bless**

κατέφαγεν → κατεσθίω, *aor. act. ind. 3s,* Rev 20:9, **to devour**

κατεφίσταμαι {κατά + ἐπί + ἵστημι} ①[aai3p] Acts 18:12, **to attack**

κατέχω (17x; 10x Paul) *act.,* Luke 4:42, **to prevent**; 14:9, **to go down**; Acts 27:40, **to head for**; Rom 1:18, **to stifle** *the truth*; 1 Cor 7:30, **to hold**; 2 Thess 2:6, 7, *subst. the* **Restrainer**[NTIW 428]; Heb 3:6, **to hold on to** *courage*; *pass.,* Rom 7:6, **to be held captive**; (47x LXX; 5x 2 Sam)

κατηγορέω[con] {κατά + ἄγω} (23x; 9x Acts) Matt 12:10; Mark 15:3[2x]; John 5:45[2x]; Acts 22:30; Rom 2:15, **to accuse**; Luke 6:7, *to find* **a charge**

κατηγορία, ας, ἡ$_{1\alpha}$ {κατά + ἄγω} ❸ John 18:29; 1 Tim 5:19, **charge, accusation**; Titus 1:6, μὴ ἐν **κατηγορίᾳ,** *not* **accused** *of wildness*

κατήγορος, ου, ὁ$_2$ {κατά + ἄγω} ❹ Acts 23:30, 35; 25:16, 18, **accuser**; ❷ LXX, Prov 18:17

κατήγωρ, ορος, ὁ$_3$ {κατά + ἄγω} ①[nms] Rev 12:10, *the* **Accuser**

κατήνεγκα → καταφέρω, *aor. act. ind. 1s,* Acts 26:10, **I agreed against** *them*

κατήφεια, ας, ἡ$_{1\alpha}$ {κατά + φαίνω} ①[afs] Jas 4:9, **gloom**

κατηχέω[con] {κατά + ἠχή} ❽ Luke 1:4, **to be instructed**; Acts 21:21, **to be informed**; 1 Cor 14:19, **to communicate instruction**[NIGTC]; Gal 6:6, *mid.,* **the one who is taught**; *act.,* **the one who teaches**

κατιόω[con] {κατά + ἰός} ①[pfmi3s] Jas 5:3, **to rust**; ①[aai3s] LXX, Sir 12:11

κατισχύω {κατά + ἰσχύς} ❸ Matt 16:18, **to overpower**; Luke 21:36; 23:23, **to have strength**; (99x LXX; 31x 2 Chr, 14x Dan)

κατοικέω {κατά + οἶκος} (44x; 20x Acts, 13x Rev) Matt 2:23, **to settle**; Rev 2:13,[2x] **to live**; Eph 3:17, **to dwell**; Acts 1:19, **the inhabitants**; (641x LXX; 86x Jer, 53x Judg, 45x Josh)

κατοίκησις, εως, ἡ$_3$ {κατά + οἶκος} ①[afs] Mark 5:3, **he lived**; ❾ LXX

κατοικητήριον, ου, τό$_2$ {κατά + οἶκος} ❷ Eph 2:22; Rev 18:2, **dwelling**; (20x LXX)
κατοικία, ας, ἡ$_{1α}$ ①^{gfs} {κατά + οἶκος} Acts 17:26, *attrib. gen.*, **habitation**; (31x LXX; 7x Lev)
κατοικίζω {κατά + οἶκος} ①^{aai3s} Jas 4:5, **he made to live** *in us*[ZEC]; (45x LXX; 7x Ezek)
κατοπτρίζω {κατά + ὁράω} ①$^{pmp.nmp}$ 2 Cor 3:18, **observing . . . as in a mirror**[BEC!]
κάτω {κατά} *adv.* ❾ Matt 4:6 = Luke 4:9; John 8:6; Acts 20:9, **down**; Matt 27:51 = Mark 15:38, *from top to* **bottom**; Mark 14:66; Acts 2:19, **below**; (27x LXX; 5x Deut)
κατώτερος, ον$_{2.2}$ {κατά} *adj.* ①^{anp} Eph 4:9, **lower**
κατωτέρω {κατά} *adv.* ① Matt 2:16, *two years old and* **under**
Καῦδα, ἡ$_3$ ①^{afs} Acts 27:16, **Cauda**[LGCb 420–22]
καῦμα, ατος, τό$_3$ {καίω} ❷ Rev 7:16; 16:9, **heat**; (19x LXX) Gen 8:22; 2 Sam 4:5
καυματίζω {καίω} ❹ Matt 13:6 = Mark 4:6; Rev 16:8, 9, **to scorch**
καῦσις, εως, ἡ$_3$ {καίω} ①^{afs} Heb 6:8, *purp.*, εἰς + *acc.*, **burned**; ❼ LXX, 2 Chr 13:11; Isa 4:4, **burning**
καυσόω^{con} {καίω} ❷$^{pmp.nnp}$ 2 Pet 3:10, 12, **to melt, burn up**
καυστηριάζω {καίω} ①$^{pfpp.gmp}$ 1 Tim 4:2, **to be cauterized**[NIGTC]
καύσων, ωνος, ὁ$_3$ {καίω} ❸ Matt 20:12, **burning heat**; Luke 12:55, **hot**; Jas 1:11, **scorching wind**; (12x LXX) Hos 13:15, **burning heat**
καυχάομαι^{con} (37x; 20x 2 Cor) Rom 2:17; 2 Cor 10:8–17,^{6x} **to boast**; 1 Cor 1:29,[NIGTC] *mid.*, **to pride oneself** *before God*; 1:31, **to glory**; (40x LXX; 8x Sir, 6x 1 Sam)
καύχημα, ατος, τό$_3$ {καυχάομαι} (11x; 6x 1–2 Cor) Rom 4:2, *he has a reason for* **boasting**; 1 Cor 9:5, *invalidate my ground for* **glorying**[NIGTC]; 2 Cor 1:14, **pride**[BEC]; (24x LXX, 8x Sir)
καύχησις, εως, ἡ$_3$ {καυχάομαι} (11x; 6x 2 Cor) Rom 3:27; 1 Cor 15:31; 1 Thess 2:19, **boasting**; 2 Cor 1:12, **boast**; 7:4, **pride**; (10x LXX) 1 Chr 29:13, *your name of* **glory**
Καφαρναούμ, ἡ$_3$ (16x Gs) Matt 4:13; Mark 2:1; Luke 4:23; John 2:12, **Capernaum**
Κεγχρεαί, ῶν, αἱ$_1$ ❷^{dfp} Acts 18:18; Rom 16:1, **Cenchreae**
Κεδρών, ὁ$_3$ *indecl.* ①^{gms} John 18:1, **Kidron** *Valley*; (16x LXX) 1 Kgs 2:37; 15:13
κεῖμαι (24x; 7x John) Matt 3:10 = Luke 3:9, **laid**; Matt 5:14, **sitting**; 28:6, *where* **he lay**; Luke 23:53, **had been laid**; John 2:6, **had been set**; 20:5–12,^{4x} **lying**; (23x LXX)
κειρία, ας, ἡ$_{1α}$ {κείρω} ①^{dfp} John 11:44, **linen strips**; ①^{dfp} Prov 7:16, **bedsheet**
κείρω ❹ Acts 8:32, *subst.*, **shearer** 18:18, **to shave**; 1 Cor 11:6,^{2x} **to shave**; (21x LXX)
κέλευσμα, ατος, τό$_3$ ①^{dns} 1 Thess 4:16, **a shout**; ①^{gns} Prov 30:27, *at one* **command**
κελεύω (25x; 17x Acts, 7x Matt) Matt 8:18; Acts 12:19, *milit.*, **to give an order**; Matt 14:9; Acts 4:15, **to command**; (27x LXX; 13x 2 Macc)
κενοδοξία, ας, ἡ$_{1α}$ {κενός + δοκέω} ①^{afs} Phil 2:3, **vain conceit**[BEC]; ❸ LXX, 4 Macc 2:15
κενόδοξος, ον$_{2.2}$ {κενός + δοκέω} *adj.* ①^{nmp} Gal 5:26, **conceited**
κενός, ον$_{2.2}$ *adj.* (18x; 4x 1 Cor) Mark 12:3 = Luke 20:10, **empty-handed**; Acts 4:25, **futile things**; 1 Cor 15:10, 58, **fruitless**[NIGTC]; 1 Cor 15:14,^{2x} **hollow**[NIGTC]; 2 Cor 6:1, **in vain**; Phil 2:16,^{2x} εἰς **κενόν**, *for* **nothing**; Jas 2:20, *O* **empty-headed** *human*[KEL]; (75x LXX; 20x Job)
κενοφωνία, ας, ἡ$_{1α}$ {κενός + φωνή} ❷ 1 Tim 6:20; 2 Tim 2:16, **empty speech**
κενόω^{con} {κενός} ❺ *act.*, Phil 2:7, **to make himself nothing**[BEC]; 1 Cor 9:15, **to deprive**; *pass.*, Rom 4:14, **to render useless**; 1 Cor 1:17, **to be nullified**[NIGTC]; 2 Cor 9:3, **to make empty**[BEC]; ❷ LXX, Jer 14:2, *her gates* **were emptied**; 15:9, *she* **has wasted away**

κέντρον, ου, τό$_2$ ❹ Acts 26:14, **goad**; 1 Cor 15:55, 56; Rev 9:10, **sting**; ❻ LXX, 2x Hos

κεντυρίων, ωνος, ὁ$_3$ ❷ Mark 15:39, 44, **centurion**

κενῶς *adv.* ① Jas 4:5, **in an empty manner**; ① LXX, Isa 49:4, **in vain**

κεραία, ας, ἡ$_{1α}$ ❷ Matt 5:18 = Luke 16:17, **the smallest letter**

κεραμεύς, εως, ὁ$_3$ ❸ Matt 27:7, 10; Rom 9:21, **potter**; (17x LXX; 5x Isa, 4x Jer)

κεραμικός, ή, όν$_{2.1.2}$ {κέραμος} *adj.* ①^{nnp} Rev 2:27, *artic. subst.*, **things made of clay** ①^{gns} Dan 2:41, **made of clay**

κεράμιον, ου, τό$_2$ {κέραμος} ❷^{ans} Mark 14:13 = Luke 22:10, **jar**; ❸ LXX, Isa 5:10; 30:14

κέραμος, ου, ὁ$_2$ ①^{gmp} Luke 5:19, **potter's clay**; ①^{gms} 2 Sam 17:28

κεράννυμι ❸ Rev 14:10; 18:6,^{2x} **to mix**; ❼ LXX, Prov 9:2, 5; Isa 5:2

κέρας, ατος, τό$_3$ {κέρας} (11x; 10x Rev) Luke 1:69; Rev 5:6, **horn**; (101x LXX; 21x Dan)

κεράτιον, ου, τό$_2$ {κέρας} ①^{gmp} Luke 15:16, **pods** *the pigs were eating*

κερδαίνω {κέρδος} (17x; 6x Matt, 5x 1 Cor) Matt 16:26 = Mark 8:36 = Luke 9:25; Phil 3:8, **to gain**; Acts 27:21, *irony*, **to gain** *injury and loss*[Bruce]; 1 Cor 9:19–22,^{5x} **to win**[NIGTC]; Jas 4:13, **to make money**[EGG]; 1 Pet 3:1, **to win over**

κέρδος, ους, τό$_3$ ❸ Phil 1:21; 3:7, **gain**; Titus 1:11, *disgraceful* **profit**[ABC]

κέρμα, ατος, τό$_3$ ①^{ans} John 2:15, **coins**

κερματιστής, οῦ, ὁ$_{1>}$ {κείρω} ①^{amp} John 2:14, **moneychangers**

κεφάλαιον, ου, τό$_2$ {κεφαλή} ❷ Acts 22:28, **large sum of money**; Heb 8:1, **the main point**[EGG]; ❻ LXX, Lev 5:24, *he will pay* **the sum total**

κεφαλή, ῆς, ἡ$_1$ (75x; 19x Rev, 12x Matt, 10x 1 Cor) Ⓐ ***lit.***, Matt 27:29 = Mark 15:19 = John 19:2, **head**; Ⓑ ***metaph.***, *Jesus in contrast with church*, Eph 4:15; Col 2:10, **preeminent**; ***metaph.***, *husband and the wife*, 1 Cor 11:3[NIGTC!]; Eph 5:23, **preeminent**; (402x LXX)

κεφαλιόω^{con} {κεφαλή} ①^{aai3p} Mark 12:4, **to beat on the head**

κεφαλίς, ίδος, ἡ$_3$ ①^{dfs} Heb 10:7, **in the scroll**; (24x LXX; 16x Exod) Exod 26:24–40:18

κημόω^{con} ①^{fai2s} 1 Cor 9:9, **to muzzle** *the ox*

κῆνσος, ου, ὁ$_2$ ❹ Matt 17:25; 22:17 (= Mark 12:14); 22:19, **taxes**

κῆπος, ου, ὁ$_2$ ❺ Luke 13:19; John 18:1; 19:41, **garden**; (36x LXX; 10x Song)

κηπουρός, οῦ, ὁ$_2$ {κῆπος} ①^{nms} John 20:15, **gardener**

κήρυγμα, ατος, τό$_3$ {κηρύσσω} ❾ Matt 12:41 = Luke 11:32, *Jonah's* **preaching**; Rom 16:25; 1 Cor 2:4; 2 Tim 4:17; Titus 1:3, **proclamation**

κῆρυξ, υκος, ὁ$_3$ {κηρύσσω} ❸ 1 Tim 2:7; 2 Tim 1:11; 2 Pet 2:5, **herald**; ❹ LXX, Gen 41:43, ἐκήρυξεν . . . **κῆρυξ, a herald** *made a proclamation*; Hom. *Il.* 2.50, **public crier**

κηρύσσω (61x; 14x Mark, 9x Matt) Matt 3:1 = Mark 1:4 = Luke 3:3; Acts 8:5; Rom 10:8; 1 Cor 1:23; 2 Cor 1:19, **to proclaim**; Acts 10:37; Rom 2:21; Phil 1:15, **to preach**; (31x LXX)

κῆτος, ους, τό$_3$ ①^{gns} Matt 12:40, **great fish**; (12x LXX; 4x Jonah, 3x Job)

Κηφᾶς, ᾶ, ὁ$_{1>}$ ❾ (4x 1 Cor:Gal) John 1:42; 1 Cor 1:12; Gal 2:9, **Cephas**

κιβωτός, οῦ, ἡ$_{2ὁδός}$ ❻ Matt 24:38 = Luke 17:27; Rev 11:19, **ark**; (221x LXX; 28x Gen)

κιθάρα, ας, ἡ$_{1α}$ ❹ 1 Cor 14:7; Rev 5:8; 14:2; 15:2, **harps**; (24x LXX; 11x Pss)

κιθαρίζω {κιθάρα} ❷ 1 Cor 14:7; Rev 14:2, **play the harp**; ①^{aaimp2s} LXX, Isa 23:16

κιθαρῳδός, οῦ, ὁ$_2$ {κιθάρα + ᾄδω} ❷^{gmp} Rev 14:2; 18:22, **harpists**

Κιλικία, ας, ἡ$_{1α}$ ❽ (7x Acts) Acts 6:9; Gal 2:1, **Cilicia**; ❼ LXX, Jdt 1:7, 12; 2:21, 25

κινδυνεύω ❹ *pass.*, Luke 8:23; 1 Cor 15:30, **to be put at risk**; Acts 19:27, 40, **to be in danger**[BHGNT]; ❼ LXX, 2 Macc 15:17; Jonah 1:4; Isa 28:13

κίνδυνος, ου, ὁ$_2$ ❾ (8x 2 Cor 11:26) Rom 8:35; 2 Cor 11:26,[BEC] **danger(s)**; (12x LXX)

κινέω^{con} ❽ Matt 23:4; Rev 6:14, **to move**; Matt 27:39 = Mark 15:29, **to shake**; Acts 21:30, **was in an uproar**[BHGNT]; 24:5, **to agitate**; (47x LXX; 8x Gen, 5x Isa)

κιννάμωμον, ου, τό$_2$ ①^{ans} Rev 18:13, **cinnamon**; ❺ LXX, Exod 30:23

Κίς, ὁ$_3$ *indecl.* ①^{gms} Acts 13:21, **Kish**; (20x LXX; 12x 1 Chr, 6x 1 Sam)

κίχρημι {χράομαι} ①^{aaimp2s} Luke 11:5, **Lend** *me some bread*!

κλάδος, ου, ὁ$_2$ {κλάω} (11x; 5x Rom) Matt 13:32 = Mark 4:32 = Luke 13:19; Rom 11:16–21, **branch**; (25x LXX; 7x Sir, 6x Ezek)

κλαίω (40x; 11x Luke, 8x John, 6x Rev) Matt 2:18; 26:75 = Mark 14:72; John 11:33; Acts 9:39; Rom 12:15; Jas 5:1; Rev 18:19, **to weep**, **cry**; (138x LXX; 26x 1–2 Sam, 14x Gen)

κλάσις, εως, ἡ$_1$ ❷^{dfs} Luke 24:35; Acts 2:42, *the* **breaking** *of bread*

κλάσμα, ατος, τό$_3$ ❾ Matt 14:20 = Mark 6:43 = Luke 9:17 = John 6:12, **scraps**; ❽ LXX

Κλαυδία, ας, ἡ$_{1α}$ ①^{nfs} 2 Tim 4:21, **Claudia**

Κλαύδιος, ου, ὁ$_2$ ❸ Acts 11:28; 18:21; 23:26, **Claudius**[LGCb 274]

κλαυθμός, οῦ, ὁ$_2$ {κλαίω} ❾ (7x Matt) Matt 2:18, **weeping** (1x); **κλαυθμὸς** καὶ ὁ βρυγμὸς τῶν ὀδόντων, Matt 13:42, **weeping** *and gnashing of teeth* (6x); Luke 23:28, **weeping** *and gnashing of teeth*; Acts 20:37, *many* **tears** *were shed*; (39x LXX; 7x Jer, 6x Isa)

κλάω^{con} (14x; 8x Syn) Matt 15:36 = Mark 8:6; Matt 26:26 = Mark 14:22 = Luke 22:19; Acts 2:46; 1 Cor 10:16, **to break** *bread*; ❷ LXX, 4 Macc 9:14, **to disjoint**; Jer 16:7, **to break** *bread*

κλείς, κλειδός, ἡ$_3$ {κλείω} ❻ Matt 16:19; Luke 11:52; Rev 3:7; 9:1, **key**; ❸ LXX, Judg 3:25

κλείω (16x; 6x Rev) Matt 6:6; Luke 4:25; Acts 21:30, **to shut**; Luke 11:7; John 20:19; Acts 5:23, **to lock**; 1 John 3:17, **to shut off** *compassion*; (24x LXX; 6x Ezek, 3x Neh)

κλέμμα, ατος, τό$_3$ {κλέπτω} ①^{gnp} Rev 9:21, **thefts**; ❹ LXX, Gen 31:39[2x]

Κλεοπᾶς, ᾶ, ὁ$_{1α}$ ①^{nms} Luke 24:18, **Cleopas**

κλέος, ους, τό$_3$ ①^{nns} 1 Pet 2:20, **credit**[Keen1P]; ❷ LXX, Job 28:22; 30:8, **a report**

κλέπτης, ου, ὁ$_{1>}$ {κλέπτω} (16x; 4x John) Matt 6:19, 20; 24:43 = Luke 12:33; John 10:1; 1 Cor 6:10; 2 Pet 3:10; Rev 16:15, **thief**, **thieves**; (17x LXX) Deut 24:7, **kidnapper**

κλέπτω (13x; 5x Matt) Matt 6:19; Mark 10:19; Matt 19:18 = Luke 18:20; John 10:10; Rom 2:21 = Eph 4:28, **to steal**; (33x LXX; 7x Gen:Exod)

κλῆμα, ατος, τό$_3$ ❹ John 15:2, 4, 5, 6, **branch**; (11x LXX; 5x Ezek)

Κλήμης, εντος, ὁ$_3$ ①^{gms} Phil 4:3, **Clement**

κληρονομέω^{con} {κληρόω + νόμος} (18x; 4x 1 Cor:Heb) Matt 5:5; Mark 10:17 = Luke 10:25; 1 Cor 6:9; 1 Pet 3:9, **to inherit**; Gal 4:30, *a share in* **the inheritance**[KeenG]; (161x LXX)

κληρονομία, ας, ἡ$_{1α}$ {κληρόω + νόμος} (14x; 3x Eph) Matt 21:38 = Mark 12:7; Acts 7:5; Eph 1:18; Col 3:24; Heb 11:8, **inheritance**; (208x LXX; 30x Num, 26x Josh)

κληρονόμος, ου, ὁ$_2$ (15x; 4x Rom) Matt 21:38 = Mark 12:7 = Luke 20:14; Rom 4:13; Gal 3:29; Titus 3:7; Jas 2:5, **heir**; ❺ LXX, 2 Sam 14:7

κλῆρος, ου, ὁ$_2$ {κληρόω} (11x; 5x Acts) Matt 27:35 = Mark 15:24 = Luke 23:34 = John 19:24; Acts 1:26, *casting* **lots**; Acts 1:17; 8:21; 26:18, **a share**; Col 1:12, *epex.*, τοῦ **κλήρου**, **apportioned lot**[EGG]; 1 Pet 5:3, **has allotted an inheritance** *for you to lead*[Keen1P]; (141x LXX; 32x Josh, 29x Deut, 20x Num)

κληρόω[con] ①[apilp] Eph 1:11, **to receive an inheritance**; ❸ LXX, 1 Sam 14:42, **to select**

κλῆσις, εως, ἡ$_{3}$ {καλέω} (11x; 5x Acts) Rom 11:29; Eph 4:1; 2 Thess 1:11, **call, calling**; 1 Cor 1:26, **call** *to faith*[NIGTC]; ❸ LXX, 3 Macc 5:14, **invitations**

κλητός, ή, όν$_{2.1.2}$ {καλέω} *adj.* (10x; 4x Rom) Matt 22:14, **chosen**; Rom 1:1; 8:28; 1 Cor 1:1; Jude 1; Rev 17:14, **called**; (18x LXX; 11x Lev) Exod 12:16, **assembly**

κλίβανος, ου, ὁ$_{2}$ ❷[ams] Matt 6:30 = Luke 12:28, **furnace**; (12x LXX; 4x Lev)

κλίμα, ατος, τό$_{3}$ ❸ Rom 15:23; 2 Cor 11:10; Gal 1:21, **region**; ①[nns] LXX, Judg 20:2

κλινάριον, ου, τό$_{2}$ {κλίνω}①[gnp] Acts 5:15, **cots**

κλίνη, ης, ἡ$_{1η}$ {κλίνω} ❾ Matt 9:2 = Luke 5:18, **stretcher**; Mark 4:21, **bed**; Rev 2:22, *idiom.*, *thrown into* **a sickbed**; (45x LXX; 7x 2 Kgs)

κλινίδιον, ου, τό$_{2}$ ❷ Luke 5:19, 24, **stretcher**

κλίνω ❼ Matt 8:20 = Luke 9:58, **to lay**; Luke 24:5; John 19:30, **to bow**; Luke 24:29, *sunset* **approaches**; Heb 11:34, *setting foreign armies* **to flight**; (58x LXX; 20x Pss)

κλισία, ας, ἡ$_{1α}$ {κλίνω} ①[afp] Luke 9:14, **groups**; ①[dfp] 3 Macc 6:31

κλοπή, ῆς, ἡ$_{1η}$ ❷[nfp] Matt 15:19 = Mark 7:21, **thefts**; ❻ LXX, Gen 40:15, **kidnapped**

κλύδων, ωνος, ὁ$_{3}$ ❷[dms] Luke 8:24; Jas 1:6, **waves**; ❾ LXX, 1 Macc 6:11, **flood**

κλυδωνίζομαι {κλύδων} ①[pmp.nmp] Eph 4:14, **tossed by the waves**; ①[fpi.3p] LXX Isa 57:20

Κλωπᾶς, ᾶ, ὁ$_{1α}$ ①[gms] John 19:25, **Clopas**

κνήθω {γναφεύς} ①[ppp.nmp] 2 Tim 4:3, **being tickled** *in their hearing*[ABC]

Κνίδος, ου, ὁ$_{2}$ ①[afs] Acts 27:7, **Cnidus**; ①[afs] LXX, 1 Macc 15:23

κοδράντης, ου, ὁ$_{1>}$ ❷ Matt 5:26; Mark 12:42, **penny**

κοιλία, ας, ἡ$_{1α}$ {κοῖλος} (22x; 7x Luke) Rom 16:18, **belly**; John 3:4, **womb**; 7:38, **deep within**; Acts 3:2, *from* **birth**; 1 Cor 6:13[2x]; Rev 10:9, **stomach**; (101x LXX; 11x Lev, 10x Isa)

κοιμάομαι[con] (194x LXX; 35x 1–2 Kgs, 27x Gen, 16x Lev:Deut) Ⓐ ***physical sleep***, Gen 19:4, **went to bed**; Ⓑ ***sexual relations, coitus***, Gen 19:32–35,[7x] **to sleep with**; Ⓒ ***regnal summary obituary***,[64x] 1 Kgs 11:21, *David* **slept** *with his fathers*

κοιμάω[con] {κεῖμαι} (18x; 6x 1 Cor) **to sleep** Ⓐ ***sleep of death***, Matt 27:52; John 11:11; Acts 7:60; 1 Cor 7:39; 1 Thess 4:13; 2 Pet 3:4; Ⓑ ***physical sleep***, Luke 22:45; John 11:12; Acts 12:6; Aeschl. *Ag* 2, **spend the night on guard duty**; Hom. *Il.* 11.24, *euphem.*, **he slept** *a bronze sleep*

κοίμησις, εως, ἡ$_{3}$ {κεῖμαι} ①[gfs] John 11:13, **natural sleep**; ❷ LXX, Sir 46:19; 48:13

κοινός, ή, όν$_{2.1.2}$ *adj.* (14x; 5x Acts) Rom 14:14,[3x] **unclean**; Acts 4:32; Titus 1:4, **common**; Acts 10:14, **impure**; Heb 10:29, **profane**; Jude 3, **common** *security*; (24x LXX; 16x 1–4 Macc)

κοινόω[con] (14x; 5x Matt:Mark) Matt 15:11[2x] = Mark 7:15[2x]; Matt 15:18–20[3x] = Mark 7:18–23[3x]; Acts 21:28; Heb 9:13, **to defile**; Acts 10:15, **to call impure**; ①[aai2s] LXX, 4 Macc 7:6

κοινωνέω[con] {κοινός} ❽ Rom 12:13, *subst. ptc.*, **sharing**; Rom 15:27, **to share** *in spiritual blessings*; Gal 6:6; 1 Pet 4:13 **to share**[KeenG]; Phil 4:15, **to enter into partnership**; 1 Tim 5:22; 2 John 11, *do not* **take part** *in evil works*; (13x LXX; 4x Sir)

κοινωνία, ας, ἡ$_{1α}$ {κοινός} (19x; 4x 2 Cor:1 John) 2 Cor 13:13; 1 John 1:3,[2x] **fellowship**; 2 Cor 6:14, **a partnership**; 1 Cor 10:16,[2x] **communal participation**; Phlm 6, **fellowship**; ❸ LXX, Lev 5:21; 3 Macc 4:6; Wis 8:18

κοινωνικός, ή, όν$_{2.1.2}$ {κοινός} *adj.* ①[amp] 1 Tim 6:18, **gladly giving others a share**[*TDNT*]

κοινωνός, οῦ, ὁ$_2$ {κοινός} (10x) Matt 23:30, **shared** *with them*; Luke 5:10; Phlm 17, **partners**; 1 Cor 10:18, 20, **communal participants**[NIGTC]; 2 Cor 1:7, **share**; ❽ LXX

κοίτη, ης, ἡ$_{1η}$ {κεῖμαι} ❹ Luke 11:7, **gone to bed**; Rom 9:10, **κοίτην** ἔχουσα, *becoming* **pregnant**; 13:13, **sexual liaisons**[ZEC]; Heb 13:4, **marriage bed**; (73x LXX; 18x Lev)

κοιτών, ῶνος, ὁ$_2$ ①^{gms} Acts 12:20, *the king's* **bedroom**; (15x LXX) Gen 49:4, **bed**

κόκκινος, η, ον$_{2.1.2}$ {κόκκος} *adj.* ❻ Matt 27:28; Heb 9:19; Rev 17:3, **scarlet**; (43x LXX)

κόκκος, ου, ὁ$_2$ ❼ Matt 13:31 = Mark 4:31 = Luke 13:19; 1 Cor 15:37, **seed**; ❷ LXX

κολάζω ❷ Acts 4:21; 2 Pet 2:9, **to punish**; (22x LXX; 12x Wis)

κολακεία, ας, ἡ$_{1α}$ ①^{gfs} 1 Thess 2:5, **flattery**

κόλασις, εως, ἡ$_3$ {κωλύω} ❷^{afs} Matt 25:46; 1 John 4:18, **punishment**; (15x LXX; 6x Ezek)

Κολασσαείς, έως, ὁ$_3$ ①^{amp} Col 1:0, *to* **the Colossians**

Κολασσαί, ῶν, αἱ$_1$ ①^{dfp} Col 1:2, ἐν **Κολοσσαῖς** *at* **Colossae**

κολαφίζω ❺ Matt 26:67 = Mark 14:65, **to strike with fists**; 1 Cor 4:11, **to treat roughly**; 2 Cor 12:7; 1 Pet 2:20, **to beat**

κολλούριον, ου, τό$_2$ ①^{ans} Rev 3:18, **eye salve**[NCBC]

κολλυβιστής, οῦ, ὁ$_{1>}$ ❸^{gmp} Matt 21:12 = Mark 11:15 = John 2:15, **money changers**

κολοβόω^{con} {κωλύω} ❹ Matt 24:22^{2x} = Mark 13:20,^{2x} **to cut short**; ①^{pai3p} 2 Sam 4:12

κόλπος, ου, ὁ$_2$ ❻ Luke 6:38, **lap**; 16:22, **side**; Acts 27:39, **a bay**; (41x LXX, 6x Exod:Prov)

κολυμβάω^{con} ①^{painf} Acts 27:43, **to swim**

κολυμβήθρα, ας, ἡ$_{1η}$ ❸ John 5:2, 7; 9:7, **pool**; (10x LXX; 4x Isa) 2 Kgs 18:17; Neh 2:14

κολωνία, ας, ἡ$_{1α}$ ①^{nfs} Acts 16:12, **a Roman colony**

κομάω^{con} {κόμη} ❷^{pas3s} 1 Cor 11:14, 15, **to wear long hair**

κόμη, ης, ἡ$_{1η}$ ①^{nfs} 1 Cor 11:15, **long hair**; (11x LXX) Num 6:5

κομίζω (10x; 3x Heb) *act.*, Matt 25:27, **to receive back**; Luke 7:37, **to bring**; Eph 6:8; Heb 10:36, **to receive**; *pass.*, 2 Cor 5:10, **to be paid back**; (26x LXX; 5x 2 Macc)

κομψότερον {κομέω} *adv.* ① John 4:52, **better**

κονιάω^{con} ❷ Matt 23:27; Acts 23:3, **to whitewash**; ❸ LXX, Deut 27:2, **to plaster** *them*

κονιορτός, οῦ, ὁ$_2$ {κονιάω + ὁρμή} ❺ Matt 10:14 = Luke 9:5, **dust**; (18x LXX; 5x Isa)

κοπάζω {κόπτω} ❸^{aai3s} **ἐκόπασεν** ὁ ἄνεμος, Matt 14:32 = Mark 6:51; Mark 4:39, *the wind* **ceased**; (26x LXX; 4x Gen) Gen 8:1

κοπετός, οῦ, ὁ$_2$ {κόπτω} ①^{ams} Acts 8:2, *they made great* **lamentation**; (20x LXX; 4x 1 Macc)

κοπή, ῆς, ἡ$_{1η}$ {κόπτω} ①^{gfs} Heb 7:1, **slaughter** *of the kings*; ❸ LXX, Gen 14:17, **slaughter**

κοπιάω^{con} {κόπτω} (23x) Matt 6:28; John 4:38,^{2x} **to labor**; Matt 11:28, πάντες οἱ **κοπιῶντες**, *all* **you weary** *and burdened* **people**; Luke 5:5; Rom 16:6; 1 Cor 15:10, **to work hard**; John 4:6, **who had become tired**; (50x LXX; 17x Isa) Isa 5:27; 16:12, **to grow tired**

κόπος, ου, ὁ$_2$ {κόπτω} (18x; 6x 1–2 Cor) Matt 26:10 = Mark 14:6, **κόπους** παρέχετε, *causing* **trouble**[ZEC]; *idiom.*, Luke 18:5, παρέχειν *with* **κόπον**, *because this widow furnishes me* **with trouble**[ABC]; 1 Cor 3:8, **labor**; Gal 6:17, **hardship**; (35x LXX; 10x Pss)

κοπρία, ας, ἡ$_{1α}$ {κόπρος} ①^{ams} Luke 14:35, **manure pile**[BHGNT]; (12x LXX; 4x Neh)

κόπριον, ου, τό$_2$ {κόπρος} ①^{anp} Luke 13:8, **manure pile**[BHGNT]; ❹ LXX, 1 Macc 2:62

κόπτω ❽ Matt 11:17, **beat oneself as an act of mourning**[EGG]; Matt 21:8 = Mark 11:8, **cutting** *branches*; (84x LXX; 17x Jer, 8x Ezek, 7x 1 Kgs)

κόραξ, ακος, ὁ$_3$ ①^{amp} Luke 12:24, **ravens**; (12x LXX) Gen 8:7; Job 38:41

κοράσιον, ου, τό$_2$ {κείρω} ❽ (5x Mark) Matt 14:11 = Mark 6:28,^{2x} **girl**; (21x LXX; 7x Esth)

κορβᾶν, τό$_3$ *indecl., Aram.* קָרְבָּן ① Mark 7:11, **Corban,** *i.e.*, **offering devoted to God**^{TDNT}

κορβανᾶς, ᾶ, ὁ$_{1α}$ ①^{ams} Matt 27:6, **temple treasury**

Κόρε, ὁ$_3$ *indecl.* ①^{gms} Jude 11, **Korah**; (43x LXX; 16x Num, 11x Pss)

κορέννυμι ❷ Acts 27:38, **to eat enough**; 1 Cor 4:8, **glutted**

Κορίνθιος, ου, ὁ$_2$ ❹ Acts 18:18; 1 Cor 1:0; 2 Cor 1:0; 6:11, **Corinthian**; ①^{gms} LXX, 2 Macc 11:21

Κόρινθος, ου, ἡ$_{2ὁδός}$ ❻ Acts 18:1; 1 Cor 1:2; 2 Cor 1:1, **Corinth**

Κορνήλιος, ου, ὁ$_2$ ❽ (Acts 10:1–30) **Cornelius**

κόρος, ου, ὁ$_2$ *Heb.* כֹּר ①^{amp} Luke 16:7, **a dry measure**; (14x LXX; 5x 1 Kgs)

κοσμέω^{con} {κόσμος} (10x; 3x Matt) Ⓐ ***adorning or decorating***, Matt 23:29, **to decorate** *tombs*; 1 Tim 2:9, **to adorn** *themselves*^{PPE}; 1 Pet 3:5, *mid.*, **to adorn** *themselves by submission*^{Keen1P}; Rev 21:2, *pass.*, **adorned** *for husband*; Ⓑ ***arrangement or preparation***, Matt 12:44 = Luke 11:25, **put in order**^{ZEC}; Matt 25:7, **to trim** *their torches*; (23x LXX; 8x Sir)

κοσμικός, ή, όν$_{2.1.2}$ {κόσμος} *adj.* ❷ Titus 2:12, **worldly**; Heb 9:1, **earthly** *sanctuary*

κόσμιος, ον$_{2.2}$ {κόσμος} *adj.* ❷ 1 Tim 2:9; 3:2, **modest**

κοσμοκράτωρ, ορος, ὁ$_3$ {κόσμος + κεράννυμι} ①^{amp} *neol.*, Eph 6:12, **world powers**

κόσμος, ου, ὁ$_2$ (186x; 78x John, 23x 1 John, 21x 1 Cor)^{NTWSD} Ⓐ ***adornment, cosmetic***, 1 Pet 3:3, **fine** *clothes*; Ⓑ ***created order***, John 12:31, *the ruler of this* **world**; Ⓒ ***contextual expressions***, John 7:4, *show yourself* **to the world**; Ⓓ ***paraenetic***, 1 Cor 6:2, *I will judge* **the world**; Ⓔ ***semantic proximity to*** αἰών, 1 Cor 1:20, *this* **age**; Eph 2:2; (71x LXX; 16x Wis)

Κούαρτος, ου, ὁ$_2$ ①^{nms} Rom 16:23, **Quartus**

κοῦμ$_3$ *indecl., Aram.* קוּם ① Mark 5:41, *Talitha* **koum!** (*i.e., Little lamb,* **get up!**)^{ZEC}

κοῦμι, *indecl., Aram.* קוּם *alternate spelling of* κοῦμ^{BDAG}

κουστωδία, ας, ἡ$_{1α}$ ❸ Matt 27:65, 66; 28:11, **guards**

κουφίζω {κοῦφος} ①^{iai3p} Acts 27:38, **to lighten** *the ship*; (11x LXX; 4x 1 Kgs, 1x Jonah)

κόφινος, ου, ὁ$_2$ ❻ Matt 14:20 = Mark 6:43 = Luke 9:17 = John 6:13, **basket**; ①^{dms} LXX, Ps 80:7 (81:6)

κράβαττος, ου, ὁ$_2$ (11x) Mark 2:11 = John 5:8, **mat**; Acts 9:33, ἐπὶ κραβάττου, **bedridden**

κράζω (55x; 12x Matt, 11x Acts:Rev) Matt 8:29 = Mark 5:7; Mark 15:13; Acts 7:57, **to shout**; Mark 9:26 = Luke 9:39; John 1:15; Jas 5:4; Rev 7:10, **to cry out**; (104x LXX; 41x Pss)

κραιπάλη, ης, ἡ$_{1η}$ ①^{dfs} Luke 21:34, **drunken behavior without moral restraint**^{EGG}

κρανίον, ου, τό$_2$ ❹ Matt 27:33 = Mark 15:22 = Luke 23:33 = John 19:17, *the Place of* **the Skull**; ❷ LXX, Judg 9:53, *Abimelech's* **skull**; 2 Kgs 9:35, *Jezebel's* **skull**

κράσπεδον, ου, τό$_2$ ❺ Matt 9:20 = Luke 8:44, **fringe**; ❺ LXX, Num 15:38,^{2x} **corners**

κραταιός, ά, όν$_{2.1.2}$ {κεράννυμι} *adj.* ①^{afs} 1 Pet 5:6, **mighty**; (65x LXX; 11x Deut)

κραταιόω^{con} {κεράννυμι} ❹ Luke 1:80; 2:40, **to become strong**; 1 Cor 16:13, **increase in strength**; Eph 3:16, *pass.*, **to be strengthened**; (59x LXX; 17x Pss, 12x 2 Sam)

κρατέω^{con} {κεράννυμι} (47x; 15x Mark) Matt 9:25 = Mark 1:31; Col 2:19, **to grasp, hold**; Matt 22:6, **to seize**; Mark 7:3, **to keep** *the tradition*; 14:44–49,^{4x} **to arrest**; Luke 24:16, **to prevent, seize** (*divine pass.*)^{ZEC}; Acts 27:13, **to achieve**; (140x LXX; 31x Neh)

κράτιστος, η, ον$_{2.1.2}$ {κεράννυμι} *adj.* ❹ Luke 1:3; **excellent** Acts 23:26; 24:3; 26:25, **Excellency**

κράτος, ους, τό$_{3}$ {κεράννυμι} (12x) Acts 19:20; Jude 25, **power**; Eph 1:19; 6:10; Col 1:11, **might**; (47x LXX; 12x Jdt)

κραυγάζω {κράζω} ❾ (6x John) Luke 4:41; John 11:43, **to shout**; ①^{aai3s} LXX, Ezra 3:13

κραυγή, ῆς, ἡ$_{1η}$ {κράζω} ❻ Matt 25:6; Luke 1:42, **shout**; Acts 23:9; Eph 4:31, **shouting**; Heb 5:7, **outcry**; (65x LXX; 13x Jer) Zeph 1:16, **battle cry**

κρέας, κρέατος$^{gen.}$ // κρέως,$^{gen.}$ τό$_{3}$ ❷^{anp} Rom 14:21; 1 Cor 8:13, **meat**; (87x LXX; 50x Pent)

κρείσσων *comp. adv. of* **ἀγαθός** ❹ 1 Cor 7:38; Phil 1:23, **better** (*manner*); 1 Cor 11:17; Heb 6:9, **better** (*superior*)

κρείττων {κρατύς} (15x; 13x Heb) 1 Cor 7:9; 1 Pet 3:17, **it is better**; Heb 1:4, **superior**; 12:24, **better things**

κρεμάννυμι ❼ *act.*, Matt 18:6; 22:40, **to hang**; Luke 23:39; Acts 5:30, **hanging**; *pass.*, Gal 3:13, **who is hung** *on a tree*

κρημνός, οῦ, ὁ$_{2}$ {κρεμάννυμι} ❸ Matt 8:32 = Mark 5:13 = Luke 8:33, **steep bank**; ❷ LXX, 2 Chr 25:12^{2x}

Κρής, ῆτος, ὁ$_{3}$ ❷^{nmp} Acts 2:11; Titus 1:12, **Cretans**; ①^{gmp} LXX, Zeph 2:5

Κρήσκης, εντος, ὁ$_{2}$ ①^{nms} 2 Tim 4:10, **Crescens**

Κρήτη, ης, ἡ$_{1η}$ ❺ Acts 27:7–21^{4x}; Titus 1:5, **Crete**; ❷ LXX, 1 Macc 10:67; Zeph 2:6

κριθή, ῆς, ἡ$_{1η}$ ①^{gfp} Rev 6:6, **barley**; (35x LXX; 6x Ruth) Exod 9:31

κρίθινος, η, ον$_{2.1.2}$ {κριθή} *adj.* ❷ John 6:9, 13, **made of barley**; ❺ LXX, Num 5:15

κρίμα, ατος, τό$_{3}$ {κρίνω} (27x) Matt 7:2, **κρίματι** κρίνετε κριθήσεσθε, **by the judgment** *you judge, you will be judged*; Mark 12:40 = Luke 20:47, **judgment**; (249x LXX; 41x Pss, 25x Song)

κρίνον, ου, τό$_{2}$ ❷ Matt 6:28 = Luke 12:27, **wild lilies**^{ZEC}; (19x LXX; 8x Song)

κρίνω (114x; 21x Acts, 19x John)^{NTWSD} **to judge**; 🅐 ***critical decision***, 1 Cor 7:37; Acts 25:25; 🅑 ***accusatory***, Matt 7:1–2; Jas 4:11–12,^{4x} **judgment** = *slander*^{KEL}; 🅒 ***juridical***, Acts 25:10, *pass.*, **to be tried**; Heb 10:30, **to vindicate**^{EGG}; 🅓 ***relational***, 1 Cor 6:6, **go to law** *with a believer*; (248x LXX; 34x Pss, 19x Judg)

κρίσις, εως, ἡ$_{3}$ {κρίνω} (47x; 12x Matt) Matt 23:23; John 7:24; Heb 9:27; Jude 6, **judgment**; Acts 8:33, **justice**; (263x LXX; 47x Isa)

Κρίσπος, ου, ὁ$_{2}$ ❷ Acts 18:8; 1 Cor 1:14, **Crispus**

κριτήριον, ου, τό$_{2}$ {κρίνω} ❸ 1 Cor 6:2, 4, *to hold* **a tribunal**^{NIGTC}; Jas 2:6, **law court**; ❸ LXX, Exod 21:6, **tribunal** *of God*

κριτής, οῦ, ὁ$_{1>}$ (19x; 10x LA) Matt 5:25; Luke 11:19; Acts 18:15, **judge**; (73x LXX; 11x Deut)

κριτικός, ή, όν$_{2.1.2}$ {κρίνω} *adj.* ①^{nms} Heb 4:12, **to scrutinize**

κρούω ❾ (4x Luke) Matt 7:7 = Luke 11:9; Acts 12:13; Rev 3:20, **to knock**; ❸ LXX

κρύπτη, ης, ἡ$_{1η}$ {κρύπτω} ①^{afs} Luke 11:33, **cellar**

κρυπτός, ή, όν$_{2.1.2}$ {κρύπτω} *adj.* (17x; 5x Matt) Matt 10:26 = Mark 4:22 = Luke 8:17, **hidden**; John 7:4, **in secret**; 1 Cor 4:5, **the hidden things**; (17x LXX; 5x Sir)

κρύπτω (18x; 7x Matt) Matt 5:14; Col 3:3; John 8:59, **to hide**; John 19:38, *adv. ptc.*, *manner*, **secretly**; Rev 2:17, *attrib. pass. ptc.*, **hidden** *manna*;^{EGG} (143x LXX; 20x Job, 19x Pss)

κρυσταλλίζω {κρύσταλλος} ①$^{pap.dms}$ Rev 21:11, **crystal**

κρύσταλλος, ου, ὁ$_{2}$ ❷ Rev 4:6; 22:1, **crystal**; ❾ LXX, Job 6:16, **ice**

κρυφαῖος, α, ον$_{2.1.2}$ {κρύπτω} *adj.* ❷^{dns} Matt 6:18,^{2x} **secret**; ❹ LXX, Exod 17:16

κρυφῇ {κρύπτω} *adv.* ① Eph 5:12, **secretly**; (10x LXX; 3x Isa)

κτάομαι[con] ❼ Matt 10:9, **to acquire**; Luke 18:12, **to earn**; 21:19, **to gain**; Acts 8:20, **to buy**; 1 Thess 4:4, **to exercise control**; (101x LXX; 14x Gen, 13x Sir, 12x Jer)

κτῆμα, ατος, τό$_3$ {κτάομαι} ❹ Matt 19:22 = Mark 10:22; Acts 2:45, **possessions**; Acts 5:1, **a piece of property**; (12x LXX) Prov 12:27, **wealth**

κτῆνος, ους, τό$_3$ {κτάομαι} ❹ Luke 10:34; 1 Cor 15:39, **animal**; Acts 23:34, **mounts**[FFB]; Rev 1:13, **horses**; (259x LXX; 45x Gen)

κτήτωρ, ορος, ὁ$_3$ {κτάομαι} ①[nmp] Acts 4:34, **owners**

κτίζω (15x; 4x Eph) Matt 19:4, **to make**; Mark 13:19; 1 Cor 11:9; Eph 2:10; Col 1:16, **to create**; Rom 1:25, *subst.*, **the Creator**; (67x LXX; 23x Sir, 6x Isa)

κτίσις, εως, ἡ$_3$ {κτίζω} (19x; 7x Rom) Mark 10:6; Rom 8:19–22[4x]; 2 Pet 3:4; Rev 3:14, **creation**; 2 Cor 5:17; Gal 6:15, *spir. a new* **creation**; Heb 4:13, **creature**; 1 Pet 2:13, *human* **system**[Keen1P]; (15x LXX) 3 Macc 2:7; Wis 19:6

κτίσμα, ατος, τό$_3$ ❹ 1 Tim 4:4, **what is created**; Jas 1:18; Rev 5:13; 8:9, **creature**; ❻ LXX

κτίστης, ου, ὁ$_{1>}$ {κτίζω} ①[dms] 1 Pet 4:19, *faithful* **Creator**; ❽ LXX, 2 Sam 22:32

κυβεία, ας, ἡ$_{1α}$ ①[dfs] Eph 4:14, **trickery**; *lit.*, Xen. *Mem.* 1.2.3, **game of dice**[BWIII]

κυβέρνησις, εως, ἡ$_3$ ①[afp] 1 Cor 12:28, **ability to formulate strategies**[NIGTC]; ❸ LXX, Prov 1:5, **intelligent guidance**; Plato *Rp.* 488b, **direction** *of the ship*, **pilotage**[BrDAG]

κυβερνήτης, ου, ὁ$_{1>}$ {κυβέρνησις} ❷ Acts 27:11; Rev 18:17, **shipmaster**, **helmsman**; ❺ LXX, 4 Macc 7:1, **pilot**; Plato *Phaed.* 247c, *intellect*, **that which governs** *the soul*[BrDAG]

κυκλεύω {κυκλόω} ①[aai3p] Rev 20:9, **to surround**; ①[aai3p] 2 Kgs 3:25

κυκλόθεν {κυκλόω + θεν} *impr. prep.* ❸ Rev 4:3, 4, 8, **all around**; (90x LXX; 24x Ezek)

κυκλόω[con] ❹ Luke 21:20; John 10:24, **to surround**; Acts 14:20, **to gather around**; Heb 11:30, **to encircle**; (91x LXX; 18x Pss) Gen 2:11, 13; Ps 7:8 (7:7)

κύκλῳ[dms] {κυκλόω} ❽ *fixed dat. of place from* κύκλος; Ⓐ (3x Rev) ***prep. w/ gen.***, 4:6, **before** *or* **around** *the throne*; Ⓑ (5x) ***adv.***, Mark 3:34, *sitting* **in a circle**; Mark 6:6 = Luke 9:12, **surrounding** *villages*; ❺ LXX, 2 Chr 4:2, **circumference**; Job 37:12, **encircling**

κυλισμός, οῦ, ὁ$_2$ {κυλίω} ①[ams] 2 Pet 2:22, **wallowing** *in the mud*

κυλίω ①[imi3s] Mark 9:20, **to roll** *on the ground*; (12x LXX) Josh 10:18

κυλλός, ή, όν$_{2.1.2}$ *adj.* ❹ Matt 15:30, 31; 18:8 = Mark 9:43, **crippled**

κῦμα, ατος, τό$_3$ {κύω} ❺ Matt 8:24 = Mark 4:37; Acts 27:41, **waves**; Jude 13, *fig.*, *they are wild* **waves**; (27x LXX; 5x Pss)

κύμβαλον, ου, τό$_2$ ①[nns] 1 Cor 13:1, **cymbal**; (20x LXX; 11x 1–2 Chr)

κύμινον, ου, τό$_2$ ①[ans] Matt 23:23, **cumin**; ❸ LXX, Isa 28:5, 27[2x]

κυνάριον, ου, τό$_2$ ❹ Matt 15:26, 27 = Mark 7:27, 28, **dog**

Κύπριος, ου, ὁ$_2$ ❸ Acts 4:36; 11:20; 21:16, **Cyprus**

Κύπρος, ου, ὁ$_2$ ❺ Acts 11:19; 13:4; 15:39; 21:3; 27:4, **Cyprus**

κύπτω ❷[aap.nms] Mark 1:7; John 8:6, **to stoop down**; (11x LXX)

Κυρηναῖος, ου, ὁ$_2$ ❻ Matt 27:32 = Mark 15:21 = Luke 23:26; Acts 11:20, **Cyrene**

Κυρήνη, ης, ἡ$_{1η}$ ①[afs] **Cyrene**; ①[afs] LXX, 1 Macc 15:23

Κυρήνιος, ου, ὁ$_2$ ①[gms] Luke 2:2, **Quirinius**

κυρία, ας, ἡ$_{1α}$ ❷ 2 John 1, 5, *the elect* **lady**; ❽ LXX, 3x Gen

κυριακός, ή, όν$_{2.1.2}$ *adj.* ❷ 1 Cor 11:20, *the* **Lord's** *Supper*; Rev 1:10, *the* **Lord's** *Day*

κυριεύω ❼ 2 Cor 1:24, **to lord over**; Rom 6:9, **to rule over**; 1 Tim 6:15, κύριος **τῶν κυριευόντων**, *the Lord* **of lords**; (50x LXX; 7x 1 Macc)

κύριος, ου, ὁ$_2$ (716x; 211x LA, 95x 1–2 Cor, 80x Matt) **Lord**; Ⓐ ***human masters***, Matt 10:24; Eph 6:5; 1 Pet 3:6; Ⓑ ***God as Lord***, Rom 4:8; 1 Cor 3:20; 1 Tim 6:15; Ⓒ ***Jesus as Lord***, Mark 2:28; 1 Cor 16:22; Phil 2:11; (8,298x LXX; 818x Pss, 607x Jer)

κυριότης, ητος, ἡ$_3$ ❹ Eph 1:21; Col 1:16, **dominion**; 2 Pet 2:10; Jude 8, **authority**

κυρόω[con] 2 Cor 2:8, **to affirm**; Gal 3:15, **to be validated**; ❹ LXX, Lev 25:30, **to pass**

κύων, κυνός, ὁ$_3$ ❺ Matt 7:6; Luke 16:21; Phil 3:2; 2 Pet 2:22, **dogs**; Rev 22:15, **male cult prostitute**[NICNT]; (38x LXX; 10x 1–2 Kgs)

κῶλον, ου, τό$_2$ ①[nnp] Heb 3:17, **bodies, corpses**; ❽ LXX, Lev 26:30, **carcasses**

κωλύω (23x; 12x LA) Matt 19:14 = Mark 10:14 = Luke 18:16; 1 Cor 14:39, **to forbid**; Mark 9:38, **to stop**; Luke 6:29; Rom 1:13, **to prevent**; (31x LXX; 6x Sir)

κώμη, ης, ἡ$_{1η}$ (27x; 12x Luke) Mark 6:6; Luke 5:17; Acts 8:25, **village**; (76x LXX; 33x Josh)

κωμόπολις, εως, ἡ$_3$ {κώμη + πόλις} ①[afp] Mark 1:38, **villages**

κῶμος, ου, ὁ$_2$ {κώμη} ❸ Rom 13:13; Gal 5:21, **uninhibited partying**[KeenG]; 1 Pet 4:3, **wild partying**[Keen1P]; ❷ LXX, 2 Macc 6:4; Wis 14:23, **carousing**

κώνωψ, ωπος, ὁ$_2$ ①[ams] Matt 23:24, **gnat**

Κώς, Κῶ, ἡ$_2$ ①[afs] Acts 21:1, **Cos**; ❸ LXX, 1 Chr 4:8; 24:10; 1 Macc 15:23

Κωσάμ, ἡ$_3$ *indecl.* ①[gms] Luke 3:28, **Cosam**

κωφός, ή, όν$_{2.1.2}$ {κόπτω} *adj.* (14x; Syn) Matt 12:22 = Luke 11:14, **mute**; (13x LXX; 6x Isa)

Λ, λ [*lambda*]

Λ, λ, τό (λάμβδα *or* λάβδα) *indecl.* **lambda**, *11th letter of the Gr. alphabet* || *num.* λʹ = 30; ͵λ = 30,000

λαγχάνω ❹ Luke 1:9; John 19:24, **to select by lot**; Acts 1:17, **to have a share**; 2 Pet 1:1, **to receive**; ❷ LXX, 3 Macc 6:1; Wis 8:19

Λάζαρος, ου, ὁ$_{2}$ (15x; 11x John) **Lazarus**; Ⓐ *brother of Mary and Martha*, John 11:1, 2; 12:1; Ⓑ *a beggar*, Luke 16:20, 23, 24, 25

λάθρᾳ {λανθάνω} *adv. of manner* ❹ Matt 1:19; 2:7; John 11:28; Acts 16:37, **secretly**; ❾ LXX, Deut 13:7; Ps 100:5 (101:5), **secretly**; 1 Sam 18:22, **in private**

λαῖλαψ, απος, ἡ$_{3}$ ❸ Mark 4:37 = Luke 8:23; 2 Pet 2:17, **windstorm**; ❼ LXX, Job 21:18

λακάω^{con} ①^{aai3s} Acts 1:18, **to burst open**

λακτίζω ①^{painf} Acts 26:14, **to kick**; Aeschl. *Pr.* 881, *heart* **knocks** *at my ribs in fear*

λαλέω^{con} (296x; 90x LA, 59x John, 44x 1–2 Cor) {λάλος} Matt 9:18; 26:47 = Mark 14:43 = Luke 22:47; Jas 1:19, **to speak**; 1 Cor 14:2–39,^{24x} *two speaking gifts*; (1,127x LXX)

λαλιά, ᾶς, ἡ$_{1α}$ ❸ Matt 26:73, **accent**; John 4:42, **message**; 8:43, **manner of speech**^{EGG}; (22x LXX) 2 Macc 5:5, **rumor**; Job 7:6, *life is lighter than* **a word**

λαμβάνω (258x; 53x Matt, 46x John) Mark 10:30; John 7:39, **to receive**; Matt 8:17; Rom 1:5, **to take**; 2 Cor 12:16, **to bamboozle**^{BEC}; (1,260x LXX; 131x Gen, 85x Ezek)

Λάμεχ ①^{gms} Luke 3:36, **Lamech**; (11x LXX; 10x Gen)

λαμπάς, άδος$_{3}$ ❾ Matt 25:1–8^{5x}; John 18:3; Rev 4:5, **torch**; Acts 20:8, **lamp**; (16x LXX, 5x Judg)

λαμπρός, ά, όν$_{2.1.2}$ {λάμπω} *adj.* ❾ Luke 23:11; Rev 15:6, **bright**; Acts 10:30, **dazzling**; Jas 2:2, **splendid**^{KEL}; ❻ LXX, Wis 6:12

λαμπρότης, ητος, ἡ$_{3}$ {λάμπω} ①^{afs} Acts 26:13, **brighter**; ❺ LXX, Ps 89:17 (90:17), **favor**; Isa 60:3, **brightness**

λαμπρῶς {λάμπω} *adv.* ① Luke 16:19, **lavishly**

λάμπω ❼ Matt 5:15, 16; Luke 17:24, **to light up**; Matt 17:2; Acts 12:7; 2 Cor 4:6,^{2x} **to shine**; ❻ LXX, Prov 4:18, **radiant**; Isa 9:1, **to dawn**

λανθάνω ❻ Matt 7:24, Luke 8:47; Acts 26:26, **to escape notice**; Heb 13:2, **to be unaware**; 2 Pet 3:5, 8, **to overlook**; (17x LXX) Lev 4:13, **to escape notice**

λαξευτός, ή, όν$_{2.1.2}$ {λᾶς} *adj.* ①^{dns} Luke 23:53, **cut out of rock**; ①^{afs} Deut 4:49

Λαοδίκεια, ας, ἡ$_{1α}$ ❻ Col 2:1; 4:13, 16; Rev 1:11; 3:14, **Laodicea**^{LGCb}

Λαοδικεύς, έως, ὁ$_{3}$ ①^{gmp} Col 4:16, **Laodicean**

λαός, οῦ, ὁ$_{2}$ (142x; 84x LA) Matt 15:8 = Mark 7:6; Luke 3:21; Acts 13:15; Rom 9:25; Heb 13:12; 1 Pet 2:9; Rev 7:9, **people**; (1,966x LXX; 168x Ex, 147x Jer, 117x Pss)

λάρυγξ, λάρυγγος, ὁ$_{3}$ ①^{nms} Rom 3:13, **throat**; (17x LXX; 9x Pss) Job 6:30, **palate**

Λασαία, ας, ἡ$_{1α}$ ①^{nfs} Acts 27:8, **Lasea**

λατομέω^{con} {λᾶς + τέμνω} ❷ Matt 27:60 = Mark 15:46, **to cut out of the rock**; (11x LXX; Exod 21:33; 2 Chr 26:10, **to dig**)

λατρεία, ας, ἡ$_{1α}$ ❺ Rom 9:4, **service**; 12:1, **worship**; Heb 9:1, 6, **ministry**; ❾ LXX, Exod 12:25, **ceremony**; Josh 22:27, **worship**; 1 Chr 28:13, **service**

λατρεύω (21x; 6x Heb) Matt 4:10 = Luke 4:8; Acts 26:7; Rom 1:9; Phil 3:3; Heb 8:5, **to serve**; Acts 7:7, 42; Rev 22:3, **to worship**; (97x LXX; 25x Deut, 19x Josh)

λάχανον, ου, τό$_{2}$ ❹ Mark 4:32, **garden plants**; Luke 11:42, **herb**; Rom 14:2, **vegetables**; ❺ LXX, Gen 9:3; 1 Kgs 20:2 (21:2), **green plants**; Prov 15:17, **vegetables**

λεγιών, ῶνος, ἡ$_{3}$ ❹ Matt 26:53, **legion**; Mark 5:9 = Luke 8:30, *My name is* **Legion**; Mark 5:15, τὸν ἐσχηκότα τὸν **λεγιῶνα**, *the one who had the* **legion**

λέγω (2,353x; *narr. rich verb*; 767x LA, 105x Rev) Matt 1:16, **to be called**; 4:2 (εἰπέ^{aaimp2s}, 12x in Matt)^{EGG}; Mark 2:24; Acts 13:40; 2 Cor 4:6, **to say, speak**; (2,078x LXX; 288x Ezek, 253x Jer) *verbal formula*, τάδε **λέγει** κύριος, *this is what the Lord* **says** (324x LXX; 126x Ezek, 64x Jer)

λεῖμμα, ατος, τό$_{3}$ ①^{nns} Rom 11:5, **remnant**; ❷ LXX, 2 Sam 21:2; 2 Kgs 19:4

λεῖος, α, ον$_{2.1.2}$ *adj.* ①^{afp} Luke 3:5, **smooth**; ❺ LXX, Gen 27:11; 1 Sam 17:40; Prov 2:20

λείπω ❻ Luke 18:22, **is missing**^{ZEC}; *subst.*, Titus 1:5, *put in order* **the things that still needed doing** (TEV); *act.*, Titus 3:13, **to fall short**; Jas 1:4, 5, **to lack**; ❼ LXX, Prov 11:3, **to leave**, **regret**

λειτουργέω^{con} {λαός + ἔργον} ❸ Acts 13:2, **to worship**; Rom 15:27; Heb 10:11, **to minister**; (97x LXX; 24x Num, 16x Ezek)

λειτουργία, ας, ἡ$_{1α}$ {λαός + ἔργον} ❻ Luke 1:23; Phil 2:30; Heb 8:6, **ministry**; 2 Cor 9:12; Phil 2:17, **service**; Heb 9:21, **worship**; (47x LXX; 21x 1–2 Chr, 18x Num)

λειτουργικός, ή, όν$_{2.1.2}$ {λαός + ἔργον} *adj.* ①^{nnp} Heb 1:14, **ministering** *spirits*; ❻ LXX, Exod 31:10, *garments for* **ministry**; Num 4:12, **serving** *utensils*

λειτουργός, οῦ, ὁ$_{2}$ {λαός + ἔργον} ❺ Rom 13:6; Heb 1:7, **servant**; Rom 15:16; Phil 2:25; Heb 8:2, **minister**; (14x LXX) 2 Sam 13:18, **servant**

λεμά *Aram. translit.* ❷ Matt 27:46 = Mark 15:34, **why?**

λέντιον, ου, τό$_{2}$ ❷ John 13:4, 5, **towel**

λεπίς, ίδος, ἡ$_{3}$ ①^{nfp} Acts 9:18, **flake, scale**; ❻ LXX, Lev 11:9; Num 17:3

λέπρα, ας, ἡ$_{1α}$ {λεπίς} ❹ Matt 8:3 = Mark 1:42; Luke 5:12, 13, **leprosy**; (39x LXX; 33x Lev)

λεπρός, οῦ, ὁ$_{2}$ {λεπίς} ❾ (all in Syn) Matt 8:2 = Mark 1:40; Luke 4:27, **leprosy**; (13x LXX, 4x Lev, 2 Chr)

λεπτός, ή, όν$_{2.1.2}$ *adj.* ❸ Mark 12:42 = Luke 21:2, **small copper coin**; (28x LXX; 10x Gen) Gen 41:3–27,^{10x} *seven* **thin-fleshed (sickly)** *cows, seven* **thin** *and wind-blasted ears of corn*

Λευί *indecl.* ❽ **Levi** Ⓐ Heb 7:5, 9, *third son of Jacob and Leah*; Ⓑ Mark 2:14 = Luke 5:27, 29, *son of Alphaeus*; Ⓒ Luke 3:24, 29, *in genealogy*; (76x LXX; 17x Num:1 Chr)

Λευίτης, ου, ὁ$_{1>}$ ❸ Luke 10:32; John 1:19; Acts 4:36, **Levite**; (310x LXX; 97x 1–2 Chr)

Λευιτικός, ή, όν$_{2.1.2}$ *adj.* ①^{gfs} Heb 7:11, **Levitical**

λευκαίνω {λευκός} ❷ Mark 9:3; Rev 7:14, **to whiten**; ❺ LXX, Lev 13:19; Isa 1:18^{2x}

λευκός, ή, όν$_{2.1.2}$ *adj.* (25x; 16x Rev) Matt 5:36; 17:2 = Mark 9:3 = Luke 9:29; Rev 1:14–20:11, **white**, *most frequently mentioned color in Rev*; (31x LXX; 16x Lev)

λέων, οντος, ὁ$_{3}$ ❾ (6x Rev) 2 Tim 4:17; 1 Pet 5:8; Rev 4:7, **lion**; (142x LXX; 47x MajPr)

λήθη, ης, ἡ$_{1\eta}$ ①[afs] 2 Pet 1:9, *pred., having* **forgotten**; (11x LXX) Lev 5:15, **unaware**

λῆμψις, εως, ἡ$_{3}$ ①[gfs] Phil 4:15, **receiving**; ❹ LXX, Prov 15:27, 29, **receiver** *of bribes*

ληνός, οῦ, ἡ$_{2}$ ❺ Matt 21:33; Rev 14:19, 20[2x]; 19:5, **winepress**; (22x LXX; 3x Pss:Joel)

λῆρος, ου, ὁ$_{2}$ ①[nms] Luke 24:11, **nonsense, empty talk**; ①[ams] LXX, 4 Macc 5:11

λῃστής, οῦ, ὁ$_{1>}$ (15x; 14x Gs) Matt 21:13 = Mark 11:17 = Luke 19:46; John 10:1; 2 Cor 11:26, **robber, thief**; ❾ LXX, Hos 7:1; Obad 5, **thief**

λίαν *adv.* (12x, 4x Matt, Mark) Matt 4:8; Luke 23:8; 2 John 4, **very**; 2 Tim 4:15, **exceedingly**; (18x LXX) Gen 1:31, **indeed**; 1 Sam 11:15, **greatly**

λίβανος, ου, ὁ$_{2}$ ❷ Matt 2:11; Rev 18:13, **frankincense**; (102x LXX; 13x Isa, 10x Song)

λιβανωτός, οῦ, ἡ$_{2}$ {λίβανος} ❷ Rev 8:3, 5, **burner, censer**; ❷ LXX, 1 Chr 9:29; 3 Macc 5:2

Λιβερτῖνος, ου, ὁ$_{2}$ ①[gmp] Acts 6:9, **Freedman**, *a Latin loanword designating a slave or descendant who had been freed*[EGG]

Λιβύη, ης, ἡ$_{1\eta}$ ①[gfs] Acts 2:10, **Lybia**

λιθάζω ❾ (5x John) John 8:5; 10:31; Acts 5:26; 2 Cor 11:25, **to stone**; ❷ LXX, 2 Sam 16:6

λίθινος, η, ον$_{2.1.2}$ *adj.* ❸ John 2:6; 2 Cor 3:3; Rev 9:20, **of stone**; (22x LXX; 7x Deut)

λιθοβολέω[con] {λίθος + βάλλω} ❼ Matt 23:37 = Luke 13:34, **to stone**; (27x LXX; 17x Pent)

λίθος, ου, ὁ$_{2}$ (59x; 14x Luke, 11x Matt) Matt 4:3 = Luke 4:3; Mark 5:5; John 8:7; Acts 4:11; Rev 4:3, **stone**; 17:4, **jewel**; (292x LXX; 29x Ex, 22x Josh)

λιθόστρωτος, ον$_{2.2}$ {λίθος + στρωννύω} *adj.* ①[ans] John 19:13, **Stone Pavement** (= *Heb.* **Gabbatha**); ❸ LXX, 2 Chr 7:3; Esth 1:6; Song 2:10

λικμάω[con] ❷ Matt 21:44 = Luke 20:18, **to shatter**; (17x LXX) Job 27:21, **to winnow**

λιμήν, ένος, ὁ$_{3}$ ❸ Acts 27:8, *Fair* **Havens**[ZEC]; 27:12,[2x] **harbor**; ❾ LXX

λίμνη, ης, ἡ$_{1\eta}$ (11x; 6x Rev, 5x Luke) Luke 5:1, 2; Rev 20:14,[2x] **lake**; ❺ LXX, 2 Macc 12:16

λιμός, οῦ, ὁ$_{2}$ (12x) Matt 24:7 = Mark 13:8 = Luke 21:11; Rom 8:35, **famine**; (114x LXX)

λίνον, ου, τό$_{2}$ ❷ Matt 12:20, **wick**; Rev 15:6, **linen**; ❽ LXX, Exod 9:31; Isa 19:9, **flax**

Λίνος, ου, ὁ$_{2}$ ①[nms] 2 Tim 4:21, **Linus**

λιπαρός, ά, όν$_{2.1.2}$ {λίπος} *adj.* ①[nnp] Rev 18:14, **splendid**; ❷ LXX, Neh 9:35, **fertile**

λίτρα, ας, ἡ$_{1\alpha}$ ❷ John 12:3; 19:29, **pound**, *a Roman pound, 325 grams or 12 oz.*[NET, NTG]

λίψ, λιβός, ὁ$_{3}$ ①[ams] Acts 27:12, **southwest**; (45x LXX; 20x Josh)

λογεία, ας, ἡ$_{1\alpha}$ {λέγω} ❷ 1 Cor 16:1, 2, **collection**

λογίζομαι {λέγω} (40x; 19x Rom) Luke 22:37, **to be reckoned**; John 11:50, **to consider**; Acts 19:27, **to be looked upon** *as nothing*[ZEC]; Rom 2:3, **to think**; 2 Tim 4:16, **to count**; 1 Cor 13:5, **to keep a reckoning up** *of evil*[NIGTC]; 1 Cor 13:11, **to count values**[NIGTC]; Gal 3:6, **to be credited**; (115x LXX; 20x Wis, 15x Isa)

λογικός, ή, όν$_{2.1.2}$ {λέγω} *adj.* ❷ Rom 12:1, **reasonable**; 1 Pet 2:2, **mind-engaging**[Keen1P!]

λόγιον, ου, τό$_{2}$ {λέγω} ❹ Acts 7:38, **word**; Rom 3:2; Heb 5:12; 1 Pet 4:11, **oracle**; (35x LXX; 27x Pss) Ps 118 (119) "Psalm of the Law," (19x) **word** = *God's law*

λόγιος, α, ον$_{2.1.2}$ {λέγω} *adj.* ①[nms] Acts 18:24, **learned**[ZEC]; Aristot. *Pol.* 1267b 28, **expert**

λογισμός, οῦ, ὁ$_{2}$ {λέγω} ❷ Rom 2:15, **thought**; 2 Cor 10:4, **argument**[BEC]; (113x LXX; 73x 4 Macc, 8x Jer) 4 Macc *passim*, **the activity of thinking and reasoning**[SCS]; **God-directed reason**[Emmet]

λογομαχέω[con] {λέγω + μάχη} ①[painf] 2 Tim 2:14, **to dispute about words**

λογομαχία, ας, ἡ$_{1\alpha}$ {λέγω + μάχη} ①[afp] 1 Tim 6:4, **disputes over words**

λόγος, ου, ὁ$_2$ (330x; 129x Gs, 97x LA) Matt 13:19–23^{6x} = Mark 4:14–20^{8x} = Luke 8:11–15^{4x}; Acts 2:22, **word**; John 1:14, *the* **Word** *became flesh*; Matt 28:15, **story**; John 4:37, **saying**; Titus 2:8, **message**; Acts 14:12, *the chief* **speaker**; 18:15, **teaching**; 20:38, **statement**; 1 Cor 1:17, **rhetoric**; 1 Pet 4:5, **account**; (1,180x LXX; 170x Jer, 147x 1–2 Kgs)

λόγχη, ης, ἡ$_{1η}$ ①^{dfs} John 19:34, **spear**; (10x LXX) 1 Sam 17:7

λοιδορέω^{con} {λοίδορος} ❹ John 9:28, **to ridicule**; Acts 23:4, **to insult**; 1 Cor 4:12; 1 Pet 2:23, **to abuse**; ❽ LXX, Exod 17:2, **to complain**

λοιδορία, ας, ἡ$_{1α}$ {λοίδορος} ❸ 1 Tim 5:14, **reviling**; 1 Pet 3:9,^{2x} **insult** *for* **insult**; ❼ LXX

λοίδορος, ου, ὁ$_2$ ❷ 1 Cor 5:11; 6:10, **verbally abusive**; ❹ LXX, Prov 25:24; 27:15, **nagging** *wife*; 26:21, **quarrelsome person**

λοιμός, οῦ, ὁ$_2$ ❷ Luke 21:11; Acts 24:5, **famine**; (27x LXX; 7x 1 Sam) 1 Sam 1:16, **wretched, worthless**

λοιπός, ή, όν$_{2.1.2}$ {λείπω} *adj.* (55x) Ⓐ^{40x} ***plural form*** (οἱ λοιποί) Matt 25:11, **the remaining ones**; Ⓑ^{13x} ***adv. acc*** (τὸ λοιπόν) Mark 14:41, **still** *sleeping*; 1 Cor 4:2, (**ὧδε λοιπόν**), **now**; Ⓒ^{2x} ***adv. gen.*** (τοῦ λοιποῦ) Gal 6:17, **from now on**; Eph 6:10, **finally**; (114x LXX; 35x 1–2 Kgs)

Λουκᾶς, ᾶ, ὁ$_1$ ❸ Col 4:14; 2 Tim 4:11; Phlm 24, **Luke**

Λούκιος, ου, ὁ$_2$ ❷ Acts 13:1, **Lucius** *of Cyrene*; Rom 16:21, **Lucius**, *countryman of Paul*

λουτρόν, οῦ, τό$_2$ {λούω} ❷ Eph 5:26; Titus 3:5, **washing**; ❸ LXX, Song 4:2; 6:6

λούω ❺ John 13:10, **to bathe**; Acts 9:37; Heb 10:22, **to wash**; (45x LXX; 23x Lev)

Λύδδα, ας, ἡ$_3$ ❸ Acts 9:32, 35, 38, **Lydda**

Λυδία, ας, ἡ$_{1α}$ ❷ Acts 16:14, 40, **Lydia**

Λυκαονία, ας, ἡ$_{1α}$ ①^{gfs} Acts 14:6, **Lycaonia**

Λυκαονιστί *prop adv.* ① Acts 14:11, **Lycaonian** *language*

Λυκία, ας, ἡ$_{1α}$ ①^{gfs} Acts 27:5, **Lycia**

λύκος, ου, ὁ$_2$ ❻ Matt 7:15; Luke 10:3; John 10:12, **wolf**^{2x}; ❾ LXX, Hab 1:8, Zeph 3:3

λυμαίνω ①^{imi3s} Acts 8:3, **to ravage**; (16x LXX) Ps 79:14 (80:13), *wild boar* **ravages**

λυπέω^{con} {λύπη} (26x; 12x 2 Cor, 6x Matt) *act.*, Matt 14:9, **to regret**; 1 Thess 4:13, **to grieve**; *pass.*, Matt 17:23; 26:22, **to be distressed**; 19:22 = Mark 10:22; John 21:17; 2 Cor 2:5^{2x}; 2 Cor 7:8–9→7:8^{2x}, *act.*, **I grieved** you, the letter **grieved** you; 7:9^{3x} **ἐλυπήθητε**; *pass.*, **you were grieved** (54x LXX; 7x Tob)

λύπη, ης, ἡ$_{1η}$ (16x; 6x 2 Cor) 1 Pet 2:19; John 16:6, 20; Rom 9:2, **grief**, **sorrow**; 2 Cor 7:10,^{2x} *godly* **grief** ≠ *wordly* **grief**^{BEC}; Heb 12:11, **grievous**; (45x LXX; 14x Sir, 7x Prov)

Λυσανίας, ου, ὁ$_1$ ①^{gms} Luke 3:1, **Lysanias**

Λυσίας, ου, ὁ$_1$ ❷ Acts 23:26; 24:22, **Lysias**

λύσις, εως, ἡ$_3$ {λύω} ①^{afs} 1 Cor 7:27, *do not be seeking* **release**^{WPNT}; *do not seek* **to loose the tie**^{NIGTC}; ❸ LXX, Eccl 8:1, **interpretation** *of a matter*, **λύσιν** ῥήματος, **untie** *a word*; Dan 12:8, **outcome**

λυσιτελέω^{con} {λύω + τέλος} ①^{pai3s} Luke 17:2, **to be better**; ❹ LXX, Tob 3:6

Λύστρα, ας, ἡ$_1$ *or* **τό**$_2$ ❻ Acts 14:6, 8, 21; 2 Tim 3:11, **Lystra**

λύτρον, ου, τό$_2$ {λύω} ❷ Matt 20:28 = Mark 10:45, **ransom**; (20x LXX; 8x Num)

λυτρόω^{con} {λύω} ❸ Luke 24:21; Titus 2:14; 1 Pet 1:18, **to redeem**; (108x LXX; 27x Pss)

λύτρωσις, εως, ἡ$_3$ {λύω} ❸ Luke 1:68; 2:38; Heb 9:12, **redemption**; (12x LXX; 3x Lev)

λυτρωτής, οῦ, ὁ$_{1>}$ {λύω} ①[ams] Acts 7:35, **deliverer**; ❹ LXX, Lev 25:31, 32, **redemption**
λυχνία, ας, ἡ$_{1\alpha}$ {λύχνος} (12x; 7x Rev) Matt 5:15 = Mark 4:21 = Luke 8:16 = Luke 11:33; Rev 1:12; 11:4, **lampstand**; (35x LXX; 15x Exod)
λύχνος, ου, ὁ$_{2}$ (14x; 6x Luke) Matt 5:15 = Luke 8:16; Rev 18:23, **lamp**; (46x LXX; 11x Exod)
λύω (42x; 30x GA) *act.*, Matt 5:19; Rev 9:14, **to break**; Mark 1:7 = Luke 3:16, **to untie**; Acts 2:24, **to free**; 1 John 3:8, **to destroy**; *pass.*, 1 Cor 7:27, **to be dissolved**[NIGTC]; (29x LXX)
Λωΐς, ΐδος, ἡ$_{3}$ ①[dfs] 2 Tim 1:5, **Lois**, *Timothy's grandmother*
Λώτ, ὁ *indecl.* ❸ Luke 17:28, 32; 2 Pet 2:7, **Lot**; (36x LXX; 32x Gen)

M, μ [*mu*]

M, μ, τό (μῦ) *indecl.* **mu**, *12th letter of the Gr. alphabet* ‖ *num.* μʹ = 40; ͵μ = 40,000; *in inscr.* M = μύριοι 10,000

Μάαθ, ὁ$_3$ *indecl.* ①[gms] Luke 3:26, **Maath**; ❷ LXX, 2 Chr 29:12; 31:13

Μαγαδάν, ἡ$_3$ *indecl.* ①[gfs] Matt 15:39, **Magadan**

Μαγδαληνή, ῆς, ἡ$_{1η}$ (12x) Matt 28:1 = Mark 16:1, 9 = John 20:1, *Mary* **Magdalene**

μαγεία, ας, ἡ$_{1α}$ ①[dfp] Acts 8:11, **sorceries**

μαγεύω ①[pap.nms] Acts 8:9, **to practice sorcery**

μάγος, ου, ὁ$_2$ ❻ Matt 2:1, 7, 16,[2x] **wise men**; Acts 13:6, 8, **sorcerer**; ❷ LXX, Dan 2:2, 10

Μαγώγ, ὁ$_3$ *indecl.* ①[ams] Rev 20:8, **Magog**; ❸ LXX Gen 10:2; 1 Chr 1:5; Ezek 38:2

Μαδιάμ, ὁ$_3$ *indecl.* ①[gms] Acts 7:29, **Midian**; (56x LXX; 32x Judg) Gen 25:2; Judg 6:1–10:12, *Gideon's call and the Midianites*

μαθητεύω {μανθάνω} ❹ Matt 13:52; 28:19; Acts 14:21, **to make a disciple**

μαθητής, οῦ, ὁ$_{1>}$ {μανθάνω} (261x; 155x Syn, 78x John) Matt 9:14 = Mark 2:18[4x] = Luke 5:33; John 3:22; Acts 9:25, **disciples**

μαθήτρια, ας, ἡ$_{1α}$ {μανθάνω} ①[nfs] Acts 9:36, **disciple** *named Tabitha*

Μαθθάτ, ὁ$_3$ *indecl.* ❷[gms] Luke 3:24, 29, **Matthat**

Μαθθίας, ου, ὁ$_1$ ❷[ams] Acts 1:23, 26, **Matthias**

μαίνομαι ❺ John 10:20, **to be crazy**; Acts 26:24, **You're out of your mind!**; 26:25, **driving** *you* **insane**; 1 Cor 14:23, **you are raving and out of your mind**[NIGTC!]; ❻ LXX; 2x Jer

μακαρίζω {μακάριος} ❷ Luke 1:48, **will count me blessed**[ZEC]; Jas 5:11, **to call blessed**; (24x LXX; 6x Sir) Gen 30:13

μακάριος, α, ον$_{2.1.2}$ *adj.* (50x; 15x Luke, 13x Matt) Matt 5:3–12 (*Jesus's beatitudes*),[9x] Rev 1:3–22:14 (*John's beatitudes*),[7x] **flourishing are the** *x*[SoM 55]; 1 Cor 7:40, **happier**; (68x LXX; 25x Pss) Gen 30:13; Aristoph. *Ve.* 1292, *O you turtles* **blessed** *in your skins*

μακαρισμός, οῦ, ὁ$_2$ {μακάριος} ❸ Rom 4:6, 9; Gal 4:15, **blessing**

Μακεδονία, ας, ἡ$_{1α}$ (22x; 8x Acts) Acts 16:9, 12, **Macedonia**[LGCb 332]

Μακεδών, όνος, ὁ$_3$ ❺ Acts 16:9; 2 Cor 9:2, 4, **Macedonian**

μάκελλον, ου, τό$_2$ ①[dns] 1 Cor 10:25, **meat market**

μακράν {μακρός} *adv.* (10x) Matt 8:30; Luke 15:20, **some distance**; Mark 12:34, οὐ **μακράν**, *not* **far**; (72x LXX; 9x Prov, 7x Isa) Gen 44:4, *not* **far off**

μακρόθεν {μακρός + θεν} *adv.* (11x; 10x Syn) Matt 26:58 = Mark 14:54, **at a distance**; Rev 18:10, *stand* **far off**, (37x LXX) Gen 21:16, **far away**

μακρο**θυμέω**[con] {μακρός + θυμός} (14x) Matt 18:26, **to be patient**; Luke 18:7; 1 Cor 13:4, **to wait patiently**; (10x LXX) Prov 19:11, **to exercise patience**; Job 7:16, **leave me alone**

μακρο**θυμία, ας, ἡ**$_{1α}$ {μακρός + θυμός} (14x) Rom 2:4; 2 Cor 6:6, **patience**; ❺ LXX, 1 Macc 8:4; Prov 25:15

μακρο**θύμως** {μακρός + θυμός} *adv.* ① Acts 26:3, **patiently**

μακρός, ά, όν$_{2.1.2}$ *adj.* ❹ Mark 12:40 = Luke 20:47, **long**; Luke 15:13; 19:12, *a* **distant** *country*; (17x LXX; 9x Prov, 7x Isa) Deut 12:21, **too far**; Prov 7:19, **long** *journey*

μακροχρόνιος, ον$_{2.2}$ {μακρός + χρόνος} *adj.* ①^{nms} Eph 6:3, **long-lived** *upon the earth*; ❷ LXX, Exod 20:12

μαλακία, ας, ἡ$_{1α}$ {μαλακός} ❸ Matt 4:23; 9:35; 10:1, **sickness**; (15x LXX; 7x 2 Chr)

μαλακός, ή, όν$_{2.1.2}$ *adj.* ❹ Matt 11:8^{2x} = Luke 7:25, **soft** *finery*[ZEC]; 1 Cor 6:9, *subst.*, **those males who are sexually penetrated by males** (i.e., *womanish*)[NIGTC]; ❷ LXX, Prov 25:15; 26:22, **gentle**, **soft**; Aristot. *Metaph.* 1090b 8, **softer** *character of females*[BrDAG]

Μαλελεήλ, ὁ$_3$ *indecl.* ①^{gms} Luke 3:37, **Mahalalel**, ❻ LXX, Gen 5:12–17^{5x}; 1 Chr 1:2

μάλιστα {μᾶλλον} *adv.* (12x) Acts 20:38; Gal 6:10; Phil 4:22; 2 Pet 2:10, **most of all**, **especially**; ❻ LXX, 2 Macc 8:7, **most advantageous**; 3 Macc 5:3, **especially**

μᾶλλον *comp adv.* (81x; 23x Gs, 18x 1–2 Cor) 🅐 ***direct comp*** + ἤ, Matt 18:13; Acts 4:19, **more than**; 🅑 ***absolute*** + περισσεύω, 1 Thess 4:1, 10, **do this even more**; 🅒 μᾶλλον + ***adjective***, Mark 9:42, καλὸν . . . **μᾶλλον**, **it would be better**; 🅓 ***implied negation***, Matt 27:42; 2 Cor 5:8, **rather**[EDNT]; (46x LXX; 7x Sir) Job 30:26, *implied neg.*, **all the more**

Μάλχος, ου, ὁ$_2$ ①^{nms} John 18:10, **Malchus**

μάμμη, ῆς, ἡ$_{1η}$ ①^{dfs} 2 Tim 1:5, **grandmother**; ① LXX, 4 Macc 16:9

μαμωνᾶς, ᾶ, ὁ$_1$ ❹ Matt 6:24 = Luke 16:13, **money**; 16:9, 11, **worldly wealth**

Μαναήν, ὁ$_3$ *indecl.* ①^{nms} Acts 13:1, **Manaen**

Μανασσῆς, ῆ, ὁ$_1$ ❸ Matt 1:10^{2x}; Rev 7:6, **Manasseh**, *son of Joseph*; (29x LXX; 11x 2 Kgs, 9x 2 Chr) Judg 1:27; 2 Kgs 21:1, **Manasseh**, *son of Hezekiah, king of Judah*

μανθάνω (25x) Matt 24:32 = Mark 13:28; 2 Tim 3:14^{2x}; Rev 14:3, **to learn**; (56x LXX)

μανία, ας, ἡ$_{1α}$ ①^{afs} Acts 26:24, *is driving you* **mad**; ❻ LXX, Hos 9:7, 8, **madness**

μάννα, τό$_3$ *indecl.* ❹ John 6:31; Heb 9:4; Rev 2:17, **manna**; (10x LXX) Num 11:6

μαντεύομαι {μαίνομαι} ①$^{pmp.nfs}$ Acts 16:16, **to tell fortunes**; (12x LXX) Ezek 13:6

μαραίνω ①^{fpi3s} Jas 1:11, **to wither away**; ❹ LXX, Job 15:30, **to shrivel up**

μαργαρίτης, ου, ὁ$_{1>}$ ❾ (5x Rev) Matt 7:6; 1 Tim 2:9; Rev 17:4; 21:21,^{2x} **pearl**

Μάρθα, ας, ἡ$_{1α}$ (13x, 9x John) Luke 10:38; John 11:1; 12:2, **Martha**

Μαρία, ας, ἡ$_{1α}$ (27x; 8x Matt:Mark) **Mary** 🅐 ***mother of Jesus***, Matt 1:16; 🅑 ***Magdalene***, Matt 27:56; 🅒 ***mother of James and Joseph (the "other" Mary)***, Mark 15:40; 🅓 ***the wife of Clopas***, John 19:25; 🅔 ***mother of Mark***, Acts 12:12; 🅕 *Jewish worker who greeted Paul*, Rom 16:6[APB]

Μαριάμ, ἡ$_3$ *indecl.* (27x; 13x Luke, 10x John) **Mary** 🅐 ***mother of Jesus***, Matt 13:55; Acts 1:14; 🅑 ***of Bethany***, John 11:19; 🅒 ***Magdalene***, John 20:18; (15x LXX; 9x Num) Exod 6:20

Μᾶρκος, ου, ὁ$_2$ ❾ Acts 12:12[ZEC]; Col 4:10; Phlm 24; 1 Pet 5:13,[Keen1P] *John* **Mark**

μάρμαρος, ου, ὁ$_2$ {μαρμαίρω} ①^{gms} Rev 18:12, **marble**; ①^{gfs} LXX, Ep Jer 71

μαρτυρέω^{con} {μάρτυς} (76x; 33x John) Matt 23:31; Luke 4:22; Rev 1:2, **to testify**; John 1:7–21:24, **to give testimony**[BEC]; Acts 6:3, **of good reputation**; Heb 11:2, 4, 5, **to win approval**; (13x LXX) Gen 31:46–48, Βουνὸς **μαρτυρεῖ**, *Mound*-**Bears-Witness**

μαρτυρία, ας, ἡ$_{1α}$ {μάρτυς} (37x; 14x John, 9x Rev) Mark 14:55; 1 John 5:9–11,^{6x} **testimony**; John 1:7, **witness**; 3 John 12, **testimony** *is true*; Rev 1:2–20:4, **testimony**; (11x LXX) Exod 20:16 = Deut 5:20, *false* **testimony**

μαρτύριον, ου, τό$_2$ {μάρτυς} (19x; 9x Syn) Matt 8:4 = Mark 1:44 = Luke 5:14; Heb 3:5,

testimony; Matt 10:18, *purp.*, εἰς + *acc.*, **to bear witness**; (257x LXX; 171x Exod–Num) Gen 21:30; Exod 25:10

μαρτύρομαι {μάρτυς} ❺ Acts 20:8; Gal 5:3; Eph 4:17, **to testify**; ①[pmi1p] LXX, Jdt 7:28

μάρτυς, μάρτυρος, ὁ$_3$ (35x; 13x Acts) Matt 26:65 = Mark 14:63; Acts 1:8; Rom 1:9; 2 Cor 13:1; Rev 2:13, **witness**; (58x LXX; 10x Prov, 9x Deut) Exod 23:1

μασάομαι {μαστιγόω} ①[imi3p] Rev 16:10, **gnawed** *on their tongues*; ①[imi3p] LXX, Job 30:4, **chewed** *on tree roots*

μαστιγόω[con] ❼ Matt 10:17; 20:19 = Mark 10:34 = Luke 18:33; John 19:1, **to flog**; Heb 12:6, **to chastise**[ABC]; (31x LXX) Exod 5:14, **to beat with a whip**

μαστίζω {μαστιγόω} ①[painf] Acts 22:25, **to scourge**; ❸ LXX, Num 22:25, **to whip, lash**

μάστιξ, ιγός, ἡ$_3$ {μαστιγόω} ❻ Mark 3:10; 5:34; Luke 7:21, **affliction**; Acts 22:24, **with the scourge**; Heb 11:36, **scourgings**; (37x LXX; 8x Sir, 7x Pss) 1 Kgs 12:11, **whips**

μαστός, ου, ὁ$_2$ ❸ Luke 11:27; 23:29, **breast**; Rev 1:13, **chest**; (35x LXX; 14x Song)

ματαιο**λογία, ας, ἡ**$_{1α}$ {μάταιος + λέγω} ①[afs] 1 Tim 1:6, **empty talk**

ματαιο**λόγος, ου, ὁ**$_2$ {μάταιος + λέγω} ①[nmp] Titus 1:10, **empty talkers**

μάταιος, α, ον$_{2.1.2}$ *adj.* ❻ Jas 1:26, **worthless**; 1 Cor 3:20, **futile**; 15:17, **without effect**[NIGTC]; 1 Pet 1:18, **empty**[Keen1P]; (75x LXX) Exod 20:7 = Deut 5:11, **in an empty way**

ματαιότης, ητος, ἡ$_3$ ❸ Rom 8:20; Eph 4:17, **futility**; 2 Pet 2:18, **empty**; (54x LXX; 39x Eccl, 14x Pss) Eccl 1:2–12:8, **ματαιότης ματαιοτήτων**,[2x] **absolute futility**

ματαιόω[con] ①[api3p] Rom 1:21, **to be rendered futile**[ZEC]; ❼ LXX, 1 Sam 13:13, **to be foolish**; Jer 2:5, **to become worthless** *idols*; 23:16, **to speak empty** *visions*

μάτην {μάταιος} *adv.* ❷ Matt 15:9 = Mark 7:7, **in vain**

Ματθάν, ὁ$_3$ *indecl.* ❷ Matt 1:15,[2x] **Matthan**, *father of Jacob*; ❷ LXX, 2 Kgs 11:18

Ματταθά, ὁ$_3$ *indecl.* ①[gms] Luke 3:31, **Mattath**, *Jesus's great grandfather*

Ματταθίας, ου, ὁ$_1$ ❷ Luke 3:25, 26, **Mattathias**, *son of Semein*; (22x LXX; 13x 1 Macc)

μάχαιρα, ης, ἡ$_{1>}$ {μάχη} (29x; 15x Syn) Matt 26:51 = Mark 14:47 = John 18:11; Acts 12:2; Eph 6:17; Rev 6:4, **sword**; (187x LXX; 50x Jer, 36x Ezek) Gen 22:6; Josh 5:2, **knife**

μάχη, ης, ἡ$_{1η}$ ❹ 2 Cor 7:5, **conflict**; 2 Tim 2:23; Titus 3:9, **dispute**; Jas 4:1, **fight**; (32x LXX; 10x Prov) Gen 13:7, **quarreling**; Josh 4:13, **battle**; Prov 17:1, **strife**

μάχομαι {μάχη} ❹ John 6:52, **to argue**; Acts 7:26; Jas 4:2, **to fight**; 2 Tim 2:24, **to be quarrelsome**[NIGTC]; (21x LXX) Gen 26:20, **to quarrel**; Exod 21:22, **to fistfight**

μεγαλεῖος, α, ον$_{2.1.2}$ {μέγας} *adj.* ①[anp] Acts 2:11, **magnificent**; (15x LXX) Deut 11:2

μεγαλειότης, ητος, ἡ$_3$ {μέγας} ❸ Luke 9:43; Acts 19:27, **greatness**, **magnificence**; 2 Pet 1:16, **majesty**; ❹ LXX, Dan 7:27, **greatness**

μεγαλο**πρεπής, ές**$_{3.3}$ {μέγας + τρέπω} *adj.* ①[gfs] 2 Pet 1:17, **Majestic Glory**; ❹ LXX, Deut 33:26; 2 Macc 8:15; 15:13; 3 Macc 2:9

μεγαλύνω {μέγας} ❽ Matt 23:5 **to lengthen**; Luke 1:46, **to exalt**; 1:58, **to magnify**; Acts 5:13, **to speak well of**; 10:46, *subst. ptc.*, **greatness**; *pass.*, 2 Cor 10:15, *ministry* **will be extended**; Phil 1:20, **will be highly honored**; (79x LXX; 17x Pss)

μεγάλως {μέγας} *adv.* ① Phil 4:10, **greatly**; (20x LXX; 5x 2 Macc) Num 6:2, **especially**

μεγαλωσύνη, ης, ἡ$_{1η}$ {μέγας} ❸ Heb 1:3; 8:1, **Majesty**; Jude 25, **majesty**; (26x LXX; 4x Pss)

μέγας, μεγάλη, μέγα$_{3.1.3}$ *adj.* (243x; 80x Rev, 64x LA) Matt 2:10, *the deepest and* **most profound** *joy*[Brun1]; Heb 4:14, **great**; 9:11, **greater**; 8:11, **the greatest**; Rev 1:10, **loud**; Luke

4:38, **high** *fever*; Rom 9:12, **the older**; 1 Cor 16:9, **wide**; Rev 1:10–21:12; *often* **μέγας** *functions in the service of eschat.*[EDNT]; (850x LXX; 102x MajPr)

μέγεθος, ους, τό$_3$ {μέγας} ①[nns] Eph 1:19, **magnificence**; (18x LXX; 7x Ezek) Exod 15:16

μεγιστάν, ᾶνος, ὁ$_3$ {μέγας} ❸ Mark 6:21, **high officials**[BEC]; Rev 6:15, **officers of the court**; 18:23, **great men**[BEC]; (42x LXX; 12x Sir, 8x 1 Esd) 2 Chr 36:28, **officers**; *only two sing.*, Sir 4:7; 10:24

μεθ**ερμηνεύω** {μετά + ἑρμηνεύω} ❽ (7x[ppp.nns]) Matt 1:23; John 1:38, **which is translated**; ①[aainf] LXX, Sir 0:30, **translation**

μέθη, ης, ἡ$_{1η}$ {μεθύω} ❸ Luke 21:34; Rom 13:13; Gal 5:21, **drunkenness**; (13x LXX)

μεθ**ίστημι** {μετά + ἵστημι} ❺ Luke 16:4; Acts 13:22; 1 Cor 13:2, **to remove**; Acts 19:26, **to mislead**; Col 1:13, **to transfer**; (29x LXX) Deut 17:17; Judg 7:5; 1 Sam 6:12

μεθ**οδεία, ας, ἡ$_{1α}$** {μετά + ὁδός} ❷ Eph 4:14; 6:11, **strategy**[ZEC]

μεθύσκω {μεθύω} ❺ Luke 12:45; John 2:10; Eph 5:18, **to get drunk**; Rev 17:2, **to become drunk** *on immorality*; (37x LXX; 8x Jer) Gen 9:21; 1 Sam 1:14; Ps 22:5 (23:5)

μέθυσος, ου, ὁ$_2$ {μεθύω} ❷ 1 Cor 5:11; 6:10, **drunkards**; ❺ LXX, Prov 23:21

μεθύω ❺ Matt 24:49, *subst. ptc.*, **drunkards**; Acts 2:15, **to be drunk**; (12x LXX; 5x Isa) Job 12:25

μέλας, μέλαινα, μέλαν$_{3.1.3}$ *adj.* ❻ Matt 5:36; Rev 6:5, 12, **black**; 2 Cor 3:3; 2 John 12; 3 John 13, **ink**; ❺ LXX, Lev 13:37; Song 1:5; Zech 6:2, 6

Μελεά, ὁ$_3$ *indecl.* ①[gms] Luke 3:3, **Melea**

μέλει (10x) Matt 22:16; 1 Pet 5:7, **to care**; 1 Cor 7:21, **to worry**; 9:9, **to be concerned**

μελετάω[con] {μέλω} ❷ Acts 4:25, **to fix one's mind on**; 1 Tim 4:15, **make** *these matters* **your business**[NIGTC!]; (34x LXX; 17x Pss) Josh 1:8; Ps 1:2, **to meditate**

μέλι, ιτος, τό$_3$ ❹ Matt 3:4 = Mark 1:6; Rev 10:9, 10, **honey**; (63x LXX; 9x Deut) Gen 43:11

Μελίτη, ης, ἡ$_{1η}$ ①[nfs] Acts 28:1, **Malta**

μέλλω (109x; 34x Acts, 13x Rev)[EDNT]→ Ⓐ ***completing an action w/ inf.***, Rev 12:4, **about** *to give birth*; Ⓑ ***purpose***, Matt 2:13, *Herod* **is preparing** *to search*; Rev 3:16, **I will** *spit you out*; Ⓒ ***certainty***, John 11:51, *Jesus* **would** *die*; Ⓓ ***uncertainty***, Luke 22:23, *who* **was going** *to do this*; Ⓔ ***hesitancy***, Acts 22:16, *And now why* **do you wait**?; (43x LXX; 21x 1–4 Macc)

μέλος, ους, τό$_3$ (34x; 16x 1 Cor) Matt 5:29; Rom 6:13, **body part, member**; Rom 12:4; 1 Cor 6:15[3x]; 12:12–25,[13x] **limb, organ**[NIGTC]; (26x LXX; 5x Lev)

Μελχί, ὁ$_3$ *indecl.* ❷ Luke 3:24, 28, **Melchi**; ❾ LXX, 1 Chr 6:25; Ezra 10:25

Μελχισέδεκ, ὁ$_3$ *indecl.* ❽ (Heb) 7:1–17,[5x] **Melchizedek**; ❷ LXX, Gen 14:18; Ps 109:4 (110:4)

μεμαθηκώς → μανθάνω, *pf. act. ptc. nms*, John 7:15, **since he has** *not* **been trained**

μεμβράνα, ης, ἡ$_{1η}$ ①[afp] 2 Tim 4:13, **parchments**

μεμιαμμένοις → μιαίνω, *pf. mid. ptc. dmp*, Titus 1:15, **to those who are defiled**

Μεμφίβοσθε, ὁ$_3$ *indecl.* (29x LXX; 2 Sam) **Mephibosheth**, *son of Saul*

μέμφομαι ❷ Rom 9:19; Heb 8:8, **to find fault**; ❸ LXX, 2 Macc 2:7; Sir 11:7

μεμψ**ίμοιρος, ον$_3$** {μέμφομαι + μείρομαι} *adj.* ①[nmp] Jude 16, **malcontents**[BEC]

μέν *part.* (179x; 48x Acts)[Runge 75–83]→ Ⓐ ***emphatic untranslated***, **μέν . . . δέ**, Matt 3:11, *I baptized . . . but he will . . .*; Ⓑ ***emphatic translated***, **μέν . . . δέ**, Luke 23:41, **indeed** . . . *but*; Ⓒ ***emphatic translated extended***, **μέν . . . δέ . . . δέ**, Heb 9:1–11, ***now*** *even* (**καί**) *the first*, *but (a)... but (b)*; Matt 25:15; ❹ **μέν *solitarium*** (*no forward anticipation*), Acts 2:41–42, **μέν ... δέ**, *So* (οὖν), *those... And they were...*; (218x LXX)[GrLXX 50]

Μεννά, ὁ$_3$ *indecl.* ①[gms] Luke 3:31, **Menna**

μενοῦν *part.* ① Luke 11:28, **on the contrary**[BDAG]

μενοῦνγε *part.* ❸ Rom 9:20, **on the contrary**[EGG]; 10:18, **Of course they did**! (GNB); Phil 3:8, **but, therefore, indeed, also**[ATR 1151]

μέντοι *advers. conj.* ❽ John 4:27, **but**; 12:42, **despite**[ZEC]; Jude 8, **actually**[BHGNT]; ❺ LXX, all in Prov; 5:4; 16:25, 26; 22:9; 26:12

μένω (118x; 40x John, 24x 1 John) 2 Cor 3:11, **to remain**; John 1:38, **to dwell, stay**; 15:4 (*t.t. in John*),[ZEC] **continue to live**; 2 Tim 3:14, **to continue, abide**; (80x LXX; 15x Isa)

μερίζω {μέρος} (14x; 8x Syn) Matt 12:25–26[3x] = Mark 3:24–26[3x]; 1 Cor 1:13, **to divide**; Heb 7:2, **to apportion**; 2 Cor 10:13, **to assign**; (34x LXX) Exod 15:9, **I will divide** *spoils*

μέριμνα, ης, ἡ$_{1η}$ {μεριμνάω} ❻ Matt 13:22 = Mark 4:19 = Luke 8:14, **worry**; 2 Cor 11:28, **anxiety**; 1 Pet 5:7, **concern**[Keen1P]; (11x LXX; 5x Sir), Ps 54:23 (55:22), **care**

μεριμνάω[con] (19x) Matt 6:25–34[6x]; Phil 4:6, **to worry**; 1 Cor 7:32–34,[4x] **to have anxiety**; 12:25, **to have concern**; Phil 2:20, **to care**; ❾ LXX, Exod 5:9[2x]

μερίς, ίδος, ἡ$_3$ {μέρος} ❺ Luke 10:42, **portion**; Acts 16:12, **district**; 2 Cor 6:15, **part**; (147x LXX; 14x Josh) Gen 14:24,[2x] **part**; Lev 6:10, **portion**; Josh 18:5–7,[4x] *land* **allotment**

μερισμός, οῦ, ὁ$_2$ {μέρος} ❷ Heb 2:4, **distribution**; 4:12, **separates**[ABC]; ❷ LXX, Josh 11:23, **allotment**; Ezra 6:18, **division**

μεριστής, οῦ, ὁ$_{1>}$ {μέρος} ①[ams] Luke 12:14, **arbitrator**

μέρος, ους, τό$_3$ (43x) Matt 2:22; Rev 16:19, **region, area, parts**; Acts 23:9, **party**; Rom 11:25, ἀπὸ **μέρους**, *lit.*, **in part, a partial** *hardening*; 15:15, **on some points**[BEC]; 1 Cor 11:18, **to some extent**; 12:27, ἐκ **μέρους, part by part, individually**[NIGTC]; 13:9, **bit by bit**; 14:27, **in turns**[NIGTC]; 2 Cor 2:5, **to a certain extent**[BEC!]; 1 Pet 4:16, *by this* **name**[Keen1P]; (127x LXX; 19x Exod, 18x Josh)

μεσημβρία, ας, ἡ$_{1α}$ {μέσος + ἡμέρα} ❷ Acts 8:26, **south**[ZEC]; 22:6, **noon, midday**; (25x LXX) Gen 18:1, **midday**

μεσιτεύω {μέσος} ①[aai3s] Heb 6:17, **to confirm**; Polyb. *Hist.* 11.34.3, **to negotiate**

μεσίτης, ου, ὁ$_{1>}$ {μέσος} ❻ Gal 3:19; Heb 9:15, **mediator**; ①[nms] LXX, Job 9:33

μεσονύκτιον, ου, τό$_2$ {μέσος + νύξ} ❹ Mark 13:35; Luke 11:5; Acts 16:5; 20:7, **midnight**; ❺ LXX, Judg 16:3[2x]

Μεσοποταμία, ας, ἡ$_{1α}$ {μέσος + πόταμος} ❷ Acts 2:9; 7:2, **Mesopotamia**; (21x LXX; 13x Gen)

μέσος, η, ον$_{2.1.2}$ *adj.* (58x; 24x LA) Ⓐ ***adjectival***, Matt 25:6, **at midnight**; Acts 26:13, **at noon**; Ⓑ ***adverbial***, Luke 4:30, **through the midst** *of them*; John 8:3, 9, ἐν μέσῳ (*adverbial inclusio*), **in the midst**; Ⓒ ***impr. prep. w/ gen.***, Mark 3:3, **in the midst**; Ⓓ ***Lukan theological***, Luke 2:46; Acts 1:5, ἐν μέσῳ, **in the midst**[EDNT]; Luke 17:11, **the middle** (*through* **no-man's land**)[ZEC]; (791x LXX) ἀνὰ **μέσον** (345x), Gen 1:4,[2x] *lit.*, *God separated* **between** *the light and separated* **between** *the darkness*

μεσότοιχον, ου, τό$_2$ {μέσος + τεῖχος} ①[ans] Eph 2:14, **dividing wall** *of hostility*

μεσουράνημα, ατος, τό$_3$ {μέσος + οὐρανός} ❸ Rev 8:13, 14:6, 19:17, **midheaven**

μεσόω[con] {μέσος} ①[pap.gfs] John 7:14, **to be in the middle, halfway point**; ❻ LXX, Exod 12:29, *ptc.*, **being at midnight**; 34:22, **being in the middle** *of the year*

Μεσσίας, ου, ὁ$_1$ ❷ John 1:41; 4:25, **Messiah**, *the Christ*[ZEC]

μεστός, ή, όν$_{2.1.2}$ *adj.* ❾ Matt 22:28; John 19:29; Rom 1:29; Jas 3:8, **full**; ❹ LXX

μεστόω[con] ①ppp.nmp Acts 2:13, **They are drunk!** ❷ LXX, 3 Macc 5:2, *ptc.*, **inebriated** *elephants*

μετά, μετ', μεθ' *prep.* (469x; 128x LA, 71x Matt, 51x Rev) Ⓐ *w/gen.*, Matt 26:58; Acts 7:38; Rev 21:3, **with**; Ⓑ *w/acc.*, Matt 17:1; John 13:27; Heb 9:3, **after**; (2,322x LXX; 248x Gen, 246x 1–2 Sam)

μεταβαίνω (12x; 6x Matt) Matt 8:34; John 7:3, **to leave**; Matt 17:20, **to move**; John 5:24; 13:1, **to cross over**[EGG]; ❺ LXX, 2 Macc 6:9, **to change over**; Wis 19:19, *pass.*, **to be transformed**; Aristot. *H.A.* 588b 4, *nature* **passes** *little by little*

μεταβάλλω ①amp.nmp Acts 28:6, **they changed their minds**; (32x LXX) Exod 7:17

μετάγω {μετά + ἄγω} ❷ Jas 3:3, 4, **to guide**; (11x LXX) 1 Kgs 8:47, 48, **to transfer**; 2 Chr 6:37, **to deport**; 36:3, **to depose**

μεταδίδωμι ❺ Luke 3:11; Rom 12:8, **to share**; ❼ LXX, Prov 11:26; Job 31:17

μετάθεσις, εως, ἡ$_3$ {μετά + τίθημι} ❸ Heb 7:12, **a change**; 11:5, **before being taken**[ABC]; 12:27, **removal**; ①afs LXX, 2 Macc 11:24, **change**

μεταίρω {μετά + αἴρω} ❷aai3s Matt 13:53; 19:1, **to depart**, **leave**; ❹ LXX, 2 Kgs 16:17

μετακαλέω[con] ❹ Acts 7:14; 10:32, **to invite**; 20:17, **to call for**; 24:25, **to send for**; ❸ LXX, Hos 11:1, 2, **to call**

μετακινέω[con] ①pmp.nmp Col 1:23, **to shift**; ❼ LXX, Deut 19:14, **to take** *you with us*; Isa 54:10, *the hills* **shake**; Aristot. *E.N.* 1137b 31, **to fit** *to the shape of the rock*

μεταλαμβάνω ❼ (4x Acts) Acts 2:46, **they ate** *their meals*; 24:25, *temp. adv. ptc.*, **when I find** *time* (NASB); 27:33, 34, **to take** *food*; 2 Tim 2:6, **to receive** *a share*; (13x LXX; 12x 2–4 Macc)

μετάλημψις, εως, ἡ$_3$ {μετά + λαμβάνω} ①afs 1 Tim 4:3, **receiving**

μεταλλάσσω {μετά + ἄλλος} ❷aai3p Rom 1:25, 26, **to exchange**[EGG]; (12x LXX; 9x 2 Macc) 2 Macc 4:7, *lit.*, *when Seleucus* **quit life**; 5:5, **died**

μεταμέλομαι {μετά + μέλω} ❻ Matt 21:29, **to change one's mind**; 27:3, **to be filled with remorse**; 2 Cor 7:8, **I** *don't* **regret** *it*[BEC]; (13x LXX) 1 Sam 15:35, **to be sorry**

μεταμορφόω[con] {μετά + μορφή} ❹ *act.*, Matt 7:2 = Mark 9:2, **to transform**, **to change in form**; *pass.*, Rom 12:2; 2 Cor 3:18, **to be transformed**

μετανοέω[con] {μετά + νοῦς} (34x, 14x LA) Matt 12:41 = Luke 11:32; Mark 1:15; Acts 2:38; Rev 2:5–3:19,[8x] **to repent**; (24x LXX; 5x Jer) 1 Sam 15:29,[2x] **to change one's mind**

μετάνοια, ας, ἡ$_{1a}$ {μετά + νοῦς} (22x; 11x LA) Matt 3:8; Luke 5:32; Acts 5:31, **repentance**; ❼ LXX, Prov 14:15, **change of mind**

μεταξύ {μετά + σύν} ❾ Ⓐ ***adverbial***, John 4:31, *in the* **meantime**; Acts 13:42, *the* **next** *Sabbath*; Ⓑ ***impr. prep. w/gen.***, Matt 18:15, **between** *you and him alone*; ❹ LXX

μεταπέμπω ❾ Acts 10:5; 25:3, **to summon**[ZEC]; 12:22, **to send for**

μεταστρέφω ❷ Acts 2:20, **to turn**; Gal 1:7, **to twist**[KeenG]; (25x LXX; 5x Pss) Exod 14:5

μετασχηματίζω ❺ 1 Cor 4:6, **I have allusively applied** *these things to myself*[NIGTC!]; 2 Cor 11:13–15, **disguising themselves** . . . *Satan* **masquerades** . . . *his servants also* **masquerade**[BEC!]; Phil 3:21, **to transform**; ①ppp.nms LXX, 4 Macc 9:22, **as though transformed** *in the fire*; Jos. *A.J.* 8.11.1 (267), **to cross dress**, **masquerade**

μετατίθημι ❻ Acts 7:16, **to bring back**; Gal 1:6, **to abandon**[KeenG]; Heb 7:12, **to change**; 11:5,[2x] **was taken**; Jude 4, **to alter**; (17x LXX; 3x Isa) Ps 45:3 (46:2), **to topple**

μετατρέπω ①[apimp3s] Jas 4:9, **to be turned**; ❹ (4 Macc) LXX, 6:5, **to sway**[SCS]

μετέπειτα {μετά + εἶτα} *adv.* ① Heb 12:17, **later, afterward**; ❸ LXX, 3 Macc 3:24

μετέχω {μετά + ἔχω} ❽ 1 Cor 9:10, *result inf.*, ἐπ' ἐλπίδι **τοῦ μετέχειν**; *in hope of* **a share**; 10:17, **to share**; 10:21, **to participate**; 10:30; Heb 5:13, **to partake**; (10x LXX) 2 Macc 4:14; Prov 1:18

μετεωρίζομαι {μετέωρος} ①[pmimp2p] Luke 12:29, **to be anxious**; (10x LXX; 4x Ezek) Mic 4:1

μετοικεσία, ας, ἡ$_{1α}$ {μετά + οἶκος} ❹ Matt 1:11, 12, 17,[2x] **exile**; ❽ LXX, Judg 18:30, **exile** *from the land*; Obad 20[2x]; Nah 3:10; Ezek 12:11, **exile**

μετοικίζω {μετά + οἶκος} ❷ Acts 7:4, *God* **resettled** *Abraham*; 7:43, *God* **resettled** *Israel by exile*[Keen2]; (10x LXX) Judg 2:3, **to drive out**; 1 Chr 5:26, **to deport**

μετοχή, ῆς, ἡ$_{1η}$ {μετά + ἔχω} ①[nfs] 2 Cor 6:14, **to have in common**[BEC]; ① LXX, Ps 121:3 (122:3); Pseud., Pss. Sol. 14.6, **companion's hip**

μέτοχος, ον$_3$ {μετά + ἔχω} *adj.* ❻ (5x Heb) Luke 5:7, **partner**; Heb 1:9; 3:14, **companion, participant**; ❼ LXX, 1 Sam 20:30, **accomplice**

μετρέω[con] {μέτρον} (11x; 5x Rev) Matt 7:2[2x] = Mark 4:24[2x] = Luke 6:38[2x]; 2 Cor 10:12; Rev 21:15, 16, 17, **to measure**; ❺ LXX, Exod 16:18; Isa 40:12

μετρητής, οῦ, ὁ$_{1>}$ {μέτρον} ①[amp] John 2:6, **measures**[EGG]; ❺ LXX, 1 Kgs 18:32; Hag 2:16

μετριοπαθέω[con] {μέτρον + πάσχω} ①[painf] Heb 5:2, **to be balanced in passions**[NIGTC!]

μετρίως *adv.* ① Acts 20:12 *not* **moderately** (*i.e., greatly*); ① LXX, 2 Macc 15:38

μέτρον, ου, τό$_2$ (11x; 5x Rev) Matt 7:2 = Mark 4:24; Luke 6:38[2x]; John 3:34; 2 Cor 10:13, **measure**; (74x LXX; 31x Ezek) Ezek 40:11–48:34, *thirty-one* **measures**

μέτωπον, ου, τό$_2$ {μετά + ὁράω} ❽ (Rev) 7:3; 9:4; 13:6; 22:4, **forehead**; ❾ LXX, 1 Sam 17:49,[2x] *Goliath's* **forehead**

μέχρι (**μέχρις** *before vowels*) (17x) Ⓐ (3x) *conj.*, Mark 13:30; Gal 4:19; Eph 4:13, **until**; Ⓑ (14x) *prep. w/gen.*, Heb 12:4, **to the point** *of shedding your blood*; (60x LXX; 26x 3–4 Macc)

μή (1,042x; 204x LA) ***central meaning***, *negate non-indicative verbal forms*; Ⓐ ***main clauses***, *opt. mood without* ἄν, Rom 6:2, **μὴ** γένοιτο, **may it never be!**; *pres. imper.*, Gal 5:13, **do not!**; *subj.*, 6:9, **let us not**; Ⓑ ***subordinate clauses***, Mark 4:22, **unless**; John 3:18, *whoever* **does not**; Ⓒ ***with participles and infinitives***, Heb 12:27, **cannot** *be shaken*; Ⓓ ***emphatic negation*** (94x), οὐ **μὴ** *w/subj. or fut.*, Matt 5:18; Mark 13:2,[2x] **will certainly not**; (3,048x LXX; 627x emph. neg.) Gen 3:1, Οὐ **μὴ** φάγητε, **you will certainly not** *eat*

μηδαμῶς {μή + δέ + ἐγώ} *adv.* ❷ Acts 10:14; 11:8, **certainly not**!; (19x LXX; 7x 1 Sam) Gen 18:25,[2x] *you* **could not possibly** *do that*!

μηδέ {μή + δέ} *neg. conj.* (56x; 11x Matt) *continued negation* Ⓐ ***head of clause***, 1 Tim 1:4, **nor, not even**; Ⓑ ***internal clause***, Eph 5:3, **not even**; (136x LXX; 22x Prov, 11x Pss)

μηδείς, μηδεμία, μηδέν$_{2.1.2}$ {μή + δέ + εἷς} (90x; 22x Acts) Ⓐ ***general usage***, Matt 16:20 = Mark 8:30 = Luke 9:21, **no one**; Ⓑ ***in prohibition clauses***, Luke 3:13, **no more**; Ⓒ **μηδέν**, ***neuter gender usage***, Jas 1:6, **without** *doubt*; (53x LXX) Prov 2:12, *speaks* **nothing**

μηδέποτε {μή + δέ + ποῦ} *adv.* ① 2 Tim 3:7, **never**; ❹ LXX, 3 Macc 3:16; 7:4

μηδέπω {μή + δέ + ποῦ} *adv.* ① Heb 11:7, **not yet**

Μῆδος, ου, ὁ$_2$ ①[nmp] Acts 2:9, **Medes**; (11x LXX; 5x Dan) Isa 13:17; Dan 5:26

μηκέτι {μή + ἔτι} *adv.* (22x) Matt 21:19 = Mark 11:14; Rom 6:6; 2 Cor 5:15; Eph 4:17, **no longer**, **again**; Luke 8:49; John 5:14; Acts 4:17, **anymore**; (12x LXX) Exod 36:6

μῆκος, ους, τό$_3$ ❸ Eph 3:18; Rev 21:16,^{2x} **length**; (85x LXX; 42x Ezek, 15x Exod) Gen 6:15; Exod 25:10–37:16; Ezek 40:7–48:21; **lengths**, *construction of ark, temple, and new Jerusalem respectively*

μηκύνω {μῆκος} ①^{pms3s} Mark 4:27, **grows**; ❸ LXX, Ezek 12:25, 28, *no longer* **delay**

μηλωτή, ῆς, ἡ$_{1η}$ {μῆλον} ①^{dfp} Heb 11:37, **sheepskins**; ❺ LXX, 1 Kgs 19:13, **sheepskin**

μήν, μηνός, ὁ$_3$ (18x; 10x LA, 6x Rev) Luke 1:24; Acts 7:20; Jas 5:17; Rev 22:2, **month(s)**; (339x LXX; 38x Ezek, 29x Num) ***time period***, Gen 7:11–8:14,^{11x} **month(s)** *in ark drama*; 1 Sam 6:1, **months**

μήν *emphatic part.* ① Heb 6:14, **indeed**; ❷ LXX, ***strong affirmation***, Num 14:35; Job 1:11, **surely**

μηνύω ❹ Luke 20:37, **to reveal**; John 11:57, **to report** *it*[ZEC]; Acts 23:30; 1 Cor 10:28, **to be informed**; ❺ LXX, 2 Macc 3:7, **to be informed**

μήποτε {μή + ποῦ} (25x; 17x Syn) Matt 4:6 = Luke 4:11, **so that**; Matt 15:32, **lest**; 2 Tim 2:25, **in the hope that**[NIGTC]; Heb 4:1, **since**; (109x LXX; 22x Sir, 19x Gen)

μήπω *adv.* ❷ Rom 9:11; Heb 9:8, **not yet**

μηρός, οῦ, ὁ$_2$ ①^{ams} Rev 19:16, **thigh**; (34x LXX; 11x Gen, 6x Judg) Gen 24:2, **thigh**

μήτε *neg. corr. conj.* (34x; 14x LA) Ⓐ Matt 5:34–36,^{4x} **not . . . nor . . . nor . . . nor**[ZEC]; Ⓑ Acts 23:8,^{2x} **neither . . . nor**; Ⓒ Acts 23:21, **μήτε . . . μήτε, not . . . nor**; Ⓓ 2 Thess 2:2,^{3x} μή . . . μηδέ . . . **μήτε** διὰ πνεύματος **μήτε** διὰ λόγου **μήτε** δι᾽ ἐπιστολῆς, *not . . . nor . . .* **neither . . . nor . . . nor . . .**; Ⓔ Jas 5:12,^{3x} **neither . . . nor . . . nor**; (16x LXX; 10x 1–4 Macc)

μήτηρ, τρός, ἡ$_3$ (83x; 60x Syn) Matt 1:18; Mark 10:29; John 2:1; Acts 12:12, **mother**; (306x LXX; 38x 4 Macc, 27x Gen) Gen 2:24; Exod 20:12 = Deut 5:16

μήτι {μή + τις} (*strengthened form of* **μή**) (18x; 13x Gs) Matt 7:16, *grapes are* **not** *gathered*; Matt 26:22, **Surely not** *I, Lord*?; ① LXX, Dan 2:11, εἰ **μήτι**, **except** *some angel*

μήτρα, ας, ἡ$_{1α}$ ❷ Luke 2:23; Rom 4:19, **womb**; (33x LXX; 6x Exod) Gen 20:18; Exod 13:2

μητρολῴας, ου, ὁ$_1$ {μήτηρ + ἀλοάω} ①^{dmp} 1 Tim 1:9, **mother-murderer**

μιαίνω ❺ John 18:28; Titus 1:15^{2x}; Jude 8, **to defile**; (128x LXX; 32x Lev, 29x Ezek)

μίασμα, ατος, τό$_3$ {μιαίνω} ①^{anp} 2 Pet 2:20, **impurity**; ❼ LXX, Lev 7:18; 1 Macc 13:50

μιασμός, οῦ, ὁ$_2$ {μιαίνω} ①^{gms} 2 Pet 2:10, **defiling desire**[BEC]; ❷ LXX, 1 Macc 4:43

μίγμα, ατος, τό$_3$ {μίγνυμι} ①^{ans} John 19:39, **mixture**

μίγνυμι ❹ Matt 27:34; John 13:1; Rev 8:7; 15:2, **to mix**; ❻ LXX, Gen 30:40; Exod 20:35

μικρός, ά, όν$_{2.1.2}$ (46x; 11x John, 8x Matt:Rev) *subst.*, Matt 18:6 = Mark 9:42 = Luke 17:2, **little ones**; Mark 14:70, *after* **a little while**; Acts 8:10, **the least**; (161x LXX; 21x Isa, 12x Gen)

Μίλητος, οῦ, ἡ$_{2ὁδός}$ ❸ Acts 20:15, 17; 2 Tim 4:20, **Miletus**; ①^{gfs} LXX, Ezek 27:18

μίλιον, ου, τό$_2$ ①^{ans} Matt 5:41, **mile**

μιμέομαι^{con} ❹ 2 Thess 3:7, 9; Heb 13:7; 3 John 11, **to imitate**; ❹ LXX, 4 Macc 9:23, 13:9

μιμητής, οῦ, ὁ$_{1>}$ ❻ 1 Cor 4:16; 11:1, *take your* **cue** *from me*[NIGTC]; 1 Thess 1:6; Heb 6:12, **imitator**; Plato *Pol.* 303c, **charlatan**, **impostor**

μιμνῄσκομαι (23x; 8x LA) Matt 5:23; 16:25; John 2:17; 1 Cor 11:2, **to remember**; (262x LXX; 49x Pss, 15x Deut) Gen 8:1; 30:12; Exod 2:24; Lev 26:42

μισέω[con] (40x; 12x John) Matt 10:22 = Mark 13:13 = Luke 21:17; John 3:20; Heb 1:9, **to hate**; (177x LXX; 40x Pss, 24x Deut) Gen 29:31; Deut 7:15

μισθαποδοσία, ας, ἡ$_{1α}$ {μισθός + ἀπό + δίδωμι} ❸ (Heb) 2:2, **just punishment**; 10:35; 11:26, **reward**

μισθαποδότης, ου, ὁ$_{1>}$ {μισθός + ἀπό + δίδωμι} ①[nms] Heb 11:6, **rewarder**

μίσθιος, ου, ὁ$_2$ {μισθός} ❷ Luke 15:17, 19, **workers**; ❻ LXX, Lev 25:50; Job 7:1

μισθός, οῦ, ὁ$_2$ (29x; 10x Matt) Matt 5:12; Mark 9:41, **reward**; Matt 20:8; John 4:36, **pay**; (63x LXX; 11x Gen) Gen 15:1; Ruth 2:12, **reward**; Num 18:31; Deut 24:14, **wage**

μισθόω {μισθός} ❷ Matt 20:1, 2, **to hire**; (15x LXX) Gen 30:16; Deut 23:5; 1 Chr 19:6

μίσθωμα, ατος, τό$_3$ {μισθός} ①[dns] Acts 28:30, **rented place**[ZEC]; (13x LXX; 7x Ezek) Ezek 16:31, *you scoffed at* **payment** *to a prostitute*

μισθωτός, οῦ, ὁ$_2$ {μισθός} ❸ Mark 1:20; John 10:12, **hired hands**; (20x LXX; 5x Lev)

Μιτυλήνη, ῆς, ἡ$_{1η}$ ①[afs] Acts 20:14, **Mitylene**

Μιχαήλ, ὁ$_3$ *indecl.* ❷ Jude 9; Rev 12:7, **Michael**, *the archangel*; (13x LXX; 8x 1–2 Chr) 1 Chr 5:13, **Michael**, *son of Abichail*

μνᾶ, ᾶς, ἡ$_{1α}$ ❾ (Luke) 19:13–25, **mina**; (12x LXX) 1 Kgs 10:17; Ezra 2:69

Μνάσων, ῶνος, ὁ$_3$ ①[dms] Acts 21:16, **Mnason**, *a Cypriot Jew who lived in Jerusalem*

μνεία, ας, ἡ$_{1α}$ ❼ Rom 1:9; 1 Thess 1:2; Phlm 4, *making* **mention**; (14x LXX) Deut 7:18

μνῆμα, ατος, τό$_3$ {μιμνήσκομαι} ❽ Mark 5:3; Luke 8:27; Acts 2:29; Rev 11:9, **tomb**; (20x LXX; 6x Num, 5x Ezek) Num 33:16, **Tombs** *of Craving*

μνημεῖον, ου, τό$_2$ {μιμνήσκομαι} (40x; 23x Syn, 16x John) Matt 23:29, **monuments**; Luke 11:47; 24:24, **tomb(s)**; John 5:28 (*echo of Dan 12:2*), **graves**, *in general*; John 11:17–12:17[4x]; 19:41–20:11,[11x] *a specific* **tomb**; (16x LXX; 8x Gen) Gen 23:6,[2x] **burial place** (CSB)

μνήμη, ης, ἡ$_{1η}$ {μιμνήσκομαι} ①[afs] 2 Pet 1:5, **μνήμην** ποιεῖσθαι, *hold things* **in remembrance**[BEC!]; (17x LXX) Ps 29:5 (30:4) **mentioning**; Prov 1:12, **remembrance**

μνημονεύω {μιμνήσκομαι} (21x) Matt 16:9; 2 Thess 2:5, **to remember**; 1 Thess 1:3, **to recall**; (22x LXX) Exod 13:3, **to remember**; 2 Sam 14:11, **to mention**

μνημόσυνον, ου, τό$_2$ {μιμνήσκομαι} ❸ Matt 26:13 = Mark 14:9, *in* **memory** *of her*; Acts 10:4, **memorial** *offering*; (74x LXX; 17x Sir, 10x Exod)

μνηστεύω {μιμνήσκομαι} ❸ Matt 1:18; Luke 1:27; 2:5, **to be engaged**; ❾ LXX, Deut 20:7; Hos 2:21–22,[3x] **I will take you to be my wife** (CSB)

μογιλάλος, ον$_3$ {μόγος + λάλος} *adj.* ①[ams] Mark 7:32, **difficulty speaking**; ①[gmp] LXX, Isa 35:6, *the tongue* **of stammerers**

μόγις *adv.* ① Luke 9:39, **scarcely**; ① LXX, 3 Macc 7:6

μόδιος, ίου, ὁ$_2$ ❸ Matt 5:15 = Mark 4:21 = Luke 11:33, **basket**

μοιχαλίς, ίδος, ἡ$_3$ {μοιχός} ❼ Matt 12:39 = 16:4; Mark 9:38; Rom 7:3[2x]; Jas 4:4, **adultress**; 2 Pet 2:14, *desire for an* **adultress**; ❼ LXX, Prov 18:22; Hos 3:1

μοιχάω[con] {μοιχός} ❹ Matt 5:32; 19:9 = Mark 10:11, 12, **to commit adultery**; (10x LXX) **μοιχάομαι**, Jer 3:8; 5:7

μοιχεία, ας, ἡ$_{1α}$ {μοιχός} ❸ Matt 15:19 = Mark 7:22; John 8:3, **adultery**; ❹ LXX

μοιχεύω {μοιχός} (15x; 8x Syn) Matt 5:27, 28; 19:18 = Mark 10:19; Luke 16:18; John 8:4; Rom 2:22; Jas 2:11, **to commit adultery**; (12x LXX; 4x Lev) Exod 20:13 = Deut 5:17

μοιχός, οῦ, ὁ$_{2}$ ❸ Luke 18:11; Heb 13:4, **adulterers**; 1 Cor 6:9, **those who practice adultery**[NIGTC]; ❻ LXX, Prov 6:32; Job 24:15; Isa 57:3

μόλις *adv.* ❻ Acts 14:18; 27:16, **barely**; 27:7; 1 Pet 4:18, **difficulty**; Rom 5:7, **rarely**; ❽ LXX, 3 Macc 1:23; Prov 11:31, **scarcely**

Μολόχ, ὁ$_{3}$ *indecl.* ①[gms] Acts 7:43, **Molech**; ❸ LXX, 2 Kgs 23:10; Amos 5:26

μολύνω ❸ 1 Cor 8:7; Rev 3:4; 14:4, **to defile**; (19x LXX) Gen 37:31; Zech 14:2; Isa 65:4

μολυσμός, οῦ, ὁ$_{2}$ {μολύνω} ①[gms] 2 Cor 7:1, **impurity**; ❸ LXX, Jer 23:15

μομφή, ῆς, ἡ$_{1η}$ {μέμφομαι} ①[afs] Col 3:13, **complaint**

μονή, ῆς, ἡ$_{1η}$ {μένω} ❷ John 14:2, **room**; 14:23, **dwelling place**; ①[afs] LXX, 1 Macc 7:38, μὴ δῷς αὐτοῖς **μονήν**, *and let them have* **a place to live** (LES)

μονογενής, ές$_{3.3}$ {μόνος + γίνομαι} *adj.* ❾ Luke 7:12; 8:42, **only**; *subst.*, John 3:16, **the unique Son**[ZEC]; Heb 11:17, **only son**; (10x LXX) *subst.*, Judg 11:34, **only child**

μόνος, η, ον$_{2.1.2}$ *adj.* (114x; 45x Gs, 14x Rom) οὐ **μόνον** . . . ἀλλὰ καί,[48x] Acts 19:27; 2 Tim 4:8, *not* **only** . . . *but also*; Matt 4:4 = Luke 4:4, **alone**; Luke 9:18, **only**; Acts 11:19, *no one* **except**; (206x LXX; 42x 1–4 Macc) οὐ **μόνον** . . . ἀλλὰ καί,[46x] 3 Macc 3:1

μονόφθαλμος, ον$_{2.2}$ {μόνος + ὁράω} *adj.* ❷ Matt 18:9 = Mark 9:47, **one-eyed**

μονόω[con] {μόνος} ①[pfpp.nfs] 1 Tim 5:5, **to be left alone**

μορφή, ῆς, ἡ$_{1η}$ ❸ Mark 16:12; Phil 2:6, 7, **form**; ❼ LXX, Judg 8:18; Job 4:16; Isa 44:13

μορφόω[con] {μορφή} ①[aps3s] Gal 4:19, **is formed** *in you*

μόρφωσις, εως, ἡ$_{3}$ {μορφή} ❷[afs] Rom 2:20; 2 Tim 3:5, **embodiment**

μοσχοποιέω[con] {μόσχος + ποιέω} ①[aai3p] Acts 7:41, **to manufacture a calf**[ZEC]

μόσχος, ου, ὁ$_{2}$ ❻ Luke 15:23, 27, 30, *fattened* **calf**; Rev 4:7, **ox**; (232x LXX; 57x Num)

μουσικός, ή, όν$_{2.1.2}$ {μοῦσα} *adj.* ①[gmp] Rev 18:22, *subst.*, **musicians**; (18x LXX) Gen 31:27

μόχθος, ου, ὁ$_{2}$ {μόγος} ❸ 2 Cor 11:27; 1 Thess 2:9; 2 Thess 3:8, **hardship**; (41x LXX)

μυελός, οῦ, ὁ$_{2}$ ①[gmp] Heb 4:12, **marrow**; Theocr. 28.18, **innermost part**, **heart**, **soul**

μυέω[con] ①[pfpi1s] Phil 4:12, **I have been taught to cope**[BEC]; ①[pfpp.dmp] LXX, 3 Macc 2:30, **those who have been initiated**

μῦθος, ου, ὁ$_{2}$ ❺ 1 Tim 1:4; 2 Tim 4:4; 2 Pet 1:16, **myths**; ① LXX, Sir 20:19

μυκάομαι[con] ①[pmi3s] Rev 10:3, **roaring** *lion*

μυκτηρίζω ①[pmi3s] Gal 6:7, **to turn up the nose** *in contempt*[NIGTC]; (15x LXX), 1 Kgs 18:27

μυλικός, ή, όν$_{2.1.2}$ {μύλη} *adj.* ①[nms] Luke 17:2, λίθος **μυλικός**, **millstone**

μύλινος, η, ον$_{2.1.2}$ {μύλη} *adj.* ①[ams] Rev 18:21, *subst.* **millstone**

μύλος, ου, ὁ$_{2}$ {μύλη} ❹ Matt 18:6 = Mark 9:42; Matt 24:41, **millstone**; Rev 18:22, **mill**; ❼ LXX, Exod 11:5; Num 11:8, **mill**, **millstone**

Μύρα, τά$_{3}$ *indecl.* ①[anp] Acts 27:5, **Myra**

μυριάς, άδος, ἡ$_{3}$ {μυρίος} ❽ Luke 12:1, **many thousands**[ZEC]; Acts 19:19, *fifty* **thousand** *silver coins*; Heb 12:22, **myriads**; Jude 14, **thousands of thousands**; (44x LXX; 10x 2 Macc)

μυρίζω {μύρον} ①[aainf] Mark 14:8, **to anoint**

μύριοι, αι, α$_{2.1.2}$ {μυρίος} *adj.* ①[gnp] Matt 18:24, **ten thousand**; (12x LXX) Judg 20:10

μυρίος, α, ον$_{2.1.2}$ *adj.* ❷[amp] 1 Cor 4:15, **thousands**; 14:19, **thousands upon thousands**[NIGTC]; ①[anp] LXX, 3 Macc 3:21, **innumerable**

μύρον, ου, τό$_{2}$ (14x; 13x Gs) Matt 26:7 = Mark 14:3 = Luke 7:37 = John 12:3, **fragrant oil**; Rev 18:13, **perfumed ointment**; (16x LXX) Exod 30:25, **aromatic perfume**

Μυσία, ας, ἡ$_{1α}$ ❷[afs] Acts 16:7, 8, **Mysia**

μυστήριον, ου, τό$_2$ {μύω} (28x; 6x 1 Cor:Eph, 4x Col) Matt 13:11 = Mark 4:11 = Luke 8:10, **secret**; Rom 11:25; Rev 1:20, **mystery**; (20x LXX; 8x Dan) Dan 2:27–47,[6x] **mystery**

μυωπάζω {μύω + ὁράω} ①[pap.nms] 2 Pet 1:9, **to be shortsighted**

μώλωψ, ωπος, ὁ$_3$ ①[dms] 1 Pet 2:24, **wounds**; ❾ LXX, Gen 4:23; Exod 21:25; Isa 1:6; 53:5

μωμάομαι[con] {μῶμος} ❷ 2 Cor 6:3, *so the ministry is not* **criticized**; 8:20, **to criticize** *us*[BEC]; ❸ LXX, Prov 9:7, **to find fault**

μῶμος, ου, ὁ$_2$ ①[nmp] 2 Pet 2:13, **blemishes**; (22x LXX; 10x Lev) Lev 21:17–24:20

μωραίνω {μωρός} ❹ Matt 5:13 = Luke 14:34, **to lose its taste**; Rom 1:22, **to become fools**; 1 Cor 1:20, **to make a fool**; ❺ LXX, Jer 10:14, *every person* **was stupid**

μωρία, ας, ἡ$_{1α}$ {μωρός} ❺ 1 Cor 1:18, 21, 23, **foolishness**; ❷[afs] LXX, Sir 20:31; 41:15

μωρολογία, ας, ἡ$_{1α}$ {μωρός + λέγω} ①[nfs] Eph 5:4, **foolish talking**

μωρός, ά, όν$_{2.1.2}$ *adj.* (12x; 6x Matt, 4x 1 Cor) Matt 5:12; 7:28; 1 Cor 1:27; 2 Tim 2:23; Titus 3:9, **foolish**; *subst.*, 1 Cor 1:25, **foolishness**; 4:10, **fools**; (36x LXX; 26x Sir) Deut 32:6; Job 16:7

Μωϋσῆς, έως, ὁ$_3$ (80x; 29x LA) Matt 8:4; John 7:19; Acts 7:31, **Moses**; (819x LXX; 297x Exod, 238x Num)

N, ν [*nu*]

Ν, ν, τό (νῦ) *indecl.* **nu**, *13th letter of the Gr. alphabet* || *num.* ν′ = 50; ͵ν = 50,000
Ναασσών, ὁ$_3$ *indecl.* ❸ Matt 1:4^{2x}; Luke 3:32, **Nahshon**; (13x LXX) Exod 6:23; Num 1:7
Ναγγαί, ὁ$_3$ *indecl.* ①^{gms} Luke 3:25, **Naggai**
Ναζαρά, ἡ$_3$ *indecl.* (12x; 9x Syn) Matt 4:13; Luke 4:16; Acts 10:38, **Nazareth**
Ναζαρέθ, ἡ$_3$ *indecl.* ❻ Matt 21:11; Luke 1:26; 2:4; Acts 10:38, **Nazareth**
Ναζαρέτ, ἡ$_3$ *indecl.* ❹ Matt 2:23; Mark 1:9; John 1:45, 46, **Nazareth**
Ναζαρηνός, ή, όν$_{2.1.2}$ *adj.* ❻ Mark 1:24 = Luke 4:34; Mark 14:67, *Jesus* **of Nazareth**
Ναζωραῖος, ου, ὁ$_2$ (13x; 8x LA) Matt 2:23, **Nazarene**; Acts 2:22, *Jesus* **of Nazareth**
Ναθάμ, ὁ$_3$ *indecl.* ①^{gms} Luke 3:31, **Nathan**
Ναθαναήλ, ὁ$_3$ *indecl.* ❻ John 1:45–49,^{5x} **Nathanael**; (13x LXX; 5x Num) Num 1:8
ναί (33x) Matt 5:37; 15:27 = Mark 7:28, **yes**; ❼ LXX, Gen 17:19; Job 19:4; Isa 48:7
Ναιμάν, ὁ$_3$ *indecl.* ①^{gms} Luke 4:27, **Naaman** *the Syrian*; (15x LXX) 2 Kgs 5:1–27
Ναΐν, ἡ$_3$ *indecl.* ①^{afs} Luke 7:11, **Nain**
ναός, οῦ, ὁ$_2$ (45x; 16x Rev) Matt 27:51 = Mark 15:38 = Luke 23:45; Acts 17:24; 1 Cor 3:16–17^{3x}; Rev 21:22, **temple**; (114x LXX; 13x Pss, 12x 2 Chr) 2 Chr 15:8, **shrine**
Ναούμ, ὁ$_3$ *indecl.* ①^{gms} Luke 3:25, **Nahum**; ❷ LXX, Neh 7:7; Nah 1:1, *Hebrew prophet*
νάρδος, ου, ἡ$_2$ ❷ Mark 14:3; John 12:3, **nard**; ❸ LXX, Song 1:12; 4:13, 14
Νάρκισσος, ου, ὁ$_2$ ①^{gms} Rom 16:11, **Narcissus**
ναυαγέω^{con} {ναῦς + ἀξίνη} ❷ 2 Cor 11:25, **shipwreck**; 1 Tim 1:19, *spir.* **shipwreck**
ναύκληρος, ου, ὁ$_2$ {ναῦς + κληρόω} ①^{dms} Acts 27:11, **ship-owner**
ναῦς, νεώς, ἡ ①^{afs} Acts 27:41 **ship**; (16x LXX; 9x 1 Kgs) 1 Kgs 9:26; Job 9:26
ναύτης, ου, ὁ$_{1>}$ {ναῦς} ❸ Acts 27:27, 30; Rev 18:17, **sailors**
Ναχώρ, ὁ$_3$ *indecl.* ①^{gms} Luke 3:34, **Nahor**; (19x LXX; 16x Gen) Gen 11:22
νεανίας, ου, ὁ$_1$ {νέος} ❸ Acts 7:58, 20:9, 23:17, **young man**; (32x LXX; 6x 2 Macc)
νεανίσκος, ου, ὁ$_2$ {νέος} (13x) Matt 19:20; Mark 16:5; Acts 2:17; 1 John 2:13, **young man**; (94x LXX; 13x Jer, 8x Isa) Gen 4:23; Jer 6:11
Νέα πόλις, ἡ$_3$ ①^{afs} Acts 16:11, **Neapolis**
νεκρός, ά, όν$_{2.1.2}$ *adj.* (128x; 31x LA, 13x Rev) *subst.*, Matt 8:22^{2x}; 11:5 = Luke 7:22; John 2:22; Acts 4:10; 1 Cor 15^{13x}; Rev 1:5, **the dead**; (83x LXX; 11x Sir, 8x Gen) Gen 23:3–15
νεκρόω^{con} {νεκρός} ❸ *subst.*, Rom 4:19, **dead as it was**^{ZEC}; Col 3:5, **to put to death**; Heb 11:12, *ptc.*, **one as good as dead** (CSB)
νέκρωσις, εως, ἡ$_3$ {νεκρός} ❷ Rom 4:19, **deadness**; 2 Cor 4:10, **death**
νεομηνία, ας, ἡ$_{1α}$ {νέος + μήν} ①^{gfs} Col 2:16, **new moon**; (10x LXX) Num 28:11
νέος, α, ον$_{2.1.2}$ *adj.* (23x; 7x Luke) Matt 9:17 = Mark 2:22 = Luke 5:37, **new**; Luke 15:12, 13; John 21:18; 1 Pet 5:5, **younger**; (118x LXX; 28x Gen) Gen 9:24; Num 28:26, **new** *things*
νεότης, ητος, ἡ$_3$ {νέος} ❹ Mark 10:20 = Luke 18:21; Acts 26:4; 1 Tim 4:12, **youth**; (64x LXX; 9x Pss) Gen 8:21; Lev 22:13; 2 Sam 19:8

νεόφυτος, ον$_3$ {νέος + φύω} *adj.* ①[ams] 1 Tim 3:6, *subst.*, **new convert**; ❺ LXX, Ps 127:3 (128:3), **shoots** *of olives*; 143:12 (144:12), **young** *plants*; Job 14:9, **newly planted**

νεύω ❷ John 13:24; Acts 24:10, **to motion**; ❷ LXX, Prov 4:25; 21:1, **to incline to**

νεφέλη, ης, ἡ$_{1η}$ {νέφος} (25x; 7x Rev) Matt 17:5 = Mark 9:7 = Luke 9:34; Acts 1:9; 1 Thess 4:17; Rev 1:7, **cloud**; (133x LXX; 21x Exod, 20x Num) Gen 9:13; Exod 19:9

Νεφθαλίμ, ὁ$_3$ *indecl.* ❸ Matt 4:13, 15; Rev 7:6, **Naphtali**; ❾ LXX, Judg 5:18; Isa 8:23

νέφος, ους, τό$_3$ ①[ans] Heb 12:1, **cloud**; (26x LXX; 16x Job) Prov 3:20; Job 7:9

νεφρός, οῦ, ὁ$_2$ ①[amp] Rev 2:23, **minds**; (31x LXX; 14x Lev) Job 16:13; Jer 12:2, **kidneys**

νεωκόρος, ου, ὁ$_2$ {ναός + κόρος} ①[ams] Acts 19:35, **guardian**

νεωτερικός, ή, όν$_{2.1.2}$ {νέος} *adj.* ①[afp] 2 Tim 2:22, **youthful**; ①[gfs] LXX, 3 Macc 4:8

νή *prep. w/acc.* ① 1 Cor 15:31, **by**[NIGTC]; ❷ LXX, Gen 42:15, 16

νήθω {νέω} ❷ Matt 6:28 = Luke 12:27, **to spin**; (10x LXX; all in Exod) 26:31, *subst.*, **spun** *linen*

νηπιάζω {νήπιος} ①[pai2p] 1 Cor 14:20, **to be a child**[NIGTC]

νήπιος, α, ον$_{2.1.2}$ *adj.* (15x; 6x 1 Cor) *subst.*, Matt 11:25 = Luke 10:21; Eph 4:14, **infants**; (46x LXX; 7x Pss, 5x Jdt:Lam)

Νηρεύς, έως, ὁ$_3$ ①[ams] Rom 16:15, **Nereus**

Νηρί, ὁ$_3$ *indecl.* ①[gms] Luke 3:27, **Neri**; ❷ LXX, Jer 28:59 (51:29); Bar 1:1, **Neriah**

νησίον, ου, τό$_2$ {νῆσος} ①[ans] Acts 27:16, **island**

νῆσος, ου, ἡ$_2$ (9x) Acts 28:7, **island**; Rev 1:9, **island** *called Patmos*; (39x LXX; 14x Isa)

νηστεία, ας, ἡ$_{1α}$ {νηστεύω} ❺ Luke 2:37; Acts 14:23; 27:9, *with* **fasting**; 2 Cor 6:5; 11:27, **hunger**; (31x LXX; 14x Isa) 2 Sam 12:16, *David fasted* **a fast**; Zeph 7:5, *fasted* **a fast**

νηστεύω (20x; 18x Syn) Matt 9:14–15[3x] = Mark 2:18–20[6x] = Luke 5:33–35[3x]; Acts 13:2, **to fast**; (27x LXX; 7x 1–2 Sam) Exod 38:26 (38:8); 2 Sam 1:12

νῆστις, ιδος, ἡ$_3$ {νη- + ἐσθίω} ❷ Matt 15:32 = Mark 8:3, *subst.*, **hungry**; ①[nfs] LXX, Dan 6:19

νηφάλιος, α, ον$_{2.1.2}$ {νήφω} *adj.* ❸ 1 Tim 3:2; 3:11; Titus 2:2, **sober**, **prudent**

νήφω ❻ 1 Thess 5:6, 8; **to exercise self-control**; 1 Pet 1:13; 5:8, **to be disciplined**[Keen1P]; 4:7, **to think in a sober way**[Keen1P]

Νίγερ, ὁ$_3$ *indecl.* ①[nms] Acts 13:1, **Niger**

Νικάνωρ, ορος, ὁ$_3$ ①[ams] Acts 6:5, **Nicanor**; (43x LXX; 42x 1–2 Macc) 2 Macc 8:23

νικάω[con] {νίκη} (28x; 17x Rev) 1 John 4:4, **to conquer**; Rom 12:21,[2x] *don't* **be conquered** *by . . . but* **conquer**; Rev 2:7–3:21, ὁ νικῶν,[5x] *the one who* **conquers**; (26x LXX; 14x 4 Macc)

νίκη, ης, ἡ$_{1η}$ ①[nfs] 1 John 5:4, **victory**; (10x LXX; 4x 2 Macc) Prov 22:9

Νικόδημος, ου, ὁ$_2$ ❺ John 3:1, 4, 9; 7:50; 19:39, **Nicodemus**

Νικολαΐτης, ου, ὁ$_{1>}$ ❷[gmp] Rev 2:6, 15, **Nicolaitans**

Νικόλαος, ου, ὁ$_2$ ①[ams] Acts 6:5, **Nicolaus**

Νικόπολις, εως, ἡ$_3$ ①[afs] Titus 3:12, **Nicopolis**

νῖκος, ους, τό$_3$ ❹ Matt 12:20; 1 Cor 15:54, 55, 57, **victory**; (10x LXX) 2 Sam 2:26

νιπτήρ, ῆρος, ὁ$_3$ {νίπτω} ①[ams] John 13:5, **basin**

νίπτω (17x; 13x John) Matt 15:2 = Mark 7:3; John 9:7, 11, **to wash**; (23x LXX) Gen 18:4

νοέω[con] {νοῦς} (14x; 8x Gs) Matt 15:17 = Mark 7:18; Heb 11:3, **to understand**; Rom 1:20, **because they are perceived**[ZEC]; (31x LXX; 11x Prov) 1 Sam 4:20; Prov 1:2, **to understand**

νόημα, ατος, τό$_3$ {νοῦς} ❻ (5x 2 Cor)[BEC] 2 Cor 2:11, *we know* **the way he thinks**; 3:14; Phil 4:7, **mind**; 2 Cor 10:5; 11:3, **thought**; ❷ LXX, 3 Macc 5:30

νόθος, η, ον$_{2.1.2}$ *adj.* ①^{nmp} Heb 12:8, **illegitimate children**; ①^{gnp} LXX, Wis 4:3, *seedlings*

νομή, ῆς, ἡ$_{1\eta}$ {νέμω} ❷ John 10:9, **a pasture**; 2 Tim 2:17, **νομὴν** ἕξει, *lit.*, *will have* **pasture** → *gangrenous teaching* **will graze** *until it razes the church*; (36x LXX; 8x Jer, 6x Ezek) Amos 1:2; Joel 1:18; Isa 49:9; Jer 10:21, **pasture**; Xen. *An.* 3.5.2, **grazing** *cattle*[BrDAG]

νομίζω {νόμος} (15x; 7x Acts) Matt 5:17; Luke 2:44; Acts 7:25; 1 Cor 7:36, **to think**, **assume**, **suppose**; (15x LXX; 8x 4 Macc) 2 Macc 4:32; 4 Macc 4:7, **to think**, **to consider**

νομικός, ή, όν$_{2.1.2}$ {νόμος} *adj.* ❾ (6x Luke) Luke 7:30, *subst.*, **law scholars**[ZEC]; Titus 3:9, **legal** *battles*; 3:13, *appositive adj.*, *Zenas*, **the lawyer**; ①^{nms} LXX, 4 Macc 5:4

νομίμως {νόμος} *adv.* ❷ 1 Tim 1:8; 2 Tim 2:5, **lawfully**; ① LXX, 4 Macc 6:18

νόμισμα, ατος, τό$_3$ {νόμος} ①^{ans} Matt 22:19, **coin**; ❷ LXX, Ezra 8:36; 2 Macc 15:6

νομοδιδάσκαλος, ου, ὁ$_2$ {νόμος + διδάσκω} ❸ Luke 5:17; Acts 5:34; 1 Tim 1:7, **teacher of the law**

νομοθεσία, ας, ἡ$_{1\alpha}$ {νόμος + τίθημι} ①^{nfs} Rom 9:4, **the giving of the law**; ❸ LXX, 2 Macc 6:23, θεοκτίστου **νομοθεσίας**, *God*-**given law**; 4 Macc 5:35, 17:16, **law code**

νομοθετέω^{con} {νόμος + τίθημι} ❷^{pfpi3s} Heb 7:11; 8:6, *the people* **received the law**[EGG]; (11x LXX; 7x Pss) Exod 24:12, *that I have subscribed* **to instruct** *them*; Ps 24:8 (25:8), **to show** *sinners the way*

νομοθέτης, ου, ὁ$_{1>}$ {νόμος + τίθημι} ①^{nms} Jas 4:12, **lawgiver**; ①^{ams} LXX, Ps 9:21 (9:20)

νόμος, ου, ὁ$_2$ (194x; 74x Rom, 32x Gal) **law**; Ⓐ ***general***, 1 Tim 1:9; Ⓑ ***Mosaic decrees***; Acts 15:5; Heb 7:16; Ⓒ ***the Law***, Matt 5:18; Heb 10:1; Ⓓ ***ideal***, Rom 13:8; Jas 1:25; 2:12; Ⓔ ***the Law of Sinai***, Rom 3:27; Phil 3:5; (425x LXX; 104x 1–4 Macc, 35x Pss)

νοσέω^{con} {νόσος} ①$^{pap.nms}$ 1 Tim 6:4, **having morbid interests**[NIGTC]; ❷ LXX, Wis 17:8^{2x}, *subst.*, **sick**; *verb*, **they were sick**

νόσος, ου, ἡ$_2$ (11x; 10x Syn) Matt 4:23; 8:17 = Luke 4:40; Mark 1:34; Acts 19:12, **disease**; (11x LXX; 3x Deut) Exod 15:26; Deut 7:15; Ps 102:3 (103:3)

νοσσιά, ᾶς, ἡ$_{1\alpha}$ {νέος} ①^{afs} Luke 13:34, **chicks**; (18x LXX) Gen 6:14; Deut 22:6, **nest**

νοσσίον, ου, τό$_2$ {νέος} ①^{anp} Matt 23:37, **chicks**; ①^{anp} LXX, Ps 83:4 (84:3), **nest**

νοσσός, οῦ, ὁ$_2$ {νέος} ①^{amp} Luke 2:24, **young**

νοσφίζω ❸ Acts 5:2, 3; Titus 2:10, *mid.*, **to put aside** *for themselves*; ❷ LXX, Josh 7:1

νότος, ου, ὁ$_2$ ❼ Matt 12:42 = Luke 11:31, *Queen* **of the South**; Rev 21:13, **south**; (85x LXX; 25x Ezek) Exod 10:13; Ezek 27:26; 40:24–48:33,^{24x} **south**, *facing* **south**

νουθεσία, ας, ἡ$_{1\alpha}$ {νοῦς + τίθημι} ❸ 1 Cor 10:11; Eph 6:4; Titus 3:10, **warnings**; ①^{afs} LXX, Wis 16:6

νουθετέω^{con} {νοῦς + τίθημι} ❽ Acts 20:31; Rom 15:14; 1 Cor 4:14, **to warn**; (13x LXX; 8x Job) Job 4:3

νουνεχῶς {νοῦς + ἔχω} *adv.* ① Mark 12:34, **wisely**

νοῦς, νοός, ὁ$_3$ (24x; 6x Rom) Luke 24:45; Rom 1:28; 12:2; 1 Cor 14:14; Rev 17:9, **mind**; 1 Cor 1:10, **mindset**[NIGTC]; (30x LXX; 9x 4 Macc) Exod 7:23; 4 Macc 1:15; Prov 29:7

νύμφη, ης, ἡ$_{1\eta}$ ❽ Matt 10:35 = Luke 12:53, **daughter-in-law**; John 3:29; Rev 18:23, **bride**; (44x LXX; 7x Ruth) Ruth 4:15, **daughter-in-law**; 2 Sam 17:3, **bride**

νυμφίος, ου, ὁ$_2$ {νύμφη} (16x; 6x Matt) Matt 9:15^{2x} = Mark 2:19–20^{3x} = Luke 5:34–35;^{2x} Rev 18:23, **groom**; (14x LXX, 4x Jer); Neh 13:28, **son-in-law**; Joel 2:16, **bridegroom**

νυμφών, ῶνος, ὁ$_3$ ❸ Matt 9:5 = Mark 2:19 = Luke 5:34, **groom**; ❷ LXX, Tob 6:14, 17

νῦν (147x; 39x LA, 29x John) Ⓐ ***temporal adverb***, Acts 2:33, **now** (*at this very moment*); Jas 4:16, *but* **now** (*reflective antithesis*); John 11:8, *just* **now** (*the immediate past*); Phil 1:20, *and* **now**[NIGTC] (*the immediate future*); Ⓑ ***transitional particle***, Luke 2:29, **now** (*present condition*); Rom 8:1, **now** *therefore* (*sweeping inference*); Jas 4:13, **now** (*exhortation of immediacy*); (624x LXX; 83x 1–2 Sam, 52x Isa, 49x Gen)

νυνί {νῦν} = **νῦν** + ι *for emph.* (20x, 6x Rom) Ⓐ ***temporal adverb***, Phlm 9, *just* **now** (*the immediate past*); 2 Cor 8:11, *but* **now** (*reflective antithesis*)[BEC]; Heb 11:16, **now** *if* (*the immediate future*); Ⓑ ***transitional particle***, Rom 7:17, **now** (*present condition*); (18x LXX)

νύξ, νυκτός, ἡ$_1$ (61x) John 3:2; Acts 5:19; Rom 13:12; 1 Thess 3:10, **night**; (265x LXX)

νύσσω ①[aai3s] John 19:34, **to pierce**; ❹ LXX, 3 Macc 5:14, **to give a nudge**

νυστάζω ❷ Matt 25:5, **to become drowsy**; 2 Pet 2:3, **has** *not* **been sleeping**; (12x LXX) 2 Sam 4:6, **to become drowsy**; Ps 120:3 (121:3), **to slumber**

νυχθήμερον, ου, τό$_2$ {νύξ + ἡμέρα} ①[ans] 2 Cor 11:25, **night and day**

Νῶε, ὁ$_3$ *indecl.* ❽ Matt 24:37 = Luke 17:26, **Noah**; (51x LXX; 43x Gen) Gen 5:29; 10:32

νωθρός, ά, όν$_{2.1.2}$ *adj.* ❷[nmp] Heb 5:11; 6:12, **lazy**; ❸ LXX, Prov 22:29; Sir 4:29; 11:12

νῶτος, ου, ὁ$_2$ {νῶτον} ①[ams] Rom 11:10, **back**; (14x LXX) 1 Sam 4:18, *broken* **back**

Ξ, ξ [*xi*]

Ξ, ξ, τό (ξῖ) *indecl.* **xi**, *14th letter of the Gr. alphabet* || *num.* ξʹ= 60; ͵ξ = 60,000

ξενία, ας, ἡ$_{1α}$ {ξένος} ❷ Acts 28:23; Phlm 22, **guest room**

ξενίζω {ξένος} (10x) Acts 10:6; 21:16, **to lodge**, **stay**; 10:23, **to give lodging**; Acts 28:7, **to entertain** *lavishly*; 17:20, **to introduce foreign ideas**^{ZEC}; 1 Pet 4:4, 12, *pass.*, **to be surprised**; Heb 13:2, **to entertain a guest**; ❹ LXX, 2 Macc 9:6, *attrib. ptc.*, **strange** *inflictions*

ξενο**δοχέω**^{con} {ξένος + δέχομαι} ①^{aai3s} 1 Tim 5:10, **to show hospitality**

ξένος, η, ον$_{2.1.2}$ *adj.* (14x) *subst.*, Matt 25:35, 44; Heb 11:13, **stranger**; Matt 27:7; Acts 17:18, 21, **foreigner**; Rom 16:23, **host**; 1 Pet 4:12, **strange**; (20x LXX) *subst.*, Ruth 2:10, **foreigner**

ξέστης, ου, ὁ$_{1>}$ ①^{gmp} Mark 7:4, **pot**, **sextarius**; *Anthalogia Palatina* 11.298.5, **vessel**, **cup**

ξηραίνω {ξηρός} (15x; 6x Mark) *act.*, Jas 1:11, **to wither**; *pass.*, Mark 5:29, *hemorrhage* **stopped**; 9:18, *teeth* **became rigid**; Rev 14:15, **to be fully ripe**; 16:12, **to dry up**; (57x LXX; 14x Isa) *act.*, Nah 1:4, **to dry up**; *pass.*, Zech 10:2, **to wander**

ξηρός, ά, όν$_{2.1.2}$ *adj.* ❽ Matt 12:10 = Mark 3:3 = Luke 6:6, **withered**; John 5:3, **paralyzed**; Heb 11:20, **dry**; (39x LXX; 7x Exod) Ezek 37:2, 4, 11, *Valley of* **Dry** *Bones*

ξύλινος, η, ον$_{2.1.2}$ {ξύλον} *adj.* ❷ 2 Tim 2:20; Rev 9:20, **wooden**; (28x LXX; 10x Ep Jer)

ξύλον, ου, τό$_{2}$ (20x, 7x Rev) Matt 26:55 = Mark 14:48 = Luke 22:52, **club**; Acts 5:30; Gal 3:13; 1 Pet 2:24, **tree** *of crucifixion*; Acts 16:24, **the stocks**; 1 Cor 3:12; Rev 18:12,^{2x} **wood**; 2:7; 22:2, 14, 19, **tree** *of life*; (291x LXX; 31x 1–2 Kgs, 25x Gen) Gen 3:17

ξυράω^{con} {ξύω} ❸ Acts 21:24; 1 Cor 11:5, 6, **to shave** *the head*; (27x LXX; 8x Lev)

O, o [*omicron*]

O, o, τό (ὂ μικρόν) *indecl.* **omicron**, *15th letter of the Gr. alphabet* || *num.* o′ = 70; ͵o = 70,000

ὁ, ἡ, τό, *pl.* **οἱ, αἱ, τά**$_{2.1.2}$ *art.* (19,865x; 9,135x Gs, 2,709x Acts, 1,889x Rev) **the**[GDG 153–62]→ Ⓐ ***w/ substantives***, Matt 2:2, **he**; John 1:21, **the** *Prophet*; John 4:11, **that** *living water*; Ⓑ ***as a pronoun***, Matt 2:5, **they** *told him*; Luke 15:12, **his** *property*; Ⓒ ***special rules***, **1. *Granville Sharp***,[Wall 270–90] Titus 2:13[PPE]; **2. *Colwell's Rule***,[Wall 256–70] John 1:1[BHGNT]; **3. *Apollonius's Corollary***,[Wall 250–52] John 10:34; (83,317 LXX; 19,278 Pent, 5,694x Pss, 4,330x Ezek)

ὀγδοήκοντα {ὀκτώ} ❷ Luke 2:37, **eighty**-*four*; 16:7, **eighty**; (37x LXX) Gen 16:16

ὄγδοος, η, ον$_{2.1.2}$ {ὀκτώ} *adj.* ❺ Luke 1:59; Acts 7:8; Rev 17:11; 21:20, **eighth**; 2 Pet 2:5, *Noah as the* **eighth**, *Noah and seven others*[BHGNT]; (45x LXX; 10x Lev)

ὄγκος, ου, ὁ$_2$ ①[ams] Heb 12:1, **hindrance**; Hom. *Il.* 4.151, **hook**, **barb**, *of an arrow*

ὅδε, ἥδε, τόδε {ὅς} (10x) Luke 10:39, **she**; Acts 21:11, **thus**; Jas 4:13, εἰς **τήνδε**, *to* **such and such** *a city*; Rev 2:1–3:14,[7x] ***formula***, **Τάδε** λέγει, **This** *is what* ***x*** *says*[NIGTC]; (449x LXX; 126x Ezek) ***formula***, **Τάδε** λέγει κύριος, **This** *is what the Lord says* (68x Ezek, 22x Jer)

ὁδεύω {ὁδός} ①[pap.nms] Luke 10:33, **to travel**; ①[iai3p] LXX, Tob 6:6

ὁδηγέω[con] {ὁδός + ἄγω} ❺ Matt 15:14 = Luke 6:39; John 16:13; Acts 8:31; Rev 7:17, **to guide**, **lead**; (44x LXX; 27x Pss) Exod 13:7; Deut 1:33

ὁδηγός, οῦ, ὁ$_2$ {ὁδός + ἄγω} ❺ Matt 15:14; 23:16; Acts 1:16; Rom 2:19, **guide**; ❺ LXX

ὁδοιπορέω[con] {ὁδός + πορεύομαι} ①[pap.nms] Acts 10:9, **to travel**

ὁδοιπορία, ας, ἡ$_{1α}$ {ὁδός + πορεύομαι} ❷ John 4:6; 2 Cor 11:26, **journey**; ❹ LXX

ὁδός, οῦ, ἡ$_2$ (101x; 58x Syn, 20x Acts) Matt 2:12, **route**; 3:3 = Mark 1:3 = Luke 3:4 = John 1:23, **way** *for the Lord*; Matt 7:13, **road**; Rom 3:16, **path**; (845x LXX; 94x Prov)

ὀδούς, ὀδόντος, ὁ$_3$ (12x; 8x Matt) Matt 5:38, **tooth** *for a* **tooth**; Luke 13:28; Matt 8:12–25:30,[6x] *formula*, *weeping and gnashing of* **teeth**; Acts 7:54; Rev 9:8, **teeth**; (55x LXX)

ὀδυνάω[con] ❹ *pass.*, Luke 2:48, **to be in anguish**; 16:24, 25, **to suffer pain**; Acts 20:38, **to be** *especially* **pained**; (11x LXX; 3x Isa) Prov 29:21, **will come to a bad end** (Tanakh)

ὀδύνη, ης, ἡ$_{1η}$ ❷ Rom 9:2, **distress**; 1 Tim 6:10, **harm**; (67x LXX) Job 3:7, **pain**

ὀδυρμός, οῦ, ὁ$_2$ {ὀδύρομαι} ❷ Matt 2:18; 2 Cor 7:7, **mourning**; ❷ LXX, 2 Macc 11:6

Ὀζίας, ου, ὁ$_1$ ❷ Matt 1:8, 9, **Uzziah**; (37x LXX; 13x 2 Chr)

ὄζω ①[pai3s] John 11:39, **to stink**; ①[aai3s] LXX, Exod 8:10 (8:14)

ὅθεν {ὅς + θεν} *adv.* (15x; 6x Heb) Luke 11:24, **from which**; 14:7, **for this reason**; 25:24, 26, **where**; Heb 2:17, *infer. conj.*, **for which reason**[EGG]; 1 John 2:18, **and so**; (43x LXX)

ὀθόνη, ης, ἡ$_{1η}$ ❷[afs] Acts 10:11; 11:5, **sheet**

ὀθόνιον, ου, τό$_2$ {ὀθόνη} ❺ Luke 24:12; John 20:5, 6, 7, **cloth**; ❷ LXX, Hos 2:7, 11 (2:5, 9)

οἶδα (318x; 84x John, 44x LA, 13x 1 Thess) Matt 24:36 = Mark 13:32; Luke 8:53; John 1:26; 1 Cor 3:16; Col 4:1; Rev 19:12, **to know**; (285x LXX; 49x Job, 20x Deut)

οἰκεῖος, ου, ὁ$_2$ ❸ Gal 6:10; Eph 2:19; 1 Tim 5:8, **household**; (19x LXX; 6x Lev)

οἰκετεία, ας, ἡ$_{1α}$ {οἶκος} ①[gfs] Matt 24:45, **household**

οἰκέτης, ου, ὁ$_{1>}$ {οἶκος} ❹ Luke 16:13; Acts 10:7; Rom 14:4; 1 Pet 2:18, **servant**; (52x LXX)

οἰκέω^{con} {οἶκος} ❾ (5x Rom) Rom 7:17, **to dwell** (*sin*); 1 Cor 3:16, **to dwell** (*the Spirit*); 7:12, **to live** (*phys.*); 1 Tim 6:16, *the only One* **dwelling**; (85x LXX; 16x Gen)

οἴκημα, ατος, τό$_{3}$ {οἶκος} ①^{dns} Acts 12:7, **cell**; ❸ LXX, Ezek 16:24, **οἴκημα** πορνικόν, **house** *of prostitution*[NICOT]

οἰκητήριον, ου, τό$_{2}$ ❷ 2 Cor 5:2, *our* **habitation** *from heaven*[BEC]; Jude 6, *angels abandoned their* **home**; ①^{ans} 2 Macc 11:2, **city**

οἰκία, ας, ἡ$_{1\alpha}$ {οἶκος} (93x; 67x Syn) Matt 7:24–27^{4x}; 12:29 = Mark 3:27; Luke 15:8; Acts 4:34, **house**; Phil 4:22, **household**; 2 Cor 5:1,^{2x} **residence** *of a tent*; (254x LXX; 110x Pent)

οἰκιακός, οῦ, ὁ$_{2}$ ❷ Matt 10:25, 36, **members of a household**

οἰκοδεσποτέω^{con} {οἶκος + δέω} ①^{painf} 1 Tim 5:14, **to manage a household**

οἰκοδεσπότης, ου, ὁ$_{1>}$ {οἶκος + δέω} (12x; 7x Matt) Matt 10:25; Luke 14:21, **master of the house**; Matt 20:11, **landowner**; 24:43, **homeowner**

οἰκοδομέω^{con} {οἶκος + δῶμα} (40x; 12x Luke) Matt 21:33 = Mark 12:1; Acts 7:47, **to build**; Matt 21:42, *subst.*, **the builders**; (449x LXX; 69x 1 Kgs, 32x 1 Macc)

οἰκοδομή {οἶκος + δῶμα} (18x; 9x 1–2 Cor) Matt 24:1 = Mark 13:1; 2 Cor 5:1, **building**; *purp.* Rom 14:19; 5:2, *for* **edification**; 1 Cor 14:3–26^{5x}; Eph 4:12, *for* the **edification** *of the church*; 2 Cor 13:10, *for* **building you up**[BEC]; (16x LXX) 1 Chr 26:27, **repair**

οἰκοδόμος, ου, ὁ$_{2}$, {οἶκος + δῶμα} ①^{gmp} Acts 4:11, **builder**; (10x LXX; 3x 1–2 Chr)

οἰκονομέω^{con} {οἶκος + νόμος} ①^{painf} Luke 16:2, *compl. inf.*, **to manage** ❸ LXX, Ps 111:5 (112:5), **to lend**

οἰκονομία, ας, ἡ$_{1\alpha}$ {οἶκος + νόμος} ❾ Luke 16:2–4,^{3x} **management**; 1 Cor 9:17, **task**[NIGTC]; Eph 1:10, **plan**; 3:2, **administration**; Col 1:25, **commission**; 1 Tim 1:4, *God's way of* **ordering things**[ABC]; ❷ LXX, Isa 22:19, 21, **stewardship, office**

οἰκονόμος, ου, ὁ$_{2}$ {οἶκος + νόμος} (10x) Luke 12:42; 1 Cor 4:1, **manager**; Gal 4:2, **estate manager**[KeenG]; Titus 1:7, *God's* **household**; 1 Pet 4:10, **steward**; (15x LXX; 3x 1–2 Kgs:Isa)

οἶκος, ου, ὁ$_{2}$ (114x; 58x LA, 11x Heb) Matt 9:6 = Mark 2:11 = Luke 5:24; Phlm 2, **home**; Luke 11:51, **sanctuary**[ZEC]; John 2:16; Acts 2:36; Heb 3:2–6,^{6x} **house**[EGG]; (1,968x LXX; 329x 1–2 Kgs, 327x 1–2 Chr, 170x Ezek) *form.*, *the* **house** *of the Lord*; *the* **house** *of God*[NIDNTT]

οἰκουμένη, ης, ἡ$_{1\eta}$ {οἶκος} (15x) Matt 24:14; Heb 1:6; Rev 3:10, **world**; (49x LXX; 17x Pss, 16x Isa)

οἰκουργός, όν$_{2.2}$ {οἶκος + ἔργον} *adj.* ①^{afp} Titus 2:5, **homemaker**

οἰκτιρμός, οῦ, ὁ$_{1}$ {οἰκτίρω} ❺ Rom 12:1; 2 Cor 1:3; Heb 10:28, **mercy**; (31x LXX; 11x Pss)

οἰκτίρμων, ον$_{3.3}$ {οἰκτίρω} *adj.* ❸ Luke 6:36^{2x}; Jas 5:11, **merciful**; (16x LXX) *in tandem with* ἐλεήμων,^{12x} **merciful** *and gracious*, Ps 85:15 (43:3)

οἰκτίρω ❷ Rom 9:15, **I will have compassion** *on whom* **I have compassion**; (36x LXX; 13x Pss) Ps 4:2 (4:1), **to extend grace**

οἰνοπότης, ου, ὁ$_{1>}$ {οἶνος + πίνω} ❷ Matt 11:19 = Luke 7:34, **drunkard**; ①^{nns} LXX, Prov 23:20, **wine-bibber** (RSV)

οἶνος, ου, ὁ$_{2}$ (34x; 21x Gs, 8x Rev) John 2:3; 1 Tim 3:8; Rev 6:6, **wine**; (235x LXX; 19x Isa)

οἰνοφλυγία, ας, ἡ$_{1\alpha}$ {οἶνος + φλύαρος} ①^{dfp} 1 Pet 4:3, **drunkenness**[Keen1P]

οἴομαι ❸ John 21:25; Phil 1:17; Jas 1:7, **to suppose**; (22x LXX; 6x Job) Job 34:12, **indeed**

οἶος, α, ον$_{2.1.2}$ {ὅς} *rel. pron.* (14x) Matt 24:21 = Mark 13:19, **such as**; Rom 9:6, **as though**; 2 Cor 10:11, **what**; 1 Thess 1:5, **what sort of men** *we were*; (17x LXX; 3x 1 Macc)

οἴσει → **φέρω**, *fut. act. ind. 3s*, John 21:18, *someone* **will carry**

ὀκνέω^{con} {ὄκνος} ①$^{\text{aas2s}}$ Acts 9:38, μὴ **ὀκνήσῃς**, *without* **delay**^{ZEC}; ❼ LXX, Judg 18:9

ὀκνηρός, ά, όν$_{2.1.2}$ {ὄκνος} *adj.* ❸ Matt 25:26, **lazy**; Rom 12:11, **don't be lazy** *in diligence*^{ZEC}; Phil 3:1, *not* **troublesome**^{BEC}; (15x LXX; 12x Prov) Prov 6:6, **sluggard** (NIV)

ὀκταήμερος, ον$_{2.2}$ {ὀκτώ + ἡμέρα} *adj.* ①^{nms} Phil 3:5, **eighth day**

ὀκτώ ❽ Luke 2:21, **eight**; John 5:5, *thirty*-**eight**; (78x LXX; 11x Neh)

ὄλεθρος, ου, ὁ$_{2}$ {ὄλλυμι} ❹ 1 Cor 5:5; 1 Thess 5:3; 2 Thess 1:9, **destruction**; 1 Tim 6:9, **ruin**; (24x LXX) 1 Kgs 13:34, εἰς **ὄλεθρον**, *led to* **destruction**

ὀλιγοπιστία, ας, ἡ$_{1\alpha}$ {ὀλίγος + πείθω} ① Matt 17:20, **little faith**

ὀλιγόπιστος, ον$_{2.2}$ {ὀλίγος + πείθω} *adj.* ❺ Matt 6:30 = Luke 12:28; Matt 16:8, *subst.*, **you of little faith**

ὀλίγος, η, ον$_{2.1.2}$ *adj.* (40x; 16x LA) Matt 15:34 = Mark 8:7, **few**; Mark 6:31, *adv.* **a little while**^{BHGNT}; Luke 7:47^{2x}; 2 Cor 8:15, **little**; Acts 27:20, *no* **small** *storm*^{ABC}; (99x LXX)

ὀλιγόψυχος, ον$_{2.2}$ {ὀλίγος + ψύχω} *adj.* ①^{amp} 1 Thess 5:14, **fainthearted**; ❻ LXX

ὀλιγωρέω^{con} {ὀλίγος} ①$^{\text{pai3s}}$ Heb 12:5b = Prov 3:11, **to take lightly**; ❷ LXX, Prov 3:11

ὀλοθρευτής, οῦ, ὁ$_{1>}$ {ὅλος + ὄλλυμι} ①^{gms} 1 Cor 10:10, **destroyer**

ὀλοθρεύω {ὅλος + ὄλλυμι} ①$^{\text{pap.nms}}$ *subst.*, Heb 11:28, **the destroyer**

ὁλοκαύτωμα, ατος, τό$_{3}$ {ὅλος + καίω} ❸ Mark 12:33; Heb 10:6, 8, **(whole) burnt offering**; (198x LXX; 55x Lev, 37x Num)

ὁλοκληρία, ας, ἡ$_{1\alpha}$ {ὅλος + κληρόω} ①^{afs} Acts 3:16, **health**

ὁλόκληρος, ον$_{2.2}$ {ὅλος + κληρόω} *adj.* ❷ 1 Thess 5:23; Jas 1:4, **complete**; ❾ LXX

ὀλολύζω ①$^{\text{pap.nmp}}$ Jas 5:1, *onoma.*, **to wail, howl with grief**^{WPNT}; (21x LXX; 13x Isa) *only in prophetic judgment subgenre*, Hos 7:14; Isa 23,^{4x} **to wail**; Hom. *Od.* 3.450, **to shout with piercing cries**, *usu. of women invoking gods*

ὅλος, η, ον$_{2.1.2}$ *adj.* (109x; 57x Syn, 18x Acts) Matt 1:22; Luke 8:43, **all**; Matt 5:29; 1 Cor 5:6; Jas 3:2, **whole**; 2 Cor 1:1, **throughout**; Gal 5:3, **entire**; (256x LXX; 39x Pss, 20x Deut)

ὁλοτελής, ες$_{3.3}$ {ὅλος + τέλος} *adj.* ①^{amp} 1 Thess 5:23, **completely**

Ὀλυμπᾶς, ᾶ, ὁ$_{1}$ ①^{ams} Rom 16:15, **Olympas**

ὄλυνθος, ου, ὁ$_{2}$ ①^{amp} Rev 6:13, **new figs**; ①^{amp} LXX, Song 2:13

ὅλως {ὅλος} *adv.* ❹ Matt 5:34, **at all**; 1 Cor 5:1, *it is* **actually** *reported*; 6:7, **without qualification**^{NIGTC}; 15:29, **really**

ὄμβρος, ου, ὁ$_{2}$ ① Luke 12:54, **rainstorm**; ❻ LXX, Deut 32:2, **gentle rain** (LES)

ὁμείρομαι {ἵμερος} ①$^{\text{pmp.nmp}}$ 1 Thess 2:8, **ὁμειρόμενοι** ὑμῶν, **feeling kindly** *toward you*; ①$^{\text{pmi3p}}$ LXX, Job 3:21, **to long** *for death*

ὁμιλέω^{con} {ὁμός + εἴλω} ❹ Luke 24:14, 15; Acts 20:11; 24:26, **to converse**; (10x LXX)

ὁμιλία, ας, ἡ$_{1\alpha}$ {ὁμός + εἴλω} ①^{nfp} 1 Cor 15:33, **ὁμιλίαι** κακαί, *bad* **gangs**^{NIGTC}; ❹ LXX, Exod 21:10, **conjugal rights** (LES); Prov 7:21, **pleading**

ὁμίχλη, ης, ἡ$_{1\eta}$ ①^{nfp} 2 Pet 2:17, **mist**; (10x LXX) Ps 147:5 (147:16), **fog**

ὄμμα, ατος, τό$_{3}$ {ὁράω} ❷ Matt 20:34; Mark 8:23, **eye**; (10x LXX; 5x Prov)

ὄμνυμι ①^{painf} Mark 14:71, **to swear**; (179x LXX; 35x Deut, 14x Jer)

ὀμνύω (25x; 13x Matt, 8x 23:18–22) Matt 5:34; Heb 3:11; Jas 5:12; Rev 10:6, **to make an oath**

ὁμοθυμαδόν {ὁμός + θυμός} *adv.* (11x; 10x Acts) Acts 1:14; 5:12; 8:6; Rom 15:6, **with one mind**; Acts 2:46; 4:24, **unanimously**; 7:57, 12:20, **together**[ZEC]; (36x LXX; 14x Job)

ὁμοιοπαθής, ές$_{3.3}$ {ὁμός + πάσχω} *adj.* ❷ Acts 14:15; Jas 5:17, **like**; ❷ LXX, 4 Macc 12:13

ὅμοιος, α, ον$_{2.1.2}$ {ὁμός} *adj.* (45x; 21x Rev) Matt 11:16 = Luke 7:31; Rev 4:3, **like**; (86x LXX)

ὁμοιότης, ητος, ἡ$_{3.3}$ {ὁμός} *adj.* ❷ Heb 4:15, **as**; 7:15, **like**[EGG]; ❹ LXX, Gen 1:11, 12

ὁμοιόω[con] {ὁμός} (15x; 8x Matt) Matt 6:8; 7:24; Heb 2:17, **to be like**; Luke 7:31, **to compare**; Acts 14:11, **ὁμοιωθέντες** ἀνθρώποις, *in human* **form**; (40x LXX; 9x Pss)

ὁμοίωμα, ατος, τό$_3$ {ὁμός} ❻ Phil 2:7; **likeness**; Rev 9:7, **appearance**; (40x LXX; 15x Ezek, 11x Deut)

ὁμοίως {ὁμός} *adv.* (30x; 11x Luke) Matt 22:26; Mark 15:31; Rom 1:27; Jas 2:25; 1 Pet 3:7; Jude 8, **same**; John 5:19; 1 Cor 7:22, **likewise**; 7:3, 4, **similarly**[NIGTC]; (20x LXX)

ὁμοίωσις, εως, ἡ$_3$ {ὁμός} ①[afs] Jas 3:9, **likeness**; ❼ LXX, Gen 1:26; Ezek 1:10

ὁμολογέω[con] {ὁμός + λέγω} (26x; 10x Gs) Matt 7:23; Rom 10:9; 1 John 1:9, **to confess**; Luke 12:8, **to bear testimony**[ZEC]; Acts 7:17, *promise that God* **made**[ZEC]; (11x LXX)

ὁμολογία, ας, ἡ$_{1α}$ {ὁμός + λέγω} ❻ 2 Cor 9:13; 1 Tim 6:12; Heb 3:1, **confession**; ❼ LXX, Lev 22:18; Amos 4:5, **a thank offering** (Tanakh)

ὁμολογουμένως {ὁμός + λέγω} *adv.* ① 1 Tim 3:16, **undeniably**[NIGTC]; ❸ LXX (4 Macc)

ὁμότεχνος, ον$_{2.2}$ {ὁμός + τίκτω} *adj.* ①[ams] Acts 18:3, **having the same occupation**

ὁμοῦ {ὁμός} *adv.* ❹ John 4:36; 20:4; 21:2; Acts 2:1, **together**; (14x LXX; 12x 2–4 Macc)

ὁμόφρων, ον$_{3.3}$ {ὁμός + φρήν} *adj.* ①[nmp] 1 Pet 3:8, **likeminded**, *unity of purpose*[EGG]

ὅμως {ὁμός} *adv.* ❸ John 12:42, **nevertheless**; 1 Cor 14:7, **similarly**[NIGTC]; Gal 3:15, **like**[KeenG]; ❻ LXX, 2 Macc 2:27; 4 Macc 15:11, **nevertheless**

ὄναρ, ατος, τό$_3$ ❻[ans] κατ' **ὄναρ**, Matt 1:20; 2:12, 13, 19, 22; 27:19, *in a* **dream**

ὀνάριον, ου, τό$_2$ {ὄνος} ①[ans] John 12:14, **young donkey**

ὀνειδίζω {ὄνειδος} ❾ (6x Syn) Matt 5:11 = Luke 6:22, **to insult**; Matt 11:20, **to denounce**; Jas 1:5, **to mock**; 1 Pet 4:14, **to vilify**[BEC]; (55x LXX) 1 Sam 17:45, **to defy** *death*

ὀνειδισμός, οῦ, ὁ$_1$ {ὄνειδος} ❺ Rom 15:3; 1 Tim 3:7; Heb 10:33; 11:26; 13:13, **taunt, insult**; (73x LXX; 13x Jer, 10x Pss) Josh 5:9; Isa 4:1, **disgrace**; Neh 3:36, **insult**

ὄνειδος, ους, τό$_3$ ①[ans] Luke 1:25, **disgrace**; (52x LXX; 12x Pss)

Ὀνήσιμος, ου, ὁ$_2$ ❷ Col 4:9; Phlm 10, **Onesimus**

Ὀνησίφορος, ου, ὁ$_2$ ❷ 2 Tim 1:16; 4:19, **Onesiphorus**

ὀνικός, ή, όν$_{2.1.2}$ {ὄνος} *adj.* ❷ Matt 18:6 = Mark 9:42, *large* **millstone**; *lit.*, **"a donkey-millstone"**[NICNT]; **associated with a donkey**[EGG]

ὀνίνημι ①[amo1s] Phlm 20, **may I benefit**; ❷ LXX, Tob 3:8; Sir 30:2, **to benefit**

ὄνομα, ατος, τό$_3$ (230x; 97x Gs, 60x Acts, 38x Rev) Ⓐ Eph 5:20 = Col 3:17, **name**; Ⓑ Mark 6:14, **reputation**; Ⓒ Acts 1:15, ὄχλος **ὀνομάτων**, *a crowd* **of names**; **people**;[BEC] Ⓓ Acts 8:9, *man* **by the name** *of Simon*; Ⓔ *crasis*, **τοὔνομα**,[nns] Matt 27:57, *a man* **named** *Joseph*; Ⓕ *in relation to Sardis*, Rev 3:1, **reputation**[BEC]; 3:4, **people**; 3:5, **name**; (995x LXX; 113x Pss)

ὀνομάζω {ὄνομα} (10x; 3x Eph) Rom 15:20, **to name**; Acts 19:13, **to pronounce** *the* **name**; 2 Tim 2:19, *all who* **call on the name** *of the Lord*; *pass.*, 1 Cor 5:11, *verb. adj.*, **to accept the name** *of Christian*[NIGTC]; Eph 5:3, **to be characterized by**; (24x LXX; 4x Jer)

ὄνος, ου, ὁ$_2$ *or* **ἡ**$_{2\text{όδός}}$ ❺ Matt 21:2, 5, 7; Luke 13:15; John 12:15, **donkey**; (109x LXX; 18x Num)

ὄντως {εἰμί} *adv.* (11x; 4x 1 Tim) John 8:36; **truly**; 1 Cor 14:25, **is indeed really**[NIGTC]; Gal 3:21, **certainly**; 1 Tim 5:16, **genuine**; 2 Pet 2:18, **really and truly**; ❺ LXX, Num 22:37

ὄξος, ους, τό$_3$ ❻ {ὀξύς} Matt 27:48 = Mark 15:36 = Luke 23:36, **sour wine**; ❺ LXX

ὀξύς, εῖα, ύ$_{3.1.3}$ ❽ Rom 3:15, **quick**; Rev 1:16; 2:12; 14:14, 18,[2x] **sharp**; (19x LXX)

ὀπή, ῆς, ἡ$_{1\eta}$ ❷ Heb 11:38, **cave**; Jas 3:11, **opening**; ❼ LXX, Exod 33:22; Judg 15:11

ὄπισθεν {ὀπίσω + θεν} ❼ Ⓐ ***spatial adv.***, Matt 9:20 = Mark 5:27 = Luke 8:44, **from behind**; Rev 4:6, **back**; 5:1, *within and* **behind**; Ⓑ **ὄπισθεν** ***w/ gen.***, Matt 15:23 **after** *us*; Luke 23:26, **behind** *Jesus*; (19x LXX) 2 Chr 13:13

ὀπίσω (35x; 26x Gs) Ⓐ ***spatial adv.***, **ὀπίσω** ***w/ gen.***, Matt 3:11 = Mark 1:7, **after** *me*; Matt 16:23, **behind** *me*; Ⓑ ***positional adv.***, (2x) Matt 24:18, *to turn* **back**; Luke 7:38, *to stand* **behind**; Ⓒ ***subst.***, (7x) **τὰ ὀπίσω**, Luke 9:62; Phil 3:13, *what* **lies behind**; (346x LXX; 125x 1–2 Sam + 1–2 Kgs)

ὁπλίζω ①[amimp2p] {ὅπλον} 1 Pet 4:1, *milit.*, **to arm oneself**[Keen1P]; Xen. *Cyr.* 6.4.4, **when he had donned these arms**; **Hoplite**, *an arms-bearing foot soldier in the Greek army*[ABC]

ὅπλον, ου, τό$_2$ ❻ John 18:3; Rom 6:13; 13:12; 2 Cor 6:7; 10:4, **weapon**; (67x LXX)

ὁποῖος, α, ον$_{2.1.2}$ {ὅς + ποῦ} *adj.* ❺ 1 Cor 3:13; 1 Thess 1:9; Jas 1:24, **what kind**; Gal 2:6, **whatever** *they once were*; ① LXX, 2 Macc 11:37, **what**

ὅπου {ποῦ} *adv.* (82x; 30x John) Matt 6:19–21[5x]; John 3:8; Acts 17:1; Rev 11:8, **where**; **ὅπου ἐάν**,[8x] Matt 8:19; **ὅπου ἄν**,[2x] Rev 14:4, **wherever**; John 4:20, **where** *it is necessary*; (22x LXX) **ὅπου ἐάν**, Ruth 1:16, **wherever**

ὀπτάνομαι {ὁράω} ①[pmp.nms] Acts 1:3, **to appear**; ❷ LXX, 1 Kgs 8:8; Tob 12:19

ὀπτασία, ας, ἡ$_{1\alpha}$ {ὁράω} ❹ Luke 1:22; 24:33; Acts 26:19; 2 Cor 12:1, **vision**; ❹ LXX

ὀπτός, ή, όν$_{2.1.2}$ *adj.* ①[gms] Luke 24:42, **broiled, roasted**; ❷ LXX, Exod 12:8, 9, **roasted**

ὀπώρα, ας, ἡ$_{1\alpha}$ ①[nfs] Rev 18:14, **fruit**; ❸ LXX, Jer 47:10 (40:1), **summer fruit**

ὅπως {ποῦ} *subord. conj.* (53x; 17x Matt, 14x Acts) Ⓐ ***purpose clause***, Acts 8:15; 2 Cor 8:14, **so that**; Mark 3:6, **to** *kill him*; Ⓑ ***causal compl.***, Matt 9:38, *ask* **to** *send*; (239x LXX; 36x Ezek)

ὅραμα, ατος, τό$_3$ {ὁράω} (12x; 11x Acts) Matt 17:9, **vision**; Acts 7:31, **sight**; (42x LXX)

ὅρασις, εως, ἡ$_3$ {ὁράω} ❹ Acts 2:17; Rev 9:17, **vision**; 4:3,[2x] **appearance**; (106x LXX; 34x Ezek, 18x Dan)

ὁρατός, ή, όν$_{2.1.2}$ {ὁράω} *adj.* ①[nnp] Col 1:16, **visible**; ❹ LXX, 1 Chr 11:23, **impressive** *man*

ὁράω[con] (455x; 270x Gs, 66x Acts, 63x Rev) Ⓐ (*most common*) Matt 2:2–16[5x]; Mark 9:9; Rom 11:22, **to see**; **ὤφθη**[api3s], *occurs* 18x; Ⓑ Luke 1:1; Acts 7:2; 1 Cor 15:5–8[4x]; Rev 11:19, **to appear**, **εἶδον**[aai], *occurs* 45x; Luke 21:29; Gal 6:11; Rev 4:1, **to look**; (1,394x LXX)

ὀργή, ῆς, ἡ$_{1\eta}$ (36x; 12x Rom) Matt 3:7; Luke 3:7; John 3:36; Eph 2:3; 1 Thess 1:10, **wrath**; Mark 3:5; Heb 3:11; Jas 1:19; Rev 16:19, **anger**; (298x LXX; 44x Pss, 25x Job)

ὀργίζω {ὀργή} ❽ Matt 5:22; Luke 15:28; Eph 4:26; Rev 12:17, **to be angry**; (75x LXX)

ὀργίλος, η, ον$_{2.1.2}$ {ὀργή} *adj.* ①[ams] Titus 1:7, **hot-tempered**; ❹ LXX, Ps 17:4; *subst.*, **adversary**

ὀργυιά, ᾶς, ἡ$_{1\alpha}$ {ὀργή} ❷ Acts 27:28,[2x] **fathom**

ὀρέγω ❸ 1 Tim 3:1; Heb 11:16, **to strive for**; 1 Tim 6:10, **to pursue**

ὀρεινός, ή, όν$_{2.1.2}$ {ὄρος} *adj.* ❷ Luke 1:39, 65, **hill country**; (40x LXX; 18x Jdt, 13x Josh)

ὄρεξις, εως, ἡ$_3$ {ὀρέγω} ①[dfs] Rom 1:27, **lust**; ❽ LXX, 4 Macc 1:33, **appetite**

ὀρθοποδέω[con] {ὀρθός + πούς} ①[pai3p] Gal 2:14, **to walk in the straight way**[KeenG]

ὀρθός, ή, όν$_{2.1.2}$ *adj.* ❷ Acts 14:10, *stand* **upright**!; Heb 12:13, **straight**; (26x LXX)

ὀρθοτομέω^{con} {ὀρθός + τομός} ①$^{pap.ams}$ 2 Tim 2:15, *metaph.*, **to accurately delineate** (*lit.*, **to cut or divide something in a straight line)**[PPE]; ❷ LXX, Prov 3:6, **to make straight**; 11:5, **to clear** *a path*

ὀρθρίζω {ὀρθρός} ①^{iai3s} Luke 21:38, **to get up early in the morning**; (55x LXX)

ὀρθρινός, ή, όν$_{2.1.2}$ {ὀρθρός} *adj.* ①^{nfp} Luke 24:22, **early**; ❹ LXX, Hos 6:4, **morning** *mist*

ὄρθρος, ου, ὁ$_2$ ❸ Luke 24:1; John 8:2; Acts 5:21, **dawn**; (32x LXX) Gen 19:15

ὀρθῶς *adv.* ❹ Mark 7:35, **clearly**; Luke 7:43; 10:28; 20:21, **correctly**; (16x LXX) Gen 4:7

ὁρίζω {ὅρος} ❽ (6x LA) Luke 22:22, **to determine**; Acts 10:42; Rom 1:4, *subst.*, **the appointed One**; Heb 4:7, **to specify**; (21x LXX; 10x Num) Num 30,^{9x} **to obligate oneself**

ὅριον, ου, τό$_2$ {ὅρος} (12x) Matt 2:16; Mark 5:17; Acts 13:50, **region**; (284x LXX; 87x Josh)

ὁρκίζω {ὅρκος} ❷ Mark 5:7, **to swear**; Acts 19:13, **to adjure**, **command**; (29x LXX)

ὅρκος, ου, ὁ$_2$ (10x) Matt 14:9 = Mark 6:26; Acts 2:30; Jas 5:12, **oath**; (58x LXX; 13x Gen)

ὁρκωμοσία, ας, ἡ$_{1α}$ {ὅρκος + ὀμνύω} ❹ Heb 7:20,^{2x} 21, 28, **oath**; ❸ LXX; 2x Ezek

ὁρμάω^{con} {ὁρμή} ❺ Matt 8:32 = Mark 5:13 = Luke 8:33; Acts 7:57, **to rush**; (16x LXX)

ὁρμή, ῆς, ἡ$_{1η}$ ❷ Acts 14:5, **attempt**; Jas 3:4, **will**; (10x LXX; 3x 3 Macc)

ὅρμημα, ατος, τό$_3$ {ὁρμή} ①^{dns} Rev 18:21, **violence**; (11x LXX) Exod 32:22, **evil**; Deut 28:49, like **the attack** of an eagle

ὄρνεον, ου, τό$_2$ {ὄρνις} ❸ Rev 18:2; 19:17, 21, **bird**; (34x LXX; 6x Gen) Gen 6:20; 9:2

ὄρνις, ιθος, ἡ$_3$ ❷ Matt 23:37 = Luke 13:34, **hen**; ❷ LXX, 1 Kgs 5:3 (4:23), **fowl**

ὁροθεσία, ας, ἡ$_{1α}$ {ὅρος + τίθημι} ①^{afp} Acts 17:26, **boundary**

ὄρος, ους, τό$_3$ (63x) Matt 4:8; 1 Cor 13:2; Rev 8:8, **mountain**; Matt 18:12, **hillside**; Matt 21:1 = Mark 11:1 = Luke 19:29, **Mount** *of Olives*; Gal 4:24, **Mount** *Sinai*; (642x LXX)

ὀρύσσω {ὄρνις} ❸ Matt 21:33 = Mark 12:1; Matt 25:18, **to dig**; (34x LXX; 10x Gen)

ὀρφανός, ή, όν$_{2.1.2}$ *adj.* ❷ John 14:18; Jas 1:27, fatherless; (52x LXX; 11x Deut) Deut 10:18

ὀρχέομαι {ὄρχος} ❹ Matt 11:17 = Luke 7:32; Matt 14:6 = Mark 6:22, **to dance**; ❼ LXX

ὅς, ἥ, ὅ$_{2.1.2}$ *rel. pron.* (1,399x; 780x GA) Ⓐ ***pure relative pronoun***, Matt 1:16; Mark 16:9; Acts 2:36; Rom 7:15–16,^{4x} **who**, **which**, **what**; Ⓑ ***with prep.***, Acts 7:18, ἄχρι **οὗ**, **while**; Rom 5:12, ἐφ᾽ **ᾧ**, **whereupon** *all sinned*[ZEC]; 2 Cor 5:4, ἐφ᾽ **ᾧ**, **because**; Ⓒ ***consecutive sense***, 1 Cor 2:16, **so that** *he could teach him*; (4,743x LXX; 386x Deut, 325x Jer)

ὁσάκις {ὅς} *adv.* ❸ 1 Cor 11:25, 26, **as often as**; Rev 11:6, **whenever**

ὅσιος, α, ον$_{2.1.2}$ *adj.* ❽ *subst.*, Acts 2:27; Rev 16:5, *the* **Holy One**; Acts 13:34, *the assured* **holy things** *of David*; 1 Tim 2:8; Rev 15:4, **holy**; (77x LXX; 26x Pss) Deut 32:4, **upright**

ὁσιότης, ητος, ἡ$_3$ {ὅσιος} ❷ Luke 1:75; Eph 4:24, **holiness**; ❾ LXX, 1 Kgs 9:4, **integrity**

ὁσίως {ὅσιος} *adv.* ① 1 Thess 2:10, **devoutly**, **holily**

ὀσμή, ῆς, ἡ$_{1η}$ {ὄζω} ❻ John 12:3; 2 Cor 2:14, 16, **aroma**; Eph 5:2; Phil 4:18, **fragrant**; (77x LXX; 20x Num, 19x Lev) **ὀσμὴ(ν)** εὐωδίας,^{48x} **smell** *of fragrance* (sacrifices)

ὅσος, η, ον$_{2.1.2}$ {ὅς} *correl. pron.* (110x; 66x GA) Ⓐ ***extension of space or time***, Rev 21:16, **the same** *size*; Rom 7:1, **as long as**; Ⓑ ***numbers***, ***quantity***, John 6:11, **as much as**; Luke 4:40, *all* **who** *had*; Ⓒ ***proportional comparisons***, Mark 7:36, **the more** . . . *the more*; Ⓓ ***ascensive***, Heb 10:25, **all** *the more*[NIGTC]; Ⓔ ***rhetorical device***, Phil 4:8,^{6x} **whatever**[BEC]; (597x LXX; 246x Pent, 56x 2 Kgs)

ὀστέον, ου, τό$_2$ ❹ Matt 23:27; Luke 24:39; John 19:36; Heb 11:22, **bone**; (127x LXX)

ὅστις, ἥτις, ὅ τι$_{2.1.2}$ {ὅς, ἥ, ὅ + τίς, τί} (152x; 44x LA, 30x Matt) Ⓐ ***common use***, Matt 7:24, **who**; Col 3:17, **whatever** *you do*; **ὅτι** *not in neuter form*; *but* **ὅ τι** *appears* (8x), *half in John* (2:5; 8:25; 14:13; 15:16), **whatever**; Ⓑ ***qualitative use***, Matt 7:15, **those who** (*wolves*); Rom 16:4, **who** (*beloved coworkers*); (119x LXX; 18x Deut, 15x Lev)

ὀστράκινος, η, ον$_{2.1.2}$ {ὄστρακον} *adj.* ❷ 2 Cor 4:7; 2 Tim 2:20, **clay**; (15x LXX; 5x Lev)

ὄσφρησις, εως, ἡ$_3$ {ὄζω} ①[nfs] 1 Cor 12:17, **sense of smell**

ὀσφῦς, ύος, ἡ$_3$ ❽ Matt 3:4 = Mark 1:6, **waist**; Luke 12:35, *gird your* **loins**; Acts 2:30; Heb 7:5, **descendant**, *lit.*, *from the fruit of his* **loin**; Heb 7:10, **ancestor**, *lit.*, *in the* **loin** *of the father*; 1 Pet 1:13, *gird the* **loins** *of your mind*; (65x LXX; 13x Ezek) Gen 35:11; Isa 15:4

ὅταν {ὅς + ἄν} *temp. part.* (123x; 86x Gs) Ⓐ ***w/ subj.***, Matt 15:2; John 9:5; 2 Cor 13:9, **whenever**; Matt 26:29, **when** *I drink it* (*future event*); Ⓑ ***w/ impf.***, Rev 4:9, **whenever**; Ⓒ ***cause, reason w/ subj.***, 1 Cor 15:27, **when**[NIGTC]; (202x LXX; 21x Isa, 20x Pss, 19x Exod)

ὅτε {ὅς + τέ} *conj.* (103x; 67x GA, 13x Rev) Matt 7:28; John 1:19; Acts 1:13; Rev 1:17, **when**; Titus 3:4, **but**; Rev 6:1, 12; 10:10, **then**; (138x; 12x Gen, 10x Job)

ὅτι (*orig. neut. form of* **ὅστις**) *conj.* (1,293x; 271x John, 64x Rev) Ⓐ ***intro. content clause***, Matt 5:17; Phil 2:11; Ⓑ ***intro. direct speech***, Matt 7:23; 2 Thess 3:10; ***quotation of Scripture***, Matt 4:6; 1 Cor 14:21; Ⓒ ***subordinate causal clause***, Matt 11:23; 1 Cor 1:25, **because**, **since**; Matt 5:3–12,[9x] **for** (*light subordination*)[EDNT]; Ⓓ ***explanatory clause***, Rom 8:29[IHR 156] **you see** (= γάρ); (3,781x LXX; 432x Pss)

οὗ {ὅς} *loc. adv.* (24x) Matt 2:9; 18:20; Acts 1:13; Rev 17:15, **where**; (64x LXX)

οὐ, οὐκ, οὐχ (1,624x; 285x LA, 282x John) Ⓐ ***basic negation***, Matt 1:12; Mark 2:17; Luke 9:53, **not**; Ⓑ ***emphatic negation***, οὐ μὴ + *subj.* (89x, 60x Gs), **never**; (6,077x LXX; 1,220x Pent)

οὐά *interj.* ① Mark 15:29, **Ha!**

οὐαί *interj.* (46x; 13x Matt; 15x Luke; 14x Rev) Matt 23:13–29,[7x] **Woe!**; Rev 8:13, **Woe! Woe! Woe!**; (66x LXX; 22x Isa)

οὐδαμῶς {ὅς + δέ} *adv.* ① Matt 2:6, **by no means**; ❼ LXX (2–4 Macc) **not in any way**

οὐδέ {ὅς + δέ} *neg. conj.* (143x; 33x LA, 27x Matt) Matt 5:15, **nor**; 6:15; John 8:11, **neither**; Matt 6:20, 26, οὔτε . . . **οὐδέ**, *neither* . . . **nor**; Mark 5:3; 14:25, (*triple neg.*) **οὐδέ** . . . οὐκέτι οὐδείς, **not even**, *no one* . . . *no longer*, (*unusually emphatic*); Rev 5:3, **οὐδέ . . . οὐδέ**, **neither . . . nor**; 1 Cor 2:6, **not**; (572x LXX; 109x Isa, 43x Deut, 40x Ezek)

οὐδείς, οὐδεμία, οὐδέν$_{3.1.3}$ {οὐ + δέ + εἷς} (227x; 156x GA, 12x Rev) Ⓐ ***adj. w/ subst.***, 1 Cor 8:4, **no** *God*; Ⓑ ***abs. sense***, Eph 5:29, **no one**; Ⓒ **οὐδέν**, ***neut. abs.***, Matt 10:26; Gal 2:6, **nothing**; (178x LXX; 16x Isa, 15x Job)

οὐδέποτε {οὐ + δέ + ποῦ} (16x; 5x Matt) Matt 7:23; Heb 10:11, **never**; Matt 9:33, **nothing** *like this has* **ever** *been seen*; ❹ LXX, Exod 10:6

οὐδέπω *temp. adv.* ❹ John 7:39; 20:9; Acts 8:16, **not yet**; ① LXX, Exod 9:30

οὐθείς {οὐ + εἷς} = **οὐδείς** ❼ (5x LA) Ⓐ ***in result clause***, Acts 19:27, *come* **to ruin**; Ⓑ ***emphatic position***, 1 Cor 13:2, **οὐθέν** εἰμι, *I am* **nothing**[NIGTC]; (81x LXX; 8x Gen:Job:Jer)

οὐκέτι {οὐ + ἔτι} *temp. adv.* (47x; 12x John) Matt 19:6; Luke 15:21; John 4:42; 17:11; 2 Cor 5:16; Gal 2:20; Rev 10:6, **no longer**; 2 Cor 1:23, **not**; (105x LXX; 23x Isa, 22x Ezek)

οὐκοῦν {οὐ + οὖν} *infer. interrog.* ① John 18:37, **so then**[EGG]

οὖν *coord. conj.* (498x; [200x John «» 1x 1–3 John], 94x LA) Ⓐ ***inferential***, Matt 3:8; 7:24; 12:12; Rom 11:11, **therefore**; Ⓑ ***resumptive***, Matt 10:32; Luke 3:7; 1 Cor 8:4, **so** (= *as I* *was saying*); 🅒 ***intro. to new topic*** (*esp. in John*), John 6:19; 7:25,^{ZEC} **then**; (247x LXX; 42x Gen, 29x Exod, 26x 2 Macc)

οὔ**πω** {οὐ + πω} *temp. adv.* (26x; 11x John) 🅐 ***strictly temporal***, Matt 24:6 = Mark 13:7; John 3:24, **not yet**; 🅑 ***theologically temporal***, John 2:4; 7:6; 8:20, *his hour had* **not yet** *come*; ❽ LXX, 3x Gen

οὐρά, ας, ἡ$_{1\alpha}$ ❺ Rev 9:10,^{2x} 19^{2x}; 12:4, **tail**; ❼ LXX, Deut 28:13; Job 40:17; Isa 9:13

οὐράνιος, ον$_{2.2}$ {οὐρανός} *adj.* ❾ (7x Matt) Matt 5:48; 6:32; Luke 2:13; Acts 26:19, **heavenly**; Matt 23:9, **in heaven**; ❼ LXX (6x 2–4 Macc) 1 Esd 6:14, *the Lord of Israel who is* **in heaven**

οὐρανό**θεν** {οὐρανός + θεν} *adv.* ❷ Acts 14:17, 26:13, **from heaven**; ① LXX, 4 Macc 4:10

οὐρανός, οῦ, ὁ$_2$ (273x; 82x Matt, 61x LA, 52x Rev) Matt 3:2–25:1, ***formulaic***, βασιλεία τῶν **οὐρανῶν**,^{17x} *kingdom* **of heaven**; Matt 8:20; 24:29, **sky**; 24:30,^{2x} 31; Rom 1:18; Rev 4:1, 8:1, **heaven**; (621x LXX; 79x Pss, 46x Deut, 44x Gen)

Οὐρβανός, οῦ, ὁ$_2$ ①^{ams} Rom 16:9, **Urbanus**

Οὐρίας, οῦ, ὁ$_1$ ①^{gms} Matt 1:6, **Uriah**

οὖς, ὠτός, τό$_3$ (36x; 18x Syn, 8x Rev) Matt 13:9 = Luke 8:8; Matt 13:43; Luke 14:35; Rev 2:7–3:22,^{7x} ***formula***: *the one who has* **ears**; Mark 8:18; 1 Cor 2:9; **ear**; (179x LXX; 24x Jer, 20x Pss)

οὐσία, ας, ἡ$_{1\alpha}$ {εἰμί} ❷ Luke 15:12, 13, **estate**; ❷ LXX, 3 Macc 3:28, **property**

οὔ**τε** {οὐ + τέ} *coord. conj.* (87x) 🅐 ***compact coord.***, Matt 6:20; Rev 3:15, **οὔτε . . . οὔτε**,^{47x} **neither . . . nor**; 🅑 ***extended coord.***, 1 Cor 6:9–10,^{7x} **neither**^{1x} **. . . nor**^{6x}; **οὔτε** *translated* **neither** *as head of list, then* **οὔτε** *translated as* **nor** *creating an exclusive list*; Rev 21:4, **nor . . . nor . . . nor**; (122x LXX; 25x LetJ, 17x Wis)

οὗτος, αὕτη, τοῦτο$_{2.1.2}$ *near demonstr. pron.* (1,387x; 465x LA, 147x Matt) 🅐 Matt 3:17 = John 1:34; Jas 4:15, **this**; 🅑 1 Cor 4:4, **ἐν τούτῳ**, (32x in GNT); **by this**; 🅒 Matt 1:20; John 21:24; 1 Cor 9:15, **ταῦτα**, **these things** (207x in GNT); (4,236x LXX; 331x Jer, 327x Gen, 230x Ezek)

οὕτως {οὗτος} *adv.* (208x; 32x Matt, 31x 1 Cor) 🅐 ***foregoing ref.***, Luke 11:30, *as Jonah was to Nineveh*, **similarly**, *the Son of Man will be to this generation*; Acts 8:32, **so** *he did not open his mouth*; 🅑 ***consecutive, leading to what follows***, Luke 24:24, *they found it* **just as**; 🅒 ***extent or degree***, Gal 3:3, *are you* **so** *foolish*; John 3:16, *for God* **so** *loved the world*; (830x LXX; 109x Jer, 79x Isa)

οὐχί (*emph. form of* **οὐ**) (54x; 18x Luke, 12x 1 Cor) 🅐 ***simple negation***, John 13:11, **not**; 🅑 ***interrog. expecting affirm. response***, Rom 3:29, *Is he* **not** *the God of gentiles*? (184x LXX)

ὀφειλέτης, ου, ὁ$_{1f}$ {ὀφείλω} ❼ Matt 6:12, **debtors**; 18:24, εἷς **ὀφειλέτης**, **a debtor**; Luke 13:4, *were greater* **offenders**;^{ZEC} Rom 1:14, *I am* **a debtor**

ὀφειλή, ῆς, ἡ$_{1\eta}$ ❸ Matt 18:32; Rom 13:7; 1 Cor 7:3, **debt**

ὀφείλημα, ατος, τό$_3$ {ὀφείλω} ❷ Matt 6:12; Rom 4:4, **debt**; ❹^{nns} LXX, Deut 24:10^{2x}

ὀφείλω (35x) 🅐 ***w/ dir. object***, Phlm 18, **to owe**; 1 Cor 5:10, **to be obliged**^{NIGTC}; 🅑 ***w/ inf.***, 1 Cor 7:36, *and* **it seems** (*to be*) *the right thing*^{NIGTC}; (16x LXX; 3x 1 Macc)

ὄφελον {ὀφείλω} *interj. of unfulfilled wish*^{EGG} ❹ 1 Cor 4:8; 2 Cor 11:1; Gal 5:12; Rev 3:15, **I wish**; ❼ LXX, Job 14:13, **Oh that** *you had kept me in Hades* (NETS)

ὄφελος, ους, τό$_3$ {ὠφελέω} ❸ 1 Cor 15:32, *what* **profit** *for me?*^{NIGTC}; Jas 2:14, 16, *what* **good is it?** ①^{nns} LXX, Job 15:3, *no* **good purpose**

ὀφθαλμο**δουλία, ας, ἡ**$_{1α}$ {ὁράω + δοῦλος} ❷ Eph 6:6 = Col 3:22, *not* **serving to be seen**

ὀφθαλμός, οῦ, ὁ$_2$ {ὁράω} (100x; 24x Matt, 18x John) Matt 5:29; 7:3–5 = Luke 6:41–42^{6x}; Matt 26:43 = Mark 14:40; John 9:14; Acts 9:8; Rev 1:14, **eye**; (637x LXX; 58x Pss, 46x 2 Kgs)

ὀφθέντες → ὁράω, *aor. pass. ptc. nmp*, Luke 9:31, **they appeared** *in glory*

ὄφις, εως, ὁ$_3$ (14x) Matt 7:10 = Luke 11:11; John 3:14; 1 Cor 10:9; Rev 9:19, **snake**; 2 Cor 11:3; Rev 12:9; 20:2, **serpent**; (40x LXX; 7x Gen:Num) Gen 3:1–14,^{6x} **serpent**

ὀφρῦς, ύος, ἡ$_3$ ①^{gfs} Luke 4:29, **edge**; ①^{afp} LXX, Lev 14:9, **eyebrow**

ὀχλέω^{con} {ὄχλος} ①$^{ppp.amp}$ Acts 5:16, *subst.*, **troubled**; ❸ LXX, Tob 6:8^{2x}; 3 Macc 5:41

ὀχλο**ποιέω**^{con} {ὄχλος + ποιέω} ①$^{aap.nfp}$ Acts 17:5, **to gather a crowd**

ὄχλος, ου, ὁ$_2$ (175x; 171x GA) Matt 4:25 = Mark 3:7 = John 6:2, **crowd**; (49x LXX)

ὀχύρωμα, ατος, τό$_3$ {ἔχω} ①^{gnp} 2 Cor 10:4, **stronghold**; (70x LXX; 27x 1 Macc) Gen 39:20, **prison**; 2 Sam 22:2, **fortress**; Job 19:6, **siege works** (Tanakh)

ὀψάριον, ου, τό$_2$ ❺ John 6:9, 11; 21:9, 10, 13, **fish**

ὀψέ ❸ Ⓐ ***prep. w/ gen.***, Matt 28:1, **after**; Ⓑ ***adv***, Mark 11:19, *when* **evening** *came*; 13:35, ἢ ὀψέ, *whether* **evening**; ❹ LXX, Gen 24:11; Exod 30:8; Isa 5:11; Jer 2:23, *in the* **evening**

ὀψία, ας, ἡ$_{1α}$ {ὀψέ} (15x) Matt 8:16 = Mark 1:32, **evening**; ①^{nfs} LXX, Jdt 13:1

ὄψιμος, ου, ὁ$_2$ {ὀψέ} ①^{ams} Jas 5:7, **spring rain**; ❼ LXX, Deut 11:14; Zech 10:1

ὄψις, εως, ἡ$_3$ {ὁράω} ❸ John 7:24, **outward appearances**; 11:44; Rev 1:16, **face**; (57x LXX; 13x Lev) Gen 24:16, **fair** *to look upon*; 39:6, **handsome**; Exod 10:15, **face** *of the earth*

ὄψονται → ὁράω, *fut. mid. ind. 3p*, Matt 5:8, **they will see** *God*

ὀψώνιον, ου, τό$_2$ ❹ Luke 3:14; Rom 6:23; **wage**; 1 Cor 9:7, **provision**^{NIGTC}; 2 Cor 11:8, **resources**^{BEC}; ❸ LXX, 1 Macc 3:28; 14:32, **provisions**

Π, π [*pi*]

Π, π, τό (πεῖ) *indecl.* **pi**, *16th letter of the Gr. alphabet* || *num.* π′ = 80; ͵π = 80,000

παγιδεύω {τήγνυμι} ①[aas3p] Matt 22:15, **to entrap**; ❷ LXX, 1 Sam 28:9, **to lay a snare**

παγίς, ίδος, ἡ$_{3}$ {τήγνυμι} ❺ Luke 21:35; Rom 11:9; 1 Tim 3:7; 2 Tim 2:26, **snare**, **trap**; (62x LXX; 21x Pss) Josh 23:13; Ps 9:16 (9:15), **trap**, **snare**, **net**

πάγος, ου, ὁ$_{2}$ ❷ Ἄρειον **πάγον**, Ἀρείου **πάγου** Acts 17:19, 22, **Areopagus** *or* **Hill of Ares**; ❻ LXX, Nah 3:17; Zech 14:6, **cold**; Hes. *Sc.* 439, **high point**; Soph. *Ph.* 293, **ice**, **frost**

παθεῖν → πάσχω, *aor. act. inf.*, Matt 16:21, **to suffer**

πάθημα, ατος, τό$_{3}$ {πάσχω} (16x; 4x 1 Pet) Rom 7:5; Gal 5:24, **passion**; Rom 8:18; 2 Cor 1:5; Col 1:24; 1 Pet 5:9, **suffering**

παθητός, ή, όν$_{2.1.2}$ {πάσχω} *adj.* ①[nms] Acts 26:23, *subject* **to suffer**[EGG]

πάθος, ους, τό$_{3}$ {πάσχω} ❺ Rom 1:26; Col 3:5; 1 Thess 4:5, **passion**, (64x LXX, 62x 4 Macc[SCS]); Job 30:31, **mourning**; Prov 25:20, **heavy**

παιδαγωγός, οῦ, ὁ$_{2}$ {παίζω + ἄγω} ❸ 1 Cor 4:15, *metaph.*, *thousands of* **people** *in Christ to correct you*; Gal 3:24, 25, **custodian**[WLC 53]; Hdt. *Hist.* 8.75.1, **slave who accompanies boys**

παιδάριον, ου, τό$_{2}$ {παῖς} ①[nns] John 6:9, **boy**; (212x LXX; 96x 1–2 Sam, 56x 1–2 Kgs)

παιδεία, ας, ἡ$_{1α}$ {παῖς} ❻ Heb 12:5, **discipline**; Eph 6:4; 2 Tim 3:16, **training**; (110x LXX; 34x Sir, 26x Prov)

παιδευτής, οῦ, ὁ$_{1>}$ {παῖς} ❷ Rom 2:20, **teacher**; Heb 12:9, **correction**; ❺ LXX, 4 Macc 9:6, **instructor**; Plato *Rp.* 493c, **master**, **preceptor**, **instructor**

παιδεύω {παῖς} (13x; 4x LA) *act.*, Luke 23:16, **to flog**; Rev 3:19, **to discipline**; *pass.*, Acts 7:22; 1 Tim 1:20, **to be instructed**; Acts 22:3, **educated** *strictly at the feet of Gamaliel*; 2 Cor 6:9, **to be disciplined**[BEC]; (88x LXX; 12x Pss, Prov); Soph. *fr.* 648, **to be nourished** *on white milk*

παιδιόθεν {παῖς + θεν} *adv.* ① Mark 9:21, ἐκ **παιδιόθεν**, *from* **infancy**, **childhood**

παιδίον, ου, τό$_{2}$ {παῖς} (53x; 43x Syn) Matt 2:8; Mark 5:39; Luke 1:59; John 16:21, **little child**, **newborn**; 1 Cor 14:20, *Eng. idiom*, **children born yesterday**; **childish self-concern**[NIGTC]; 1 John 2:14; 3:7, **children**; (124x LXX; 33x Gen, 20x Tob)

παιδίσκη, ης, ἡ$_{1η}$ {παῖς} (13x; 5x Gal) Matt 26:69 = Mark 14:66 = Luke 22:56 = John 18:17; Acts 16:16; Gal 4:22, 23, 30,[2x] **slave-girl**; (88x LXX; 37x Gen) Gen 16:1–8[6x]

παίζω {παῖς} ①[painf] 1 Cor 10:7, *rose up* **to virtual orgy**[NIGTC!]; (20x LXX), Zech 8:5, **to play** (*children*); Judg 16:25, **to entertain** *drunkards*; Exod 32:1–6 (*1 Cor 10:7*), **to indulge in pagan revelry**[NIGTC!]; Isa 3:16, **to jingle** *their ankle bracelets*[NAC!]

παῖς, παιδός, ὁ$_{3}$ (24x, GA) Matt 2:16; John 4:51, **child**; Matt 8:6–13[3x]; Luke 1:54; Acts 3:13, **servant**; Matt 17:18; Luke 2:43, **boy**; (460x LXX; 166x 1 Sam–2 Chr, 94x Gen)

παίω ❺ Matt 26:68 = Luke 22:64, **to strike**; Rev 9:5, **to sting**; (25x LXX; 6x 1–2 Sam) Judg 14:19, **to kill**; Eur. *Or.* 1472, **to sink** *the black sword into the throat*

πάλαι {παλαιός} *adv.* ➐ Matt 11:21 = Luke 10:13; Heb 1:1; Jude 4, **long ago**; Mark 15:44, **for some time**; 2 Cor 12:19, **all this time**[BEC]; 2 Pet 1:9, **past**; ➑ LXX, Isa 37:26, **long ago**

παλαιός, ά, όν$_{2.1.2}$ *adj.* (19x; 11x Syn) Matt 9:16 = Mark 2:21 = Luke 5:36, **old** *cloak*; Rom 6:6, Col 3:9, **old** *self*; 2 Cor 3:14, **old** *covenant*; 1 John 2:7, **old** *commandment*; (24x LXX; 7x Lev)

παλαιότης, ητος, ἡ$_3$ {παλαιός} ①^{dfs} Rom 7:6, **old, obsolete**; Eur. *Hel.* 1056, **antiquity**

παλαιόω^{con} {παλαιός} ➍ Luke 12:33; Heb 1:11, **to wear out**; 8:13$^{2\text{x}}$, **to make obsolete**; (26x LXX; 5x Job) Job 9:5, **to remove** *mountains*; Plato *Symp.* 208b, **to lose vigor**

πάλη, ης, ἡ$_{1\eta}$ ①^{nfs} Eph 6:12, **struggle**; Hom. *Il.* 23.635, **wrestling**

παλιγγενεσία, ας, ἡ$_{1\alpha}$ {πάλιν + γίνομαι} ➋ Matt 19:28, **renewal** *of the world*; Titus 3:5, **rebirth**; MAur. 11.1, *Stoic philosopher*, **palingenesis, rebirth**

πάλιν *adv.* (141x; 45x John, 28x Mark) Matt 4:7, **on the other hand**[BDAG 753–54]; Matt 4:8; 19:24, **once more**[BHGNT]; Rom 8:15, **again**; Gal 1:9, **repeat**; (82x LXX; 10x 2 Macc, 9x Gen)

παμπληθεί {πᾶς + πληρόω} *adv.* ① Luke 23:18, **all together**

Παμφυλία, ας, ἡ$_{1\alpha}$ ➎ Acts 5:10; 13:13; 14:24; 15:38; 27:5, **Pamphylia**

πανδοχεῖον, ου, τό$_2$ {πᾶς + δέχομαι} ①^{ans} Luke 10:34, **inn**; Aristoph. *Ran.* 550, **hotel**

πανδοχεύς, εως, ἡ$_3$ {πᾶς + δέχομαι} ①^{dms} Luke 10:35, **inn-keeper**; Lyc. 655, Ἅιδης **πανδοκεῦς** (*alt. spell.*, χ → κ) πάντα, *Hades*, **who receives everyone**[BrDAG]

πανήγυρις, εως, ἡ$_3$ {πᾶς + ἄγω} ①^{dfs} Heb 12:22, **joyful gathering**; ➍ LXX, Amos 5:21; Ezek 46:11, **festival**; Aeschl. *Ag.* 845, **congress**

πανοικεί {πᾶς + οἶκος} *adv.* ① Acts 16:34, **with one's entire household**

πανοπλία, ας, ἡ$_{1\alpha}$ {πᾶς + ὅπλον} ➌^{afs} Luke 11:22, *Satan's* **panoply of armor**[ZEC]; Eph 6:11, 13, **whole armor**; (11x LXX) Job 39:20, *have you clad him* **in perfect armor?**[SeptJob]

πανουργία, ας, ἡ$_{1\alpha}$ {πᾶς + ἔργον} ➎ Luke 20:23; 1 Cor 3:19, **craftiness**[NIGTC]; ➑ LXX, Num 24:22, **shrewdness**; Men. *Perin.* 11, *pos.* **sagacity**; Aeschl. *Sept.* 603, *neg.* **malice, evil**

πανοῦργος, ον$_{2.2}$ {πᾶς + ἔργον} *adj.* ①^{nms} 2 Cor 12:16, **devious** *me, I bamboozled you!*[BEC]; (19x LXX; 13x Prov) Prov 12:16, **cloaking**; Job 5:12, **crafty**

πανταχῇ {πᾶς} *adv.* ① Acts 21:28, **everywhere**; ➌ LXX, 2 Macc 8:7; Isa 24:11

πανταχοῦ {πᾶς} *adv.* ➐ Mark 1:28; 16:20; Luke 9:6; Acts 17:30, **everywhere**

παντελής, ές$_{3.3}$ {πᾶς + τέλος} *adj.* ➋^{ans} Luke 13:11, **completely**; Heb 7:25, **to the uttermost**; ①^{afs} LXX, 3 Macc 7:16, **even to the point** *of death*

πάντη {πᾶς} *adv.* ① Acts 24:3, **in every way**; ➋ LXX, 3 Macc 4:1, **everywhere**

πάντοθεν {πᾶς + θεν} *adv.* ➌ Mark 1:45; Luke 19:43; Heb 9:4, **on all sides, from every quarter**; (10x LXX) 2 Sam 24:14, **on every side**; Jer 20:9, **everywhere**

παντοκράτωρ, ορος, ὁ$_3$ {πᾶς + κεράννυμι} (10x; 9x Rev) 2 Cor 6:18; Rev 1:8; 21:22, **the Almighty**; (181x LXX; 55x Zech, 25x Mal) Orph. *H.* 18.17, **ruler of the universe**

πάντοτε {πᾶς + ὅς + τέ} *adv.* (41x; 9x 1–2 Thess, 7x John) Matt 26:11 = Mark 14:7$^{2\text{x}}$ = Luke 15:31; John 7:6; 1 Thess 1:2; 2 Thess 1:3, **always, constantly**; ➋ LXX, Wis 11:21; 19:18

πάντως {πᾶς} *adv.* ➑ Luke 4:23, **doubtless**; Acts 28:4, **must**; 1 Cor 5:10, **in no way**; 9:22, **through every possible means**; 16:12, **fully** *determined*[NIGTC]; ➌ LXX, 2 Kgs 5:11, **surely**

παρά, παρ᾽ *prep.* (194x; 58x LA, 35x John) Ⓐ ***w/ gen.***, Mark 14:43, **from**; 16:9, **out of**; Ⓑ ***w/ dat.***, Luke 9:47, **next**; 1 Cor 7:4, **before**; Rev 2:13, **among**; Ⓒ ***w/ acc.***, Matt 4:18, **alongside**; Heb 11:12, **on**; (831x LXX; 225x Pent, 43x Pss, 42x Prov) παραβαίνω ❸ Matt 15:2, 3, **to transgress**[ZEC]; Acts 1:25, **to deviate**; (64x LXX; 8x Num)

παραβάλλω ①[aai1p] Acts 20:15, **to cross over**; (10x LXX) Ruth 2:16[2x]; Prov 2:2[2x], **inclining** *your heart to understanding and* **making** *your ear* **attentive** *to wisdom*

παράβασις, εως, ἡ$_3$ {παρά + βαίνω} ❼ Rom 2:23; Heb 9:15, **transgression**, **deviation**; ❸ LXX, Ps 100:3 (101:3); Plut. *QCon.* 649b, **distortion** *or* **curvature** *of wood*

παραβάτης, ου, ὁ$_{1>}$ (παρά + βαίνω) ❺ Rom 2:25; Gal 2:18; Jas 2:9, **transgressor**; Hom. *Il.* 23.132, **warrior who fights next to the charioteer**; Aeschl. *Eum.* 553, **violator**[BrDAG]

παραβιάζομαι (παρά + βία) ❷ Luke 24:29; Acts 16:15, **to urge strongly**; ❼ LXX, Amos 6:10, **to act defiantly**; Jonah 1:13, **to try hard** (Heb. *the men* **dug in their oars**)

παραβολεύομαι {παρά + βάλλω} ①[amp.nms] Phil 2:30, **to put** *one's life* **at risk**[NIGTC]

παραβολή, ῆς, ἡ$_{1η}$ {παρά + βάλλω} (50x; 48x Syn) Matt 13:3 = Mark 4:2; Matt 13,[12x] **parable**; Heb 9:9; 11:19, **symbol**, **type**[NIGTC]

παραγγελία, ας, ἡ$_{1α}$ {παρά + ἄγγελος} ❺ Acts 5:28, **παραγγελίᾳ** παρηγγείλαμεν, *emph. Sem. idiom*, **strictly charged** *you*[EGG]; Acts 16:24; 1 Thess 4:2; 1 Tim 1:5, 18, **instruction**, **order**

παραγγέλλω {παρά + ἄγγελος} (32x; 15x LA) Matt 15:35 = Mark 8:6; Acts 1:4; 1 Cor 7:10; 1 Thess 4:11, **to command**; (21x LXX), Ezra 1:1; Jer 26:14 (46:14), **to proclaim**

παραγίνομαι (37x; 28x LA, 33x[aormid]) Matt 2:1; Acts 5:21–28:21,[20x] **to arrive**; (174x LXX)

παράγω {παρά + ἄγω} (10x) Matt 9:9 = Mark 2:14, **to leave**, **go**; John 9:1, **to pass by**; 1 Cor 7:31, **to slip away**[NIGTC]; 1 John 2:8, 17, **to pass away**[ZEC]; (14x LXX)

παραδειγματίζω {παρά + δείκνυμι} ①[pap.amp] Heb 6:6, **to disgrace publicly**[BDAG]; ❻ LXX, Num 25:4, **to execute** (HCSB); Jer 13:22, **to strip off**

παράδεισος, ου, ὁ$_2$ *Persian term* ❸ Luke 23:43; 2 Cor 12:4[BEC]; Rev 2:7, **paradise**; (34x LXX; 14x Gen); Gen 2:8, **garden**; Neh 2:8, *the king's* **forest** *or* **park**; Xen. *An.* 1.2.7, **park**, *area planted with trees and stocked with game*[BrDAG]

παραδέχομαι ❻ Mark 4:20; 1 Tim 5:19; Heb 12:6, **to accept**; Acts 15:4, **to welcome**; 16:21, **to adopt**; ❸ LXX, Exod 23:1, **to spread**; Prov 3:12, **to delight in**

παραδίδωμι (119x; 96x GA, 31x Matt) Ⓐ ***neg. sense***, Matt 10:4–21,[4x] *act.*, **to hand over**; Matt 26:45 = Mark 14:41, *pass.*, *Jesus* **being delivered over**[Spicq] *t.t.*; Ⓑ ***pos. sense***, *act.*, Matt 25:14, *all things* **have been entrusted** *to me*; 1 Cor 11:23, **to pass on** *the tradition*; *pass.*, Rom 6:17, **to be committed to**[NIGTC]; (248x LXX; 27x Judg); *120+ instances*, **deliver into the hands**[NIDNTT]

παράδοξος, ον$_{2.2}$ {παρά + δοκέω} *adj.* ①[anp] Luke 5:26, *subst.*, **incredible things**; ❽ LXX, 2 Macc 9:24, **unexpected**; Xen. *Cyr.* 7.2.16, **contrary to opinion**

παράδοσις, εως, ἡ$_3$ {παρά + δίδωμι} (13x; 5x Mark) Matt 15:2 = Mark 7:5; 1 Cor 11:2; Gal 1:14, **tradition**; ❸[dfs] LXX, Jer 39:4 (32:4), 41:2 (34:2), **παραδόσει** παραδοθήσεται ...[2x] "*I am going to give this city* **in surrender** ..."

παραζηλόω[con] {παρά + ζέω} ❹ Rom 10:19; 11:11, 14, **to make jealous**; 1 Cor 10:22, **to arouse** *the Lord's* **jealousy**[NIGTC]; (10x LXX) Deut 32:21; 1 Kgs 14:22; Ps 36:1 (37:1)

παραθαλάσσιος, ου, ὁ$_2$ {παρά + ἅλας} ①[afs] Matt 4:13, **by the sea**; ❻ LXX

παραθεωρέω[con] {παρά + θεάομαι} ①[imi3p] Acts 6:1, **to neglect**

παραθήκη, ης, ἡ$_{1η}$ {παρά + τίθημι} ❸ 1 Tim 6:20; 2 Tim 1:12, 14, **the deposit**, **that which has been entrusted**; ❷ LXX, Lev 5:21, 23

παραινέω[con] {παρά + αἶνος} ❷ Acts 27:9, 22, **to urge strongly**; ❹ LXX, 2 Macc 7:25

παραιτέομαι[con] {παρά + αἰτέω} (12x) Mark 15:6; Heb 12:19, **to request**; Luke 14:18, **to make excuse**; Acts 25:11, **to decline**; 2 Tim 2:23, **to avoid**; ❽ LXX, Esth 4:8

παρακαθέζομαι {παρά + κατά + ἕζομαι} ①[app.nfs] Luke 10:39, **to sit beside**

παρακαλέω[con] (109x; 22x Acts, 18x 2 Cor) Matt 2:18, **to comfort**; 18:32; Phil 4:2,[2x] **to beg**; Titus 1:9, **to proclaim**; 1 Thess 3:2; Heb 10:25, **to encourage**; Acts 28:14, **to invite**; ***spec. emph.*** 2 Cor 1:4,[3x] 6; 2:7; 7:6,[2x] **to console**[BEC]; Phlm 9, **to exhort** *to action*[BEC]; (137x LXX; 28x Isa, 21x 2 Macc)

παρακαλύπτω ①[pfmp.nns] Luke 9:45, **to conceal**; ❷ LXX, Ezek 22:26, **to cover** *their eyes*

παράκειμαι ❷ Rom 7:18, 21, **to lie close at hand**; (10x LXX; 5x 2–3 Macc)

παρακεκαλυμμένον → **παρακαλύπτω**, *pf. mid. ptc. nns*, Luke 9:45, **concealed**

παράκλησις, εως, ἡ$_{3}$ {παρά + καλέω} (29x; 11x 2 Cor) Luke 2:25; 2 Cor 1:3–7,[6x] **comfort**[*DJG* 272]; Acts 4:36; Phlm 7, **encouragement**; Rom 12:8; Heb 13:22, **exhortation**; (16x LXX) Job 21:2, **consolation**; Iambl. *Myst.* 4.3, **invocation** *of the gods*

παράκλητος, ου, ὁ$_{2}$ {παρά + καλέω} ❺ John 14:16, 26; 15:26; 16:7, **Paraclete** (*Holy Spirit*)[ZEC]; 1 John 2:1, **Paraclete** (*Jesus*); ①[nmp] LXX[Theodotion] Job 16:2, *mischievous* **counselors**[ZEC]; Demosth. 19.1, **defender**; Philo *Spec.* 1.237, *irreproachable* **mediator**[*BrDAG*]

παρακοή, ῆς, ἡ$_{1η}$ {παρά + ἀκούω} ❸ Rom 5:19; 2 Cor 10:6; Heb 2:2, **disobedience**; Plato *Epist.* 341b, **echo, mediated message**; *medic.*, Gal. *U.P.* 4.764, **error in comprehension**; 7.108, **poor hearing**[*BrDAG*]

παρακολουθέω[con] {παρά + ἀκόλουθος} ❹ Mark 16:17, **to accompany**; Luke 1:3, **to stay actively informed**[ICC]; 1 Tim 4:6, **to study diligently**; 2 Tim 3:10, **to study at close quarters**; ❷ LXX, 2 Macc 8:11; 9:27, **to follow closely**

παρακούω {παρά + ἀκούω} ❸ Matt 18:17,[2x] **to refuse to listen**; Mark 5:36, **to overhear**; ❼ LXX, Esth 3:3, **to disobey**; Hdt. *Hist.* 3.129.3, **to hear in passing**

παρακύπτω ❺ Luke 24:12 = John 20:5; 20:11, **to peer into**[BEC]; Jas 1:25, **to gaze**; 1 Pet 1:12, **to peer into**[EGG]; ❼ LXX, Gen 26:8; Judg 5:28, **to look out** *the window*

παραλαμβάνω (49x; 16x Matt) Matt 1:20–27:27, **to take**[15x]; Matt 12:45 = Luke 11:26, **to bring**; John 1:11, **to accept**; 1 Cor 11:23; Phil 4:9; Heb 12:28, **to receive**; (38x LXX)

παραλέγομαι {παρά + λέγω} ❷ Acts 27:8, 13, **to sail**

παράλιος, ου, ἡ$_{2ὁδός}$ {παρά + ἅλας} ①[gfs] Luke 6:17, **seacoast**; (12x LXX) Deut 1:7

παραλλαγή, ῆς, ἡ$_{1η}$ {παρά + ἄλλος} ①[nfs] Jas 1:17, **change** *or* **shadow** *of turning*[KEL]; ①[dfs] LXX, 2 Kgs 9:20, **to ride furiously**[KEL]; Chrysip. 3.125.20, **mental deviancy**[*BrDAG*]

παραλογίζομαι {παρά + λέγω} ❷ Col 2:4; Jas 1:22, **to deceive**; (14x LXX) Gen 29:25

παραλυτικός, οῦ, ὁ$_{2}$ {παρά + λύω} (10x) Matt 4:24; Mark 2:3, **paralytic**

παραλύω ❺ Luke 5:18, 24; Acts 8:7; 9:33, **to be paralyzed**; Heb 12:12, **to be weak**; (24x LXX) Deut 32:36, **to lose power**; Hdt. *Hist.* 3.136, **to unfasten** *the rudders of a ship*

παραμένω ❹ 1 Cor 16:6, **to stay**; Phil 1:25, μενῶ καὶ **παραμενῶ**, *I will stay and* **remain**[BEC]; Heb 7:23, **to continue in office**; Jas 1:25, **to persevere**; ❽ LXX, Prov 12:7, **to withstand** *the onslaught of evil*; Hom. *Il.* 13.151, **to remain at one's post**

παραμυθέομαι[con] {παρά + μύθος} ❹ John 11:19, 31, **to console**; 1 Thess 2:12; 5:14, **to encourage**; ①[pmp.nms] LXX, 2 Macc 15:9, **to encourage**

παραμυθία, ας, ἡ$_{1α}$ {παρά + μύθος} ①[afs] 1 Cor 14:3, **consolation**; ❷ LXX, Wis 19:12

παραμύθιον, ου, τό$_{2}$ {παρά + μύθος} ①[nns] Phil 2:1, **consolation**; ①[ans] LXX, Wis 3:18

παρα**νομέω**[con] {παρά + νόμος} ①[pap.nms] Acts 23:3, **to violate**[Keen3]; (10x LXX) Job 34:18

παρα**νομία, ας, ἡ**$_{1\alpha}$ {παρά + νόμος} ①[afp] 2 Pet 2:16, **transgression**; (11x LXX; 1x Ps)

παρα**πεσόντας** → παρα**πίπτω**, *aor. act. ptc. amp*, Heb 6:6, **who have fallen away**

παρα**πικραίνω** {παρά + πικρός} ①[aai3p] Heb 3:16, **to rebel**; (43x LXX; 20x Ezek, 12x Pss) Deut 31:27, *ptc.*, **rebellious**; ➠**Ezekiel**, διότι οἶκος **παραπικραίνων** ἐστίν[8x], "though they are a **rebellious** breed" (Tanakh)

παρα**πικρασμός, οῦ, ὁ**$_2$ {παρά + πικρός} ❷[dms] Heb 3:8, 15, **rebellion**, *quoting Ps 94:8*; ①[dms] LXX, Ps 94:8 (95:8)

παρα**πίπτω** ①[aap] Heb 6:6, **to fall away**; ❽ LXX (5x Ezek), Ezek 15:8, **to act faithlessly**

παρα**πλέω**[con] ①[aainf] Acts 20:16, **to sail by**

παρα**πλήσιος, α, ον**$_{2.1.2}$ *adj.* ①[ams] Phil 2:27, **close**; Hdt. *Hist.* 4.128.3, **just about equal**

παρα**πλησίως** {παρά + πλησίον} *adv.* ① Heb 2:14, **likewise**

παρα**πορεύομαι** ❺ Matt 27:39, **to pass by**; Mark 2:23, **to pass through**; (36x LXX)

παρά**πτωμα, ατος, τό**$_3$ {παρά + πίπτω} (19x; 9x Rom) Rom 4:25; Gal 6:1; Eph 2:5 = Col 2:13, **trespass**; (19x LXX; 9x Ezek) Wis 3:13, **defilement**; Ezek 3:20, **iniquity**

παρα**ρρέω**[con] {παρά + ῥέω} ①[apslp] Heb 2:1, **to drift away**; ❷ LXX, Prov 3:21, **to forget**

παρά**σημος, ον**$_{2.2}$ {παρά + σημεῖον} *adj.* ①[dns] Acts 28:11, **figurehead**; ①[dns] LXX, 3 Macc 2:29, **symbol**

παρα**σκευάζω** {παρά + σκεῦος} ❸ Acts 10:10; 1 Cor 14:8, **to prepare**; 2 Cor 9:2, 3, **to be anxious to participate**[BEC]; (15x LXX; 5x Jer) 1 Sam 24:4 (24:3), **to make oneself ready**, i.e., **to empty the bowels**[BrDAG]; Prov 15:18, **to stir up**; Plato *Ap.* 39d, **to make himself** *the best*

παρα**σκευή, ῆς, ἡ**$_{1\eta}$ {παρά + σκεῦος} ❻ Matt 27:62 = Mark 15:42 = Luke 23:54 = John 19:14, 31, 42, **day of Preparation** (ESV); ❸ LXX, Jdt 2:17; 4:5; 2 Macc 15:12

παρα**τείνω** ①[iai3s] Acts 20:7, **to extend**; ❼ LXX, Ezek 27:13, **to stretch out**

παρα**τηρέω**[con] ❻ Mark 3:2 = Luke 6:7, **to watch**; 14:1; 20:20, **to watch** *closely*[ZEC]; Acts 9:24, **to stand guard**[ZEC]; Gal 4:10, **to observe**; ❷ LXX, Ps 36:12 (37:12), **to scheme**

παρα**τήρησις, εως, ἡ**$_3$ {παρά + τηρέω} ①[gfs] Luke 17:20, **something observable**[EGG]; Polyb. *Hist.* 16.22.8, **to observe** *with ill intent*[BrDAG]

παρα**τίθημι** (19x; 9x LA) Matt 13:24, 31, **to place before**, *teaching*; Mark 6:41 = Luke 9:16, **to set before**, *feeding*; Luke 12:48, **to entrust**; (37x LXX) Gen 18:8; Deut 4:44

παρα**τυγχάνω** ①[pap.amp] Acts17:17, **those who happened to be there**[ZEC]

παρ**αυτίκα** {παρά + αὐτός} *temp. adv.* ① 2 Cor 4:17, **momentary**[BEC]; ❷ LXX, Ps 69:4 (70:3), **immediately**; Aeschl. *Suppl.* 767, **on the spur of the moment**[BrDAG]

παρα**φέρω** ❹ Mark 14:36 = Luke 22:42, **to remove**; Heb 13:9; Jude 12, *mid.*, **to be carried away**; ❸ LXX, 1 Sam 21:14 (21:13), **to gesture madly**; Hp. *Prorrh.*1.21, **to go crazy**

παρα**φρονέω**[con] {παρά + φρήν} ①[pap.nms] 2 Cor 11:23, **to be out of one's mind**[BEC]; ①[pap.ams] LXX, Zech 7:11, **to turn his back** *in foolishness*[BrDAG]

παρα**φρονία, ας, ἡ**$_{1\alpha}$ {παρά + φρήν} ①[ams] 2 Pet 2:16, **madness**

παρα**χειμάζω** {παρά + χιών} ❹ Acts 27:12; 28:11; 1 Cor 16:6; Titus 3:12, **to winter**

παρα**χειμασία, ας, ἡ**$_{1\alpha}$ {παρά + χιών} ①[afs] Acts 27:12, **wintering**

παρα**χρῆμα** {παρά + χράομαι} *temp. adv.* (18x; 16x LA) Matt 21:19, 20, **at once**; Luke 1:64–22:60;[10x] Acts 3:7–16:33,[6x] **immediately, at that moment**; (17x LXX) Num 6:9

πάρδαλις, εως, ἡ$_3$ ①^{dfs} Rev 13:2, **leopard**

παρ**εδρεύω** {παρά + ἕζομαι} ①$^{pap.nmp}$ 1 Cor 9:13, **to officiate** *at the altar*[NIGTC]; ❷^{pai3s} LXX, Prov 1:21; 8:3, **to sit beside**

πάρ**ειμι** {παρά + εἰμί} (24x) Matt 26:50; Luke 13:1; 2 Cor 10:2, **to be present**; Acts 10:33, **to be here**; Heb 13:5, *ptc.*, **with what one has**; 2 Pet 1:9, *whoever does not* **have** *them*; Hom. *Od.* 1.140, **disposable goods**; Rev 17:8, *the beast* **is to come**; (59x LXX; 20x 1–4 Macc, 8x Wis)

παρ**εισάγω** {παρά + εἰς + ἄγω} ①^{fai3p} 2 Pet 2:1, **to bring in**, **introduce** (*not necessarily by stealth*)[BEC]; Polyb. *Hist.* 2.7.8, **to introduce furtively**

παρ**είσακτος, ον**$_{2.2}$ {παρά + εἰς + ἄγω} *adj.* ①^{amp} Gal 2:4, *false siblings* **who snuck in**[KeenG]

παρ**εισδύνω** ①^{aai3p} Jude 4, **to weasel one's way in**[BEC]

παρεισενέγκαντες → **παρεισφέρω**, *aor. act. ptc. nmp*, 2 Pet 1:5, **do one's best to**

παρ**εισέρχομαι** {παρά + εἰς + ἔρχομαι} ❷ Rom 5:20; Gal 2:4, **to enter**

παρ**εισφέρω** ①$^{aap.nmp}$ 2 Pet 1:5, *idiom.* **do one's best to**[BHGNT]

παρ**εκτός** {παρά + ἐκ} ❸ *impr. prep.*, Matt 5:32; Acts 26:29, **except**; *adv.* 2 Cor 11:28, χωρὶς τῶν **παρεκτός**, *apart from* **other things**[BEC]

παρ**εμβάλλω** {παρά + ἐν + βάλλω} ①^{fai3p} Luke 19:43, *milit.*, **to set up** *siege works*; (186x LXX; 81x Num) 2 Kgs 25:1, **to lay siege**; Ps 33:8 (35:7), *angel of the Lord* **encamps**

παρ**εμβολή, ῆς, ἡ**$_{1η}$ {παρά + ἐν + βάλλω} (10x; 6x Acts) Acts 23:16, **barracks**; Heb 11:34, *to put* **armies** *to flight*; Rev 20:9, **camp**; (300x LXX; 64x 1 Macc, 51x Num), *mostly milit.*, **encampment**, **company**, **army**; Gen 32:2; Polyb. *Hist.* 11.32.6, **battle line**

παρ**ενοχλέω**^{con} {παρά + ἐν + ὄχλος} ①^{painf} Acts 15:19, **to cause trouble**; Judg 14:17, **to nag**; (14x LXX) Job 16:3, **to provoke**

παρ**επίδημος, ου, ὁ**$_2$ {παρά + ἐπί + δῆμος} ❸ Heb 11:13; 1 Pet 1:1; 2:11, **foreigners**, **exiles**; ❷ LXX, Gen 23:4; Ps 38:13 (39:12)

παρ**έρχομαι** (29x; 23x Syn) Matt 24:34 = Mark 13:30 = Luke 21:32; 12:37, **to come**; Mark 6:48[*CMG* 226–27!]; Acts 16:8, **to pass by**; 2 Cor 5:17; Jas 1:10; 1 Pet 4:3; 2 Pet 3:10, **to pass away**; (148x LXX; 15x Deut, 11x Isa) *usu.* **to pass by**, Exod 33:19, 22[2x]

πάρ**εσις, εως, ἡ**$_3$ {παρά + ἵημι} ①^{afs} Rom 3:25, **dismissal**[ZEC]

παρ**έχω** (16x; 9x LA) Matt 26:10 = Mark 14:6, **to trouble**; Luke 6:29, **to offer**; Acts 16:16, **to bring**; Titus 2:7, **to show**; Gal 6:17, κόπους . . . **παρεχέτω**, **to make further trouble**[KeenG]; Col 4:1; 1 Tim 6:17, **to provide**; (15x LXX) Job 34:29, **to maintain**

παρ**ηγορία, ας, ἡ**$_{1α}$ {παρά + ἄγω} ①^{nfs} Col 4:11, **comfort**; ❷ LXX, 4 Macc 6:1

παρθενία, ας, ἡ$_{1α}$ {παρθένος} ①^{gfs} Luke 2:36, **marriage**[ZEC]; (11x LXX) Deut 22:14, 17,[2x] 20, **evidence of virginity**

παρθένος, ου, ἡ$_{2όδός}$ (15x; 6x 1 Cor 7) Matt 1:23; Luke 1:27, **virgin**; Matt 25:1, **young women**[ZEC]; Acts 21:9, **unmarried daughters**; 1 Cor 7:25, **those not yet married** (*m or f*); 7:28, **a woman not yet married**; 7:34, **a woman never married**; 7:36, 38, **betrothed**; 7:37, **virginity**[NIGTC!]; 2 Cor 11:2, *pure* **virgin**; Rev 14:4, *metaph.* **virgin**[NIGTC]; (64x LXX; 7x Gen:Jer:Lam) Gen 24:23; Isa 7:14, **unmarried virgin**; Jer 2:32; Joel 1:8, **bride**

Πάρθοι, ων, οἱ$_2$ ①^{nmp} Acts 2:9, **Parthians**

παρ**ίημι** {παρά + ἵημι} ❷ Luke 11:42, **to neglect**; *pass.*, Heb 12:12, *adj. ptc.*, **weakened** *hands*; (20x LXX; 5x Sir) *pass.*, 2 Sam 4:1, **to be dismayed** παρ**ίστημι** {παρά + ἵστημι} (41x; 13x Acts) Matt 26:53, **to send**; Mark 4:29, **to arrive**; Acts 1:10, **to stand nearby**; Rom 14:10, **who stands** *before God*; Eph 5:27 = Col 1:22, **to present**; Acts 23:33, **to provide**; 1 Cor 8:8, **will not bring us** *to God's judgment*[NIGTC]; (90x LXX; 8x 1 Kgs)

Παρμενᾶς, ᾶ, ὁ$_3$ ①[ams] Acts 6:5, **Parmenas**

πάρ**οδος, ου, ἡ**$_{2ὁδός}$ ①[dfs] 1 Cor 16:7, *idiom.* ἄρτι ἐν **παρόδῳ**, **just in passing**[NIGTC]; ❽ LXX, Gen 38:14, **road**; Xen. *An.* 4.7.4, **mountain pass**

παρ**οικέω**[con] {παρά + οἶκος} ❷ Luke 24:18, μόνος **παροικεῖς**, **Are you the only visitor?**; Heb 11:9, **to sojourn**; (64x LXX; 14x Gen), *usu. alien residency*, Gen 35:27, **they sojourned**

παρ**οικία, ας, ἡ**$_{1α}$ {παρά + οἶκος} ❷ Acts 13:17, **sojourner**; 1 Pet 1:17, **resident foreigner**[Keen1P]; (20x LXX; 5x Pss) Ps 33:5 (34:4), **terror** (LEB); Ps 119:5 (120:5), **alien**

πάρ**οικος, ου, ὁ**$_2$ ❹ Acts 7:6, 29; Eph 2:19; 1 Pet 2:11, **sojourner**, **alien**; (32x LXX; 8x Lev)

παρ**οιμία, ας, ἡ**$_{1α}$ ❺ John 10:6; 16:25[2x]; 2 Pet 2:22, **figure of speech**, **proverb**; ❼ (5x Sir) LXX, Prov 1:1, **Παροιμίαι** Σολωμῶντος, **The Proverbs of Solomon**; 26:7, **proverb**

παρ**οιμιάζω** {παρά + οἶμος} ①[iai3s] LXX, **to recount a proverb**

πάρ**οινος, ου, ὁ**$_2$ ❷[ams] 1 Tim 3:3[ABC]; Titus 1:7, **drunkard**

παρ**οίχομαι** ①[pfmp.dfp] Acts 14:16, *in* **past** *generations*

παρ**ομοιάζω** {παρά + ὁμός} ①[pai2p] Matt 23:27, **to resemble**

παρ**όμοιος, ον**$_{2.2}$ {παρά + ὁμός} *adj.* ①[anp] Mark 7:13, **like**, **similar**

παρ**οξύνω** {παρά + ὀξύς} ❷ *pass.*, Acts 17:16, **to be provoked to anger**; 1 Cor 13:5, **to become exasperated into resentment**[NIGTC]; (52x LXX) Isa 63:10, **to grieve** *his holy spirit*

παρ**οξυσμός, οῦ, ὁ**$_2$ {παρά + ὀξύς} ❷ *neg.*, Acts 15:39, *pred. nom.*, *they had such a* **sharp disagreement**[ZEC]; *pos.*, Heb 10:24, εἰς **παροξυσμόν**, εἰς + *acc.* = *purp. cl.*, **to stimulate** *one another to good works*[NIGTC]; ❷ LXX, *neg.*, Deut 29:28, **fury**; Jer 39:37, **indignation**

παρ**οργίζω** {παρά + ὀργή} ❷ Rom 10:19; Eph 6:4, **to provoke to anger**; (57x LXX; 16x 1–2 Kgs)

παρ**οργισμός, οῦ, ὁ**$_2$ {παρά + ὀργή} ①[dms] Eph 4:26, **anger**, **wrath**; ❼ LXX, Neh 9:18, **blasphemy**; Jer 21:5, *great* **wrath**

παρ**οτρύνω** ①[aai3p] Acts 13:50, **to incite**

παρ**ουσία, ας, ἡ**$_{1α}$ {παρά + εἰμί} (24x) Matt 24:3; 1 Cor 15:23; 1 Thess 2:19; 2 Pet 3:12, **coming** *of the Lord*; 2 Cor 7:6 **arrival** (*of coworkers*); 2 Cor 10:10, Phil 2:12 *physical* **presence**; 2 Thess 2:8, **coming** *of the lawless one*; ❹ LXX, Jdt 10:18, **arrival**

παρ**οψίς, ίδος, ἡ**$_3$ {παρά + ὀψάριον} ①[gfs] Matt 23:35, **plate**, **dish**[BHGNT]

παρ**ρησία, ας, ἡ**$_{1α}$ {παρά + ῥῆμα} (31x; 9x John) Mark 8:32, **παρρησίᾳ** τὸν λόγον **plainly**; Col 2:15, ἐν **παρρησίᾳ**, **public**, **publicly**; Heb 4:16, **boldness**; 2 Cor 7:4, **openness**; (12x LXX) 1 Macc 4:18, **boldness**

παρ**ρησιάζομαι** {παρά + ῥῆμα} ❾ (7x Acts) 1 Thess 2:2, **to speak boldy**; Acts 26:26, **to speak openly**; ❺ LXX, Sir 6:11, **they brag openly**

παρῳχημέναις → παρ**οίχομαι**, *pf. mid. ptc. dfp*, Acts 14:16, **in past generations**

πᾶς, πᾶσα, πᾶν$_{3.1.3}$ *adj.* (1,243x; 329x LA, 129x Matt) Matt 4:23, **each**, **every**; 1 Cor 1:2, **whole**, **entire**, **all**; Rom 3:23, 1 Cor 6:12[3x], **all**; Matt 17:11, **all things**; Rom 3:4, **everyone** (6,396x LXX; 1,599x Pent, 926x MajP, 340x Pss)

πάσχα, τό$_3$ *indecl.* (29x; 10x John) Matt 26:2 = Mark 14:1 = Luke 22:1 = John 2:13 = Acts 12:4, **Passover**; 1 Cor 5:7, *Christ, our* **paschal lamb**; (43x LXX; 14x 1 Esd, 10x Num)

πάσχω (42x; 12x 1 Pet, 11x LA) Matt 16:21 = Mark 8:31 = Luke 9:21; Heb 5:8, **to suffer** = *Jesus's Passion* (*synecdoche*); Luke 13:2, *because* **they suffered** *these things*; Acts 28:5; 1 Pet 2:19–23,[4x] **to suffer**; Phil 1:29; 2 Tim 1:12; Rev 2:10, **to suffer** *persecution*; Heb 13:12, **to suffer** (*crucifixion*); (19x LXX) Esth 9:26 (*see Luke 13:2*)

Πάταρα, ων, τά$_2$ ①[anp] Acts 21:1, **Patara**

πατάσσω (10x) Matt 26:31 = Mark 14:27; Luke 22:49; Rev 11:6, **to strike**; Acts 12:7, **to tap**; (404x LXX; 74x 1–2 Sam, 67x 1–2 Kgs) Exod 3:20–32:35,[22x] **to strike** *down*

πατέω[con] ❺ Luke 10:19; 21:24; Rev 11:2; 19:15, **to tread, to trample**; (18x LXX; 7x Isa)

πατήρ, πατρός, ὁ$_3$ (413x; 137x Syn, 136x John)[DJG2 316] (264x God, 150x man) Matt 6:9, *our* **Father**; 10:21, **father**; (1,738x LXX; 218x Gen)

Πάτμος, ου, ὁ$_2$ ① Rev 1:9, **Patmos**[LGCb 619]

πατριά, ᾶς, ἡ$_{1α}$ {πατήρ} ❸ Luke 2:4; Acts 3:25; Eph 3:15, **family**; (172x LXX; 55x 1 Chr)

πατριάρχης, ης, ἡ$_{1η}$ {πατήρ + ἄρχω} ❹ Acts 2:29; 7:8, 9; Heb 7:4, **patriarch**; ❼ LXX

πατρικός, ή, όν$_{2.1.2}$ {πατήρ} *adj.* ①[gmp] Gal 1:14, **ancestral**; (13x LXX; 4x 1 Chr)

πατρίς, ίδος, ἡ$_3$ {πατήρ} ❽ Matt 13:57 = Mark 6:4 = Luke 4:24 = John 4:44; Heb 11:14, **country**, **homeland**; (24x LXX; 10x 2 Macc) 1 Chr 5:7, **family**

Πατροβᾶς, ᾶ, ὁ$_{1α}$ {πατήρ} ①[ams] Rom 16:14, **Patrobas**

πατρολῴας, ου, ὁ$_2$ {πατήρ + ἀλοάω} ①[dmp] 1 Tim 1:9, **father-murderer**; *cf.* Aristoph. *Nub.* 1327, **parricide**

πατροπαράδοτος, ον$_{2.2}$ {πατήρ + παρά + δίδωμι} *adj.* ①[gms] 1 Pet 1:18, **passed down from your ancestors**[Keen1P]

πατρῷος, α, ον$_{2.1.2}$ {πατήρ} *adj.* ❸ Acts 22:3; 24:14; 28:17, **ancestral**; (11x LXX; 9x 2–4 Macc)

Παῦλος, ου, ὁ$_2$ (158x; 128x Acts) *the apostle* **Paul**; *only one other Paul*, Acts 13:7, *Sergius* **Paulus**, Σεργίῳ **Παύλῳ**

παύω (15x; 9x LA) Luke 5:4; 1 Cor 13:8, **to stop**; 1 Pet 3:10, **to keep** *one's tongue from evil*; (77x LXX; 15x Isa, 12x Jer), Isa 1:16, **to stop** *doing evil*

Πάφος, ου, ἡ$_{2ὁδός}$ ❷ Acts 13:6, 13, **Paphos**

παχύνω {παχύς} ❷[api3s] *pass.*, Matt 13:15; Acts 28:27, **to grow thick, dull**; ❻ LXX, *act.*, 2 Sam 22:12, **to grow thick**; Isa 6:10, *pass.*, **to become insensitive, obtuse, stupid**[BrDAG]

πέδη, ης, ἡ$_{1η}$ {πούς} ❸ Mark 5:4[2x] = Luke 8:29, **fetter**; (15x LXX) Judg 16:21

πεδινός, ή, όν$_{2.1.2}$ {πούς} *adj.* ①[gms] Luke 6:17, **level**; (22x LXX); Josh 9:1, **lowland**

πεζεύω {πούς} ①[painf] Acts 20:13, **to travel overland**

πεζῇ {πεζεύω} *adv.* ❷ Matt 14:13; Mark 6:33, **by foot**

πειθαρχέω[con] {πείθω + ἄρχω} ❹ Acts 5:29, 32; Titus 3:1 **to obey**; Acts 27:21, **to follow advice**; ❸ LXX, Dan 7:27, **to obey**

πειθός, ή, όν$_{2.1.2}$ {πείθω} *adj.* ①[dmp] 1 Cor 2:4, **enticing**[NIGTC]

πείθω (52x; 17x Acts) *act.*, Matt 27:20, **to persuade**; 2 Cor 1:9, **to trust**; Jas 3:3, **to obey**; Acts 12:20, **to win over**; *pass.*, Acts 26:26, **to be certain**; Rom 8:38, **to be convinced**; Phlm 21, **to be confident**; (175x LXX; 36x Isa, 19x Jer)

πεινάω[con] (23x; 9x Matt) Matt 4:2 = Luke 4:2; John 6:35, **to hunger**; (49x LXX; 15x Isa)

πεῖρα, ας, ἡ$_{1\alpha}$ ❷[afs] Heb 11:29, **test, experiment**[NIGTC]; 11:36, **experience**; ❻ LXX, Deut 28:56, **attempt**; Wis 18:20, **experience**

πειράζω {πεῖρα} (38x; 19x GA) Matt 4:1 = Luke 4:2; 1 Cor 7:5, **to tempt**; Acts 9:26, **to attempt**; 2 Cor 13:5, **to test yourself**[BEC]; 1 Thess 3:5,[2x] **the tempter tempted** *you*; Heb 4:14; Jas 1:13–14[4x]; Rev 2:10, *pass.*, **to be tempted, tested**; (48x LXX; 7x Wis)

πειρασμός, οῦ, ὁ$_2$ {πεῖρα} (21x; 6x Luke) Matt 6:13; 1 Tim 6:9, **temptation**; Acts 20:19; Jas 1:2; Rev 3:10, **trial**; 1 Cor 10:13,[2x] **testing**; (14x LXX; 6x Sir, 5x Deut)

πειράω[con] {πεῖρα} ①[imi3p] Acts 26:21, **to attempt** *to kill*; ❼ LXX, Judg 6:29

πεισμονή, ῆς, ἡ$_{1\eta}$ {πείθω} ①[nfs] Gal 5:8, **contrary persuasion**[KeenG]

πέλαγος, ους, τό$_3$ ❷ Matt 18:6, **depth** *of the sea*; Acts 27:5, **sea**; ❷ LXX, 2 Macc 5:21; 4 Macc 7:1

πέμπτος, η, ον$_{2.1.2}$ {πέντε} *adj.* ❹ Rev 6:9; 21:20, **fifth**; (61x LXX; 10x 1 Chr)

πέμπω (79x; 32x John) Rom 8:3, **to send** *his Son*; 2 Thess 2:11, **to send** *a powerful delusion*; *with* **ἀποστέλλω**,[28x] John 20:21, *the Father* **ἀ.** *me, I* **π.** *you*; (22x LXX; 11x 2 Macc)

πένης, ητος, ὁ$_3$ {πόνος} ①[dmp] 2 Cor 9:9, **day-laborer, poor person**; (78x LXX; 33x Pss)

πενθερά, ᾶς, ἡ$_{1\alpha}$ {πενθερός} ❻ Matt 8:14 = Mark 1:30 = Luke 4:38, *Simon Peter's* **mother-in law**; (13x LXX; 11x Ruth!)

πενθερός, οῦ, ὁ$_2$ ①[nms] John 18:13, **father-in-law**; (10x LXX) Gen 38:13

πενθέω[con] {πένθος} (10x) Matt 5:4; Mark 16:10; Rev 18:19, **to mourn**; (64x LXX; 12x Isa) Gen 50:3, **to weep**; Amos 1:2; Isa 16:8, **to wither**; Isa 66:10; Jer 4:28, **to mourn**

πένθος, ους, τό$_3$ ❺ Jas 4:9; Rev 18:7,[2x] 8; 21:4, **mourning** (53x LXX; 7x Gen) Gen 27:41

πενιχρός, ά, όν$_{2.1.2}$ {πόνος} *adj.* ①[afs] Luke 21:2, **poor**; ❸ LXX, Exod 22:25; Prov 28:15; 29:17, **poor**

πεντάκις {πέντε} *adv.* ① 2 Cor 11:24, **five times**; ① LXX, 2 Kgs 13:19

πεντακισχίλιοι, αι, α$_{2.1.2}$ {πέντε + χίλιοι} *adj.* ❻ Matt 14:21 = Mark 6:44 = Luke 9:14 = John 6:10; Matt 16:19 = Mark 8:19, **five thousand**; (19x LXX) 1 Chr 29:7; 2 Chr 35:9

πεντακόσιοι, αι, α$_{2.1.2}$ {πέντε + ἑκατόν} *adj.* ❷ Luke 7:42; 1 Cor 15:6, **five hundred**; (63x LXX; 19x Num)

πέντε *indecl. adj.* (38x; 12x Matt) Matt 14:17; Acts 20:6, **five**; (271x LXX; 50x Num, 36x Ezek)

πεντεκαιδέκατος, η, ον$_{2.1.2}$ *adj.* ①[dns] {πέντε + καί + δέκα} Luke 3:1, **fifteenth**; (22x LXX)

πεντήκοντα$_3$ {πέντε} *indecl. adj.* ❼ Mark 6:40 = Luke 9:14, **fifty**; John 21:11, *one hundred and* **fifty**-*three*; (163x LXX; 27x Num, 18x 2 Kgs) Gen 6:15; Exod 26:5[2x]

πεντηκοστή, ῆς, ἡ$_{1\eta}$ {πέντε} ❸ Acts 2:1; 20:16; 1 Cor 16:8, **Pentecost**

πεπιεσμένον → **πιέζω**, *pf mid. ptc. ans*, Luke 6:38, **pressed down**

πεποίθησις, εως, ἡ$_3$ {πείθω} ❻ (4x 2 Cor) 2 Cor 1:15; 3:4; 8:22; 10:2, **bold confidence**[BEC]; Eph 3:12; Phil 3:4, **confidence**; ① LXX, 2 Kgs 18:19

πεπόνθασιν → **πάσχω**, *pf act. ind. 3p*, Luke 13:2; Esth 9:26, **suffered** *these things*

πεπραγμένον → **πράσσω**, *pf mid. ptc. nns*, Luke 23:15, **he has done** *nothing*

πέπωκαν → **πίνω**, *pf. act. ind. 3p*, Rev 18:3, *the nations* **have drunk**

περαιτέρω {πέραν} *comp. adv.* ① Acts 19:39, **further**

πέραν (23x; 15x Syn, 8x John, all in Gs) Matt 8:18 = Mark 4:35 = Luke 8:22; John 6:22, (10x) *to the* **other side**; Matt 4:15; 19:1; Mark 10:1 (8x) **beyond** *the Jordan*; (99x LXX; 26x Josh)

πέρας {πέραν} ❹ Matt 12:42 = Luke 11:31; Rom 10:18 = Ps 19:5; *spatial*, **ends** *of the earth*; Heb 6:16, *log.*, **end** *of a dispute*; (40x LXX; 12x Pss)

Πέργαμος, ου, ἡ$_{2>}$ ❷ Rev 1:11; 2:12, **Pergamum**

Πέργη, ης, ἡ ❸ Acts 13:13, 14; 14:25, **Perga**

περί {πέριξ} *prep.* (333x; 117x LA, 67x John) Ⓐ (294x) ***w/ gen.***, 1 Thess 4:13; 1 John 2:27, **about**, **concerning**; Ⓑ (39x) ***w/ acc.***, Mark 1:6, **around**; Jude 7, **surrounding**; Ⓒ (12x LA) **τὰ περί**, Luke 24:19; *the things* **concerning**; Ⓓ **περί** ***w/ cmpds.***, **around**, **about**[PrTh]; (811x LXX)

περι**άγω** ❻ Matt 4:23; Acts 13:11, **go around**, **about**; 1 Cor 9:5, **to go through life with**[NIGTC]; ❼ LXX, Isa 28:27, **to roll over**; Ezek 37:2, **to lead around**

περι**αιρέω**[con] ❺ Acts 27:20, **to give up**; 27:40, **to cast off** *the anchors*; 28:13, **to weigh anchor**[ZEC]; 2 Cor 3:16, **to remove**; Heb 10:11, **to take away**; (60x LXX; 12x Lev)

περι**άπτω** ①[aap.gmp] Luke 22:55, **to kindle** *a fire*; ①[aai3p] LXX, 3 Macc 3:7, **they attached** (NETS)

περι**αστράπτω** {περί + ἀστραπή} ❷ Acts 9:3; 22:6, **to flash around**; ①[pap.nmp] 4 Macc 4:10, **with lightning flashing** *from their weapons*

περι**βάλλω** (23x; 12x Rev) Matt 6:29 = Luke 12:27, **to clothe**; Luke 23:11 = John 19:2, **to dress**; Acts 12:8, **to wrap**; Rev 3:5; 4:4,[NIGTC] **to be dressed** *in white garments*[7x]; (69x LXX)

περι**βλέπω** ❼ (6x Mark) (5x, **περιβλεψάμενος**[amp.nms]) Mark 3:34; 5:32; 9:8; 10:23; Luke 6:10 = Mark 3:5, **to look around**; ❾ LXX, 1 Kgs 21:40 (20:40), **was busy** (HCSB)

περι**βόλαιον, ου, τό**$_2$ {περί + βάλλω} ❷ 1 Cor 11:15, **covering**; Heb 1:12, **cloak**; (10x LXX) Job 26:6, *Abaddon has no* **covering**; Eur. *H.F.* 549, **wrapping**, *flesh around the body*

περι**δέω**[con] ①[pfmi3s] John 11:44, **was wrapped**; ①[aai3s] LXX, Job 12:18, **to fasten**, **bind**; Plut. *Praec.* 825e, **to bind** *the hands with boxing gloves*

περιέδραμον → **περιτρέχω**, *aor. act. ind. 3p*, Mark 6:55, **to run throughout**

περιενέγκασαν → **περιφέρω**, *aor. act. ptc. ams*, 2 Macc 7:27, **carried** *you in the womb*

περι**εργάζομαι** {περί + ἔργον} ①[pmp.amp] 2 Thess 3:11, *they are not busy, but* **busybodies**; ①[pmimp2s] LXX, Sir 3:23, **to meddle**

περί**εργος, ου, ὁ**$_2$ {περί + ἔργον} ❷ Acts 19:19, **magic**[Keen3]; 1 Tim 5:13, **busybodies**[PPE]

περι**έρχομαι** ❸ Acts 19:13, **itinerant**; 1 Tim 5:13, **περιερχόμεναι** τὰς οἰκίας, **to go around** *from house to house* (*gossipers*); Heb 11:37, **to wander about**; (14x LXX; 8x Josh)

περι**έχω** ❷ Luke 5:9, **to seize**; 1 Pet 2:6, **to trust** *in Scripture*[Keen1P]; (34x LXX) 1 Kgs 6:30

περι**ζώννυμι** ❻ Luke 12:35; 17:8, **to make oneself ready**; Eph 6:14, **by strapping** *truth*; Rev 1:13; 15:6, **to clothe**; (περιζωννύω, 40x LXX), Exod 12:11, **to gird** *one's loins*

περί**θεσις, εως, ἡ**$_3$ {περί + τίθημι} ①[gfs] 1 Pet 3:3, **the donning** *of gold*[Keen1P]

περι**ΐστημι** ❹ John 11:42; Acts 25:7, **to stand around**; *mid.*, 2 Tim 2:16; Titus 3:9, **to avoid**, **shun**; ❼ LXX, Josh 6:3, **to march around**

περι**κάθαρμα, ατος, τό**$_3$ {περί + καθαρός} ①[nnp] 1 Cor 4:13, **scum**[NIGTC]; ①[nns] LXX, Prov 21:18, **a lawless person** (NETS)

περι**καλύπτω** ❸ Mark 14:65 = Luke 22:64, **to blindfold**; Heb 9:4, **to overlay**, **cover**; ❹ LXX, 1 Kgs 7:5 (7:17), **to cover** *w/ latticework*

περί**κειμαι** ❺ Acts 28:20, *mid.*, **to wear**; Heb 5:2, *mid.*, **is subject** *to weakness*; Heb 12:1,

we are surrounded; Mark 9:42 = Luke 17:2; *pass.*, **to be bound**; **is subject to**; ❸ LXX, 4 Macc 12:2, *pass.*, **to be bound** *in fetters*

περι**κεφαλαία, ας, ἡ**$_{1α}$ {περί + κεφαλή} ❷[afs] Eph 6:17; 1 Thess 5:8, *fig.*, **helmet**; (10x LXX; 3x 1 Sam:Ezek) 1 Sam 17:5, 38, 49, *lit.*, **helmet**

περι**κρατής, ές**$_{3.3}$ {περί + κεράννυμι} *adj.* ①[nmp] Acts 27:16, **under control**

περι**κρύβω** {περί + κρύπτω} ①[iai3s] Luke 1:24, **περιέκρυβεν** ἑαυτήν *kept herself* **in seclusion**[EGG]

περι**κυκλόω**[con] ①[fai3p] Luke 19:43, **to surround**; (16x LXX) Ps 17:6 (18:5), **to entangle**

περι**λάμπω** ❷ Luke 2:9; Acts 26:13, **to shine around**

περι**λείπομαι** {περί + λείπω} ❷[pmp.nmp] 1 Thess 4:15, 17, **to remain**; ❹ LXX

περί**λυπος, ον**$_{2.2}$ *adj.* ❺ Matt 26:38 = Mark 14:34, **deeply grieved**[BHGNT]; Luke 18:23, 24, **very sad**; ❼ LXX, Dan 2:12, **furious rage**; Aristot. *E.N.* 1124a 16, **great anguish**

περι**μένω** ①[painf] Acts 1:4, **to wait**; ❷ LXX, Gen 49:18; Wis 8:12

πέριξ {περί} *adv.* ① Acts 5:16, **around**

περι**οικέω**[con] {περί + ἶκος} ①[pap.amp] Luke 1:65, **the neighbors**

περί**οικος, ου, ὁ**$_{2}$ ①[nmp] Luke 1:58, **neighbor**; ❺ LXX, Gen 19:25, **inhabitant**

περι**ούσιος, ον**$_{2.2}$ {περί + εἰμί} *adj.* ① Titus 2:14, λαὸν **περιούσιον**,[ams] *people* **for his own possession**[NIGTC]; ❺ LXX, λαὸς **περιούσιος**, Exod 19:5; 23:22; Deut 7:6; 14:2

περι**οχή, ῆς, ἡ**$_{1η}$ {περί + ἔχω} ①[nfs] Acts 8:32, *Scripture* **passage**; (25x LXX) 1 Sam 22:4, **enclosure**, **stronghold**; 2 Kgs 25:2, *under* **siege**

περι**πατέω**[con] (95x; 17x John, 8x Acts:Eph) 🅐 ***lit.***, Matt 14:25 = Mark 6:48, 49 = John 6:19; Acts 14:8, **to walk**; John 11:9–10, **to live** *in faith*; 🅑 ***fig.***, Rom 6:4; 2 Cor 4:2, **to behave**; Gal 5:16, **to live**; Eph 2:2, 10, **to live/walk**; 2:10 → ***expanded illustrations of how* περιπατέω *is applied***, 4:1, 17; 5:2, 8, 15; 🅒 ***lit. and fig.***, 1 Pet 5:8, **prowling around**; Rev 2:1, *Jesus* **walks** *among the lampstands*; (34x LXX; 5x Sir)

περι**πείρω** ①[aai3p] 1 Tim 6:10, **to pierce through, impale**[NIGTC]

περι**πίπτω** ❸ Luke 10:30; Jas 1:2, **to encounter**[NIGTC]; Acts 27:41, **to run aground**; ❾ LXX, 2 Sam 1:6, **to happen**

περι**ποιέω**[con] ❸ Luke 17:33, **to preserve**; Acts 20:28, **to acquire**; 1 Tim 3:13, **to gain** *for oneself*; (30x LXX) Judg 21:11, **to devote to destruction**

περι**ποίησις, εως, ἡ**$_{3}$ {περί + ποιέω} ❺ Eph 1:14; 1 Pet 2:9, **possession**; 1 Thess 5:9; 2 Thess 2:14, **to obtain**; Heb 10:39, **to preserve** *their souls*; ❸ LXX, Hag 2:9; Mal 3:17

περι**ρήξαντες** → περι**ρήγνυμι**, *aor. act. ptc. nmp*, Acts 16:22, **to strip off** *clothing*

περι**σπάω**[con] ①[imi3s] Luke 10:40, **to be distracted**; ❺ LXX, 2 Sam 6:6

περισσεία, ας, ἡ$_{1α}$ {περί} ❹ Rom 5:17; 2 Cor 8:2, **effusive**, **unreserved**[BEC]; 2 Cor 10:15, **tremendously**[BEC]; Jas 1:21, **abundance**; (LXX, 12x all in Eccl) 1:3, **profit**

περίσσευμα, ατος, τό$_{3}$ {περί} ❺ Matt 12:34 = Luke 6:45; 2 Cor 8:14,[2x] **oversupply**[BEC]; Mark 8:8, **leftover**; ①[gns] LXX, Eccl 2:15, **excess**

περισσεύω {περί} (39x; 13x 1–2 Cor) 🅐 Matt 5:20, *act.*, **to surpass**; 🅑 Matt 13:12, *pass.*, **to be given abundantly**; 🅒 Luke 15:17, *act.*, **to have more than enough**; 🅓 Matt 14:20 = Luke 9:17 = John 6:12, *act.*, **to be left over**; 🅔 1 Cor 8:8, *act.*, **to gain advantage**; 🅕 2 Cor 8:7,[2x] *act.*, **to excel**; 🅖 1 Cor 15:58, *act.*, **to abound more and more without**

measure[NIGTC!]; Ⓗ 2 Cor 1:5, *act.*, **to overflow**; 9:8, **to lavish**; 9:12, **broader effect**[BEC!]; ❼ LXX, 1 Sam 2:33, *all* **the increase** *in your house* (Tanakh)

περισσός, ή, όν$_{2.1.2}$ {περί} *adj.* (15x) Mark 12:33; Luke 12:4, **more**; 12:40, **greater**; John 10:10, **in abundance**; 1 Cor 12:23,[2x] 24, **greater**; 2 Cor 2:7, **overwhelming**; 9:1, **redundant**[BEC]; (19x LXX; 5x Eccl, 4x Ezek) Exod 10:5, **the surviving** *remnant* (Tanakh)

περισσότερος, ον$_{2.2}$ {περί} *adj.* ❼ Matt 11:9 = Luke 7:26, **more than**; 1 Cor 15:10, **harder than**; 2 Cor 10:8, **a bit more about**; Heb 6:17; 7:15, **all the more**

περισσοτέρως {περί} *adv.* (12x; 7x 2 Cor) 2 Cor 1:12, **especially**; 2:4, **very great** *love*; 7:13, **more**; Gal 1:14, *showing* **far more** *zeal*; Heb 2:1, **much closer** *attention*

περισσῶς {περί} *adv.* ❹ Matt 27:23 = Mark 15:14, **all the more**; Mark 10:26, **exceedingly**; Acts 26:11, **furiously**; ❷ LXX, Ps 30:24 (31:23), **abundantly** *repays*

περιστερά, ᾶς, ἡ$_{1α}$ (10x) Matt 3:16 = Mark 1:10 = Luke 3:22 = John 1:32, **dove** *at Jesus's baptism*; (36x LXX; 9x Lev, 8x Song), Gen 8:8–12,[5x] **dove** *from Noah's ark*

περι**τέμνω** {περί + τέμνω} (17x) Luke 1:59; Gal 5:2, *lit.*, **to circumcise**; Col 2:11, *fig.*, **to circumcise** *without hands*; (39x LXX) Jer 4:4, *fig.*, **to circumcise** *the foreskin of your heart*

περι**τίθημι** ❽ Matt 21:33 = Mark 12:1, **to put up** *a fence*; Matt 27:28 = Mark 15:17; Mark 15:36 = John 19:29, **to put on**; 1 Cor 12:23, **to invest**[NIGTC]; (52x LXX; 7x Job)

περι**τομή, ῆς, ἡ**$_{1η}$ {περί + τομός} (36x; 15x Rom) Acts 11:2; Titus 1:10, **circumcision** *party*; Rom 2:25–28,[5x] *lit.*, **circumcision**; 2:29, *fig.*, *heart* **circumcision**; Phil 3:3, *we are the* **circumcision**; ❹ LXX, Jer 11:16, *noise of (olive tree)* **being lopped**

περι**τρέπω** ①[pai3s] Acts 26:24, **to make go** *crazy*; ①[fai3s] LXX, Wis 5:23, **to overturn**

περι**τρέχω** ①[aai3p] Mark 6:55, **to run** *throughout the region*; ❷ LXX, Amos 8:12, **to roam**

περι**φέρω** ❸ Mark 6:55, **to bring**; 2 Cor 4:10; Eph 4:14, **to carry around, about**; ❹ LXX, Josh 24:33, **to be engulfed** (BrLXX); 2 Macc 15:30, **to bring**

περι**φρονέω**[con] {περί + φρήν} ①[paimp3s] Titus 2:15, **to disregard**; ❸ LXX, 4 Macc 6:9; 7:16; 14:1, **to despise**; Thuc. 1.25.4, **to watch with disdain**

περί**χωρος, ου, ἡ**$_{2όδός}$ {περί + χωρέω} ❾ (6x LA) Matt 3:5 = Mark 1:28; Acts 14:6, **surrounding region, country**; (22x LXX; 8x Neh) Gen 13:10, **country round about** *Jordan*

περί**ψημα, ατος, τό**$_{3}$ {περί + φρήν} ①[nns] 1 Cor 4:13, **the world's scum, the scrapings from everyone's shoes**[NIGTC]; ①[nns] LXX, Tob 5:19, **off-scouring** (LES)

περπερεύομαι {πέρπερος} ①[pmi3s] 1 Cor 13:4, **to boast, to brag**[NIGTC]

Περσίς, ίδος, ἡ$_{3}$ ①[afs] Rom 16:12, **Persis**

πέρυσι {πέραν} *adv.* ❷ 2 Cor 8:10; 9:2, **last year, a year ago**

πετεινόν, οῦ, τό$_{2}$ {πέτομαι} (14x; 10x Syn) Matt 6:26 = Luke 12:24; Jas 3:7; Rom 1:23, **bird**; ❾ LXX; 5x Sir

πέτομαι ❺ Rev 4:7; 8:13; 12:14; 14:6; 19:17, **to fly**; (13x LXX; 4x Isa) Job 9:26, **to swoop**

πέτρα, ας, ἡ$_{1}$ (15x; 5x Matt) Matt 7:24 = Luke 6:48, **rock**; Rom 9:33; 1 Pet 2:8, **rock** *of offense*; 1 Cor 10:4,[2x] *spiritual* **rock** *was Christ*; (101x LXX; 17x Isa) Isa 2:10, **rock**[Mot]

Πέτρος, ου, ὁ$_{2}$ (158x; 75x LA, 34x John) Matt 14:28, **Peter**; 16:18, **Peter** = *rock*; 16:23, **Peter** = *Satan*

πετρώδης, ες$_{3.3}$ *adj.* ❹ *subst.*, Matt 13:5 = Mark 4:5; Matt 13:20 = Mark 4:16, **rocky** *areas*[EGG]

πήγανον, ου, τό$_{2}$ ①[ans] Luke 11:42, **rue**, *a scented herb*

πηγή, ῆς, ἡ$_{1η}$ (11x; 5x Rev) Mark 5:29, **flow**; John 4:6,[2x] **well**; 4:14; Jas 3:11; Rev 7:17, **spring** *of water*; (96x LXX; 14x Prov, 13x Gen)

πήγνυμι ①[aai3s] Heb 8:2, **to pitch** *a tent*; (36x LXX; 5x Job) Gen 26:25

πηδάλιον, ου, τό$_{2}$ ❷ Acts 27:40; Jas 3:4, **rudder**

πηλίκος, η, ον$_{2.1.2}$ {ἡλικία} ❷ Gal 6:11, **large**; Heb 7:4, **great**; ❸ LXX, Zech 2:6[2x] **how long** *the width*, **how long** *the length*?; 4 Macc 15:22, **how great** *was the mother's torment*?

πηλός, οῦ, ὁ$_{2}$ ❻ John 9:6,[2x] 11, 14, 15, **mud**; Rom 9:21, **clay**; (31x LXX; 7x Job:Isa)

πήρα, ας, ἡ$_{1α}$ ❻ Matt 10:10 = Mark 6:8 = Luke 9:3, **bag**; *traveler's knapsack*; ❸ LXX

πῆχυς, εως, ὁ$_{3}$ ❹ Matt 6:27 = Luke 12:25; **arm, cubit**; John 21:8; Rev 21:17, **cubits**; (241x LXX; 96x Ezek, 38x Exod, 36x 1 Kgs)

πιάζω {πιέζω} (12x; 8x John 7:30–11:57) Acts 12:4; Rev 19:20, **to arrest**; John 21:3, 10, **to catch** *fish*; Acts 3:7, **to take** *by the hand*; ❷ LXX, Song 2:15, **to catch** *foxes*

πιέζω ①[pfmp.ans] Luke 6:38, **to press down**; ①[fai2s] LXX, Mic 6:15, **to tread** *grapes*; Hom. *Il.* 16.510, **to constrict** *a part of the body*

πιθανολογία, ας, ἡ$_{1α}$ {πείθω + λέγω} ①[dfs] Col 2:4, **speculative argument**[NIGTC]; Plato *Theaet.* 162c, **appealing arguments**; *distinguishes from* ἀπόδειξις, 162e, **compelling conclusion**

πικραίνω {πίκρος} ❹ Col 3:19, *pass.*, **to be harsh**; Rev 8:11; 10:9, 10, **to make bitter**; (12x LXX) Exod 16:20, **to be angry**

πικρία, ας, ἡ$_{1α}$ {πίκρος} ❹ Acts 8:23; Rom 3:14; Eph 4:31; Heb 12:15, **bitterness**; (27x LXX; 5x Job); Exod 15:23; Num 33:8, 9, **bitter**, **Marah** (Heb.)

πικρός, ά, όν$_{2.1.2}$ *adj.* ❷ Jas 3:11, 14, **bitter**; (36x LXX; 7x 4 Macc) Judg 18:25, **angry**

πικρῶς {πίκρος} *adv.* ❷ Matt 26:75 = Luke 22:62, **bitterly**; ❼ LXX, Isa 33:7, *weep* **bitterly**

Πιλᾶτος, ου, ὁ$_{2}$ (55x; 20x John) Matt 27:2–65[9x], **Pilate**, *the governor*

πίμπλημι {πληρόω} (24x; 22x LA) Matt 22:10; Luke 1:15, 41; Acts 5:17, **to fill**; Luke 1:23; 2:22, **to fulfill**; (116x LXX; 15x Prov, 14x Ezek)

πίμπρημι ①[ppinf] Acts 28:6, **to swell up**; Hom. *Il.* 1.481, **to swell** *the sail with wind*

πινακίδιον, ου, τό$_{2}$ {πίναξ} ①[ans] Luke 1:63, **a small writing tablet**

πίναξ, ακος, ὁ$_{3}$ ❺ Matt 14:8, 11 = Mark 6:25, 28, *John the Baptist's head on a* **platter**; Hom. *Od.* 12.67, **plank** *for building ships*

πίνω (73x; 20x LA, 14x 1 Cor) Ⓐ ***lit.***, Matt 6:25, 31; John 4:7; 1 Cor 11:22, **to drink**; Ⓑ ***fig.***, Mark 10:38–39,[3x] *the cup of crucifixion*; 1 Cor 11:25–29,[6x] *the cup of the new covenant*;[NIGTC] Rev 14:10, *the wine of God's wrath*; (270x LXX; 24x Isa, 23x 1 Kgs)

πιπράσκω ❾ *act.*, Matt 13:46; Acts 2:45, **to sell**; *pass.*, Rom 7:14, **to be sold** *into slavery under sin*; (32x LXX; 7x Lev) *pass.*, Lev 27:27, *if an unclean animal is not redeemed*, **it will be sold**[NIDNTT]

πίπτω (90x) Matt 2:11, **to kneel down**; 7:25, **to collapse**; 1 Cor 10:8, **to die**; Matt 26:39 = Mark 14:35, **he threw himself down**; 1 Cor 14:25, **to bow down**; Rev 7:16, **to strike down**; (390x LXX; 48x Ezek, 38x 1 Macc, 30x Isa)

Πισιδία, ας, ἡ$_{1α}$ ①[afs] Acts 14:24, **Pisidia**

Πισίδιος, α, ον$_{2.1.2}$ *adj.* ①[afs] Acts 13:14, **Pisidian**

πιστεύω (243x; 98x John) Ⓐ ***objective***, (45x; 36x John, **πιστεύω** εἰς) Matt 18:6 = Mark 9:4; John 1:12, **to believe** *in*; Ⓑ ***purposive***, (1x, **πιστεύω** . . . εἰς τὸ) Rom 15:13, **to believe** . . .

so that; Ⓒ ***credal formula***, (25x, 13x John, πιστεύω ὅτι) 1 Thess 4:14, **to believe** *that*; (81x LXX; 11x Sir, 8x Exod)

πιστικός, ή, όν$_{2.1.2}$ {πίστις} *adj.* ❷ Mark 14:3; John 12:3, **genuine**, **pure**

πίστις, εως, ἡ$_{3}$ (243x; 40x Rom, 32x Heb, 27x 1–2 Tim) 1 Cor 15:14; Gal 5:22, **faith**; Rom 3:22, **faith**[NIGTC!]; 2 Tim 3:8, *counterfeit* **faith**; (59x LXX) Deut 32:30, **faithfulness**

πιστός, ή, όν$_{2.1.2}$ {πείθω} *adj.* (67x; 11x 1 Tim, 8x Rev) Matt 24:45 = Luke 12:42; 1 Cor 1:9; Rev 19:11, **faithful**; Acts 10:45, **believers**; (69x LXX; 13x Sir, 10x Prov)

πιστόω[con] {πείθω} ①[api2s] 2 Tim 3:14, **to firmly believe**; (16x LXX) 2 Sam 7:16

πλανάω[con] {πλάνη} (39x) Matt 18:12–13,[3x] **to go astray**; Matt 22:29 = Mark 12:24, **to be wrong**; Rev 2:20, **to lead astray**; Jas 1:16, **to be deceived**; (119x LXX; 31x Isa)

πλάνη, ης, ἡ$_{1\eta}$ (10x) Matt 27:64, **deception**; Rom 1:27, **perversion**[NIGTC]; Eph 4:14, **deceit**; 2 Pet 2:18; Jude 11, **error**; ❻ LXX, Prov 14:8, **adverse**; Eur. *I.T.* 417, **vagabond**

πλανήτης, ου, ὁ$_{1>}$ {πλάνη} ①[nmp] Jude 13, **wandering**; ①[nmp] LXX, Hos 9:17, **wanderers**; Plato *Tim.* 38, **planets**

πλάνος, ον$_{2.2}$ {πλάνη} *adj.* ❺ Matt 27:63; 2 Cor 6:8; 2 John 7,[2x] **deceiver**; ❷ LXX, Job 19:4

πλάξ, πλακός, ἡ$_{3}$ ❸ 2 Cor 3:3[2x]; Heb 9:4, **tablet**; (33x LXX; 16x Deut, 14x Exod) Exod 31:18–34:29; Deut 4:13–10:5, *Ten Commandments' narratives*

πλάσμα, ατος, τό$_{3}$ {πλάσσω} ① Rom 9:20, **what is molded**[EGG]; ❺ LXX, Job 40:19, **works** *of the Lord*

πλάσσω ❷ Rom 9:20, **to mold**; 1 Tim 2:13, **to form**; (52x LXX; 12x Isa, 10x Pss)

πλαστός, ή, όν$_{2.1.2}$ {πλάσσω} *adj.* ①[dmp] 2 Pet 2:3, **made-up** *stories*

πλατεῖα, ας$_{1\alpha}$ {πλατύς} ❾ Matt 6:5; Acts 5:15; Rev 11:8, **street**; ❸ LXX

πλάτος, ους, τό$_{3}$ {πλατύς} ❹ Eph 3:18; Rev 20:9; 21:16,[2x] **breadth**; (55x LXX; 18x Ezek)

πλατύνω {πλατύς} ❸ *act.*, Matt 23:5, **to make wide**; *pass.*, 2 Cor 6:11, *our heart* **stands wide open**; 2 Cor 6:13, **make room** *for us*; (24x LXX); Exod 34:24, **to enlarge** *your borders*

πλατύς, εῖα, ύ$_{3.1.3}$ *adj.* ①[nfs] Matt 7:13, **wide**; (61x LXX) Gen 19:2, *subst.*, **street**; Soph. *Ajax*, 1250, **broad**-*shouldered man*

πλέγμα, ατος, τό$_{3}$ ①[dnp] 1 Tim 2:9, *adorn themselves . . . with modesty and wisdom, not in* **braids**[PPE] Gal. *U.P.* 9.4, *medic.* **network** *of blood vessels around the veins*

πλέκω ❸[aap.nmp] Matt 27:29 = Mark 15:17 = John 19:2, **to weave**; ❷ LXX, Exod 28:14

πλεονάζω {πληρόω} ❾ Rom 5:20,[2x] **to increase**; 2 Cor 4:15, **πλεονάσασα** . . . πλειόνων, **to spread** *dynamically*[BEC]; 8:15, **to have too much**[BEC]; Phil 4:17, *the profit* **that is increasing** *to your account*[EGG]; (27x LXX; 6x Num, 4x Exod)

πλεονεκτέω[con] {πληρόω + ἔχω} ❺ 2 Cor 2:11, **to exploit**; 7:2, **to take advantage**; 12:17,[2x] **to cheat**[BEC]; 1 Thess 4:6, *to transgress* **by taking advantage** (*hendiadys*)[ZEC]; ❷ LXX

πλεονεξία, ας, ἡ$_{1\alpha}$ {πληρόω + ἔχω} (10x) Mark 7:22; Luke 12:15, **acts of greed**; 2 Cor 9:5, **expression of greediness**; Col 3:5; 2 Pet 2:14, **greed**; ❽ LXX, Judg 5:19, **spoils**

πλευρά, ᾶς, ἡ$_{1\alpha}$ ❺ John 19:34; 20:20, 25, 27; Acts 12:7, **side**; (29x LXX) Gen 2:21

πλέω[con] ❻ (5x LA) Luke 8:23; Acts 21:3, **to set sail**[Keen3]; Rev 18:17, **seafarers**; ❻ LXX

πληγή, ῆς, ἡ$_{1\eta}$ {πλήσσω} (22x; 16x Rev) Acts 16:23; 2 Cor 11:23, **a severe beating**; Acts 16:33, **wounds**; Rev 9:18; 15:1, **plague**[14x]; Rev 13:3, 12, *death* **blow**; (94x LXX; 11x Isa)

πλῆθος, ους, τό$_{3}$ {πληρόω} (31x; 24x LA) Mark 3:7; 1 Pet 4:8, **multitude**; Luke 5:6, **so many**; Acts 2:6, **crowd**; 6:5, **community**; (281x LXX; 35x 1–2 Chr)

πληθύνω {πληρόω} (12x) Matt 24:12, **to increase**; 2 Cor 9:10, **to greatly multiply**; Heb 6:14,[2x] **πληθύνων πληθυνῶ, multiplying, I will multiply** *you*; 1 Pet 1:2; 2 Pet 1:2, Jude 2, **πληθυνθείν,**[apo3s] **to be in abundance**; (199x LXX) Gen 3:16[2x] = Gen 22:17[2x] = Heb 6:14[2x]

πλήκτης, ου, ὁ$_{1>}$ {πλήσσω} ❷ 1 Tim 3:3; Titus 1:7, **given to violence, a giver of blows**[BNTC]; Aristot. *E.E.* 1221b 14, *he showed himself* **violent**

πλήμμυρα, ης, ἡ$_{1>}$ {πληρόω} ①[gfs] Luke 6:48, **flood**; ① LXX, Job 40:23

πλήν {πληρόω} (31x; 15x Luke) Ⓐ ***advers. conj.***, Luke 12:31, **instead**; 22:42, **nevertheless**; Ⓑ ***prep. w/ gen.***, Acts 15:28, **apart from**; (230x LXX; 38x 1–2 Kgs, 23x Num)

πλήρης, ες$_{3.3}$ {πληρόω} *adj.* (16x; 8x Luke) Matt 14:20; Luke 4:1; 2 John 8, **full**; (119x LXX)

πληροφορέω[con] {πληρόω + φέρω} ❻ *act.*, 2 Tim 4:5, **to carry out fully**; *pass.*, Luke 1:1, **to bring to completion**[ZEC]; Rom 4:21; 14:5, **to convince fully**; Col 4:12, **to be fully assured**; 2 Tim 4:17, **bear the fullness**[PPE]; ①[api3s] LXX, Eccl 8:11, **fullness**

πληροφορία, ας, ἡ$_{1α}$ {πληρόω + φέρω} ❹ Col 2:2, **full assurance**; Heb 6:11; 10:22; 1 Thess 1:5, **conviction**

πληρόω[con] (86x; 16x Matt, Acts, 15x John) Matt 1:22; Mark 1:15; John 3:29; **to fulfill**; John 12:3; Acts 2:2; 2 Tim 1:4, **to fill**; John 15:11; Rev 6:11, **to complete**; (106x LXX; 13x Pss)

πλήρωμα, ατος, τό$_3$ {πληρόω} (17x) Matt 9:16 = Mark 2:21, **patch**; Mark 8:20, **that which is enough to fill**[BDAG 829c]; John 1:16; Rom 11:12, **fullness**; (15x LXX; 5x Pss) Ps 23:1 (24:1), **fullness**

πλησίον *adv.* (17x) Matt 5:43; Luke 10:29; Jas 2:8; *adv. of place or proximity*, **neighbor**; John 4:5, **neighboring** *city*; (214x LXX; 61x Pent, 27x Sir, 16x Jer); Exod 2:13, **fellow** *Hebrew*; Lev 25:14[3x], **neighbor, neighbor, one another**; Jonah 1:7, **to one another (near** *each other on the boat*); Zech 3:8, **colleague**

πλησμονή, ῆς, ἡ$_{1η}$ {πληρόω} ①[gfs] Col 2:23, **gratification** *of the flesh*[ZEC]; (28x LXX)

πλήσσω ①[api3s] Rev 8:12, **to strike**; (28x LXX; 5x Isa), Exod 16:3

πλοιάριον, ου, τό$_2$ {πλέω} ❺ Mark 3:9; John 6:22–24[3x]; 21:8, **small boat**

πλοῖον, ου, τό$_2$ {πλέω} (67x; 27x LA) Matt 4:21 = Mark 1:19; Luke 8:37; John 6:17, **boat**; Acts 20:13–28:11[19x Keen3]; Jas 3:4; Rev 8:9, **ship**; (41x LXX; 10x Isa)

πλόος, ου, ὁ$_2$ {πλέω} ❸ Acts 21:7; 27:9, 10, **sea voyage**[Keen3–4]

πλούσιος, α, ον$_{2.1.2}$ {πλοῦτος} *adj.* (28x; 11x Luke) Matt 19:23 = Mark 10:25 = Luke 18:25; 2 Cor 8:9; Jas 2:5; Rev 2:9, **rich**; (55x LXX; 17x Sir, 10x Prov) 2 Sam 2:10, **powerful**

πλουσίως {πλοῦτος} *adv.* ❹ Col 3:16; 1 Tim 6:17; Titus 3:6; 2 Pet 1:11, **richly**

πλουτέω[con] {πλοῦτος} (12x; 5x Rev) Luke 1:53; 1 Cor 4:8; 2 Cor 8:9; Rev 18:3, **to be rich**; Rom 10:12, **to show generosity**; Rev 3:17, **to prosper**; (13x LXX) Gen 30:43

πλουτίζω {πλοῦτος} ❸ 1 Cor 1:5; 2 Cor 6:10; 9:11, **to enrich, make rich**; (13x LXX)

πλοῦτος, ου, ὁ$_2$ (22x) Matt 13:22 = Mark 4:19 = Luke 8:14; Rom 2:4; Eph 1:7; Jas 5:2, **riches**; 2 Cor 8:2, **extravagant**; Heb 11:26, **wealth**; (97x LXX; 19x Prov, 12x Sir:Isa)

πλύνω ❸ Luke 5:2; Rev 7:14; 22:14, **to wash**; (52x LXX) Lev 1:9–17:15[35x]

πνεῦμα, ατος, τό$_3$ {πνέω} (379x; 146x Paul) Ⓐ **breath**, John 3:8; Rev 11:11; Ⓑ **spirit, essence of life**, Matt 23:46; John 6:63; Ⓒ **rational spirit**, 1 Cor 2:14; Ⓓ **inward person** *or* **the heart**, Matt 5:3[SoM] Ⓔ **Spirit of God**, Acts 8:18; 2 Cor 12:12; (350x LXX; 39x Isa)

πνευματικός, ή, όν$_{2.1.2}$ {πνέω} *adj.* (26x; 15x 1 Cor) Rom 1:11; 1 Cor 2:15; Gal 6:1, **spiritual**

πνευματικῶς {πνέω} *adv.* ❷ 1 Cor 2:14, **spiritually** *discerned*[NIGTC!]; Rev 11:8, **figuratively** *called Sodom and Egypt*[TNTC]

πνέω[con] ❼ Matt 7:25, 27; John 3:8; Acts 27:40; Rev 7:1, **to blow**; ❻ LXX, 2 Macc 9:7, **to breathe** *fire of rage*; Isa 40:24, **to blow**

πνίγω ❸ Matt 13:7; 18:28, **to choke**; Mark 5:13, **to drown**; ❷ LXX, 1 Sam 16:14, 15, *evil spirit from the Lord* **to torment** *Saul*

πνικτός, ή, όν$_{2.1.2}$ {πνίγω} *adj.* ❸ Acts 15:20, 29; 21:25, **strangled**

πνοή, ῆς, ἡ$_{1η}$ {πνέω} ❷ Acts 2:2, **wind**; 17:25, **breath**; (24x LXX; 5x Job)

ποδήρης, ους, ὁ$_3$ {πούς} ①[ams] Rev 1:13, **foot-length robe**; (12x LXX; 5x Exod)

πόθεν {πω + ὅς + θεν} *interrog. adv.* (29x; 13x John) Matt 13:27 = Mark 6:2; Luke 13:25; John 3:8; 6:5; Jas 4:1, **where?**; (42x LXX) Job 1:7; 2:2

ποιέω[con] (568x; 156x LA, 110x John) Matt 4:19 = Mark 1:17; Acts 7:50; **to do**, **make**; Luke 13:9, **to bear** *fruit*[ZEC]; Acts 15:3, **to bring**; 15:33, **after spending** *some time*[ZEC]; 16:21, **to practice**; (3,208x LXX; 284x Exod, 188x Ezek)

ποίημα, ατος, τό$_3$ {ποιέω} ❷ Rom 1:20; Eph 2:10, **creation**; (28x LXX; 20x Eccl)

ποίησις, εως, ἡ$_3$ {ποιέω} ①[dfs] Jas 1:25, **what one does**; (10x LXX); Exod 28:8, **workmanship**; Aristoph. *Th.* 38, **poetic art**

ποιητής, οῦ, ὁ$_{1>}$ {ποιέω} ❻ Acts 17:28, **poet**; Rom 2:13; Jas 1:22, 23, **doer**; ①[amp] LXX, 1 Macc 2:67, **observer** *of the law*

ποικίλος, η, ον$_{2.1.2}$ *adj.* (10x) Matt 4:24; Luke 4:40; 2 Tim 3:6; Heb 2:4; Jas 1:2, **various**; (26x LXX; 10x Gen) Zech 6:3, **dappled-gray** *horses*

ποιμαίνω {ποιμήν} (11x; 4x Rev) Matt 2:6; John 21:16; Acts 20:28; 1 Pet 5:2; Rev 7:17, **to shepherd**; (54x LXX; 10x Pss, 7x Jer) Ps 22:1 (23:1), *the Lord is the one* **shepherding** *me*

ποιμήν, ένος, ὁ$_3$ (18x; 6x John) Matt 9:36 = Mark 6:34; Luke 2:18; John 10[6x]; Eph 4:11; Heb 13:20; 1 Pet 2:25, **shepherd**, **pastor**; (81x LXX; 19x Jer, 17x Ezek) Jer 3:1, 3, **lover**[NAC]

ποίμνη, ης, ἡ$_{1η}$ {ποιμήν} ❺ Matt 26:31; Luke 2:8; John 10:16; 1 Cor 9:7, **flock**; ❷ LXX, Gen 32:17, μέσον **ποίμνης** καὶ **ποίμνης**, *between* **the herds**

ποίμνιον, ου, τό$_2$ {ποιμήν} ❺ Luke 12:32; Acts 20:28; 1 Pet 5:2, 3, **flock**; (73x LXX; 17x 1 Sam)

ποῖος, α, ον$_{2.1.2}$ {οἷος} (33x; 19x Syn) Matt 19:18, **what**, **which**, **what kind of?**; (36x LXX)

πολεμέω[con] {πόλεμος} ❼ (6x Rev) Jas 4:2; Rev 2:16; 12:7[2x]; 17:14, **to wage war**, **to fight**; (221x LXX; 55x 1 Macc, 31x Judg)

πόλεμος, ου, ὁ$_2$ (18x; 9x Rev) Matt 24:6 = Mark 13:7 = Luke 21:9; Jas 4:1, **war**, **battle**; Rev 11:7; 12:17; 19:19, ποιήσει . . . **πόλεμον**, *to make* **war**; (380x LXX; 136x 1 Sam–2 Chr)

πόλις, εως, ἡ$_3$ (163x; 82x LA) Matt 2:23; Heb 11:16; Rev 3:12, **town**, **city**; (1,472x LXX)

πολιτάρχης, ου, ὁ$_{1>}$ {πόλις + ἄρχω} ❷ Acts 17:6, 8, **city official**

πολιτεία, ας$_{1α}$ {πόλις} ❷ Acts 22:28; Eph 2:12, **citizenship**; ❽ LXX (2–4 Macc), 2 Macc 4:1, **civic institution**

πολίτευμα, ατος, τό$_3$ {πόλις} ①[nns] Phil 3:20, **citizenship**; ①[ans] LXX, 2 Macc 12:7

πολιτεύομαι {πόλις} ❷ Acts 23:1; Phil 1:27, **to exercise one's citizenship**[ABC]; ❽ LXX (7x 2–4 Macc)

πολίτης, ου, ὁ$_{1>}$ {πόλις} ❹ Luke 15:15; Acts 21:39; Heb 8:11, **citizen**; Luke 19:14, **subjects** (17x LXX; 9x 2 Macc) 2 Macc 5:8, **compatriot**

πολλάκις *adv.* (18x; 5x 2 Cor) Matt 17:15; 2 Cor 8:22, **often**; ❾ LXX (5x 1–4 Macc)

πολλα**πλασίων, ον**$_{3.3}$ {πολύς} *adj.* ①^{anp} Luke 18:30, **many more times**; Plato *Rp.* 587e; Aristot. *Pol.* 1308b 5, **multiplication**

πολυ**λογία, ας, ἡ**$_{1\alpha}$ {πολύς + λέγω} ①^{dfs} Matt 6:7, **many words**; ①^{gfs} LXX, Prov 10:19

πολυ**μερῶς** *adv.* ① Heb 1:1, **long ago**

πολυ**ποίκιλος, ου, ὁ**$_2$ {πολύς + ποικίλος} ①^{nfs} Eph 3:10, **beautifully complex**[BEC]

πολύς, πολλή, πολύ$_{3.1.3}$ (416x; 186x Syn) (*comp. adv.*, **πλείων, πλεῖον**, 18x) Ⓐ ***adj.***, Matt 2:18, **great**; Ⓑ ***adv.***, Matt 9:14, **often**; Acts 27:14, *but before* **long**; 28:6, *after* **a long time**; Ⓒ ***comp. adv***., Matt 5:20, **greatly**; 12:41, **greater**; Luke 3:13, *don't collect* **any more than**; Rev 2:19, **greater than**; (865x LXX; 160x 1–4 Macc)

πολύ**σπλαγχνος, ον**$_{2.2}$ {πολύς + σπλάγχνον} *adj.* ①^{nms} Jas 5:11, **greatly compassionate**

πολυ**τελής, ες**$_{3.3}$ {πολύς + τέλος} *adj.* ❸ Mark 14:3; 1 Tim 2:9, **expensive**; 1 Pet 3:4, **invaluable**[Keen1P]; (15x LXX; 5x Prov) Prov 1:13, **valuable property**

πολύ**τιμος, ου, ὁ**$_2$ {πολύς + τιμή} ❸ Matt 13:46, **great value**; John 12:3, **expensive**; 1 Pet 1:7, **worth far more**[Keen1P]

πολυ**τρόπως** {πολύς + τρέπω} *adv.* ① Heb 1:1, **in many forms**[ABC]

πόμα, ατος, τό$_3$ {πίνω} ❷ 1 Cor 10:4; Heb 9:10, **drink**; ❹ LXX, 3 Macc 5:2

πονηρία, ας$_{1\alpha}$ {πόνος} ❼ Matt 22:18, **wickedness**; Mark 7:22, **evil actions**; Luke 11:39; Rom 1:29; 1 Cor 5:8; Eph 6:12, **evil**; Acts 3:26, **evil ways**; (62x LXX; 13x Sir, 12x Jer)

πονηρός, ά, όν$_{2.1.2}$ *adj.* (78x; 26x Matt, 13x Luke) Matt 5:11; Luke 11:26; Eph 5:16, **evil**; Matt 5:37, **evildoer**; 6:13, **the evil one**; Mark 7:22, **envy**, *lit.*, **evil** *eye*[ZEC]; (369x LXX; 33x Jer)

πόνος, ου, ὁ$_2$ ❹ Col 4:13, *he has* **labored** *much*; Rev 16:10, 11; 21:4, **pain**; (93x LXX; 21x 4 Macc)

Ποντικός, ή, όν$_{2.1.2}$ *adj.* ①^{ams} Acts 18:2, *native* **of Pontus**

Πόντιος, ου, ὁ$_2$ ❸ Luke 3:1; Acts 4:27; 1 Tim 6:13, **Pontius** *Pilate*

Πόντος, ου, ὁ$_2$ ❷ Acts 2:9; 1 Pet 1:1, **Pontus**

Πόπλιος, ου, ὁ$_2$ ❷ Acts 28:7, 8, **Publius**

πορεία, ας$_{1\alpha}$ ❷ Luke 13:22, **way**; Jas 1:11, **daily life**[ZEC]; (32x LXX) Num 33:2

πορεύομαι (154x; 88x LA, 29x Matt) Ⓐ ***emph.***, πορευθέντες + **verb**, Matt 2:8, **go** *and search*; Ⓑ ***ethical like Paul's* περιπατέω,** *pos.*, Luke 1:6; Acts 9:31, **to walk** *in the fear of the Lord*; *neg.*, 1 Pet 4:3, **to follow** *the polluting desires*; Jude 11, **to go** *the way of Cain*; (1,116x LXX; 311x 1 Sam–2 Kgs, 65x Gen, 58x Jer)

πορθέω[con] ❸ Acts 9:21, **to cause havoc**[ZEC]; Gal 1:13, 23, **to destroy**; ❷ LXX, 4 Macc 4:23

πορισμός, οῦ, ὁ$_2$ ❷ 1 Tim 6:5, 6, **gain**; ❷ LXX, Wis 13:19, **money-making**

Πόρκιος, ου, ὁ$_2$ ①^{ams} Acts 24:27, **Porcius**

πορνεία, ας, ἡ$_{1\alpha}$ {πόρνη} (25x; 7x Rev) Matt 5:32; 2 Cor 12:21; 1 Thess 4:3; Rev 2:21, **sexual immorality**; (49x LXX; 22x Ezek) Hos 1:2,^{2x} **promiscuity**

πορνεύω {πόρνη} ❽ 1 Cor 6:18; 10:8; Rev 2:14, 20; 17:2, **to commit sexual immorality**; (18x LXX; 5x Hos) Hos 3:3, **to be promiscuous**; Amos 7:17, **to play the prostitute**

πόρνη, ης, ἡ$_{1\eta}$ (12x; 5x Rev) Matt 21:31; Luke 15:30; Rev 17:15, **prostitute**; (42x LXX)

πόρνος, ου, ὁ$_2$ {πόρνη} (10x; 4x 1 Cor) 1 Cor 5:9–11^{3x}; Rev 21:8, **sexually immoral**; ❷ LXX

πόρρω {πρό} *adv.* ❹ Matt 15:8 = Mark 7:6; Luke 14:32; 24:28, **faraway**; (17x LXX; 5x Isa)

πόρρωθεν *adv.* ❷ Luke 17:12; Heb 11:13, **a distance**; (16x LXX; 8x Isa)

πορφύρα, ας, ἡ$_{1\alpha}$ ❹ Mark 15:17, 20; Luke 16:19; Rev 18:12, **purple cloth**, **garment**; (46x LXX; 22x Exod) Exod 25:4–39:12, **purple** *appointments for proper Yahweh worship*[Vogt]

πορφυρόπωλις, ιδος, ἡ$_3$ {πορφύρα + πωλέω} ①^{nfs} Acts 16:14, **dealer in purple cloth**

πορφυροῦς, ᾶ, οῦν$_{2.1.2}$ *adj.* ❹ John 19:2, 5, **purple**; Rev 17:4; 18:16, *dressed in* **purple**

ποσάκις {ὅς} *adv.* ❸ Matt 18:21, **how many times?**; 23:37; Luke 13:34, **how often?**; ❺ LXX, Ps 77:40 (78:40), **how often!**

πόσις, εως, ἡ$_3$ {πίνω} ❸ John 6:55; Col 2:16, **drink**; Rom 14:17, **drinking**; ①^{afs} LXX, Dan 1:10, **drink**

πόσος, η, ον$_{2.1.2}$ {ὅς} (27x; 20x Syn) Matt 6:23; 7:11 = Luke 11:33; 2 Cor 7:11; Phlm 16, **how much** *more*?; Luke 15:17; Acts 21:20, **how many?**; (12x LXX) Gen 47:8

ποταμός, οῦ, ὁ$_2$ {πίνω} (17x; 8x Rev) Matt 3:6 = Mark 1:5, *Jordan* **River**; Matt 7:25, 27 = Luke 6:48; Rev 8:10, **river**; John 7:38, **stream**; (241x LXX; 27x Isa, Ezek, 26x Exod)

ποταμοφόρητος, ον$_{2.2}$ {πίνω + φέρω} *adj.* ①^{afs} Rev 12:15, **swept away by a river**

ποταπός, ή, όν$_{2.1.2}$ {ποῦ + ἀπό} ❼ Matt 8:27; Luke 1:29, **what kind of?**; Mark 13:1, **What magnificent** *stones and* **what magnificent** *buildings*![ZEC]; 2 Pet 3:11, **what sort**; 1 John 3:1, **what great** *love*; ①^{dms} LXX, Sus 54, **in what part** *of the garden* . . . ?

πότε {ποῦ} *interrog. adv.* (19x; 18x Gs) Matt 17:17; Mark 9:19; Luke 9:41; John 10:24; Rev 6:10, ἕως πότε, **how long?**; Matt 24:3; 25:44, **when?** (45x LXX; 19x Pss, 5x Jer)

ποτέ {ποῦ} *enclitic part.* (29x) Gal 1:23,^{2x} *inclusio* (**ποτέ**) *who* **formerly** *persecuted*, (**νῦν**) *now preaches the good news* . . . *he* (**ποτέ**) **formerly** *tried to destroy*; Eph 2:2, **previously**; 2 Pet 1:21, **ever**; Phlm 11, **once**; 1 Pet 3:5, **in the past**; (130x LXX; 21x Pss)

πότερον {ποῦ + ἕτερος} *coord. conj.* ① John 7:17, **whether**; (12x LXX; all in Job), 4:6–31:15, *signals rhetorical questions that reveal evidence in Job's legal case*; 4:6; 7:1; 21:22; 22:2, 5, **Is not . . . ?**; 4:12, **Am I . . . ?**; 15:2, **Will not . . . ?**; 31:15, **Were not . . . ?**

ποτήριον, ου, τό$_2$ {πίνω} (31x; 18x Syn) Matt 10:42 = Mark 9:41, **cup** *of water*; Matt 20:22, 23 = Mark 10:38, 39, **cup** = *suffering*; Matt 26:27 = Mark 14:23 = Luke 22:17; 1 Cor 11:25, **cup** *of blessing*; Rev 14:10, **cup** *of wrath*; (33x LXX; 7x Jer) Jer 30:6; 32:15

ποτίζω {πίνω} (15x; 5x Matt:1 Cor) Matt 10:42; 25:35, **to give a drink**; Luke 13:15; Rom 12:20; Rev 14:18, **to drink**; 1 Cor 3:6, **to water**; (65x LXX; 20x Gen)

Ποτίολοι, ων, ὁ$_2$ ①^{amp} Acts 28:13, **Puteoli**, *town in Italy*

πότος, ου, ὁ$_2$ {πίνω} ①^{dmp} 1 Pet 4:3, **wild partying**[Keen1P]; (34x LXX; 7x Esth) Gen 19:3

ποῦ *interrog. adv.* (45x; 19x John) John 1:38, **where?**; 1 Cor 1:20,^{3x} **Where is** *the wise*? **Where is** *the scribe*? **Where is** *the debater*?; (121x LXX; 10x Gen) Gen 3:9, **Where** *are you*?

πού *enclitic adv.* ❼ Acts 27:29, *lest* **somewhere** *we run aground* (LEB); Rom 4:19, **since**; Heb 2:6, **πού** τις, *someone* **somewhere**; ❹ LXX, 1 Kgs 10:12; Prov 29:39

Πούδης, εντος, ὁ$_2$ ①^{nms} 2 Tim 4:21, **Pudens**

πούς, ποδός, ὁ$_3$ (93x; 38x LA, 11x Rev) Matt 4:6 = Luke 4:11; 1 Cor 12:15, **foot**; Luke 7:38–46$^{amp\ 7x}$; Rev 1:15, *Jesus's* **feet**; Heb 1:13, ὑποπόδιον τῶν **ποδῶν**, **footstool**; (279x LXX; 35x Pss, 18x Isa:Ezek) ὑποπόδιον τῶν **ποδῶν**,^{2x} Ps 109:1 (110:1); Isa 66:1

πρᾶγμα, ατος, τό$_3$ {πράσσω} (11x; 3x Heb) 1 Thess 4:6, **matter**; Luke 1:1, **events**; Acts 5:4, **thing**; 1 Cor 6:1, **case**, **matter**; Jas 3:16, **practice**; (121x LXX; 48x 1–4 Macc)

πραγματεία, ας, ἡ$_{1\alpha}$ {πράσσω} ①^{dfp} 2 Tim 2:4, **concern**; ❼ LXX, 1 Kgs 9:1

πραγματεύομαι {πράσσω} ①[amimp2p] Luke 19:13, **to conduct business**; ❷ LXX, Dan 8:27, **to go about the business** *of the king*

πραιτώριον, ου, τό$_2$ ❽ Matt 27:27 = Mark 15:16 = John 18:28, **residence**, **headquarters**; Acts 23:35, **palace**; Phil 1:13, **imperial guard**

πράκτωρ, ορος, ὁ$_3$ {πράσσω} ❷ Luke 12:58,[2x] **bailiff**; ①[nmp] LXX, Isa 3:12, **rulers**

πρᾶξις, εως, ἡ$_3$ {πράσσω} ❼ Matt 16:27; Luke 23:51; Rom 8:13, **deed**, **action**; Acts 1:0, **Πράξεις** Ἀπόστολων, **Acts** *of the Apostles*; Col 3:9, **practices**; Rom 12:4, **function**; (20x LXX) 2 Chr 13:22, **Acts** *of Abijah*; 27:27, **Acts** *of Jotham*

πρασιά, ᾶς, ἡ$_{1α}$ {πράσσω} ❷ Mark 6:40, **πρασιαὶ πρασιαί**,[nfp] **group by group** *for ease of distribution*, **forming clusters**[BrDAG]; ①[afs] LXX, Sir 24:31; Hom. *Od.* 7.127, **flowerbed**

πράσσω (39x; 13x Acts, 10x Rom) Luke 3:13, **to collect**; 22:23; 2 Cor 5:10, **to do**; Acts 16:26, **to harm**; 19:19, **to practice**; Rom 2:25, **to do**, **practice**; 1 Thess 4:11, **to tend to**; (20x LXX; 9x Prov, 8x Job) Job 5:27, **to know**

πραϋπάθεια, ας, ἡ$_{1α}$ {πραΰς + πείθω} ①[afs] 1 Tim 6:11, **gentleness**

πραΰς, πραεῖα, πραΰ$_{3.1.3}$ *adj.* ❹ Matt 5:5; 11:29; 21:5; 1 Pet 3:4, **humble**, **gentle**; (16x LXX)

πραΰτης, ητος, ἡ$_3$ {πραΰς} (11x) 1 Cor 4:21; 2 Cor 10:1; Gal 5:23; Jas 3:13, **gentleness**; ❾ LXX, Ps 89:10 (90:10), **humility** *has come upon us* (LES)

πρέπω ❼ Matt 3:15, **it is fitting**; 1 Cor 11:13, **is it appropriate?**[NIGTC]; 1 Tim 2:10, **is proper**; Titus 2:1, **is sound**; Heb 7:26, **precisely appropriate**[WBC]; (10x LXX; 4x 3 Macc, 3x Pss)

πρεσβεία, ας, ἡ$_{1α}$ {πρεσβύτης} ❷[afs] Luke 14:32; 19:14, **emissary**; ①[afs] 2 Macc 4:11

πρεσβεύω {πρεσβύτης} ❷ 2 Cor 5:20; Eph 6:20, **to be an ambassador**

πρεσβυτέριον, ου, τό$_2$ {πρεσβύτης} ❸ Luke 22:66; Acts 22:5; 1 Tim 4:14, **elders**

πρεσβύτερος, α, ον$_{2.1.2}$ *adj.* (66x; 18x Acts, 12x Matt) εἴκοσι τέσσαρας **πρεσβυτέρους**, Rev 4:4–19:4,[12x] *the twenty-four* **elders**; *subst.*, Matt 15:2 = Mark 7:5; 2 John 1; 3 John 1, **elder**; John 8:9, **oldest** *in the group*; Acts 2:17, **old men**; 1 Tim 5:1, *an* **older man**; Heb 11:2, **ancestor**; (202x LXX; 20x Gen)

πρεσβύτης, ου, ὁ$_{1>}$ ❸ Luke 1:18; Titus 2:2; Phlm 9, **old (older, elderly) man**; (38x LXX)

πρεσβῦτις, ιδος, ἡ$_3$ {πρεσβύτης} ①[afp] Titus 2:3, **older women**; ①[vfs] LXX, 4 Macc 16:14, **elderly woman**

πρηνής, ές$_{3.3}$ {πρό} *adj.* ①[nms] Acts 1:18, **headfirst**; ❹ LXX, 3 Macc 6:23, **to fall headlong**

πρίζω {πρίων} ①[api3p] Heb 11:37, **to saw in two**; ①[iai3p] LXX, Amos 1:3

πρίν, πρὶν ἤ {πρό} *conj.* (13x) Matt 1:18; Acts 2:20, **before**; (55x LXX; 12x Isa)

Πρίσκα, ας, ἡ$_1$ ❸ Rom 16:3; 1 Cor 16:19; 2 Tim 4:19, **Prisca**

Πρίσκιλλα, ης, ἡ$_{1,p>}$ ❸ Acts 18:2, 18, 26, **Priscilla**

πρό *prep.* (47x; 29x GA) Ⓐ ***w/gen.***, Matt 5:12; Luke 2:21; 1 Cor 4:5, **before**; Acts 5:36, *some time* **ago**; 2 Cor 12:2, *fourteen years* **ago**; 1 Pet 4:8, **above all**; Ⓑ (9x) **πρὸ τοῦ** + ***inf.***, Matt 6:8; John 1:48, **before** (*acc. functions as the subj. of the inf.*); (244x LXX; 31x Deut)

προάγω (20x; 12x Syn) Matt 2:9[SiM 18–25]; Mark 10:32, **to go before**; Acts 16:30, **to bring**; 1 Tim 1:18, **to make previously**; 2 John 9, **to go beyond**; (13x LXX; 3x Deut:3 Macc)

προαιρέω[con] ①[pfmi3s] 2 Cor 9:7, **to determine**; (14x LXX) Gen 34:8, **to set** *one's heart*

προαιτιάομαι {πρό + αἰτία} ①[amiIp] Rom 3:9, **to charge beforehand**

προακούω ①[aai2p] Col 1:5, **to hear before**

προαμαρτάνω ❷ 2 Cor 12:21, **to persist in sin**[BEC]; 13:2, **to sin before**

προαύλιον, ου, τό$_2$ {πρό + αὐλή} ①^{ans} Mark 14:68, **entryway**

προβαίνω ❺ Matt 4:21 = Mark 1:19, **to go on**; Luke 1:7, 18; 2:36 (*pf ptc.*), **to be advanced in age**; (17x LXX) Gen 18:11, **advanced** *in days*; Exod 19:19, **grew** *louder*

προβάλλω ❷ Luke 21:30, **to sprout leaves**; Acts 19:33, **to push forward**; ❽ LXX, Judg 14:12, **to pose** *a riddle*; Prov 26:18, **to put** *arguments* **forward**

προβατικός, ή, όν$_{2.1.2}$ *adj.* {πρό + βαίνω} ①^{dfs} John 5:2, *subst.*, **Sheep Gate**; ❸ LXX, Neh 3:1, 32; 12:39

πρόβατον, ον, τό$_2$ {πρό + βαίνω} (39x; 19x John, 11x Matt) Matt 26:31 = Mark 6:34; John 2:14; 10:1–26,^{15x} **sheep**; (295x LXX; 59x Gen, 33x Ezek, 29x Exod)

προβιβάζω {πρό + βαίνω} ①$^{app.nfs}$ Matt 14:8, **to be directed**; ❷ LXX, Exod 35:34

προβλέπω ①$^{amp.gms}$ Heb 11:40, **to provide**; ①^{pai3s} LXX, Ps 36:13 (37:13)

προγίνομαι ①$^{pfap.gnp}$ Rom 3:25, **to commit previously**; ❸ LXX, 2 Macc 14:3

προγινώσκω ❺ Acts 26:5, **to know** *for a long time*; Rom 8:29; 11:2; 1 Pet 1:20; **to foreknow**; 2 Pet 3:17, **to know in advance**; ❸ LXX, Wis 6:13; 8:8, **to know beforehand**

πρόγνωσις, εως, ἡ$_3$ ❷ Acts 2:23; 1 Pet 1:2, **foreknowledge**; ❷ LXX, Jdt 9:6; 11:19

πρόγονος ❷ 1 Tim 5:4, **parent**; 2 Tim 1:3, **ancestor**; (11x LXX) 2 Macc 8:19, **ancestor**

προγράφω ❹ *act.*, Rom 15:4; Eph 3:3, **to write beforehand**; Gal 3:1, **to depict**[KeenG]; *pass.*, Jude 4, **to be marked out**[BEC]; ❷ LXX, 1 Macc 10:36, **to enroll**

πρόδηλος, ον$_{2.2}$ *adj.* ❸ 1 Tim 5:24,^{2x} **obvious**; Heb 7:14, **evident**; ❸ LXX, Jdt 8:29

προδίδωμι ①^{aai3s} Rom 11:35, **to advance a sum**[ZEC]; ❸ LXX, 2 Kgs 6:11, **to take a stand with**; 2 Macc 7:37, **to sacrifice** *body and life*; 4 Macc 4:1, **to betray**

προδότης, ου, ὁ$_{1>}$ {πρό + δίδωμι} ❸ Luke 6:16; Acts 7:52; 2 Tim 3:4, **traitor**; ❹ LXX

πρόδρομος, ου, ὁ$_2$ {πρό + τρέχω} ① Heb 6:20, **going before**[NIVAC]; ❸ LXX, Num 13:20, **first ripe** *grapes*; Wis 12:8, **forerunner** *of your army*; Isa 28:4, **ripe** *fig*

προελπίζω {πρό + ἐλπίς} ① Eph 1:12, **have placed their hope firmly** *in Christ*

προενάρχομαι {πρό + ἐν + ἄρχω} ❷ 2 Cor 8:6, **καθὼς προενήρξατο**, *since* **he started**[BEC]; 8:10, **to take the initiative**

προεπαγγέλλω {πρό + ἐπί + ἄγγελος} ❷ Rom 1:2; 2 Cor 9:5, **to promise previously**

προέρχομαι ❾ Matt 26:39 = Mark 14:35; 2 Cor 9:5, **to go ahead**; Luke 1:17, **to go before**; 22:47, **to lead**; Acts 12:10, **to pass**; (10x LXX) Gen 33:3; Jdt 15:13; Prov 8:24

προετοιμάζω {πρό + ἕτοιμος} ❷ Rom 9:23; Eph 2:10, **to prepare beforehand**; ❷ LXX, Wis 9:8; Isa 28:24

προευαγγελίζομαι {πρό + εὖ + ἄγγελος} ①^{ami3s} Gal 3:8, **to announce the good news in advance**[KeenG]

προέχω ①^{pai1p} Rom 3:9, **to be surpassed**[ZEC!]; ①^{aas2s} LXX, Num 16:15, **to respect**

προηγέομαι^{con} {πρό + ἄγω} ①$^{pmp.nmp}$ Rom 12:10, **to lead the way**; (13x LXX) Deut 20:9

προηλπικότας → **προελπίζω**, *pf. act. ptc. amp*, Eph 1:12, **those who placed their hope in** *the Messiah*

πρόθεσις, εως, ἡ$_3$ {πρό + τίθημι} (12x) Matt 12:4 = Mark 2:26 = Luke 6:4; Heb 9:2, *bread of the* **Presence**; Acts 11:23, **devoted** *hearts*; 27:13; Eph 1:11, **plan**; Rom 8:28; 9:11, **purpose**; (18x LXX) Exod 39:17, *bread of the* **Presence**

προθεσμία, ας, ἡ$_{1α}$ {πρό + τίθημι} ①^{afs} Gal 4:2, **the time appointed**[KeenG]

προ**θυμία, ας, ἡ**$_{1α}$ {πρό + θυμός} ❺ Acts 17:11, **good will**[ZEC]; 2 Cor 8:11, 12, **eager**; 8:19, **readiness**; 9:2, **zeal**[BEC]; ①[gfs] LXX, Sir 45:23, **courage**

πρό**θυμος, ον**$_{2.2}$ *adj.* ❸ Matt 26:41 = Mark 14:38, **willing**; Rom 1:15, **eager**[EGG]; LXX, Hab 1:8, *the eagle* **swift** *to devour*

προ**θύμως** *adv.* ① 1 Pet 5:2, **eagerly**; ❻ LXX, 2 Chr 29:34, **conscientious**

προϊδών → προοράω, *aor. act. ptc. nms*, Acts 2:31, **he foresaw**

πρό**ϊμος, ου, ὁ**$_{2}$ {πρό + ὕω → **to rain**} ①[ams] Jas 5:7, **early** *rains*; ❽ LXX, Zech 10:1, **spring rain**; Hos 9:10, **first fruit** *on a fig tree*; Isa 58:8, **dawn**

προ**ΐστημι** ❽ Rom 12:8; 1 Thess 5:12, **to lead**; 1 Tim 3:4, 5, 12, **to manage**; Titus 3:8, **to take the lead**[ABC]; ❽ LXX, 1 Macc 5:19, **to take charge**

προ**καλέω**[con] ①[pmp.nmp] Gal 5:26, **to challenge**[KeenG]; ①[pmp.nms] LXX, 2 Macc 8:11, **to invite**

προ**καταγγέλλω** {πρό + κατά + ἄγγελος} ❷ Acts 3:18, **to announce beforehand**; Acts 7:52, **to predict**

προ**καταρτίζω** {πρό + κατά + ἄρτι} ①[aas3p] 2 Cor 9:5, **to organize in advance**[BEC]

πρό**κειμαι** ❺ 2 Cor 8:12, *act.*, **to exist**[BEC]; Heb 6:18, *mid.*, **to set before**; *mid*, 12:1, 2, **to lie before**; Jude 7, *mid.*, **to put on public display**[BHGNT]; (11x LXX) Esth 1:7, *without* **restraint**

προ**κηρύσσω** ①[aap.gms] Acts 13:24, **to proclaim previously**

προ**κοπή, ῆς, ἡ**$_{1η}$ {πρό + κόπτω} ❸ Phil 1:12, **advance**; 1:25, *make* **progress**; 1 Tim 4:15, **progress**; ❷ LXX, 2 Macc 8:8, *moving toward* **progress**

προ**κόπτω** ❻ Luke 2:52; Gal 1:14, **to advance**; 2 Tim 2:16, **to advance** *in godlessness*

πρό**κριμα, ατος, τό**$_{3}$ {πρό + κρίνω} ①[gns] 1 Tim 5:21, **prejudice**

προ**κυρόω**[con] {πρό + κύριος} ①[pfmp.afs] Gal 3:17, **has already validated**[KeenG]

προ**λαμβάνω** ❸ Mark 14:8, **to do ahead of time**; 1 Cor 11:21, **to devour**[NIGTC!]; Gal 6:1, *pass.*, **to be overtaken by surprise**[KeenG]; ①[app.nms] LXX, Wis 17:16, **to be overtaken suddenly**

προ**λέγω** (15x) Matt 24:25, **to tell beforehand**; Acts 1:16; Jude 17, **to predict**; 2 Cor 7:3, **to condemn**; Gal 5:21,[2x] **to warn**; ①[pap.nms] LXX, Isa 41:26, **to declare**

προ**μαρτύρομαι** {πρό + μάρτυς} ①[pmp.nns] 1 Pet 1:11, **to testify in advance**[Keen1P]

προ**μελετάω**[con] {πρό + μέλω} ①[painf] Luke 21:14, **to plan ahead of time**

προ**μεριμνάω**[con] ①[paimp2p] Mark 13:11, **to worry beforehand**

προ**νοέω**[con] {πρό + νοῦς} ❸ Rom 12:17; 2 Cor 8:21, **to give careful consideration**; 1 Tim 5:8, **to perceive ahead of time**; ❾ LXX, Prov 3:4, **to provide**

πρό**νοια, ας, ἡ**$_{1α}$ {πρό + νοῦς} ❷ Acts 24:2, **foresight**; Rom 13:14, **provision**; ❾ LXX

προ**οράω**[con] ❹ Acts 2:25, **to see always**; 2:31; **to foresee**; 21:29, **to see earlier**; Gal 3:8, **to see in advance**[KeenG]; ❹ LXX, Gen 37:18; 4 Macc 4:25

προ**ορίζω** {πρό + ὅρος} ❻ Acts 4:28; Rom 8:29; 1 Cor 2:7, **to decide beforehand**

προ**πάσχω** ①[aap.nmp] 1 Thess 2:2, **to suffer previously**

προ**πάτωρ, ορος, ὁ**$_{3}$ {πρό + πατήρ} ①[ams] Rom 4:1, **forefather**; ①[nms] LXX, 3 Macc 2:21, *God,* **the first father** *of all*

προ**πέμπω** ❾ Acts 15:3; 2 Cor 1:16; 3 John 6, **to send on one's way**; Acts 20:38; 21:5; Rom 15:24, **to accompany**; ❺ LXX, 1 Macc 12:4; 2 Macc 6:23

προ**πετής, ές**$_{3.3}$ {πρό + πίπτω} *adj.* ❷ Acts 19:36; 2 Tim 3:4, **reckless**; ❸ LXX, Prov 10:14

προ**πορεύομαι** ❷ Luke 1:76; Acts 7:40, **to go before**; (34x LXX; 8x Exod)

πρός *prep.* (714x; 299x LA, 102x John)[PrTh] Ⓐ (1x) ***w/ gen.***, Acts 27:34, **for**; Ⓑ (7x) ***w/ dat.***, Mark 5:11, **on** *the hillside*; Rev 1:13, **around** *his chest*; Ⓒ (691x) ***w/ acc.***, Matt 26:57, **to** *Caiaphas*; Mark 11:31, **among** *themselves*; Ⓓ (3x) ***unique texts*:** John 1:1, **with** *God*; 2 Cor 5:6–8, *at home* **with** *the Lord*[BEC]; 1 John 5:16–17,[4x] **leads to** *death*[NIDNTT, ZEC]; (4,096x LXX; 963x Pent, 721x MajPr)

προ**σάββατον, ον, τό**$_2$ ① Mark 15:42, **day before Sabbath**; ❷ LXX, Jdt 8:6

προσ**αγορεύω** ①[app.nms] Heb 5:10, **to declare**; ❼ LXX, 1 Macc 14:40

προσ**άγω** ❹ Luke 9:41; Acts 16:20; 27:27; 1 Pet 3:18, **to bring**; (172x LXX; 43x Lev)

προσ**αγωγή, ῆς, ἡ**$_{1η}$ {πρός + ἄγω} ❸ Rom 5:2; Eph 2:18; 3:12, **to have access**

προσ**αιτέω**[con] ①[pap.nms] John 9:8, **to beg**; ①[fai3p] LXX, Job 27:14, **to beg**

προσ**αίτης, ου, ὁ**$_{1>}$ ❷ Mark 10:46; John 9:8, **beggar**

προσ**αναβαίνω** ①[aaimp2s] Luke 14:10, **to go up**; ❾ LXX, Exod 19:23, **to come up**

προσ**αναλόω**[con] {πρός + ανα + λόω} ①[aap.nfs] Luke 8:43, **though she had spent**

προσ**αναπληρόω**[con] ❷ 2 Cor 9:12, **to meet**; 11:9, **to provide**[BEC]; ①[aas3p] LXX, Wis 19:4

προσ**ανατίθημι** ❷ Gal 1:16, **to check**; 2:6, **to add** *nothing*[KeenG]

προσ**απειλέω**[con] {πρός + ἀπ + εἰλέω} ①[amp.nmp] Acts 4:21, **to threaten further**

προσ**δαπανάω**[con] ①[aas2s] {πρός + δαπάνη} Luke 10:35, **to spend in addition**

προσ**δέομαι** ①[pmp.nms] Acts 17:25, **to need**; ❻ LXX, Prov 12:9, **to want**

προσ**δέχομαι** (14x; 7x LA) Mark 15:43; Luke 12:36, **to wait for**; 2:25, 38, **to look forward to**; Rom 16:2, **to welcome**; Heb 10:34, **to accept**; (47x LXX; 4x Job:Wis:Isa:Ezek)

προσ**δοκάω**[con] {πρός + δοκέω} (16x; 11x LA) Matt 11:3 = Luke 7:19; Acts 10:24, **to expect**; Luke 1:21, **to wait for**; (13x LXX) Deut 32:2, **to come down (to be received)**

προσ**δοκία, ας, ἡ**$_{1α}$ ❷ Luke 21:26; Acts 12:11, **expectation**; ❾ LXX, Gen 49:10

προσ**εάω**[con] ①[pap.gms] Acts 17:25, **to allow**

προσ**εργάζομαι** ①[ami3s] Luke 19:16, **to produce**

προσ**έρχομαι** (86x; 51x Matt, 20x LA) Matt 4:3, **to approach**; 4:11; John 12:21, **to come**

προσ**ευχή, ῆς, ἡ**$_{1η}$ {πρός + εὔχομαι} (36x; 12x LA) Matt 21:13 = Mark 11:17 = Luke 19:46; Rom 1:10; Phil 4:6; Phlm 4; Rev 5:8, **prayer**; (109x LXX; 28x Pss)

προσ**εύχομαι** (85x; 44x Syn) Matt 5:44; Acts 1:24; Eph 6:18; Jude 20, **to pray**; (100x LXX)

προσ**έχω** (24x; 10x LA) Matt 6:1; Acts 5:35, **to be careful**; Matt 7:15, **to beware**; 1 Tim 1:4; 2 Pet 1:19, **to pay attention**; (120x LXX; 24x Pss, 14x Deut)

προσ**ηλόω**[con] ①[aap.nms] Col 2:14, **to nail to**; ①[pfpp.nmp] LXX, 3 Macc 4:9, **to fasten**

προσ**ήνεγκαν** → προσ**φέρω**, *aor. act. ind. 3p*, Matt 2:11; 4:24, **presented**

προσ**ήλυτος, ου, ὁ**$_2$ {πρός + ἔρχομαι} ❹ Matt 23:15; Acts 2:11; 6:5; 13:43, **proselyte**; (84x LXX; 22x Lev:Deut) Lev 19:33–34,[3x] **alien**

πρόσ**καιρος, ον**$_{2.2}$ *adj.* ❹ Matt 13:21 = Mark 4:17, **short-lived**; 2 Cor 4:18, **here today and gone tomorrow**[BEC]; Heb 11:25, **fleeting**; ❸ LXX, 4 Macc 15:2, 8, 23, **temporary**

προσ**καλέω**[con] (29x) Matt 10:1 = Mark 3:13, **to summon**; Mark 8:34; Jas 5:14, **to call**

προσ**καρτερέω**[con] {πρός + κεράννυμι} (10x; 6x Acts) Mark 3:9, **to make ready**; Acts 2:42, **to devote oneself to**; 8:13, **to follow intently**; Rom 12:12, **to be persistent**; ①[aap.nmp] LXX, Num 13:20, **to be boldly resolute**

προσ**καρτέρησις, εως, ἡ**$_3$ {πρός + κεράννυμι} ①[dfs] Eph 6:18, **perseverance**

προσκεφάλαιον, ου, τό$_2$ {πρός + κεφαλή} ①[ans] Mark 4:38, **cushion**; ❸ LXX, Ezek 13:18, 20, *sewing* **bands** *on wrists associated with "binding magic"*[NICOT!]

προσκληρόω[con] ①[api3p] Acts 17:4, **to associate**

προσκλίνω ①[api3s] Acts 5:36, **to join**; ①[plpfpi3s] LXX, 2 Macc 14:24, **to be attached to**

πρόσκλισις, εως, ἡ$_3$ ①[afs] 1 Tim 5:21, **favoritism**

προσκολλάω[con] ❷[fpi3s] Mark 10:7; Eph 5:31, **to be united** *to his wife*; (17x LXX; 3x Deut)

πρόσκομμα, ατος, τό$_3$ {πρό + κόπτω} ❻ Rom 9:32; 14:13; 1 Cor 8:9[NIGTC]; 1 Pet 2:8, **stumbling block**; (11x LXX; 5x Sir) Exod 23:33, **snare**

προσκοπή, ῆς, ἡ$_{1η}$ {πρό + κόπτω} ①[afs] 2 Cor 6:3, **to offend**[BEC]

προσκόπτω ❽ Matt 4:6 = Luke 4:11, **to strike** *your foot*; Matt 7:27, **to pound**; John 11:9; Rom 14:21; 1 Pet 2:8, **to stumble**; (17x LXX; 4x Sir)

προσκυλίω ❷ Matt 27:60 = Mark 15:46, **to roll** *a great stone* **against**

προσκυνέω[con] (60x; 24x Rev) Matt 2:2; Matt 4:9, 10 = Luke 4:7, 8; John 4:20, **to worship**; Mark 5:6, **to kneel down**; Rev 3:9, **to bow down**; (206x LXX; 23x Gen, 18x Pss, 14x Dan)

προσκυνητής, ῆς, ἡ$_{1η}$ {πρός + κυνέω} ①[nmp] John 4:23, **worshiper**

προσλαλέω[con] ❷ Acts 13:43; 28:20, **to speak**; ❷ LXX, Exod 4:16; Wis 13:17, **to speak to**

προσλαμβάνω (12x; 5x Acts) Matt 16:22 = Mark 8:32, **to take aside**; Acts 17:5, **to bring together**; Acts 27:33, 36, **to take** *food*; Phlm 17, **to welcome**; ❽ LXX, Wis 17:10, **to receive**

πρόσλημψις, εως, ἡ$_3$ {πρός + λαμβάνω} ① Rom 11:15, **acceptance**

προσμένω ❼ Matt 15:32 = Mark 8:2, **to remain with**; Acts 11:23, **to remain steadfast**; 13:43, **to continue**; 18:18, **to stay**[ZEC]; ❸ LXX, Judg 3:25, **to wait**

προσορμίζω ①[api3p] Mark 6:53, **to cast anchor**

προσοφείλω ①[pai2s] Phlm 19, **to owe**

προσοχθίζω {πρός + ὀχθέω} ❷ Heb 3:10, 17, **to be angry**; (21x LXX; 8x Lev), Gen 27:46, **to grow weary**; Lev 18:25, 28, *the land* **vomited out** *its inhabitants*; Num 21:5, **to detest**

πρόσπεινος, ον$_{2.2}$ {πρός + πεινάω} *adj.* ① Acts 10:10, **hungry**

προσπήγνυμι ①[aap.nmp] Acts 2:23, **to be fixed on, to crucify**

προσπίπτω ❼ Matt 7:25, **to beat**; Mark 3:11; Luke 5:8, **to fall down**; (23x LXX; 7x 2 Macc)

προσποιέω[con] ①[ami3s] Luke 24:28, **to give the impression that**[EGG]; ❹ LXX, Job 19:14

προσπορεύομαι ①[pmi3p] Mark 10:35, **to approach**; (18x LXX; 12x Pent)

προσρήσσω {πρός + ῥήγνυμι} ❷[aai3s] Luke 6:48, 49, **to burst against**

προστάσσω ❼ Matt 1:24; 8:4 = Mark 1:44 = Luke 5:14; Acts 10:33, **to command**; 17:26, **to determine**; (72x LXX; 10x 1 Esd:3 Macc)

προστάτις, εως, ἡ$_3$ {πρό + ἵστημι} ①[nfs] Rom 16:2, **benefactor**

προστίθημι (18x; 13x LA) Matt 6:27 = Luke 12:25; Mark 4:24; Acts 2:41, 47; Gal 3:19, **to add**; Luke 17:5, **to increase**; 20:11, **to proceed**; Acts 13:36, **to gather**; *pass.*, Heb 12:19, μὴ **προστεθῆναι** αὐτοῖς λόγον, **any further** *message* **be given** *to them*[ABC]; (285x LXX; 35x 1–2 Sam, 18x Isa)

προστρέχω ❸ Mark 9:15; 10:17; Acts 8:30, **to run up**; ❻ LXX, Gen 18:2; 33:4

προσφάγιον, ου, τό$_2$ {πρός + φάγος} ①[ans] John 21:5, **cooked fish**[ZEC]

πρόσφατος, ον$_{2.2}$ {πρός + φόνος} *adj.* ①[afs] Heb 10:20, **freshly killed**, **newly made**;[WPNT] ❻ LXX, Num 6:3, **fresh**; Deut 32:17, **new** *gods*; Hom. *Il.* 24.757, **not yet decomposed**

προσφάτως {πρός + φόνος} *adv.* ① Acts 18:2, **recently**; ❺ LXX, Deut 24:5; Jdt 4:3

προσ**φέρω** (47x; 20x Heb, 15x Matt) Matt 2:11, **to present**; 4:24, **to bring**; 5:23; 8:4 = Mark 1:44 = Luke 5:14, **to offer**; Heb 5:1–11:17,[19x] **to offer** *in sacrificial sense*; 12:7, (*only mid. in NT*) **to deal with**, *w/ dat.*; (161x LXX; 69x Lev)

προσ**φιλής, ές**$_{3.3}$ {πρός + φίλος} *adj.* ①[nnp] Phil 4:8, **lovely**; ❸ LXX, Esth 15:5; Sir 4:7; 20:13

προσ**φορά, ᾶς, ἡ**$_{1\alpha}$ {πρός + φέρω} ❾ (5x Heb 10) Acts 21:26; Rom 15:16; Eph 5:2; Heb 10:5, **offering**; (15x LXX; 9x Sir)

προσ**φωνέω**[con] ❼ Matt 11:16 = Luke 7:32, **to call out**; Acts 21:40; 22:2, **to address**; ❹ LXX, 1 Esd 6:21, **to send** *directions*; 2 Macc 15:15, **to address**

πρόσ**χυσις, εως, ἡ**$_3$ {πρός + χάρις} ①[afs] Heb 11:28, **sprinkling**

προσ**ψαύω** {πρός + ψάω} ①[pai2p] Luke 11:46, **to touch**

προσ**ωπολημπτέω**[con] {πρός + ὁράω + λαμβάνω} ①[pai2p] Jas 2:9, **to show favoritism**

προσ**ωπολήμπτης, ου, ὁ**$_{1>}$ {πρός + ὁράω + λαμβάνω} ①[nms] Acts 10:34, **one who shows favoritism**

προσ**ωπολημψία, ας, ἡ**$_{1\alpha}$ {πρός + ὁράω + λαμβάνω} ❹ Rom 2:11; Eph 6:9; Col 3:25; Jas 2:1, **favoritism**

πρόσ**ωπον, ου, τό**$_2$ {πρός + ὁράω} (76x; 25x LA, 12x 2 Cor) 1 Cor 13:12, **face**; Luke 9:51, **ahead**; 2 Cor 5:12, **appearance**; Mark 12:14, *idiom.*, *does not show favoritism*; Mark 14:65, *covered his* **face** (= *blindfolded*); 2 Cor 1:11, *many* **people**[BEC]; 2:10, **presence**; Gal 1:22, **personally**; (1,242x LXX; 104x Ezek, 103x Jer, 94x)

προ**τείνω** ①[aai3p] Acts 22:25, **to stretch out**; ❼ LXX, 2 Macc 3:20, **to stretch forth**

πρότερος, α, ον$_{2.1.2}$ *adj.* (11x) John 6:62, **before**; 7:50, **previously**; 2 Cor 1:15, **first**; Eph 4:22; 1 Pet 1:14, **former**; (108x LXX; 23x 1 Macc, 10x Isa)

προ**τίθημι** ❸ Rom 1:13, **to plan**; 1:25, **to display publicly**; Eph 1:9, **to design**; (12x LXX)

προ**τρέπω** ①[amp.nmp] Acts 18:27, **to encourage**; ❺ LXX, 4 Macc 12:7

προ**τρέχω** ❷ Luke 19:4; John 20:4, **to run ahead**; ❸ 1 Sam 8:11, **to run before**

προ**ϋπάρχω** {πρό + ὑπό + ἄρχω} ❷ Luke 23:12, *imperf. periphr.* **προϋπῆρχον** γὰρ ἐν ἔχθρᾳ ὄντες πρὸς αὐτούς, *for* **previously they had been** *in a state of enmity*[BHGNT]; Acts 8:9, **was formerly** *practicing magic*[EGG]; ①[iai3s] LXX, Job 42:17, *he* **was previously** *named Jobab*

πρό**φασις, εως, ἡ**$_3$ {πρό + φαίνω} ❻ Mark 12:40 = Luke 20:47, **for show**[ZEC]; John 15:22, **excuse**; Acts 27:30, **on the pretext**[Herm]; Phil 1:18, **pretense**[BEC]; 1 Thess 2:5, **false motive**; ❸ LXX, Ps 140:4 (141:4), **wicked**; Hos 10:4, *false* **allegations**

προ**φέρω** ❷ προφέρει,[pai3s] Luke 6:45, **to produce, to bring out**; ❻ LXX, 3 Macc 1:12

προ**φητεία, ας, ἡ**$_{1\alpha}$ {πρό + φημί} (19x; 7x Rev, 5x 1 Cor) Matt 13:14; Rom 12:6; 1 Cor 12:10; 14:6; 1 Thess 5:20; Rev 22:19, **prophecy**; (16x LXX; 7x Sir)

προ**φητεύω** {πρό + φημί} (28x; 11x 1 Cor, 6x LA) Matt 7:22; 15:7 = Mark 7:6; 14:65; John 11:51; Acts 2:17; 1 Cor 11:4; 14:1–39,[8x] **to prophesy**; (117x LXX; 40x Jer; 38x Ezek)

προ**φήτης, ου, ὁ**$_{1>}$ {πρό + φημί} (144x; 59x LA, 37x) 1 Cor 12:28; Eph 4:11, **prophet**; (323x LXX; 81x 1–2 Kgs; 48x Jer)

προ**φητικός, ή, όν**$_{2.1.2}$ {πρό + φημί} *adj.* ❷ Rom 16:26; 2 Pet 1:19; **prophetic**

προ**φῆτις, εως, ἡ**$_3$ {πρό + φημί} ❷ Luke 2:36, *Anna*, **prophetess**; Rev 2:20, *Jezebel*, *false* **prophetess**; ❺ LXX, Judg 4:4, *Deborah*; 2 Kgs 22:14 = 2 Chr 34:22, *Huldah*; Isa 8:3

προ**φθάνω** ①[aai3s] Matt 17:25, **to anticipate**[EGG]; (20x LXX; 11x Pss) 2 Sam 22:6; 1 Macc 10:4

προ**χειρίζω** {πρό + χείρ} ❸ Acts 3:20; 22:14; 26:16, **to appoint**

προχειροτονέω[con] {πρό + χείρ + τείνω} ①[pfmp.dmp] Acts 10:41, **to choose beforehand**

Πρόχορος, ου, ὁ$_{2}$ ①[ams] Acts 6:5, **Prochorus**

πρύμνα, ης, ἡ$_{1η>}$ ❸ Mark 4:38; Acts 27:29, 41, **stern** *of a boat*

πρωΐ {πρό} *adv.* (12x; 6x Mark) Matt 16:3; Mark 1:35; John 18:28, **early morning**; Acts 28:23, **dawn**; (185x LXX; 28x Exod, 19x Gen) Gen 1:5–31[6x]; Exod 16:7–24,[10x] **morning**

πρωΐα, ας, ἡ$_{1α}$ {πρό} ❷ Matt 27:1; John 21:4; (10x LXX), 2 Sam 23:4

πρωϊνός, ή, όν$_{2.1.2}$ *adj.* ❷ Rev 2:28; 22:16, **Morning** *Star*; (12x LXX) **morning**

πρῷρα, ης, ἡ$_{1η>}$ ❷ Acts 27:30, 41, **bow** *of a ship*

πρωτεύω {πρό} ①[pap.nms] Col 1:18, **to have first place**; ❸ LXX, Esth 5:11; 2 Macc 6:18

πρωτοκαθεδρία, ας, ἡ$_{1α}$ {πρό + κατά + ἕζομαι} ❹ Matt 23:6 = Mark 12:39 = Luke 11:43; 20:46, **the front seat**

πρωτοκλισία, ας, ἡ$_{1α}$ {πρό + κλίνω} ❺ Matt 23:6 = Mark 12:39 = Luke 14:7; 20:46, **place of honor**

πρῶτος, η, ον$_{2.1.2}$ {πρό} *adj/adv.* (157x; 76x Gs, 36x LA) Ⓐ ***position, order, time***, Eph 6:2; Phil 1:15; 1 Tim 5:2; Rev 2:4, **first of all**; Ⓑ ***adv.***, John 1:41; Acts 26:2, **first**; Ⓒ ***fig.***, ***ranking***, Matt 20:27; Luke 19:47; Acts 16:12, *to be* **first** (226x LXX; 31x 1–2 Chr)

πρωτοστάτης, ου, ὁ$_{1>}$ {πρό + ἵστημι} ①[ams] Acts 24:5, **ringleader**; ①[nms] LXX, Job 15:24

πρωτοτόκια, ας, ἡ$_{1α}$ {πρό + τίκτω} ①[anp] Heb 12:16, **birthright**; ❼ LXX (5x Gen), Gen 25:31–34[4x]; Deut 21:17, **firstborn**

πρωτότοκος, ον$_{2.2}$ *adj.* ❽ Luke 2:7; Rom 8:29; Col 1:15; Rev 1:5, **firstborn**; (132x LXX)

πρώτως {πρό} *adv.* ① Acts 11:26, **first** *called Christians at Antioch*

πταίω ❺ Rom 11:11, **to stumble**; Jas 2:10; 2 Pet 1:10, *milit.*, **to fall**[KEL]; (15x LXX) 1 Sam 4:10, *milit.*, **to be defeated**; Aristot. *Pr.* 875b 19, *the tongues of drunken men* **stumble**

πτέρνα, ης, ἡ$_{1η>}$ ①[afs] John 13:18, **heel**; (11x LXX; 3x Gen) Gen 3:15

πτερύγιον, ου, τό$_{2}$ {πέτομαι} ❷ Matt 4:5 = Luke 4:9, **pinnacle** *of the temple*; (18x LXX)

πτέρυξ, υγος, ἡ$_{3}$ {πέτομαι} ❺ Matt 23:37 = Luke 13:34; Rev 4:8; 12:14, **wings**; (78x LXX; 20x Ezek, 11x Pss)

πτηνός, οῦ, τό$_{2}$ {πέτομαι} ①[gnp] 1 Cor 15:39, **bird**

πτοέω[con] ❷ Luke 21:9; 24:37, **to be terrified, startled**; (37x LXX; 11x Jer) Exod 19:16

πτόησις, εως, ἡ$_{3}$ {πτοέω} ①[gnp] 1 Pet 3:6, **terror**[Keen1P]; ①[afs] LXX, Prov 3:25, **intimidation**

πτύον, ου, τό$_{2}$ ❷ Matt 3:12 = Luke 3:17, *winnowing* **shovel**

πτύρω ①[pmp.nmp] Phil 1:28, *ptc.*, **to frighten**

πτύσμα, ατος, τό$_{3}$ {πτύω} ①[gns] John 9:6, **spittle, saliva**

πτύσσω {πτύω} ①[aap.nms] Luke 4:20, **to roll up**

πτύω ❸ Mark 7:33; 8:23; John 9:6, **to spit**; ❷ LXX, Num 12:14; Sir 28:12

πτῶμα, ατος, τό$_{3}$ {πίπτω} ❼ Matt 14:12 = Mark 6:29; Rev 11:8–9,[3x] **corpse**; (22x LXX; 8x Job) Judg 14:8, **carcass** *of a lion*

πτῶσις, εως, ἡ$_{3}$ ❷ Matt 7:27; Luke 2:34, **collapse, fall**; (36x LXX; 7x Ezek)

πτωχεία, ας, ἡ$_{1α}$ ❸ 2 Cor 8:2, 9; Rev 2:9, **poverty**; (19x LXX; 7x Sir, 5x Pss)

πτωχεύω {πτωχός} ①[aai3s] 2 Cor 8:9, **to become poor**; ❻ LXX, Judg 6:6

πτωχός, ή, όν$_{2.1.2}$ *adj.* (28x; 10x Luke) Matt 5:3; Mark 12:42; Luke 16:20; John 12:5; 2 Cor 6:10; Jas 2:2–6[4x]; Rev 3:17; 13:16, **poor**; (122x LXX; 34x Pss, 22x Prov, 11x Isa)

πυγμή, ῆς, ἡ$_{1η}$ {πύξ} ①[dfs] Mark 7:3, *to wash* **with a handful** *of water*, **or with a cupped**

hand[ZEC!]; ❷ LXX, Exod 21:18; Isa 58:4, **fist**; Plato *Leg.* 795b, **boxing**; Thphr. *H.P.* 9.11.5, **arm**, *measuring from the elbow to a fisted first-finger joint*[BrDAG]

πύθων, ωνος, ὁ$_3$ ①[ams] Acts 16:16, *had a spirit of* **divination**; Πύθων = **Python**, *refers to the huge female dragon (or snake) called Python, which Apollo killed near Delphi*[BrDAG]

πυκνός, ή, όν$_{2.1.2}$ {πύξ} *adj.* ❸ Luke 5:33; Acts 24:26; 1 Tim 5:23, **often, frequent**; ❼ LXX

πυκτεύω {πυκνός} ①[pai1s] 1 Cor 9:26, **one who shadowboxes** *into empty air*[NIGTC]

πύλη, ης, ἡ$_{1η}$ (10x) Matt 7:13–14[3x]; Luke 7:12; Heb 13:12, **gate**; Acts 3:10, *Beautiful* **Gate**; (365x LXX; 99x Ezek, 36x 1–2 Chr, 35x Neh, 27x Jer)

πυλών, ῶνος, ὁ$_2$ (18x) Luke 16:20; Rev 21:12–22:14,[12x] **gate, gateway**; (30x LXX; 6x Ezek)

πυνθάνομαι (12x; 7x Acts) Matt 2:4; Luke 15:26; John 4:52; Acts 23:34, **to ask**; (13x LXX)

πῦρ, ος, τό$_3$ (71x; 26x Rev, 12x Matt) Matt 3:10 = Luke 3:9; Jas 3:5, 6, **fire**; 1 Cor 3:13–15,[3x] *will be saved . . . as through* **fire**[NIGTC]; Heb 1:7; Rev 1:14; 10:15, **fiery**; (502x LXX; 107x Pent)

πυρά, ᾶς, ἡ$_{1α}$ {πῦρ} ①[afs] Acts 28:2, **fire**; ❼ LXX, 2 Macc 1:22; 7:5

πύργος, ου, ὁ$_2$ ❹ Matt 21:33 = Mark 12:1, **watchtower**; Luke 13:4; 14:28, **tower**; (76x LXX; 9x Neh:1 Macc) Gen 11:4, 5, 8, **tower**

πυρέσσω {πῦρ} ❷ Matt 8:14 = Mark 1:30, *act.*, *in bed* **with a fever**

πυρετός, οῦ, ὁ$_2$ {πῦρ} ❻ Matt 8:15 = Mark 1:31 = Luke 4:38, 39; John 4:52; Acts 28:8, **fever**; ①[dms] LXX, Deut 28:22

πύρινος, η, ον$_{2.1.2}$ {πῦρ} *adj.* ①[amp] Rev 9:17, **fiery red**; ❸ LXX, Sir 48:9; Ezek 28:14, **fiery**

πυρόω[con] {πῦρ} ❻ 1 Cor 7:9; 2 Cor 11:29, **to burn**; Eph 6:16, *subst. ptc.*, **flaming**; 2 Pet 3:12, *will be destroyed* **by fire**; Rev 3:18, **to be refined** *by fire*; (26x LXX; 11x *pf. pass. ptc.*) Ps 11:7 (12:6)

πυρράζω {πῦρ} ❷ Matt 16:2, 3, *the sky* **is red**

πυρρός, ά, όν$_{2.1.2}$ {πῦρ} *adj.* ❷ Rev 6:4; 12:3, **fiery**; ❽ LXX, Zech 1:8[2x]; 6:2, **chestnut** *horses*

Πύρρος, ου, ὁ$_2$ {πῦρ} ① Acts 20:4, **Pyrrhus**

πύρωσις, εως, ἡ$_3$ {πῦρ} ❸ 1 Pet 4:12, *fiery* **burning**[Keen1P]; Rev 18:9, 18, **burning**; ❷ LXX, Prov 27:21, **burning**; Amos 4:9, **fever** (LES)

πωλέω[con] (22x; 20x GA) Matt 21:12 = Mark 11:15 = Luke 19:45 = John 2:14; Acts 4:34; 5:1; 1 Cor 10:25; Rev 13:17, **to sell**; (16x LXX) Gen 41:56; Exod 21:8; Neh 13:16

πῶλος, ου, ὁ$_2$ (12x; 11x Syn) Matt 21:2 = Mark 11:2 = Luke 19:30, **donkey**; ❼ LXX

πώποτε *adv.* ❻ (4x John) Luke 19:30; 1 John 4:12, **ever**; ❸ LXX, 1 Sam 25:28, **at any time**

πωρόω[con] ❺ Mark 6:52; John 12:40; Rom 11:7, **to harden**; ①[pfpi3p] LXX, Job 17:7, **to dim**

πώρωσις, εως, ἡ$_3$ {πωρόω} ❸ Mark 3:5; Rom 11:25; Eph 4:18, **hardness**

πῶς {ὅς} *interrog.* (103x; 20x John) Rom 4:10, **in what way?**; John 9:10, 19, 26, **how?**; 1 Cor 15:35, **How** *are the dead raised?*; (132x LXX; 17x Jer)

πώς {ὅς} *enclitic part.* (15x) Ⓐ (4x) εἴ **πως**, Acts 27:12; Rom 1:10; Phil 3:11, **somehow**; Ⓑ (11x) *w/* μή, 1 Cor 8:9, **lest somehow**; 2 Cor 2:7; 9:4, **perhaps**

Ρ, ρ [*rhō*]

Ρ, ρ, τό {ῥῶ} *indecl.* **rho**, *17th letter of the Gr. alphabet* || *num.* ρʹ = 100; ͵ρ = 100,000

Ῥαάβ, ἡ *indecl.* ❷ Heb 11:31; Jas 2:25, **Rahab**, ἡ πόρνη; *see below* **Ῥαχάβ, ἡ**$_3$ (12x LXX; 6x Rahab of NT)

ῥαββί *also* ῥαββεί (15x; 8x John) Matt 23:7; Mark 9:5; John 1:38–11:8, **Rabbi**

ῥαββουνί ❷ Mark 10:51; John 20:16, **teacher, Rabbouni** (***my teacher***)

ῥαβδίζω {ῥάβδος} ❷ Acts 16:22; 2 Cor 11:25, **to beat with a rod**; ❷ LXX, Judg 6:11

ῥάβδος, οῦ, ἡ$_{2\text{ὁδός}}$ (12x; 4x Heb, Rev) Matt 10:10 = Mark 6:8 = Luke 9:3, **staff**; 1 Cor 4:21, **stick**; Heb 1:8,^{2x} **scepter**; Rev 11:1, **a measuring rod**; (117x LXX; 22x Exod:Lev)

ῥαβδοῦχος, ου, ὁ$_2$ {ῥάβδος + ἔχω} ❷ Acts 16:35, 38, **police**

Ῥαγαύ, ὁ$_3$ *indecl.* ①^{gms} Luke 3:35, **Reu**; ❼ LXX, Gen 11:18, 24, **Reu**

ῥᾳδιούργημα, ατος, τό$_3$ {ῥᾴδιος + ἔργον} ①^{nns} Acts 18:14, **ῥᾳδιούργημα** πονηρόν, **serious piece of villainy** (NET); **wicked crime**[EGG]

ῥᾳδιουργία, ας, ἡ$_{1\alpha}$ ①^{gfs} Acts 13:10, **thoroughgoing fraud**[ABC]

Ῥαιφάν, ὁ *indecl.* ①^{gms} Acts 7:43, **Rephan**; ①^{gms} LXX, Amos 5:26

ῥακά, *also* **ῥαχά** ① Matt 5:22, **Raca**, *or* **empty-headed fool**[ZEC]

ῥάκος, ους, τό$_3$ ❷ Matt 9:16 = Mark 2:21, **piece of cloth, rag**; ❸ LXX, Isa 64:6

Ῥαμά, ἡ *indecl.* ①^{dfs} Matt 2:18, **Ramah**[*LCGa*]; (25x LXX; 8x 1 Sam) Jer 38:15 (31:15)

ῥαντίζω {ῥαίνω} ❹ Heb 9:13, 19, 21; 10:22, **to sprinkle**; ❸ LXX, 2 Kgs 9:33, **to splatter**

ῥαντισμός, οῦ, ὁ$_2$ {ῥαίνω} ❷ Heb 12:24; 1 Pet 1:2, **sprinkled**; ❺ LXX, Num 19:9

ῥαπίζω {ῥαπίς} ❷ Matt 5:39; 26:67, **to slap**; ❸ LXX, Judg 16:25, **to insult**; Hos 11:4, **to lift** *an infant* **to the cheek**; Hdt. *Hist.* 8.59, *the ones who jump the start signal* **are struck**[*BrDAG*]

ῥάπισμα, ατος, τό$_3$ {ῥαπίς} ❸ Mark 14:65 = John 18:22; 19:3, *with* **blows**: *club, whip, or slaps*; ①^{apn} LXX, Isa 50:6, **blows** *on the cheeks*

ῥαφίς, ίδος, ἡ$_3$ {ῥάπτω → **to stitch**} ❷ Matt 19:24 = Mark 10:25, **needle**; Aristot. *fr.* 294, *ichthyology*, **garfish**

Ῥαχάβ, ἡ$_3$ *indecl.* ①^{gfs} Matt 1:5, **Rahab**; *see above*, **Ῥαάβ, ἡ**

Ῥαχήλ, ἡ$_3$ *indecl.* ①^{nfs} Matt 2:18, **Rachel**; (50x LXX; 47x Gen) Gen 29:6–48:7

Ῥεβέκκα, ας, ἡ$_{1\alpha}$ ①^{nfs} Rom 9:10, **Rebecca**; (34x LXX, all in Gen) Gen 22:23–49:31

ῥέδη, ης, ἡ$_{1\eta}$ ①^{gfp} Rev 18:13, **four-wheeled carriage, chariot**

ῥέω^{con} ①^{fai3p} John 7:38, **to flow**; (41x LXX; 20x Pent) Exod 3:8, *land* **flowing** *with milk and honey*; Lev 15:19, **to discharge**; Zech 14:12, *eyes* **to melt out** (Heb. *rot*)

Ῥήγιον, ου, τό$_2$ ①^{ans} Acts 28:13, **Rhegium**[*LGCb*]

ῥῆγμα, ατος, τό$_3$ {ῥήγνυμι} ① Luke 6:49, **ruin**; ❺ LXX, 1 Kgs 11:30; 2 Kgs 2:12, **torn piece**; Hp. *Aër.* 4, *medic.* **fracture**; Aristot. *H.A.* 635a 4, **laceration, tear**

ῥήγνυμι ①^{pmi3p} Matt 9:17, **to burst, rupture**[EGG]; (38x LXX; 8x Job:Isa) Gen 7:11, *fountains of the great deep* **burst forth**; Jer 46:2 (39:2), *the city* **was breached**

ῥηθείς → λέγω, *aor. pass. ptc. nms*, Matt 3:3, *who* **said**

ῥηθέν → λέγω, *aor. pass. ptc. nns*, Matt 3:15, *who* **said**

ῥῆμα, ατος, τό$_3$ (68x; 33x LA) John 6:68, **word**; Luke 2:17, **thing(s) spoken**; 1:37, ὅτι οὐκ ἀδυνατήσει παρὰ τοῦ θεοῦ πᾶν ῥῆμα; *lit., not impossible will be* **word (or thing)** *with God*[ABC]; 7:1, **sayings**; Acts 2:14, **what** *I say*; Rom 10:37, **message**; 2 Cor 12:4, ἄρρητα ῥήματα, *unutterable* **words**; Jude 17, *prophetic* **message**[BEC]; (517x LXX; 164x Pent)

Ῥησά, ὁ$_3$ *indecl.* ①[gms] Luke 3:27, **Rhesa**

ῥήσσω {ῥήγνυμι} ❻ Matt 7:6, **to maul**; Mark 2:22 = Luke 5:37; Gal 4:27, **to burst**; Mark 9:18 = Luke 9:42, *it* **throws** *him down*

ῥήτωρ, ορος, ὁ$_3$ {ῥῆμα} ①[gms] Acts 24:1, **attorney**; Eur. *Hec.* 124, **public speaker**

ῥητῶς {ῥῆμα} *adv.* ① 1 Tim 4:1, **expressly**

ῥήξει → ῥήγνυμι, *fut. act. ind. 3s*, Luke 5:37, *the new wine* **will burst** *the wineskins*

ῥίζα, ης, ἡ$_{1>}$ (17x) Matt 3:10 = Luke 3:9, **taproot**[EGG]; Rom 15:12, *the* **root** *of Jesse*; 1 Tim 6:10, **root** *of all kinds of evil*; (56x LXX; 10x Job) Job 13:27, **soles** *of my feet*

ῥιζόω[con] {ῥίζα} ❷[pfpp.nmp] Eph 3:17 = Col 2:7, **to take root**; ❺ LXX, Isa 40:24; Jer 12:2, **to take root**; Hdt. *Hist.* 1.60.1, *he had a sovereignty that was not yet firmly* **rooted**

ῥιπή, ῆς, ἡ$_{1η}$ {ῥίπτω} ①[dfs] 1 Cor 15:52, **blinking** *of an eye*; Hom. *Il.* 16.589, *poet.* **force** *of a hurled object*; Aeschl. *Ag.* 893, *awoken by the faint* **buzz** *of mosquito's wings*[BrDAG]

ῥιπίζω {ῥίψ} ①[ppp.dms] Jas 1:6, **to be tossed about**[KEL]; ①[aai3s] LXX, Dan 2:35, **to carry away**; Aristoph. *Ec.* 842, *the fish* **is on** *the flame*

ῥιπτέω[con] ①[pap.gmp] Acts 22:23, **to take off**; Dion. *Rom. Ant.* 5.46, **to fling oneself** *into the enemy*

ῥίπτω ❼ Matt 9:36, **to be worn out**; 15:30, **to place**; Luke 4:35, **to throw down**; Acts 27:29, **to let down** *four anchors*; (103x LXX; 11x Ex:2 Kgs:Jer); Job 16:11, **to cast**

Ῥοβοάμ, ὁ$_3$ *indecl.* ❷ Matt 1:7,[2x] **Rehoboam**; (62x LXX; 30x 1 Kgs, 28x 2 Chr)

Ῥόδη, ης, ἡ$_1$ ①[nfs] Acts 12:13, **Rhoda**, *female name*

Ῥόδος, ου, ἡ$_2$ ①[afs] Acts 21:1, **Rhodes**; ①[afs] LXX, 1 Macc 15:23

ῥοιζηδόν *adv.* ① 2 Pet 3:10, **with a roar**[BEC]; Lyc. 66, **with hissing**, **violently**

ῥομφαία, ας, ἡ$_{1α}$ ❼ Luke 2:35; Rev 1:16, **sword**; (236x LXX; 46x Ezek, 20x 1 Sam)

Ῥουβήν, ὁ *indecl.* ①[gms] Rev 7:5, **Reuben**, *oldest son of Jacob and Leah*; (87x LXX)

Ῥούθ, ἡ *indecl.* ①[gfs] Matt 1:5, **Ruth**, *a Moabite, the wife of Boaz*; (19x LXX, Ruth)

Ῥοῦφος, ου, ὁ$_2$ ❷ Mark 15:21; Rom 16:13, **Rufus**

ῥύμη, ης, ἡ$_{1η}$ ❹ Matt 6:2; Luke 14:21; Acts 9:11; 12:10, **street**; ❸ LXX, Isa 15:3

ῥύομαι (17x) Matt 6:13; Rom 7:24; 1 Thess 1:10; 2 Pet 2:9; 2 Cor 1:10,[3x BEC!] **to rescue**, **deliver**; Rom 11:26, *subst. ptc.*, *the* **Deliverer**; (180x LXX; 62x Pss, 26x Isa)

ῥυπαίνω {ῥύπος} ①[apimp3s] Rev 22:11, **to be filthy**, **impure**

ῥυπαρία, ας, ἡ$_{1α}$ {ῥύπος} ①[afs] Jas 1:21, **moral filth**

ῥυπαρός, ά, όν$_{2.1.2}$ {ῥύπος} *adj.* ❷ Jas 2:2; Rev 22:11, **dirty**, **filthy**; ❷ LXX, Zech 3:3, 4, **filthy** *so a change for vestments is required for service to Yahweh*[ABC]

ῥύπος, ου, ὁ$_2$ ①[gms] 1 Pet 3:21, **dirt**, **moral filth**;[BEC] ❹ LXX, Job 11:15, **blemish**

ῥύσις, εως, ἡ$_3$ {ῥέω} ❸ Mark 5:25 = Luke 8:43, 44, **hemorrhage**; (19x LXX; 16x Lev) Lev 15:2–20:18, *laws concerning* **discharge**, **period**, **blood flow**

ῥυτίς, ίδος, ἡ$_3$ ①[afs] Eph 5:27, **fold**, **wrinkle**; Plato *Symp.* 190e, **crease**, **wrinkle**

Ῥωμαϊστί, *adv.* ① John 19:20, **in Latin, in the Roman language**; Plut. *Fort. Rom.* 318d, **in Latin**; Ῥωμαϊστής, IG 11.2.133.81, **actor in Latin comedy**

Ῥωμαῖος, α, ον$_{2.1.2}$ *adj.* (13x; 11x Acts) *subst.*, John 11:48; Acts 2:10, **Rome**; 16:21, **Romans**; Rom 1:0, Πρὸς **Ῥωμαίους**; (11x LXX; 10x 1–2 Macc) **Rome**, **Romans**; Dan 11:30

Ῥώμη, ης, ἡ$_{1η}$ ❽ (5x Acts) Acts 18:2; Rom 1:7; 2 Tim 1:17, **Rome**; (15x LXX; 12x 1 Macc)

ῥώννυμι ①^{pfpimp2p} Acts 15:29, **farewell, be strong**^{WPNT}; (10x LXX) 2 Macc 11:21, **farewell**

Σ, σ, ς [*sigma*]

Σ, σ *and* **ς, τό** (σίγμα *or* σῖγμα) *indecl.* **sigma**, *18th letter of the Gr. alphabet; in the form* **ς** *at the end of a word* ‖ *num.* σʹ = 200; ͵σ = 200,000

σαβαχθάνι *Aram.* ❷ Matt 27:46 = Mark 15:34, *Why* **have you abandoned me**?

Σαβαώθ, ὁ$_3$ *and* **τό**$_3$ *Heb. indecl.* ❷ Rom 9:29; Jas 5:4, **hosts, armies**; (64x LXX; 53x Isa)

σαββατισμός, οῦ, ὁ$_2$ {σάββατον} ①^{nms} Heb 4:9, **Sabbath rest, observance**

σάββατον, ου, τό$_2$ (68x; 66x GA) Matt 12:1 = Mark 2:23 = Luke 6:1; John 5:9; Acts 1:12; 1 Cor 16:2; Col 2:16, **Sabbath, week**^{NIDNTT}; (130x LXX; 21x Lev)

σαγήνη, ης, ἡ$_{1\eta}$ ①^{dfs} Matt 13:47, **dragnet**; **fishing-net**; (7x LXX) Hab 1:15

Σαδδουκαῖος, ου, ὁ$_2$ (14x; 7x Matt) Matt 3:7 = Luke 20:27; Acts 23:6, **Sadducee(s)**

Σαδώκ, ὁ$_3$ *indecl.* ❷ Matt 1:14,^{2x} **Zadok**; (42x LXX; 15x 1 Chr) 2 Sam 15:24; 1 Chr 15:11

σαίνω ①^{painf} 1 Thess 3:3, **to disturb**; Hes. *Th.* 771, *Cerberus, monster dog guarding Hades,* **fawns** *with his tail*; Hom. *Od.* 10.219, **wagging** *long tails*

σάκκος, ου, ὁ$_2$ ❹ Matt 11:21 = Luke 10:13; Rev 6:12; 11:3, **sackcloth**; (62x LXX; 9x Isa)

Σαλά, ὁ$_3$ *indecl.* ❷^{gms} Luke 3:32, 35, **Shelah**; ❼ LXX, Gen 10:24^{2x}

Σαλαθιήλ, ὁ$_3$ *indecl.* ❸ Matt 1:12; Luke 3:27, **Shealtiel**^{BEC}; (16x LXX; 6x Hag) Hag 1:1

Σαλαμίς, ῖνος, ἡ$_3$ ①^{dfs} Acts 13:5, **Salamis**

Σαλείμ, τό$_3$ *indecl.* ①^{gns} John 3:23, **Salim**; ①^{ams} LXX, Josh 19:22

σαλεύω {σάλος} (15x; 8x LA) *act.*, Matt 24:29 = Mark 13:25, **to shake**; Acts 17:13, **to stir up**; *pass.*, Heb 12:27,^{2x} *evil powers* **to be shaken**^{NICNT}; 2 Thess 2:2, *to have* **unshaken** *composure*; (76x LXX; 34x Pss); Xen. *Oec.* 8:17, *pass.*, **to be tossed around violently** *on a ship*

Σαλήμ, ἡ$_3$ *indecl.* ❷^{gfs} Heb 7:1, 2, **Salem**; ❹ LXX, Gen 14:18; 33:18

Σαλμών, ὁ$_3$ *indecl.* ❷ Matt 1:4, 5, **Salmon**, *son of Nahshon, father of Boaz*; *echoing* 1 Kgs 2:11; ❸ LXX, Num 25:14; 1 Chr 4:11

Σαλμώνη, ης, ἡ$_{1\eta}$ ①^{afs} Acts 27:7, **Salmone**

σάλος, ου, ὁ$_2$ ①^{gms} Luke 21:25, **surging wave**; ❾ LXX, Jonah 1:15, **raging** *sea*

σάλπιγξ, ιγγος, ἡ$_3$ {σαλπίζω} (11x; 6x Rev) Matt 24:31; 1 Cor 14:8; 15:52; 1 Thess 4:16; Rev 1:10; 4:1; 8:2; 9:14, **trumpet**; (95x LXX; 12x 2 Chr) 2 Chr 5:12

σαλπίζω (12x; 10x Rev) 1 Cor 15:52; Rev 8,^{5x} **to sound a trumpet**; (61x LXX; 10x Num)

σαλπιστής, οῦ, ὁ$_{1>}$ {σαλπίζω} ①^{gmp} Rev 18:22, **trumpeter**

Σαλώμη, ης, ἡ$_1$ ❷^{nfs} Mark 15:40, 16:1, **Salome**

Σαμάρεια, ας, ἡ$_{1\alpha}$ (11x; 7x Acts) Luke 17:11 = John 4:4; Acts 9:31, **Samaria**; (114x LXX)

Σαμαρίτης, ου, ὁ$_{1>}$ ❾ Matt 10:5; Luke 10:33; John 4:39; Acts 8:25, **Samaritan**

Σαμαρῖτις, ιδος, ἡ$_3$ ❷ John 4:9,^{2x} **Samaritan** *woman* ❸ LXX, 1 Macc 10:30

Σαμοθρᾴκη, ης, ἡ$_{1\eta}$ ①^{afs} Acts 16:11, **Samothrace**

Σάμος, ου, ὁ$_2$ ①^{ams} Acts 20:15, **Samos**; ①^{ams} LXX, 1 Macc 15:23

Σαμουήλ, ὁ$_3$ *indecl.* ❸^{gms} Acts 3:24; 13:20; Heb 11:32, **Samuel**; (147x LXX; 133x 1 Sam)

Σαμψών, ὁ$_3$ *indecl.* ①^{gms} Heb 11:32, **Samson**; (45x LXX; 45x Judg) Judg 13:24–16:30

σανδάλιον, ου, ὁ$_2$ ❷ Mark 6:9; Acts 12:8, **sandal**; ❹ LXX, Josh 9:11; Isa 20:2
σανίς, ίδος, ἡ$_3$ ①^{dfp} Acts 27:44, **board**, **plank**; ❷ LXX, Song 8:9; Ezek 27:5
Σαούλ, ὁ$_3$ *indecl.* ❾ Acts 9:4; 22:7; 26:14, **Σαοὺλ, Σαούλ**; 9:17, 22:13, **Saul** *of Tarsus*; 13:21, *King* **Saul**, *first Israelite king* (381x LXX; 270x 1 Sam, 66x 2 Sam)
σαπρός, ά, όν$_{2.1.2}$ {σήπω} *adj.* ❽ Matt 7:17, 18 = Luke 6:43^{2x}; Matt 12:33, **unhealthy**, **rotten**; Eph 4:29, **evil**; Aristoph. *Ach.* 1095, **stale**
σάπφειρος, ου, ἡ$_{2ὁδός}$ ①^{dfs} Rev 21:19, **sapphire**; (13x LXX) Isa 54:11
Σάπφιρα, ης, ἡ$_1$ ①^{dfs} Acts 5:1, **Sapphira**
σαργάνη, ης, ἡ$_{1η}$ ①^{dfs} 2 Cor 11:33, **basket**
Σάρδεις, εων, ἡ$_3$ ❸ Rev 1:11; 3:1, 4, **Sardis**
σάρδιον, ου, ὁ$_2$ ❷ Rev 4:3; 21:20, **carnelian**; ❼ LXX (4x Exod)
σαρδόνυξ, υχος, ὁ$_3$ {σάρδιον} ①^{nms} Rev 21:20, **onyx**
Σάρεπτα, ων, τά$_3$ ①^{anp} Luke 4:36, **Zarephath**; ❸ LXX, Obad 20
σαρκικός, ή, όν$_{2.1.2}$ {σάρξ} *adj.* ❼ Rom 15:27, *subst.*, **things of the flesh**; 1 Cor 3:3, **moved by human compulsion**^{NIGTC}; 2 Cor 1:12; 10:4, **merely human**^{BEC}; 1 Pet 2:11, **carnal**
σάρκινος, η, ον$_{2.1.2}$ {σάρξ} *adj.* ❹ Rom 7:14; 1 Cor 3:1, **unspiritual**, **of the flesh**; 2 Cor 3:3, **fleshy**; Heb 7:16, **physical**, ❺ LXX, 2 Chr 32:8; Prov 24:22; Ezek 36:26
σάρξ, σαρκός, ἡ$_3$ (147x; 91x Paul: 26x Rom) 🅐 ***sinful humanity/flesh***: Matt 26:41 = Mark 14:38; 1 Cor 5:5^{NIGTC}; 🅑 ***human flesh***: Matt 16:7; Rev 19:21; 🅒 ***human standards***: 2 Cor 10:3^{BEC}; Gal 2:20; Jude 8; 🅓 ***human nature***: Gal 4:29; 2 John 7; 🅔 ***humanity***: Acts 2:17; 🅕 ***worldly perspective***: 2 Cor 5:16^{BEC}; 🅖 ***everyday life***: Heb 5:7; (208x LXX; 32x Gen, 23x Sir)
σαρόω^{con} ❸ Matt 12:44 = Luke 11:25; 15:8, **to sweep** *in a house*
Σάρρα, ας, ἡ$_{1α}$ ❹ Rom 4:19; 9:9; Heb 11:11; 1 Pet 3:6, **Sarah**; (65x LXX; 52x Gen)
Σαρών, ῶνος, ὁ$_3$ ①^{ams}Acts 9:35, **Sharon**; ❸ LXX, Josh 12:18; 1 Chr 5:16; Isa 33:9
Σατανᾶς, ᾶ, ὁ$_1$ (36x; 15x Syn, 1x John) Matt 4:10; 16:23; Mark 1:13; John 13:27; Acts 5:3; 2 Cor 11:14; 1 Thess 2:18; Rev 2:9–20:7,^{8x} **Satan**; ①^{ams} LXX, Sir 21:27, **adversary**
σάτον, ου, τό$_2$ ❷ Mark 13:33 = Luke 13:21, **measure**; ❷ LXX, Hag 2:16^{2x}
Σαῦλος, ου, ὁ$_2$ (15x, Acts) 7:58, **Saul**, *Hebrew name of the apostle Paul*
σβέννυμι {ἄ + σβεστος} ❻ Matt 12:20, **to smolder**; 25:8, **to flicker**; Mark 9:48; Eph 6:16; 1 Thess 5:19; Heb 11:34, **to quench**; (44x LXX; 8x Job) Job 4:10, **to break**
σεαυτοῦ, ῆς {σύ + αὐτός} *refl. pron.* (43x; 9x John) Matt 4:6 = Luke 4:9; Matt 19:19 = Rom 13:9 = Gal 5:14; 2 Tim 4:11; Titus 2:7, **yourself**; Phlm 19, **your own self** (230x LXX)
σεβάζομαι {σέβω} ①^{api3p} Rom 1:25, **to worship**
σέβασμα, ατος, τό$_3$ {σέβω} ❷ Acts 17:23; 2 Thess 2:4, **object of worship**; ❷ LXX
Σεβαστός, ή, όν$_{2.1.2}$ {σέβω} *adj.* ❸ Acts 25:21, 25, equiv. to Lat. *Augustus*, so **Emperor**; 27:1, *the* **Augustan Cohort**
σέβω (10x *pres. mid.*; 8x Acts) Matt 15:9 = Mark 7:7; Acts 18:13; 19:27, **to worship**; 18:7, **worshiper**; 13:43, 50; 17:4, 17; 18:7, **devout**; (20x LXX) Josh 4:24
σειρά, ᾶς, ἡ$_{1α}$ ①^{dfp} 2 Pet 2:4, **chain**; ❹ LXX, Judg 16:13, *seven* **locks** *of Samson's hair*
σεισμός, οῦ, ὁ$_2$ {σείω} (14x) Matt 8:24, **windstorm**^{KeenM}; Matt 24:7 = Mark 13:8; Acts 16:26; Rev 6:12–16:18,^{7x} **earthquake**; (15x LXX) Nah 3:2, *the* **rumble** *of the wheel*
σείω ❺ *act.*, Matt 27:51, Heb 12:26, **to shake** *the earth, ground*; Matt 28:4, **to tremble**; *pass.*,

Matt 21:10, **to be in turmoil**; Rev 6:13, **when shaken** *by a gale* (42x LXX); *medic.*, Aristoph. *Nub.* 1276, *pass.*, *brain* **is shaken**; *medic.*, Hp. *Prorrh.* 1.143 *subst.*, **seizures** *in the head*[BrDAG]; Xen. *Hel.* 4.7.4, *the god* **made the earth tremble**

Σεκοῦνδος, ου, ὁ ①[nms] Acts 20:4, **Secundus**; Eus. *Hist. eccl.* 3.33.3; Jos. *B.J.* 2.205

Σελεύκεια, ας, ἡ$_{1α}$ ①[afs] Acts 13:4, **Seleucia**; ①[gfs] LXX, 1 Macc 11:8

σελήνη, ης, ἡ$_{1η}$ ❾ Matt 24:29 = Luke 21:25; Acts 2:20; Rev 6:12, **moon**; (41x LXX; 9x Pss)

σεληνιάζομαι {σελήνη} ❷ Matt 4:24; 17:15, **to be an epilectic,**[BN] **to be moonstruck**

Σεμεΐν, ὁ$_{3}$ *indecl.* ①[gms] Luke 3:26, **Semein**, *in Jesus's genealogy*

σεμίδαλις, εως, ἡ$_{3}$ ①[afs] Rev 18:3, **fine wheat flour**; (65x LXX; 27x Num)

σεμνός, ή, όν$_{2.1.2}$ {σέβω} *adj.* ❹ Phil 4:8, **honorable**; 1 Tim 3:8, 11; Titus 2:2, **dignified**; ❾ LXX, Prov 8:6, **noble**; Aeschl. *Ag.* 519, **majestic, worthy of respect**

σεμνότης, τητος, ἡ$_{3}$ {σέβω} ❸ 1 Tim 2:2; 3:4; Titus 2:7, **moral earnestness**; ①[dfs] LXX, 2 Macc 3:12, **sanctity**; Plato *Menex.* 235b, **gravitas**

Σέργιος, ου, ὁ$_{2}$ ①[dms] Acts 13:7, **Sergius** *Paulus, Paul's first named convert*

Σερούχ, ὁ$_{2}$ *indecl.* ①[gms] Luke 3:35, **Serug**, *son of Reu*; ❼ LXX, Gen 11:20–23[4x]

Σήθ, ὁ$_{3}$ *indecl.* ①[gms] Luke 3:38, **Seth**, *son of Adam*; (10x LXX; 7x Gen 4–5)

Σήμ, ὁ$_{3}$ *indecl.* ①[gms] Luke 3:36, **Shem**, *son of Noah*; (17x LXX; 14x Gen)

σημαίνω {σημεῖον} ❻ John 12:33; 18:32; 21:19; Acts 25:27, **to indicate**; 11:28, **to predict**; Rev 1:1, **to signify**; (25x LXX) Num 10:9, **to give a signal**

σημεῖον, ου, τό$_{2}$ (77x; 61x GA, 17x John) Matt 12:38; Mark 13:22; Luke 2:12; Acts 2:19; Rom 4:11; 2 Cor 12:12; 2 Thess 2:9; Rev 12:1–19:20,[7x] **sign**; (116x LXX; 19x Exod, 15x Isa)

σημειόω[con] ①[pmimp2p] 2 Thess 3:14, **to take note of**; ❷ LXX, Ps 4:7, **to look**

σήμερον {ἡμέρα} *adv.* (41x; 20x LA) Matt 6:11, **daily**; 6:30, Mark 14:30; 2 Cor 3:14; **day**; Luke 19:5; Heb 1:5; 4:7[2x]; Jas 4:13, **today**; (283x LXX; 68x 1–2 Sam, 67x Deut)

σήπω {σαπρός} ①[pfai3s] Jas 5:2, **to cause to rot**[KEL] ❽ LXX (4x Job), *pass.*, Job 33:21, *their flesh is* **wasted**; Hom. *Il.* 19.27; Aristot. *An.* 411b, **to go septic**, *of corpses* (*with pf. act.*)

σής, σητός, ὁ$_{3}$ ❸[nms] Matt 6:19, 20 = Luke 12:33, **moth** (10x LXX; 3x Job)

σητόβρωτος, ον$_{2.2}$ {σής + βιβρώσκω} *adj.* ①[nnp] Jas 5:2, **moth-eaten**; ①[nns] LXX, Job 13:28

σθενόω[con] {σθένος} ①[fai3s] 1 Pet 5:10, **to fortify**[Keen1P]; ①[iai3p] LXX, 3 Macc 3:8

σιαγών, όνος, ἡ {ψίω} ❷[afs] Matt 5:39 = Luke 6:29, **cheek, jaw**; (21x LXX; 8x Judg)

σιγάω[con] {σιγή} (10x; 6x LA) Luke 9:36; 1 Cor 14:28, 30, **to be silent**; Acts 15:13, **to stop speaking**; 1 Cor 14:34, **to allow for silence**[NIGTC]; (18x LXX; 5x Pss) Amos 6:10, **Hush!**

σιγή, ῆς, ἡ$_{1η}$ {σιγάω} ❷ Acts 21:40; Rev 8:1, **silence**; ❷ LXX, Wis 18:14; 3 Macc 3:23

σίδηρος, ου, ὁ$_{2}$ {σιδηροῦς} ①[gms] Rev 18:12, **iron**; (68x LXX; 8x Dan, 7x Job)

σιδηροῦς, ᾶ, οῦν$_{2.1.2}$ {σίδηρος} *adj.* ❺ (4x Rev) Acts 12:10; Rev 2:27; 9:9, **made of iron** (38x LXX)

Σιδών, ῶνος, ἡ$_{3}$ ❾ Matt 11:21 = Luke 10:13, Acts 27:3, **Sidon**; (23x LXX; 4x Ezek, 3x Deut)

Σιδώνιος, ία, ιον$_{2.1.2}$ *adj.* ❷ Luke 4:26; Acts 12:20, **of Sidonia, Sidonian** (15x LXX; 5x Judg)

σικάριος, ου, ὁ$_{2}$ ①[mgp] Acts 21:38, **terrorist**[Keen3]; (19x Jos. ***Sicarii***)

σίκερα, τό$_{3}$ *indecl.* ① Luke 1:15, **fermented drink**; (12x LXX; 6x Isa) Lev 10:9, **beer**

Σιλᾶς, α or **Σίλας, ᾶ, ὁ**$_{1}$ (12x, only in Acts) Acts 15:22–18:5, **Silas**

Σιλουανός, οῦ, ὁ$_{2}$ ❹ *Latinized form of* Σίλας, 2 Cor 1:19; 1 Thess 1:1; 2 Thess 2:1; 1 Pet 5:12, **Silvanus**, *probably same as* Σίλας[NIGTC]

Σιλωάμ, ὁ$_3$ *indecl.* ❸ Luke 13:4; John 9:7, 11, **Siloam**[LGCa]

σιμι**κίνθιον, ου, το$_2$** ①[anp] *from Latin semicinctium*,[ZEC] Acts 19:12, **apron**[Keen3]

Σίμων, ωνος, ὁ$_3$ (75x) **Simon**: Ⓐ *Peter, Jesus's disciple* (29x), Matt 4:18; Ⓑ *eight other less prominent men named Simon in NT*; (80x LXX; 78x 1–4 Macc)

Σινά, τό$_3$ *indecl.* ❹ Acts 7:30, 38; Gal 4:24, 25, *Mount* **Sinai**; (38x LXX; 14x Exod, 13x Num)

σίναπι, εως, ἡ$_3$ ❺[gns] Matt 13:31; 17:20; Mark 4:31; Luke 13:19; 17:6, **mustard plant**

σινδών, όνος, ἡ$_3$ ❻ Matt 27:59; Mark 14:51, **linen cloth**; ❸ LXX, Judge 14:12

σινιάζω ①[aainf] Luke 22:31[NIGTC] **to sift**

σιρικός, ή, όν$_{2.1.2}$ *adj.* ①[gns] Rev 18:12, **silk**

σιτευτός, ή, όν$_{2.1.2}$ {σιτίζω} *adj.* ❸ Luke 15:23, 27, 30, **fattened** *calf*; ❷ LXX, 1 Kgs 4:23

σιτίον, ου, τό$_2$ {σιτίζω} ①[anp] Acts 7:12, **grain**; ①[gnp] LXX, Prov 24:57 **food**

σιτιστός, ή, όν$_{2.1.2}$ {σιτίζω} *adj.* ①[nnp] Matt 22:4, **fattened animals**

σιτο**μέτριον, ου, τό$_2$** {σιτίζω + μέτρον} ①[ans] Luke 12:42, **ration of grain**

σῖτος, ου, ὁ$_2$ (14x) Matt 3:12; Acts 27:38; Rev 6:6, **wheat**; (79x LXX; 13x Gen)

Σιών, ἡ$_3$ *indecl.* ❼ Matt 21:5; Rom 9:33; 1 Pet 2:6; Rev 14:1, **Zion**[LGCb]; (184x LXX; 54x Isa)

σιωπάω[con] {σιωπή} (10x; 5x Mark) Matt 20:31; 26:63; Mark 3:4; Luke 1:20; Acts 18:9, **to be silent, quiet**; (35x LXX) Job 18:3, **to be stupid** (NRSV)

σκανδαλίζω {σκάνδαλον} (29x) Matt 18:6 = Mark 9:42 = Luke 17:2 Matt 5:29, 30, **to fall away**; Matt 26:31, **to run away** (HCSB); Mark 9:42–47[DGNT2]; 1 Cor 8:13, **to trip one up**[NIGTC]; 2 Cor 11:29, **to lead into sin**[BEC]; ❺ LXX, Dan 11:41, **to fall victim**

σκάνδαλον, ου, τό$_2$ {σκανδαλίζω} (15x) Matt 13:41, *all* **causes of sin**[BHGNT]; 16:23, *Peter,* **a big problem**[Brun2]; 18:7,[3x] **that which trips up another's faith**[Brun2]; Rev 2:14, **stumbling stone**; Gal 5:11, *the* **offense** *of the cross*; (22x LXX; 7x Pss) Lev 19:14, **stumbling block**; Ps 69:22 (68:23), **snare**

σκάπτω ❸ Luke 6:48; 13:8; 16:3, **to dig**; ①[aps3s] LXX, Isa 5:6, **to hoe** *its ground*

σκάφη, ης, ἡ$_{1η}$ {σκάπτω} ❸ Acts 27:16, 30, 32, **boat**; ①[dfs] LXX, Bel 33

σκέλος, ους, τό$_3$ ❸ John 19:31, 32, 33, **legs**; (10x LXX)

σκέπασμα, ατος, τό$_3$ ①[anp] 1 Tim 6:8, **clothing**; Plato *Pol.* 279d, **protection**, *i.e., shoes*

Σκευᾶς, ᾶ, ὁ$_1$ ①[gms] Acts 19:14, **Sceva**

σκευή, ῆς, ἡ$_{1η}$ ①[afs] Acts 27:19, *ship's* **tackle**[Keen4]; ❼ LXX, Ezra 1:6, *silver* **vessels**

σκεῦος, ους, τό$_3$ (23x; 5x Acts) Matt 12:29 = Mark 3:27, **property**; John 19:29, **jar**; 2 Tim 2:20, **utensil**; 2 Cor 4:7, *clay* **jars**; 1 Thess 4:4, *euph.* **body**, **sexuality**, **genitalia**[NIGTC]; (300x LXX; *esp.* historical books) 1 Sam 21:5, **vessels**; Ael. *N.A.* 17.11, **penis**

σκηνή, ῆς, ἡ$_{1η}$ (20x; 10x Heb) Matt 17:4; **shelter**; Acts 7:43; Heb 8:2–13:10, **tent**; Rev 13:6; 15:5; 21:3, **tent**, **tabernacle** *in heaven*; (423x LXX; 112x Num, 96x Exod)

σκηνο**πηγία, ας, ἡ$_{1α}$** {σκηνόω + πήγνυμι} ①[nfs] John 7:2, *Festival of* **Tabernacles**, ❾ LXX, Deut 16:16, *Festival of* **Shelters**; *feast of* **tent pitching** (NETS)

σκηνο**ποιός, οῦ, ὁ$_2$** {σκηνή + ποιέω} ①[nmp] Acts 18:3, **tentmaker**, *by ext.* **tanner**; Com. 806, **theater set-designer**

σκῆνος, ους, τό$_3$ {σκηνόω} ❷ 2 Cor 5:1, 4, **a tent**[BEC]; ①[nns] LXX, Wis 9:15

σκηνόω[con] {σκῆνος} ❺ John 1:14, **to dwell**, **pitch a tent**; Rev 7:15; 12:12; 21:3, *subst. ptc.*, **those tabernacling**, *whether God or his people*; ❹ LXX, Judg 8:11, *subst. ptc.*, *the way of* **the tent dwellers**

σκήνωμα, ατος, τό$_3$ {σκηνόω} ❸ Acts 7:46, **dwelling place**; 2 Pet 1:13, **body, temporary dwelling**; 2 Pet 1:14, *the laying aside of my* **temporary dwelling** (= *death*); (78x LXX; 26x Pss) 2 Sam 19:9 (19:8), **home, tent**

σκιά, ᾶς, ἡ$_{1\alpha}$ ❼ Matt 4:16; Mark 4:32; Luke 1:79; Acts 5:15; Col 2:17; Heb 8:5; 10:1, **shadow, shade**; (52x LXX; 10x Job:Pss) Ps 106:14 (107:14), **gloom**

σκιρτάω^{con} ❸ Luke 1:41, 44; 6:23, **to leap**; ❼ LXX, Gen 25:22, **to struggle** *in the womb*; Plato *Rp.* 571c, *the beastly and wild part of the soul* **jumps playfully**

σκληρο**καρδία, ας, ἡ**$_{1\alpha}$ ❸ Matt 19:8 = Mark 10:5; Matt 19:8; **hard-hearted**; Mark 16:14, **stubbornness**; ❷ LXX, Deut 10:16; Jer 4:4, **the hardness of your heart**

σκληρός, ά, όν$_{2.1.2}$ {σκληρύνω} *adj.* ❺ Matt 25:24; Jas 3:4; Jude 15, **harsh**; John 6:60; Acts 26:14, **difficult, hard**; (57x LXX; 11x Isa) Isa 48:4, **obstinate**; Hp. *Aph.* 3.25, **constipated**

σκληρότης, ητος, ἡ$_3$ {σκληρός} ①^{afs} Rom 2:5, **stubbornness**; ❹ LXX, 2 Sam 22:6, **snares** *of death*; Isa 4:6, **storm**; Thphr. *C.P.* 6.14.12, **harshness** *of wine*

σκληρο**τράχηλος, ον**$_{2.2}$ *adj.* ①^{vmp} Acts 7:51, **stiff-necked**; ❽ LXX, Exod 33:3

σκληρύνω {σκληρός} ❻ Acts 19:9, **to be hardened**; Rom 9:18, **to harden**; Heb 3:8, 13, 15; 4:7, **to harden** *one's heart*; (37x LXX; 14x Exod) Exod 4:21–14:17, *comb. of* 4:21, *God* **will harden** *Pharaoh's heart*; 8:15, *Pharaoh* **hardens** *his own heart*; and 7:13, *Pharaoh's heart* **was hardened**

σκολιός, ά, όν$_{2.1.2}$ *adj.* ❹ Luke 3:5; Acts 2:40; Phil 2:15, **crooked, corrupt**; 1 Pet 2:18, **abrasive, harsh**; (23x LXX; 11x Prov) Prov 2:15, **crooked**; Pind. *P.* 2.85, **twisting** *paths*

σκόλοψ, οπος, ὁ$_3$ ①^{nms} 2 Cor 12:7, **splinter, thorn**; ❹ LXX, Hos 2:6, **brier**; Eur. *I.T.* 1430, *to impale on a* **stake**

σκοπέω^{con} {σκοπός} ❻ 2 Cor 4:18; Phil 3:17, **to pay careful attention**; Rom 16:17, **to look out for**; Phil 2:4, **to be concerned about**; ❷ LXX, 2 Macc 4:5, **to have in view**

σκοπός, οῦ, ὁ$_2$ ①^{ams} Phil 3:14, **goal**; (27x LXX; 7x 2 Sam) 2 Sam 18:24–27,^{5x} **watchman**; Job 16:13 (16:12), **target**

σκορπίζω ❺ Matt 12:30 = Luke 11:23; Matt 12:30; John 10:12; 2 Cor 9:9, **to scatter**; (26x LXX) Neh 4:13 (4:19), **to separate**

σκορπίος, ου, ὁ$_2$ ❺ Luke 10:19; 11:12; Rev 9:3, 5, 10, **scorpion**; (10x LXX) 2 Chr 10:14, **barbed whips**; *cf.* 1 Macc 6:51, *milit.*, **σκορπίδιον, siege engine**

σκοτεινός, ή, όν$_{2.1.2}$ *adj.* ❸ Matt 6:23 = Luke 11:34, 36, **darkness, dark**

σκοτία, ας, ἡ$_{1\alpha}$ {σκότος} (16x; 8x John, 6x 1 John) Matt 10:27 = Luke 12:3; 1 John 1:5–2:11,^{3x} **darkness**; ❸ LXX, Job 28:3, **gloom**; Mic 3:6; Isa 16:3; Ap. 4.1698, **darkness** *of death*

σκοτίζω {σκότος} ❺ Matt 24:29; Rom 1:21; 11:10, **to be dark, darkened**; Ps 68:24 (69:3); ❻ LXX, 3 Macc 4:10, **to darken, grow dim**

σκότος, ους, τό$_3$ {σκοτία} (31x; 7x Matt) Matt 27:45 = Mark 15:33 = Luke 23:44; John 3:19; Acts 2:20; 2 Cor 4:6; Eph 6:12; 2 Pet 2:17, **darkness**; (112x LXX; 24x Job)

σκοτόω^{con} {σκοτόω} ❸ Eph 4:18; Rev 9:2; 16:10, *pass.*, **to become dark, be darkened**; ❻ LXX, Job 3:9, **to grow dark**; Soph. *Ai.* **to blind**; Plato *Prot.* 339e, **to have a dizzy spell**

σκύβαλον, ου, τό$_2$ ①^{anp} Phil 3:8, **excrement**; ①^{nnp} LXX, Sir 27:4, **refuse**, *poet. w/* **faults**; Leon. 6.302.6, **residue, rubbish**; Plut. *Isid.* 352d, **excrement**

Σκύθης, ου, ὁ$_{1>}$ ①^{nms} Col 3:11, **Scythian**; ①^{gmp} LXX, Jdt 3:10

σκυθρωπός, ή, όν$_{2.1.2}$ {σκυθρός + ὁράω} *adj.* ❷ Matt 6:16, **sad-faced** (HCSB); Luke 24:17, **glum, gloomy-faced**[ZEC]; ❷ LXX, Gen 40:7, *faces* **downcast**; Demosth. 45.68, **severe**

σκύλλω ❹ Mark 5:35 = Luke 8:49; Matt 9:36; Luke 7:6, **to be troubled**

σκῦλον, ου, τό$_{2}$ {σκύλλω} ①[anp] Luke 11:22, **plunder**; (96x LXX; 17x 1, 2 Sam) 1 Sam 14:30, **spoil, plunder**; Soph. *Ph.* 1428, *usu. pl.* **armaments** *of a slain enemy*

σκωληκόβρωτος, ον$_{2.2}$ {σκώληξ + βιβρώσκω} ①[nms] Acts 12:23, **eaten by worms**

σκώληξ, ηκος, ὁ$_{3}$ ①[nms] Mark 9:48, **worm**; (18x LXX) Ps 21:7 (22:6)

σμαράγδινος, η, ον$_{2.1.2}$ {σμάραγδος} *adj.* ①[dms] Rev 4:3, **made of emerald**

σμάραγδος, ου, ὁ$_{2}$ ①[nms] Rev 21:19, **emerald**; (10x LXX; 6x Exod)

σμύρνα, ης, ἡ$_{1>}$ ❷ Matt 2:11; John 19:3, *botan.* **myrrh**; (10x LXX; 7x Song) Exod 30:23

Σμύρνα, ης, ἡ$_{1>}$ ❷ Rev 1:11; 2:8, **Smyrna**

σμυρνίζω {σμύρνα} ①[pfpp.ams] Mark 15:23, **to flavor with myrrh**

Σόδομα, ων, τά$_{2}$ ❾ Matt 10:15; 11:23 = Luke 10:12; **Sodom**; (40x LXX; 21x Gen)

Σολομῶν, ῶνος, ὁ$_{2}$ (12x; 5x Matt) Matt 1:6; 12:42 = Luke 11:31; John 10:23; Acts 3:11; 7:47, **Solomon**; (343x LXX; 175x 1 Kgs)

σορός, οῦ, ἡ$_{2όδός}$ ①[gfs] Luke 7:14, **bier**[EGG]; ❷ LXX, Job 21:32, **grave**; Hdt. *Hist.* 1.68.3, **coffin, sarcophagus**; *fig. comparison* Aristoph. *Ve.* 1365, **old ghost**, *nickname of old men*[BrDAG]

σός, σή, σόν$_{2.1.2}$ {σύ} *adj.* (25x; 8x Matt) Matt 7:3; Mark 2:18 = Luke 5:33; Luke 15:31; John 17:10; Phlm 14, **your** (135x LXX; 68x Prov)

σουδάριον, ου, τό$_{2}$ ❹ Luke 19:2; John 11:44; 20:7; Acts 19:12, **cloth**

Σουσάννα, ης, ἡ$_{1>}$ ① Luke 8:3, **Susanna**, *a woman who traveled with Jesus*[ZEC]; ❹ LXX, Sus 2, 29, 30, **Susanna**, *wealthy Jewish woman who lived in Babylon during the exile*

σοφία, ας, ἡ$_{1α}$ (51x; 17x 1 Cor) Matt 13:54 = Mark 6:2; Acts 6:3; Eph 3:10, **wisdom** *from God*; 1 Cor 1:17, *eloquent* **wisdom**; 1:30, **wisdom** *from God*; 1:17–3:19;[NIGTC] 2 Cor 1:12, *earthly* **wisdom**; Jas 3:15, *devilish* **wisdom** ≠ 3:17, **wisdom** *from above*; Rev 13:18; 17:9, **wisdom** *required to decipher 666* (246x LXX; 176x WisLit)

σοφίζω {σοφός} ❷ 2 Tim 3:15, **to teach, make wise**; 2 Pet 1:16, **to devise cleverly**; (21x LXX; 10x Sir) Ps 18:8 (19:7); Sir 10:36, **to flaunt wisdom**

σοφός, ή, όν$_{2.1.2}$ {σοφίζω} *adj.* (20x; 11x 1 Cor) Matt 11:25 = Luke 10:21; Rom 1:14; 1 Cor 1:26; 3:18–20,[4x] **wise** *by human measures*; 3:10, **skilled**; 6:5; Eph 5:15; Jas 3:13, **wise, mature**; (186x LXX; 115x Wis. Litt.)

Σπανία, ας, ἡ$_{1α}$ ❷ Rom 15:24, 28, **Spain**; ①[gfs] LXX, 1 Macc 8:3

σπαράσσω {σπάω} ❸ Mark 1:26; 9:26; Luke 9:39, **to throw into convulsions**; ❹ LXX, 2 Sam 22:8; Jer 4:19; Aeschl. *Pr.* 1018, **to rend**, *of thunder*; Eur. *Med.* 1217, **to tear in pieces**

σπαργανόω[con] {σπάργω} ❷ Luke 2:7, *act.*, **to wrap in cloth**, 2:12, *mid.*, *a child* **wrapped**; ❷ LXX, Job 38:9

σπαταλάω[con] {σπατάλη} ❷ 1 Tim 5:6; Jas 5:5, **to live in pleasure**; ❷ LXX, Sir 21:15; Ezek 16:49, **to live in comfortable security**; Polyb. *Hist.* 36.17.7, **to give in to excess**

σπάω[con] ❷ Mark 14:47; Acts 16:27, **to draw** *a sword*; (23x LXX) Num 22:23; Aeschl. *Ch.* 533, **to suck** *clotted blood with milk*[BrDAG]

σπεῖρα, ας, ἡ$_{1α}$ ❼ Matt 27:27 = Mark 15:16; John 18:3; Acts 27:1, **a detachment of soldiers** (*one tenth of a legion; about 600 men*); ❹ LXX, 2 Macc 8:23, **band** *of soldiers*; Hp. *Morb.* 2.33, **coil, winding**; Theocr. 22.80, *leather* **thongs** *or* **straps** *used as boxing gloves*

σπείρω (52x; 17x Matt) Matt 13:3–23 = Mark 4:3–20 = Luke 8:5–15, **to sow**; 1 Cor 15:36–44,[7x] **to sow** *a bare grain*[NIGTC]; Gal 6:7–8, **to sow** *to the flesh or Spirit*[ABC]; (60x LXX)

σπεκουλάτωρ, ορος, ὁ$_3$ ①[ams] Mark 6:27, **executioner**[Herm]

σπένδω ❷ Phil 2:17; 2 Tim 4:6, **to offer a libation**, **drink offering**; (20x LXX; 7x Jer)

σπέρμα, ατος, τό$_3$ {σπείρω} (43x; 9x Rom) Matt 22:24 = Mark 12:19 = Luke 20:28, **seed**; Mark 12:19–22,[4x] **child, children**; Luke 1:55; 2 Cor 11:22, **descendants**; Gal 3:16,[3x] **offspring**; Heb 11:11, **procreation**; 1 John 3:9, *God's* **seed**; (265x LXX; 60x Gen)

σπερμολόγος, ον$_{2.2}$ {σπείρω + λέγω} *adj.* ① Acts 17:18,[Keen3] *subst.* **scavenger**, **gossip**,[ZEC] **a bird-brain devoid of method**[Spicq]; Aristoph. *Av.* 232, **pecks at seeds**

σπεύδω {σπουδή} ❻ Luke 2:16; 2 Pet 3:12, **to hasten**; Luke 19:5, 6, **to hurry**; (64x LXX)

σπήλαιον, ου, τό$_2$ ❻ Matt 21:13 = Mark 11:17 = Luke 19:46, **den**; Heb 11:38; Rev 6:15, **cave**; (54x LXX; 15x Gen)

σπιλάς, άδος, ἡ$_3$ {σπιλόω} ① Jude 12, **hidden reefs**[NAC]; Polyb. *Hist.* 1.37.2[BrDAG]

σπίλος, ου, ὁ$_2$ {σπιλόω} ❷ Eph 5:27; 2 Pet 2:13, **stain**, **impurity**

σπιλόω[con] {σπίλος} ❷ Jas 3:6; Jude 23, **to stain**, **defile**; ①[app.nns] LXX, Wis 15:4

σπλαγχνίζομαι {σπλάγχνον} (12x, Syn) Matt 9:36 = Mark 6:34; 1:41; Luke 15:20, **to have compassion**; ①[painf] LXX, 2 Macc 6:8

σπλάγχνον, ου, τό$_2$ {σπλαγχνίζομαι} (11x) Luke 1:78; 1 John 3:17, **compassion**; Acts 1:18, **bowels** *gushed out*; 2 Cor 7:15, **affection**[BEC]; Phlm 7, 12, 20, **heart**; (17x LXX) 4 Macc 5:30–15:29,[8x] **entrails**; Aristoph. *Ran.* 1006, **guts** *are seething with indignation*[BrDAG]

σπόγγος, ου, ὁ$_2$ ❸ Matt 27:48 = Mark 15:36 = John 19:29, **sponge**

σποδός, οῦ, ἡ$_{2όδός}$ ❸ Matt 11:21 = Luke 10:13; Heb 9:13, **ashes**; (37x LXX) Gen 18:27

σπορά, ᾶς, ἡ$_{1α}$ {σπείρω} ①[gfs] 1 Pet 1:23, **seed**; ❷ LXX, 2 Kgs 19:29, **sowing**

σπόριμος, ον$_{2.2}$ {σπείρω} *adj.* ❸[gnp] Matt 12:1 = Mark 2:23 = Luke 6:1, **grain field**; ❸ LXX

σπόρος, ου, ὁ$_2$ {σπείρω} ❻ Mark 4:26, 27 = Luke 8:5, 11; 2 Cor 9:10, **seed**; (11x LXX)

σπουδάζω (11x) Gal 2:10, **to be eager**; Eph 4:3; Heb 4:11, **to make every effort**; 1 Thess 2:17, **to long for intensely**; 2 Pet 3:14, **to be thoughtfully efficient**; (11x LXX)

σπουδαῖος, α, ον$_{2.1.2}$ {σπεύδω} *adj.* ❸ 2 Cor 8:17, **earnest**; 8:22,[2x] **more earnest than ever**[BEC]; ①[nnp] LXX, Ezek 41:25, *wooden* **canopy** (*Heb. meaning is obscure*)

σπουδαίως *adv.* ❹ Luke 7:4; Phil 2:28; 2 Tim 1:17; Titus 3:13, **earnestly**; ① LXX, Wis 2:6

σπουδή, ῆς, ἡ$_{1η}$ {σπεύδω} (12x) Mark 6:25, *with* **haste**; Rom 12:8, *in* **diligence**; 2 Cor 7:11, *your* **eagerness**[BEC]; Jude 3, *pred.*, *while making all* **haste** *to write to you* (NET)

σπυρίς, ίδος, ἡ$_3$ ❺ Matt 15:37 = Mark 8:8; Matt 16:10; Acts 9:25, **basket**

στάδιον, ου, τό$_2$ {ἵστημι} ❼ Matt 14:24 = John 6:19; Matt 14:24; Luke 24:13, **stadia**; 1 Cor 9:24, **stadium**; ❽ (6x 2 Macc) LXX, 2 Macc 11:5; 12:9

σταθήσεται → ἵστημι, *fut. pass. ind. 3s*, Matt 12:25, 26, **stood**

στάμνος, ου, ἡ$_{2όδός}$ {ἵστημι} ① Heb 9:4, **jar**; ❺ LXX, 1 Kgs 12:24

στάς → ἵστημι, *aor. act. ptc. nms*, Matt 20:32, **stopped**

στασιαστής, οῦ, ὁ$_{1>}$ {ἵστημι} ①[gmp] Mark 15:7 = Luke 23:19, **rebel**, **insurrectionist**; Dion. *Rom. Ant.* 6.70.1, **one who stirs up discord**; Chio 7.1, **acting hostile** *to all*

στάσις, εως, ἡ$_3$ {ἵστημι} ❾ (7x LA) Mark 15:7 = Luke 23:19, **insurrection**; Acts 15:2; 23:7; 24:5, **dissension**; Heb 9:8, *to have* **standing**; (25x LXX)

στατήρ, ῆρος, ὁ$_3$ {ἵστημι} ①[ams] Matt 17:27, *meas.* **stater** (*a silver coin worth*)[EGG]

σταυρός, οῦ, ὁ$_2$ {σταυρόω} (27x) **cross** Ⓐ ***willingness to die***,[ZEC] Matt 16:24 = Mark 8:34 = Luke 9:23; Matt 10:38; Ⓑ ***phys.***, Mark 15:32; Ⓒ ***subject of proclamation***,[NIGTC] 1 Cor 1:17, 18; Ⓓ ***Jesus's passion***,[ZEC] Eph 2:16; Ⓔ ***instrument of warfare***,[NIGTC] Col 1:20; Ⓕ ***where the indictment is crucified***,[NIGTC] Col 2:14

σταυρόω[con] (46x; 35x Gs) Matt 27:22 = Mark 15:13 = Luke 23:21 = John 19:6; Matt 28:5; Luke 23:21–24:20[6x]; John 19:6–41[11x]; Gal 3:1, **to crucify**; ❷ LXX, Esth 7:9, **to hang**

σταφυλή, ῆς, ἡ$_{1η}$ ❸ Matt 7:16 = Luke 6:44; Rev 14:18, **grape cluster**; (31x LXX)

στάχυς, υος, ὁ$_3$ ❻ Matt 12:1 = Mark 2:23 = Luke 6:1; Mark 4:28, **head of grain**, **wheat**; (17x LXX; 10x Gen)

Στάχυς, υος, ὁ$_3$ {στάχυς} ①[ams] Rom 16:9, **Stachys**

στέγη, ης, ἡ$_{1η}$ ❸ Matt 8:8 = Luke 7:6; Mark 2:4, **roof**; ❺ LXX, Gen 8:13, **covering** *of the ark*

στέγω ❹ 1 Cor 9:12, **to put up with**[NIGTC!]; 13:7, **to never tire of support**[NIGTC!]; 1 Thess 3:1, 5, **to endure**; ①[aainf] LXX, Sir 8:17, **to keep**; Thuc. 2.94.3, *ships not* **watertight**

στεῖρα, ας, ἡ$_{1α}$ ❺ Luke 1:7; 23:29; Gal 4:27; Heb 11:11, **barren**; (14x LXX) Gen 11:30; Exod 23:26, **childless**, **barren**; Hom. *Il.* 1.482; *Od.* 2.248, **front part of a ship's keel**

στέλλω ❷ 2 Cor 8:20, **we are organizing** *things in this way*;[BEC] 2 Thess 3:6, **to keep away from**, **avoid**; ❼ LXX, Hdt. *Hist.* 3.52.6, **to equip**, **outrig**, *of ships*

στέμμα, ατος, τό$_3$ {στεφανός} ①[anp] Acts 14:13, **garland wreath**

στεναγμός, οῦ, ὁ$_2$ {στενός} ❷ Acts 7:34; Rom 8:26, **groaning**; (26x LXX; 8x Pss) Gen 3:16, **pain** *in childbirth*; Exod 2:24, *God heard their* **groaning**

στενάζω {στενός} ❸ Mark 7:34, **to sigh**; Rom 8:23; 2 Cor 5:2, 4,[BEC] **to long for** *heaven*; Heb 13:17, **to be sad**; (26x LXX; 5x Job) Job 18:20, **to be appalled**

στενός, ή, όν$_{2.1.2}$ *adj.* ❸ Matt 7:13 = Luke 13:24, **narrow**; (18x LXX; 4x 1 Sam) Prov 23:27, *an adulteress is a* **narrow** *well*; Xen. *Hel.* 7.1.29, *a* **narrow** *place in the road*

στενο**χωρέω**[con] {στενός + χωρέω} ❸ 2 Cor 4:8, **to be restricted**,[BEC] **to be emotionally cramped**[BDAG]; 6:12,[2x] **to be held back**; ❹ LXX; Machon *Chr.* 396, **to be in a narrow place**

στενο**χωρία, ας, ἡ$_{1α}$** {στενός + χωρέω} ❹ Rom 2:9; 8:35, **distress**; 2 Cor 6:4; 12:10, **stressful situations**[BEC]; (13x LXX) Deut 28:53

στερεός, ά, όν$_{2.1.2}$ {στερέω} *adj.* ❹ 2 Tim 2:19; Heb 5:12, 14; 1 Pet 5:9, **solid**; (16x LXX)

στερεόω[con] ❸ Acts 3:7, 16; 16:5, **to strengthen**; (34x LXX; 10x Sir) Hos 13:4, **to make firm**

στερέωμα, ατος, τό$_3$ {στερεόω} ①[ans] Col 2:5, **firmness**; (28x LXX) Gen 1:6, **firmament**

Στεφανᾶς, ᾶ, ὁ$_1$ ❸ 1 Cor 1:16; 2 Cor 16:15, 17, **Stephanas**

Στέφανος, ου, ὁ$_2$ ❼ Acts 6:5; 7:59; 22:20, **Stephen**

στέφανος, ου, ὁ$_2$ {στεφανόω} (18x) 1 Cor 9:25; 1 Thess 2:19; 2 Tim 4:8; Jas 1:12; Rev 3:11,[L7 70–76] **crown**; Matt 27:29 = Mark 15:17 = John 19:2, **crown** *of thorns*; (51x LXX; 9x Sir)

στεφανόω[con] {στέφανος} ❸ 2 Tim 2:5; Heb 2:7, 9, *pass.*, **to be crowned**; ❽ LXX; 3x Pss

στῆθος, ους, τό$_3$ ❺ Luke 18:13; John 13:25; Rev 15:6, **chest**; ❽ LXX; 3x Exod

στήκω {ἵστημι} (10x) Mark 3:31, **to stand**; John 8:44, **stand** *in the truth*

στηριγμός, οῦ, ὁ$_2$ {στηρίζω} ①[gms] 2 Pet 3:17, **proper constancy**[ABC]

στηρίζω (13x) Luke 9:51, **to resolve firmly**[BHGNT]; 22:32; Rom 1:11; Jas 5:8, **to strengthen**; (53x LXX; 10x Ezek) Ezek 6:2; Gem. 12.23, *astr.* **stationary** *planetary phases*

στιβάς, άδος, ἡ$_3$ ①[afs] Mark 11:8, **branches**

στίγμα, ατος, τό$_3$ {στίζω} ①[anp] Gal 6:17, **marks**; ①[gnp] LXX, Song 1:11

στιγμή, ῆς, ἡ$_{1\eta}$ {στίζω} ①[dfs] Luke 4:5, **moment**; ❷ LXX, Isa 29:5; 2 Macc 9:11

στίλβω ①[pap.nnp] Mark 9:3, **glistening**[BEC]; ❽ LXX, 1 Esd 8:56, **gleaming**

στοά, ᾶς, ἡ$_{1\alpha}$ {ἵστημι} ❹ John 5:2; 10:23, **colonnade**; ❹ LXX, 1 Kgs 6:33, **porticoes**

Στοϊκός, ή, όν$_{2.1.2}$ *adj.* ①[gmp] Acts 17:18, *subst.*, **Stoics**

στοιχεῖον, ου, τό$_2$ {στοιχέω} ❼ Gal 4:3; Col 2:8, **elemental entities**[KeenG]; 2 Pet 3:10, **elements**; ❸ LXX, Wis 7:17; 4 Macc 12:13

στοιχέω[con] {στοιχεῖον} ❺ Acts 21:24, **to conform**[BEC]; Rom 4:12; ①[fai3s] LXX, Eccl 11:6

στολή, ῆς, ἡ$_{1\eta}$ {στέλλω} ❾ (5x Rev) Mark 12:38 = Luke 20:46, **robe** (95x LXX; 22x Exod)

στόμα, ατος, τό$_3$ (78x; 22x Rev, 21x LA) Matt 12:34 = Luke 6:45; Rev 1:16 **mouth**; 2 Cor 6:11, *idiom.*, **we have spoken** *openly*[BEC]; 13:11, **utterance**[BEC]; Heb 11:33, 34, **the mouths** *of lions*, **the edge** *of the sword*; 2 John 12, **face-*to*-face**; (457 LXX; 66x Pss, 45x Prov)

στόμαχος, ου, ὁ$_2$ {στόμα} ①[ams] 1 Tim 5:23, **stomach**

στρατεία, ας, ἡ$_{1\alpha}$ {στρατία} ❷ 2 Cor 10:4, **warfare**; 1 Tim 1:18, **fight**; ①[afs] LXX, 4 Macc 9:24, **fight**

στράτευμα, ατος, τό$_3$ {στρατία} ❽ (4x Rev) Matt 22:7; Luke 23:11, **soldiers, troops**; ❼ LXX, 1 Macc 9:34, **army**

στρατεύω {στρατία} ❼ Luke 3:14, **soldiers**; 2 Tim 2:4, **to serve in the army**; 1 Pet 2:11, **to wage war**; 1 Tim 1:18, **to fight**; ❼ LXX, 2 Sam 15:28, **to be poised for war**

στρατηγός, οῦ, ὁ$_2$ {στρατία + ἄγω} (10x LA) Luke 22:4; Acts 4:1, **officer**; (55x LXX; 24x 1–4 Macc)

στρατιά, ᾶς, ἡ$_{1\alpha}$ {στρατεύομαι} ❷ Luke 2:13; Acts 7:42, **army** *of heaven*; (42x LXX; 10x 1–2 Chr)

στρατιώτης, οῦ, ὁ$_1$ (26x; 13x Acts) Matt 8:9 = Luke 7:8; John 19:2, **soldiers**; ❻ LXX

στρατολογέω[con] {στρατία + λέγω} ①[aap.dms] 2 Tim 2:4, **soldier on active duty**[NIGTC]

στρατόπεδον, ου, τό$_2$ {στρατιά + πούς} ①[gnp] Luke 21:20, **foot soldiers**; ❼ LXX

στρεβλόω[con] {στρέφω} ①[fai3p] 2 Pet 3:16, **to twist**; ❻ LXX, 2 Sam 22:27; 4 Macc 9:17

στρέφω (21x; 10x LA) Matt 5:39; Rev 11:6, **to turn**; Acts 7:39, **to turn back**; (40x LXX)

στρηνιάω[con] ❷ Rev 18:7, 9, **to indulge, live in luxury**

στρῆνος, ους, τό$_3$ ①[gns] Rev 18:3, **luxurious**; ①[nns] LXX, 2 Kgs 19:28, **wantonness**

στρουθίον, ου, τό$_2$ {στρουθός} ❹ Matt 10:29, 31 = Luke 12:6, 7, **sparrow** (13x LXX)

στρωννύω ❻ Matt 21:8 = Mark 11:8, **to spread**; Mark 14:15, **to furnish**; Acts 9:34, **to make your bed**; Hdt. *Hist.* 7.54, στόρνυμι, **to spread** *clothes over a bed*[BrDAG]

στυγητός, ή, όν$_{2.1.2}$ {στυγέω} *adj.* ①[nmp] Titus 3:3, **hated**

στυγνάζω {στυγέω} ❷ Matt 16:3, **to threaten**; Mark 10:22, **to be shocked**; ❷ LXX

στῦλος, ου, ὁ$_2$ ❹[nmp] Gal 2:9; 1 Tim 3:15; Rev 3:12; 10:1, **pillar**; (150x LXX; 66x Exod)

σύ, *see* **ἐγώ** *2 pers. pron.* (2,907x; 1,741 LA) (13,166 LXX; 1,597x Deut, 1,351x Pss) **you**

συγγένεια, ας, ἡ$_{1\alpha}$ {σύν + γίνομαι} ❸ Luke 1:61; 7:3, 14, **relative** (40x LXX; 14x Num)

συγγενής, ῆς, ἡ$_{1\eta}$ {σύν + γίνομαι} (11x) Mark 6:4; Luke 1:58, **relative** (20x LXX)

συγγενίς, ίδος, ἡ$_3$ {σύν + γίνομαι} ①[nfs] Luke 1:36, **relative**

συγγνώμη, ης, ἡ$_{1\eta}$ {σύν + γινώσκω} ①[afs] 1 Cor 7:6, **concession**; ❷ LXX, Sir 3:13

συγκάθημαι {σύν + κατά + ἧμαι} ❷ Mark 14:54; Acts 26:30, **to sit with**; ①[aminf] LXX, Ps 100:6 (101:6)

συγκαθίζω {σύν + κατά + ἵζω} ❷ Luke 22:55, **to sit down**; Eph 2:6, **to seat**; ❻ LXX, Gen 15:11, *the birds* **descended**; Num 22:27, *the donkey* **settled down** *under Balaam*

συγκακοπαθέω[con] {σύν + κακός + πάσχω} ❷ 2 Tim 1:8; 2:3, **to share in suffering**

συγκακουχέομαι {σύν + κακός + ἔχω} ①[pminf] Heb 11:25, **to be maltreated with**[ABC]

συγκαλέω[con] {σύν + καλέω} ❽ (7x LA) Mark 15:16; Luke 9:1; Acts 10:24, **to call together**; 5:21, **to convene**; (13x LXX; 5x Josh)

συγκαλύπτω {σύν + καλύπτω} ①[pfmp.nns] Luke 12:2, **to cover completely**; (19x LXX)

συγκάμπτω {σύν + κάμπτω} ①[aaim2s] Rom 11:10, **to bend**; ❸ LXX, 2 Kgs 4:35

συγκαταβαίνω {σύν + κατά + βαίνω} ①[aap.nmp] Acts 25:5, **to go down with**; ①[fmi3s] LXX, Ps 48:18 (49:17); Aristot. *Meteor.* 358b 32, **to descend together**

συγκατάθεσις, εως, ἡ$_3$ {σύν + κατά + τίθημι} ①[nfs] 2 Cor 6:16, **mutual agreement**

συγκατατίθημι {σύν + κατά + τίθημι} ①[pfmp.nms] Luke 23:51, **to agree with**; ❷[fmi2s] LXX, Exod 23:32, **to establish** *a covenant*

συγκαταψηφίζομαι {σύν + κατά + ψάω} ①[api3s] Acts 1:26, **to be included**

συγκεράννυμι {σύν + κεράννυμι} ❷ 1 Cor 12:24, *God* **puts together** *the body*[NIGTC!]; Heb 4:2, **to blend**[EGG]; ❷ LXX, 2 Macc 15:39, **to mix together**; Plato *Tim.* 35a, **to mix together** *diff. elements into a single form*

συγκινέω[con] {σύν + κινέω} ①[aai3p] Acts 6:12, **to stir up**; Aristot. *Pr.* 949a19, **to excite**

συγκλείω {σύν + κλείω} ❹ Luke 5:6, **to enclose** *fish in a net*; Rom 11:32 (*God is jailor*); Gal 3:23 (*law is warden*), **to imprison**; (44x LXX) 1 Sam 1:6, **to close the womb**

συγκληρονόμος, ον$_{2.2}$ {σύν + κληρόω + νόμος} *adj.* ❹ Rom 8:17; Eph 3:6; Heb 11:9; 1 Pet 3:7, **joint**, **fellow heirs**

συγκοινωνέω[con] {σύν + κοινός} ❸ Eph 5:11, **to have fellowship**; Phil 4:14, **to share**; Rev 18:4, *do not* **partake** *of her sins*; Alexis 167.5, **to divide up** *something*

συγκοινωνός, οῦ, ὁ$_2$ {σύν + κοινός} ❹ Rom 11:17; 1 Cor 9:23, **sharer**; Phil 1:7, **partaker**; Rev 1:9, **fellow partaker**

συγκομίζω {σύν + κομίζω} ①[aai3p] Acts 8:2, **to bury** *Stephen*; ①[app.nfs] LXX, Job 5:26, **to come to the grave**; Xen. *Cyr.* 8.2.24, **to gather** *the best doctors around himself*

συγκρίνω {σύν + κρίνω} ❸ 1 Cor 2:13, **to interpret**[NIGTC]; 2 Cor 10:12,[2x] **to compare**[BEC]; (12x LXX; 7x Gen) Gen 40:8; Polyb. *Hist.* 14.3.7, **to interpret**

συγκύπτω {σύν + κύπτω} ①[pap.nfs] Luke 13:11, **to bend over**; ❸ LXX, Job 9:27; Sir 19:26, *the villain* **bowed down** *with mourning*; Hdt. *Hist.* 3.82, *they act* **in concert**

συγκυρία, ας, ἡ$_{1\alpha}$ {σύν + κυρέω} ①[afs] Luke 10:31, **by chance**

συγχαίρω {σύν + χάρις} ❼ Luke 1:58; 15:6; 1 Cor 12:26, Phil 2:17, **to rejoice with**; ①[fmi3s] LXX, Gen 21:6, **to laugh with**; Aeschl. *Ag.* 793, **to be glad together**

συγχέω[con] {σύν + χέω} ❺ Acts 2:6, **to be bewildered**; 9:22, **to confound**; 21:31, **to be confused**; 21:27, **to stir up**; (16x LXX; 6x MinPr) Amos 3:15, **I will wreck** *the winter house*

συγχράομαι ①[pmi3p] John 4:9, **to associate**

σύγχυσις, εως, ἡ$_3$ {σύν + χέω} ①[gfs] Acts 19:29, **confusion**; ❹ LXX, Gen 11:9, *is called* **Confusion** (*Babel*, בבל); Epiph. *Haer.* 76.34.8, **union** *of two natures of Christ*

συζάω[con] {σύν + ζάω} ❸ Rom 6:8; 2 Cor 7:3; 2 Tim 2:11, **to live with**

συζεύγνυμι {σύν + ζυγός} ❷[aai3s] Matt 19:6 = Mark 10:9, **to join together**; ①[pmp.nfp] LXX, Ezek 1:11, **to adjoin**

συζητέωcon {σύν + ζητέω} (10x) Mark 1:27, **to discuss**; Acts 6:9; 9:29, **to argue**BEC
συζητητής, οῦ, ὁ$_{1>}$ {σύν + ζητέω} ①nms 1 Cor 1:20, **debater**; Ign. *Eph.* 18.1
σύζυγος, ου, ὁ$_2$ ①vms Phil 4:3, **companion**; Aristot. *H.A.* 610b, **yoked, united**
συζωοποιέωcon {σύν + ζάω + ποιέω} ❷aai3s Eph 2:5 = Col 2:13, **to make alive with**ZEC
συκάμινος, ου, ἡ$_{2ὁδός}$ ①dfs Luke 17:6, **black mulberry tree**ZEC; ❻ LXX, 1 Kgs 10:27
συκῆ, ῆς, ἡ$_{1η}$ {σῦκον} (16x) Luke 13:6; John 1:48; Jas 3:12; Rev 6:13, **fig tree**; (27x LXX)
συκομορέα, ας, ἡ$_{1α}$ {σῦκον + μείρομαι} ①afs Luke 19:4, **sycamore tree**
σῦκον, ου, τό$_2$ ❹ Matt 7:16 = Luke 6:44; Mark 11:13, Jas 3:12, **fig**; (12x LXX)
συκοφαντέωcon {σῦκον + φαίνω} ❷ Luke 3:14; 19:8, **to accuse falsely**; ❾ LXX, Lev 19:11, **to lie**; Aristoph. *Ach.* 828, *intran.*, **to be a slanderer***BrDAG*
συλαγωγέωcon {συλάω + ἄγω} ① Col 2:8, **to take as plunder***BrDAG*
συλάωcon ①aai1s 2 Cor 11:8, **to rob**; ①aps3p LXX, Ep Jer 17, **to be stripped** *by robbers*
συλλαλέωcon {σύν + λάλος} ❻ Matt 17:3 = Mark 9:4 = Luke 9:30, **to talk**; 22:4; Acts 25:12, **to confer**; ❹ LXX, Jer 18:20, **to speak** *words on behalf of your life*
συλλαμβάνω {σύν + λαμβάνω} (16x; 11x LA) Matt 26:55 = Mark 14:48; Acts 1:16, **to arrest, capture, seize**; Luke 1:24; Jas 1:15, **to conceive**; Luke 5:7, Phil 4:3, **to help**; (111x LXX; 20x Gen, 18x Jer, 15x 1 Macc) 1 Kgs 18:40, **to seize** *the prophets of Baal*
συλλέγω {σύν + λέγω} ❽ (7x Matt) Matt 7:16 = Luke 6:44; Matt 13:28–30,3x **to gather**; (42x LXX; 11x Ruth, 9x Exod) Ruth 2:3, **to glean**
συλλογίζομαι {σύν + λέγω} ①ami3p Luke 20:5, **to discuss**; ❺ LXX, Lev 25:27, **to compute**; Hdt. *Hist.* 2.148.2, *if one were to* **add up** *all the buildings of the Greeks*
συλλυπέωcon {σύν + λύπη} ①pmp.nms Mark 3:5, **to grieve**
συμβαίνω {σύν + βαίνω} ❽ Mark 10:32; Luke 24:14; 1 Pet 4:12, **to happen**; Acts 21:35, **to come about**; (47x LXX; 11x 2 Macc) Gen 41:13, **to happen**; Job 42:11, **to know**
συμβάλλω {σύν + βάλλω} ❻ (LA) Luke 2:19, **to ponder**; 14:31, **to encounter**; Acts 17:18, *w/ dat.* **to debate**; 18:27, **to assist**; ❾ LXX, 2 Chr 25:19, **to provoke trouble**; *Il.* 4.447, **to set one against another**; Xen. *Lac.* 4.2, **to contest for power**
συμβασιλεύω {σύν + βασιλεύς} ❷ 1 Cor 4:8; 2 Tim 2:12, **to rule, reign with**
συμβιβάζω {σύν + βαίνω} ❼ Acts 9:22, **to prove**; 16:10, **to conclude**; 19:33, **to advise**; 1 Cor 2:16, **to instruct**; Eph 4:16 = Col 2:19, **to hold together, knit together**; ❽ LXX, Isa 40:13, **to instruct**; Aristot. *Top.* 155a 25, **to demonstrate logically**
συμβουλεύω {σύν + βούλομαι} ❹ Matt 26:4; Acts 9:23, **to conspire**; John 18:14; Rev 3:18, **to advise**; (32x LXX) Exod 18:19, **to advise**; Josh 15:18, **to urge**
συμβούλιον, ου, τό$_2$ {σύν + βούλομαι} ❽ Matt 27:1 = Mark 15:1; Matt 12:14, **to plot**; Acts 25:12, **council**; ①nns LXX, 4 Macc 17:17, **council**
σύμβουλος, ου, ὁ$_2$ {σύν + βούλομαι} ①nms Rom 11:34, **counselor**; (28x LXX) Isa 1:26
Συμεών, ὁ$_3$ *indecl.* ❼ **Simeon**: Ⓐ *Peter's Aram. name*, 2 Pet 1:1; Ⓑ *son of Jacob*, Rev 7:7; Ⓒ *man in Jerusalem*, Luke 2:25; Ⓓ *Christian surnamed Niger*, Acts 13:1; Ⓔ *son of Judah, in Jesus's genealogy*, Luke 3:30; (55x LXX; 13x Num, 11x Gen)
συμμαθητής, οῦ, ὁ$_{1>}$ {σύν + μανθάνω} ①dmp John 11:16, **fellow disciple**
συμμαρτυρέωcon {σύν + μάρτυς} ❸ Rom 2:15; 8:16; 9:1, **bears witness**
συμμερίζω {σύν + μερίζω} ①pmi3p 1 Cor 9:13, **to have a share**NIGTC
συμμέτοχος, ου, ὁ$_2$ {σύν + μετά + ἔχω} ❷ Eph 3:6; 5:7, **sharers**

συμμιμητής, οῦ, ὁ$_{1>}$ {σύν + μιμέομαι} ①[nmp] Phil 3:17, **united in imitating** *me*[NIGTC]

συμμορφίζω {σύν + μορφή} ①[pmp.nms] Phil 3:10, **to be conformed continually**[NIGTC]

σύμμορφος, ον$_{2.2}$ {σύν + μορφή} *adj.* ❷ Rom 8:29; Phil 3:21, **conformed**

συμπαθέω[con] {σύν + πάσχω} ❷ Heb 4:15, **to have sympathy**; 10:34, **to be sympathetically affected**[NIGTC]; ①[pai3s] LXX, 4 Macc 5:25, **to show sympathy**

συμπαθής, ές, ῆ$_{3}$ {σύν + πάσχω} ①[nmp] 1 Pet 3:8, **sympathetic**; ❸ LXX, 4 Macc 13:23, **more sympathetic**; Aristot. *Pol.* 1340a 13, **experiencing similar feelings**

συμπαραγίνομαι {σύν + παρά + γίνομαι} ① Luke 23:48, **to gather**; ①[ami3s] LXX, Ps 82:9 (83:8); Hdt. *Hist.* 4.199.2, **to be ready at the same time**, *of crops*; Thuc. 2.82, *milit.*, **to reinforce**

συμπαρακαλέω[con] {σύν + παρά + **καλέω**} ①[apinf] Rom 1:12, **to be mutually encouraged**; Xen. *Cyr.* 8.1.38, **to be invited** *to the hunt*

συμπαραλαμβάνω {σύν + παρά + λαμβάνω} ❹ Acts 12:25; 15:37, 38; Gal 2:1, **to take along**; ❹ LXX, Gen 19:17

συμπάρειμι {σύν + παρά + εἰμί} ①[pap.vmp] Acts 25:24, **to be present together**; ❸ LXX, Tob 11:11; Prov 8:27; Wis 9:10

συμπάσχω {σύν + πάσχω} ❷ Rom 8:17; 1 Cor 12:26, **to suffer together**

συμπέμπω {σύν + πέμπω} ❷[aai1p] 2 Cor 8:18, 22, **to send with**; Aeschl. *Suppl.* 493, **to dispatch together**

συμπεριλαμβάνω {σύν + περι + λαμβάνω} ①[aap.nms] Acts 20:10, **to take in one's arms**; Hp. *Fist.* 4, **to encircle**

συμπίνω {σύν + πίνω} ①[aai1p] Acts 10:41, **to drink with**; ①[aainf] LXX, Esth 7:1, **to feast with**

συμπίπτω {σύν + πίπτω} ①[aai3s] Luke 6:49, **to fall**; (15x LXX) 1 Sam 17:32, *a heart* **to fail**; Eur. *H.F.* 905, **to collapse** (*a structure*); Thuc. 8.41.2, *earthquake* **demolished** *a city*

συμπληρόω[con] {σύν + πληρόω} ❸ Luke 8:23, *boat* **to fill** *with water*; Luke 9:51, **to draw near**; Acts 2:1, **to arrive**; Plato *Symp.* 202e, **to fill to the brim**

συμπνίγω {σύν + πνίγω} ❺ Matt 13:22 = Mark 4:7, 19, **to choke**; Luke 8:42, **to press**; Thphr. *C.P.* 6.11.6, *pass.*, **to be snuffed out**

συμπολίτης, ου, ὁ$_{1>}$ {σύν + πολίτης} ①[nmp] Eph 2:19, **fellow citizen**

συμπορεύομαι {σύν + πορεύομαι} ❹ Mark 10:1, **to gather**; Luke 7:11; 14:25; 24:15, **to travel, go**; (25x LXX; 9x Pent, 6x Tob)

συμπόσιον, ου, τό$_{2}$ {σύν + πόσιον} ❷ Mark 6:39,[2x] **συμπόσια συμπόσια**, **party by party, dining groups**[ZEC]; (10x LXX) Esth 7:7, **feast**

συμπρεσβύτερος, ου, ὁ$_{2}$ {σύν + πρεσβύτης} ①[nms] 1 Pet 5:1, **fellow elder**

συμφέρω {σύν + φέρω} (15x; 4x John) John 11:50, **it is better**; Acts 19:19, **to collect**; 1 Cor 6:12, **it is permissible**; 12:7, *pred. ptc.*, *for the* **common good**; (11x LXX) Prov 19:10

σύμφημι {σύν + φημι} ①[pai1s] Rom 7:16, **to agree**; ❷ LXX, Dan 2:9; Sus 38

σύμφορος, ον$_{2.2}$ {σύν + φέρω} *adj.* ❷ 1 Cor 7:35; 10:33, **profitable, advantageous, helpful**; ①[ans] LXX, 2 Macc 4:5, **welfare**; Aristoph. *Pl.* 1162, **suitable**

συμφυλέτης, ου, ὁ$_{1>}$ {σύν + φύω} ①[gmp] 1 Thess 2:14, **fellow countryman**

σύμφυτος, ον$_{2.2}$ {σύν + φύω} *adj.* ①[nmp] Rom 6:5, *pred.*, εἰ γὰρ **σύμφυτοι** γεγόναμεν, *we are* **united with**; ❸ LXX, Amos 9:13, *pred.*, **σύμφυτοι** ἔσονται *will* **flow with**; Zech 11:2, *pred.*, ὁ δρυμὸς ὁ **σύμφυτος**, *thick forest* **has been felled**; Aristot. *Top.* 145b, **that which grows together**

συμ**φύω** ①[app.nfp] Luke 8:9, **to grow with**; ①[pfap.ans] LXX, Wis 13:13, **to be full of** *knots*

συμ**φωνέω**[con] {σύν + φωνή} ❻ Matt 18:19; Acts 5:9, **to agree**; Luke 5:36, **to match**; ❹ LXX, Isa 7:2, **to ally oneself**, **itself**; Plato *Lach.* 193e, *actions do not* **accord** *with words*

συμ**φώνησις, εως, ἡ**$_3$ {σύν + φωνή} ①[nfs] 2 Cor 6:15, *theol.*, What **harmony** is there between Christ and Beliar?[BEC!]; *gramm.*, AG Ox. 4.326, **synizesis**[BrDAG]; *also.*, **synesis**, *notional concord*[AGG.479]; John 1:12, **τοις πιστεύουσιν**, *full pronunciation combines and simplifies into a smoother form when spoken*; **the accord between two voices singing together**[Spicq]

συμ**φωνία, ας, ἡ**$_{1α}$ {σύν + φωνή} ①[gfs] Luke 15:25, **music**; ❷ LXX, Dan 3:5, **symphony** (NETS); Aristot. *Cael.* 290b 22, **harmony**, *as in Pythagorean doctrine*

σύμ**φωνος, ον**$_{2.2}$ {σύν + φωνή} *adj.* ①[gns] 1 Cor 7:5, **mutual agreement**[NIGTC]; ❷ LXX, 4 Macc 7:7, **in harmony** *with the law*; Soph. *Ichn.* 319, *a melodious* **song**

συμ**ψηφίζω** {σύν + ψάω} ①[aai3p] Acts 19:19, **to assess**[ZEC]

σύμ**ψυχος, ον**$_{2.2}$ {σύν + ψύχω} *adj.* ①[nmp] Phil 2:2, **in full accord**

σύν *prep. w/dat.* (128x; 74x LA, *most common NT prep. in forming compounds*) [PrTh]→ Ⓐ ***mainly physical proximity***: Matt 27:28 = Mark 15:27 = Luke 23:32, **with**; Ⓑ ***intimate personal union***: Rom 6:8; 8:32; 2 Cor 4:14; 1 Thess 4:17b, **with**; (221x LXX; 34x Eccl, 27x 2 Macc)

συν**άγω** (59x; 24x Matt) Matt 3:12 = Luke 3:17; John 4:36; 1 Cor 5:4; Rev 16:14, **to gather**, **assemble**, **meet** (360x LXX; 37x Isa, 31x 1 Macc)

συν**αγωγή, ῆς, ἡ**$_{1η}$ {σύν + ἄγω} (56x; 34x LA) Matt 10:17 = Mark 13:9 = Luke 21:12; Rev 2:9; 3:9, **synagogue**; Jas 2:2, **assembly**[KEL]; (221x LXX; 89x Num) Gen 1:9,[2x] **be gathered**

συν**αγωνίζομαι** {σύν + ἀγών} ①[aminf] Rom 15:30, **to join in an epic struggle**[NIGTC!]; Xen. *Cyr.* 4.5.49; Thuc. 5.109, **to fight on the same side**, **be allied**

συν**αθλέω**[con] {σύν + ἀθλέω} ❷ Phil 1:27; 4:3, **to strive along with**, **struggle together**

συν**αθροίζω** {σύν + α + θρόος} ❷ Acts 12:12; 19:25, **to gather**; (33x LXX; 11x 1–2 Sam)

συν**αίρω** ❸ Matt 18:23, 24; 25:19, **to reckon**, **settle accounts**

συν**αιχμάλωτος, ου, ὁ**$_2$ {σύν + αἰχμή + ἅλωσις} ❸[amp] Rom 16:7; Col 4:10; Phlm 23, **fellow prisoner**

συν**ακολουθέω**[con] {σύν + ἀκόλουθος} ❸ Mark 5:37; 14:51; Luke 23:49, **to follow**; ❷ LXX, 2 Macc 2:4, **to follow**

συν**αλίζω** {σύν + ἅλας} ①[pmp.nms] Acts 1:4, **to stay**; ①[pmimp2s] LXX, Prov 22:24, **to associate**

συν**αλλάσσω** {σύν + ἄλλος} ①[iai3s] Acts 7:26, **try to reconcile**; Aeschl. *Sept.* 597, **to bring into relation**; Soph. *Ai.* 493, *spouses* **having sexual relations**

συν**αναβαίνω** ❷ Mark 15:41; Acts 13:31, **to go up with**; (11x LXX) Gen 50:7, 9, 14

συν**ανάκειμαι** ❼ (all in Syn) Matt 9:10 = Mark 2:15, **to recline with**; Matt 14:9; Luke 14:15, *subst.*, *one of* **the dinner guests**; ①[pmp.nmp] LXX, 3 Macc 5:39, **to recline with**

συν**αναμίγνυμι** ❸ 1 Cor 5:9, 11, **to mix indiscriminately with**[NIGTC!]; 2 Thess 3:14, *not* **to associate with**; ①[amimp2p] LXX, Ezek 20:18, **to observe**; Hp. *Nat. Mul.* 97, **to mix together**

συν**αναπαύομαι** {σύν + ἀνά + παύω} ①[ams1s] Rom 15:32, **to be refreshed**; ①[fmi3s] LXX, Isa 11:6, **to lie down**; Dion. *Rom. Ant.* 9.4, **to sleep together**

συν**αντάω**[con] {σύν + ἀντί} ❻ Luke 9:37; Acts 10:25; Heb 7:1, **to meet**; (58x LXX; 8x 1 Macc) Josh 11:20, **to come against**; Judg 8:21, **to fall upon**

συν**αντιλαμβάνομαι** {σύν + ἀντί + λαμβάνω} ❷ Luke 10:40; Rom 8:26, **to help**; ❸ LXX, Exod 18:22, **to bear the burden** (ASV)

συναπάγω ❸ Rom 12:16, *pass.*, **to be carried away** *with humble concerns*[ZEC]; Gal 2:13; 2 Pet 3:17, **to be carried away** *by hypocrisy or error*; ①[aai3s] LXX, Exod 14:6, **to take**

συναποθνῄσκω ❸ Mark 14:31; 2 Cor 7:3; 2 Tim 2:11, **to die with**; ①[aaimp3s] LXX, Sir 19:10, **to perish with**; Plato *Phaed.* 88d, *the soul does not* **die with** *him*

συναπόλλυμι {σύν + ἀπό + ὄλλυμι} ①[ami3s] Heb 11:31, **to perish together**; (10x LXX) Dan 2:13, **to execute**

συναποστέλλω ①[aai1s] 2 Cor 12:18, **to send**; ❸ LXX, Exod 33:2, 12, **to send** *an angel*

συναρμολογέω[con] {σύν + ἁρμόζω + λέγω} ❷ *neol.*, Eph 2:21; 4:16, **to be fitted together**[ZEC!]

συναρπάζω ❹ Luke 8:29; Acts 6:12, **to seize**; 19:29, **to drag**; 27:15, *a ship* **caught** *in the wind*; ❹ LXX, Prov 6:25, **to captivate** *with eyelashes*; Aeschl. *Pers.* 195, **to snatch**

συναυξάνω ①[pminf] Matt 13:30, **to increase together**; ❷ LXX, 2 Macc 4:4, **to intensify**

σύνδεσμος, ου, ὁ$_2$ {σύν + δέω} ❹ Acts 8:23, **captive**; Eph 4:3; Col 3:14, **bond**; 2:19, **ligament**; ❽ LXX, 1 Kgs 14:24, **male prostitutes**; 2 Kgs 11:14[2x], **Treason! Treason!**; 2 Kgs 12:21, **conspiracy**; Job 41:6 (41:15), **pericardium**[BrDAG]; Plato *Rp.* 520a, *fig.*, **the bond** *that holds the city together*; Hippar. 1.11.20, *astron.*, **the Knot**, *in the constellation Pisces*

συνδέω[con] ①[pmp.gmp] Heb 13:3, **to fasten together, prisoners**; ❽ LXX, Exod 14:25, **to clog**

συνδοξάζω {σύν + δοκέω} ①[apsIp] Rom 8:17, **to glorify with**

σύνδουλος, ου, ὁ$_2$ (10x; 5x Matt) Matt 18:28, 29, 31, 33, **fellow slaves**; Col 1:7; 4:7; Rev 6:11, **fellow servant**; (8x LXX; all in Ezra) Ezra 4:7; 5:3; 6:6, **companion**, **associate**

συνδρομή, ῆς, ἡ$_{1η}$ {σύν + τρέχω} ①[nfs] Acts 21:30, ἐγένετο **συνδρομὴ** τοῦ λαοῦ, **a tumultuous concourse** *of* people; ❷ LXX, Jud 10:18, **tumultuous mob**

συνεγείρω ❸ Eph 2:6 = Col 2:12; 3:1, **to raise together with**; ❸ LXX, Exod 23:5, **to rescue**; 4 Macc 2:14, *subst.*, **helping raise up**; Isa 14:9, **to stir up**

συνέδραμεν → **συντρέχω**, *aor. act. ind. 3s*, Acts 3:11, **ran toward**

συνέδριον, ου, τό$_2$ {σύν + ἕζομαι} (22x; 14x Acts) Matt 10:17 = Mark 13:9; Acts 4:15, **council**, **court**, **Sanhedrin**; (12x LXX; 8x Prov) Prov 22:10, **scoffer**; Hdt. *Hist.* 8.56, **congress**

συνείδησις, εως, ἡ$_3$ {σύν + εἶδος} (30x; 11x 1–2 Cor) Rom 2:15; 1 Cor 8:7–12[3x]; 10:25–29[5x]; 2 Cor 1:12; 1 Tim 1:5; 1 Pet 2:19, **conscience**; ❷ LXX, Eccl 10:20, **thoughts**

σύνειμι[α] ❷ Luke 9:18; Acts 22:11, **to be with, come together**; ❺ LXX, Jer 3:20, *as a faithless wife leaves* **the one who is with** *her* (i.e., *her husband*); Aristoph. *Ec.* 619, **to have sexual relations**; *Ve.* 236, **to pass one's life together**

σύνειμι[β] ①[pap.gms] Luke 8:4, **to gather**; ❺ LXX, 1 Esd 6:2, **to assist**

συνεισέρχομαι ❷ John 6:22; 18:15, **to board** *the boat*; ❺ LXX, Exod 21:3, **to go out**

συνέκδημος, ου, ὁ$_2$ ❷ Acts 19:29; 2 Cor 8:19, **travel companion**

συνεκλεκτός, ή, όν$_{2.1.2}$ {σύν + ἐκ + λέγω} *adj.* ①[nfs] 1 Pet 5:13, *subst.*, *your* **fellow-chosen**[Keen1P]

συνεπιμαρτυρέω[con] {σύν + ἐπί + μάρτυς} ①[pap.gms] Heb 2:4, **to corroborate the testimony**[ABC]; Aristot. *Mund.* 400a 15, **to attest together**

συνεπιτίθημι ①[ami3p] Acts 24:9,[ZEC] **to join in a verbal attack**; ❼ LXX, Num 12:11, **to punish**; Ps 3:7 (3:6); Xen. *Cyr.* 4.2.3, **to come into conflict**, **clash**

συνέπομαι {σύν + ἕπω} ①[ami3p] Acts 20:4, **to accompany**, **follow**; ❸ LXX, 2 Macc 15:2

συνεργέω[con] ❺ Mark 16:20; Rom 8:28[IHR 157]; 1 Cor 16:16; 2 Cor 6:1, **to work together**; Jas 2:22, *faith* **was active with** *his works*; ❷ LXX, 1 Esd 7:2, **to assist** *the elders*; Xen. *Mem.* 3.5.16, **to accomplish what is fitting for one another**

συνεργός, οῦ, ὁ$_{2}$ (13x) Rom 16:3; 2 Cor 1:24; Phlm 1; 3 John 8, **fellow worker**; ❷ LXX, 2 Macc 8:7, **more advantageous** (*nighttime attacks*); Eur. *Or.* 1446, **one who joins forces**

συνέρχομαι (30x; 16x Acts) Matt 1:18, **to come together**; Acts 28:17, **to assemble**; John 11:33, **to come with**; Acts 1:21, **to accompany**; 1 Cor 11:17, 18, 20, 33, 34; 14:23, 26, **to come together** *for church*; (19x LXX) Exod 32:26, **to gather**; Jer 3:18, **to go together**

συνεσθίω ❺ Luke 15:2; Acts 10:41; Gal 2:12, **to eat with**; 1 Cor 5:11, **to share a table**[NIGTC]; ❹ LXX, Ps 100:5 (101:5), *this I will not* **tolerate**

σύνεσις, εως, ἡ$_{3}$ {σύν + ἵημι} ❼ Mark 12:33; Eph 3:4; 2 Tim 2:7, **discernment**; (119x LXX; 35x *with* σοφία in Proverbs) Prov 1:7, **knowledge**; Hom. *Od.* 10.515, **confluence** *of rivers*

συνετός, ή, όν$_{2.1.2}$ {σύν + ἵημι} *adj.* ❹ Matt 11:25 = Luke 10:21; Acts 13:7, **intelligent, discerning**; 1 Cor 1:19, **shrewd**[NIGTC]; (51x LXX; 16x Sir) Prov 12:8; Sir 19:2, **intelligent**

συνευδοκέω[con] ❻ Luke 11:48; Acts 8:1; 22:20; Rom 1:32; 1 Cor 7:12, 13, **to applaud**; ❸ LXX, 1 Macc 1:57, **to adhere to**; Demad. 17, **to agree, consent**

συνευωχέομαι {σύν + εὖ + ἔχω} ❷[ppp.nmp] 2 Pet 2:13; Jude 12, **to feast with**

συνεφάγομεν → **συνεσθίω**, *aor. act. ind. 1p*, Acts 10:41, **to eat with**

συνεφίστημι {σύν + ἐπί + ἵστημι} ①[aai3s] Acts 16:22, **join to attack**[ZEC]

συνέχω (12x; 9x LA) *act.*, Luke 8:45, **to pressure**; 19:43, *milit.*, **to hem in**; 22:63, **to hold in custody**; 2 Cor 5:14, **to constrain**[BEC]; *pass.*, Luke 12:50, **to be distressed**; Acts 18:5, **to be occupied**; 28:8, **to be afflicted with disease**; Phil 1:23, **to be in dire straits**[BEC]; (49x LXX; 10x Job) Job 2:9, **to persist**; Hdt. *Hist.* **to be entangled** *w/ a violent-tempered father*[CGL]

συνήδομαι ①[pmi1s] Rom 7:22, **to delight**; Plato *Rp.* 462e, **to rejoice**

συνήθεια, ας, ἡ$_{1α}$ {σύν + ἔθος} ❸ John 18:39; 1 Cor 11:16, **custom**; 8:7, **force of habit**[NIGTC]; ❹ LXX, 4 Macc 2:12; 6:13, **companionship**

συνηλικιώτης, ου, ὁ$_{1>}$ {σύν + ἡλικία} ①[amp] Gal 1:14, **peers**

συνθάπτω ❷ Rom 6:4; Col 2:12, **to be buried with**

συνθλάω[con] ❷[fpi3s] Matt 21:44 = Luke 20:18, **to be broken to pieces, shatter**; ❽ LXX

συνθλίβω ❷ Mark 5:24, 31, **to crowd, press in**; ❷ LXX, Sir 31:14; 1 Macc 15:14, *he* **pressed** *the town hard*; Aristot. *Rh.* 1361b 17, **to press together**

συνθρύπτω {σύν + τρυφή} ①[pap.nmp] Acts 21:13, **to break** *my heart*

συνιδόντες → **συνοράω**, *aor. act. ptc. nmp*, Acts 14:6, **they found out about it**

συνίημι (26x; 22x SynA) Matt 13:13–51[6x]; Luke 8:10; 24:45; Rom 3:11; **to understand**; 2 Cor 10:12, οὐ **συνιᾶσιν**, *they* **are clueless**[BEC]; (97x LXX; 27x Pss)

συνίστημι (16x; 9x 2 Cor, 1x GA) Luke 9:32, **those standing with** *him*; Rom 3:5; 5:8, **to demonstrate**; Rom 16:1; 2 Cor 3:1, **commend**; Gal 2:18, **to show**; 2 Pet 3:5, **has come to exist**[BHGNT]; Col 1:17, **to hold together**; (42x LXX; 23x 1–3 Macc)

συνοδεύω {σύν + ὁδός} ①[pap.nmp] Acts 9:7, **to travel with**; ①[fai1s] LXX, Wis 6:23

συνοδία, ας, ἡ$_{1α}$ {σύν + ὁδός} ①[dfs] Luke 2:44, **caravan**; ❸ LXX, Neh 7:5, 64

σύνοιδα ❷ Acts 5:2, **knowledge**; 1 Cor 4:4, **conscience**[NIGTC]; ❷ LXX, Lev 5:1; Job 27:6

συνοικέω[con] {σύν + οἶκος} ①[pap.nmp] 1 Pet 3:7, **to live together** *with*; (14x LXX; 5x Sir)

συνοικοδομέω[con] {σύν + οἶκος + δῶμα} ①[pmi2p] Eph 2:22, **being built together**; ①[fai1p] LXX, 1 Esd 5:65, **we will build along with** *you*

συνομιλέω[con] {σύν + ὁμός + εἴλω} ①[pap.nms] Acts 10:27, **to talk with**

συνομορέω[con] {σύν + ὁμός + ὅρος} ①[pap.nfs] Acts 18:7, **to be next door**

συνοράω ❷ Acts 12:12; 14:6, **to realize**; (16x LXX; 15x 1–3 Macc) 1 Macc 4:21; 2 Macc 4:4

συνοχή, ῆς, ἡ$_{1η}$ {σύν + ἔχω} ❷ Luke 21:25; 2 Cor 2:4, **anguish** ❹ LXX, Jer 52:5, **siege**

συντάσσω ❸ Matt 21:6; 26:19; 27:10, **to direct**; (124x LXX; 38x Exod, 28x Num) Gen 18:19

συνταφέντες → **συνθάπτω**, *aor. pass. ptc. nmp*, Col 2:12, **you were buried with** *him*

συντέλεια, ας, ἡ$_{1α}$ {σύν + τέλος} ❻ (5x Matt) Matt 13:39, 40; Heb 9:26, *the* **end** *of the age*; (81x LXX; 23x Dan, 16x Sir)

συντελέω[con] {σύν + τέλος} ❻ Mark 13:4, **to be accomplished**; Luke 4:2, **to be completed**; 4;13, **to finish**; Rom 9:28, *to act* **conclusively**; (193x LXX; 15x 1 Kgs)

συντέμνω ①[pap.nms] Rom 9:28, *to act* **decisively**; ❺ LXX, Isa 10:22; 28:22

συντετρῖφθαι → **συντρίβω**, *pf. mid. inf.*, Mark 5:4, **to crush**

συντηρέω[con] ❸ Matt 9:17, **to preserve**; Mark 6:20, **to protect**; Luke 2:19, **to treasure**; (34x LXX; 14x Sir, 11x 1–2 Macc) 1 Macc 8:11

συντίθημι ❸ Luke 22:5; John 9:22; Acts 23:20, **to agree**; ❾ LXX, 1 Sam 22:13, **to conspire**

συντόμως *adv.* ❷ Mark 16:20; Acts 24:4, **briefly**; ❸ LXX, Prov 23:28, **suddenly**

συντρέχω ❸ Mark 6:33; Acts 3:11, **to run**; 1 Pet 4:4, **to join**[Keen1P]; ❼ LXX, Jdt 6:16

συντρίβω {σύν + τρίβος} ❼ Matt 12:20, **to bruise**; Mark 5:4, **to smash**; 14:3, **to break**; Luke 9:39, **to beat severely**[EGG]; (219x LXX; 30x Jer) Jer 2:13, *adj. ptc.*, **cracked** *cisterns*

σύντριμμα, ατος, τό$_3$ {σύν + τρίβος} ①[nns] Rom 3:16, **ruin**; (35x LXX; 9x Jer, 8x Isa)

σύντροφος, ον$_3$ {σύν + τρέφω} *adj.* ①[nms] Acts 13:1, **close friend**; ❹ LXX, 1 Kings 12:24

συντυγχάνω ①[aainf] Luke 8:19, **to join**[ZEC]; ①[aainf] LXX, 2 Macc 8:14, **to meet**

Συντύχη, ης, ἡ$_{1η}$ ①[afs] Phil 4:2, **Syntyche**

συνυποκρίνομαι {σύν + ὑπό + κρίνω} ①[api3p] Gal 2:13, **to join in hypocrisy**

συνυπουργέω[con] {σύν + ὑπό + ἔργον} ①[pap.gmp] 2 Cor 1:11, **to join in helping**

συνωδίνω {σύν + ὠδίν} ①[pai3s] Rom 8:22, **to suffer birth pangs together**[ZEC]

συνωμοσία, ας, ἡ$_{1α}$ {σύν + ὀμνύω} ①[afs] Acts 23:13, **plot, conspiracy**

Συράκουσαι, ῶν, αἱ$_1$ ①[afp] Acts 28:12, **Syracuse**

Συρία, ας, ἡ$_{1α}$ ❽ Matt 4:24; Luke 2:2; Acts 15:23, 41, **Syria**; (143x LXX; 62x 1–2 Kgs)

Σύρος, ου, ὁ$_2$ ①[nms] Luke 4:27, **Syrian**; (32x LXX; 11x 1 Chr)

Συροφοινίκισσα, ης, ἡ$_{1η}$ ①[nfs] Mark 7:26, **Syrophoenician**

Σύρτις, εως, ἡ$_3$ ①[afs] Acts 27:17, **Syrtis**

σύρω ❺ John 21:8; Acts 8:3; 14:19; 17:6, **to drag**; Rev 12:4, **to sweep away**; ❽ LXX, Deut 32:24, **to slither**

συσπαράσσω {σύν + σπάω} ❷[aai3s] Mark 9:20 = Luke 9:42, **to throw into convulsions**

σύσσημον, ου, τό$_2$ {σύν + σημεῖον} ①[ans] Mark 14:44, **signal**; ❸ LXX, Isa 5:26; 49:22

σύσσωμος, ον$_3$ {σύν + σῶμα} *adj.* ①[anp] Eph 3:6, *prob. neol.*, **members in the same body**[ABC]; **one who receives a possession together with someone else**[EGG]; **united in a single body**[BrDAG]

συστατικός, ή, όν$_{2.1.2}$ {σύν + ἵστημι} *adj.* ①[gfp] 2 Cor 3:1, **recommendation** *letters*

συσταυρόω[con] {σύν + σταυρόω} ❺ Matt 27:44 = Mark 15:32; John 19:32; Rom 6:6; Gal 2:19, **to crucify with**

συστέλλω {σύν + στέλλω} ❷ Acts 5:6, **to wrap up**; 1 Cor 7:29, **limits have been placed**[NIGTC]; ❺ LXX, 1 Macc 3:6, **to draw back**

συστενάζω {σύν + στένος} ①^{pai3s} Rom 8:22, **to groan together**

συστοιχέω^{con} {σύν + στοιχέω} ①^{pai3s} Gal 4:25, **to correspond to**

συστρατιώτης, ου, ὁ$_{1>}$ {σύν + στρατία} ❷ Phil 2:25; Phlm 2, **fellow soldier**

συστρέφω {σύν + στρέφω} ❷ Matt 17:22; Acts 28:3, **to gather**; (19x LXX) 2 Sam 16:51, **conspirators**

συστροφή, ῆς, ἡ$_{1η}$ {σύν + στρέφω} ❷ Acts 19:40; 23:12, **disturbance**; (11x LXX) Judg 14:8, **swarm**; 2 Kgs 15:15, **conspiracy**

συσχηματίζω {σύν + ἔχω} ❷ Rom 12:2; 1 Pet 1:14, **to conform to**

Συχάρ, ἡ$_3$ *indecl.* ①^{afs} John 4:5, **Sychar**

Συχέμ ❷ Acts 7:16, **Shechem**; (29x LXX; 16x Gen) Gen 12:6

σφαγή, ῆς, ἡ$_{1η}$ ❸ Acts 8:32; Rom 8:36; Jas 5:5, **slaughter**; (24x LXX; 7x Jer)

σφάγιον, ου, τό$_2$ {σφάζω} ①^{anp} Acts 7:42, **animals**; ❺ LXX, Lev 22:23; Amos 5:25

σφάζω (10x; 8x Rev) 1 John 3:12, **to murder**; Rev 5:6, 9, *subst. ptc.*, **slaughtered**; 6:4, **to slaughter**; (84x LXX; 39x Lev) Gen 22:10, **to kill**; Lev 1:5–22:28, *passim*, **to slaughter**

σφόδρα *adv.* (11x; 7x Matt) Matt 2:10, **χαρὰν** μεγάλην **σφόδρα**, *Hebraism*, **very** *great joy*; 17:6, **completely** *terrified*; (396x LXX; 37x 1 Macc, 36x Pss) Gen 7:19, **σφόδρα** σφοδρῶς, **very greatly**

σφοδρῶς *adv.* ① Acts 27:18, **violently**^{EGG}; ❹ LXX, Josh 3:16, μακρὰν σφόδρα **σφοδρῶς**, *very*, **very** *far off* (NETS)

σφραγίζω {σφραγίς} (14x; 8x Rev) Matt 27:66; John 3:33; Rev 7:3, **to seal**; (26x LXX)

σφραγίς, ῖδος, ἡ$_3$ (16x; 13x Rev) Rom 4:11; 1 Cor 9:2; Rev 5:1, **seal**; (26x LXX; 9x Sir)

σφυδρόν, οῦ, τό$_2$ ①^{nnp} Acts 3:7, **ankles**

σχεδόν *adv.* ❸ Acts 13:44; 19:26; Heb 9:22, **almost**, ❸ LXX, 2 Macc 5:2; 3 Macc 5:14

σχῆμα, ατος, τό$_3$ ❷ 1 Cor 7:31; Phil 2:7, **form**; ①^{ans} LXX, Isa 3:17

σχίζω (11x) Matt 27:51 = Mark 15:38 = Luke 23:45, **to split**; (11x LXX)

σχίσμα, ατος, τό$_3$ ❽ Matt 9:16 = Mark 2:21, **a rip**; John 7:43, **divided**; 1 Cor 1:10; 11:18; 12:25, **division**

σχοινίον, ου, τό$_2$ ❷ John 2:15; Acts 27:32, **cords**; (28x LXX)

σχολάζω {σχολή} ❷ Matt 12:44, **unoccupied**^{ZEC}; 1 Cor 7:5, **to find unhurried time**$^{NIGTC!}$; ❸ LXX, Exod 5:8, 17, **they have spare time** (NETS); **they are slackers** (CSB)

σχολή, ῆς, ἡ$_{1η}$ {σχολάζω} ①^{dfs} Acts 19:9, **hall, leisure time lecture**^{ZEC}; ❸ LXX, Gen 33:14, *idiom* κατὰ **σχολήν**, **slowly**

σχῶμεν → **ἔχω**, *aor. act. subj. 1p*, Matt 21:38, **take**

σῴζω (106x; 47x Syn, 13x Acts) Ⓐ **to rescue**, *phys.*, Matt 16:25; **to be rescued**, *phys.*, Acts 27:20; Ⓑ **to be saved**, *spir.*, Matt 10:22 = Mark 13:13; **to save**, *spir.*, Jas 4:12; Ⓒ *hol.*, **to heal**, *phys.* «» *spir.*, Luke 8:48 *hol.*, **to be healed**, *phys.* «» *spir.*, Acts 14:9; (340x LXX; 70x Pss, 37x Isa, 28x Jer)

σῶμα, ματος, τό$_3$ (142x; 46x 1 Cor) **body**; Ⓐ ***phys.***, Matt 5:29; 1 Cor 12^{15x}; Eph 5:28; Ⓑ ***church***, 1 Cor 10:16; Ⓒ ***Jesus's body as the temple***, John 2:21; Ⓓ ***earthly vs. heavenly***, 1 Cor 15:37–44^{8x}; Ⓔ ***corpse***, Acts 9:40; (128x LXX; 20x Lev)

σωματικός, ή, όν$_{2.1.2}$ *adj.* ❷ Luke 3:22; 1 Tim 4:8, **bodily**, ❷ LXX, 4 Macc 1:32; 3:1

σωματικῶς *adv.* ① Col 2:9, **bodily**

Σώπατρος, ου, ὁ$_2$ ①^{nms} Acts 20:4, **Sopater**

σωρεύω ❷ Rom 12:20, **to pile**; 2 Tim 3:6, **to be overwhelmed**; ❷ LXX, Prov 25:22

Σωσθένης, ους, ὁ$_3$ ❷ Acts 18:17; 1 Cor 1:1, **Sosthenes**

Σωσίπατρος, ου, ὁ$_2$ ①^{nms} Rom 16:21, **Sosipater**; ❷ LXX, 2 Macc 12:19, 24

σωτήρ, ῆρος, ὁ$_3$ {σῴζω} (24x; 6x Titus, 5x 2 Pet) Luke 1:47; John 4:42; Titus 1:3, **Savior**; (38x LXX; 9x Pss) Deut 32:15, **salvation**

σωτηρία, ας, ἡ$_{1\alpha}$ {σῴζω} (46x; 10x LA) Luke 1:69; John 4:22; Acts 4:12; Rom 10:10, **salvation**; Acts 27:34, **survival**; (150x LXX; 34x Pss, 16x Isa)

σωτήριος, ον$_{2.2}$ {σῴζω} *adj.* ①^{nfs} Titus 2:11, **salvation**; ❺ LXX, 3 Macc 6:31

σωφρονέω^{con} {σῶς + φρήν} ❻ Mark 5:15 = Luke 8:35; 2 Cor 5:13, **to be in a right mindset**; Rom 12:3, **to think sensibly**; 1 Pet 4:7, **to be of sound mind**^{EGG}

σωφρονίζω {σῶς + φρήν} ①$^{\text{pas3p}}$ Titus 2:4, **to encourage**

σωφρονισμός, οῦ, ὁ$_2$ {σῶς + φρήν} ①^{gms} 2 Tim 1:7, **sound judgment**

σωφρόνως {σῶς + φρήν} *adv.* ① Titus 2:12, **wisely**; ① LXX, Wis 9:11

σωφροσύνη, ῆς, ἡ$_{1\eta}$ {σῶς + φρήν} ❸ Acts 26:25, **reasonable**; 1 Tim 2:9, 15, **good sense**; ❾ LXX (6x 4 Macc)^{SCS}

σώφρων, ον$_{2.2}$ *adj.* ❹ 1 Tim 3:2; Titus 1:8; 2:2, 5, **sensible**; ❽ LXX (4 Macc)^{SCS}

T, τ [*tau*]

Τ, τ, τό (ταῦ) *indecl.* **tau**, *19th letter of the Gr. alphabet* ‖ *num.* τʹ = 300; ͵τ = 300,000

Ταβέρναι, ῶν, αἱ$_1$ ① Τριῶν **ταβερνῶν**[gfp] Acts 28:15, *Three* **Taverns**[Hem]

Ταβιθά, ἡ$_1$ ❷ Acts 9:36, 40, **Tabitha**

τάγμα, ατος, το$_3$ {τάσσω} ①[dns] 1 Cor 15:23, **proper arranged order**[NIGTC]; (15x LXX; 11x Num) Num 2:10, **unit, division**; Xen. *Mem.* 3.1.11, *milit.*, *t.t.* **band** *of troops*

τακτός, ή, όν$_{2.1.2}$ {τάσσω} *adj.* ①[dfs] Acts 12:21, **appointed** *day*; ①[ams] LXX, Job 12:5, **time**

ταλαι**πωρέω**[con] {τάλας + πείρω} ①[aai2p] Jas 4:9, **to be distressed** *over one's sins*[KEL]; (60x LXX; 6x Jer) Jer 4:13; 12:12, **to endure ruin, destruction**

ταλαι**πωρία, ας, ἡ**$_{1\alpha}$ {τάλας + πείρω} ❷ Rom 3:16; Jas 5:1, **misery**; (29x LXX; 7x Pss)

ταλαί**πωρος, ον**$_{2.2}$ {τάλας + πείρω} *adj.* ❷ Rom 7:24, *I am a* **miserable** *human being*![ZEC]; Rev 3:17, **wretched**; (10x LXX) Judg 5:27; 3 Macc 5:22, **in such distress**

ταλαντιαῖος, α, ον$_{2.1.2}$ {τάλαντον} *adj.* ①[nfs] Rev 16:21, **weighing a talent**[NIGTC]

τάλαντον, ου, τό$_2$ (14x, all in Matt) Matt 18:24; 25:15–28,[13x] **talent**, *Greek coin worth 5–6,000 denarii*; (72x LXX; 19x 1–2 Chr) Exod 25:39; 1 Chr 19:6

ταλιθά *Aram.* ① Mark 5:41, **little girl**, *Jairus's daughter*

ταμεῖον, ου, τό$_2$ {τέμνω} ❹ Matt 6:6; 24:26; Luke 12:3, 24, **inner room**, **closet**

τάξις, εως, ἡ$_3$ {τάσσω} ❾ (5x Heb) Luke 1:8; Col 2:5, **order**; Heb 5:6, 10; 6:20; 7:11, 17, **order** *of Melchizedek*; (19x LXX; 5x 2 Macc, 4x Job) Judg 5:20, **course**

ταπεινός, ή, όν$_{2.1.2}$ *adj.* ❽ Matt 11:29; Rom 12:16; Jas 4:6; 1 Pet 5:5, **humble**, **lowly**; Jas 1:9, **poor**; (66x LXX; 12x Isa, 8x Lev) Lev 13:20, *comp.*, (7x) **deeper** (Tanakh); Lev 27:8 (1x) **cannot afford**; Isa 11:4[2x], *subst.*, **the poor, the meek**

ταπεινο**φροσύνη, ης, ἡ**$_{1\eta}$ {ταπεινός + φρήν} ❼ Acts 20:19; Eph 4:2; Col 2:18; 1 Pet 5:5, **humility**[NIDNTT]

ταπεινό**φρων, ον**$_{3.3}$ {ταπεινός + φρήν} *adj.* ①[nmp] 1 Pet 3:8, **humble**; ①[amp] LXX, Prov 29:23

ταπεινόω[con] {ταπεινός} (14x) Matt 23:12 = Luke 14:11; Phil 2:8; Jas 4:10; 1 Pet 5:6, **to humble** *oneself*; (167x LXX; 32x Pss, 26x Isa) Deut 22:24, **to dishonor**, **use violence** *against a woman*; Lam 5:11, **to rape** *the women* (NLT); Plato *Lys.* 210e, **to lessen**, **humble**, **mistreat**

ταπείνωσις, εως, ἡ$_3$ {ταπεινός} ❹ Luke 1:48, **humble station**[ZEC]; Acts 8:33, **humilation**; Phil 3:21, **characterized by humility**[BEC]; Jas 1:10, **of humble circumstances**; (42x LXX; 10x Pss) 1 Sam 1:11, **affliction** *that prompted Hannah's prayer*

ταράσσω (17x; 6x John) Matt 2:3; John 5:7,[LGCa] **to stir up**; 11:33, **to be deeply troubled**; 14:1, **to be frightened**[ZEC]; Acts 15:24, *to throw into* **confusion**, **disturbed**[ZEC]; Gal 1:7; 5:10, οἱ ταράσσοντες, **the "disturbers"**; 1 Pet 3:14, **to agitate**[EGG]; (114x LXX; 35x Pss, 11x Isa) Ps 17:8 (18:7), *the mountains* **trembled**

τάραχος, ου, ὁ$_2$ {ταράσσω} ❷ Acts 12:18; 19:23, **commotion**; ❹ LXX, 1 Sam 5:9

Ταρσεύς, έως, ὁ$_3$ ❷ Acts 9:11; 21:39, **Tarsus**, *hometown of the apostle Paul*

Ταρσός, ου, ὁ$_2$ ❸ Acts 9:30; 11:25; 22:3, **Tarsus**

ταρταρόω[con] ①[aap.nms] 2 Pet 2:4, **to put into hell**; Hom. *Il.* 8.13, 481, **deep abyss**[NIDNTT]

τάσσω ❽ Matt 28:16, **to direct**; Acts 15:2, **to appoint**; Rom 13:1, **to be appointed**; Acts 28:23, **to arrange**; 1 Cor 16:15, **to assign**[NIGTC]; (80x LXX) Gen 3:24, **to station**

ταῦρος, ου, ὁ$_{2}$ ❹ Matt 22:4; Acts 14:13; Heb 9:13; 10:4, **bull**, **ox**; (36x LXX; 14x Exod)

ταφή, ῆς, ἡ$_{1η}$ {θάπτω} ①[afs] Matt 27:7, **burial place**; (14x LXX) Gen 50:3; Job 17:1

τάφος, ου, ὁ$_{2}$ {θάπτω} ❼ (6x Matt) Matt 23:27; 28:1; Rom 3:13, **grave**, **burial place**; (58x LXX; 19x 1–2 Sam + 1–2 Kgs, 6x Pss) Gen 23:4, **burial** *property*

τάχα {ταχύς} *adv.* ❷ Rom 5:7; Phlm 15, **perhaps**; ❷ LXX, Wis 13:6; 14:19

ταχέως {ταχύς} *adv.* (15x) Luke 14:21; John 11:31; Gal 1:6, **quickly**; 1 Cor 4:19; Phil 2:19, **soon**; 2 Thess 2:2, **easily**[NAC]; *comp. adv.* **τάχιον**, John 13:27; Heb 13:19, **quickly**; (29x LXX; 9x 2 Macc) Judg 9:48

ταχινός, ή, όν$_{2.1.2}$ {ταχύς} ❷ 2 Pet 1:14, *adv.*, **suddenly**[TNTC]; 2:1, *adj.*, **rapid** *ruin*[ABC]; ❻ LXX, Prov 1:16, *they* **hurry**; Hab 1:6, **impetuous** *nation*

τάχος, ους, τό$_{3}$ {ταχύς} ❽ Luke 18:8; Rom 16:20; Rev 1:1; 22:6, **ἐν τάχει**, **quickly**

ταχύς, εῖα, ύ$_{3.1.3}$ (13x; 6x Rev) 12x *in the neut. sing. as the* ***adv.*** **ταχύ**; Matt 5:25; John 11:29, **quickly**; Rev 2:16–22:20, **soon**; 1x *as adj.*, Jas 1:19, ταχὺς εἰς τὸ ἀκοῦσαι, **quick** *to hear*,[PNTC] (45x LXX; 7x Pss, Isa) Gen 27:20, **quickly**; Hom. *Il.* 13.819, *horses* **swifter** *than hawks*

τέ *enclitic coord. conj., always postpositive* (215x; 151x Acts!) [EDNT]→ Ⓐ ***indep. part.***, (13x) Matt 27:48; Jude 6; (95x Acts) 2:33; 5:19; 20:35; 23:10, **and**; Ⓑ ***in conj.*** *with* **καί**, Luke 2:16, **both** *Mary* **and** *Joseph*, **and** *the baby*; Ⓒ ***ambiguous cases***, Luke 21:11[BHGNT]; Acts 2:43, 46; 22:7[EGG]; Ⓓ **τέ . . . τέ** (*rare*), Rom 14:8; Acts 26:16, **both . . . and**; Ⓔ ***intensifier***; Luke 14:26, *and* **even** *his own life*[BHGNT!]; (266x LXX; 88x 1–4 Macc, 21x Exod)

τεθλιμμένη → **θλίβω**, *pf. pass. ptc. nfs*, Matt 7:14, *the way* **is difficult**

τεῖχος, ους, τό$_{3}$ {τοῖχος} ❾ (6x Rev 21) Acts 9:25 = 2 Cor 11:33, *lit.*, **wall**; Heb 11:30, *lit.*, **the walls** *of Jericho fell* «» Rev 21:12, 14, 17, *sym.*, **the walls** *of eternal security/salvation*[NIGTC]; Pseud., 2 En. 65.10, *a great, indestructible* **wall**; (191x LXX; 31x Neh, 28x 1–2 Macc, 17x Isa) 2 Macc 12:15

τεκμήριον, ου, τό$_{2}$ {τέκμαρ} ①[dnp] Acts 1:3, **convincing proof**; ❸ LXX, 3 Macc 3:24

τεκνίον, ου, τό$_{2}$ {τίκτω} *diminutive* ❼ John 13:33; 1 John 2:1–5:21,[6x] **little children**

τεκνο**γονέω**[con] {τίκτω + γίνομαι} ①[painf] 1 Tim 5:14, **to bear children**

τεκνο**γονία, ας, ἡ**$_{1α}$ {τίκτω + γίνομαι} ①[gfs] 1 Tim 2:15, **bearing of children**, **childbearing**

τέκνον, ου, τό$_{2}$ {τίκτω} (99x; 14x Matt:Luke) Ⓐ Matt 7:11 = Luke 11:13, **child**; Ⓑ Matt 23:37, **citizens** *of Jerusalem*; Ⓒ Gal 4:31, **descendant**; Luke 15:1, **son**; Ⓓ 1 Tim 1:2; 2 Tim 1:2, **child** *in the faith*; Ⓔ 1 John 3:1–2, 10, **children** *of God and* **children** *of the devil*[NIDNTT]; (303x LXX; 46x Sir, 45x 1–4 Macc, 21x Gen, 18x Isa)

τεκνο**τροφέω**[con] {τίκτω + τρέφω} ①[aai3s] 1 Tim 5:10, **to nurture or raise children**

τέκτων, ονος, τό$_{3}$ {τίκτω} ❷ Matt 13:55 = Mark 6:3, **woodworker**, **joiner**, **carpenter**; (30x LXX) 1 Sam 13:19, **craftsman** *of iron*; **blacksmith**; 2 Sam 5:11, **craftsmen** *of wood and stone*; **carpenters** *and* **stonemasons**

τέλειος, α, ον$_{2.1.2}$ {τέλος} *adj.* (19x; 5x Jas) Matt 5:48,[2x] *emph. subst.*, *be* **complete** (*in the reach of your goodness*); 19:21, **ethically complete**[ZEC]; Rom 12:2, **perfect**; 1 Cor 14:20, *subst.*, **mature adults** *in thinking*[NIGTC]; 1 Cor 2:6; Jas 1:4, *the* **mature**; 1 Cor 13:10, *eschat.*, *when* **completeness** *comes*; (17x LXX) Gen 6:9, **blameless**; 1 Kgs 11:4, *he was not* **wholeheartedly devoted**

τελειότης, ητος, ἡ$_3$ {τελέω} ❷ *adj.*, Col 3:14, *love—the* **perfect** *bond of unity* (HCSB); Heb 6:1, **maturity**; ❹ LXX, Judg 9:16, 19, **loyally** (Tanakh)

τελειόω[con] {τελέω} (23x; 9x Heb) Luke 2:43, **to complete**; 13:32; Phil 3:12, **to reach a goal, to accomplish a mission**[ZEC!]; John 19:28, **to make come true**; Heb 2:10–12:23 (*major theme*), **to bring to perfection, to fulfill God's purpose**[EGG]; Jas 2:22, *pass.*, *faith* **brought to completion** *through works*[KEL]; (21x LXX; 4x Exod:Lev) Exod 29:9, **to ordain**

τελείως {τέλος} *adv.* ① 1 Pet 1:13, (*emph.*) **all** *your future expectation*[Keen1P]; ❹ LXX

τελείωσις, εως, ἡ$_3$ {τέλος} ❷ Luke 1:45; Heb 7:11, **fulfillment**; (17x LXX) Exod 29:22, *a ram* **for ordination**

τελειωτής, οῦ, ὁ$_{1>}$ {τέλος} ①[ams] Heb 12:2, **perfecter**

τελεσ**φορέω**[con] {τέλος + φέρω} ①[pai3p] Luke 8:14, **mature fruit**; ①[app.nmp] LXX, 4 Macc 13:20, **to be brought to full term**, *of children in the mother's womb*

τελευτάω[con] {τέλος} (11x; 7x Syn) Matt 15:4 = Mark 7:10; Heb 11:22, **to die**; (91x LXX)

τελευτή, ῆς, ἡ$_{1η}$ {τέλος} ①[gfs] Matt 2:15, **death**; (26x LXX; 9x Sir) Gen 27:2; Sir 1:13

τελέω[con] {τέλος} (28x; 8x Rev, 7x Matt) Matt 7:28; 26:1, **to conclude** *teaching*; 10:23, **to complete your mission**[WBC]; 17:24, **to pay** *a tax*; Rom 2:27, **to satisfy**[NIGTC]; 2 Cor 12:9, **to perfect**; Luke 12:50; Rev 1:7–20:7,[8x] **to finish**; (24x LXX)

τέλος, ους, τό$_3$ (40x; 13x Syn) Ⓐ Matt 24:6 = Mark 13:7 = Luke 21:9; Rev 22:13, *eschat.*, **the end**; Ⓑ Matt 17:25, *poll*-**tax**; Ⓒ Rom 13:7,[2x] **tribute money** (*see* **τελώνης**); Ⓓ Matt 26:58, **outcome**; Ⓔ Rom 10:4, **climax**[NICNT]; Ⓕ 2 Cor 1:13, **ἕως τέλους**, *idiom.*, **fully**[BEC]; Ⓖ 2 Cor 3:13, **εἰς τὸ τέλος**,[1x] *to the* **designed end**[BEC!]; Ⓗ Jas 5:11, **purpose** *of the Lord*; (154x LXX; 76x Pss) Εἰς τὸ **τέλος**, (56x Pss), Ps 4:1 (4:0 LXX), **permanence, may the psalm serve its purpose** *translating* Heb. נצח, *for the* **choir director** (CSB); *for the* **leader** (Tanakh)

τελ**ώνης, ου, ὁ$_{1>}$** {τέλος + ὠνέομαι} (21x Syn; 10x Luke) Matt 5:46; Mark 2:15–16[3x]; Luke 3:12, **tax collector**; Matt 10:3; Luke 5:27, **the tax collector** *Matthew/Levi*; Aristoph. *Eq.* 248 (*insulting term in 5th–4th BCE*)[BrDAG]

τελώνιον, ου, τό$_2$ {τέλος + ὠνέομαι} ❸ Matt 9:9 = Mark 2:14 = Luke 5:27, **tax office**

τέρας, ατος, τό$_3$ (16x; 9x Acts, *pl. only, always* + σημεῖον) **wonders** Ⓐ Matt 24:24 = Mark 13:22; 2 Thess 2:9, *by false prophets and the lawless one*; Ⓑ Acts 2:19–15:12; 2 Cor 12:12, *by God, Jesus, Moses, Stephen, and the apostles*; (47x LXX; 10x Deut, 6x Exod)

Τέρτιος, ου, ὁ$_2$ ①[nms] Rom 16:22, **Tertius**, *one of Paul's amanuenses*

Τέρτυλλος, ου, ὁ$_2$ ❷ Acts 24:1, 2, **Tertullus**

τέσσαρες, α$_{3.3}$ *adj.* (41x; 29x Rev) Matt 24:31 = Mark 13:27; John 11:17; Acts 10:11; Rev 7:1; 9:13, **four**; 4:4; 7:4; 21:7, *in larger numbers*; (224x LXX; 43x Ezek, 31x 1 Chr)

τεσσαρεσ**καιδέκατος, η, ον$_{2.1.2}$** {τέσσαρες + καί + δέκα} *adj.* ❷ Acts 27:27, 33, **fourteenth**; (29x LXX; 8x Esth)

τεσσαρά**κοντα**[LXX] {τέσσαρες + ἑκατόν} *adj.* (141x; 19x Num, 16x Gen) Gen 5:13; Exod 16:35; Num 13:25, **forty**; Num 1:31–2:28,[7x] *part of a larger number*

τεσσεράκοντα {τέσσαρες + ἑκατόν} *indecl. adj.* (22x; 8x Acts) Matt 4:2 = Mark 1:13 = Luke 4:2; Acts 1:3; 2 Cor 11:24, **forty**; Rev 7:4–21:17, **forty**; 14:1, 3, *in 144,000*

τεσσερακοντα**ετής, ές$_{3.3}$** {τέσσαρες + ἑκατόν + ἔτος} *adj.* ❷ Acts 7:23; 13:18, **forty years old**

τέταγμέναι → **τάσσω**, *pf pass. ptc. nfp*, Rom 13:1, **being appointed** *by God*
τεταρταῖος, α, ον$_{2.1.2}$ {τέσσαρες + ἔτος} *adj.* ①[nms] John 11:39, *on the* **fourth** *day*
τέταρτος, η, ον$_{2.1.2}$ {τέσσαρες} *adj.* (10x; 7x Rev) Matt 14:25 = Mark 6:48; Rev 6:7–8[3x]; 8:12; 16:8; 21:19, **fourth**; Acts 10:30, **four**; (94x LXX; 16x 1 Chr, 9x Num)
τετρα**αρχέω**[con] {τέσσαρες + ἄρχω} ❸[pap.gms] Luke 3:1,[3x] **to be tetrarch**
τετρα**άρχης, ου, ὁ**$_{1>}$ {τέσσαρες + ἄρχω} ❹ Matt 14:1; Luke 3:19; 9:7; Acts 13:1, *Herod the* **Tetrarch**
τετρά**γωνος, ον**$_{2.2}$ {τέσσαρες + γωνία} *adj.* ①[nfs] Rev 21:16, **four-cornered**, **in a square** (*echo from Ezek 41:21)*[NIGTC]; (10x LXX; 4x Exod:Ezek); (Gk. Classics; 1,100+; *geom.* 1,000+ Eucl. *El.*)
τετράδιον, ου, τό$_2$ {τέσσαρες} ①[dnp] Acts 12:4, **squad of four soldiers**
τετρα**κισχίλιοι, αι, α**$_{2.1.2}$ {τέσσαρες + χίλιοι} *adj.* ❺ Matt 15:38; 16:10 = Mark 8:9; Acts 21:36, **four thousand**; ❾ LXX, 1 Chr 12:27, **four thousand** *six hundred*
τετρα**κόσιοι, αι, α**$_{2.1.2}$ {τέσσαρες + ἑκατόν} *adj.* ❹ Acts 5:36; 7:6; 13:20; Gal 3:17, **four hundred**; (64x LXX; 14x Num) Gen 11:13, **four hundred** *and three years*
τετρά**μηνος, ον**$_{2.2}$ {τέσσαρες + μήν} *adj.* ① John 4:35, *subst.*, **the period of four months**[EGG]; ❷ LXX, Judg 19:2
τετραπλοῦς, ῆ, οῦν$_{2.1.2}$ {τέσσαρες} *adj.* ①[ans] Luke 19:8, **fourfold**[ZEC]; Xen. *An.* 7.6.7, **quadruple** *reward for killing a general*
Τετραπλᾶ, **Tetrapla**, *compilation of four Greek versions of the Bible*
τετρά**πους, ποδος, τό**$_3$ {τέσσαρες + πούς} ❸ Acts 10:12; 11:6; Rom 1:23, **quadrupeds**[ZEC]; (13x LXX; 5x Exod, 4x Lev) Exod 9:9, **beasts**
τεφρόω[con] {τύφω} ①[aap.nms] 2 Pet 2:6, **to reduce to ashes**[BEC, *WPNT*]
τεχθείς → **τίκτω**, *aor. pass. ptc. nms*, Matt 2:2, *he who* **has been born**
τέχνη, ης, ἡ$_{1η}$ {τίκτω} ❸ Acts 17:29, **skill**; 18:3, **trade**; Rev 18:22, **artisan**; (10x LXX)
τεχνίτης, ου, ὁ$_{1>}$ {τίκτω} ❹ Acts 19:24, 38; Rev 18:22, **craftsman**; Heb 11:10, **designer**; (12x LXX; 3x Jer) Jer 10:9, **craftsmen** *adorned with blue and scarlet*
τήκω ①[pmi3s] 2 Pet 3:12, **to melt**; (50x LXX) Deut 28:65, **to languish**; Zech 14:12,[2x] **to rot**
τηλαυγῶς {τῆλε + αὐγή} *adv.* ① Mark 8:25, *to see* **clearly**
τηλικοῦτος, αύτη, οῦτο$_{2.1.2}$ {τῆλε + οὗτος} *adj.* ❹ 2 Cor 1:10, **so horrible** *a death*; Heb 2:3, **so great** *a salvation*; Jas 3:4, *ships are* **so large**; Rev 16:18, **so terrible** *of an earthquake*[NIGTC]; ❸ LXX, 2 Macc 12:3, *did* **so** *ungodly a deed*
τηρέω[con] (70x; 18x John, 11x Rev, 7x 1 John) *act.*, John 2:10, **to keep**; Jude 6, **to guard**, **keep watch**; 1 Thess 5:23, **to preserve**; Eph 4:3, **to maintain**; 2 Cor 11:9; Jude 21, **to persist**; Jas 1:27, **to guard** *oneself*; John 2:10–17:5, **to remain committed**; Jude 13, *pass.*, **to be reserved** *forever*; (37x LXX) Gen 3:15, **to strike**; Xen. *Cyn.* 6.1, **to control** *hunting dogs*
τήρησις, εως, ἡ$_3$ {τηρέω} ❸ Acts 4:3, **custody**; 5:18, **public jail**; 1 Cor 7:19, **keeping**[NIGTC]; ❺ LXX, Sir 32:23, *the* **keeping** *of the commandments*
Τιβεριάς, άδος, ἡ$_3$ ❸ John 6:1, 23, *city of* **Tiberias**; 21:1, *Sea of* **Tiberias**
Τιβέριος, ου, ὁ$_2$ ①[gms] Luke 3:1, **Tiberius** *Caesar*
τίθημι (100x; 39x LA) Ⓐ Mark 12:36; Rom 4:17; Heb 1:13, **to appoint**, **arrange**; Ⓑ 2 Cor 5:19, **to instill** *the message of reconciliation in us*[BEC]; Ⓒ Luke 6:48; John 19:19; Rom 14:13; Rev 10:2, **to put**, **place**; Ⓓ John 10:11; 1 John 3:16, **to lay down** *a life*; Ⓔ Acts 5:4,

to contrive, resolve; 🅕 1 Cor 9:18, **I make** *the gospel free of charge*; 🅖 1 Pet 2:8, *pass.*, *a destiny to which* **they have been consigned**[Keen1P]; (527x LXX; 67x Pss, 43x Isa, 34x Ezek, 33x Job) Gen 1:17, 2:8, **to place**

τίκτω (18x; 9x nativity texts) Matt 1:21; Luke 1:31; John 6:21; Gal 4:27, **to give birth to a child**; Heb 6:7, **to produce** *a crop*; Jas 1:15, **to give birth** *to sin*; Rev 12:2, 4, 13, *fig.*, **to give birth**[NIGTC]; (236x LXX; 81x Gen, 43x Isa, 34x Ezek, 33x Job)

τίλλω ❸ Matt 12:1 = Mark 2:23 = Luke 6:1, **to pluck**; ❹ LXX, Ezra 9:3

Τιμαῖος, ου, ὁ$_2$ ①[gms] Mark 10:46, **Timaeus**, *father of Bartimaeus*

τιμάω[con] {τιμή} (21x; 16x Gs) Matt 19:19 = Mark 10:19 = Luke 18:20 = Eph 6:2, **to honor** *your father and mother*; John 5:23[4x]; 1 Pet 2:17, **to honor**; (46x LXX) Exod 20:12

τιμή, ῆς, ἡ$_{1η}$ {τιμάω} (41x) Matt 27:6, **money**; 1 Cor 6:20; 7:23, **price**; John 4:44; 1 Tim 6:16; Rev 4:9, **honor**; Acts 4:34; 5:2, **proceeds**; Acts 28:10, **τιμαῖς** ἐτίμησαν, *they honored us* **with honors (greatly)**; (71x LXX) Lev 27:2–17,[16x] **assessment** *of vows*

τίμιος, α, ον$_{2.1.2}$ {τιμή} *adj.* (13x; 6x Rev) Acts 5:34; Heb 13:4, **held in honor**; Acts 20:24; 1 Cor 3:12; Jas 5:7; 2 Pet 1:4; Rev 17:4, **precious**; (40x LXX) 1 Chr 20:2, **precious** *stones*

τιμιότης, ητος, ἡ$_3$ {τιμάω} ①[gfs] Rev 18:19, **wealth**, **abundance**

Τιμόθεος, ου, ὁ$_2$ {τιμή + θεός} (26x) Acts 16:1; Phil 2:19; Phlm 1; Heb 13:23, **Timothy**

Τίμων, ωνος, ὁ$_3$ ①[ams] Acts 6:5, **Timon**

τιμωρέω[con] {τιμή + αἴρω} ❷ Acts 22:5 = 26:11, **to punish**, **torment**[Keen3]; (11x LXX; 4x 4 Macc) 2 Macc 7:7, **to suffer as a martyr**

τιμωρία, ας, ἡ$_{1α}$ {τιμή + αἴρω} ①[gfs] Heb 10:29, **punishment**; (15x LXX; 4x 3 Macc) 1 Esd 8:24, **death penalty**; Hdt. *Hist.* 5.63, *they were making ready for* **vengeance**

τίνω ①[aai3p] 2 Thess 1:9, **to pay the penalty** *of eternal destruction*[NIGTC]; ❹ LXX, Prov 27:12

τίς, τί$_{3.3}$ *interrog. pron./adj.* (552x; 358x Gs) Matt 3:7, **who?**; Luke 17:7, **which?**; 20:17, **what?**; (1,466x LXX; 249x MajPr)

τις, τι$_{3.3}$ *indef. pron.* (537x; 200x LA, 161x Paul) Luke 19:39, **some**; Acts 10:47, **anyone**; 21:37, **something**; (280x LXX; 70x Pent)

Τίτιος, ου, ὁ$_2$ ①[gms] Acts 18:7, **Titius** *Justus, a worshiper of God*

τίτλος, ου, ὁ$_2$ ❷ John 19:19, 20, **inscription**, **notice**

Τίτος, ου, ὁ$_2$ (14x; 9x 2 Cor) 2 Cor 2:13; Gal 2:1, 3; 2 Tim 4:10; Titus 1:4, **Titus**

τοιγαροῦν {τοι + γάρ + οὖν} *intensive part.* ❷ 1 Thess 4:8; Heb 12:1, **for that very reason**[NIGTC]; (11x LXX; 4x 4 Macc) Job 22:10; 24:22, **therefore**; Eus. *Hist. eccl.*[6x]

τοίνυν {τοι + νῦν} *conj.* ❸ Luke 20:25; 1 Cor 9:26; Heb 13:13, **for that reason**

τοιόσδε, τοιάδε, τοιόνδε$_{2.1.2}$ {τοι + ὁ + δέ} ① 2 Pet 1:17, **this**; ❷ LXX, 2 Macc 11:17

τοιοῦτος, τοιαύτη, τοιοῦτον$_{2.1.2}$ {τοι + οὗτος} (57x; 10x 1 Cor:2 Cor) 🅐 ***corr. pron.***, Matt 9:8; 2 Cor 2:6[2x]; Gal 5:23; Heb 7:26; 3 John 8, **such**, **such a one**; 🅑 ***adj.***, 1 Cor 5:5; 2 Cor 12:2; Gal 5:21, **this**, **this man**, **this one**; (80x LXX; 8x Job:Jer)

τοῖχος, ου, ὁ$_2$ {τεῖχος} ①[vms] Acts 23:3, **wall**; (76x LXX; 22x Ezek) Ezek 12:5, 7

τόκος, ου, ὁ$_2$ {τίκτω} ❷ Matt 25:27 = Luke 19:23, *money with* **interest**

τολμάω[con] (16x; 4x 2 Cor) Mark 15:43; Rom 5:7; Jude 9,[ABC] **to be brave**, **dare**; 1 Cor 6:1, **to have the affrontery**[SacPag]; 2 Cor 10:2, **to have bold confidence**[BEC]; ❼ LXX, Job 15:12

τολμηρός, ά, όν$_{2.1.2}$ {τολμάω} *adj.* ① *comp. adv.* τολμηρότερον Rom 15:15, **quite boldly**; ❸ LXX, Sir 8:15; 19:2, 3, *warnings conc. the* **reckless**; Thuc. 2.87.5, **greater courage**[BrDAG]

τολμητής, οῦ, ὁ$_{1>}$ {τολμάω} ①^{nmp} 2 Pet 2:10, **audacious**[ABC]; Thuc. 1.70.3, **bold**
τομός, ή, όν$_{2.1.2}$ {τέμνω} *adj.* ① *comp. adj.* τομώτερος Heb 4:12, **sharper**; ❷ LXX
τόξον, ου, τό$_2$ ①^{ans} Rev 6:2, *an archer's* **bow**; (78x LXX) Gen 9:13, 16, **rainbow**
τοπάζιον, ου, τό$_2$ {τόπαζος} ① Rev 21:20, **topaz**; ❺ LXX, Exod 28:17
τόπος, ου, ὁ$_2$ (94x; 37x LA) **place**: Ⓐ ***general location***, Luke 2:7, *in the inn*; 4:37, *in the region*; Ⓑ ***specific ref.***, Luke 4:17, *in the scroll*; 14:9–10,^{3x} *at the table*; Ⓒ ***positional***, Acts 1:25, **place** *of responsibility*; 1 Cor 14:16; Ⓓ ***favor. circum.***, Acts 25:16; Eph 4:27; Heb 12:17, **opportunity**; (587x LXX) *assoc. w/ toponyms*, Gen 12:6
τοσοῦτος, τοσαύτη, τοσοῦτον$_{2.1.2}$ {οὗτος} *corr. adj.* (20x) Matt 8:10, **such**; 15:33,^{2x} **so great**; Gal 3:4, **so many**; Heb 4:7, **τοσούτῳ** χρόνῳ, **so long**; 1:4; Rev 18:17, **so much**; Heb 10:25, **τοσούτῳ** μᾶλλον, **all the more**; (24x LXX; 16x 1–4 Macc)
τότε {ὅς + τέ} *temp. adv.* (160x; 142x GA, 90x Matt) Ⓐ ***narrative***,[Runge sec. 2.4] Matt 2:7–28:10; Acts 1:12–28:1, **then**; Matt 4:5, **afterward**[EGG]; Ⓑ ***summative***, 1 Cor 4:5; 15:54; 1 Thess 5:3; Heb 10:7; 2 Pet 3:6, **then**; Ⓒ ***temporal***, Matt 3:13, **at that time**[BHGNT]; 1 Cor 16:2; Gal 4:8, 29; Col 3:4, **when**; (246x LXX; 39x Dan)
τοὐναντίον {ὁ + ἀντί, ***crasis***} ❸ 2 Cor 2:7; Gal 2:7; 1 Pet 3:9, **on the contrary**
τοὔνομα {ὁ + ὄνομα, ***crasis***} ①^{nns} Matt 27:57, **named**
τράγος, ου, ὁ$_2$ {τρώγω} ❹^{gmp} Heb 9:12,^{2x} 19; 10:4, **male goat**; (32x LXX; 13x Num)
τράπεζα, ης, ἡ$_{η>}$ {τέσσαρες + πούς} (15x; 4x Luke) Matt 15:27 = Mark 7:28; Luke 16:21; John 2:15; Heb 9:2, **table**; 1 Cor 10:21,^{2x} **table** *of the Lord*, **table** *of demons*[NIGTC]; (77x LXX; 16x Exod, 9x Ezek) Exod 25:23–30:28,^{8x} *construction and use of* **the table**[TOTC]
τραπεζίτης, ου, ὁ$_{1>}$ {τέσσαρες + πούς} ①^{dmp} Matt 25:27, **banker**, **money changer**
τραῦμα, ατος, τό$_3$ ①^{anp} Luke 10:34, **wound**; (17x LXX) Exod 21:25^{2x}
τραυματίζω {τραῦμα} ❷ Luke 20:12; Acts 19:16, **to wound**; (10x LXX; 5x Ezek) Isa 53:5
τραχηλίζω {τράχηλος} ①$^{pfpp.nnp}$ Heb 4:13, *pass.*, **to be exposed**, **to lay bare**; Plato *Am.* 132c, **to be thrown to the ground** *in wrestling*; Philo *Mut. Nom.* 81, *metaph.*, **to wrestle** (*in phil. debate*) *against the* (*hostile*) *reasonings*; Strabo *Geogr.* 6.2.3, *boats* **overcome** *by a storm*
τράχηλος, ου, ὁ$_2$ ❼ Matt 18:6 = Mark 9:42 = Luke 17:2; Acts 15:10; Rom 16:4, **neck**; Luke 15:20, *embraced him about the* **neck**[BEC]; Acts 20:37, *fell upon his* **neck**, **to embrace**[Keen3]; (76x LXX; 12x Jer) Jer 7:26, *hardened their* **necks**
τραχύς, εῖα, ύ$_{2.1.2}$ *adj.* ❷ Luke 3:5; Acts 27:29, **rough**, **rocky**; ❼ LXX, Deut 21:4; Isa 40:4
Τραχωνῖτις, ιδος, ἡ$_3$ ①^{gfs} Luke 3:1, **Trachonitis**
τρεῖς, τρία$_{3.3}$ *adj.* (69x; 47x LA) Matt 12:40^{4x}; 17:4 = Mark 9:5 = Luke 9:33; John 2:19; Acts 9:9; Jas 5:17; Rev 21:13,^{4x} **three**; (353x LXX; 48x 1–2 Chr, 30x Exod)
Τρεῖς ταβέρναι, *see* **Ταβέρναι**
τρέμω ❸ Mark 5:33 = Luke 8:47; 2 Pet 2:10, **to tremble**; (11x LXX) Isa 66:2; Hom. *Il.* 13.18, *the imposing mountains and the forest* **trembled** *at the immortal footsteps*[BrDAG]
τρέφω ❾ Matt 6:26 = Luke 12:24, **to feed**; Luke 4:16; **to raise**, **nourish**; Luke 23:29, **to nurse**; Acts 12:20, διὰ τὸ **τρέφεσθαι**, **for food**[EGG]; Jas 5:5, **to fatten**[KEL]; Rev 12:6, 14, **to sustain** *the messianic community of faith*[NIGTC]; (22x LXX)
τρέχω (20x; 8x Gs) Matt 27:48 = Mark 15:36, **to run**; Rom 9:16, **to put forth effort**[ABC]; 1 Cor 9:24,^{3x} **runners**, **race**, **run**; Heb 12:1, *metaph.*, **to run**; 2 Thess 3:1, **run swiftly**; Rev 9:9, **to rush**; (63x LXX) Ps 147:4 (147:15), *his word* **runs swiftly**

τρῆμα, ατος, τό$_3$ ①^{gns} Luke 18:25^{EGG}, **eye** *of a needle*; Aristoph. *Ve.* 141, **mouth**; Gal. *U.P.* 2.838, **blind foramen** *of the skull*; Amips. 19, **a point**, *marked on the sides of dice, one to six*

τριάκοντα {τρεῖς + ἑκατόν} *adj.* (11x; 5x Matt) Matt 13:8 = Mark 4:8; Matt 13:23 = Mark 4:20; Matt 26:15; 27:3; Luke 3:23; Gal 3:17, **thirty**; (167x LXX; 30x Num, 21x Gen) Gen 5:5

τριακόσιοι, αι, α$_{2.1.2}$ {τρεῖς + ἑκατόν} *adj.* ❷ Mark 14:5; John 12:5, **three hundred**; (80x LXX; 11x 1–2 Chr, 8x Gen) Gen 5:23; Judg 7:6

τρί**βολος, ου, ὁ$_2$** {τρεῖς + βάλλω} ❷ Matt 7:16; Heb 6:8, **thistle**; ❹ LXX, Gen 3:19

τρίβος, ου, ὁ$_2$ {τρίβω → ***to rub***} ❸ Matt 3:3 = Mark 1:3 = Luke 3:4, **path**

τρι**ετία, ας, ἡ$_{1α}$** {τρεῖς + ἔτος} ①^{afs} Acts 20:31, **period of three years**

τρίζω ①^{pai3s} Mark 9:18, **to grind one's teeth**; Zeux. 10, **to trumpet**, *elephant*; Hom. *Il.* 23.101, **to squeak and gibber**, *ghost noises*; Eup. 120, **crackling** *of a burning person*

τρίμηνος, ον$_{2.2}$ {τρεῖς + μήν} *adj.* ①^{ans} Heb 11:23, **period of three months**; ❹ LXX

τρίς {τρεῖς} *indecl. adj.* (12x) Matt 26:34 = Mark 14:30 = Luke 22:34 = John 13:38, **three**; (12x LXX)

τρί**στεγον, ου, τό$_2$** {τρεῖς + στέγω} ①^{gns} Acts 20:9, **third floor**

τρισ**χίλιοι, α, ον$_{2.1.2}$** {τρεῖς + χίλιοι} *adj.* ①^{nfp} Acts 2:41, **three thousand**; (35x LXX)

τρίτος, η, ον$_{2.1.2}$ *adj.* (57x; 23x Rev) Matt 16:21 = Luke 9:22 = 1 Cor 15:4; John 21:14, 17^{2x}; 2 Cor 12:14; 3 John 0; Rev 4:7; 21:19, **third**; (167x LXX; 28x 1–2 Chr) Gen 1:13; 2:14

τρίχινος, η, ον$_{2.1.2}$ {θρίξ} *adj.* ①^{nms} Rev 6:12, **made of hair**, **hairy**; ❷ LXX, Exod 26:7, *curtains* **of goat hair**; Zech 13:4, **hairy** *cloak*; Xen. *An.* 4.8.3, *soldiers with* **hair** *tunics*

τρόμος, ου, ὁ$_2$ {τρέμω} ❺ Mark 16:8; 1 Cor 2:3; Eph 6:5; Phil 2:12, **trembling**; (11x LXX) Gen 4:12

τροπή, ῆς, ἡ$_{1η}$ {τρέπω} ①^{gfs} Jas 1:17, **turning**, **change**; (11x LXX) Exod 32:18, **defeat**

τρόπος, ου, ὁ$_2$ {τρέπω} (13x) Matt 23:37 = Luke 13:34; Acts 1:11; 2 Tim 3:8, ὃν **τρόπον**, *in the same* **way** *as*; Rom 3:2; Phil 1:18; 2 Thess 2:3; 3:16, *in every or any* **way**; Heb 13:5,^{EGG} *let your* **manner of life** *be*^{WPNT}; Jude 7, **likewise**; (233x LXX; 26x Josh)

τροπο**φορέω**^{con} {τρέπω + φέρω} ①^{aai3s} Acts 13:18, **to tolerate the character**, **endure the habits**; (*alt. form*, LXX, Deut 1:31, ἐτροφοφόρησεν, **to carry**)

τροφή, ῆς, ἡ$_{1η}$ {τρέφω} (16x; 7x Acts) Matt 3:4; 6:25 = Luke 12:23; Acts 2:46; Jas 2:15, *physical* **food**; Heb 5:12, 14, *solid* **food** *for the mature*

Τρόφιμος, ου, ὁ$_2$ ❸ Acts 20:4; 21:29; 2 Tim 4:20, **Trophimus**

τροφός, ου, ἡ$_1$ {τρέφω} ①^{afs} 1 Thess 2:7, *as a* **nursing mother** *cherishes her own children*^{BEC}; ❹ LXX, Isa 49:23, *their queens will be your* **nursing mothers**

τροχιά, ᾶς, ἡ$_{1α}$ {τρέχω} ①^{afp} Heb 12:13, **path**; ❻ LXX, Prov 2:15; 4:26, 27

τροχός, οῦ, ὁ$_2$ {τρέχω} ①^{ams} Jas 3:6,^{KEL} **wheel** *or* **cycle** *of nature*; (57x LXX; 28x Ezek, 10x 4 Macc) 1 Sam 7:17–19,^{5x} *a* **wheel** *on a cart*; Prov 20:20 (20:26), *wise king crushes the wicked with the* **wheel**; Aristoph. *Pl.* 875, *to be tortured on the* **wheel**^{BrDAG}

τρύβλιον, ου, τό$_2$ ❷ Matt 26:23 = Mark 14:20, **bowl**; (19x LXX; 15x Num) Num 4:7; 7:13–84,^{13x} **bowl**

τρυγάω^{con} {τρύγη} ❸ Luke 6:44; Rev 14:18, 19, **to gather**; (14x LXX) Lev 25:11

τρυγών, όνος, ἡ$_3$ {τρύγη} ①^{gfp} Luke 2:24, **turtledove**; (15x LXX; 9x Lev) Gen 15:9

τρυμαλιά, ᾶς, ἡ$_{1α}$ ①[gms] Mark 10:25, **eye** *of a needle*[ZEC]; ❸ LXX, Jer 13:4; 16:16; 30:10 (29:16), **cleft** *of the rock*; Sotad. 1, **hole** *in the center*

τρύπημα, ατος, τό$_3$ {τρυμαλιά} ①[gns] Matt 19:24, **eye** *of a needle*; Aristoph. *Pax* 1234, **holes** *on a ship for oars*; Poll. 9.95, **point** *marked on the faces of dice*

Τρύφαινα, ης, ἡ$_{1>}$ ① Τρύφαιναν,[afs] Rom 16:12, **Tryphaena**

τρυφάω[con] {τρυφή} ①[aai2p] Jas 5:5, **to live indulgently**; ❸ *positive in* LXX, Neh 9:25; Isa 66:11, **to delight oneself**; Plato *Men.* 76b, **the spoiled**; Eur. *Bac.* 969, **to live wantonly**; Eur. *Ion* 1376, **to live softly** *in the arms of one's mother*

τρυφή, ῆς, ἡ$_{1η}$ ❷ Luke 7:25, **luxury**; 2 Pet 2:13, **carousing**; (25x LXX; 6x Ezek) Gen 3:23, 24 (3:24, 25), *drive you out of* **the garden of delight**; Eur. *Or.* 1113, *Trojan* **luxuries**

Τρυφῶσα, ης, ἡ$_{1>}$ ①[afs] Rom 16:12, **Tryphosa**

Τρῳάς, άδος, ἡ$_3$ ❻ Acts 16:8; 2 Cor 2:12; 2 Tim 4:13, **Troas**

τρώγω ❻ Matt 24:38, **to eat**; John 6:54, 56[3x]; 13:18, ὁ τρώγων, **the one eating**

τυγχάνω {τύπος} (12x; 5x Acts) Luke 20:35, **to experience**; Acts 19:11; 28:2, **extraordinary** *kindness*; 27:3, **to care for**; 1 Cor 14:10, **it may be**[NIGTC]; 2 Tim 2:10; Heb 11:35, **to obtain**; (28x LXX; 12x 2 Macc) Deut 19:5, **to strike**

τυμπανίζω {τύπος} ①[api3p] Heb 11:35, **to be tortured**; ①[iai3s] LXX, 1 Sam 21:13, **to scribble** *as a madman*; Eup. 77, **to beat a drum**

τυπικῶς {τύπος} *adv.* ① 1 Cor 10:11, **formative models of broader patterns**[NIGTC!]; Orib. 8.47.11, *medic.* **sculpted in a typical process**[BrDAG]

τύπος, ου, ὁ$_2$ {τύπτω} (15x) John 20:25,[2x] **mark** *of the nails*; Acts 7:43, **image**; 23:25, **effect**; Rom 6:17, **form**; 1 Cor 10:6, **formative models** *for us*[NIGTC]; 1 Pet 5:3, **role model**[Keen1P]; 1 Thess 1:7; Titus 2:7, **example**; Heb 8:5, **pattern**; ❹ LXX

τύπτω {τύπος} (13x; 9x LA) Matt 24:49 = Luke 12:45; Acts 18:7; 21:35, **to inflict blows**; 1 Cor 8:12, **to inflict damaging blows on their self-awareness**[NIGTC]; (40x LXX) Exod 2:11, **to strike**; 2:13, **to attack**; Xen. *Hel.* 4.2.12, *pass.*, **to be stung** *by many wasps*;[BrDAG]

Τύραννος, ου, ὁ$_2$ ①[gms] Acts 19:9, **Tyrannus**

Τύριος, ου, ὁ$_2$ ①[dms] Acts 12:20, **Tyrian**; ❽ LXX, 2 Kgs 2:13; Hdt. *Hist.* 2.112

Τύρος, ου, ἡ$_{2δδός}$ (11x; GA) Matt 15:21; Mark 3:8; Acts 21:3, 7, **Tyre**; (41x LXX; 6x Isa)

τυφλός, ή, όν$_{2.1.2}$ {τυφλόω} *adj.* (50x; 18x John, 17x Matt) Matt 9:27; Mark 10:49, 51; Luke 4:18; John 9:13–32[4x], *subst.*, **blind person**; Matt 15:14 = Luke 6:39; Rev 3:17, *spiritually* **blind**; (25x LXX) Isa 29:18, *the eyes of the* **blind** *shall see*

τυφλόω[con] {τυφλός} ❸ John 12:40; 2 Cor 4:4, **to blind**; ①[api3p] LXX, Isa 42:19, **blinded**

τυφόω[con] ❸ 1 Tim 3:6; 6:4; 2 Tim 3:4, **to be puffed up, conceited**

τύφω ①[ppp.ans] Matt 12:20, **smoldering** *wick*

τυφωνικός, ή, όν$_{2.1.2}$ *adj.* ①[nms] Acts 27:14, **violent wind, northeaster**[Keen4]

Τυχικός, οῦ, ὁ$_2$ ❺ Acts 20:4; Eph 6:21; Col 4:7; 2 Tim 4:12; Titus 3:12, **Tychicus**

Y, υ [*upsilon*]

Y, υ, τό (ὖ ψιλόν) *indecl.* **upsilon**, *20th letter of the Gr. alphabet* || *num.* υʹ = 400; ͵υ = 400,000

ὑακίνθινος, ίνη, ινον$_{2.1.2}$ {ὑάκινθος} *adj.* ①^{amp} Rev 9:17, **dark blue**; (26x LXX)

ὑάκινθος, ου, ὁ$_2$ ①^{nms} Rev 21:20, **jacinth**; (34x LXX; 24x Exod) Exod 25:4, *cloth* **of hyacinth color**

ὑάλινος, η, ον$_{2.1.2}$ {ὕαλος} *adj.* ❸ Rev 4:6; 15:2,^{2x} *sea of* **glass**

ὕαλος, ου, ἡ$_2$ ❷ Rev 21:18, 21, **clear glass**; ①^{nfs} LXX, Job 28:17

ὑβρίζω {ὕβρις} ❺ Matt 22:6; Luke 11:45; 18:32; Acts 14:5; 1 Thess 2:2, **to treat shamefully, insult**; ❻ LXX, Isa 13:3, *act.*, **to exult** 2 Macc 14:42, *pass.*, **to suffer outrages** *unworthy of his noble birth*

ὕβρις, εως, ἡ$_3$ ❸ Acts 27:10, 21, **damage**, **heavy loss**^{ZEC}; 2 Cor 12:10, **insult**, **harsh treatment**^{BEC}; (62x LXX; 11x Prov, 10x Isa) 3 Macc 3:25, **harsh treatment**; Isa 9:8, **pride**

ὑβριστής, οῦ, ὁ$_{1>}$ {ὑβρίζω} ❷ Rom 1:30, **arrogant**; 1 Tim 1:13, **violent man**; ❽ LXX; Prov 27:13, **a scorner** (BLXX); Hes. *Th.* 307, **insolent**, **arrogant**

ὑγιαίνω {ὑγιής} (12x; 8x PE) Luke 5:31; 3 John 2, **to enjoy good health**; Luke 7:10, **healthy** *by healing*; 15:27, **safe and sound**^{ZEC}; 1 Tim 1:10, **healthy** *teaching*; (62x LXX)

ὑγιής, ές$_{3.3}$ {ὑγιαίνω} *adj.* (11x; 6x John) Matt 15:31; John 5:6–15,^{5x} **healed**; Mark 5:34, **be cured**, **be free**; Acts 4:10, **healthy**; Titus 2:8, **healthy** *instruction*; ❾ LXX (4x Lev)

ὑγρός, ά, όν$_{2.1.2}$ {ὕω} *adj.* ①^{dns} Luke 23:31, **green**; ❹ LXX, Judg 16:7, 8, **fresh**

ὑδρία, ας, ἡ$_1$ {ὕδωρ} ❸ John 2:6, 7; 4:28,^{ZEC} **water jar**; (18x LXX; 9x Gen) Gen 24:14

ὑδροποτέω^{con} {ὕδωρ + πίνω} ①^{paimp2s} 1 Tim 5:23, **to drink water exclusively**; ①^{painf} LXX, Dan 1:12

ὑδρωπικός, ή, όν$_{2.1.2}$ {ὕδωρ} *adj.* ①^{nms} Luke 14:2, **swollen with fluid**; Polyb. *Hist.* 13.2.2, **suffering from dropsy**

ὕδωρ, ατος, τό$_3$ (76x; 21x John) Matt 3:11; Acts 1:5; 1 Pet 3:20; Rev 1:15, **water**; Acts 8:38; Rev 11:6, **body of water**; John 4:10, 11, 14; 7:38, *living* **water**; Rev 1:15; 14:2; 17:1; 19:6, **rushing waters**; (657x LXX; 215x Pent) Gen 6:17–9:15, *flood narrative*

ὑετός, οῦ, ὁ$_2$ {ὕω} ❺ Acts 14:17; 28:2; Heb 6:7; Jas 5:18; Rev 11:6, **rain**; (83x LXX)

υἱοθεσία, ας, ἡ$_1$ {υἱός + τίθημι} ❺ Rom 8:15, 23; 9:4; Gal 4:5; Eph 1:5, **adoption**

υἱός, οῦ, ὁ$_2$ (377x; 277x GA, 89x Matt) Matt 1:21; Luke 1:13, **son**; Heb 12:6, **child** *of God*; Acts 13:10, **son** *of the devil*; 2 Thess 2:3, **son** *of destruction*; Mark 3:17, *Boanerges, the* **Sons** *of Thunder*; Mark 8:38; Acts 7:56, *the* **Son** *of Man*; Rev 21:12, *Israel's* **sons**, cf. Dan 7:13–14; Mark 2:19, οἱ υἱοὶ τοῦ νυμφῶνος, *the bridegroom's* **attendants** (4,914x LXX; 844x 1–2 Chr, 481x Num, 340x Gen) Gen 4:17, **son**; Ezek 2:1–47:6^{94x}; Dan 8:17, **Υἱὲ ἀνθρώπου**, **Son** *of Man*

ὕλη, ης, ἡ$_{1η}$ ①^{afs} Jas 3:5, **forest**; ❽ LXX, Job 38:40, **thicket**

ὑμεῖς, *s.v.* ἐγώ

Ὑμέναιος, ου, ὁ$_2$ ❷ 1 Tim 1:20; 2 Tim 2:17, **Hymenaeus**

ὑμέτερος, α, ον$_{2.1.2}$ {σύ} *poss. adj.* (11x) Luke 6:20; John 7:6; 8:17; 15:20; Acts 27:34; Rom 11:31; 1 Cor 15:31; 2 Cor 8:8; Gal 6:13, **your, yours**; ❹ LXX, Gen 9:5

ὑμνέω^{con} {ὕμνος} ❹ Matt 26:30 = Mark 14:26, **to sing psalms**; Acts 16:25; Heb 2:12, **to sing hymns**; (65x LXX; 35x Pr Azar) Isa 42:10; Pr Azar (*all occurrences*), *form.*, **ὑμνεῖτε** καὶ ὑπερυψοῦτε αὐτὸν εἰς τοὺς αἰῶνας, **sing praise** *to him and highly exalt him forever*

ὕμνος, ου, ὁ$_{2}$ ❷^{dmp} Eph 5:19 = Col 3:16, **hymn**; (32x LXX; 13x Pss) 2 Chr 7:6; Neh 12:46

ὑπάγω {ὑπό + ἄγω} (79x; 32x John; 19x Matt, 15x Mark) Mark 1:44; Luke 8:42; John 3:8; 21:3; Jas 2:16; 1 John 2:11; Rev 17:11, **to go away**; Matt 5:24; John 7:3; Rev 14:4, **to go**; Matt 16:23 = Mark 8:33, **Get** *behind me, Satan!*; Matt 26:24, **to die**; ❷ LXX, Exod 14:21, **to drive back**

ὑπακοή, ῆς, ἡ$_{1\eta}$ {ὑπό + ἄγω} (15x; 7x Rom) Rom 1:5; 2 Cor 7:15; Phlm 21; Heb 5:8; 1 Pet 1:22, **obedience**; ①^{nfs} LXX, 2 Sam 22:36

ὑπακούω {ὑπό + ἀκούω} (21x) Matt 8:27 = Mark 4:41; Luke 17:6; Rom 6:12; Eph 6:1; Phil 2:12; 2 Thess 1:8; Heb 11:8; 1 Pet 3:6, **to obey**; Acts 12:13, **to answer** *a door*; (58x LXX; 9x Prov, 7x Deut) Gen 16:2, **to listen**; Hom. *Od.* 14.485, **to listen, give ear**

ὕπανδρος, ον$_{2.2}$ {ὑπό + ἀνήρ} *adj.* ①^{nfs} Rom 7:2, **married**; ❹ LXX, Num 5:20, 29

ὑπαντάω^{con} {ὑπό + ἀντί} (10x, *aor. act*) Matt 8:28 = Mark 5:2 = Luke 8:27; Acts 16:16, **to oppose** *demons, adversary*; Matt 28:9; John 4:51; 12:18, **to meet** *cordially*; ❻ LXX

ὑπάντησις, εως, ἡ$_{3}$ {ὑπό + ἀντί} ❸ Matt 8:34; 25:1; John 12:13, **meeting**

ὕπαρξις, εως, ἡ$_{3}$ {ὑπό + ἄρχω} ❷ Acts 2:45; Heb 10:34, **possession**; τῶν ὑπαρχόντων–**ὕπαρξις**, *play on words—temporary earthly vs. permanent heavenly* **possessions**[NIGTC]; (10x LXX; 4x Prov) Prov 8:21

ὑπάρχω {ὑπό + ἄρχω} (60x; 40x in LA) **τὰ ὑπάρχοντα**,^{6x} Matt 19:21; Heb 10:34, **possessions**; **ὑπάρχω** = εἰμί, Luke 7:25; Gal 1:14; 2 Pet 2:19, **it is, it exists**; Acts 3:6; 4:32, 34, 37, **to have, possess**; (143x LXX; 17x Gen) Ps 36:10 (37:10), **will** *in no way* **survive**

ὑπαχθείς → ὑπάγω, *aor. pass. ptc. nms*, 4 Macc 4:13, **moved** *by these words*[SCS]

ὑπείκω ①$^{\text{pai2p}}$ {ὑπέρ + εἴκω} Heb 13:17, **to give way, yield**; ①^{painf} LXX, 4 Macc 6:35

ὑπεναντίος, α, ον$_{2.1.2}$ {ὑπό + ἐν + ἀντί} *adj.* ❷ Col 2:14, **hostile**; Heb 10:27, **those who stand in opposition**; (43x LXX; 6x Isa) Isa 26:11, **enemies, adversaries**

ὑπενεγκεῖν → ὑποφέρω, *aor. act. inf.*, 1 Cor 10:13, **to endure**

ὑπέρ *prep.* (150x; 101x in Paul, 34x 2 Cor) 🅐 ***w/ gen.*** Matt 5:44; 2 Cor 5:12–21^{5x}; Heb 2:9–13:17^{9x}; 3 John 7, **for, on behalf of, in the place of**; 2 Cor 13:8, **in the interest of**; 🅑 ***w/ acc.*** Matt 10:24, **above**, 1 Cor 4:6, **beyond**; Heb 4:12, *sharper* **than** *any double-edged sword*; 🅒 ***adv.***[BDAG] 2 Cor 11:23, **superior to**[BEC]; 2 Cor 12:13, **other**; (416x LXX; 58x Pss, 34x Sir)

ὑπεραίρω ❷ 2 Cor 12:7, **to be consumed with self-importance**[BEC]; 2 Thess 2:4, **to exalt oneself**; ❻ LXX, 2 Chr 32:23, **to be exalted**; 2 Macc 5:23, **to lord over**

ὑπέρακμος, ον$_{2.2}$ {ὑπέρ + ἀκή} *adj.* ① 1 Cor 7:36, *subst.*, **matter of undue strain**[NIGTC]; **heightened desire for sexual intercourse, full of sexual passion**[BEC]

ὑπεράνω {ὑπέρ + ἀνά} *impr. prep. w/gen.* ❸ Eph 1:21; 4:10; Heb 9:5, **up above, high above**; (20x LXX) Deut 26:19, **elevate**; 28:1, **far above**; Hag 2:15, **beyond**

ὑπεραυξάνω ①$^{\text{pai3s}}$ 2 Thess 1:3, **to grow abundantly**; Andoc. *Alc.* 24, *the soldiers guarding the city* **increased abundantly**

ὑπερ**βαίνω** ①[painf] 1 Thess 4:6, **to wrong, to overstep the bounds**[PNTC]; (17x LXX)

ὑπερ**βαλλόντως** {ὑπέρ + βάλλω} *adv.* ① 2 Cor 11:23, **much worse**[BEC]; ① LXX, Job 15:11, *spoken* **exceedingly much**; Plato *Rp.* 492b, **excessively**

ὑπερ**βάλλω** ❺[pap] 2 Cor 3:10, **superabundance** *of glory*; 9:14, **extraordinary** *grace*[BEC]; Eph 1:19; 2:7, **outstripping**[BEC]; 3:19, **surpasses**[ABC]; ❻ LXX, 3 Macc 2:23, **exceedingly** *great fear*

ὑπερ**βολή, ῆς, ἡ**$_{1η}$ {ὑπέρ + βάλλω} ❽ καθ' **ὑπερβολήν**[5x], Rom 7:13, **beyond measure**; 1 Cor 12:31, **greater** *way*[NIGTC]; 2 Cor 1:8, **extraordinary degree**[BEC]; Gal 1:13 καθ' **ὑπερβολὴν** εἰς **ὑπερβολήν**, 2 Cor 4:17[2x] (*only Paul uses this class. phrase in NT*); καθ' **ὑπερβολὴν** εἰς **ὑπερβολήν**, *in a way* **both breathtaking and immeasurable**[BEC]; Gal 1:13, **viciously** *persecuting God's community, and trying to wipe it out*[KeenG]; ①[afs] LXX, 2 Macc 7:22, **extreme** *tortures*

ὑπερ**έκεινα** {ὑπέρ + ἐκεῖ} *adv.* ① 2 Cor 10:16, *regions* **beyond** *you*[BEC, NIGTC]

ὑπερ**εκπερισσοῦ** {ὑπέρ + ἐκ + περί} *adv.* ❸ Eph 3:20; 1 Thess 3:10, 5:13 **quite beyond all measure, infinitely more than** (*the highest form of comparison imaginable*)[ZEC]; Origen, *On Prayer* 6.58 (*only occurrence outside NT*)

ὑπερ**εκτείνω** ①[pailp] 2 Cor 10:14, **to stretch out beyond**[BEC]

ὑπερ**εκχύννω** {ὑπέρ + ἐκ + χέω} ①[ppp.ans] Luke 6:38, **to overflow, to gush over**[ZEC]; Clem. Al. *Quis. div.* 33, *quoting and commenting on Luke 16:19–31.*

ὑπερ**εντυγχάνω** {ὑπέρ + ἐν + τυγχάνω} ①[pai3s] Rom 8:26, *the Spirit* **to intercede** *for us*[NICNT 2nd ed]; Origen, *On Prayer*[8x]

ὑπερ**έχω** ❺[pap] Rom 13:1, **governing authorities**; Phil 2:3, **to consider more important**; 3:8; 4:7, **to surpass**; 1 Pet 2:13, **to surpass in power, extent, and value**[EGG]; (11x LXX) Dan 5:11, *King Nebuchadnezzar* **appointed** *him* **chief** *over the diviners*

ὑπερη**φανία, ας, ἡ**$_{1α}$ {ὑπέρ + φαίνω} ① Mark 7:22, **pride**; (57x LXX; 9x Pss) Lev 26:19; Num 15:30

ὑπερή**φανος, ον**$_{2.2}$ {ὑπέρ + φαίνω} *adj.* ❺ Luke 1:51; Rom 1:30; 2 Tim 3:2; Jas 4:6; 1 Pet 5:5, **proud, arrogant**; (41x LXX; 12x Sir, 11x Pss) 4 Macc 4:15

ὑπεριδών → ὑπεροράω, *aor. act. ptc. nms*, Acts 17:30, **to overlook**

ὑπερ**λίαν** *adv.*❷ 2 Cor 11:5; 12:11, τῶν **ὑπερλίαν** ἀποστόλων, *the* **super***apostles*[BEC]

ὑπερ**νικάω** {ὑπέρ + νίκη} ①[pailp] Rom 8:37, **to be completely victorious**[EGG]; Diod. Sic. *Bib. Hist.* 9.15, *hero who could* **outstrip** *fast-moving chariots*[NIDNTT]

ὑπέρ**ογκος, ον**$_{2.2}$ *adj.* ❷[anp] 2 Pet 2:18 = Jude 16, **pompous, boastful**; ❻ LXX, Exod 18:22, 26, **hard, important** *cases*; Deut 30:11, **difficult** *command*

ὑπερ**οράω**[con] ①[aap.nms] Acts 17:30, **to overlook, pay no attention to, disdain**[NIDNTT]; (42x LXX) Lev 20:4, **to stumble**

ὑπερ**οχή, ῆς, ἡ**$_{1η}$ {ὑπέρ + ἔχω} ❷ 1 Cor 2:1, **ὑπεροχὴν** λόγου, **high-sounding** *rhetoric*[NIGTC]; 1 Tim 2:2, **position of authority, prominence**; ❺ LXX, Jer 52:22, **height, projection**

ὑπερ**περισσεύω** {ὑπέρ + περί} ❷ Rom 5:20, **to superabound**; 2 Cor 7:4, **to be ecstatic**[BEC]

ὑπερ**περισσῶς** {ὑπέρ + περί} *adv.* ① Mark 7:37, **beyond all measure**[Herm, WPNT]

ὑπερ**πλεονάζω** {ὑπέρ + πληρόω} ①[pai3s] 1 Tim 1:14, **to overflow**; Pseud., Pss. Sol. 5.16, **to abound too much**

ὑπερ**υψόω**[con] {ὑπέρ + ὕψος} ①[aai3s] Phil 2:9, **to raise above all heights**; (37x LXX; 35x Pr Azar)

Pss 36:35 (37:35); 96:9 (97:9), **to highly exalt**; Pr Azar (*all occurrences*), *form.*, ὑμνεῖτε καὶ **ὑπερυψοῦτε** αὐτὸν εἰς τοὺς αἰῶνας, *sing praise to him and* **highly exalt** *him forever*
ὑπερ**φρονέω**con {ὑπέρ + φρήν} ①painf Rom 12:3, **to think too highly**; ❸ LXX, 4 Macc 16:2, **to despise** *the fiercest tortures*
ὑπερ**ῷον, ου, τό**$_2$ {ὑπέρ} ❹ Acts 1:13; 9:37, 39; 20:8, **upstairs room**; (21x LXX)
ὑπ**έχω** {ὑπό + ἔχω} ①pap.nfp Jude 7, **to suffer** *a punishment*; ❹ LXX, 2 Macc 4:48
ὑπ**ήκοος, ον**$_{2.2}$ {ὑπό + ἀκούω} *adj.* ❸ Acts 7:39; 2 Cor 2:9; Phil 2:8, **obedience**; ❺ LXX
ὑπ**ηρετέω**con {ὑπέρ + ἐρέσσω} ❸ Acts 13:36; 20:34; 24:23, **to serve**; ❺ LXX
ὑπ**ηρέτης, ου, ὁ**$_{1>}$ {ὑπέρ + ἐρέσσω} (20x; 9x John) Matt 5:25, 26:58, **officer, servant of the court**; Mark 14:54; John 7:32; Acts 26:16; 1 Cor 4:1,[NIGTC] **servant**; Mark 14:65, **guard**; Luke 1:2, **minister** (Plato *Leg.* 773e, **ministers** *of a god*); Luke 4:20, **synagogue attendant**; Acts 5:22, 26, **officer**; ❹ LXX, Prov 14:23, **servant**
ὕπνος, ου, ὁ$_2$ ❻ Matt 1:24; Luke 9:32; John 11:13; Rom 13:11, **sleep**; (56x LXX; 10x Gen)
ὑπό, ὑπ', ὑφ' *prep.* (220x; 72x in LA) Ⓐ ***w/ gen.***, Matt 1:22, 4:1; 1 Cor 1:11, **by**; Ⓑ ***w/ acc.***, Matt 8:8 = Luke 7:6; 1 Cor 15:25; 1 Pet 5:6, **under**; (481x LXX; 33x Eccl:Job)
ὑπο**βάλλω** ①aai3p Acts 6:11, **to instigate secretly**[EGG]; ①pmi3p LXX, 1 Esd 2:17, **to lay the foundations**
ὑπο**γραμμός, ου, ὁ**$_2$ {ὑπό + γράφω} ①ams 1 Pet 2:21, **example**; ①dmp LXX, 2 Macc 2:28, **outline, pattern**
ὑπό**δειγμα, ατος, τό**$_3$ {ὑπό + δείκνυμι} ❻ John 13:15, **a rule** *of life*[ECBC]; Heb 4:11; 2 Pet 2:6, **example**; Heb 8:5; 9:23, **earthly copy of a heavenly reality**[NIGTC]; ❺ LXX
ὑπο**δείκνυμι** ❻ Matt 3:7 = Luke 3:7, **to warn**; Luke 6:47; 12:5; Acts 9:16; 20:35, **to show**; (45x LXX; 12x Dan) Dan 11:2, **to impart** *the truth*
ὑπο**δέχομαι** ❹ Luke 10:38; 19:6; Acts 17:7; Jas 2:25, **to welcome as a guest**; ❹ LXX
ὑπο**δέω**con ❸ Mark 6:9; Acts 12:8; Eph 6:15, **to put on** *sandals*; ❷ LXX, 2 Chr 28:15
ὑπό**δημα, ατος, τό**$_3$ {ὑπό + πούς + δέω} (10x) Matt 3:11; 10:10; Luke 3:16; 22:35; John 1:27; Acts 7:33; 13:35, **sandal**; (26x LXX) Exod 3:5; Deut 25:9
ὑπό**δικος, ον**$_{2.2}$ {ὑπό + δική} *adj.* ①nms Rom 3:19, **liable to be brought to trial**[NIDNTT]
ὑπο**δραμόντες** → ὑπο**τρέχω** *aor. act. ptc. nms*, Acts 27:16, **after running under**
ὑπο**ζύγιον, ου, τό**$_2$ {ὑπό + ζυγός} ❷ Matt 21:5; 2 Pet 2:16, **donkey**; (28x LXX)
ὑπο**ζώννυμι** ①pap.nmp Acts 27:17, **to undergird** *a ship*[Keen4]
ὑπο**κάτω** {ὑπό + κατά} *prep. w/ gen.* (11x) Matt 22:44; Mark 6:11; Heb 2:8; Rev 5:3, 13; 6:9; 12:1, **under**; (84x LXX; 11x Ezek) Gen 1:7; Amos 2:13; Ezek 6:13
ὑπο**κρίνομαι** {ὑπό + κρίνω} ①pmp.amp Luke 20:20, **to play the role, act as if**[ZEC]; (10x LXX) 2 Macc 5:25, **to pretend**
ὑπό**κρισις, εως, ἡ**$_3$ {ὑπό + κρίνω} ❻ Matt 23:28; Mark 12:15; Gal 2:13; 1 Tim 4:2; 1 Pet 2:1, **hypocrisy**; ❷ LXX, 2 Macc 6:2; Aristot. *E.N.* 1118a, **to play a role in a drama**
ὑπο**κριτής, οῦ, ὁ**$_{1>}$ {ὑπό + κρίνω} (17x Syn; 13x in Matt) Matt 6:2; 24:51; Mark 7:6; Luke 6:42; 12:56; 13:15, **hypocrite**; ❷ LXX, Job 34:30; 36:13
ὑπο**λαμβάνω** ❺ Luke 7:43, **to suppose**; 10:30, **to answer**; Acts 1:9, **to take away**; 3 John 8, **to support**; (50x LXX; 26x Job), Job 2:4, *Satan* **answered** *the Lord*
ὑπό**λειμμα, ατος, τό**$_3$ {ὑπό + λείπω} ① Rom 9:27, **remnant**; ❽ LXX, Mic 4:7; 5:7
ὑπο**λείπω** ①api1s Rom 11:3, **to be left alone**; (84x LXX; 10x Exod) Gen 30:36, **the remaining**

ὑπο**λήνιον, ου, τό**$_2$ {ὑπό + ληνός} ①[ans] Mark 12:1, **trough placed under a wine press**; ❹ LXX, Joel 3:13; Hag 2:16; Zech 14:10; Isa 16:10, **wine press**

ὑπο**λιμπάνω** {ὑπό + λείπω} ①[pap.nms] 1 Pet 2:21, **to leave** *you an example*

ὑπο**μένω** (17x; 4x Heb) Matt 10:22 = Mark 13:13; Matt 24:13, *eschat.*, **to endure**, **stand fast**; *act.*, Acts 17:14, **to stay behind**, **remain**; 1 Cor 13:7; Heb 10:32; Jas 1:12; 1 Pet 2:20,[2x] **to endure**; *pass.*, Rom 12:12, **to be patient**; (82x LXX); Isocr. *Archid.* 70, **weathering** *the hardships of war*[NIDNTT]

ὑπο**μιμνήσκω** {ὑπό + μιμνήσκομαι} ❼ Luke 22:61, **to remember**; John 14:26; 2 Tim 2:14; Titus 3:1; 2 Pet 1:12; 3 John 10; Jude 10, **to remind**; ❹ LXX, 1 Kgs 4:3, **recorder**

ὑπό**μνησις, εως, ἡ**$_3$ {ὑπό + μιμνήσκομαι} ❸ 2 Tim 1:5; 2 Pet 1:13; 3:1, **remembrance**, **reminder**; ❷ LXX, 2 Macc 6:17; Wis 16:11

ὑπο**μονή, ῆς, ἡ**$_{1η}$ {ὑπό + μένω} (32x; 7x Rev) Luke 8:15, *with* **patient endurance**; Rom 2:7–15:5[6x]; 2 Cor 1:6; Rev 1:9–14:12,[7x] **steadfast endurance**; (25x LXX; 11x 4 Macc[SCS])

ὑπο**νοέω**[con] {ὑπό + νοῦς} ❸ Acts 13:25, **to suppose**; *jur.*, 25:18, **to expect**; *naut.*; 27:27, **to suspect**[ZEC]; ❸ LXX, Jdt 14:14; Tob 8:16, **to expect**

ὑπό**νοια, ας, ἡ**$_{1α}$ {ὑπό + νοῦς} ①[nfp] 1 Tim 6:4, **suspicion**; ❹ LXX, Dan 4:16, **thought**

ὑπο**πλέω**[con] ❷[aai1p] Acts 27:4, 7, **to be under the shelter (protection) of**[Keen4]

ὑπο**πνέω**[con] ①[aap.gms] Acts 27:13, **to blow gently**

ὑπο**πόδιον, ου, τό**$_2$ {ὑπό + πούς} ❼ Jas 2:3; Acts 7:49 (*quot.* LXX, Isa 66:1, 2), **footstool**; Luke 20:43 = Acts 2:35 = Heb 1:13, *make your enemies your* **footstool**; ❹ LXX

ὑπό**στασις, εως, ἡ**$_3$ {ὑπό + ἵστημι} ❺ 2 Cor 9:4; 11:17,[BEC!] **stratagem, project, undertaking**[TDNT, NIDNTT]; Heb 1:3, **real essence** *of the Son*[ECBC]; 3:14; 11:1, **confidence, assurance**[ABC]; (22x LXX) Deut 1:12, **burden**; Judg 6:4, **to leave** *nothing* **alive**

ὑπο**στέλλω** ❹ Acts 20:20, **to keep silent**; 20:27, **to hesitate**; Gal 2:12, *Peter* **drew back**; Heb 10:38, **to turn back**; ❻ LXX, Exod 23:21, **he won't carry** *your rebellions* (TFT); Deut 1:17, **you will be in dread** *of no one's person* (TFT); Hp. *Aph.* 1.11, **to restrict**

ὑπο**στολή, ῆς, ἡ**$_{1η}$ {ὑπό + στέλλω} ①[gfs] Heb 10:39, **cowardice, timidity**; Ap. Dys. *Pron.* 94.1, *gramm.* **suppression** *of a letter or a sound in a word.*

ὑπο**στρέφω** (35x; 33x LA) Luke 1:56; 24:52; Acts 1:12; Gal 1:17; Heb 7:1, **to return**; Acts 13:34, *fig.*, **to return** *to the corruption of the grave*; 2 Pet 2:21, *fig.*, **to turn back** *from the holy commandment*; (12x LXX) Gen 8:7, **to return**

ὑπο**στρωννύω** ①[iai3p] Luke 19:36, **to spread out**

ὑπο**ταγή, ῆς, ἡ**$_{1η}$ {ὑπό + τάσσω} ❹[dfs] 2 Cor 9:13; Gal 2:5[KeenG]; 1 Tim 2:11; 3:4, **subjugation**

ὑπο**τάσσω** (38x; 9x 1 Cor) Luke 2:51; 10:17, **to be submissive**; Rom 8:7, *unable* **to submit itself**; Rom 8:20, *creation* **subjected to** *futility*; 10:3; 1 Cor 14:32, **to subject oneself under control**; 14:34, **let them maintain their order**[NIGTC!]; Eph 5:21, 24 = Col 3:18 = 1 Pet 3:1, 5; Rom 13:1, **to submit oneself**; 1 Cor 15:27–28[6x]; Eph 1:22; 1 Pet 3:22, *eschat.*, *God* **puts** *all things* **under subjection** *to Christ*; (28x LXX; 9x Pss)

ὑπο**τίθημι** ❷ Rom 16:4, τράχηλον **ὑπέθηκαν**, **to lay down** *one's neck* (= **to risk** *one's neck*); 1 Tim 4:6, *mid.*, **to point out**; (13x LXX; 4x Exod) Exod 17:12, **to put under**

ὑπο**τρέχω** ①[aap.nmp] Acts 27:16, **to run under the shelter of**

ὑπο**τύπωσις, εως, ἡ**$_3$ {ὑπό + τύπος} ❷[afp] 1 Tim 1:16; 2 Tim 1:13, **example**[ABC]

ὑπο**φέρω** ❸ 1 Cor 10:13; 2 Tim 3:11; 1 Pet 2:19, **to bear up under**; (20x LXX; 4x Job)

ὑποχωρέω[con] ❷ Luke 5:16; 9:10, **to withdraw**; ①[pap] LXX, Sir 13:9, **to be reserved**

ὑπωπιάζω {ὑπό + ὁράω} ❷ Luke 18:5, *metaph.* **to annoy thoroughly**; 1 Cor 9:27, *metaph.* **to treat roughly**[NIGTC]; Aristoph. *Pax* 541, *lit.*, **to strike under the eye**

ὗς, ὑός, ἡ ① 2 Pet 2:22, **sow, pig**; ❻ LXX, Lev 11:7

ὕσσωπος, ου, ἡ$_2$ ❷ John 19:29[ZEC]; Heb 9:19, **hyssop**; (10x LXX; 5x Lev)

ὑστερέω[con] {ὕστερος} (16x; 6x 1–2 Cor) Matt 19:20 = Mark 10:21; Rom 3:23[ZEC]; 1 Cor 1:7, **to fall short**[NIGTC]; Luke 15:14, **to suffer from want** (*prodigal son*); Phil 4:12, **to be in need**; John 2:3, **to run dry** (*the wine*); 1 Cor 8:8, **to be worse off**; 12:24, **to be less honorable**; Heb 12:1, **to be inferior**; (19x LXX; 6x Sir) Ps 22:1 (23:1), **I don't lack**

ὑστέρημα, ατος, τό$_3$ {ὕστερος} ❾ Luke 21:4, **poverty**; Phil 2:30; Col 1:24,[NIGTC] **absence, lack, deficiency**; 2 Cor 8:14, **shortfall**[BEC]; 9:12, **need**; 1 Thess 3:10, τὰ **ὑστερήματα**, **the things lacking** *in your faith*; ❻ LXX, Judg 18:10, **lack**

ὑστέρησις, εως, ἡ$_3$ {ὕστερος} ❷ Mark 12:44, **poverty**; Phil 4:11, **because of need**

ὕστερος, α, ον$_{2.1.2}$ *adj.* (12x; 7x Matt) Matt 4:2, **afterward**[EGG]; 25:11; Heb 12:11, **later**; Matt 21:37; Luke 20:32, **at last, finally**; 1 Tim 4:1, **latter, last**; (20x LXX; 5x Jer) Jer 47:1 (40:1)

ὑφαντός, ή, όν$_{2.1.2}$ {ὑφαίνω} *adj.* ① John 19:23, **woven**; ❾ LXX (Exod), 26:31, 36:12

ὑψηλός, ή, όν$_{2.1.2}$ {ὕψος} *adj.* (11x) Matt 17:1 = Mark 9:2, **high**; Luke 16:15, **exalted**; Acts 13:17, **mighty**; Rom 12:16, **proud**; Heb 1:3, ἐν **ὑψηλοῖς** = ἐν τοῖς οὐρανοῖς (Heb 8) = ἐν ὑψίστοις (Luke 2:14) = ἐν τοῖς ἐπουρανίοις (Eph 1:20), **in the heavens**; (214x LXX)

ὑψηλοφρονέω[con] {ὕψος + φρήν} ①[painf] 1 Tim 6:17, **to be high-minded** (*cf.* **ὑψηλὰ** φρόνει *in Rom 11:20*)[NIDNTT]

ὕψιστος, η, ον$_{2.1.2}$ {ὕψος} *adj.* (13x; 9x LA) Luke 19:38, **in the highest heaven**; 1:32; Acts 7:48; Heb 7:1, *subst.*, *the* **Most High** *God*; (124x LXX; 47x Sir, 25x Pss) Sir 4:10, *subst.*, *the* **Most High**

ὕψος, ου, τό$_3$ ❻ Luke 1:78; Eph 4:8, *on* **high**; 3:18; Rev 21:16, **height**; Jas 1:9, **high position**; (122x LXX; 13x Isa, 11x 1 Kgs:Pss) Isa 2:11, **loftiness**

ὑψόω[con] {ὕψος} (20x; 9x LA) Ⓐ *act.*, John 3:14a, **to lift up** *the serpent*; Acts 2:33; 5:31, **to exalt**[ZEC]; 2 Cor 11:7, **to enhance**[BEC]; Ⓑ *pass.*, Matt 23:12 = Luke 14:11,[2x] **to be exalted**; 8:28, *the Son of Man* **to be lifted up**; (192x LXX; 51x Pss, 25x Isa)

ὕψωμα, ατος, τό$_3$ {ὕψος} ❷[ans] Rom 8:39, **height**; 2 Cor 10:5, *fig.*, **rampart, a defensive wall of a fortress**[BEC]; ❹ LXX, Job 24:24; Plut. *Symp.* 149a, *astr.* **rising** *of the stars*

Φ, φ [*phi*]

Φ, φ, τό (φεῖ *or* φῖ) *indecl.* **phi**, *21st letter of the Gr. alphabet* || *num.* φ′ = 500; ͵φ = 500,000

φαγεῖν → **ἐσθίω,** *aor. act. inf.*, Matt 12:4, **to eat**

φάγος, ου, ὁ$_2$ ❷ Matt 11:19 = Luke 7:34, **glutton**

φαιλόνης, ου, ὁ$_{1>}$ ①[ams] 2 Tim 4:13, **cloak**

φαίνω {φαίνω} (31x; 13x Matt) Ⓐ *act.*, Matt 1:20, **to appear**; Matt 24:27, *lightning* **to flash**; Phil 2:15, **to shine**; Rev 18:23, οὐ μὴ **φάνῃ**, *light* **will never shine**; Ⓑ *pass.*, Matt 9:33, **to be seen**; 2 Cor 13:7, **to be recognized**[BEC]; Heb 11:3, **to be observed**; 1 Pet 4:18, **to become visible**; (65x LXX; 24x 1–4 Macc)

Φάλεκ, ὁ *indecl.* ①[gms] Luke 3:35, **Peleg**

φανερός, ά, όν$_{2.1.2}$ {φαίνω} *adj.* (18x) Rom 2:28, **evident**, **known**; Mark 3:12, *make Jesus* **known** = *blow his cover*[NIGTC]; Luke 8:17; Phil 1:13, *become* **plain**, **clear**; (19x LXX)

φανερόω[con] (49x; 9x John:2 Cor, 29x *aor. pass.*) Ⓐ *act.*, John 7:4, **to show** *yourself*[ZEC]; 1 Cor 4:5, **to disclose**; 2 Cor 5:10, **to appear**; 1 Cor 4:5, **to disclose**; 1 John 4:9, **to express**[ZEC]; Ⓑ *mid.*, 1 John 1:2[2x], 4:9, **was revealed**[BHGNT]; Ⓒ *pass.*, 2 Cor 5:11[2x], **πεφανερώμεθα**, *our lives* **stand open** *before God*[BEC]; **πεφανερῶσθαι** *I hope* **to be well known**[BHGNT]; 1 John 2:19, **to be revealed**; ①[fai3s] LXX, Jer 40:6 (33:6), **to be evident**

φανερῶς {φαίνω} *adv.* ❸ Mark 1:45; John 7:10; Acts 10:3, **openly**; ① LXX, 2 Macc 3:28

φανέρωσις, εως, ἡ$_3$ {φαίνω}❷ 1 Cor 12:7, **manifestation**; 2 Cor 4:2, **public proclamation** *in contrast to secrets, deceit, and trickery*[BEC]

φανός, οῦ, ὁ$_2$ {φαίνω} ①[gmp] John 18:3, **lantern**

Φανουήλ, ὁ$_2$ *indecl.* ①[gms] Luke 2:36, **Phanuel**

φαντάζω {φαίνω} ①[pmp] Heb 12:21, *so terrifying was* **the sight**[NIGTC]; ❷ LXX, Wis 6:16

φαντασία, ας, ἡ$_{1a}$ {φαίνω} ①[gfs] Acts 25:23, **pomp**, **grandeur**; ❻ LXX (MT, ירה) Hab 2:18, **φαντασίαν** ψευδῆ, **a teacher** *of lies* (HCSB); 2:19, *Can it* **teach?** (HCSB), *thus* **deceptive representation**, **appearance** *with respect to lifeless idols*[NICOT]; *phrase communicates astonishment at such a delusion*[BCOT]

φάντασμα, ατος, τό$_3$ {φαίνω} ❷ Matt 14:26 = Mark 6:49, **ghost**; ① LXX, Wis 17:15, **monstrous specters** (NRSV); Plato *Phaed.* 81d, **shadowy phantoms of souls**[BrDAG]

φάραγξ, αγγος, ἡ$_3$ ①[nfs] Luke 3:5, **ravine**, **valley**; (85x LXX; 18x Isa)

Φαραώ, ὁ$_3$ *indecl.* ❺ Acts 7:10; Rom 9:17; Heb 11:24, **Pharaoh**, *at the time of Joseph and Moses*; (292x LXX; 122x Exod, 94x Gen, 23x 1–2 Kgs) Gen 41:1–55[34x]; Exod 2:5–15[8x]

Φαρές, ὁ$_3$ *indecl.* ❸ Matt 1:3[2x]; Luke 3:33, **Perez**

Φαρισαῖος, ου, ὁ$_2$ (98x; 88x Gs, 9x Acts) Matt 9:11 = Mark 2:16 = Luke 5:30; John 8:3; Acts 23:6–9[6x]; Phil 3:5, **Pharisee**

φαρμακεία, ας, ἡ$_{1a}$ {φάρμακος} ❷ Gal 5:20; Rev 18:23, **sorcery**; ❽ LXX, Exod 7:11, 22; 8:3 (8:7), 8:14 (8:18); Wis 12:4; 18:13; Isa, 47:9, 12, **magical arts**, **sorcery**

φάρμακον, ου, τό$_{2}$ {φάρμακος} ①[gnp] Rev 9:21, **sorcery, magic arts**; ❼ LXX, Nah 3:4, *mistress of* **sorcery**; 2 Kgs 9:22, **witchcraft** *from your mother Jezebel*

φάρμακος, ου, ὁ$_{2}$ ❷ Rev 21:8; 22:15, **sorcerer**; (12x LXX) Deut 18:10, **sorcerer**

φάσις, εως, ἡ$_{3}$ {φαίνω} ① Acts 21:31, **report**

φάσκω {φαίνω} ❸ Acts 24:9; 25:19; Rom 1:22, **to assert**; ❺ LXX, Gen 26:20

φάτνη, ης, ἡ$_{1\eta}$ ❹ Luke 2:7, 12, 16; 13:15, **feeding trough**[*TDNT*]; ❽ LXX, 2 Chr 32:28

φαῦλος, η, ον$_{2.1.2}$ *adj.* ❻ John 3:20; Rom 9:11; 2 Cor 5:10; Jas 3:16, **evil**; (10x LXX; 5x Prov) Prov 5:3, **forbidden** *woman*

φέγγος, ους, τό$_{3}$ ❷[ans] Matt 24:29 = Mark 13:24, **light**; (25x LXX; 5x Job)

φείδομαι (10x) Acts 20:29; Rom 8:32; 2 Cor 1:23; 2 Pet 2:4, 5, **to spare**; (95x LXX)

φειδομένως {φείδομαι} *adv.* ❷ 2 Cor 9:6,[2x] **sparingly**; Plut. *Alex.* 25.5, **tight-fisted**

φέρω (66x; 17x John, 15x Mark) Ⓐ *act.*, 2 John 10, **to bring**; John 20:27,[2x] **to put, place**; 15:2–16,[7x] **to produce** *fruit*; 2 Pet 2:17, **to come**; Ⓑ *pass.*, Heb 9:16, *death* **to be proved**[BDAG]; Acts 2:2, *ptc.*, *violent* **rushing** *wind*; 27:15, **to be driven along** *by the wind*; Heb 1:3, **to bear up, sustain**[NIGTC]; 6:1, **to move on** *with swift energy*,[NICNT, Bruce] **to press on**[*WPNT*]; 2 Pet 1:21, **to be moved**; (273x LXX; 22x Lev:2 Chr, 21x Exod:Isa)

φεύγω {φευγή} (29x; 7x Matt, 27x act. voice) Matt 2:13; Mark 5:14; Rev 16:20; **to flee**; 1 Cor 6:18; 10:14, **to run away from**[NIGTC]; Heb 11:34, **to escape**; (230x LXX; 36x 1 Macc, 35x 1–2 Sam)

Φῆλιξ, ικος, ὁ$_{3}$ ❾ (Acts) 23:24–25:14, **Felix**[Keen4]

φήμη, ης, ἡ$_{1\eta}$ {φημί} ❷ Matt 9:26 = Luke 4:14, **report, news**; ❹ LXX, 2 Macc 4:39

φημί (66x; 33x LA, 16x Matt) Matt 4:7; 27:65; Luke 7:40; 23:40; Acts 2:38; 26:32; 1 Cor 6:16; Heb 8:5, **to say**; (74x LXX; 26x Jer, 14x 4 Macc) Job 24:25

Φῆστος, ου, ὁ$_{2}$ (13x, all in Acts) 24:27–26:32, **Festus**[Keen4]

φθάνω ❼[aor.act.] Matt 12:28 = Luke 11:20, **to come**; 2 Cor 10:14, **to reach**; 1 Thess 2:16, **to overtake**[PNTC]; 1 Thess 4:15, **to precede**; Rom 9:31; Phil 3:16, **to attain**; (14x LXX)

φθαρτός, ή, όν$_{2.1.2}$ {φθείρω} *adj.* ❻ 1 Cor 9:25, **perishable**; 15:53, 54, **subject to decay**[NIGTC]; Rom 1:23; 1 Pet 1:18, 23, **corruptible, perishable**; ❹ LXX, Isa 54:17, **artificial**

φθέγγομαι ❸ Acts 4:18; 2 Pet 2:16, 18, **to emit a sound, speak**; (15x LXX) Job 13:7

φθείρω ❾ *act.*, 1 Cor 3:17,[2x] **to destroy**,[NIGTC] **to disintegrate**[EEE]; 1 Cor 15:33, **to ruin**; 2 Cor 7:2, **to corrupt**[BEC]; *pass.*, 2 Pet 2:12, *in their destruction* **they will be destroyed**; Jude 10, **to destroy themselves**; 2 Cor 11:3, *thought processes* **might be ruined**[BEC]; Eph 4:22, *continually* **being corrupted**; (20x LXX; 6x Dan, 3x Isa)

φθινοπωρινός, ή, όν$_{2.1.2}$ {φθίνω + ὀπώρα} *adj.* ①[nnp] Jude 12, **autumnal**

φθόγγος, ου, ὁ$_{2}$ {φθέγγομαι} ❷ Rom 10:18, **voice**; 1 Cor 14:7, **sound**; ❷ LXX, Ps 18:5 (19:4), **message**

φθονέω[con] {φθόνος} ①[pap.nmp] Gal 5:26, **to envy** *one another*; ❷ LXX, Tob 4:7, 16

φθόνος, ου, ὁ$_{2}$ {φθονέω} ❾ Matt 27:18 = Mark 15:10; Rom 1:29; Gal 5:21; Phil 1:15; 1 Tim 6:4; Titus 3:3; Jas 4:5; 1 Pet 2:1, **jealousy, envy**; ❹ LXX, 1 Macc 8:16

φθορά, ᾶς, ἡ$_{1\alpha}$ {φθείρω} ❾ Rom 8:21; 1 Cor 15:42, *body* **corruption**; 2 Pet 1:4, 2:19, **moral corruption**; Gal 6:8; 2 Pet 2:12,[2x] **decomposition**; (11x LXX) Ps 102:4 (103:4)

φιάλη, ης, ἡ$_{1\eta}$ (12x, all in Rev) 5:8–21:9, **bowl**; (35x LXX; 15x Num) Num 7:13, **basin**

φιλάγαθος, ον$_{2.2}$ {φίλος + ἀγαθός} *adj.* ①^{ams} Titus 1:8, **loving what is good**; ①^{ams} Wis 7:22

Φιλαδέλφεια, ας, ἡ$_{1α}$ {φίλος + ἀδελφός} ❷ Rev 1:11; 3:7, **Philadelphia**[LGCb 674]

φιλαδελφία, ας, ἡ$_{1α}$ {φίλος + ἀδελφός} ❻ Rom 12:10; 1 Thess 4:9; Heb 13:1; 2 Pet 1:7,[2x] **brotherly affection**; ❸ LXX, 4 Macc 13:23, 26; 14:1, **brotherly love**

φιλάδελφος, ον$_{2.2}$ {φίλος + ἀδελφός} *adj.* ①^{nmp} 1 Pet 3:8, **loving fellow believers**; ❸ LXX

φίλανδρος, ον$_{2.2}$ {φίλος + ἀνήρ} *adj.* ①^{amp} Titus 2:4, **loving one's husband**; Soph. *fr.* 1111, **that loves masculine habits**; Plato *Symp.* 191e, **lewd woman**

φιλανθρωπία, ας, ἡ$_{1α}$ {φίλος + ἄνθωπος} ❷ Acts 28:2, **unusual kindness**[ZEC]; Titus 3:4, **love for humanity**; ❺ LXX, Add Esth 16:11 (cp. 8:11 MT); 2 Macc 6:22; 3 Macc 3:15

φιλανθρώπως {φίλος + ἄνθωπος} *adv.* ① Acts 27:3, **kindly**; ❻ LXX, 2 Macc 9:27, **kindness**; Men. *Sam.* 35; Polyb. *Hist.* 1.68.13 = Titus 3:4[BrDAG]

φιλαργυρία, ας, ἡ$_{1α}$ {φίλος + ἄργυρος} ①^{nfs} 1 Tim 6:10, **lover of money**; ①^{nfs} LXX, 4 Macc 1:26, **covetousness**[SCS]

φιλάργυρος, ον$_{2.2}$ {φίλος + ἄργυρος} *adj.* ❷^{nmp} Luke 16:14; *subst.*, 2 Tim 3:2, **lovers of money**; ①^{nms} LXX, 4 Macc 2:8

φίλαυτος, ον$_{2.2}$ {φίλος + αὐτός} *adj.* ①^{nmp} 2 Tim 3:2, **self-centered**, **selfish**

φιλέω^{con} {φίλος} (25x) Matt 10:37; Rev 22:15, **to love**; 1 Cor 16:22 (*NT hapax phrase*), **to love** *the Lord*[NIGTC!]; Matt 26:48 = Mark 14:44 = Luke 22:47, **to kiss**; (32x LXX)

φιλήδονος, ον$_{2.2}$ {φίλος + ἡδονή} *adj.* ①^{nmp} 2 Tim 3:4, **lover of pleasure**

φίλημα, ατος, τό$_3$ {φιλέω} ❼ Luke 7:45; 22:48, **kiss** *of betrayal*; *w/* ἐν ἁγίῳ, Rom 16:16; 1 Cor 16:20; 1 Thess 5:26, **a holy kiss**; 1 Pet 5:14, **kiss of love**; ❷ LXX, Prov 27:6

Φιλήμων, ονος, ὁ$_3$ ①^{dms} Phlm 1, **Philemon**

Φίλητος, ου, ὁ$_2$ ①^{nms} 2 Tim 2:17; Eus. *Hist. eccl.* 6.21.2, **Philetus**

φιλία, ας, ἡ$_{1α}$ {φίλος} ①^{nfs} Jas 4:4, **friendship**; (36x LXX) Prov 7:18, **lovemaking**

Φιλιππήσιος, ου, ὁ$_2$ ①^{vmp} Phil 4:15, **Philippian**

Φίλιπποι, ων, οἱ$_2$ ❹ Acts 16:12; 20:6; Phil 1:1; 1 Thess 2:2, **Philippi**

Φίλιππος, ου, ὁ$_2$ (36x; 18x LA) **Philip:** Ⓐ *one of the twelve apostles*, Matt 10:3 = Mark 3:18 = Luke 6:14; John 1:43–14:9[12x]; Ⓑ *son of Herod the Great*, Luke 3:1; Ⓒ *one of the seven "deacons,"* Acts 6:5; 8:5–40[13x]; Ⓓ *first husband of Herodias*, Matt 14:3; (11x LXX, all in 1–2 Macc) **Philip** *of Macedon*

φιλόθεος, ον$_{2.2}$ {φίλος + θεός} *adj.* ①^{nmp} 2 Tim 3:4, **loving God**

Φιλόλογος, ου, ὁ$_2$ {φίλος + λέγω} ①^{ams} Rom 16:15, **Philologus**

φιλονεικία, ας, ἡ$_{1α}$ {φίλος + νεῖκος} ①^{nfs} Luke 22:24, **a quarrel**[ZEC]; ❸ LXX

φιλόνεικος, ον$_{2.2}$ {φίλος + νεῖκος} *adj.* ①^{nms} 1 Cor 11:16, *minded to be* **contentious**,[NIGTC!] **want to make an issue of this**[Wire]; ① LXX, Ezek 3:7, **hardheaded**

φιλοξενία, ας, ἡ$_{1α}$ {φίλος + ξένος} ❷ Rom 12:13; Heb 13:2, **hospitality**

φιλόξενος, ον$_{2.2}$ {φίλος + ξένος} *adj.* ❸ 1 Tim 3:2; Titus 1:8; 1 Pet 4:9, **hospitable**

φιλοπρωτεύω {φίλος + πρό} ①$^{pap.nms}$ 3 John 9, **to be ambitious**[BrDAG]

φίλος, ή, όν$_{2.1.2}$ *adj.* (29x; 18x LA) Matt 11:19; Luke 7:6; 15:9; John 3:29–19:12[6x]; Acts 10:24; 3 John 14, **friend**; (180x LXX; 47x Sir) Judg 5:30, **ladies in waiting**[ABC]

φιλοσοφία, ας, ἡ$_{1α}$ {φίλος + σοφία} ①^{gfs} Col 2:8, **love of wisdom**, *empty and deceitful* **philosophy**, καί *is epexegetical* (*i.e., not all philosophy*)[ZEC]; ❺ LXX, 4 Macc 1:1

φιλόσοφος, ου, ὁ$_2$ {φίλος + σοφία} ①^{gmp} Acts 17:18, **philosopher**; ❹ LXX, 4 Macc 1:1

φιλόστοργος, ον$_{2.2}$ {φίλος + στέργω} *adj.* ①[nmp] Rom 12:10, **authentically loving**[ZEC]; ①[vns] LXX, 4 Macc 15:13, **parental love**; Xen. *Cyr.* 1.3.2, **tender affection**

φιλότεκνος, ον$_{2.2}$ {φίλος + τίκτω} *adj.* ①[afp] Titus 2:4, **lovers of children**; ❸ LXX, 4 Macc 15:4, *parents* **who love their children**; 15:5, *mothers are* **more devoted to their children**[SCS]; *see* Xen. *Oec.* 7.24, *implanted in the woman* **a larger share of affection for the newborn child**

φιλοτιμέομαι[con] {φίλος + τιμή} ❸ *w/ inf.* Rom 15:20,[ZEC] **to be eager**; 2 Cor 5:9,[BEC] **to consider** *it* **an honor**; 1 Thess 4:11,[ZEC] **to aspire to**

φιλοφρόνως {φίλος + φρήν} *adv.* ① Acts 28:7, **hospitably**; ❷ LXX, 2 Macc 3:9

φιμόω[con] {φιμός} ❼ 1 Pet 2:15, **to silence**; Mark 1:25; 4:39 = Luke 4:35, **Be quiet!**; 1 Tim 5:18, *do not* **muzzle** *the ox*; ❸ LXX 4 Macc 1:35, **to bridle**; Aristoph. *Nub.* 592, **to squeeze the throat** *with wood* (φιμός); *cf.* **φιμός**, Aeschn. 1.59, **box** *or* **cup** *for dice*

Φλέγων, οντος, ὁ$_3$ ① Rom 16:14, **Phlegon**

φλογίζω {φλόξ} ❷ Jas 3:6,[2x] **to enflame, set ablaze**; ❻ LXX, Exod 9:24, **to burn**

φλόξ, φλογός, ἡ$_3$ ❼ Luke 16:24; Acts 7:30; 2 Thess 1:8; Rev 1:14, **flame**; (51x LXX)

φλυαρέω[con] {φλύαρος} ①[pap.nms] 3 John 10, **to gossip**

φλύαρος, ον$_{2.2}$ *adj.* ①[nfp] 1 Tim 5:13, *subst.*, **nonsense talkers**;[PPE] ①[gfs] LXX, 4 Macc 5:10, *avoid the* **nonsense**[SCS]; Plato *Ax.* 369a, **one who speaks without reflection**

φοβέομαι[con] {φόβος} (95x; 62x GA, *aor. pass.*) Matt 28:10; John 6:19; 2 Cor 11:3; Rev 1:17, **to fear**; Matt 27:54, **ἐφοβήθησαν** σφόδρα, **to be terrified**; Luke 2:9; Mark 4:41, **ἐφοβήθησαν** φόβον μέγαν, **to fear** *a great fear* (= Jonah 1:10, 16); Eph 5:33, **to respect**

φοβερός, ά, όν$_{2.1.2}$ {φόβος} *adj.* ❸ Heb 10:27, 31; 12:21, **fearful**, **terrifying**; (36x LXX; 12x Pss) Gen 28:17, **afraid**; Ps 65:3 (66:3), **awe-inspiring**

φόβητρον, ου, τό$_2$ {φοβέομαι} ①[nnp] Luke 21:11, **dreadful event**; ①[ans] LXX, Isa 19:17, **terrifying**; Luc. *Alex.* 25, **terror**

φόβος, ου, ὁ$_2$ {φοβέομαι} (47x; 12x LA) Matt 14:26; John 7:13; 2 Cor 7:5; Jude 23; Rev 11:11, *emotional* **fear**; Luke 5:26; Acts 5:5; 2 Cor 5:11; Phil 2:12; 1 Pet 1:17, *reverential* **fear**; Rom 13:3, **threat**; Polyb. *Hist.* 11.30.2, **sheer terror** *of witnessing an execution*; 1 Pet 3:14, *don't fear their* **fear** (*i.e.*, **what they threaten**[BEC]); (198x LXX; 31x Sir, 23x Job)

Φοίβη, ης, ἡ$_{1η}$ ①[afs] Rom 16:1, **Phoebe**, *a deaconess at Cenchrea*

Φοινίκη, ης, ἡ$_{1η}$ ❸ Acts 11:19; 15:3; 21:2, **Phoenicia**[LGCb]

φοῖνιξ, ικος, ὁ$_3$ ❷ John 12:13; Rev 7:9, **palm branch**; (40x LXX; 12x Ezek)

Φοῖνιξ, ικος, ὁ$_3$ ①[ams] Acts 27:12, **Phoenix**, *a harbor of Crete*

φονεύς, έως, ὁ$_2$ {φονεύω} ❼ Matt 22:7; Acts 3:14; 1 Pet 4:15; Rev 21:8; 22:15, **murderer**; ①[amp] LXX, Wis 12:5

φονεύω {φόνος} (12x) Matt 5:21; 19:18 = Mark 10:19 = Luke 18:20; Rom 13:9 = Jas 2:11; Matt 23:31, **to murder**, **kill**; (49x LXX; 13x Num, 11x Josh) Exod 20:15 = Deut 5:18

φόνος, ου, ὁ$_2$ ❾ Matt 15:19 = Mark 7:21; Heb 11:37; Rev 9:21, **murder**; (24x LXX)

φορέω[con] ❻ Matt 11:8; Jas 2:3, **to wear**; Rom 13:4; 1 Cor 15:49, **to bear**; ❻ LXX, Prov 3:16, *she* **carries** *law and mercy on her tongue* (LES)

φόρον, ου, ὁ$_2$ ①[gns] Acts 28:15, **forum** *of Appius and Three Taverns*

φόρος, ου, ὁ$_2$ {φέρω} ❺ Luke 20:22; 23:2; Rom 13:6, 7, **tax, tribute**; (46x LXX; 10x 1 Macc) Judg 1:28, **forced labor**; *cf.* **Φόρος** (9x) 1 Esd 9:26; Ezra 2:3, **Parosh**

φορτίζω {φέρω} ❷ Matt 11:28; Luke 11:46, **to burden**; ①[iai2s] LXX, Ezek 16:33

φορτίον, ου, ὁ$_2$ {φέρω} ❻ Matt 11:30; 23:4 = Luke 11:46; Gal 6:5, **burden**; Acts 27:10, **cargo** *on a ship*; ❽ LXX, Judg 9:48; Job 7:20

Φορτουνᾶτος, ου, ὁ$_2$ ①[gms] 1 Cor 16:17, **Fortunatus**

φραγέλλιον, ου, τό$_2$ ①[ans] John 2:15, **whip**

φραγελλόω[con] {φραγέλλιον} ❷ Matt 27:26 = Mark 15:15, **to scourge**, **whip**

φραγμός, ου, ὁ$_2$ {φράσσω} ❹ Matt 21:33 = Mark 12:1, **fence**; Luke 14:23, **hedges**[*NIDNTT*]; Eph 2:14, *the mid-wall of the* **fence**[ZEC]; *ethnic* **barrier**[*NIDNTT*]; (21x LXX) Gen 38:29, **barrier**; Thuc. 4.13.4, **an obstruction** *used to block inlets to a harbor*

φράζω ①[aaimp2s] Matt 15:15, **to explain**; ❸ LXX, Dan 2:4, **to interpret**

φράσσω ❸ Rom 3:19; Heb 11:33, **to shut**; 2 Cor 11:10, *pass.*, *Paul's boast not* **being silenced**, **blocked**[BEC]; ❻ LXX, Dan 8:26, *the vision* **is sealed**

φρέαρ, φρέατος, τό$_3$ ❼ Luke 14:5, **well**; Rev 9:1–2,[3x] **shaft** *to abyss*; (58x LXX; 36x Gen)

φρεναπατάω[con] {φρήν + ἀπάτη} ①[pai3s] (only 2 occ. in all Gk. litt.) Gal 6:3; Ign. *Trall.* 6, **to deceive one's own mind**,[NIGTC] *lit.*, **to walk one's mind away**

φρεναπάτης, ου, ὁ$_{1>}$ {φρήν + ἀπάτη} ①[nmp] Titus 1:10, **deceiver of souls**[*BrDAG*]

φρήν, ένος, ἡ$_3$ {φρονέω} ❷ 1 Cor 14:20,[2x] *pl.* **matters of the mind**[NIGTC]; (12x LXX; 8x Prov); Plut. *Mor.* 116a, *the sphere of* **thinking**, *or* **judgment**, *or* **understanding**[*TDNT*]

φρίσσω ①[pai3p] Jas 2:19, **to tremble, to shudder**[KEL]; ❸ LXX, Job 4:15, *hair* **stood up**

φρονέω[con] {φρήν} (26x; 10x Phil, 9x Rom) Matt 16:23 = Mark 8:33; Rom 12:3,[2x] **to think**; Rom 12:16, **to live** *in harmony*; Phil 4:2, **to agree**; Gal 5:10, **to think** *no differently*[NIGTC]; Phil 4:10,[2x]; Col 3:2, **keep your minds fixed on** *things above*; (16x LXX) Deut 32:29, **to have sense**; 1 Macc 10:20, **to think**

φρόνημα, ατος, τό$_3$ {φρήν} ❹ Rom 8:6–7,[3x] 27, **mind**; ❷ LXX, 2 Macc 13:9, *barbarous* **arrogance**; Plato *Rp.* 573b–c, τυραννικὸν **φρόνημα**, *tyrannical* **temper**[*BrDAG*]

φρόνησις, εως, ἡ$_3$ {φρήν} ❷[dfs] Luke 1:17; Eph 1:8, **wisdom, insight**; (58x LXX)

φρόνιμος, ον$_{2.2}$ {φρήν} *adj.* (14x; 7x Matt) Matt 7:24; 24:45 = Luke 12:42; 1 Cor 4:10, **wise**; Luke 16:8, **shrewd**; 1 Cor 10:15, *subst.*, **sensible people**[NIGTC]; (40x LXX; 16x Prov)

φρονίμως {φρήν} *adv.* ① Luke 16:8, **shrewdly, wisely**; Jos. *A.J.* 19.112

φροντίζω {φρήν} ①[pas3p] Titus 3:8, **to concentrate upon**[NIGTC]; (15x LXX) 2 Macc 2:25

φρουρέω[con] {ὁράω} ❹ 2 Cor 11:32; Phil 4:7, **to guard**, **protect**; Gal 3:23, **to be guarded** *and locked up*[KeenG]; 1 Pet 1:5, *pass.*, **to be guarded** *by God's power*[Keen1P]; ❸ LXX, Jdt 3:6

φρυάσσω ①[aai3p] (4x in all Gk. litt.) Acts 4:25; Ps 2:1; 3 Macc 2.2; Eus. *Hist. eccl.* 1.3.6, **to neigh like a horse**, **to prance** *or* **stamp the ground**; *hence* **to rage**

φρύγανον, ου, τό$_2$ ①[gnp] Acts 28:3, **stick**; ❻ LXX, Isa 41:2, **stubble**

Φρυγία, ας, ἡ$_{1α}$ ❸ Acts 2:10; 16:6; 18:23, **Phrygia**

Φύγελος, ου, ὁ$_2$ ①[nms] 2 Tim 1:15, **Phygelus**

φυγή, ῆς, ἡ$_{1η}$ ①[nfs] Matt 24:20, **flight**, **escape**, *esp. in battle*; (15x LXX) 2 Macc 4:42

φυλακή, ῆς, ἡ$_{1η}$ {φυλάσσω} (47x; 16x Acts, 10x Matt) 2 Cor 6:5; **prison**, **jail**; Matt 14:25 = Mark 6:48, *fourth* **watch**, *3–6 a.m.*; Matt 24:43, **time**; Luke 2:8, **the night watch**; Acts 12:10, *first and second* **guard posts**; Matt 5:25 = Luke 12:58, **prison** = **place for those waiting future judgment**[*NIDNTT*]; Rev 18:2,[3x] **dwelling place** *of demons*,[NIGTC, ZEC] (119x LXX)

φυλακίζω {φυλάσσω} ①[pap.nms] Acts 22:19, **to imprison**; ①[apinf] LXX, Wis 18:4

φυλακτήριον, ου, ὁ$_2$ {φυλάσσω} ①[anp] Matt 23:5, **phylactery**

φύλαξ, ακος, ὁ$_3$ {φυλάσσω} ❸ Acts 5:23; 12:6, 19, **watchman**, **guard**; (16x LXX)

φυλάσσω (31x; 14x LA) Matt 19:20 = Mark 10:20 = Luke 18:21; **to keep** *the commandments, law*; Acts 16:4, **to obey** *decisions*; 2 Tim 1:14; 2 Thess 3:3; Jude 24, **to guard**; Luke 12:15, **to take a guarded stance** *against greed*; 2 Tim 4:15; 1 John 5:21, **to avoid** *false teachers and idols*; (457x LXX; 65x Pss, 55x Deut, 31x Prov)

φυλή, ῆς, ἡ$_1$ {φύω} (31x; 21x in Rev) Matt 19:28; Luke 2:36; Rom 11:1; Phil 3:5; Heb 7:13; Jas 1:1; Rev 5:5, **tribe**; Matt 24:30; Rev 1:7, **people**; (410x LXX; 101x Num)

φύλλον, ου, τό$_2$ ❻ Matt 21:19 = Mark 11:13; Matt 24:32 = Mark 13:28, **leaf**; Rev 22:2, **leaves** *on the tree of life have healing properties* (*cf.* Ezek 47:12); (18x LXX; 5x Neh)

φύραμα, ατος, τό$_3$ {φύρω} ❺ Rom 9:21, **lump of clay** *for potter*; Rom 11:16; 1 Cor 5:6, 7,[NIGTC] *the whole* **mixed lump**; Gal 5:9, **batch of dough**[NIDNTT]; ❹ LXX, Exod 12:34

φυσικός, ή, όν$_{2.1.2}$ {φύω} ❸ Rom 1:26, 27, **natural**; 2 Pet 2:12, *creatures* **of instinct**[PNTC]

φυσικῶς {φύω} *adv.* ① Jude 10, **instinctual**, **unreasoning**[BEC]

φυσιόω[con] {φύω} ❼ (6x 1 Cor) 1 Cor 4:6; 5:2; 13:4; Col 2:18, **to be puffed up**, **arrogant**

φύσις, εως, ἡ$_3$ {φύω} (14x; 7x Rom) Rom 1:26, τὴν παρὰ φύσιν, **unnatural relations**[NIGTC!] *i.e., contrary to nature*; Rom 11:21, *with* **no human interference**; 1 Cor 11:14, **the ordering of how things are**[NIGTC]; 2 Pet 1:4, **instinctively**; Gal 2:15, **by birth**; Rom 2:27, *the uncircumcision* **by nature**; 11:24, *Israelites* **physically** (κατὰ **φύσιν**) *descended from Abraham versus gentiles wild and contrary to* **nature** (παρὰ **φύσιν**); Jas 3:7, **species**; (18x LXX; 8x 4 Macc)

φυσίωσις, εως, ἡ$_3$ ①[nfp] 2 Cor 12:20, **swelled heads**[BEC]; Gal. *U.P.* 14.386, **swelling**[BrDAG]

φυτεία, ας, ἡ$_{1α}$ {φύω} ① Matt 15:13, **plant**; ❹ LXX, 2 Kgs 19:29, **planting**

φυτεύω {φύω} (11x) Matt 15:13; Luke 17:28; 20:9; 1 Cor 3:6; 9:7, **to plant**; *pass.*, Luke 13:6; 17:6, **to be planted**; (50x LXX; 9x Jer, 7x Isa) Gen 2:8; Isa 5:2, **to plant**

φύω ❸ Luke 8:6, 8; Heb 12:15, **to grow**; (14x LXX; 2x Dan) 4 Macc 1:20, **to pertain** *by nature* (NETS)

φωλεός, οῦ, ὁ$_2$ ❷[amp] Matt 8:20 = Luke 9:58, **hole**, **lair**

φωνέω[con] {φωνή} (43x; 42x GA) Matt 20:32; John 4:16; Acts 10:7, **to call**; Matt 26:34 = Mark 14:30 = Luke 22:34 = John 13:38, **to crow** (*the rooster* **sounded**); Mark 1:26, **to shout**; Luke 14:12,[2x] **to invite**; (24x LXX; 5x Isa)

φωνή, ῆς, ἡ$_{1η}$ {φωνέω} (139x; 55x Rev, 41x LA) Ⓐ **voice(s)**, Matt 3:3 = Mark 1:3 = Luke 3:4 = John 1:23; Rev 1:10 21:3[36x]; Ⓑ **voice** *of God*, Matt 3:17 = Mark 1:11 = Luke 3:22 (*Jesus's baptism, transfig., and crucif.*); Ⓒ **sound**, 1 Cor 14:7; Ⓓ **complex**, Mark 1:26, φωνῆσαν **φωνῇ** μεγάλῃ, **shrieking loudly**; 1 Cor 14:10, 11, **language**; (600x LXX; 80x Jer)

φῶς, φωτός, τό$_3$ {φαίνω} (73x; 23x John) Ⓐ ***active use***, Matt 5:14; Acts 9:3–26:23[8x]; 2 Cor 4:6; Eph 5:14, **light**; Ⓑ ***descriptive use***, Acts 26:18; 1 Pet 2:9, *transfer from darkness to* **light**; Rom 13:12, *donning the armor of* **light**; 2 Cor 11:14, *Satan mimicking an angel of* **light**[BEC]; (165x LXX; 32x Isa; 23x Job) Gen 1:3, *let there be* **light**

φωστήρ, ῆρος, ὁ$_3$ {φαίνω} ❷ Phil 2:15, **star**; Rev 21:11, **radiance**; ❾ LXX, Gen 1:14

φωσφόρος, ον$_{2.2}$ {φαίνω + φέρω} *adj.* ①[nns] 2 Pet 1:19,[L7 125] *eschat.*, **morning star**[BNTC, BEC]

φωτεινός, ή, όν$_{2.1.2}$ {φαίνω} *adj.* ❺ Matt 6:22 = Luke 11:34, 36,[2x] **full of light**; ❷ LXX

φωτίζω {φαίνω} (11x) Luke 11:36; John 1:9; 1 Cor 4:5; Eph 3:9; Rev 21:23; 22:5, **to shed light on**, **to illustrate**; Eph 1:18; Heb 6:4; 10:32, *pass.*, **to be enlightened**; 2 Tim 1:10, **to bring** *life and immortality* **to light**; Rev 18:1, **to make bright**; (40x LXX)

φωτισμός, οῦ, ὁ$_2$ {φαίνω} ❷[ams] 2 Cor 4:4, 6, **enlightenment**[*NIDNTT*] ❻ LXX

X, χ [*chi*]

X, χ, το, (χεῖ *or* χῖ) *indecl.* **chi**, *22nd letter of Gr. alphabet* || *num.* χʹ = 600; ͵χ = 600,000; *but in inscr.*, X = χίλιοι, 1,000

χαίρω (74x; 19x LA) Matt 2:10; Acts 5:41; 2 Cor 2:3–13:11[8x]; Phil 1:18–4:10[9x]; 2 John 4, **to rejoice**; Matt 26:49; Jas 1:1, **Greetings!**; 2 John 10, *grant no* **welcome**; Luke 23:8, *Herod evilly* **glad**;[ZEC] Rev 11:10, **to gloat**; (76x LXX; 11x 1 Macc) 1 Macc 12:6, **greeting** *in a letter*

χάλαζα, ης, ἡ$_1$ ❹ (Rev) 8:7; 11:19; 16:21,[2x] **hail**; (39x LXX; 19x Exod), Exod 9:18

χαλάω[con] ❼ Mark 2:4; Luke 5:4; Acts 9:25; 2 Cor 11:33, **to lower**; ❹ LXX, Exod 36:28

Χαλδαῖος, ου, ὁ$_2$ ①[gmp] Acts 7:4, **Chaldean**; (90x LXX; 41x Jer) Jer 21:4

χαλεπός, ή, όν$_{2.1.2}$ *adj.* ❷ Matt 8:28, *extremely* **violent**; 2 Tim 3:1, **difficult**; (11x LXX)

χαλιναγωγέω[con] {χαλάω + ἄγω} ❷ Jas 1:26; 3:2, **to bridle**

χαλινός, οῦ, ὁ$_2$ {χαλάω} ❷ Jas 3:3; Rev 14:20, **bit, bridle**; ❼ LXX, 2 Kgs 19:28, **hook**

χαλκεύς, έως, ὁ$_2$ {χαλκός} ①[nms] 2 Tim 4:14, **coppersmith**, **metalworker**; ❼ LXX, Gen 4:22, **χαλκεὺς** χαλκοῦ, **forger** *of bronze*; Job 32:19, **blacksmith**

χαλκηδών, όνος, ὁ$_3$ {χαλκός} ①[nms] Rev 21:19, **chalcedony, agate**

χαλκίον, ου, τό$_2$ {χαλκός} ①[gnp] Mark 7:4, **copper**; ①[ans] LXX 1 Sam 2:14; Aristoph. *fr.* 231, **copper cup** *used for playing kottabos, a sordid Greek drinking game*[BrDAG]; cf. 2 Tim 4:14, *Alexander, the coppersmith*[ABC]

χαλκολίβανον, ου, τό$_2$ {χαλκός + λείβω} ❷[dns] Rev 1:15; 2:18, **burnished bronze**[L7 111–17]

χαλκός, οῦ, ὁ$_2$ ❺ Matt 10:9, *don't ever try to win* (κτάομαι) *gold or silver or* **copper**[Brun1] (*i.e., don't charge for your services*) = Mark 6:8, *take* (αἴρω) *nothing, no* **coins**; Mark 12:41, **money**; 1 Cor 13:1; Rev 18:12, **brass, bronze**; (55x LXX; 8x Exod) Exod 25:3

χαλκοῦς, ῆ, οῦν$_{2.1.2}$ {χαλκός} *adj.* ①[anp] Rev 9:20, **made of bronze**; (101x LXX; 26x Exod)

χαμαί *adv.* ❷ John 9:6, **on the ground**; 18:6, **to the ground**; ❼ LXX, Job 1:20; Dan 8:18

Χανάαν, ἡ$_1$ *indecl.* ❷ Acts 7:11; 13:19, **Canaan**; (97x LXX; 48x Gen) Gen 9:18

Χαναναῖος, α, ον$_{2.1.2}$ *adj.* ① Matt 15:22, **Canaanite** *woman* (58x LXX; 16x Josh:Judg)

χαρά, ᾶς, ἡ$_{1\alpha}$ {χάρις} (59x; 12x LA) Matt 2:10; Mark 4:16; Phlm 7, **joy**; (44x LXX)

χάραγμα, ατος, τό$_3$ {χαράσσω} ❽ (7x Rev) Acts 17:29, **image**[ZEC]; Rev 13:16; 20:4, *fig.*, **mark** *of the beast*[NIGTC]

χαρακτήρ, ῆρος, ὁ$_3$ {χαράσσω} ① Heb 1:3, **exact representation**[NIGTC]; ❸ LXX, Lev 13:28, **scar** *from a burn*; 2 Macc 4:10, *Greek* **way of life**; 4 Macc 15:4, **likeness**

χάραξ, ακος, ὁ$_3$ {χαράσσω} ①[ams] Luke 19:43, *milit.*, **siege ramp**; (15x LXX) Isa 29:3, **ramparts**; Jos. *B.J.* 5.262ff., 491ff. *destruction of Jerusalem*, AD 70[DJG2]

χαρίζομαι {χάρις} (23x) Luke 7:21; Rom 8:32; Gal 3:18; Phil 1:29, **to give graciously**; Luke 7:42; Eph 4:32 = Col 3:13, **to forgive graciously**[BDAG]; Acts 25:11, **to hand over** *for trial*; Phlm 22, *pass.*, **graciously to be given**

χάριν {χάρις} *impr. prep. w/ gen.* ❾ Luke 7:47, **because** *of this*; Eph 3:1; Titus 1:5, **for** *this* *reason*; 1 John 3:12, **why?**; Jude 16, **for** *their own advantage*; 1 Tim 5:14, *noun used as a fixed form as a prep.*,[PPE!] **on account** *of slander* (29x LXX; 15x Sir, 9x 1 Macc)

χάρις, ιτος, ἡ$_3$ (155x; 100x Paul, 25x LA, 24x Rom) Luke 1:30, **favor**; 2:40; John 1:14; 1 Cor 3:10, **grace**; 10:30, **thanksgiving**; Col 3:16, **gratitude**; (132x LXX; 26x Sir, 20x Prov)

χάρισμα, ατος, τό$_3$ {χάρις} (17x; 16x Paul) Rom 1:11, **spiritual gift**; 5:15; 12:6; 1 Cor 1:7–12:31[7x]; 2 Cor 1:11; 1 Tim 4:14; 2 Tim 1:6; 1 Pet 4:10, **gift(s)**

χαριτόω[con] {χάρις} ❷ Luke 1:28, *subst. ptc.*, **greatly favored one**; Eph 1:6, **he graced** *us* **with**; ①[ppp.dms] LXX, Sir 18:17, **a favored man**

Χαρράν, ἡ$_3$ *indecl.* ❷[dfs] Acts 7:2, 4, **Haran**; (14x LXX; 9x Gen) Gen 11:31

χάρτης, ου, ὁ$_{1>}$ {χαράσσω} ①[gms] 2 John 12, **paper**; ①[nms] LXX, Jer 43:23 (36:23)

χάσμα, ατος, τό$_3$ {χάσκω → **to yawn, gape**} ①[nns] Luke 16:26, **chasm**; ①[ans] LXX, Sam 18:17, *large* **pit**; Eur. *Ph.* 1605, *the abyssal* **chasms** *of Tartaros*

χεῖλος, ους, τό$_3$ ❼ Matt 15:8 = Mark 7:6; 1 Cor 14:21; 1 Pet 3:10, **lip**; Heb 11:12, **shore**, *i.e., the* **lip** *of the sea*; (172x LXX; 43x Prov, 28x Pss) Gen 11:1, **language** *and vocabulary* (φωνή); 1 Kgs 7:10 (7:23), *basin called the Sea from* **brim** *to* **brim**

χειμάζω {χειμῶν} ①[ppp.gmp] Acts 27:18, **to be severely battered** *by waves*[Keen4]; ①[ppi3s] LXX, Prov 26:10

χειμάρρος, ου, ὁ$_2$ {χεῖμα + ῥέω} ①[gms] John 18:1, *the Kidron* **Valley**; (95x LXX; 11x Deut)

χειμών, ῶνος, ὁ$_2$ ❻ Matt 16:3, Acts 27:20, **stormy, storm**; Matt 24:20 = Mark 13:18; John 10:22; 2 Tim 4:21, **winter**; ❼ LXX, Job 37:6,[2x] **torrential rains**

χείρ, χειρός, ἡ$_3$ (177x; 91x in Gs, 45x in Acts) Matt 3:12 = Luke 3:17; Mark 7:32; John 3:35; Rom 10:21, **hand**; Luke 15:22, *ring for his* **hand**; Gal 6:11, **handwriting**; (1,812x LXX; 117x Pss) Exod 4:4, *stretch out your* **hand** (9x Exod)

χειραγωγέω[con] {χεῖρ + ἄγω} ❷ Acts 9:8,[pap.nmp] **to take by the hand**; 22:11,[ppp.nms] **to be led by the hand** *due to Saul's blindness*; ①[pap.ams] LXX, Judg 16:26, *Samson* **being led by the hand**

χειραγωγός, ου, ὁ$_2$ {χεῖρ + ἄγω} ①[amp] Acts 13:11, **guide** *for blinded Elymas*; Plut. *An Seni* 21, **to be led**, *of a soldier after losing eyes*; *Mor.* 10, *blind* **guides**

χειρόγραφον, ου, τό$_2$ {χεῖρ + γράφω} ①[ans] Col 2:14, *leg.* **a bill of indictment**[ABC]; ❷ LXX, Tob 5:3, 9:5; Polyb. *Hist.* 30.8.4, **incriminating record**, *coll.* **rap sheet**

χειροποίητος, ον$_{2.2}$ {χεῖρ + ποιέω} *adj.* ❻ Mark 14:58; Acts 7:48; 17:24; Eph 2:11; Heb 9:11, 24, **handmade**; (14x LXX; 7x Isa) Lev 26:1, **idols** (*always pejorative*)

χειροτονέω[con] {χείρ + τείνω} ❷ Acts 14:23; 2 Cor 8:19, **to appoint**[BEC]

χείρων, ον$_{3.3}$ *adj.* (11x) Matt 9:16 = Mark 2:21; Matt 12:45 = Luke 11:26; Mark 5:26; John 5:14; 1 Tim 5:8; 2 Tim 3:13; 2 Pet 2:20; Heb 10:29, **worse**

Χερούβ, τό$_2$ ①[nnp] Heb 9:5, **cherubim**; (83x LXX; 27x Ezek)

χήρα, ας, ἡ$_{1\alpha}$ (26x; 12x in LA) Mark 12:42; Luke 4:25; 1 Cor 7:8; 1 Tim 5[6x]; Jas 1:27; Rev 18:7, **widow**; (68x LXX; 12x Deut) Gen 38:11; Exod 22:21; Num 30:10

χιλίαρχος, ου, ὁ$_2$ {ἄρχω + χίλιοι} (21x) Mark 6:21; John 18:12; Acts 21:31–25:23[17x]; Rev 6:15; 19:18, **commander of a thousand, commanders**

χιλιάς, άδος, ἡ$_3$ {χίλιοι} (23x) Luke 14:31; Acts 4:4; 1 Cor 10:8; Rev 5:11–21:16,[19x] **a thousand, group of one thousand**; (320x LXX; 95x 1–2 Chr, 30x Ezek)

χίλιοι, αι, α$_{2.1.2}$ *adj.* (11x) 2 Pet 3:8; Rev 11:3–20:7,[10x] **a thousand**; (116x LXX)

Χίος, ου, ἡ$_2$ ①[gfs] Acts 20:15, **Chios**

χιτών, ῶνος, ὁ$_3$ (11x; 9x Gs) Matt 10:10 = Mark 6:9 = Luke 9:3; John 19:23; Acts 9:39; Jude 23, **undergarment**, **tunic**; (36x LXX; 8x Gen:Exod)

χιών, όνος, ἡ$_3$ ❷ Matt 28:3; Rev 1:14, **snow**; (25x LXX) 2 Sam 28:20, **snowy**

χλαμύς, ύδος, ἡ$_3$ ❷[afs] Matt 27:28, 31, **cloak**; ①[gfs] LXX, 2 Macc 12:35

χλευάζω ①[iai3p] Acts 17:32, **to sneer**; ❸ LXX, 2 Macc 7:27; 4 Macc 5:22, **to scoff**, **deride**

χλιαρός, ά, όν$_{2.1.2}$ *adj.* ①[nms] Rev 3:16, **lukewarm**, **tepid**, **emetic**;[NIGTC] *Colossae*[LGCb 586] *had cold, pure, drinkable waters, while Hierapolis*[LGCb 686] *had hot, medicinal waters—retention of both properties were lost when piped in to Laodicea*[ACNT, NIGTC]

χλόη, ης, ἡ$_{1\eta}$ ①[gfs] 1 Cor 1:11, **Chloe**

χλωρός, ά, όν$_{2.1.2}$ {χλόη} *adj.* ❹ Mark 6:39; Rev 8:7; 9:4, **green**, *color of life*; Rev 6:8, **pale green**, *color of disease and death, corpse-like*[BEC]; (15x LXX; 4x Gen) Exod 10:15

χοϊκός, ή, όν$_{2.1.2}$ {χέω} *adj.* ❹ 1 Cor 15:47–49,[4x] **made of dust**

χοῖνιξ, ικος, ἡ$_3$ ❷ Rev 6:6,[2x] **quart**; ❸[nfs] LXX, Ezek 45:10–11,[3x] **measure**

χοῖρος, ου, ὁ$_2$ (12x) Matt 8:30, 31, 32 = Mark 5:11, 12, 13, 16 = Luke 8:32, 33, **pig**

χολάω[con] {χολή} ①[pai2p] John 7:23, **to be angry**

χολή, ῆς, ἡ$_{1\eta}$ ❷ Matt 27:34, **drugged wine**[NICNT]; Acts 8:23, **poison**; (17x LXX; 6x Tob)

Χοραζίν, ἡ$_1$ ❷[vfs] Matt 11:21 = Luke 10:13, **Chorazin**

χορηγέω[con] {χορός + ἄγω} ❷ 2 Cor 9:10, **to provide**; 1 Pet 4:11, **to supply**; (18x LXX; 5x Sir)

χορός, οῦ, ὁ$_2$ ①[gmp] Luke 15:25, **dancing** *upon return of the lost son*; (22x LXX)

χορτάζω {χόρτος} (16x; 12x Syn) 14x, *mid./pass.*, Matt 14:20 = Mark 6:42 = Luke 9:17 = John 6:26; Luke 15:16; Jas 2:16, **to be filled**, **satisfied**; Phil 4:12, **to be well-fed**; Rev 19:21, *birds of prey* **will be gorged**; 2x, *act.*, Matt 15:23 = Mark 8:4, **to feed**; (13x LXX; 9x Pss) Ps 16:14 (17:14), **to be fed**

χόρτασμα, ατος, τό$_3$ {χόρτος} ①[anp] Acts 7:11, **food for humans**[NIDNTT]; ❾ LXX

χόρτος, ου, ὁ$_2$ (15x) Matt 14:19 = Mark 6:39 = John 6:10; Rev 8:7, **grass**; Matt 13:26; Mark 4:28, **growing plant**; 1 Cor 3:12, **hay** *as combustible building material*[NIGTC]; Jas 1:10; 1 Pet 1:24, **wildflower**, **grass**, *metaph.*, *transience of human life*; (45x LXX; 11x Pss)

χουζᾶς, ᾶ, ὁ$_1$ ①[gms] Luke 8:3, **Chuza**, *Herod's steward*

χοῦς, χοός, ὁ$_3$ {χέω → **to pour**} ❷[ams] Mark 6:11; Rev 18:19, **dust**; (52x LXX; 10x Pss)

χράομαι (11x; 7x 1–2 Cor) Acts 27:3, **to treat**; 1 Cor 7:21, **make positive use** *of the present*-[NIGTC]; 7:31, *ptc.*, **those who deal with** *the world*[NIGTC]; 1 Tim 1:8; 5:23, **employ**; 2 Cor 3:12, **to conduct ministry**; 13:10, *I may not have* **to deal** *harshly with you*[BEC!]

χρεία, ας, ἡ$_{1\alpha}$ {χράομαι} (49x; 26x in GA) Matt 9:12 = Mark 2:17 = Luke 5:31; John 2:25; Acts 2:45; Rom 12:13; 1 Cor 12:21[2x]; 1 John 3:17, **need(s)**; (52x LXX) 1 Macc 11:63, **position**

χρεοφειλέτης, ου, ὁ$_{1>}$ {χράομαι + ὀφείλω} ❷ Luke 7:41; 16:5, **debtor**; ❷ LXX

χρή *impers. verb*[EGG] {χράομαι} ①[pai3s] Jas 3:10, **οὐ χρή** *w/ acc. + inf.*,[NIDNTT] **it ought not to be**[ABC]; ①[pai3s] LXX, Prov 25:27, **it is not good**

χρῄζω {χράομαι} ❺ Matt 6:32 = Luke 12:30; Rom 16:2; 2 Cor 3:1, **to need**

χρῆμα, ατος, τό$_3$ {χράομαι} ❻ Mark 10:23 = Luke 18:24, **wealth**; Acts 4:37; 8:18; 24:26, **money**; (41x LXX; 15x Sir) Josh 22:8; Prov 17:6

χρηματίζω {χράομαι} ❾ *pass.*, Matt 2:12; Heb 8:5; 11:7; 12:25, **to be warned**; Luke 2:26, **to be made known**; Acts 10:22, **to be directed**; 11:26; Rom 7:3, **to be called**; (10x LXX; 8x Jer) Job 40:8, **to deal with**; Jer 33:2[2x] (26:2), **to give an oracle**

χρηματισμός, οῦ, ὁ$_2$ {χράομαι} ①[nms] Rom 11:4, **divine reply**[TDNT]; ❸ LXX

χρήσιμος, η, ον$_{2.1.2}$ {χράομαι} *adj.* ①[ans] 2 Tim 2:14, **ἐπ᾽οὐδὲν χρήσιμον, is useless**, CSB; *this is in no way* **beneficial**, LEB; (13x LXX; 3x Sir, 2x Wis)

χρῆσις, εως, ἡ$_3$ {χράομαι} ❷[afs] Rom 1:26, 27, **intimate involvement**[EGG]; ❹ LXX, 1 Sam 1:28, *given to God for his* **use**; Plato *Leg.* 841a, **the use** *of what belongs to Aphrodite, i.e.,* **sexual relations**; Xen. *Symp.* 8.28, **use** *of the body*

χρῆσον → **κίχρημι**, *aor. act. imp. 2s*, Luke 11:5, **Lend** *me three loaves of bread*!

χρηστεύομαι {χράομαι} ①[pmi3s] 1 Cor 13:4, *love shows* **kindness**; Pseud., Pss. Sol. 9.6

χρηστολογία, ας, ἡ$_{1α}$ {χράομαι + λέγω} ①[gfs] Rom 16:18, **smooth talk**[NIDNTT]

χρηστός, ή, όν$_{2.1.2}$ {χράομαι} *adj.* ❼ Matt 11:30, **easy to wear**[Brun1]; Luke 5:39, **pleasing**; Eph 4:32; 1 Pet 2:3, **kind**; 1 Cor 15:33, **reputable** *lifestyles*[NIGTC]; (39x LXX; 14x Pss)

χρηστότης, ητος, ἡ$_3$ {χράομαι} (10x; 5x Rom) Rom 11:22[3x]; 2 Cor 6:6 (*of God and believers*)[BEC]; Eph 2:7; Col 3:12, **kindness**; Titus 3:4, **goodness**; (26x LXX; 15x Pss)

χρῖσμα, ατος, τό$_3$ {χρίω} ❸[ans] 1 John 2:20, 27,[2x] **anointing**

Χριστιανός, οῦ, ὁ$_2$ {χρίω} ❸ Acts 11:26; 26:28; 1 Pet 4:16, **Christian**

Χριστός, οῦ, ὁ$_2$ {χρίω} (529x; 382x in Paul, 54x Gs, 25x Acts) Matt 16:16 = Mark 8:29 = Luke 9:20 = John 1:41, **Christ, Messiah, the Anointed One**; (51x LXX; 18x 1–2 Sam, 10x Pss) Lev 4:5, *the* **anointed** *priest*; 1 Sam 2:10; Ps 27:8 (28:8), *his* **anointed one**; Aeschl. *Pr.* 480, **ointment**; *cf.* Aristot. *Gen. an.* 747a9, **ἔγχριστος, rubbed in**[NIDNTT]

χρίω ❺ Luke 4:18; Acts 4:27; 2 Cor 1:21; Heb 1:9, **to rub, anoint**; (76x LXX)

χρονίζω ❺ Matt 24:48 = Luke 12:45; Matt 25:5; Heb 10:37, **to delay**; (23x LXX) 2 Sam 20:5, **to be late**; Hp. *Aph.* 3.28, **to become chronic**, *of diseases*[BrDAG]

χρόνος, ου, ὁ$_2$ (54x; 24x in LA) Matt 25:19; Gal 4:4; Rev 2:21, **time**; Mark 2:19; Gal 4:1, **as long as**; Mark 9:21, **How long . . . ?**; Rev 10:6, **delay**[NIGTC]; Matt 2:7, **time, instant**; Luke 8:29, **on many occasions**[NIGTC]; John 12:35, **just a little longer**; Acts 7:23; 13:18, *for forty* **years**; (134x LXX; 19x Isa, 12x Job) Gen 26:1

χρονοτριβέω[con] {χρόνος + τρίβος} ①[aainf] Acts 20:16, **to waste time,**[ABC] **to lose time**[ZEC]; Plut. *CMi.* 53, **to draw out** *the war*

χρυσίον, ου, τό$_2$ {χρυσός} (12x; 5x Rev) Acts 3:6; 1 Tim 2:9; Heb 9:4; 1 Pet 1:7; Rev 3:18; 21:21, **gold**; (290x LXX; 51x Exod, 37x 2 Chr, 27x 1 Kgs)

χρυσοδακτύλιος, ον$_{2.2}$ {χρυσός + δείκνυμι} *adj.* ①[nms] Jas 2.2, **wearing a gold ring**

χρυσόλιθος, ου, ὁ {χρυσός + λίθος} ①[nms] Rev 21:20, **chrysolite**, *yellow topaz*; ❸ LXX, Exod 28:20; 36:20; Ezek 28:13, **chrysolite**

χρυσόπρασος, ου, ὁ$_2$ {χρυσός + πρασία} ①[nms] Rev 21:20, **chrysoprase**, *green quartz*

χρυσός, οῦ, ὁ (18x; 5x Matt) Matt 2:11; Acts 17:29; Jas 5:3; Rev 9:7, **gold**; (13x LXX)

χρυσοῦς, ῆ, οῦν$_{2.1.2}$ {χρυσός} *adj.* (*contractions*, **εος, εα, εον**) (18x; 15x Rev) 2 Tim 2:20; Heb 9:4; Rev 1:12, **golden, gold**; (206x LXX; 45x Exod) Gen 24:22; Exod 3:22; 20:23

χρυσόω[con] ❷[pfpp.nfs] Rev 17:4; 18:16, **glittering** *with gold*; ❽ LXX, Exod 25:12; 38:18

χρώς, χρωτός, ὁ$_3$ ①[gms] Acts 19:12, **skin**; (15x LXX; 14x Lev) Lev 13:21, **flesh**

χωλός, ή, όν$_{2.1.2}$ *adj.* (14x, 5x Matt) Matt 11:5, **lame**; 18:8 = Mark 9:45 (*wordplay*; καλόν→ χωλόν; *better*→ **lame**)[DGNT2]; Luke 7:22; Heb 12:13, **lame**; (12x LXX; 5x 2 Sam)

χώρα, ας, ἡ$_{1α}$ {χωρέω} (28x; 17x LA) Matt 4:16, *in the* **land** *and shadow of death*; Mark 5:1;

Luke 2:8; Acts 13:49, **region**, **country**; Luke 12:16; John 4:35; Jas 5:4, **field**, **land**; Acts 27:27, *approaching* **land**, **shore**; (232x LXX; 51x 1 Macc)

χωρέω[con] (10x; 4x Matt) Matt 15:17, **to proceed**; 19:11, **to grasp**; Mark 2:2; John 2:6; 8:37, **to have space**; 2 Cor 7:2, **make room for** *us*[BEC]; John 21:25, **to contain**; 2 Pet 3:9, **to come to**; (10x LXX) Gen 13:6, **to support**; 2 Macc 15:37, **to be ruled**

χωρίζω {χωρίς} (13x; 4x 1 Cor) Matt 19:6 = Mark 10:9; Phlm 15; Heb 7:26, **to divide**; Acts 1:4, **to depart**; 1 Cor 7:10, 11, 15, **to separate**[NIGTC]; (21x LXX) Lev 13:46

χωρίον, ου, τό {χωρέω} (10x; 7x Acts) Matt 26:36 = Mark 14:32, **a place** *called Gethsemane*; John 4:5, **plot**; Acts 1:18–28:7,[7x] **field**, **land**; ❻ LXX; 3x 2 Macc

χωρίς *impr. prep. w/gen.* (41x; 13x Heb, 6x Rom) Matt 13:34; 1 Tim 2:8; Phlm 14; Jas 2:18, 26, **without**; Heb 9:18, οὐδὲ . . . **χωρὶς** αἵματος, *not* **without** *blood*; Matt 14:21, **besides**, **not counting**; John 1:3; Rom 7:8, 9, **apart**; John 20:7, *adv.* **by itself**; (20x LXX) Gen 26:1

Ψ, ψ [*psi*]

Ψ, ψ (ψεῖ *or* ψῖ) *indecl.* **psi**, *23rd letter of the Gr. alphabet* || *num.* ψʹ = 700; ͵ψ = 700,000; *in inscr.* **Ψ**= 10 drachmas

ψάλλω {ψαλμός} ❺ Rom 15:9; 1 Cor 14:15^{2x}; Eph 5:19; Jas 5:13, **to sing praise**; (58x LXX; 45x Pss) Judg 5:3; Ps 17:50 (18:49), **I will sing praise**

ψαλμός, οῦ, ὁ$_2$ {ψάλλω} ❽ Luke 20:42; Acts 1:20, *book of* **Psalms**; 1 Cor 14:26; Eph 5:19 = Col 3:16, **hymn**, **psalm**; (92x LXX; 72x Pss) 1 Sam 16:18, *he knows* **music** (LES); Pss 3:1–142:1,^{35x} **ψαλμὸς** τῷ Δαυιδ, **a psalm** *by David*

ψευδ**άδελφος, ου, ὁ**$_2$ {ψεύδομαι + ἀδελφός} ❷ 2 Cor 11:26; Gal 2:4, **false brother**

ψευδ**απόστολος, ου, ὁ**$_2$ {ψεύδομαι + ἀπό + στέλλω} ①^{nmp} 2 Cor 11:13, **false apostle**, *intense appositional description follows in vv. 13–15*^{BEC}

ψευδής, ές$_{3.3}$ {ψεύδομαι} *adj.* ❸ Acts 6:13; Rev 2:2, **false**; 21:8, **liar**; (95x LXX; 20x Jer)

ψευδο**διδάσκαλος, ου, ὁ**$_2$ {ψεύδομαι + διδάσκω} ①^{nmp} 2 Pet 2:1, **false teacher**

ψευδο**λόγος, ου, ὁ**$_2$ {ψεύδομαι + λέγω} ①^{gmp} 1 Tim 4:2, **liar**

ψεύδομαι {ψευδής} (12x) Matt 5:11; Acts 5:3, 4; Rom 9:1; 2 Cor 11:31; Gal 1:20; Col 3:9; 1 Tim 2:7; Heb 6:18; Jas 3:14; 1 John 1:6; Rev 3:9, **to lie, speak falsely**; (35x LXX; 8x Pss:Job)

ψευδο**μαρτυρέω**^{con} {ψεύδομαι + μάρτυς} ❺ Matt 19:18 = Mark 10:19 = Luke 18:20; Mark 14:56, **to testify falsely**; ❷ LXX, Exod 20:16 = Deut 5:20, *do not* **give false testimony**

ψευδο**μαρτυρία, ας**$_{1α}$ {ψεύδομαι + μάρτυς} ❷ Matt 15:19; 26:59, **false witness**

ψευδό**μαρτυς, υρος, ὁ**$_3$ {ψεύδομαι + μάρτυς} ❷ Matt 26:60; 1 Cor 15:15, **false witness**; ①^{amp} LXX, Sus 60, **false witnesses**

ψευδο**προφήτης, ου, ὁ**$_{1>}$ {ψεύδομαι + πρό + φημί} (11x) Matt 7:15; 24:11, 24 = Mark 13:22; Luke 6:26; Acts 13:6 (*of Bar-Jesus*); 2 Pet 2:1; 1 John 4:1; Rev 16:13; 19:20; 20:10, **false prophet**; (10x LXX; 9x Jer) Zech 13:2; Jer 6:13, **pseudo-prophet**

ψεῦδος, ους, τό$_3$ (ψεύδομαι) (10x) John 8:44; Rom 1:25; Eph 4:25; 2 Thess 2:9, 11; 1 John 2:21; Rev 14:5, **lie**, **falsehood**; (46x LXX; 9x Jer) Ps 4:3 (4:2); Prov 24:22, **falsehood**

ψευδό**χριστος, ου, ὁ**$_2$ {ψεύδομαι + χρίω} ❷ Matt 24:24 = Mark 13:22, **false messiah**

ψευδ**ώνυμος, ον**$_{2.2}$ {ψεύδομαι + ὀνομάζω} *adj.* ①^{gfs} 1 Tim 6:20, **falsely called**^{NIGTC}

ψεῦσμα, ατος, τό$_3$ {ψεύδομαι} ①^{dns} Rom 3:7, **lie**

ψεύστης, ου, ὁ$_{1>}$ {ψεύδομαι} (10x) John 8:44, 55; Rom 3:4; 1 Tim 1:10; Titus 1:1; 1 John 1:10; 2:4, 22; 4:20; 5:10, **liar**; ❹ LXX, Prov 19:22

ψηλαφάω^{con} {ψάω} ❹ Luke 24:39; Heb 12:18; 1 John 1:1, **to touch**; Acts 17:27, **to feel around**^{ZEC}; (15x LXX) Gen 27:12, 21, 22, **to touch**

ψηφίζω {ψώχω} ❷ Luke 14:28, **to count up**^{ZEC}; Rev 13:18, **to calculate** *the beast's number*; Hdt. *Hist.* 9.55.2, ψήφῳ **ψηφίζεσθαι**, **to vote** *with a pebble*

ψῆφος, ου, ἡ$_2$ {ψώχω} ❸ Acts 26:10, **vote**, *a pebble used in voting: black for conviction, white for acquittal*^{ZEC}; Rev 2:17,^{2x} *white* **stone**$^{BEC, NET}$ ❺ LXX, 4 Macc 15:26, *two* **ballots**

ψιθυρισμός, οῦ, ὁ$_{2}$ {ψιθυρίζω} ①^{nmp} 2 Cor 12:20, **whispery gossip**[BEC]; ①^{dms} LXX, Eccl 10:11, *snake charmer's* **whispers**[BEC]; Plut. *Mor.* 1.13, **whispering** *during lecture*

ψιθυριστής, οῦ, ὁ$_{1>}$ {ψιθυρίζω} ①^{amp} Rom 1:29, **gossip, tale-bearer**; Dem. 59.39, **ψιθυριστὴν** Ἑρμῆν, **the whispering** *Hermes*

ψιχίον, ου, τό$_{2}$ {ψίξ, ψιχός} ❷^{gnp} Matt 15:27 = Mark 7:28, **crumbs**

ψυχή, ῆς, ἡ$_{1\eta}$ {ψύχω} (103x; 63x GA) Matt 10:28 = Mark 12:30 = Luke 10:27; Eph 6:6 = Col 3:23, **soul**, **heart**; John 10:11–15:13[7x]; Acts 15:26–27:22,[5x] **life**; John 10:24, *take away our* **life**[ABC]; Acts 2:41, **people**; 15:24, *peace of* **mind**[ABC]; (954x LXX; 149x Pss)

ψυχικός, ή, όν$_{2.1.2}$ {ψύχομαι} *adj.* ❻ 1 Cor 2:14, **the animated** *human being*;[ABC] *living on an entirely human level*[NIGTC]; 15:44,[2x] 46, **ordinary human** *body*; Jas 3:15 (cf. Jude 19), *of false teachers*, **devoid of the Spirit** + *earthly* + *demonic* = *evil triad rooted in Gehenna*; ①^{nfp} LXX, 4 Macc 1:32, **natural**[SCS]

ψῦχος, ους, τό$_{3}$ {ψύχομαι} ❸ John 18:18; Acts 28:2; 2 Cor 11:27, **cold**; ❽ LXX, 2x Dan

ψυχρός, ά, όν$_{2.1.2}$ {ψύχομαι} *adj.* ❹ Matt 10:42; Rev 3:15,[2x] 16, **cold**; ❸ LXX, Gen 8:22

ψύχω {ψύχομαι} ①^{fpi3s} Matt 24:12, *love* **will grow cold**; ❻ LXX, 2 Sam 17:19, **to spread out**; Jer 6:7, *as a cistern* **cools** *water, so wickedness* **refreshes** *her* (LES)

ψωμίζω {ψώχω} ❷ Rom 12:20, **to feed**; 1 Cor 13:3, **to give away**; (20x LXX)

ψωμίον, ου, τό$_{2}$ {ψώχω} ❹ John 13:26,[2x] 27, 30, **morsel, piece of bread**

ψώχω {ψωμίζω} ①$^{pap.nmp}$ Luke 6:1, **to rub**

Ω, ω [*ōmega*]

Ω, ω, τό (ὦ μέγα) *indecl.* **omega**, *24th and last letter of the Greek alphabet*; **(3x)** Rev 1:8; 21:6; 22:13, **omega**; *completes the verbal merism* τὸ Ἄλφα καὶ τὸ Ὦ, **the Alpha and the Omega**[NIGTC] || *num.* ω′ = 800; ͵ω = 800,000

ὦ, *interj.* (20x) Matt 15:28; Gal 3:1; 1 Tim 6:20; Jas 2:20, **O!**; (88x LXX; 36x 4 Macc)

Ὠβήδ[LXX] *indecl.* (14x; 10x 1–2 Chr) Ruth 4:17; 1 Chr 5:13; 2 Chr 23:1, **Obed**

ὧδε *adv.* (61x; 50x GA) Matt 8:29; John 11:32; 1 Cor 4:2; Rev 13:18, **here**; Heb 7:8, **ὧδε μέν, in the one case**[NIGTC]; Rev 14:12, **this requires**; (79x LXX; 12x Gen)

ᾠδή, ῆς, ἡ$_{1η}$ {ᾄδω} ❼ Eph 5:19 = Col 3:16; Rev 5:9; 14:3; 15:3, **song**; (85x LXX; 44x Pss)

ὠδίν, ῖνος, ἡ$_{3}$ ❹ Matt 24:8 = Mark 13:8c; 1 Thess 5:3, **birth pangs**; Acts 2:24, *freeing him from the* **agonies** *of death, Hades birthed Jesus*[Keen1]; (35x LXX) 2 Sam 22:6, **snares**

ὠδίνω {ὠδίν} ❸ Gal 4:19, *intran.* **to suffer horrid labor pains**; Gal 4:27; Rev 12:2, **to experience the pain of childbirth**; (22x LXX; 3x Isa); Hom. *Il.*11.269, *Agamemnon's wounds compared to the Eileithuiai, goddesses of childbirth,* **dispensers of cruel pain**[ABC]

ὤζεσεν → **ὄζω**, *aor. act. ind. 3s*, Exod 8:10, *the land* **stinks**

ὦμος, ου, ὁ$_{2}$ ❷ Matt 23:4; Luke 15:5, **shoulder**; (52x LXX; 8x Exod:Isa)

ὤμοσεν → **ὀμνύω**, *aor. act. ind. 3s*, Luke 1:73, **to promise**

ὠνέομαι[con] ①[ami3s] Acts 7:16, **to buy**

ᾠόν, οῦ, τό$_{2}$ ①[ans] Luke 11:12, **egg**; ❻ LXX, Deut 22:6; Job 39:14

ὥρα, ας, ἡ$_{1α}$ (106x; 50x Syn, 26x John) Ⓐ ***length of time***, Matt 27:46; 1 Cor 15:30; Rev 18:10, **hour**; Ⓑ ***immediacy of time***, Matt 26:55; Rev 3:3; Acts 16:18, *that very* **hour**[ZEC]; Ⓒ ***Johannine appointed crucifixion time***, John 2:4, 7:30, 17:1; Ⓓ ***critical time markers***, Mark 15:25; Luke 22:14; John 4:6; Ⓔ ***narrative neutral time***, Matt 14:15; Acts 2:15; (66x LXX; 14x Pent, 13x Dan); Gen 18:10, *about this* **time** *next year*[Waltke]

ὡραῖος, α, ον$_{2.1.2}$ *adj.* ❹ Matt 23:27, **beautiful**; Acts 3:2, 10, **Beautiful** *Gate*; Rom 10:15, **timely** *the arrival of the feet*[ABC]

ὠρύομαι ①[pmp.nms] 1 Pet 5:8, **roar** *of lions*; (11x LXX; 3x Pss) Zeph 3:3

ὡς *adv.* (504x; 114x LA, 71x Rev, 37x 1–2 Pet) Ⓐ ***basic usage***, 2 Thess 2:2, **as, like** Ⓑ ***compar. part.***, 1 Cor 3:15; Eph 5:33, **like**; Ⓒ ***temp. conj.***, Luke 1:23, **when**; 24:32, **while**; Ⓓ ***consec. conj.***, Heb 3:11, **so that**; John 1:39, **about**[EDNT]; (1,965x LXX; 252x Isa, 134x Pss)

ὡσαννά *indecl. interj.* ❻ Matt 21:9[2x] = Mark 11:9, 10 = John 12:13, **Hosanna!**

ὡσαύτως *adv.* (17x; 9x Syn) Matt 20:5; 21:30; Mark 14:31, **same**; Matt 25:17; Mark 12:21; Luke 22:20; 1 Tim 2:9; 3:8; Titus 2:3, 6, **likewise**; Luke 13:5; Rom 8:26; 1 Cor 11:25, **just as, in the same way**; 1 Tim 5:25, **so also**; (37x LXX; 7x Exod)

ὡσεί *part.* (21x; 15x LA) Ⓐ ***compar.***, (11x) Matt 9:36; Mark 9:26; Acts 2:3; 6:15; Rom 6:13; Heb 1:12, **like**; Ⓑ ***indef.***, (10x) Matt 14:21; Luke 3:23; Acts 1:15, **about**; (186x LXX; 67x Pss)

Ὡσηέ, ὁ$_{2}$ *indecl.* ①[dms] Rom 9:25, **Hosea**; (14x LXX; 8x 2 Sam)

ὥσπερ *comp. adv.* (36x) Matt 6:2; Luke 17:24; 2 Cor 8:7; Heb 7:27, **as**; Matt 6:7; Rev 10:3, **like**; John 5:21; Rom 5:12; Jas 2:26, **just as**; (262x LXX; 81x Job, 49x Prov)

ὡσπερεί ① 1 Cor 15:8, **as if**; Pseud., 1 En. 5.2; Ezek. Trag. 1.132

ὥστε *conj.* (83x; 21x 1–2 Cor, 15x Matt) Matt 8:24; 1 Cor 1:7, **so that**; Matt 10:1, **to**; 12:12; John 3:16; 1 Cor 3:7, **so**; Acts 15:39; 2 Cor 1:8, **that**; Phil 2:12; 4:1, **therefore**; 1 Thess 1:7, **with the result that**[ABC]; (178x LXX; 25x Exod)

ὠτάριον, ου, τό$_2$ {οὖς} ❷[ans] Mark 14:47; John 18:10, **ear**

ὠτίον, ου, τό$_2$ {οὖς} ❸ Matt 26:51; Luke 22:51; John 18:26, **ear**; (17x LXX; 8x 1–2 Sam)

ὠφέλεια, ας, ἡ$_{1\alpha}$ {ὠφελέω} ❷ Rom 3:1; Jude 16, **advantage**, **gain**; (13x LXX; 3x Sir:Jer)

ὠφελέω[con] {ὄφελος} (15x; 9x Gs) Matt 16:26 = Mark 8:36 = Luke 9:25, **to benefit**; Mark 5:26, μηδὲν **ὠφεληθεῖσα**, *instead of* **getting better**[ZEC]; (28x LXX; 7x Jer)

ὠφέλιμος, ον$_{2.2}$ {ὠφελέω} *adj.* ❹ 1 Tim 4:8,[2x] (1st occur.) *limited* **beneficial value**; (2nd occur.) *totally* **beneficial**; 2 Tim 3:16; Titus 3:8, **profitable**